KARL MARX'S THEORY OF REVOLUTION

KARL MARX'S THEORY OF REVOLUTION

by Hal Draper

with the assistance of Stephen F. Diamond

VOLUME III
THE DICTATORSHIP
OF THE PROLETARIAT'

MONTHLY REVIEW PRESS
NEW YORK

Copyright © 1986 by Hal Draper
All rights reserved

Library of Congress Cataloging-in-Publication Data
Draper, Hal.
  Karl Marx's theory of revolution.

  Includes bibliographies and indexes.
    Contents: v. 1. State and bureaucracy. v. 2. The politics of social classes. v. 3. The "dictatorship of the proletariat."
    1. Marx, Karl, 1818-1883. 2. Revolutions and socialism, I. Title.
JC233.M299D7   321.09   76-40467

ISBN: 978-0-85345-674-2

Monthly Review Press
146 West 29th Street, Suite 6W
New York, NY 10001
www.monthlyreview.org

CONTENTS

Foreword   1

    PART I:
    DICTATORSHIP:
    ITS MEANING IN 1850

1. **From Rome to Robespierre**   11
   1. The Roman *Dictatura* (12) 2. Survival of the *Dictatura* (13) 3. Early Allusions (16) 4. The Great French Revolution (18) 5. Marat and Dictatorship (22) 6. The "Terrible Use" (25)

2. **Socialism and Dictatorship: The Beginning**   28
   1. Testimony of Words (28) 2. The Beginning: Babeuf and Buonarroti (29) 3. The Blanquist Myth (34) 4. Utopians and Dictators (39) 5. Dezamy, Morrison, and Young Engels (42)

3. **Dictatorship in 1848**   45
   1. Even Louis Blanc . . . (45) 2. The Cavaignac Dictatorship (48) 3. Cavaignac as Prelude (51) 4. Weitling and Dictatorship (53) 5. Bakunin and Dictatorship in 1848 (55)

4. **The Dictatorship of the Democracy: Marx in 1848**   58
   1. The Case of Proudhon (58) 2. Toward the Rule of the Democracy (59) 3. What Marx Proposed (61) 4. Dictatorial Measures (65)

5. **The "Dictatorship of the People": Conservative Version**   68
   1. "Popular Despotism" and Guizot (68) 2. The "Fearful Word" of Donoso Cortes (70) 3. Stein's "Social Dictatorship" (71)

PART II:
THE TERM 'DICTATORSHIP'
IN MARX AND ENGELS

6. **The Spectrum of 'Dictatorship'**   77
   1. 'Despotism' and 'Class Despotism' (77) 2. The Dim Side of the Spectrum (80) 3. Military Dictators and Dictatorships (82) 4. Some Nondictatorial Dictators (84) 5. The "Dictators" of the Democracy (88)

7. **Some Dictators over the Proletariat**   93
   1. Bakunin and the "Secret Dictatorship" of Anarchy (93) 2. Marx on Bakunin's Dictatorship (96) 3. Lassalle as "Workers' Dictator" (98) 4. The Apprentice Dictators (101) 5. A Clutch of Dictators (104)

PART III:
PRELIMINARIES:
THE "MARX-BLANQUIST" MYTH

8. **Introduction to the Investigation**   111
   1. Periodization (111) 2. The 'Rule of the Proletariat' (112) 3. The Concept of Class Rule (115) 4. The Word in 1850: Cabet Again (117)

9. **Marx and Blanqui**   120
   1. Marx and Babouvism (120) 2. The Blanquist Tendency (124) 3. Marx and Blanqui: The Revolutionary (127) 4. Marx and Blanqui: The Defense Movement (131) 5. Marx and Blanqui: Personal Relations (133) 6. Marx and Blanqui: The United Front (140)

10. **Marx Versus Blanquism**   145
    1. Early Years (145) 2. Lessons of the Brussels Period (148) 3. The Question of Allies in the Manifesto (150) 4. Revolution and Restraint (153) 5. Retrospection in the Fifties (158) 6. Marx's 1850 Attack on Blanquism (160) 7. The Rest of 1850 (163) 8. Through the Fifties (168)

PART IV:
'DICTATORSHIP OF THE PROLETARIAT'
IN MARX AND ENGELS

11. **Marx's *Class Struggles in France***   175
    1. 'Dictatorship' Times Five (175) 2. Locus 1: Three Passages (178) 3. Blanqui as Bogey (181)

12. **The SUCR Episode**   184
    1. Locus 2: The SUCR Statutes and the Signers (184) 2. The Blanquist Refugees and the "Alliance" (188) 3. Why SUCR Collapsed (193) 4. The Trouble with Nicolaievsky's Fabulation (199) 5. The Simple Solution (206) 6. Our Central Thesis (211)

13. **Reverberations in 1850: The *NDZ* Exchange**   214
    1. "Proletarian Ascendancy" (214) 2. Otto Luning and the *NDZ* (216) 3. Luning Lifts a Lance (219) 4. Locus 3: Lüning Versus Marx (220) 5. Marx's Equation (224)

14. **More Reverberations**   227
    1. Miquel's "Dictatorship" (227) 2. Enter Hooligan, Raving (229) 3. Willich's "Dictatorship" (232) 4. Techow's "Dictatorship" (236) 5. Eccarius, the "Vrai Peuple," and a Near-Locus (238)

15. **From Weydemeyer to Vogt**   242
    1. Introducing Weydemeyer (242) 2. Weydemeyer's Article on "Dictatorship" (244) 3. Locus 4: Marx's Letter (246) 4. Echo in *Herr Vogt* (248) 5. More Echoes (251)

16. **The Many Dictatorships of Moses Hess**   253
    1. Introducing Hess (253) 2. Lassalle as Hess' Dictator (256) 3. Messianic Interlude (259) 4. Hess in the International (260)

17. **The Second Period of the 'Dictatorship of the Proletariat'**   264
    1. Marx Versus Blanquism—Continued (264) 2. The Paris Commune (269) 3. Blanquists in the Commune (274)

18. **Marx and the Blanquists After the Commune**   279
    1. The Blanquists and the International (279) 2. Marx and the Émigrés (280) 3. The Blanquist Split (282) 4. The New Blanquist Formulations (284) 5. Delahaye's Formulation (286)

19. **Marx and Engels in the Second Period**   289
    1. The Case of Vermersch (289) 2. Locus 5: Marx's Banquet Speech (292) 3. Locus 6: Marx on Political Indifference (295)

4. Locus 7: Engels on the Housing Question (296) 5. Marx's Notes on Bakunin's Book (298) 6. Locus 8: Engels on the Blanquist Refugees (302) 7. Locus 9: Marx on the Gotha Program (303)

20. **The Third Period of the Dictatorship of the Proletariat** 307
1. Lafargue's Landmark (307) 2. Locus 10: Engels' Letter to Schmidt (309) 3. Second Round on the Gotha Program (310) 4. Rumpus in the Reichstag (312) 5. Locus 11: Engels on the Paris Commune (315) 6. Locus 12: Engels on the Erfurt Program (317) 7. Engels' Talk with Voden on Plekhanov (323)

SPECIAL NOTES

A. **Marxologists at Work** 329
1. Surveys (329) 2. Marxological Mentions (332)

B. **Fabrication of a Fable: The "Marx-Blanquist" Myth** 337
1. Bernstein's Case (338) 2. Lichtheim's Putsch Against Marx (343) 3. Decrying Wolfe (347) 4. Tarradiddles and Sciolists (353) 5. The Case of Ernst Schraepler (357)

C. **The Meaning of 'Terror' and 'Terrorism'** 360
I. Marx on the Jacobin Terror (361) 2. Marx on 'Revolutionary Terrorism' (367) 3. Terrorism'After 1848 (371)

D. **Ghosts, Goblins, and Garbles** 375
1. Ghost-Locus: Feuer out of Mayer (375) 2. Ghost-Locus: Iring Fetscher (377) 3. Ghost-Locus: Georges Gurvitch (378) 4. Ghost-Locus: Easton-Guddat (378) 5. The Goblins of Locus 1c (379) 6. The Miquel Goblin (380) 7. Ectoplasmic Quotes: Dommanget (381) 8. Questions about MECW Translations (383)

E. **Marx-Engels Loci: Summary List** 385

Reference Notes 387

Bibliography (Works Cited) 421

Index 443

FOREWORD

This volume of *Karl Marx's Theory of Revolution* (KMTR) is not about the dictatorship of the proletariat. It is about the 'dictatorship of the proletariat'. That is, it is about the term. The difference takes us to the very heart of the present work. Let me explain.

1

This volume of KMTR is a bridge between the first two volumes and the next two. As presently planned, Volume 4 will take up Marx's views on other socialisms and on the "road to power"; Volume 5, workers' state and socialist society, that is, postrevolutionary problems.* My original intention was to discuss the 'dictatorship of the proletariat' in the last volume, since it is properly related to the workers' state period. This is entirely proper in terms of the real meaning of 'dictatorship of the proletariat', but it is unsatisfactory if we are to deal with the way 'dictatorship of the proletariat' has actually figured in the history of Marxist thought.

It is going to be our conclusion (this can be revealed in advance) that Marx used the term to mean nothing less *and nothing more* than a workers' state—what he commonly called the "conquest of political power by the proletariat." The period following a socialist revolution had several interchangeable labels in Marx's writings: 'workers' state', the 'political ascendancy (or sway, *Herrschaft)* of the proletariat', 'workers' political (or state) power', the 'rule *(Herrschaft)* of the proletariat', and some others; and one of these, used in certain contexts, was the 'dictatorship of the proletariat'.

---

*It will be evident to readers of previous volumes that the plan of KMTR has changed and expanded since my original description in Volume 1. As apology or explanation, I need only say that the project has taken shape in the making.Obviously, references in Volumes 1 and 2 to material planned for forthcoming volumes need amendment.

1

But this simple view has not been the usual one, as we will see. One of the problems is the persistent raising of the wrong questions. Thus, it has been written a thousand times, in complaint, condemnation or regret, that Marx "failed" to describe his 'dictatorship of the proletariat' in any detail. But this assumes that there is something *special* to describe, other than the workers' state in general; and this is precisely what is untrue. Of course, it is quite in order to complain that Marx did not write more fully on what a workers' state would or should look like, though here the reasons for his reluctance are better known. But in any case, the two complaints are one: there is no *special* revelation about the dictatorship of the proletariat' (properly understood) that he could have made.

Marx, contrary to myth, had a good deal to say about the problems of the postrevolutionary period. There is the problem of defending the workers' state against counterrevolution; of using force against enemies; of rooting out (or "smashing") the old state machinery; of recasting governmental forms so as to maximize democratic control; and so on. All of these problems and more are raised by the term 'workers' state' or its equivalents. Some of these problems have already been touched on in the first two volumes of KMTR, and, as mentioned, the postrevolution period as a whole will be the subject of the last volume.

The present volume, then, does not have the task of setting forth Marx's positive views in this very important area. It does something else: it undertakes to clear away the underbrush that stands in the way of understanding Marx's ideas.

I said that many problems are *raised* by the term 'workers' state', but no one would suggest that the term itself provides answers. The case is different with the term 'dictatorship of the proletariat'. *Is it not true that this term was invented precisely because it points to special policies, policies that are specially dictatorial in some way? Do you not have a 'dictatorship of the proletariat' only if you do something sturdily dictatorial like, say, disfranchising the bourgeoisie, or giving double voting rights to certified proletarians, or at least occasionally throwing a brace of your critics into jail...?*

This is the sort of assumption that confers a special freight of meaning on 'dictatorship of the proletariat', a burden that none of the other terms is thought to carry. This is the assumption that has been so thoroughly embedded in all literature about Marxism that it is seldom even discussed.

We know why this state of affairs persisted. The well-known fact is that the term 'dictatorship of the proletariat' became a political football as soon as the Russian Revolution of 1917 presented its new state as a dictatorship of the proletariat. Communists and social-democrats, flanked by historians, scholars, and exegetes, launched into a bitter controversy, decade after decade, purporting to argue about what Marx meant by the 'dictatorship of the proletariat'.

In reality, the debate was usually over something else, revolving around the Soviet state and its course of development, finally around the counterrevolution represented by the rise of Stalinism. I grant that this *something else* was of the greatest importance; but it was not clarified by a camouflaged assault on another front. The phrase 'dictatorship of the proletariat' acquired the status of a shibboleth—a code word for both sides.

After most of a century of this sort of disputation, *Marx's* ideas on the subject were buried under the mass of burnt-out squibs, dud cannonballs, and fizgigs exploded during this ideological warfare. Few of the controversialists even cared much about what old Marx thought of it all, so long as a point could be scored in the real battle: the battle over the Russian Revolution and, later, over its corpse embalmed by Stalin.

This battle is not waged in the present volume. We will deal with the history of the question only through Marx's and Engels' lifetime, that is, to 1895. For the rest of this history, see Section 4 below.

2

As a result of the ideological wars, at almost every stage of the present investigation we have to strike down myths about Marx's and Engels' relationship to this and allied questions. In doing so, we have to deal with many statements that are—well, untrue. Now English is tricky about words like 'false', 'falsity', 'falsehood', 'falsification', and the like. The first two, says Merriam-Webster's, do not necessarily imply conscious desire to deceive; the other two do. Now I happen to believe, with Dr. Johnson, that deliberate deceit in this area is rare: "It is more from carelessness about truth than from intentional lying that there is so much falsehood in the world," said the great lexicographer, using 'falsehood' neutrally. Carelessness is not the main point: most people are so expert at sincerely believing whatever is convenient that simple mendacity is unnecessary; self-deception is the most effective kind.

In no case, then, will I imply that falsity involves falsification; but still a term is needed for this neutral 'falsehood'. I have a lexicographical proposal. The word 'fiction' already signifies the relation of nonfacts without intention to deceive. Fables are surely a form of fiction, rather than falsification: when we come across cases of fabulation, let us call it *falsifiction*.

We need not, then, inquire into the subjective intentions of the fabulists. But their falsifictions will be a recurring motif of this study.

3

In 1962 I published a longish essay on "Marx and the Dictatorship of the Proletariat" which introduced the innovative method of setting down and examining what Marx and Engels had actually written or said about the 'dictatorship of the proletariat', in order to determine what they meant.* This method was unorthodox, indeed singular, in comparison with the common procedure of the marxologists, which is to quote a snatch from Marx or Engels and then construct the corpus of "Marxism" by extrapolation, much as a paleontologist may invent a dinosaur from a single bone. But my eccentric procedure had the advantage of being fruitful.

The present volume is based in part on that seventy-page study, but a great deal of material has been added, and the scope has been substantially enlarged.

Part I, which examines the history of the word 'dictatorship', is not a philological excursion. It is basically an attempt to answer the following question: When in 1850 Marx first set down the phrase 'dictatorship of the proletariat', what did the word 'dictatorship' (by itself) mean, not only to him but to the socialist movement and, indeed, to the general political public?

This part, therefore, is not a history of dictatorship (whatever the *thing* dictatorship is taken to be) but rather a history of *the term as a political statement.* To be sure, the distinction sometimes blurs in practice, as usual, but it is always the latter history that is the guiding aim. When the readers of Marx's magazine, the *Neue Rheinische Zeitung/Revue,* first saw the words "dictatorship of the proletariat" in 1850, they responded with contemporaneous consciousness, not with our twentieth-century notions about the meaning of 'dictatorship'.

Part II performs the task of relating this history to the writings of Marx and Engels: it surveys how they used the word 'dictatorship' *tout court.* In this connection a great deal of ancillary political material comes to light, in particular on the dictatorial hankerings of certain socialist figures, some of whom are enshrined by marxologists as paladins of democracy and freedom.

Part III takes up the subject which is, in general, the secondary theme of the entire volume, viz., the relation of Marx to Blanqui and Blanquism. (It was represented in my 1962 essay by only a short passage.) The mass of literature on Marx's 'dictatorship of the proletariat' is permeated, saturated, and waterlogged with the myth (or falsifiction) that this phrase had some special origin in Blanqui or the Blanquist movement, and that Marx was, for some short or long time, a Blanquist in some sense, including the Pickwickian. It is

---

*This essay was published, in English, in the Paris journal *Etudes de Marxologie* (No. 6, September 1962), edited by Maximilien Rubel, who had been helpful in getting me started on this project. A summary, only about a third of the whole, was publised in *New Politics* (New York), Summer 1962.

not just a question of establishing historical truth, though this is necessary; no one who is victimized by this falsification can understand Marx's views.

Part III therefore presents a searching investigation of Marx's relation to Blanqui and the Blanquists. My aim has been to make it the most thoroughgoing available. In this respect, too, the present volume is a bridge to the volumes that follow. A positive presentation of Marx's views on force and violence in the social struggle will be made in Volume 4, but here we have to clear away some rubbish. This is also the function of the Special Note on the meaning of the term 'terror(ism)'—not only in Marx but in all the literature of the mid-nineteenth century—for few terms have rivaled this one in its capacity for obfuscation.

Part IV presents and examines every use by Marx and Engels of the term 'dictatorship of the proletariat' or its equivalent. It covers the ground to which my 1962 essay was mainly devoted; but much has been added.* In particular, there are new sections on documents and episodes involving Marx or Engels which I would call *near-loci*. Special attention has been paid to cases where the term 'dictatorship of the proletariat' or something like it showed up in the writings of others.

In the course of Part IV I have taken advantage of the subject to cover some matters that might otherwise have been left out of KMTR as digressive, but which (even if *really* digressive!) have the habit of cropping up in marxological works. Thus, the "SUCR episode" of 1850 has been referred to in countless books, with various imaginative interpretations, but the whole story (that is, as much of it as we know) has never been presented. Here it is, in Chapter 12. Chapter 16 on Moses Hess may appear to be digressive; but there is no better way of showing what ideas about dictatorship were prevalent in the movement *alongside* Marx—by figures hostile to him. Hess's dictatorial conceptions are all the more important because Hess has a right to be called the father of social-democratic reformism. The split in the Paris Commune over dictatorship is rarely mentioned, but it should be seen as part of the total picture. For a final example: the most amazing thing about Engels' condemnation of Plekhanov's interpretation of 'dictatorship of the proletariat' (Chapter 20) is that it is virtually unknown; yet here the Marx-Engels tradition voiced its flat repudiation of the whole future course of the movement on this question.

The complete picture of Marx's political thought—the overall aim of KMTR—would be unfinished without these episodes, vignettes, and case studies.

*Locus 5, Marx's banquet speech of 1871, was not included in the 1962 essay; I published a supplementary note about it in *New Politics*, Summer 1962, page 130. (The rest of the locus numbers, therefore, are changed from the 1962 list.)

6   Foreword

4

For interested readers, additional material on the subject of this volume is available from other sources.

(1) Some documentation, for example, has been left out of this volume purely for space considerations. The Special Notes should have included two studies which I published in periodicals, but they have been regretfully omitted. These are:

• "Karl Marx and Simón Bolívar: A Note on Authoritarian Leadership in a National Liberation Movement"—an essay on Marx's analysis of Bolívar as a Bonapartist dictator.

• "Joseph Weydemeyer's 'Dictatorship of the Proletariat' "—in particular its translation (full text) of the first article ever entitled "The Dictatorship of the Proletariat," written by Marx's friend Weydemeyer in 1852.

The background of these articles is explained in this text; their publication data are given in the Bibliography. Copies of these articles are obtainable, at nonprofit reproduction rates, from the Center for Socialist History (Berkeley), which I helped to found in order to facilitate historical research on the socialist movement.*

(2) As mentioned, this volume ends with 1895. The rest of the history of the 'dictatorship of the proletariat' will be the subject of a separate work, tentatively titled *The 'Dictatorship of the Proletariat' from Marx to Lenin*. This will trace the question through the Second International, in the Russian movement (particularly in Plekhanov and Lenin), during the First World Revolution of 1918-1921, and up through the Year One of the Russian Revolution, that is, until November 1918. The subsequent utilization of the term by Stalinism, as the label for a species of noncapitalist totalitarianism, is of no separate theoretical interest.

5

This volume is the same as previous volumes in format and other technical respects. The following reminders may be useful.

• *Notes.* There is a sharp distinction between *reference notes*, which are relegated to the back of the book, and *footnotes*, which are intended to be read as part of the text. The general reader is advised to ignore all the superscript numbers that pepper the pages: the reference notes mainly offer information

---

*For information and rates, address the Center for Socialist History, 2633 Etna, Berkeley, CA 94704, enclosing a self-addressed stamped envelope.

on sources and some other technical matters, but never affect the line of thought.

- *Quotes.* Inside quoted passages, all emphasis is in the original, and all [bracketed words] represent my own interpolations.
- *Degree-mark symbol.* This unorthodox sign is used to indicate that certain quoted words or passages are in *English in the original.* A double degree mark (°°) at the beginning of a quotation means that the whole passage was originally written in English. Inside a quotation, words or phrases originally in English are marked off using the symbol like quotation marks, °as here.° (This is done only when necessary, not in every case.)
- *Translations.* Where possible, I have used English translations from the volumes so far published of the Marx-Engels *Collected Works* (MECW) or from the three-volume Marx-Engels *Selected Works* (MESW). All translations or revisions of translations not otherwise ascribed are my own responsibility.
- *Single quotes.* These, with the punctuation outside, are used to indicate that a word is being exhibited—that a term is being used as a term—rather than being either quoted or used as an integral part of the sentence.

I | DICTATORSHIP: ITS MEANING IN 1850

1 | FROM ROME TO ROBESPIERRE

The question is: what did the word 'dictatorship' *(dictature, Diktatur,* etc.) mean in the year 1850, when Marx first used the term 'dictatorship of the proletariat'?

The assumption of the marxologists, it seems, has always been that it meant exactly the same thing that we mean by it in the late twentieth century. Few people, to be sure, will admit making this assumption consciously; but all have incorporated it into their argumentation; and in any case no marxologist has ever questioned it.*

But the present-day meaning of 'dictatorship' does not go back to the beginning of time; in fact, it is relatively recent. The first warning of this fact that I came across was sounded by Henry R. Spencer in 1931 in the *Encyclopaedia of the Social Sciences:* "Dictatorship is a term which has undergone notable change in meaning." He explained its original meaning, and added that, while modern times have seen absolutism, despotism and tyranny,

> the concept of dictatorship has until recently been kept separate and history has used it to designate an emergency assumption of power....
> In the decade following the [First] World War, however, there was a widespread tendency to use the term dictatorship as synonymous with absolutism or autocracy.[1]

Actually, the change must have begun before the First World War, in the last decades of the nineteenth century. There is often a period in which new and old meanings jostle in the public consciousness; Spencer's date probably marked the end of the jostling.† But his essential point is true and important: the present-day aura around the word 'dictatorship' is relatively modern.

---

* I must explain that I use the term 'marxologist' only pejoratively, much as others use 'kremlinologist.' *I* do not do 'marxology'; my subject is Marxism.

† For example, in 1906 Lenin, discussing the 'dictatorship of the proletariat', showed awareness of a terminological problem: "The idea that there can be a dictatorship without any police, or that dictatorship need not be a police dictatorship, seems strange to [people]," he remarked.[2]

1. THE ROMAN *DICTATURA*

To understand what 'dictatorship' meant in the middle of the nineteenth century, we must go back to Rome. The reason is not antiquarian: the old Roman meaning was not dead in 1850.

During most of that century, 'dictatorship' still retained a great deal of its original reference to the institution called the *dictatura* in the constitution of the classical Roman Republic, an institution that lasted for centuries. It had three main features:

(1) It was constitutional and legal. The constitution itself provided for the naming—in time of invasion or civil disorder, that is, of crisis and emergency—of a one-man ruler who united specially extended powers in his hands.

(2) It was temporary. The maximum duration was six months, but usually the dictator handed his power back sooner, whenever the emergency ended.

(3) It was limited in significant ways. Most particularly, while the laws were temporarily abrogated, the dictatorship could not make *new* laws. The dictator's jurisdiction was primarily not civil but military, whether against an external foe or internal dissension. Money had to be voted; the Senate held the purse strings. The dictator's authority was confined to Italy. Power of life and death over citizens was early limited by law. And in fact, in the course of time, changes were made in the limitations and conditions of the *dictatura*, precisely because it was not conceived to be an independent autocracy, and because there was an obvious danger that this institution would be put to unintended use.

It worked—for three centuries: that means it worked. For centuries the practice of the *dictatura* stayed within the constitutional, legal framework of the Republic and did not degenerate into tyranny. The first *dictatura* was said to have been established in 501 B.C.; the last of the general dictators (leaving aside a minor type *of dictatura* I have not mentioned) took office in 216 B.C.

Finally, like all other institutions, this one broke down. When Sulla and Caesar had themselves appointed "perpetual dictators," this meant the scrapping of the constitutional *dictatura.* Even so, Sulla laid down the office after a few years and retired. Caesar instituted a dictatorship in our current sense as a result of destroying the institution in the original Roman sense—and incidentally gave rise to a whole family of new terms (Caesarism, kaiser, czar, etc.).

Was the *dictatura* the cause of the phenomenon that came to be called Caesarism? When first Sulla, then Caesar, wanted to establish his personal Imperium, the *dictatura* was invitingly at hand. It was the obvious institution for them to seize on and abuse. Therefore, in 44 B.C.—after the assassination of Caesar—a law was adopted abolishing the *dictatura* as part of the constitution.

1. From Rome to Robespierre 13

The far-from-world-shaking result was that, when Augustus took over and returned to republican forms, he called himself not dictator but Number One or Número Uno—depending on your translation of *princeps civitatis* or *princeps*. It was not the *dictatura* that created Caesarism or the Caesarist type of dictatorship; it was Caesarism that bent the *dictatura* to its purpose. If not that, something else would have been found, as always. Significantly, this prefigured the fate of 'dictatorship of the proletariat'.

2. SURVIVAL OF THE *DICTATURA*

Something like the Roman *dictatura* still exists in the contemporary world. It is called martial law (on the Continent, state of siege), a form of crisis government or emergency regime. It has the essential features of the Roman device: behind martial law is understood a framework of constitutional law, not tyranny; it is temporary; it can abrogate laws (temporarily) but cannot legally impose new laws or constitutions.

Modern history, which has seen many invocations of martial law, shows that it does not *necesearily* lead to tyranny, though it can be abused. It is not regarded as *ipso facto* undemocratic, though a particular invocation may be so, of course. It is not only consistent with democratic institutions but, when it is directed against a threat to these institutions, it appears as a veritable democratic bulwark.

An academic conservative, Clinton Rossiter, has offered an extensive examination of martial-law forms of government as the modern incarnation of the Roman *dictatura*, in a book called *Constitutional Dictatorship: Crisis Government in the Modern Democracies* (1948). The best-known example of such a "constitutional dictatorship" was provided for by Article 48 in the Weimar Constitution of pre-Hitler Germany, a constitution sometimes called the most democratic in the world. This offers the classic case of what may be called the political version of Murphy's Law: viz., *if anything can be abused, it will be*.

Between 1919 and 1925 this "constitutional dictatorship" was invoked 135 times,[3] by Social-Democratic and other governments pledged to combat "Marxism" and revolution. Although Article 48 gave the president of the republic authority to issue emergency decrees in face of a threat to public order, it was actually used frequently to impose economic and other measures for which popular democratic sanction was lacking. When the economic situation eased up, in 1925-1930, it was invoked only nineteen times. By 1930 it was used by Chancellor Brüning to maintain his government, with the support of the Social-Democrats, on the basis of an economic program of cuts in welfare that could not get a majority vote in the Reichstag. The historian

Arthur Rosenberg sees this situation as the death of the Weimar Republic: "The Reichstag thus abandoned the struggle with the unconstitutional dictatorship of Brüning and his friends by a majority vote."[4] The republic then collapsed from one dictatorship into another, the Nazi dictatorship coming as the end term. In 1931-1932 Article 48 was invoked 101 times.

It is usually argued that the "constitutional dictatorship," that is, Article 48, was not used but misused; no doubt. But the situation would not have been different if there had been no convenient Article 48 to abuse. The real history of Weimar was a struggle of social forces, not an exercise in political forms. Still, we have to understand the political forms of the struggle.

Professor Rossiter had no doubt that "dictatorship" might be needed to defend "democracy"—constitutional dictatorship, that is. Constitutional dictatorship, he wrote, has been used "in all free countries, and by all free men." Indeed

> It is in this twentieth century and indeed in these very days that the age-old phenomenon of constitutional dictatorship has reached the peak of its significance.

And

> Our problem is to make that power [of the United States government] effective and responsible, to make any future dictatorship a constitutional one. No sacrifice is too great for our democracy, least of all the temporary sacrifice of democracy itself.[5]

Rossiter, a democrat and a patriotic American, would know what to think if he heard a *dictator* talking about "temporarily" sacrificing democracy in order to save it. Yet this would not shake his view that a democracy must have this device at its disposal. Obviously, any particular invocation of a "constitutional dictatorship" can be justified only by a specific sociopolitical analysis; nor can it be impugned simply by pointing with alarm.

Twelve years after publishing his *Constitutional Dictatorship* Rossiter crowned his labors of erudition with a work, *Marxism: The View from America* (1960), in which he did not fail to pay the usual respects to Marx's 'dictatorship of the proletariat.' Only somehow, in the intervening years, Rossiter had forgotten all about his insight into the concept of 'dictatorship' and the survival of the Roman meaning. His new book had not a single sentence showing awareness that 'dictatorship' did not always mean what it means now to any newspaper reader. In fact, in at least one passage he lightly takes it for granted that 'dictatorship' means only "absolute power,"[6] and that it meant this to Marx, as to anyone else, at any time and place. Elsewhere, in a genial moment, he credits Marx with a thought about "this proletariat, operating through the famous dictatorship...."[7] This breezy reference is to the dictatorship made "famous" by one ignorant book after another, not to the 'dictatorship' discussed by Rossiter in 1948.

There is another piquant example of the fixed idea that 'dictatorship' is historically immutable: a multivolume reference work with the notable title, *Dictionary of the History of Ideas,* edited by P. P. Wiener. History of ideas: that is exactly what we need! It has, for instance, a long historical article on the career of the word 'despotism'. But there is no article on 'dictatorship', and among all mentions of the term that can be traced through the index, there is not a single sentence to intimate that this word has not always meant what it does now.

On the other hand, there are some different cases: modern political scientists who understand that the Roman meaning of 'dictatorship' still has life. For example, Charles . Merriam explained in 1939 that it was a misnomer to call the Nazi regime a dictatorship. His discussion shows, not a softer view of Nazism, but a reminiscence of the classical 'dictatorship', and a feeling that it was still viable for him.[8]

In the same year, the theoretician of liberalism R. M. MacIver published a discussion of dictatorship in which he thought it useful to point out that the old Roman sense "is not unknown in the modern world." He was referring to the Weimar constitution. Then he linked this thought with Marx as follows:

> The original Marxist doctrine of the "dictatorship of the people" *[sic]* had in it something akin to the Roman idea. It was to be a temporary and exceptional form of government to prepare the way for the inauguration of a new dictatorless—in fact, stateless—order.[9]

Clearly, like Rossiter in 1948, MacIver did not think that the Roman *dictatura* was quite as dead as a doornail, and also had a glimmering of the situation in the nineteenth century.

Third example (to make a trio): Elie Halévy, in his much-praised book *The Era of Tyrannies* (1938), explains why he uses the word 'tyranny' instead of 'dictatorship':

> The Latin word 'dictatorship' implies a provisional regime, leaving intact in the long run a regime of liberty which, in spite of everything, is considered normal . . .

unlike the Greek 'tyranny'.[10] He was not motivated by any special knowledge about Marx's use of 'dictatorship of the proletariat', for on this point he displays the usual ignorance.[11]

I am not citing these three cases to show that the Roman meaning of *dictatura* has been common coin in our century. On the contrary: by their own time these writers were exceptional—more than a bit archaizing. True, exceptions still occur: for example, the *Columbia Encyclopedia* speaks of Abraham Lincoln's "wise control that amounted practically to dictatorship."[12] This language no doubt reflects Lincoln's ignoring of legalities in order to impose emergency measures. But while the Roman meaning shows only twitching signs of life in this century, we must be prepared for the news that it was in flourishing health early in the previous century.

And that is the point.

Thus, in 1855 the New *York Daily Tribune* carried an editorial titled "British Disaster in the Crimea" which talked of "dictatorship" by a commander in chief on the field of battle. The thought not only made the term 'dictatorship' equivalent to the Roman *dictatura*, it made the connection explicitly. The subject was the disastrously inept organization of the British army, revealed in the war. "But what was to be done?"

> ... there is only one remedy. This is the assumption by the General-in-Chief of the expedition upon his own authority, and his own responsibility, of that dictatorship over all the conflicting and contending departments of the military administration which every other General-in-Chief possesses, and without which he cannot bring the enterprise to any end but ruin. That would soon make matters smooth; but where is the British General who would be prepared to act in this Roman manner, and on his trial defend himself, like the Roman, with the words, "Yes, I plead guilty to having saved my country"?[13]

The author of this article was Friedrich Engels. The article made it plain that nothing startling was being proposed, for "every other General-in-Chief" had this power, which of course operated only in the theater of war and remained subordinate to the home government. The link to the Roman *dictatura* was assumed to be clear. This is all the more noteworthy since the term 'dictatorship of the proletariat' had been used for the first time only five years before.

3. EARLY ALLUSIONS

Through the first half of the nineteenth century the language of politics in all of Europe was French: the French usually invented the new words and established the connotations. But *dictature* and *dictateur* were not new terms. *Dictateur* went back to the thirteenth century, *dictature* to the fourteenth.

In Italy, Niccolò Machiavelli—in an essay more democratic in mood than *The Prince*—gave a glowing picture of the Roman *dictatura*. A republic, he argued in the 1510s, is not harmed by "power that comes in lawful ways; it is apparent that never in Rome during so long a course of time did any dictator do the republic anything but good."[14]

In conclusion, therefore, I say that those republics that cannot against
impending danger take refuge under a dictator or some such authority
will in serious emergencies always be ruined.[15]

Spinoza, on the other hand, took a dim view of the institution, considering
resort to it a danger to the state.[16] (During his Berlin student days, Marx,
writing in his 1840-1841 notebooks, made extensive excerpts from the work by
Spinoza just quoted.[17]) This positive-negative pairing can be found elsewhere.
Of the two poets who died in 1674 Milton used 'dictatorship' only for Satan,[18]
never for his rival; but Robert Herrick's laudatory poem "To Sir John
Berkley, Governor of Exeter" referred to his subject's "great Dictator-ship"
without derogation. Certainly the word had no hard-and-fast pejorative
connotation.

Algernon Sidney attacked Filmer's attempt in 1680 to justify royal
absolutism by referring to the dictatorship. In his reply Sidney praised the
Roman *dictatura* because it did *not* confer absolute power and because the
people remained sovereign:

Though I do therefore grant, that a power like to the dictatorian,
limited in time, circumscribed by law, and kept perpetually under the
supreme authority of the people, may, by virtuous and well-disciplined
nations, upon some occasions, be prudently granted to a virtuous man,
it can have no relation to our author's monarch, whose power is in
himself, subject to no law, perpetually exercised by himself, and for his
own sake . . . nothing being more unreasonable than to deduce consequences from cases, which in substance and circumstances are
altogether unlike.[19]

No doubt all of the writers cited above believed that they were using
'dictatorship' to mean the Roman *dictatura,* but in fact a certain imprecision
had made itself felt through the lapse of centuries. This is scarcely surprising.
As a model to copy, the *dictatura* was a little blurry around its edges, as the
Romans found out.

Dictionary-makers groped. In 1691, the French dictionary by Furetière[20]
gave only the Roman meaning of *dictature.* The first edition of the French
Academy's dictionary in 1694 purported to do so too, but it omitted any
mention of the temporary nature of the *dictatura,* and the sole example it gave
was—Julius Caesar![21] Plainly, a piece of the picture had gotten lost. In 1734
the *Dictionnaire de Trevoux* added, to the Roman meaning, a figurative one:
"pour signifier l'empire et la domination."[22] Empery and domination: this is
broad enough to cover a multitude of political sins.

In the 1750s Diderot's great Encyclopedia knew *dictature* only as a temporary
Roman institution, and it echoed Machiavelli: "nothing better and more
wisely established; the republic felt its benefits for a long time."[25] Rousseau's

opinion in the 1760s was similar, emphasizing the limitations of the institution. In a chapter of the *Social Contract* devoted to "The Dictatorship" (coordinate with one on the offices of tribune and censor respectively) he judged that the later Republic's fear of the institution was unjustified: "that a dictator might, in certain cases, defend the public liberty, but could never endanger it; and that the chains of Rome would be forged, not in Rome itself, but in her armies." He saw that Caesarism, which utilized the institution, came from outside it, from the application of armed force.[24]

In America, the two men whose names are supposed to stand for opposite approaches to politics did not express opposite points of view on this question. Alexander Hamilton, arguing in the 1780s for a one-man executive, adduced

> how often that [Roman] republic was obliged to take refuge in the absolute power of a single man, under the formidable title of dictator...[25]

Thomas Jefferson likewise did not always exclude the need for a dictatorship, as he understood the term. In a letter written shortly after the acquittal of the Aaron Burr conspirators, he remarked:

> Should we have ever gained our Revolution, if we had bound our hands by manacles of the law, not only in the beginning, but in any part of the revolutionary conflict? There are extreme cases where the laws become inadequate even to their own preservation, and where the universal resource is a dictator, or martial law.[26]

To be sure, Jefferson did not allow consistency to be a hobgoblin, and at other times he had other things to say about dictatorship.[27] Perhaps the most interesting thing about his statement, quoted above, is its last three words: here we find, perhaps for the first time, an identification of dictatorship with martial law, viewed favorably.

In all these allusions, so far, references to 'dictatorship' have been incidental. Like all the basic elements of modern politics, 'dictatorship' did not take center-stage until the Great French Revolution.

4. THE GREAT FRENCH REVOLUTION

It was in the Great French Revolution that, for the first time, the word 'dictatorship' became a political football in a big arena. As partisan charges were hurled back and forth, other terms too were affected. When dire things happen to people, mere words are pummeled out of shape.

It has been observed that there was a terminological link between the French Revolution and Roman times. E. B. Bax remarked that this was indicated even in people's names: Anacharsis Cloots, Anaxagoras Chaumette, Gracchus Babeuf, etc. "Everyone with the smallest smattering of education talked Roman History, just as in the English political movements of the preceding century everyone talked Old Testament."[28] In *The Eighteenth Brumaire,* Marx wrote that

> the Revolution of 1789 to 1814 draped itself alternately as the Roman republic and the Roman empire, and the Revolution of 1848 knew nothing better to do than to parody, now 1789, now the revolutionary tradition of 1793 to 1795.... Camille Desmoulins, Danton, Robespierre, Saint-Just, Napoleon, the heroes as well as the parties and the masses of the old French Revolution, performed the task of their time in Roman costume and with Roman phrases, the task of unchaining and setting up modern *bourgeois* society.[29]

"Roman costumes and phrases": we are, of course, concerned precisely with one of these phrases. Marx then underlined a key point:

> The new social formation once established, the antediluvian Colossi disappeared and with them resurrected Romanity—the Brutuses, Gracchi, Publicolas, the tribunes [add also: the dictators], the senators, and Caesar himself. . . [I]n the classically austere traditions of the Roman republic, its [the bourgeoisie's] gladiators found the ideals and the art forms, the self-deceptions that they needed in order to conceal from themselves the bourgeois limitations of the content of their struggles ....[30]

The key point was this: the forms (such as "tribunes," etc.) looked like something from the past, but the contents were new and different. The words and terms used came from the historical model, but these bottles were filled with new wine.

This happened in two periods. In the first, the actors in the Great French Revolution spoke lines they thought came from the Roman drama; in the second, the "heroes" of 1848 stalked about thinking they were assaulting the Bastille or orating in the Convention. Engels reminisced:

> When the February Revolution broke out, all of us... were under the spell of previous historical experience, particularly that of France.... It was, therefore, natural and unavoidable that our conceptions of the nature and the course of the "social" revolution proclaimed in Paris in February 1848, of the revolution of the proletariat, should be strongly colored by memories of the prototypes of 1789 and 1830.[31]

Just as generals are usually accused of getting ready to fight the last war all over again, so too revolutionary movements.

If the word 'dictatorship' was in bad odor among the orators and publicists of the French Revolution, this was less because of any alleged antidemocratic connotation than because of another aspect of the Roman meaning: whatever a dictatorship was, it was something wielded by *one man*. If one of the actors was charged with wanting a dictatorship, *this* was the accusation.

The main target was Robespierre, who indeed made the nearest approach to concentrating personal power in his own hands. For this very reason Robespierre was more emphatic than anyone else in denouncing dictatorship and would-be dictators.[32] Like everyone else, he sought to turn the charge against his critics. In an attack on Lafayette published June 18, 1792, he wrote that the general was "not yet dictator of France," nor "arbiter of the state," questioned the patriotism of this *"dictateur présomptif,"* and sarcastically called him *"general-dictateur."*[33] Lafayette was vulnerable.* The label was just as handy inside the Jacobins. When Doppet proposed appointment of a committee to sift charges before they came to the floor, Robespierre opposed the motion as dictatorial: it would be "a committee outfitted as a supreme dictator."[35]

The "dictatorship" charge was a stand-by of the Girondins. But it would be a mistake to believe that the charge was inspired simply by fear of one-man rule or by reminiscences of the Roman *dictatura*. In the first place, the Girondin leader Brissot was just as violently denunciatory of the idea of a "tribunate": tribunes, he declared, were the most dangerous enemies of the people—"men who flatter the people in order to subjugate them, who tyrannize over opinion under the name of liberty." He equated the Roman institution with the Cromwellian "protectorate." Condorcet attacked Robespierre for inspiring Marat to agitate for a *tribunate*.[36] Brissot linked the dirty word 'dictatorship' with whatever he was against. In speeches of July 25-26, 1792, he spoke against the establishment of the republic. The Robespierrists, he said, were a faction of regicides "who want to create a dictator and establish the republic." He advised against dethroning the king, naming dictators, and convoking the representative assemblies.[37] It was one integrated thought. The old Roman institutions jostled in his mind side by side with the institutions of popular sovereignty, even while he advocated the retention of the present one-man rule called monarchy.

The following month, Brissot dotted the i's. The attack on "dictatorship" became an attack on the Commune of Paris, that is, on the organized revolutionary democracy of Paris. In articles in late August he conceded that the commune's revolutionary powers had been necessary, but they were now getting dangerous: "these powers can only be a dictatorship"; "a long dictatorship, a dictatorship even of several days, can only be the tomb of liberty." The Eternal Laws "governing everything in the Moral Order" told him that "the

---

* Marat too took advantage of Lafayette's vulnerability: he accused the Girondins of wanting to make Lafayette "dictateur suprême, sous le nom de protecteur."[34] But for Marat, as we will see, this was a *tu quoque* response.

dictatorial commission of the Commune of Paris" was dangerous because "it would prolong the revolutionary means beyond the moment of crisis that had made them necessary." Other Brissotins, like Girey-Dupré, likewise attacked the "dictatorship" of the commune; and Delacroix warned that if Paris "invested a provisional council with dictatorial authority" it would be isolated from the country.[38]

We will likewise meet with references to the "dictatorship of the National Convention," the most democratically elected assembly of the age. Plainly, these were efforts to displace the odium that attached to one-man rule: to shift the odium from the "one man" to the "rule"; to mix up the meaning so that any strong revolutionary coercion would seem illegitimate. The result, which will be visible later on, was the weakening of the one-man meaning of the Roman term.

Brissot was not the only politician engaged in this operation. Mirabeau probably anticipated him when, in late July 1789, the Assembly published a proclamation urging the cessation of some recent public disorders. Mary Wollstonecraft's history of the Revolution relates that Mirabeau took the floor:

> After endeavoring to excuse the violence, or, more properly speaking, to account for it, Mirabeau observed to the Assembly, "that they ought to be thoroughly convinced, that the continuation of this formidable dictator would expose liberty to as much risk as the stratagems of her enemies. Society," he continues, "would soon be dissolved, if the multitude, accustomed to blood and disorder, placed themselves above the magistrates, and braved the authority of the law." [39]

The reference is none too clear, but Mirabeau was apparently calling the "multitude" a *dictator*—doubtless as the wielder of extralegal coercion.

One of the works on the French Revolution that the young Marx studied with the greatest care was the memoirs of the Jacobin Convention deputy René Levasseur; we have Marx's detailed notes on it. Levasseur noted (in passages excerpted by Marx) the attacks directed against the Paris commune and against a number of Paris deputies "for seeking to organize a dictatorship." The accusation was reprised later: "Indirect accusations that the Commune of Paris is striving for a dictatorship." Two Girondin deputies "name Robespierre as the candidate of the dictatorship." [40]

We see, then, that the meaning of 'dictatorship', while still linked to its Roman origins, has expanded to cover the possibility *of l'empire et la domination* not of one man but indeed of the most democratic and representative bodies then in existence. Even the accusations about the "dictatorship of Robespierre" or the "dictatorship of the Committee of Public Safety" often meant in reality the "dictatorship" of the revolutionary democracy if accompanied by resolute and energetic action.

5. MARAT AND DICTATORSHIP

Thus far we have seen a political game of mutual recrimination around a cuss-word. But did anyone actually propose a "dictatorship"?

Perhaps Saint-Just did. He is quoted as saying that "In every revolution a dictator is necessary to save the state by force or Censors to save it by virtue."[41] But Saint-Just does not seem to have pressed this view. Note that his statement brought up still another of ancient Rome's magistracies: the office of the two Censors, who supervised the census and public morality, wielding certain arbitrary powers.

The proposal of a dictatorship *was* put forward by Marat. It is difficult to discuss his role briefly because his name has been covered by thick deposits of historical slander, a miasma of falsifiction about his alleged bloodthirsty desire for mass murder—the same libelous operation that has made a farce of much history-writing about the "Enragés." All we can do is make clear what his view of dictatorship really was.

In their efforts to paint Marat as a gory wild man, historians often neglect to mention that he was one of the more erudite men of his society. Trained as a physician, he early became a scientific authority on optics and electricity; while practising medicine in London, in 1773 he published (in English) a *Philosophical Essay on Man*—which "shows a wonderful knowledge of English, French, German, Italian and Spanish philosophers"[42]—and other works on philosophy, politics, criminology and medicine. He became one of the prominent scientific men in France—before the Revolution transformed his and everyone's life.

I bring this up to stress that, to this eminent savant, there can be no doubt that *dictature* meant the old *dictatura* and not the blurry simulacrum of dirty politics that the Girondins and Jacobins were kicking back and forth in the modern manner.*

In an early pronouncement, Marat raised the question of how to save the "innocent" from revolutionary suspicion. He suggested a way: "It is to name, for a short time, a supreme dictator, arm him with public power, and put him in charge of punishing the guilty."[44] But this was only one formulation of his

---

* L. R. Gottschalk, whose 1927 biography of Marat is still considered the standard one in English, thought that Marat must have gotten the idea from Rousseau's *Social Contract*—for this historian had evidently never heard of the Roman *dictatura*. He literally did not know what the argument was about. The positive side of Gottschalk's work was his refutation of the lies and calumnies invented or retailed by Brissot, Michelet, et al.; also he finally did make clear that Marat's "dictatorship" was "not of the Caesarian or Napoleonic type," and was "undeserving of the condemnation that it has brought upon Marat."[43] This will do until someone publishes a half-decent work on Marat in English.

proposal. In a 1792 speech he complained that enemies "ascribe ambitious views to me by distorting my opinions on the need for a military tribune, a dictator, or a triumvirate to punish the intriguers..." He denied that this was the proposal of a "faction":

> These opinions [wrote Marat] are my personal ones, and I have often reproached ardent patriots for rejecting this salutary measure, though every man who knows the history of revolutions feels its indispensable need, a measure that could be taken without any drawbacks by limiting its duration *to a few days,* and by limiting the mission of the officials in charge to the *summary punishment* of the intriguers; for there is nobody in the world who is more revolted than I am by the establishment of an arbitrary authority entrusted even to the purest hands for a period of some duration.[45]

Repeatedly Marat sought to make his proposal explicit and clear as to its limited character:

> After July 14, '89, if there had been a single statesman in the nation's senate, he would have asked for the institution of the office of dictator, elected by the people in *times of crisis,* whose authority would *last only three days,* and whose duty would be to *punish* the bad citizens who endangered the public safety.[46]

It must be understood that this kind of talk—the need to punish the counter-revolutionary intriguers—was commonplace on all sides; what was particular to Marat was his proposal for the appointment, or election, of a special agent armed with special power to get this done. Those named to wield the power of tribune, dictator, triumvirate (choose your own Roman term) "did not have to be clothed with any authority; their mission to beat down the criminal heads of conspirators raised above the sword of the laws did not have to last more than a day. After this ephemeral existence they would be forever lost in the crowd."[47]

The National Convention, starting its existence in late September 1792— after the "September massacres" which Marat did *not* instigate—saw the launching of a regular anti-Marat lynching bee by the Girondins, who called for his execution (being themselves, of course, humane opponents of bloodthirsty politics). Danton and Robespierre sought to head off the dogs snapping at their own heels by joining in the cry against "dictatorship" and in the demands for guillotining its advocates; thus they stabbed Marat in the back as he stood at bay. Robespierre naturally knew that he was the Girondins' target. Barbaroux shouted, "The plan for a dictatorship does exist!" and pointed over Marat's head to the Commune of Paris. Marat took the floor amidst this tumult and cries for his blood, and, when his speech was finished, the lynchers had stopped shouting.[48]

On the "dictatorship" issue, Marat proudly stood up alone:

> They [my enemies] have dared to accuse me of aspiring to the tribunate ... Well, I must injustice declare that my colleagues, namely Robespierre, Danton, and all the rest, have continually disapproved of the idea of either a tribunate or a triumvirate or a dictatorship. If anyone is guilty of having flung these ideas out among the public, it is I.

He added: "I believe I am the first political writer, perhaps the only one in France since the Revolution," to make this proposal.[49] In the same vein, he assumed that "the people" was itself a "dictator":

> ... if you impute criminal conduct to me, the people would contradict you; for, obedient to my voice, it felt that the means I proposed was the sole way of saving the country, and, having itself become dictator, it was able to get rid of traitors.

The connotation of 'dictatorship', one sees, was emergency authority outside of normal forms. Marat continually used all the old magistracies interchangeably: "I have several times proposed to give immediate authority to a wise and strong man, under the appellation of tribune of the people, dictator, etc.: this bootless title is of no account." In summary he said:

> If it was a crime to propose dictatorship in the conditions I laid down, I alone am responsible for this proposal, for I alone have made the proposal, and supported it; I alone still support it.

In April 1793 Marat was hauled before a court in the Girondin drive to murder him legally, but he successfully defended himself against the charge of being (as he put it) "a factionalist, an anarchist, a bloodthirsty and ambitious man who aimed to get supreme power under the title of tribune, triumvir, dictator ..." But the drive got him murdered nonetheless: Charlotte Corday told her interrogators that she had not killed a man but a "ferocious beast," who "undertakes civil war in order to get named dictator."[50] She knew that because she had read it in the papers.

Marat's repeated limitation of his proposed "tribune, triumvir, dictator," or whatever, to a matter of days, with restricted authority, was more significant than may appear. An examination of his statements on the question indicate strongly that *he never envisioned this proposed official as the head of government in any sense,* including a temporary one. Yet historians have tended to assume that 'dictatorship' means dictatorship means dictatorship, and that Marat was proposing what Robespierre was actually doing while, unlike Marat, renouncing the word.

Marat liked to put things as strongly as possible, that is, as openly and starkly as can be—not, I think, a bad habit when everyone else is dodging behind words.

It is by violence [said Marat] that liberty ought to be established, and the moment has come to organize temporarily the despotism of liberty in order to wipe out the despotism of kings.[51]

"Despotism"—a word with as checkered a history as 'dictatorship'—meant coercion, extralegal coercion, in this context, not tyranny; and unquestionably Marat had in mind the use of all means of coercion to enforce the "despotism" (or dictatorship) of "liberty."* It was not this that separated him from his colleagues; rather it was his call for the vesting of this power in the hands of a single appointed agent. If Jacques Roux is accurately quoted as saying that "Dictatorship is the annihilation of liberty,"[52] it was undoubtedly one-man rule that he especially feared.

6. THE "TERRIBLE USE"

There is still another contrast to be made in order to bring out the meaning of 'dictatorship'.

As we have discussed, the close modern analogue of the Roman dictatorship is martial law. At the same time that the right wing of the French Revolution expressed horror at Marat's call for an energetic special power to repress counterrevolution, it instituted in practice the form of the *dictatura* called martial law—as an antidemocratic device. In the months after the fall of the Bastille, the Council of Three Hundred, running the Paris municipality, seized the pretext of a baker's murder to get martial law established by the Assembly. A municipal officer could invoke martial law by hoisting a red flag, after which an assemblage of citizens ("crowd") had to disperse or get shot on the spot; ringleaders could be jailed for years or executed.

In all of the Paris press, densely populated by souls horrified by calls for "dictatorship," only Marat protested this law; in the Assembly, Robespierre (but not as a matter of principle).[53] In 1791, in response to an incident ("rowdy" demonstration) in a working-class area, Bailly and Lafayette decided to make an example: the martial-law flag was hoisted; the bourgeoisie's National Guardsmen invaded the Champ-de-Mars, and opened fire; a number

---

* It was Robespierre who is best known for the statement, "The government of the Revolution is the despotism of liberty over tyranny. Was force meant only to protect crime?" (Report to the Convention, February 5, 1794.) He was justifying "terror" as an instrument of liberty or tyranny. "Terror" is one of the "fearful words" that are completely misunderstood nowadays: in the context it meant the use of coercive force by the authorities to inspire fear in malefactors. The various ways in which it might be implemented are not a part of the definition of the term. It is further discussed in Special Note C.

were killed or wounded, and many were jailed.⁵⁴ This, of course, was not "dictatorship" but the maintenance of Law and Order—by ruthless bloodletting. There is no record that the bloodthirsty monster Marat ever had anyone shot.

As mentioned, Robespierre himself regularly denounced dictatorship and dictators. Finally, in his speech of self-exoneration on the 8th Thermidor, with his neck already on the block, he had some interesting words to say about the aura of the word *dictature:*

> However, this word 'dictatorship' has magical effects; it stigmatizes liberty; it vilifies the government; it destroys the Republic; it degrades all the revolutionary institutions, which are presented as if the work of a single man; it traduces national justice, which is presented as if instituted for the ambition of a single man; it concentrates at one point all the hatreds and all the daggers of fanaticism and the aristocracy. What terrible use the enemies of the Republic have made of just the name of a Roman magistracy! And if their erudition is so fatal to us, what about their treasuries and intrigues?⁵⁵

The double reference to "a single man" indicates that Robespierre's repudiation of dictatorship was based on the one-man definition of the term. The closing reference to "erudition" emphasized that the term appeared to him as essentially historical. The "terrible use" to which it was put was largely effected by an exercise in meaning-shift through political demagogy directed *against democracy,* not against dictatorship in our modern sense.

Over a half-century later, Marx wrote (in a letter to Engels) as if the men of the French Revolution used the term 'dictatorship' in a way similar to his own. He was discussing the fact that the Robespierrist government and its Committee of Public Safety mistrusted the Polish national-revolutionary leaders:

> In 1794 [Marx wrote] they summoned the representative of the Polish insurgents before them and put the following questions to this *"citoyen":*
> "How does it happen that your Kosciuszko is a popular dictator and [yet] tolerates a king at his side, one moreover who, he must be aware, was put on the throne by Russia? How does it happen that your dictator does not carry out a levy en masse of the peasants...?" [And soon, with an indictment of the Polish leadership.]⁵⁶

In viewing the national-revolutionary Kosciuszko as a "popular dictator" in a benign sense—that is, a leader who has assumed popular power through emergency forms of government—Marx was using the term in a fashion that had *not* been adopted by the French Revolution, but which had become familiar in Marx's own time. It came into use after the rise of the socialist movement in the early nineteenth century, and then suffered virtual oblivion in the twentieth.

We will now see that the history of self-conscious "revolutionary dictatorship" begins with Babeuf, that is, at the very same moment that modern socialism begins.

2 | SOCIALISM AND DICTATORSHIP: THE BEGINNING

We are going to see, in the next chapter, that 1848 was the turning point in the history of the term 'dictatorship', or rather the starting point of its modern history. But even in that year, naturally, it did not appear out of nowhere. Let us see what led up to 1848.

1. TESTIMONY OF WORDS

Dictionaries can give only an approximate idea of how a word was actually used at a given time, but the main trouble is that they run ten to twenty years behind usage. Following the French Revolution, French dictionaries continued to give only the Roman meaning *of dictature,* as if nothing had happened. The formulations of the pre-Revolutionary lexicographers were repeated by Laveaux in 1820[1] and by Philipon de La Madeline's 1823 abridgment of the Academy's dictionary.[2]

If we look ahead, we find the pre-1848 changes reflected in the post-1848 dictionaries, though we have to keep in mind that their compilers had seen much nonlexical action in the meantime. For what it is worth, we can note that in 1863 Littré recorded the fact that *dictature* had a second meaning in addition to the Roman one:

(2) In modern times, absolute power placed temporarily in the hands of a man or an assembly. *La dictature de la Convention.*[3]

Still looking ahead: by 1870 Larousse's *Grand Dictionnaire* will have an article on *dictature* which is a political essay embracing modern history, emphasizing the institution's temporary and emergency nature and distinguishing it sharply from despotism.[4] Littré's example, "the dictatorship of the National Convention" of the French Revolution, is sufficient to show how the meaning had shifted from the original Roman conception of one-man rule to something its very opposite: the "dictatorship" of a popular body. By the time this appeared in Littré, it had in fact expanded to embrace the "dictatorship" of a whole section of the people, indeed of the majority of the people.*

In the mid-1830s great prominence was given to the tradition of the Roman *dictatura* by a novel that gained so much popularity, and was translated so widely into the European languages, that it can be treated as an event in its own right. This was Bulwer-Lytton's *Rienzi* (which inspired young Engels to start writing an opera libretto about a year before Wagner did the job). The entranced public read about the man who clothed his rule in Rome first with the title tribune, then senator, both as reminiscences of the ancient empire. Of the "proud name of Senator," the novelist wrote, "The authority attached to the name seems to have had no definite limit; it was that of a stern dictator, or an indolent puppet, according as he who held it had the power to enforce the dignity he assumed." Later on, the populace wants to crown Rienzi king; he rejects the title in the name of "liberty." One of the "people's" leaders says, "But... Rome must endow you with a legal title—if not that of King, deign to accept that of Dictator or of Consul." Rienzi rejects these too: "Dictator and Consul are the appellations of patricians." He assumes the title of tribune—and it is perfectly clear that whatever the title, dictator or tribune or senator or whatever, the power would be the same. There was no special virtue or vice in "dictator." Further on, the pope is referred to as the dictator of Rome.[6]

2. THE BEGINNING: BABEUF AND BUONARROTI

But of course we are specially interested here in how the term 'dictatorship' was used by the early socialists and communists. This part of the history begins exactly where the history of the socialist movement begins: with Babeuf's "Conspiracy of the Equals," the first organized socialist or communist group. Now the importance of this episode, for our present purposes, does not lie with the Babouvist enterprise itself, but with the book which told about it, and thus educated a generation of Jacobin-communist activists who populated the secret societies of the 1830s and 1840s. In 1828—in good time for the revolution of 1830—Buonarroti, one of Babeuf's lieutenants, published his

---

* In spite of all the events of the twentieth century, this meaning is with us still. While working on some aspects of the present work in 1974, I listened to a news broadcast on television, which reported that Vice-President Gerald Ford was telling Republican gatherings that if the Democrats elected a "veto-proof" Congress the result would be a "legislative dictatorship," by which he meant that the legislature would become more powerful than the executive. No one thought that his language was odd. I dare say that this usage can be heard quite often. It is the "dictatorship of the majority of people" all over again, invented by the right wing of the French Revolution to attaint the democracy.[5]

account of the movement; and in 1836 the Chartist leader Brontenre O'Brien published an English translation.

Buonarroti's report on the internal discussions of the "Secret Directorate" of the Babouvist movement laid sharply before its readers the question of a transitional revolutionary regime. He provided the first textbook on this question; for a long time, the only one. Its great significance cannot be exaggerated.

The existing government must be overthrown; the aim is the establishment of the 1793 constitution, the most democratic so far devised—agreed. But the directorate had to resolve the "thorny" question: "what form of authority would be immediately substituted for the authority whose destruction was intended." It was agreed that the "primary assemblies" called for by the constitution could not be immediately called into being; between the insurrection and their installation there had to be an interval; yet "it would be extremely imprudent to leave the nation for a moment without director and guide." It was not just a question of how long it would necessarily take to convoke the assembly; there was another consideration—and this lies at the center of our interest.

The Secret Directorate was convinced of the following proposition:

> ... history and the experience of the French Revolution had taught it that the sure effect of inequality is to divide the community, create opposing interests, foment hostile passions, and subject the multitude, whom it makes ignorant, credulous, victimized by excessive toil, to a small number of trained and skillful men who, abusing the preference they were able to win, worked only to preserve and reinforce, in the distribution of goods and advantages, the order that is exclusively favorable to them; from which it concluded that a people so strangely kept away from the natural order was scarcely capable of making useful choices, and had need of an extraordinary means that would return it to a state of affairs where it would be possible for it to exercise the plenitude of sovereignty effectively and not fictitiously.
>
> From this way of thinking arose the plan to replace the existing government by a revolutionary and provisional authority, constituted in such a way as to forever shield the people from the influence of the natural enemies of equality, and give it the necessary will for the adoption of republican institutions.[7]

You have just read the basic formulation of the socialist theory that dominated a whole sector of the movement for the next century and a half—and still does to an appreciable extent. It can be called the theory of the "educational dictatorship"—an educational dictatorship over the people to do them good. The people who worked it out, in the very first days of socialism as a movement, were not demagogues nor interested in deceiving anyone: they

2. Socialism and Dictatorship: The Beginning 31

simply faced a problem and devised an honest solution. The social order was bad because it corrupted the people, and one consequence of this was that the people could not emancipate themselves but had to be emancipated from above, from outside, by a band of liberators who themselves had somehow remained uncorrupted.

Buonarroti himself not only reported this "way of thinking" but strongly agreed with it. In his own name he formulated it even more sharply:

> The experience of the French Revolution and most particularly the troubles and vicissitudes of the National Convention have, it seems, sufficiently shown that a people whose opinions have been formed under a regime of inequality and despotism is not well suited at the beginning of a regenerating revolution to designate the men charged with leading and consummating that revolution. This task can belong only to wise and courageous citizens....

It was necessary for the revolutionary leadership, "even out of respect for the real [in the Platonic sense] sovereignty of the people," to be concerned not with "getting the votes" but rather with "making sure that the supreme authority falls, as little arbitrarily as possible, into the hands of wise and strong revolutionists."[8]

When the Secret Directorate asked what form should be taken by the revolutionary authority whose task it was to superintend the new order, they debated three answers: (1) the recall of a rump National Convention; (2) the creation of a dictatorship; and (3) the establishment of a new ruling body. It was easy to reject the first. By the second, "dictatorship," they meant one-man rule; and they rejected this term. Their decision fell to the third, which meant that the Provisional Authority would be named by "the Paris insurgents," that is, by the revolutionary band in the capital—thereby incidentally implementing the Babouvist-Blanquist tradition favoring the dictatorship of Paris over France. At all the steps in ratiocination, they were concerned to argue that "This system was in harmony with the sovereignty of the people." This sovereignty, however, was temporarily in hock, and only the revolutionary band held the ticket. Buonarroti was aware that enemies would not see it precisely the right way: "It was foreseen that the cunning enemies of equality would try to raise the inhabitants of the departêments [the provinces] against what they would not fail to call *the trampling by the Paris brigands over the rights of the sovereign.*"[9]

The two who proposed a dictatorship *sans phrase*, Debon and Darthé, argued from essentially the same ground as the majority. Buonarroti reported their views with a great deal of sympathy. There are few passages in early socialist history more important than the following:

Debon and Darthé, who proposed dictatorship, attached to this word the idea of an extraordinary authority, entrusted to a single man, charged with the double function of *proposing to the people simple legislation suitable for assuring it equality and the real exercise of sovereignty,* and of *provisionally dictating the preparatory measures that inclined the nation to take it on.* In their view, a task so important and audacious, which could not be fulfilled except by dint of a perfect unity of thought and action, must be conceived and executed by a single head. In support of their view, they invoked the example of the peoples of antiquity, and recalled the fatal consequences of plurality, of which they saw recent evidence in the divisions within the Committee of Public Safety.

It seemed to them that the dangers of the abuse that might result from such a magistracy could be easily avoided by the well-known virtue of the citizen who would assume it [i.e., Babeuf], by the clear and legal exposition of the aim to be attained, and by the limits set to its duration in advance.

In this system the task of the Secret Directorate would be reduced to sketching the aim of the reform in a few articles, fixing a term to the new magistracy, searching out the most virtuous citizen of the republic, and getting its plan adopted by the Parisian insurgents.

The link with the Roman example was quite clear. To the above exposition of the views of Debon and Darthé, Buonarroti added a note of his own, whose words still reverberate down the history of socialism:

> To what must one reasonably attribute the loss of democracy and liberty in France if not to the diversity of views, the opposition of interests, the lack of virtue, unity and perseverance in the National Convention? It is not, it seems to me, to preserve but to establish equality among a corrupt nation that one needs a strong and irresistible authority. It is to be presumed that if, in the years II and III [1793-1795], one had had the wisdom to invest a man of Robespierre's stamp with the dictatorship proposed by Debon and Darthé, the revolution would have achieved its true aim.[10]

According to Buonarroti, the Secret Directorate *did* recognize the validity of the argument in favor of a dictatorship, but drew back before "the difficulty of choice, the fear of abuse, the apparent resemblance of this magistracy to royalty, and, above all, the general prejudice that it seemed impossible to be victorious." It took care of the corrupt people in other ways—for example, with planned decrees on freedom of the press, including the following two:

(1) No one can put forward opinions contrary to the sacred principles of equality and the sovereignty of the people....

(4) Every writing is printed and distributed if the conservators of the national Will judge that its publication can be useful to the republic.[11]

2. Socialism and Dictatorship: The Beginning   33

It must be understood that there was no demagogic talk by Buonarroti or the other Babouvists about a dictatorship *of* the People, Populace, Proletariat or other appellation for the corrupted population that was to be weaned to socialism. They knew that they were for a Socialism from Above, and they confronted their own views without hypocrisy.

Even more than Babeuf, it was Buonarroti who exemplified this pattern most plainly—and it must be remembered that it was Buonarroti whose career constituted the real link between the Babouvist episode of 1796 and the burgeoning of the Jacobin-communist secret societies after 1830. E. L. Eisenstein, who has given us the most detailed portrait of "the first professional revolutionist," emphasized that for Buonarroti "the working population played a subordinate and even an incidental role" in his revolutionary plan. The "proletariat" meant the mass of the poor ("the most numerous class")—a good reservoir for barricade-fodder, for the troops who were to be wielded by the revolutionary elite. He rejected the idea of basing the cause on class interest; he had no confidence whatever in the capacity of these proles to emancipate themselves; the "Fourth Estate" had to be appealed to in terms of *(ugh!)* material interest because of the corruption enforced by centuries of servitude.[12]

In Buonarroti's view, experience had shown

> that the people are incapable of either regenerating themselves or of designating the people who must direct the regeneration. That before thinking of a Constitution or of fixed laws, it is necessary to establish a reforming or revolutionary government on other bases than those of a regular and peaceful liberty.[13]

This provided the *theory* of the Educational Dictatorship:

> Midst the collapse of free institutions, midst the general corruption of sentiments one cannot find . . . . future regeneration save in a secret corps guided by a pure and dictatorial authority. . . .[14]

His model in political theory was explicitly the Jesuits, who (he argued) have used their methods for Evil, while we must use them for Good. "The Jesuitical congregation can be compared to an army full of enthusiasm and submissive by conviction to a homogeneous and absolute authority." He advocated "an equivalent army" which however would fight against tyranny rather than for it. He denounced "tolerance" for "the liberty of *all* opinions" just as if his name were Herbert Marcuse.[15]

In short, the political theory and practice on which Jacobin-communism was founded by the movement from Babeuf to Buonarroti had nothing to do with a 'dictatorship of the proletariat'. Babouvism consciously and honestly advocated an Educational Dictatorship over the corrupted mass ("proletariat").

34 Part I: Dictatorship: Its Meaning in 1850

This is not said censoriously. We are, after all, dealing with the infancy of a movement, and to say that this movement had an infantile view of dictatorship is no more to condemn it than to point to a baby's difficulty with toilet training. If, a century and a half later, a movement still holds to the same infantilism, the solution is still not simply to condemn it but to provide diapers.

3. THE BLANQUIST MYTH

The Babouvist movement was the first incarnation of the Jacobin-communist current in the pre-1848 blossoming of all the socialist-communist tendencies. This was the current that was typically organized in the communist secret societies that proliferated, especially in France, under leaders like Blanqui and Barbès.

The Jacobin-communist groups adopted the Babouvist idea of dictatorship as their orthodoxy. One can read in a communist catechism of 1839 (used by the prosecution at the trial following the putsch of that year led by Blanqui and Barbès):

> It is unquestionable that after a revolution accomplished in behalf of our ideas, there will be created a dictatorial power whose mission it will be to direct the revolutionary movement. This dictatorial power will of necessity base itself on the assent of the armed population, which, acting in the general interest, will evidently represent the enlightened will of the great majority of the nation.
> To be strong, to act quickly, the dictatorial power will have to be concentrated in as small a number of persons as possible.[16]

Particularly in later historians' shorthand, this tendency has come to be called "Blanquist" as a generic name. As a label for the type, "Blanquist" is unobjectionable, provided one is not led to think that a "Blanquist" was necessarily a follower of Auguste Blanqui. Barbès, for example, became a bitter enemy of Blanqui; others simply organized separately.

One of our problems is the fact that the "Blanquist" label was given much of its currency around the end of the nineteenth century by the Bernsteinian revisionist campaign to pin a derogatory label on Marx's early revolutionary views. According to this historiographic mode, the revolutionary currents of the thirties and forties were Blanquist, therefore Blanquism was revolutionism, and it follows ineluctably that revolutionism was Blanquism; hence if Marx was a revolutionary when he wrote the *Communist Manifesto,* the Manifesto was "Blanquist"—Q.E.D. You will find this contribution to socialist history in

2. Socialism and Dictatorship: The Beginning 35

Bernstein's *Evolutionary Socialism*.[17] It is the starting point of the Blanquist myth.

One of the consequences of this line of thought is that historians knew just where to look for the origins of the 'dictatorship of the proletariat' concept: Blanqui. Blanquism stood for dictatorship, didn't it? So Blanqui must have invented it. And since we have just learned that Marx used to be a "Blanquist," there can be no doubt where he got it from ...

The only trouble with this proposition is that, factually speaking, every word is false: the "dictatorship of the proletariat" cannot be found anywhere in Blanqui either as a term or an idea. But the lack of a single validating fact has stopped no one from making the standard claim that the dictatorship of the proletariat is "Blanquist" in origin.

G. D. H. Cole, for example, asserted that Blanqui "stated the doctrine of the dictatorship of the proletariat much more clearly than Marx ever did..." even though he knows of nowhere that Blanqui ever stated this "doctrine" at all (as his failure to annotate indicates).[18] Isaiah Berlin went even further: "The dictatorship of the proletariat was adumbrated by Babeuf in the last decade of the eighteenth century, and was explicitly [note: *explicitly*] developed in the nineteenth in different fashions by Weitling and Blanqui ...." No note, no facts.[19] In his well-known *Era of Tyrannies*, Halévy took a special tack—he merely asked questions:

> The Marxist doctrine of the dictatorship of the proletariat comes, does it not, in a straight line from Babeuf, the last survivor of Robespierrism? Was not Karl Marx, in Paris before 1848, very definitely influenced by Blanqui, who revived the theory of Babeuf?[20]

The answer is: no and no; but Halévy, you see, had not committed himself. Did Halévy know that Marx "in Paris before 1848" never met Blanqui, who furthermore was not in Paris but in prison? Never mind, the "Blanquist" spirit was hovering over the rooftops of Paris, tainting everything with "Blanquism" that came within spitting range.

Sombart likewise was too clever to commit himself: in unusually vulgar terms, he spoke of "that crazy notion, worthy only of a Blanqui, of the dictatorship of the proletariat." Lewis L. Lorwin was one of the few who purported to point to a definite locus in Blanqui, viz., his famous *Instructions pour une Prise d'Armes:* "According to this program the workers were to arm themselves, seize the government, disarm the bourgeoisie, and establish a proletarian dictatorship." But in this entire document (written moreover in 1868-1869, and circulated only in some manuscript copies) there was *no* mention of "proletarian dictatorship," term or idea; in fact, being explicitly military-technical in content, it never even approached the political questions involved, let alone the answer of dictatorship.[21]

Real authorities on Blanqui's writings have left no doubt about the facts. Alan Spitzer, the American authority on Blanqui, writes: "Blanqui had often been credited with coining the phrase, 'the dictatorship of the proletariat', but no one has ever been able to document his use of it upon any occasion."[22] The leading European authority is Maurice Dommanget, who has devoted several books to a minute examination of Blanqui's works, including his unpublished manuscripts. Besides, Dommanget is generally anxious to turn Blanqui into a proto-Marxist at any cost, and would be delighted to turn up even a microscopic piece of evidence to prove Blanqui's priority.* But Dommanget has to report that "dictatorship of the proletariat" is "a term that Blanqui does not use." Disappointed, he adds that Blanqui's "London friends" used the term "jointly with Marx" in 1850 (we will describe this usage in Chapter 12, locus 2)—but Marx had already used it previously. So not only does Dommanget know no use of the term by Blanqui, he also knows of none by any other Blanquist, other than the cases involving Marx which we will discuss.[23] It can be added: outside of the word 'dictatorship' itself, he clearly knows of no formulation by Blanqui that can be pummeled into the shape of 'dictatorship of the proletariat'.

The ideological drive behind the Blanqui myth has been explained, but such myths also need a starting point, after which they are copied from one work to another. The starting point in the present case may well have been R. W. Postgate's lively book of socialist historical sketches *Out of the Past* (1923), which contains the longest attempt I know of to make a case for the claim that Blanqui "was the first to formulate and act upon the theory of proletarian dictatorship."[24] Postgate's evidence dissolves on examination. His key statement is that he dates Marx's first use of the term at 1875 (*Critique of the Gotha Program*, locus 9), whereas "Blanqui's advocacy is to be dated in the 1860s." Neither statement is true. Marx's first use was in 1850; as for the occurrences of the term between 1850 and 1875, Postgate is ignorant of some and dismisses others on incomprehensible grounds that are of no interest now except to document his unreliability. As for Blanqui: Postgate's ascription of the term to him "in the 1860s" is simply an error. Here is his case:

> Where he [Blanqui] described this as the first duty of the revolution is uncertain. [In other words, Postgate doesn't know.] It is quoted as his in an *Histoire des Blanquistes* (Ch. Da Costa. 1912), between two other phrases which are easily traceable as his. But this author gives no authorities for his quotations, and I have not been able to trace it in the incomplete works of Blanqui which I have been able to search. Nevertheless, there is no reason to doubt Da Costa's good faith, nor can the

---

* For a note on the nature of Dommanget's tendentiousness, see Special Note D, Section 7.

2. Socialism and Dictatorship: The Beginning 37

words have been written much after 1870 (probably much earlier), in which case I imagine Blanqui's claim to have formulated first the most deadly point in the modern Bolshevik programme is established.[25]

The original claim about "the 1860s" fades out almost as soon as stated. But as a matter of fact Charles Da Costa's history *Les Blanquistes* (to give it its correct title) does not contain any statement answering Postgate's description. What it does contain (as we will report latter) is a statement by a group of Blanquist refugees from the Paris Commune, in London, using the term. Obviously it had to date from the 1870s. Undated in Da Costa—hence Postgate's vagueness perhaps—it was actually published in 1874. It is harder to explain, even as a mistake, Postgate's reference to something "between two other phrases." Perhaps this reflects the fact that the Blanquist statement of 1874 does indeed revolve around three phrases which give the document its structure: *we are atheists, we are communists, we are revolutionists*, proclaim the Blanquists, and they devote a section to each. The passage mentioning the dictatorship of the proletariat is in the third section. And it does not refer to Blanqui.

Postgate cites another Blanquist programmatic document from the same period, the brochure *Internationale et Révolution* (1872), which we will also not fail to describe later. While in any case the London Blanquist documents of this period have nothing to do with proving Blanqui's "priority," we will see, when we return to this material, that these London refugees had by this time taken the term from Marx, not vice-versa. Outside of Postgate there is no case for the Blanquist myth worth refuting.

But if Blanqui did not actually use the term 'dictatorship of the proletariat', isn't it true that he holds priority on the idea—for didn't he advocate *a* theory of dictatorship?

(1) He certainly did propose a dictatorship as the goal of revolutionary action, but without qualification it was the conception common to Jacobin-communism in the thirties and forties, derived from the Babouvists via Buonarroti—the conception of the Educational Dictatorship. Blanqui, who was not a theoretician and did not pretend otherwise, had no ideas on the subject of his own devising. (Postgate's passing reference to "Blanqui's claim" is another invention of his.) The only difference from the Babouvists is that the latter, remember, *rejected* the dictatorial solution insofar as it meant a one-man agency. By Blanqui's time, some such theory of "revolutionary dictatorship" was virtually standard in the milieu of the communist conspiratorial sects. There is not the slightest question of Blanqui's "priority" on this score either. When, for example, *L'Homme Libre*, a Blanquist organ of the thirties, called for "a dictatorial power with the mission of leading the revolutionary movement,"[26] it was frankly advocating, not even the dictatorship of the "revolutionary

movement," but rather the dictatorship of the leaders of the revolutionary movement.

(2) In Blanqui's view, the desired "revolutionary dictatorship" would not be "of the proletariat," in any sense of the last word. Blanqui made no hypocritical noises about implementing the rule of the masses—who, after all, would have to go through a long weaning process before their societal corruption could be burnt out. In the immediate sense, the operational sense, the dictatorship would be the rule of the conspiratorial band, just as it was for the Babouvists. When Blanqui attempted a larger view, he came up with a perspective which is clearly limned in a striking passage in his manuscripts:

> The bourgeoisie includes an elite minority ... it is the essence, the soul, the life of the Revolution .... Who has planted the flag of the proletariat? Who has rallied it after its defeats? Who leads the people to battle against the bourgeoisie?—The bourgeoisie itself. They will cease only after having led the Revolution to the victory of Equality. But what is the device on its banner? Democracy? No—the proletariat. For its soldiers are workers though the leaders are not.[27]

This was an honest statement of what a "working-class orientation" meant in the Jacobin-communist milieu: "*its soldiers are workers though the leaders are not.*" He formulated the same perspective in a passage of his *Critique Sociale:*

> Thousands of the élite live in conditions of extreme misery ... These *déclassés,* invisible agents of progress, are today the secret ferment which sustains the masses and prevents them from sinking to a condition of impotence. Tomorrow they will be the reserve force of the Revolution.[28]

This was the usual pre-Marx version of revolutionary dictatorship—the "dictatorship of the revolutionary gang." Of course, it was supposed to be a dictatorship on behalf of, or in the interest of, the People; and this too was an honestly held view, not an exercise in demagogy.

(3) Indeed, the term 'dictatorship of the *proletariat*' is irrelevant to an understanding of Blanqui. By 'proletarian' he meant virtually anyone except the small number of aristocrats and exploiting bourgeois, as Spitzer points out cogently.[29] This is what was behind Blanqui's famous reply to the court when asked his occupation: "Proletarian." He explained the term as "one of the thirty million Frenchmen who live by their labor." That population figure comprised eight-ninths of a people overwhelmingly petty-bourgeois in composition. Blanqui's heart beat for the oppressed working people, but he was no more ready than Buonarroti to turn the state over to them, comes the revolution.

Another dictatorship of which the Blanquists spoke often enough was the "dictatorship of Paris" over the country. Dommanget tells us quite clearly: "The plebeian dictatorship of which Blanqui conceived is the dictatorship of revolutionary Paris over the rest of France."[30] This concept was enough, by itself, to doom any Blanquist insurrection; it was alien to Marx and Engels. As it happened, it came up in their correspondence in 1869, when the Blanquist Gustave Tridon published his brochure *Gironde et Girondins*. "Confused," thought Engels, especially on the issue of centralization and decentralization. "Comical is the conception that the dictatorship of Paris over France, on which the first revolution [of 1789+] came to grief, could once again be carried out without ado and with some different result."[31] The troubles of the Paris Commune two years later demonstrated the principle again. In his notes preparing for the writing of his *Civil War in France*, Marx included a clipping from the Commune's *Journal Officiel* for April 1 which strongly renounced Parisian hegemony over the country and championed the aim of communal self-government and local independent autonomy.[32] This was echoed in Chapter 3 of Marx's address, with even greater emphasis and greater detail.[33]

To ascribe the "dictatorship of the proletariat" conception to Blanqui is worse than a mistake: it is an irrelevancy. We will return to Blanqui and Blanquism in Chapter 9.

4. UTOPIANS AND DICTATORS

The Babouvists, as the first socialist movement in history, hold the patent on many aspects of the socialist enterprise, but they were not in the least peculiar in linking Socialism from Above with a form of the Educational Dictatorship. Among all sorts of socialists/communists it was common—virtually standard—to believe that "Every new regime needs the nest of dictatorship in order to be hatched." (This aphorism came in 1848 from Emile de Girardin, a proto-Hearst who was about as socialistic as his successor in his radical-demagogue days.)[34]

The innovators of Utopian socialism were all inventors of Socialisms from Above, by the very nature of their approach. Saint-Simon was prolific in schemes for dictatorial regimes in which some man of power would impose the latest Saint-Simonian plan upon a happy people. If he did not use the word 'dictatorship' (I don't know) the fact is of purely lexicographical interest. Wilheim Weitling, the pioneer of early German utopian communism, was outspokenly for the dictatorship of a "messiah," whose name and address needed little divination. In his best-known work, *Guarantees of Harmony and Freedom* (1842), he testified to the prevalence of the notion of dictatorship among the communists of the time:

Communists are still pretty undecided about the choice of their form of government. A large part of those in France incline to a dictatorship, because they well know that the sovereignty of the people, as understood by republicans and politicians, is not suited for the period of transition from the old to a completely new organization. Owen, the chief of the English communists, would have the performance of specific duties allotted to men according to age, and the chief leaders of a government would be the oldest members of it. All socialists with the exception of the followers of Fourier, to whom all forms of government are the same, are agreed that the form of government which is called the sovereignty of the people is a very unsuitable, and even dangerous, sheet anchor for the young principle of communism about to be realized.[35]

We will see in Chapter 3 that Weitling was consistent: back in Germany during the 1848 revolution, he lost no time in proposing a dictatorship quite openly.

There were other, lesser figures who were just as frank: for example, "that communist ex-priest Pillot—later to be found in the ranks of Blanqui's followers—who, a few years before 1848, ended one of his books with the threat that if mankind did not want communism it would be forced to accept it, just as the inmates of an insane asylum had to take shower baths whether they wanted them or not."[36] We may remark at this point that the insane-asylum analogy was not Pillot's eccentricity. That very sensible man Robert Owen wrote that, such was the irrationality of society, the "speediest mode" to remedy things "will be to govern or treat all society as the most advanced physicians govern and treat their patients in the best arranged lunatic hospitals," naturally with all "forbearance and kindness."[37] This is not essentially different from the Babouvist view of the consequences of societal corruption. But it is doubtful whether Pillot or Owen or their like would identify this benevolent approach with the word 'dictatorship', which would be considered at all only by radicals concerned with the question of a "transitional" revolutionary regime.

The Saint-Simonian tendency led by Barthélemy Prosper Enfantin was not one of the socialistic groups intensely concerned with the "transitional" question; and as far as I know, the word 'dictatorship' seldom cropped up in their literature. (Their own terms for their Maximum Leader tended to 'pope' and 'messiah'.) But right after the "July Revolution" of 1830 which brought Louis Philippe to the throne, Bazard, then still head of the sect, was swept along to the Hotel de Ville by Enfantin, and there proposed to the liberal leader Lafayette that he "take the dictatorship" and thus make it possible to clean up the whole mess. Later, after the October 1832 trial of Enfantin and Olinde Rodrigues on trumped-up swindling charges, an unsigned article in the group's press closed with the following thought: granting that a judicial

2. Socialism and Dictatorship: The Beginning 41

system is necessary for society in order to oversee morality and ferret out evil, still–
But who today can lay claim to this permanent dictatorship?
This "dictatorship" was the judicial system itself. The link in meaning with the old *dictatura* had indeed become tenuous.[38]

Among the French utopians of the period, easily the most political of the groupings was that organized and led by Etienne Cabet. The Cabetist, or "Icarian," tendency called itself communist, since alone among the utopians it stood for a thorough sort of communal ownership of production, and it was also distinctive in orienting itself toward a working-class public. Cabet openly advocated a "dictatorship" as his proposal for a transitional regime.

Cabet's dictatorship was set forth right in the pages of his basic text, the utopian novel *Voyage en Icarie* (1840). Here the whole grand social goal is implemented by a dictator, clearly so called. He succeeds a "tyrant." "Happily, the dictator elected by the people, the good and courageous Icar, turned out to be the best of men!" As dictator, Icar proposes the Community System to his fellow citizens of Icaria. The Icarian assembly establishes festivals to commemorate the victory of the dictator over the tyrant, and the third annual fête is "that of the dictatorship." There is a long "historical" section glorifying Icar's work as dictator. At the festival of the dictatorship, a splendid agit-prop spectacle is organized on the style of Hitler's Nuremberg circuses. The grateful masses cry, "Icar the dictator!" over and over. We are triumphantly told that every detail of the show has been prescribed by law. How fortunate the Icarians were "to find a dictator who sincerely *wished* their liberty and prosperity"! "Behold Washington, the Dictator and American Icar!"

The statement that Icar was "elected" seems to be an imprecision, for the election apparently takes place by acclamation in a paroxysm of joy. The dictator issues the plan for the election of a National Assembly, and everything naturally is adopted unanimously. The plan calls for a "transitional period" of fifty years. As promised, Icar lays down the dictatorship when the Assembly is convened, but resumes it to put down a counterrevolutionary coalition. However, he refuses to be named dictator for life: "nevertheless he was the Soul, the Genius, and in reality the Dictator of the Republic." The Community System is finally voted in unanimously, which is better than Stalin was ever able to do.[39]

In his own name Cabet discusses the period of the Jacobin "dictatorship" in the French Revolution: "During this terrible dictatorship" the National Convention "pushed Democracy to the furthest limits of exaltation and enthusiasm." Don't expect me, he tells the reader, to "condemn *en masse* the Democracy, the Convention and its terrible Dictatorship."[40] It was the Democracy that exercised the dictatorship: understand this statement and you understand some of the convolutions of the term.

Cabet had written about his view a year before publication of the novel. In a note intended for circulation among colleagues, he avowed that the "patriot party" should create a shadow government prepared to take dictatorial power in case of revolution. Once the novel was published, he was committed to the "dictatorship" talk; and indeed in 1841, when an associate, Richard Lahautière, split with Cabet in the direction of a religio-mystic "communism" influenced by Pierre Leroux, Lahautière's rival journal jibed at Cabet's "dictatorial role." But later in the 1840s Cabet, feeling the pressure of "practical politics," moved toward milder language. This gave rise to internal dissension in Lyons, where the Icarian movement reached a high point in 1843-1844. The memoirs of Sébastien Commissaire report that one faction wanted to establish the Icarian society "by violence," while Cabet's group "put all their hope in pacific propaganda." The former argued à la Buonarroti that a populace miseducated by this society could not be won by propaganda; hence a revolution was necessary "to establish a dictatorship in the interests of the masses in place of a dictatorship in the interest of a small number, a family, or a single person." No doubt these leftists cited Icar.[41]

The sequel for Cabet will be seen in Chapter 8.

5. DÉZAMY, MORRISON, AND YOUNG ENGELS

To the left of Cabet, concern with the "transitional regime" problem was more general, and no doubt there was more talk of dictatorship, as the solution or one of the solutions, than I have been able to turn up. Théodore Dézamy—who, by the way, was read with great interest by the young Marx when he was just starting to study communist literature—split with Cabet on political grounds. In one of his propaganda pamphlets, Dézamy praised unity, and asked:

> But what is unity? How realize this principle? Here a mass of divergences and disagreements arise. According to some, unity is the absolute concentration of all the political and social powers in the hands of a single man, a Monarch; others see legitimate unity only in a republican dictatorship, either in the hands of a committee of public safety, or in those of a national convention; some praise the excellence of a theocratic power, organized hierarchically—of Papism, for example.

Dézamy viewed the Saint-Simonians and the Cabetists as examples of the last type; but he himself did not assume responsibility for the second. He referred hostilely to "Robespierre's pontificate, protected by the frightful laws of Prairial."[42] It would be useful if we had similar surveys of the scene by other participants.

2. Socialism and Dictatorship: The Beginning   43

But we must not give the impression that the word 'dictatorship' as such was linked only to Socialisms from Above. As before, the term was versatile. If the one-man meaning was uppermost, the consequence was of course an approach to what sounds like the modern usage, though it was not. But if the notion of *extralegal coercion*—which we have already encountered—was uppermost, then the word could tie up with really popular movements.

Take James Morrison, whose *Pioneer* was one of the best organs of Owenite cooperativism, militant trade-unionism, and profeminist agitation for women's rights and equality—all in the 1830s. He was a mild socialist, essentially reformist, and inclined to substitute trade-unionism for revolutionary politics (which has given him something of a "syndicalist" hue). In a typical editorial, Morrison stressed the need for a "general association of the people" to train them in conducting affairs. He continued:

> The growing power and growing intelligence of trades unions, when properly managed, will draw into its vortex all the commercial interests of the country, and, in so doing, it will become, by its own self-acquired importance, a most influential, we might almost say dictatorial part of the body politic. When this happens we have gained all that we want; we have gained universal suffrage....

and he looked forward to a government headed by a House of Trades instead of the House of Commons.[43] It should not be thought that Morrison was a Jacobin or "Blanquist" fire-eater; unlike Owen, with whom he eventually had to part ways, he was a thorough democrat. Well-educated, he took 'dictatorial' to mean *possessed of ruling power beyond the normal forms of government.*

As for Marx and Engels in the years before 1848, use of the word 'dictatorship' was almost nonexistent and, in a couple of cases where it shows up after a fashion, not remotely favorable. One occurrence was in an article written by Engels in 1844, before he had absorbed anything from Marx and during the short interval when he tended to echo Moses Hess's anarchoid language. Instead of taking the space for the whole passage, which has to be read to see what the article is saying, I cite only a few lines:

> Pure monarchy provokes terror—one thinks of Oriental and Roman despotism. Pure aristocracy is no less frightening... Democracy is more fearsome than either; Marius and Sulla, Cromwell and Robespierre, the bloody heads of two kings, the proscription lists and dictatorship speak loudly enough of the "horrors" of democracy.[44]

This mishmash concludes with the view that it is "the state itself" that is "the cause of all these inhumanities and is itself inhuman." But mishmash comes in all varieties, and this variety—we note with interest—mixes up "democracy" and "dictatorship" into one indistinguishable stew.

The second occurrence was in the unpublished manuscript of the *German*

Ideology—in a section very likely written by Engels—but it is quite unenlightening: it occurs in a passage quoted from someone else.[45]

While, as we have seen, the term 'dictatorship' was certainly around in the thirties and forties, its almost complete nonuse by Marx or Engels in this period contrasts sharply with their attention to it after 1848. Something must have happened ...

3 DICTATORSHIP IN 1848

Something *did* happen—in France in 1848. It was the establishment of the first modern dictatorship, under General Eugène Cavaignac. Before taking this up, however, a detail should be filled in.

By this time, the word 'dictatorship' itself was well known and unhesitatingly used. Cabetists had used it for some time; even more so had the communist and left-republican clubs and secret societies. If further evidence is needed, it is the fact that the pinkest socialist in France was willing to use it.

1. EVEN LOUIS BLANC...

Louis Blanc has *gone* down in history as one of the mildest of social-democrats, and above all a democratic socialist. In fact, his tendency was among the first to use that label. By 1848 he was famous for his brochure *The Organization of Labor* and as a leader of the left wing of the Republican party.

Revolutions have a habit of concretizing a question that previously appears to be one of fanciful theory: the nature of *transitional* regimes, the provisional-revolutionary governments of the day after the revolution. As we have seen, it is the question of the transitional regime that most insistently brings up the term 'dictatorship'. It did even for Louis Blanc, who was a serious politician.

The question was raised for Blanc by the government's decision in favor of early elections to the National Constituent Assembly, set for April 23, 1848. The large majority of all leftists, from any shade of pink to red, were for some postponement of the elections, to allow a little more time to educate the people about the issues. After all, the very possibility of being heard by the people had opened up only the day before yesterday: the mass of people, particularly the peasants and the provinces, were still blanketed by the antidemocratic propaganda of royalists and priests.

Blanc was for postponement of the elections. He thought of it as meaning that the Provisional Government set itself up as a "dictatorial authority"—and he advocated this. The Provisional Government (he wrote in a book ten years later) should "regard themselves as dictators appointed by a revolution which had become inevitable and which was under no obligation to seek the sanction of universal suffrage until after having accomplished all the good which the moment required."[1]

His conclusions under the pressure of the situation went beyond postponement. What he really sought, we are told by his biographer Leo Loubère, was "ministerial power for himself within a pliable, provisional dictatorship of a committee of public safety."[2] Not that Loubère denounces him for this peccadillo: on the contrary, he defends Blanc on the ground of his "loathing of terrorism."*

On April 16, when Blanc met with the governing Council, he again argued for postponement of the national election:

> To the numerous objections raised he admitted he wanted a dictatorship, albeit one of progress, not of reaction. He averred that no one had more respect for popular sovereignty than himself; what he dreaded was its falsification.[4]

Blanc's attitude on postponement was more extreme than that of the leftist and workers' clubs. The latter, Blanc complained, proposed a postponement of only one month, but Blanc felt this was not long enough for the provinces to overcome their long miseducation.[5] No, he insisted: the elections should be deferred "to the latest possible date."[6]

Moreover, the dictatorship that Blanc desired had deeper roots in the Jacobin tradition: he was very clear that he wanted the dictatorship of Paris over the country. Loubère gives his point of view:

> As in 1793, the struggle between rural and urban France must be resolved by the dictatorship of the capital, by the "dictatorship of progress."

The enlightened Paris minority had the right to speak and act for all France. To objectors Blanc replied that "the whole of France coming to Paris, Paris is to the provinces what the sea is to the rivers which flow into it. Through Paris it is France which speaks," and so on.[7] What he emphasized was "the numerical superiority of the ignorant people of the countryside over the enlightened people of the cities," a difference due to a half-century of mind-dulling state "corruption."[8]

---

* Loubère is defending Blanc against *Marx*, who, he says, was critical of the "little sultan" "for not setting up a personal dictatorship."[3] No note, no fact, in this book peppered with erudite reference notes. It is simply a falsifiction. One gathers that if Marx wanted him to impose a *personal* dictatorship, he was indeed a democratic paladin in wishing merely the "dictatorship of a committee of public safety."

3. Dictatorship in 1848   47

Loubère concedes that Blanc was here following a "new direction," namely, the rule of a minority. Our prototypical social-democrat was not advocating the dictatorship of the majority of the people in any sense. The Jacobin-communist perspective of Educational Dictatorship was accepted well to the right of Blanqui or Barbès, if only in somewhat attenuated form. Even if it was called the "dictatorship of progress," or if one orated, with the journalist Taxile Delord, that "the revolution of 1848 will govern by the dictatorship of liberty."[9]

The only member of the Provisional Government who agreed with Blanc on this question was a mechanic, one Albert, the governing Council's window-dressing worker-member, who had been imposed on the politicians by the vast demonstration at the Tuileries by the masses of workers who had just toppled the monarchy. (Blanc wrote of that occasion that "it was with moist eyes that I inscribed these words, 'Albert, worker,' on the list of future dictators"—i.e., the list of Provisional Government members.[10]) On the other hand, his fiercest opponent in the government was Lamartine, at whom he let fly a wicked shaft, speaking of the poet's short day of wide popularity at the outset of the republic: "He went to bed thinking he had France at his feet, he went to sleep intoxicated with himself, he dreamed of dictatorship, he awoke—he was alone."[11] We see that for Blanc there was no need of a special comment on the fact that both the extreme left and the extreme right of the Provisional Government "dreamed [or at least thought] of dictatorship."

Lamartine, who was against postponing the elections since he wanted to assure an elected assembly of the right political hue, publicly used the term 'dictatorship' not for what he dreamed about but for what he was actually doing. The Provisional Government, after all, had not been the product of the ballot box, hence in Lamartine's language it was a dictatorship. Facing a delegation from Blanqui's club asking for postponement, he righteously declared that the government had to give its power back to the nation. The *government, he* said, should not prolong, "not even for a minute, the form of dictatorship circumstances compelled us to enter upon."[12]

There was somebody else around at this time who was a little outside this right/left dichotomous line. Louis Blanc devoted a passage in his 1850 book to defending himself against the charge that he had in *fact failed* to establish his "dictatorial authority" when the gigantic mass demonstration of March 17 gave him a chance to do so; he should have utilized the imposing power of the masses to overthrow the government majority ... This charge, he tells us, came from the book *Confessions d'un Révolutionnaire* by the "anarchist" Proudhon. (We will meet this "libertarian" again in the next chapter, but at the moment we are concerned with that other whited sepulchre, Louis Blanc.)

Blanc's reply to Proudhon went this way: he, Blanc, *would* have been in favor of taking over the government if he could have convinced himself that

48   Part I: Dictatorship: Its Meaning in 1850

such action would have "saved the Republic" without "everything going up in flames."¹³ In other words, he would have obligingly made a revolution if it didn't disturb anyone unduly. But the fact that the discussion was about a dictatorial putsch did not seem to disturb either the social-democrat or the anarchist.

We now turn to what happened when this advocate of a dictatorship was confronted by a real dictatorship.

2. THE CAVAIGNAC DICTATORSHIP

The statement that Cavaignac wielded the first modern dictatorship has to be hedged with reservations, we will see, but it will serve to make a distinction. The word 'dictatorship' can be found before 1848 in private and public loci, and among the public ones there are both prominent and obscure sources; but there has as yet been no occurrence of the term in the political mainstream. When Spencer opined that the word had taken a turn after the First World War,[14] he was undoubtedly thinking of the fact that something called a fascist dictatorship burst upon world consciousness. Now in 1848, for the first time, we have a dictatorship that, as it were, made the headlines in Europe and America.

The dictatorship of General Cavaignac was the French bourgeoisie's response to the greatest workers' insurrection that had taken place up to that time: the rising of the Paris working classes of June 23-26. Agitated stirrings among the workers were becoming serious by June 19, when the government established by the February Revolution announced the impending dissolution of the National Workshops. As a make-work project (dressed up as a "socialistic" implementation of Louis Blanc's system of "Organization of Labor"), the National Workshops stood between some tens of thousands of workers and starvation. On the morning of June 22 there was a demonstration of several hundred workers before the seat of the Executive Commission, which wielded the powers of government conferred by the National Assembly. The same day the government published a decree giving young workers the option of enlisting in the army or being dismissed. Around noon, Minister of War Cavaignac put the army in Paris on a state of alert. There were scattered demonstrations and a mass meeting in the evening. The insurrection broke out early the next day, June 23, when thousands of demonstrating workers were challenged by troops.

The leading group of Republican deputies decided that the Executive Commission was incapable of handling the situation, looked around for a

Man on Horseback, and found him immediately in the Republican general who had shown he could keep the French military heel on Algeria. General Louis Eugène Cavaignac had come from Algeria, to become minister of war, only on May 17. He was available.

Cavaignac was offered the dictatorship *before* the insurrection broke out, on the 22nd. Some historians dispute the view—expressed among others by Marx[15]—that the government either provoked or smoothed the way for the cataclysm in order to administer a fatal blow to working-class pressure on the regime, which was becoming unbearable from the bourgeoisie's standpoint.* The slogan was "*Il faut en finir!*" Be that as it may, there is no question but that the leading Republicans, who had enough political clout to bring down the Executive Commission, made no effort on June 22 to head off an insurrection, but instead directed their energies to instituting the dictatorship that would crush it in blood.

On the morning of the 22nd, the Republican group agreed that the Executive Commission had to be replaced by "a more vigorous hand" in order to get "action." Garnier-Pagès, government leader and historian, related that some of these,

> enamored of the traditions of the past, believed in the necessity of an energetic dictatorship to save the Republic, and felt no repugnance in resorting to a sword that was prompt to defend and to strike if need be.[17]

One of them picked up that morning's issue of *La Presse,* and read to his colleagues a piece by publisher-editor Girardin (the proto-Hearst) that was going the rounds of the city. It represented two government leaders in conversation:

> *Short dialogue:* Things have to start going even worse. — Now, why? — Because we now have only one way to hold on to the power that is slipping from our hands. — What way? — It's by making General Cavaignac's dictatorship necessary...[18]

Girardin had divined exactly what they were up to. The group assigned three

---

* You can feel this standpoint in the words of a French historian, who explained that the *government* forces wanted "to defend a society threatened at its base by anarchical doctrines, and to end the insupportable dictatorship which the perpetual insurrection of the Paris workers made possible over the political life of the country."[16] Of the "perpetual" insurrections that the workers had made, the last *one* had been the February revolt which put into *office* the very forces who were now chafing at the working classes' influence over political life, which belonged exclusively to the bourgeoisie, in their view. The historian, writing a century later, uses 'dictatorship' with the same irritation at extralegal coercion which motivated his brothers in 1848.

colleagues to feel out Cavaignac, who immediately agreed provided he was given a free hand—not an unreasonable request from a prospective dictator. A monarchist spokesman also assured Cavaignac of support.[19]

Next morning: the insurrection. The cannon were booming when good citizens awoke. On this June 23 Cavaignac was endowed by the Assembly with the unified military command of all armed forces in Paris. In the morning, in a conversation with the president of the Assembly, Cavaignac insisted on the proclamation of a state of siege.[20] On the 24th, the dictatorship was rammed through the National Assembly, in an interesting scene.

The Republican deputy Pascal Duprat, a member of the executive board of the social-democratic organ *La Réforme*, made the proposal: "Paris is placed in a state of siege; all powers are concentrated in the hands of General Cavaignac."

The Nièvre deputy Dupin immediately protested: "The Assembly does not intend to confer a dictatorship; it does not intend to give up its rights; it intends to delegate only the executive power." Duprat conceded the amending of "powers" to "executive powers," while the assembled statesmen were already yelling "Vote! Vote!" Deputy Larabit supported the delegation of powers but declared: "I oppose the state of siege; I oppose the dictatorship; the laws are sufficient... We do not have to suspend the laws." In answer, the statesmen yelled "Vote! Vote!" Deputy Nachet took the tribune: "I rise to protest with all my strength against the declaration of a state of siege over Paris." He appealed to the memory of 1832 when the Republican deputies had fought against the establishment of a state of siege by the monarchists. At this point Jules Bastide, cabinet member and editor of *Le National*, sought to stampede the vote by yelling that the insurrection was on the point of overrunning the Hôtel de Ville (a warning which he had just invented). Deputy Larabit tried to speak again; there was a tumult as the assembled defenders of Law and Order rushed to prevent him from occupying the tribune. In the tumult, the president declared a *clôture*. "What!" cried poor Larabit, as he quit the tribune, "so one doesn't have the right to express his opinions!" Not one man rose to explain why a state of siege was necessary to defend the Hôtel de Ville when all military power was already concentrated in the hands of the republican general.

The state of siege was voted by "an immense majority" in an atmosphere of hooligan intimidation, calculated to prevent all but the lionhearted from standing up for the laws of France. Only after the vote could deputy Germain Sarrut be heard to exclaim: "In the name of the memory of 1832, we protest against the state of siege"—while cries of "Order!" drowned him out. There were continued cries of protest against the state of siege—for example, by deputy Charles Lagrange. As Lagrange protested, the president suspended the session to shut opposition off.[21]

As a historian has said: "the fear that gripped the upper classes was like that in Rome at the invasion of the barbarians."[22]

3. CAVAIGNAC AS PRELUDE

Cavaignac's operation in crushing the insurrection is not our subject. There has been much controversy about it; but if we give Cavaignac the benefit of all doubts, there is no doubt that his policy was to treat the revolt like a foreign foe, a purely military strategy. If he made no move to prevent the building of massive barricades, it was so that his own centralized operations could destroy it all equally massively—with a consequent maximum of slaughter and destruction.

Just as the scenario had called on June 24 for a National Assembly show in which the parliamentarians had pushed the dictatorship on a reluctant general—who had arranged for the show two days before—so too on June 26, the insurrection sputtering out, the dictator came before the Assembly to strike a republican pose and lay his dictatorial powers at their feet. There are still plenty of historical accounts that exhibit this charming picture.[23] The truth was that Cavaignac merely wanted to be reinvested with the dictatorship— that is, the state of siege and delegation of powers—by a *normal* act of the Assembly, without resting on the authority of the June 24 day of hysteria. He virtually told them *so* on June 26 when he came before the deputies:

> He was confident [a historian relates] that the Assembly would retain him in power, but he wanted to receive a new vote of confidence and to change the legal basis of his authority, so that it would derive "not from the kind of proclamation by the Assembly on June 24, but following mature deliberation."[24]

On June 28 this scenario was acted out: the dictator went through the motions of "laying down his powers," and the deputies made not the least pretence of mature deliberation in scrambling to give them back. Cavaignac had demanded that the state of siege was to stand indefinitely, and this was done.

For weeks the "dictatorship of the saber" rounded up thousands of prisoners *after* the insurrection had been controlled; there were courts martial of alleged leaders; transportation without trial to overseas penal colonies; army patrols in the working-class areas making arbitrary searches, arrests, and confiscations, as the victorious soldatesca baited the defeated enemy:

> Only four or five hundred of the rebels appear to have perished on the barricades, but more than three thousand were massacred by the soldiers of the *Garde Mobile* and the regular army after the fighting was over.[25]

The dictatorship closed down all workers' clubs, sealed up eleven newspaper presses; jailed even Girardin until July 5, for he had committed the crime of telling the truth for once; fifty thousand troops were concentrated around the capital. Leftists like Louis Blanc who had pusillanimously supported the suppression of the insurrection were jailed and hounded into exile.

While the good Republicans of the National Assembly had already resolved to shut down the National Workshops in some diplomatic (i.e., cowardly) fashion, Cavaignac showed what dictatorships are good for: he dissolved the whole institution with a wave of his saber. A whole series of social reforms, inaugurated after the February Revolution, led by the ten-hour day, were killed by the Assembly, shielded by the good right arm of the Republican savior of Law and Order. In July and August the government put through a number of laws which seriously undercut the freedoms of press and assembly won in February by the same working-class fighters who had just been cut down by the beneficiaries. By this time, still, no one had explained why a state of siege was necessary; but by this time perhaps it was the question that was unnecessary.[26]

To do justice to Cavaignac, it must be made clear that he had no intention of exercising a permanent dictatorship. A permanent dictatorship was a contradiction in terms, anyway, for anyone who still felt the link with the Roman *dictatura*. Cavaignac sometimes used 'dictatorship' to stand for the "permanent" meaning only, or at least he sounded that way. When Bastide urged him to assume full dictatorial powers and use them to strike against the reaction *on the right*, the general remembered that he had principles. "It's a coup d'état that you ask!" he exclaimed. "A dictatorship! You shouldn't dream of it."[27]

By July, when some deputies were getting uneasy especially about the continued suppression of the press, Cavaignac conceded that "the state of siege is in fact a terrible weapon in the hands of the power that wields it," but pleaded the "rectitude of my intentions." (The Babouvist advocates of dictatorship had likewise argued that the dictator's "virtue" was the shield of liberty.) The Assembly agreed to Cavaignac's insistence on indefinite maintenance of the state of siege. Victor Hugo, a deputy, protested against it and hinted that Cavaignac sought dictatorship (meaning, presumably, *permanent* dictatorship). The general denied that he had really wielded a dictatorship—for it had never officially received this name—but added: "If there was a dictatorship, I only recall with what patriotic zeal I came to lay it down before the Assembly."[28] Since we know this reply was mere demagogy, we can see how the virtuous general of the republic had come to be replaced by the sinuous politician.

Even when the Assembly faced the agenda of discussing and adopting the Constitution of the republic, Cavaignac insisted on continuing the state of siege. In a reminiscence of a previous revolution, he argued that it was "the law of public safety," a mild counterpart of the Terror. Instead of proscribing men, he proscribed ideas, political ideas . .[29] Yet the Assembly voted to maintain the state of siege even while debating the Constitution. When the state of siege actually ended on October 19, it is likely that Cavaignac yielded to pressure. To do him justice again, he was not really the stuff real dictators are made of; his rigidity was brittle.

Another way of doing justice to Cavaignac is to make clear that he conceived of his extended powers as police power, not legislative power. He did not in fact try to decree any new laws. In this he continued the tradition of the Roman *dictatura*.

We see, then, why serious qualifications have to be attached to the claim that Cavaignac's was the first modern dictatorship. It would be better to say, perhaps, that it was the prelude to the modern history of dictatorship. It made dictatorship a European institution, even if it was as different from what dictatorships were going to become as it itself was from the Roman variety. It provided the basis, first, for the state-of-siege provision put into the French Constitution of November 4, 1848, as Article 106, which in turn spawned the law of August 9, 1849, still in force in the twentieth century as the fundamental law of "constitutional dictatorship" in France.[30] It provided the model, next, for the martial-law institutions established in Berlin and Vienna later in the year. And it cleared the way for Bonaparte's dictatorship, which had a different label altogether.

In his last year of life, Engels referred to "dictatorship" as the Bismarck government's likely response to continued victories by the Social-Democratic movement within the legal framework. *Gentlemen*! advised Engels, *you must face the music: "breach of the constitution, dictatorship, return to absolutism . . . !*"[31] Politically this was a point he had made before: it is better if the ruling class makes the first move to break through this legality which is killing it. Terminologically Engels was thinking of the recourse to dictatorship against revolution that had been Cavaignac's contribution to history.

4. WEITLING AND DICTATORSHIP

For another leftist who openly advocated a dictatorship in 1848 we go to Germany, to meet Wilhelm Weitling again. We have already seen that his frank proposal of a messianic dictatorship was his regular stock-in-trade, no conjunctural aberration.[32] On the outbreak of the 1848 revolution, Weitling, who had been living in the United States since the end of 1846, hied himself to Berlin, where he made unsuccessful attempts to establish a paper. In the last week of June, he turned up in Cologne, where Marx's *Neue Rheinische Zeitung* group was the leading force on the left.

Meeting Hermann Becker, he sought permission to address the Democratic Association in order to explain his system of ideas. Becker informed him that no permission was necessary; the speakers' platform was freely open to all.

Still [Becker related] I introduced him to Executive members, and on June 30 [error for July 21] he explained his views. Near the meeting hall the Association had a sort of writing room; here Marx sought me out and asked: "Don't we have enough of this Gottschalk-type nonsense, do you have to bring Weitling up too?"[33]

Weitling's particular brand of nonsense on this occasion included a call for a dictatorship: he argued that the vital task of the revolution was the establishment of a dictatorial Provisional Government consisting of a limited number of "very keen people."[34] Marx at first announced he would reply; then changed his mind, postponed the answer, left the hall, and avoided a personal discussion with Weitling. He gave his response at the August 4 meeting.

The only report we have of Marx's speech comes not from his own paper but from the moderate-Democratic organ in Cologne, *Der Wachter am Rhein*, in an obviously skimpy and unreliable account. The clearest thing about it is that Marx directly confronted Weitling's proposal for a dictatorship and rejected it. As we will see, there were dictatorships and dictatorships, for Marx as for others, but there was no mistaking the nature of Weitling's dictatorial ambitions. Marx's "pithy and fairly long speech" apparently focused on the relation of social and political development to revolution "on the grounds of the historical development of the revolutions that have taken place during the last few centuries." (Truly a fit subject for a pithy speech!)

> As for the dictatorship proposed by Weitling as the most desirable constitutional form, Marx holds it on similar grounds to be impractical and quite impossible, since power cannot be established from a single class; the desire to carry through a system involving a single head in the dictatorship deserves to be called nonsense. On the contrary, the governmental power, like the Provisional Government of Paris, must be composed of the most heterogeneous elements, which then through an exchange of ideas have to agree on the most suitable kind of administration.[35]

What this reflected, in a mixed-up fashion, was Marx's view, reiterated in his paper at this time, that political power in Germany should be taken by the coalition of revolutionary classes called the Democracy (petty-bourgeoisie and peasantry led by the proletariat).[36] What Marx was actually writing about dictatorship in this connection will be the subject of the next chapter.

About a year later, Weitling returned to New York, where he published the

3. *Dictatorship in 1848* 55

weekly *Republik der Arbeiter* (1850-1855) and ran the "Communia" colony in Iowa as absentee dictator. As dissension shook the colony, Weitling took over complete dictatorial control in line with his principled commitment to "the necessity of complete submission to the single, higher will."[37] When the Prussian government executed its frameup trial of the Cologne Communists (October-November 1852) Weitling's paper retailed slanders about the Communists on trial, and Marx was privately infuriated. Sending a clipping from Weitling's organ to Engels, Marx added: "you see the venom of this king of the tailors and dictator of the 'Communia' colony over the Cologne Communist trial and the party of Marx & Co."[38] The "king of the tailors" was John of Leyden, the dictator of the famous Anabaptist community of Minister.

To wind up the case of Weitling, we can add the information that he was broadminded enough to advocate dictatorship by a "single, higher will" other than his own, namely, that of Napoleon III, "heir of Louis Blanc." Bonaparte, he thought, could provide a solid foundation for "communism" in five years; and even after his hero donned the imperial crown, he clung to the hope that the Empire would prepare the road for communism, for did not the Emperor have the workers' interests at heart? Above all, he chortled over Bonaparte's destruction of parliamentarism and "the humbug of democracy"—for "It will be easier, by revolution, to get rid of one tyrant than nine hundred" (that is, nine hundred parliamentary "talkers"). This clever nonsense has been standard among "revolutionary" cretins for a very long time. "As late as March, 1855," relates his biographer, Weitling "still hoped for a new European revolution led by a dictator who would abolish private property . . . and transform his regime into a popular government . . . ."[39]

This type of socialism never had to be repressed by the bad capitalists: it obligingly cut its own throat.

5. BAKUNIN AND DICTATORSHIP IN 1848

Of the advocates of dictatorship on the left, one of the most virulent cases was Michael Bakunin. To be sure, the myth of Bakunin's "libertarian" yearning for Freedom still marches across acres of paper, but let us leave it aside and confine ourselves to facts. In the period with which we are presently concerned, Bakunin was not yet an anarchist—he donned that ideological costume in time for his takeover drive in the International almost two decades later. In 1848 Bakunin was a revolutionary Pan-Slavist agitator with an amorphously antibourgeois set of ideas.

Later he was going to lay out his plan for an anarchist "secret dictatorship," centralized in the hands of one all-powerful dictator, in considerable detail. But most of what we know about the stage he had reached in 1848 comes from one of the most interesting documents he penned.

This is the long "Confesssion" written by Bakunin at the czar's behest, in the Peter-and-Paul Fortress in 1851. When its text was first published in 1921 (after excerpts in 1919), attention was fixed on a secondary aspect: the tone of belly-crawling before the czar that permeated this production by our hero. This reaction was understandable: many a Russian revolutionary had staunchly held up in czarist prisons under conditions of suffering such as Bakunin was *not* subjected to, and did not break. Of course, this cringing tone was assumed, but it is well established that the idea-content of the "Confession" was by and large a reliable statement of views and as accurate an account of events as Bakunin would have written if free.[40] The fact that the "Confession" belongs to his preanarchist period means little, since his later anarchism was largely an ideological superstructure added to his long-held conception of revolution.

Bakunin's views on dictatorship were set forth mainly in two passages of the "Confession." The first gave his thinking about a revolution in Russia. He explained that he rejected a "parliamentary republic," "representative rule, constitutional forms," etc.

> I thought that in Russia more than anywhere else a strong dictatorial government that would be exclusively concerned with elevating and educating the popular masses would be necessary; a government free in the direction it takes and in its spirit, but without parliamentary forms; with the printing of books free in content but without the freedom of printing...

This elocutionary invocation of Freedom to mask the repression of "printing" was a maiden effort; he got better at it.

> I told myself that the whole difference between such a dictatorship and a monarchical government would consist in this, that the former, because of the spirit in which it is established, must strive to make its existence unnecessary as soon as possible.... What there would be after the dictatorship I did not know, and I thought that no one could now foresee this. And who would be the dictator?[41]

He protested that he had no personal ambition. He may very well have believed it at the moment, since fantasists like Bakunin cannot easily be dishonest—they are too ready to believe their own tales. Anyway, in this document he had another dictator to propose: the czar. Throughout his life he appealed to one or another despot to impose the revolution from above; in the "Confession" he appealed to Nicholas I to put himself at the head of a revolutionary Pan-Slav movement, under the "Russian eagle" and "against

3. Dictatorship in 1848   57

the hated Germans," as the "savior" of Europe. (The czar wrote "no, thank you" in the margin.)[42]

In another section Bakunin described his plan for the 1848 revolution in Bohemia. Bakunin was one of the delegates to the Slav Congress in Prague when, on the last day, June 12, an uprising broke out in the city, lasting until June 16-17. His "Confession" explained his contribution: "I advised the students and other participants to overthrow the Rathaus [provisional government in the town hall], which was carrying on secret talks with Prince Windischgrätz, and to put in its place a military committee with dictatorial powers." The insurrection was defeated before his advice could be carried out.[43] He had a vast plan for the Bohemian revolution:

> The revolutionary government with unlimited dictatorial power must sit in Prague.... All clubs and journals, all manifestations of garrulous anarchy will also be destroyed, and all will be subjugated to a single dictatorial authority.

The revolution would be organized by three secret societies, unknown to each other, each with "a strict hierarchy and unconditional discipline," composed of a small number comprising "all the talented, learned, energetic, and influential people." These, "obeying central directions, would in their turn act invisibly, as it were, on the crowd."

Here we have Bakunin s'main new twist on the theory of dictatorship: the scheme for a leadership of Invisible Dictators, here worked out only in embryo. The top linkage would be made by a secret committee of Bakunin plus two or four others. Comes the revolution, this *Apparat* would not be disbanded but would expand to fill the "positions in the revolutionary hierarchy." Bakunin himself would begin by being its "secret leader": "all the main threads of the movement would have been concentrated in my hands..."[44]

The roots of this conception in Jacobin-communist conspiratorialism are evident; but it is on the way to becoming a mephitic thing of its own brand. The account of Bakunin's theory of dictatorship will be continued in Chapter 7.

4 | THE DICTATORSHIP OF THE DEMOCRACY: MARX IN 1848

To understand what happened in 1848, we have to learn a different vocabulary. We are accustomed to the counterposition "dictatorship versus democracy," which has been dinned into readers in the twentieth century. In 1848, for good or ill, dictatorship was often thought of *as an accompaniment or aspect of democracy.*

1. THE CASE OF PROUDHON

Certainly 'dictatorship' was not the word that commonly came to mind to describe absolute authority. There is a piquant way of illustrating this.

The Frenchman of 1848 who most avidly thirsted for absolute authority was P.J. Proudhon, the mythical "libertarian." Elsewhere I have filled an article with dozens of passages from his notebooks of the revolutionary period, in which he repeatedly expressed, sometimes in pathological language, his craving for mastership over organized society.[1] The word 'master' was one that he liked: France needs a "master"; we will be "absolute masters," comes the revolution; and so on. He proclaimed himself the "guide, master, and leader" of the people; the future Director of all social power; "beyond criticism," and more of the same. I need not repeat this sad stuff here, but one passage tied up closely with the real dictatorship of 1848, which was based on the use of the state of siege. This was a note which he jotted down to threaten "reprisals" when *he* got into power:

> From you [the government] we have inherited the state of siege, war councils, the High Court, the September law [against free press] restored and strengthened, arbitrary arrests, preventive arrest, convict ships and transportation: we have only the scaffold to set up.[2]

We see he was very specific about the state-of-siege mechanism to impose his Libertarian grip on society.

4. The Dictatorship of the Democracy: Marx in 1848   59

Now this same Proudhon was, at the same time, very consistent in repudiating the word 'dictatorship' even as he spelled out his yearning for mastership over the new social order. What then did 'dictatorship' connote to him? In case after case, it was linked in his mind to *extreme democracy*. (This was bad because democratic authority was the worst kind of authority.) For example:
- He jotted down a note for himself—"Protest against the theory of the omnipotence *of majorities,* which is a form of dictatorship."[3] But when he wrote down, "I have been, I still am the invisible Director of society,"[4] this had nothing to do with dictatorial aspirations—in his own vocabulary.
- He more than once denounced the "dictatorship of the democratic party" and the "dictatorship of L. Blanc and Ledru-Rollin"—citing no fact or complaint. But when he exulted, "I am right and have a will stronger than all of you!" etc., this was *not* dictatorial.[5]
- Right after the February Revolution, with political life wide open, he already announced that "a provisional dictatorship is being established"—by the Democracy, naturally. But in the same pages he deplored the overthrow of the type of dictator called a monarch, in the name of Liberty, of course.[6]
- He denounced the republican government for "usurpation of powers ... dictatorship." At the same time he confided to his notebook that "La Révolution, c'est moi!" in deliberate echo of the most extreme absolutist claim ever made.[7]

The word 'dictatorship' came to his pen in pejorative contexts just as the vocabulary of democracy did. In his peculiar way Proudhon illustrated the fact that in his thinking 'dictatorship' and 'democracy' were not opposites but cognates.

We will see that *this* peculiarity was not Proudhonian, especially when we review the writings of François Guizot, Juan Donoso Cortès, and Lorenz von Stein in 1850, in the next chapter. But at this point we are still in 1848, when talk is plentiful not only about "democracy" but especially about *"the Democracy."*

2. TOWARD THE RULE OF THE DEMOCRACY

In the political language of 1848, *the Democracy* meant the movement of The People for the democratization of political power. On its liberal side, the Democracy stood for the winning of a constitution, universal suffrage, the basic freedoms of speech, press, assembly, etc. On its social side, it demanded social reforms to ameliorate the condition of the mass of workingpeople. This was the wing of the Democracy aiming for *social* democracy.[8]

By 1847 Engels had adopted a political perspective that saw the coming revolution in Germany as first putting the Democracy in power, thus advancing the proletarian revolution to the top of the social agenda. In this view, the

Democracy was a class coalition: an alliance of proletariat, petty-bourgeoisie, and small peasantry under the leadership of the first-named class. In his draft for the *Communist Manifesto* (called *Principles of Communism*) he offered a transitional program for the government of the Democracy in power. Marx, it seems, did not embrace this view until the outbreak of the revolution itself; the Manifesto, for example, plainly did not accept it.[9]

From March 1848 on, Marx applied, as energetically as Engels, the political line that followed from this view of the revolution: on one side of the barricades, as it were, was the class alliance called the Democracy (the three working classes); on the other side, the economically dominant class of the bourgeoisie plus the state power held by the Crown-bureaucracy-army-nobility comprising the ruling class. At the same time (and here we come to a problem that Marx did not straighten out in his own mind until the last stage of the revolution and his own policy), Marx early expected that there was still enough of a revolutionary-progressive drive in the bourgeoisie to enable it to take the lead in establishing a bourgeois-democratic constitutional regime supported by the Democracy. He not only expected this to happen, but looked forward to the next step in the pattern of Permanent Revolution: the continued shift of power to the left, and the establishment of the rule of the Democracy itself in a transitional regime. This in turn would lay the basis for another transition to the left: proletarian ascendancy, the dominance of the urban workers in the regime of the Democracy.[10]

Thus for Marx, as for the entire left of 1848 in different ways, the dynamic of the revolution centered around the basic goal, which was the victory of the Democracy, the ascendancy of the Democracy, the dominance of the Democracy, or—

To use another expression representative of the time, the *dictatorship* of the Democracy.

The readers of Marx's *Neue Rheinische Zeitung* in Cologne and the Rhineland and indeed elsewhere in Germany had no difficulty in understanding this language—even those who had to have the articles read aloud in the pothouses or coffee houses. It is we, heads stuffed with a later vocabulary, who have to grasp what everyone knew then.*

* Yet, as previously mentioned, even today what is virtually the same conception is put forward under some circumstances. For example, an article by the essayist Gore Vidal, who is sophisticated in political matters, argued in the year 1981 that the American president is a dictator operating through executive decrees. Vidal made no effort to explain his use of the term, evidently assuming that the reader would understand.[11] In 1931 a Fabian tract by Sidney Webb discussed the fact that "in effect a Party Dictatorship" had been set up by the victory of the "National Government" in the election by a great majority.[12] In neither case did the train of thought entail the charge that democratic institutions had been violated; the "dictatorship" was apparently established by the exertion of power through normal forms. I think this usage is fairly frequent today, but it is not admitted into formal political analysis.

3. WHAT MARX PROPOSED

The first "dictatorship" that Marx advocated was not that of the proletariat. It was the dictatorship of the Democracy. This idea (not the term) was put forward throughout the life of his *New Rheinische Zeitung*. The basis for this political line was explained in the first issue of the *NRZ* by Engels, as he advocated the basic demand of the Democracy: a constitution based on popular sovereignty.

The first act of the National Assembly should be to proclaim this sovereignty of the German people loudly and publicly.

Its second act should be to work out the German constitution on the basis of popular sovereignty, and to eliminate from the actually existing state of affairs in Germany everything that contradicts the principle of popular sovereignty.

During its whole session, it should take the necessary measures to thwart all the attempts of the reaction, to maintain the revolutionary ground on which it stands, to safeguard the achievement of the revolution, popular sovereignty, from all attacks.[14]

While the *NRZ*'s prescription for Germany was popular sovereignty, the government that had just issued from the revolution, the Camphausen ministry, wanted only an agreement with the Crown that would give the National Assembly some limited rights. Prime Minister Camphausen's line was that nothing unusual had taken place, least of all a revolution; that 'business as usual' was the ticket. And this attitude is what he counterposed to 'dictatorship', in a speech on May 30. And so it happens that the first mention of 'dictatorship' in the *NRZ* was not by Marx but by Camphausen. Let us see what Marx reported.

The government, declared the prime minister, refused to "interpret the situation ... as if the whole governmental system of our state had been overturned, as if everything hitherto existing had lost its legitimacy, as if all conditions had to be re-established anew juridically." Therefore, he explained, the government resisted demands for any greater change, "especially to change the system of indirect voting to direct voting." *It is precisely this that Camphausen then counterposed to dictatorship:* "The government did not yield on this. The government has not exercised any dictatorship; it could not exercise any, it did not want to. The electoral law has been applied in actual fact just as it stands juridically."[14]

Camphausen's view of what would constitute 'dictatorship' is perfectly clear: the new government established by the revolution would be acting *dictatorially* if it defied the Crown and practiced popular sovereignty. The prime minister assumed, like everyone else, that 'dictatorship' meant *democratization,* in the first place the democratization of the elections.

Marx's article quoted all this from Camphausen's speech, and then proceeded to discuss, not dictatorship, but revolutionary legality. Marx's subsequent references to 'dictatorship' in the *NRZ* were completely within the framework established *by the prime minister* and, naturally, taken up by the general press.

A few days later, this was followed up by an article urging a radical program of democratization:

> A Constituent National Assembly must above all be an *active*, revolutionary-active assembly. The Assembly in Frankfurt is doing parliamentary school exercises and lets the governments [of the German states] do the acting. Granted that this learned council succeeds after the maturest deliberation in working out the best agenda and the best constitution: what is the use of the best agenda and the best constitution if the governments meanwhile have placed bayonets on the agenda?[15]

The National Assembly had to act "dictatorially" in order to make democracy possible:

> It only needed to dictatorially oppose the reactionary encroachments of the outlived governments and it would have won over the power of public opinion against which all bayonets and rifle butts would have shattered.[16]

But for Camphausen, who insisted on maintaining the juridical fiction that no revolution had taken place and the legal thread remained unbroken, any *democratic* proposal brought up visions of the guillotine at work. He argued that the assembly must not act as if "we are on the threshold of conditions such as we know from the history of the English Revolution in the 17th and the French Revolution in the 18th century, conditions whose outcome is that power passes into the hands of a dictator." In the *NRZ* Engels quoted this and replied: "Hence the Berlin revolution [of March 18] is not allowed to be a revolution since otherwise it would be obliged to engender a Cromwell or Napoleon, against which Herr Camphausen protests."[17]

But the argument was not over a "Cromwell or Napoleon," that is, over a turn to "Caesarism." One-man dictatorship was the pejorative side of 'dictatorship', in Marx's paper as elsewhere.* Toward the end of June Cavaignac's dictatorship in Paris gave the term new notoriety, in a context quite different from Camphausen's. But the Camphausen meaning still overshadowed the German situation, as we find in July in an article by Engels on Minister Kühlwetter.

In this article Engels attacked the minister's claim that the "separation of

---

* In the *NRZ*, the mayor of Trier, a king's man named Sebaldt, was called the "dictator of Trier" in passing; and the French right-wing republican Marrast was attacked for *Alleinherrschaft* (one-man rule) and "dictatorship" on a single page.[18] In addition there were references to Cavaignac's (one-man) dictatorship.

4. The Dictatorship of the Democracy: Marx in 1848 63

powers" must be assumed to exist even though no constitution existed. Kühlwetter meant the autonomy of the executive in respect to the legislative power, that is, the uncontrollability of the executive by the people. Here is Engels' rebuttal:

> On the contrary: the revolutionary provisional situation exists precisely in the fact that the separation of powers is provisionally *abolished*, that at the moment either the legislative authority usurps the executive power or else the executive authority usurps the legislative power. It makes no difference whether the revolutionary dictatorship (it is a dictatorship, however slackly it is exercised) is in the hands of the Crown or an assembly or the two together. If Herr Kühlwetter wants examples of all three cases, French history since 1789 offers a number.[19]

This passage shows, with the clarity of a textbook example, why the term 'dictatorship' could be used at the time in both a commendatory and condemnatory context. The old legality and its norms were no more; some power had to take over in the transitional exigency, whether in the name of advancing to democracy or of returning to absolutism; and such an emergency assumption of power was a 'dictatorship'—however "slackly" or energetically it was exercised. If the Frankfurt talkshop that called itself the National Assembly had screwed up its courage to assert its own legitimacy, the legitimacy of popular sovereignty, against the Crown, it would have been exercising the 'dictatorship of the Assembly' until a new constitutional regime was instituted, consolidated, and normalized.

Editor Marx and leader writer Engels were going to be disappointed and disillusioned, for the political representatives of the German bourgeoisie proved to be capable only of elocution, unwilling to enforce energetic coercive action in defense of their political rights against the absolutist Crown.

After a couple more months of this, Marx published an important series of articles called "The Crisis and the Counterrevolution." The third article of the series, on September 14, made the point:

> "Constitutional principle!" But it is precisely the gentlemen who want to save the constitutional principle at all costs who must first see that in a provisional setup it is to be saved only by energy.

Energy—energetic action—meant bold coercive action, not simply "empty talk" and the pretense that a constitutional status had been achieved, when in fact no constitution yet existed. Marx continued:

> Every provisional state setup after a revolution requires a dictatorship, and an energetic dictatorship at that. From the beginning we taxed Camphausen [the prime minister] with not acting dictatorially, with not immediately smashing and eliminating the remnants of the old institutions. So while Herr Camphausen lulled himself with constitutional

dreams, the defeated party strengthened its positions in the bureaucracy and in the army—indeed here and there even ventured on open struggle. Marx argued that there could not indefinitely coexist the dual powers of the Assembly and of the absolutist state power; continued coexistence could only lead to an irreconcilable clash, which had to be prepared for. Marx went on:

> In any nonconstitutional setup [i.e., where no constitution exists], it is not this or that principle that is decisive, but only the *salut public*, the public welfare. The cabinet could avoid a clash between the Assembly and the Crown only by recognizing the public welfare as the sole principle, even at the risk of *itself coming* into collision with the Crown. But it preferred to remain "possibilist" in Potsdam. Against the Democracy it never hesitated to employ measures of public welfare *(mesures de salut public)*, dictatorial measures. Or what else was the application of the old laws to political crimes, even when Herr Märker [minister of justice] had already recognized that these articles of the Prussian Code had to be abrogated? What else were the wholesale arrests in all parts of the kingdom?
>
> But against the counterrevolution the cabinet took good care not to intervene on public-welfare grounds!
>
> And it was precisely out of this half-heartedness of the cabinet in face of the counterrevolution that was daily becoming more menacing that there arose the necessity for the Assembly *itself* to *dictate* measures of public welfare.[20]

There was no question here of proposing that the Camphausen government establish a "dictatorship" in some formal sense, as if a dictatorship were some special form of government. A government of the Democracy that would energetically repress the counterrevolution and thus make possible the setting up of a democratic constitution—this would *be* the "dictatorship." After a further account of the abject capitulation of the Assembly in face of the Right's encroachments, Marx exclaimed:

> And yet these gentlemen talk about constitutional principle!
> To sum up:
> The inevitable clash between two powers with equal rights within a provisional setup has gotten under way. The cabinet was incapable of carrying on the government energetically enough; it failed to come up with the necessary measures of public welfare...
> Whoever has the greater courage and consistency will win.[21]

The "dictatorship" for which Marx called, then, was that of the elected representative body of the German Democracy, a dictatorship to be exercised against the counterrevolution of the temporarily defeated absolutist state power. (The 'dictatorship of the Democracy' was not the term used, but that was its political description.) The word 'dictatorship' itself played no special prescriptive role.

After the revolution Engels, looking back to the same period, used the word with the same insouciance: The National Assembly at Frankfurt "had been, in the beginning of the Revolution, the bugbear of all German Governments. They had counted upon a very dictatorial and revolutionary action on its part—on account of the very want of definiteness in which it had been found necessary to leave its competency."[22] Instead, the Assembly merely chattered about imaginary laws for an imaginary country called Germany.

The historian Franz Mehring has reported that Marx's article of September 1848 gave rise to attacks in the press, as might be expected:

> The statement in the *NRZ* about the need for a "dictatorship" by the Camphausen government brought the charge by bourgeois critics that the *NRZ* "demands the immediate installation of a dictatorship as a means of carrying out democracy."

This attack merely echoed Camphausen's original warning against "dictatorship," but Mehring did not make the connection. This "nonsense," wrote Mehring, was distilled out of the passage beginning "Every provisional state setup after a revolution requires a dictatorship" etc. Writing in 1902, long before 'dictatorship' had become a crux in politics, he scoffed at the ascription of special significance to it:

> ... in this summary version it [the *NRZ*] said nothing different than what Waldeck had said in the Berlin Assembly on June 15: If we do not demolish the dreary remains of the feudal state, we are plowing in sand and building in air; or Bucher on July 18 in the same place: We should let no day go by without demolishing a piece of the obsolete past.[23]

These were the sentiments of the left wing of the Democracy expressed in the Prussian National Assembly, of which Waldeck was vice-president. Using the language of a later time, we can say that to Mehring 'dictatorship' meant energetically (boldly, thoroughly, etc.) recasting the old state machinery.

4. DICTATORIAL MEASURES

But these "dictatorial measures" that Marx advocated: what exactly were they? What would the "dictatorship of the Democracy" have looked like, concretely?

To begin with, the short answer was already indicated in Marx's article:

"immediately smashing and eliminating the remnants of the old institutions" by "measures of public welfare" boldly carried through. The historical reference was to the "dictatorship of the Commune" or the "dictatorship of the Convention" in the French Revolution. A more complete answer was scattered through Marx's and Engels' *NRZ* articles of 1848-1849; but for a convenient summary we should turn to their historical account, *Revolution and Counterrevolution in Germany*, drafted by Engels over Marx's signature. There were three passages in this work that spelled out the bold and energetic measures the Assembly should have taken, thereby in effect describing what a "dictatorship" would have done. The first one, which can stand for all, explained that no one knew if the Frankfurt Assembly's acts were to have the force of law:

> In this perplexity, if the Assembly had been possessed of the least energy, it would have immediately dissolved and sent home the Diet—than which no corporate body was more unpopular in Germany—and replaced it by a Federal Government, chosen from among its own members. It would have declared itself the only legal expression of the sovereign will of the German people, and thus have attached legal validity to every one of its decrees. It would, above all, have secured to itself an organized and armed force in the country sufficient to put down any opposition on the part of the Governments.[24]

Behold, the dictatorship of the Democracy! Of course, the Assembly did nothing of this sort. It failed to support or recognize the revolutionary uprisings that broke out, or "to call the people to take up arms everywhere in defense of the national representation." Instead, the deputies "shrunk back from decisive action." The old governments that had expected "dictatorial" and revolutionary action from it had nothing to worry about.[25]

It should not be supposed that Marx and Engels, in the *NRZ* or anywhere else, used *dictatorship*—or any other term—with a single consistent meaning. Indeed, the word had occurred in the second article of the series on "The Crisis and the Counterrevolution," a day before the passage we quoted at length. "If the Crown wins," wrote Marx,

> then the Assembly will be dissolved, the right of association suppressed, the press muzzled; an electoral law based on property qualifications will be decreed . . .—all this under cover of military dictatorship, cannon and bayonet.[26]

The suppression of democratic rights described would not *be* the dictatorship, it would take place under *cover* of military dictatorship. The year 1849 saw many military takeovers; typically the term used by Marx and Engels was not "dictatorship" *tout court* but either "military dictatorship" or "saber dictatorship." This can be found especially in March-May 1849.[27] Of course, the Cavaignac dictatorship had made this combination particularly well known

4. The Dictatorship of the Democracy: Marx in 1848   67

in Europe. Political vocabulary now had the dichotomy: dictatorships of the left and of the right.

The two sorts of meanings jostled in the pages of the NRZ as elsewhere. We have already mentioned that Camphausen's 'dictatorship of the assembly' was not crowded out by Cavaignac's 'dictatorship of the saber': the two coexisted without trouble in Marx's and Engels' articles in the paper.*

With the defeat of the revolution of 1848-1849 there was little occasion to think about the problems of a transitional revolutionary government—until one sat down to review the whole great historical experience. That too could be done from the right as well as from the left. In the next chapter we will be concerned with how this was done from the right, for it was in this review that the term 'dictatorship' entered into the realm of political theory.

---

* For example: "Cavaignac's military dictatorship" (June 27); "the dictator Cavaignac" (June 28); "dictator of France" (September 1); "The dictatorship and the state of siege were decided ... " (June 28); "The frightened National Assembly named Cavaignac as dictator, and he, accustomed since Algeria to 'energetic' intervention, knew what was to be done" (July 2).[28]

5 | THE "DICTATORSHIP OF THE PEOPLE": CONSERVATIVE VERSION

For its supporters the revolution of 1848-49 was the revolution of the Democracy. It was no less so for the right wing of European politics. The 1850s were, among other things, a time of retrospection on the meaning of the upheaval. The word dictatorship' had become so well known a part of the everyday vocabulary that it could now be used for the time-honored practice of proving that the masses had to accept their immemorial subjection to the classes.

1. "POPULAR DESPOTISM" AND GUIZOT

The idea of the "despotism of the people" goes back very far—no doubt beyond even Plato's and Aristotle's demonstrations of the horrors of democracy*—but let us mention only some cases that came to Marx's attention in the 1850s. A couple cropped up in Marx's *New York Daily Tribune* articles. Toward the end of 1853 the London *Times* attacked the proposal to lower the franchise to £5. By this means, thundered the *Times*, "the present electors would be virtually disenfranchised, because the class to be admitted will greatly outnumber all others put together, and has only to be unanimous to be supreme." Marx commented: "In other words, enfranchising the majority even of the small trading class [i.e., the petty-bourgeoisie] would disenfranchise the minority. A very ingenious argument this."² Two months later, he reported that the president of the Manchester Commercial Association was denouncing strikes by declaiming: "as Manchester had put down royal tyranny and

---

* A Prof. A. N. Holcombe tells us that according to Aristotle

a democratic government would ordinarily, therefore, be a government dominated by the poor. If there were no restraints upon their power, he also believed, the poor would use it primarily in their own interest. Hence an Aristotelian democracy corresponds to what is now called a dictatorship of the proletariat.¹

5. The "Dictatorship of the People": Conservative Version 69

aristocratic tyranny, so it would also deal with the tyranny of Democracy," said the capitalist.[3]

Fulminations against the despotism of democracy, in the name of the despotism of capital, were perhaps routine; but similar notions emanated from liberal intellectuals. In 1856 Tocqueville, sighing that the French revolution should have been carried through by an "enlightened autocrat" instead of by "the masses on behalf of the sovereignty of the people," made another instructive contrast: the revolution constituted "a spell of anarchy and 'popular' dictatorship" and so set the stage "for a return to one-man government."[4] The "dictatorship" was that of the masses on behalf of popular sovereignty; the "one-man government" was—something else. No doubt Marx read Tocqueville's book, though he left no comment on it. In the first part of his *Democracy in America* (1835) Tocqueville had expounded his view of the dangers of "democratic despotism"—the "despotism" or "tyranny" of the majority. (In the later part, both terms were abandoned as inadequate.)

For that matter Marx might have remembered the excerpts from Hegel which he had laboriously analyzed in the summer of 1843, for Hegel had argued that despotism was a "condition of lawlessness" in which law is replaced by "the particular will as such—be it that of a monarch or a people."[5]

In 1849 an interesting book was published by Guizot, the last prime minister serving under a French king, Louis Philippe. A scholar turned politician, the revolution of 1848 had forced him to revert to his old trade. His book was *De la Démocratie en France*.

The best-known passage in Guizot's book explained that everybody is for democracy nowadays—monarchists, republicans, socialists, communists, everyone. But democracy means chaos, class war, base desires, and popular despotism. Guizot was clear enough about what he meant by popular despotism. As one of the early formulators of a class-struggle view of history, he saw there was a three-way class struggle among the aristocracy, the bourgeoisie, and the "people." Unfortunately the first two classes were minorities. His book was a warning: *You the people, do not impose your will on these sections of society, for after all they have to rule, not you; if you impose your will over them, you are instituting despotism.*

This was "popular despotism," He attacked the idea that sovereignty should flow from elections; it is an un-French idea, he explained. In the course of this warning, there is the following dictum:

> Popular tyranny or military dictatorship may be the expedient of a day, but can never be a form of government.

Dictatorship is here set side by side with "popular despotism" or "popular tyranny," by which Guizot meant democracy.

The line of thought was clear enough. Democracy meant All Power to the People. This was wrong. Power had to be shared with the aristocracy and the bourgeoisie, who had to have the lion's share. Otherwise you have tyranny, despotism, dictatorship, and of course anarchy.[6]

It is easy to translate "All power to the people." You romanize "all power" into "dictatorship," and modernize "the people" into "the proletariat," and you have—the dictatorship of the proletariat. I am now speaking of Guizot's view, not Marx's.

2. THE "FEARFUL WORD" OF DONOSO CORTÉS

Before the revolution, Juan Donoso Cortés was a minor Spanish politician, though he had already gained some notoriety as an open advocate of dictatorship. Of a provincial bourgeois family claiming nobility, he became an absentee capitalist landlord in 1829, as marquis de Valdegamas. The ruling class, he thought, should be (by coincidence) the one that he himself belonged to: namely, the propertied bourgeoisie "as a new legitimate aristocracy ruling by right of 'sovereignty of intelligence'."[7] In 1836 lectures he came out with a theory of dictatorship to answer the threat of radicalism. (How advanced he was can be indicated by the fact that even the word 'socialism' had not yet been used in Spanish.)

With recurrent political crises in Spain in 1836, 1840, 1847, and 1848, he kept returning to the need for dictatorship as the answer. In October 1847 he helped to put the authoritarian General Narváez into power, so that Spain was already ruled by a virtual dictator when the European revolution broke out a few months later. Also in 1847, he went through a spiritual crisis—perhaps in reaction to his advancing syphilis, which was to kill him a few years later—and became a Catholic zealot.

On January 4, 1849 he made a "Speech on Dictatorship" in the Spanish parliament, a speech that resounded all over Europe and the world. Overnight he became famous as the greatest orator and prophet of reaction. He said what few dared to put into words. This man had no compunction about blurting out that power belonged in the hands of bourgeois property—by right of "intelligence" (to cover the "ethical" angle) and by right of the saber (to be less philosophical about it). Legality? Bah!

> When legality suffices to save society, then legality. When it does not suffice, dictatorship.... this fearful word (which is indeed a fearful one, though not so much so as the word revolution, which is the most fearful of all)...[8]

His erudition gave class egotism a classical gloss. Every society made provision for dictatorship in crisis, he explained. There was the Roman example, of course (which he himself had absorbed from Ferguson's *History of*

5. The "Dictatorship of the People": Conservative Version   71

the Roman Republic). In Athens he found "this omnipotent power in the hands of the people, and it was called ostracism."[9] The French Revolution had produced a horrible dictatorship. The new republic in France was nothing less than "dictatorship under a republican name." The most colossal dictatorship of all existed permanently in England—democratic England, the delight of the liberals; for the British Parliament could do anything it wanted: "Who, gentlemen, has ever seen so colossal a dictatorship?" God is a dictator, for his miracles suspend the laws of nature. "Liberty is dead!"[10]

It was only a question of what sort of dictatorship you favored, or, rather, whose:

> ... it is a question of choosing between the dictatorship of the insurrection and the dictatorship of the government: then in this case, I choose the dictatorship of the government, as less burdensome and less ignominious.

This was followed by his oratorical masterpiece:

> It is a question of choosing between the dictatorship from below and the dictatorship from above: I choose the dictatorship from above, since it comes from a purer and loftier realm. It is a question of choosing, finally, between the dictatorship of the dagger and the dictatorship of the saber: I choose the dictatorship of the saber, since it is nobler.[11]

This counterposition of "the dictatorship from below and the dictatorship from above" rang out over the Continent; it was translated into many languages, and printed everywhere, to a chorus of praise and blame. It aroused even more interest in Germany than elsewhere, perhaps. For one thing, soon afterwards Donoso became Spanish ambassador in Berlin, where he exhorted the Prussian king to repress demagogues and traitors. Friedrich Wilhelm IV seems to have resented the notion that he needed urging. From March 1851, when Donoso became envoy in Paris, he conspired with Bonaparte to carry out the coup d'état establishing the Second Empire, since the choice was "military dictatorship or revolutionary despotism" again. At the same time he published a book, translated into English as *Essay on Catholicism, Liberalism and Socialism,* which philosophized about ethical principles and other noble thoughts.

3. STEIN'S "SOCIAL DICTATORSHIP"

Donoso became a celebrity of the day because he said brashly what slyer politicians confined to private mutterings. And he is now forgotten because the content of his contribution was simply open class greed. Such vulgarity is not highly thought of in retrospect. Lorenz von Stein, on the other hand, made no tremendous splash when he came out in 1850 with a new edition of an important work originally published in 1842.[13] But his *History of the Social Movement in France* was the most searching of the antirevolutionary analyses of the revolution.

Stein developed views about dictatorship and about the rule of the proletariat, and while the phrase 'dictatorship of the proletariat' did not occur in his pages, this was what he was discussing. His views were unlike Marx's, of course, but they shed light on the political thought of the time. As far as is known, neither Marx nor Engels ever commented on Stein's 1850 volume, though one supposes they read it; and there is no reason to believe that Stein influenced Marx in any way. Both of them were deriving a line of thought from the events, the experiences, the pressures, and the climate of ideas of the time: this is what made Stein interesting.

Stein was one of the first (back in 1842) to understand that the modern proletariat was an emerging new class ominous to society. Not being a majority, it can be effective only by an "alliance with the movement for political liberation," the alliance that Marx and Engels called the Democracy and urged forward throughout the revolution. Stein further understood that the proletarians' employers constitute the class that "controls the state."[13]

> Thus the belief emerges that the proletarians are called upon, and are able, to help themselves by acquiring the power of the state. Consequently, they consider themselves entitled to seize governmental power in order to realize their social ideas.[14]

But, Stein argued, control of the state by the proletariat would be bad; for when "political power accrues in the hands of a single social class," this is "contrary to the inherent nature of the state," since then the state no longer represents the "common will." The lower class is not socially able to rule because it "does not have the prerequisites of true authority; it has neither the material goods on which authority rests [i.e., private property], nor is it superior in knowledge to the property-owning class." It therefore has no *justification* for seizing political power; but can seize power only by "sheer force." "It is therefore inevitable that, with the emergence of the rule of the proletariat, the rule of force develops, a rule of force of a specific and terrible kind." The struggle turns into *terrorism*, which seeks to accomplish the impossible.[15]

Since victory was gained by force, force "eventually occupies an independent position above the two classes of society." This independent position by which force rules as such, not in the name of any social idea, is called 'dictatorship'. The really successful social revolution, therefore, always leads

5. The "Dictatorship of the People": Conservative Version 73

to a dictatorship (wielded by the counterrevolution, that is). And as this dictatorship stands *over* society, it immediately takes on the character of that power which is superior to society by its very nature. It declares itself to be *independent state power*, and invests itself with the legality and sacredness of the state.[16]

Here is a theory of dictatorship that made a complete break with the Roman model; Stein was trying to deduce the meaning of modern dictatorship from modern experience. By making the *lack* of any social content the definition of dictatorship, Stein's formulation was the opposite of Marx's. It defined dictatorship only by the force that was its method—another "force theory of history." Its interest, however, lies in the fact that it pointed to the phenomenon of the complete autonomization of the state power, associated here with dictatorship.

But following a discussion of the Napoleonic dictatorship Stein seemed to depart from his definition, as he established another type of dictatorship: the "social dictatorship."

> ... those [dictatorships] which grow organically out *of* the life of a nation are altogether different. They persist because they correspond to a definite condition of society. This type of dictatorship grows out of preceding dissolution of a social order; the beginning of a new social order usually coincides with the beginning of dictatorship. We might call it a social dictatorship. The most striking similar case of such a dictatorship is that of Cromwell. There is no doubt that any country under similar conditions will bring forth a dictator; it is an inevitable consequence of the laws of social development. Even the greatest historical figures are subject to these laws of history. "Freedom" has little meaning in this context.[17]

The dictatorship meant the concentration of power in the hands of "one individual." "A social dictatorship," Stein theorized, "usually finds the state in dissolution."[18] Society *needs* it, and this is why it succeeds in legitimizing itself. It is not instituted or installed, it "must engender itself."[19]

Stein concretized his views about the February Revolution and the June uprising in a discussion of class struggle and class consciousness, which play a vital part in his thought. The leaders of the working class, "striving for power, raised the proletariat to an awareness of its strength ..., to consider itself as a class" with intense class feeling. The leaders taught the working class "to take the law into its own hands." The working class "had to make the attempt to usurp the power of the state as a social class in order to attain its social goals." "The struggle for state control between the classes in society had become inevitable after the proletariat had become class-conscious .. ."[20]

The Provisional Government could have chosen "to establish a dictatorship

74   Part I: Dictatorship: Its Meaning in 1850

and act as the agency of the ruling class" after "a final, fierce battle with the proletariat"; but it split on the issue of postponing the election, which was an issue of class power.

> Both classes, more and more concerned with the issue, carefully gathered their strength. Social dictatorship became the slogan of the proletariat, and popular representation the slogan of the Democracy and the property owners. This struggle indicated the form in which each of the two classes began to wrestle for the control of the state.[21]

It must not be supposed that Stein had the Blanquists in mind as the advocates of "social dictatorship"; he was thinking of none other than Louis Blanc, whom he quotes. The social-democrats, said Stein, could decide to

> overthrow the government, replace it exclusively by Social Democrats, and therewith establish the rule of the proletariat. The statements by Louis Blanc who defends this position ... leave no doubt that this was really the opinion of the leaders of the proletariat.[22]

After citing Louis Blanc's statement, Stein commented that the idea of popular sovereignty was thus turned into the idea that "a Provisional Government should uphold a dictatorship until it had carried out all measures it considered necessary." This was a "liberty-defying dictatorship." "The struggle of the classes for control of the state was here clearly formulated."[23]

Stein's weakness was that he took Louis Blanc's rhetoric of desperation utterly seriously as a thought-out revolutionary policy, when in fact it was elocutionary foam on the waters. But what put him far ahead of all the bourgeois commentators of the time was that he saw clearly that the "rule of the proletariat" had come on the historical agenda, and that this rule of a *class* had some relationship to the new forms that dictatorship had assumed in the revolutionary turmoil. He saw that relationship in a way entirely different from Marx, to be sure, but he saw it. Marx worked out a relationship in his own way, and under different pressures.

II | THE TERM 'DICTATORSHIP' IN MARX AND ENGELS

6 | THE SPECTRUM OF 'DICTATORSHIP'

Before we grapple directly with Marx's use of 'dictatorship' in 'dictatorship of the proletariat', let us underline from still another side the word's mutability of meaning during most of the nineteenth century. During this century, the word made a traverse from the Roman meaning to our current meaning, and not in a straight line. In its course from one to the other, the meaning was unstable and shifting; in the midst of events that buffeted vocabulary more violently than usual, the meaning was erratic and volatile.

I am sure this could be successfully shown by tracing the use of 'dictatorship' by press, politicians, presidents, poets, or playwrights; but I have not investigated those fields; and anyway, we may find it more useful to see some examples from Marx and Engels themselves, as well as other closely related ones.

1. 'DESPOTISM' AND 'CLASS DESPOTISM'

Unlike 'dictatorship' the word 'despotism' began its life in antiquity as a designation of unbridled domination or absolute authority. It was pejorative or favorable depending on the user's view *of* despotism itself. Even in the eighteenth century, when Montesquieu made it the name of one of three basic types of government, it was a "dirty word." But it was already adopting a more varied hue: we have mentioned the use to which it was put in the French Revolution and, not long before the period we are concerned with, by Tocqueville.[1] The "despotism of liberty," the "despotism of the majority," and so on—such usages began highlighting that side of the word which emphasized the use of *forcible coercion*.[2]

Tocqueville's use had shown how the word was available to mean the coercive domination of a collectivity, apart from governmental forms or despite them. This is exactly the sense with which it is often found in Marx. Of course, the old sense still hung on, especially in combinations like 'Oriental despotism'. But in the combination 'class despotism' it was another matter. The usage can be called metaphorical, if need be.

In his *Class Struggles in France* (which will figure importantly in Chapter 11) Marx had occasion to mention another metaphorical use: the French government of the Second Republic claimed that it attacked Rome in order to fight the "despotism of anarchy." Like all convenient terms, it was now available for demagoguery. A few pages away, Marx explained what happened after the "June days" of 1849 when the government placed Paris in a state of siege (following the Cavaignac model): "the minority [the social-democracy] had gone so far as to attempt a *parliamentary insurrection*; the majority (the government] elevated its *parliamentary despotism* to law."[3] (In the preceding paragraph this "parliamentary despotism" was called "the legislative dictatorship of the united royalists.")

'Despotism' had been used in this way already in the *Communist Manifesto*, where the factory system and capitalist industry in general are called "this despotism." On the other hand, the measures of the transitional program presented at the end of Section II are described as "despotic inroads on the rights of property."[4] Plainly, the meaning that is uppermost is *coercive dominance*, whether by the "good guys" or the "bad guys."

In Marx's *Eighteenth Brumaire,* use of the term 'class despotism' came to the fore. The defeat of the June revolt of 1848 "had revealed that here *bourgeois republic* signifies the unlimited despotism of one class over other classes."[5] This was said of the parliamentary republic, hardly a 'despotism' of any sort in our modern vocabulary. Bonaparte's *coup d'état* of 1851, which overthrew this parliamentary 'class despotism', was, among other things, *"the victory... of the executive power over the legislative power."*

> France, therefore, seems to have escaped the despotism of a class only to fall back beneath the despotism of an individual...[6]

In Marx's view, the Bonaparte regime was not the despotism of a *class* because it was a state that represented an extreme form of state autonomization.[7]

In both of these passages in the *Eighteenth Brumaire*, it is clear that in 'class despotism' the component 'despotism' was far from meaning absolutist tyranny. Almost two decades later, Marx employed a similar vocabulary in *The Civil War in France*, which partly looked back on the same events. With the development of modern industry, wrote Marx, "the State power assumed more and more the character of the national power of capital over labour, of a public force organised for social enslavement, of an engine of class despotism. . . ."[8] It is especially plain here that strong words are being used with propagandistic force (e.g., "enslavement"), and that the strong term "despotism" means *coercive* rule.

In the drafts for the *Civil War in France,* Marx used these strong terms more freely than in the final version. In at least three passages, the term 'class despotism' was used in conjunction with an even stronger term, 'class terrorism'—both of them accompanying (and signifying) *class rule* in some plainly coercive form.* In the following passage of the First Draft, the target is the parliamentary Second Republic:

> [∞] ... this anonymous or republican form of the bourgeois regime—this Bourgeois Republic, this Republic of the *Party of Order* is the most *odious* of all political regimes. Its direct business, its only *raison d'être* is to crush down the people. It is the *terrorism* of class rule. . . . Of course, that spasmodic form of anonymous class despotism cannot last long, can only be a transitory phasis.[9]

Another passage in the First Draft associated "class rule" with "the *republican form* of class despotism" and both with the formulation about "the *anonymous* terrorism" or "*anonymous* terror of class rule."[10] By "anonymous" Marx meant impersonal and collective, unlike Bonaparte's personal rule—another way of emphasizing the *class* character of the "despotism" or "terrorism." He used the "anonymous" formulation elsewhere in this draft: the Second Republic was "that spasmodic form *of anonymous* class despotism," and (on the same page) "the *anonymous* form of class rule."[11]

Similarly, in the Second Draft Marx wrote that the revolution had disclosed the real social meaning of state power—

> [∞]its secret as an instrument of class despotism is laid open. . . . The parliamentary republic of the Party of Order is not only the reign of terror of the ruling class. The state power becomes in their hand[s] the *avowed instrument of the civil war*...[12]

Some of the formulations of the First Draft were repeated,[13] and one contrast was made a little more clearly:

> [∞]The Empire . . . divesting the state power from its direct form of class-despotism by br[e]aking the parliamentary and, therefore, directly political power of the appropriating classes, was the only possible state-form to secure the old social order a respite of life.[14]

Whereas in our modern vocabulary the Bonaparte regime was *more* 'despotic' than the parliamentary republic, in Marx's language it was the latter that was the "*class* despotism." In a personal letter, that is, in an informal context, Marx was quite capable of using "bourgeois despotism" virtually as a routine synonym for the bourgeois social order.[15]

Among the points that should now be clear is this: the case of 'class despotism' (and, less prominently, 'class terrorism') followed the same model that was represented by Marx's invention of that other term in which we are interested, *class dictatorship.*

* For the term 'terror (ism)', see Special Note C.

2. THE DIM SIDE OF THE SPECTRUM

But 'despotism' had no complex spectrum of meaning like 'dictatorship'. It is the latter's complexity that we now pass in review. In particular, we should not lose sight of the weakest, or dimmest, end of the spectrum. This was a meaning that barely implied some form of domineering, assertive, or "bossy" demeanor.

In a typical example, Helene Demuth ("Lenchen")—who managed the Marx household from April 1845 on, and then ran Engels' ménage until her own death—was more than once described as "dictator of the house." Liebknecht's memoirs made a distinction: "Lenchen was the dictator in the house; Mrs. Marx was the ruler; and Marx submitted like a lamb to the dictatorship."[16] Everyone knows what this sort of talk means.*

The *Oxford English Dictionary* cites a related sort of case, for example, a 1741 reference to an author who "assumes an air of sovereignty and dictatorship." There are similar citations under 'dictator', definition 2, including a "dictator" of fashions, of learning, of dress and behavior, of the racing turf, and so on. Closely related are references to "intellectual dictators"—individuals, perhaps institutions, that influence thought in some predominating way. Engels referred a couple of times to the "intellectual dictatorship" of the medieval church, and the "intellectual dictatorship" of the pope.[18] Marx reported in 1880 that anarchists were denouncing his collaborators as "Prussian agents, under the dictatorship of the 'notorious' Prussian agent—Karl Marx."[19] The ex-Saint-Simonian financier Isaac Péreire, who masterminded a couple of Bonapartist swindles, was "the inventor and dictator of the Crédit Mobilier."[20]

Not far from these cases in the spectrum of meaning is the use of 'dictator(ship)' in connection with a person in charge of some limited task or operation. In a hospital's operating theater, the surgeon is the absolute dictator; no one would cavil. On a ship on the high seas, the captain is dictator (and with some legal power behind the appellation). In a soccer game, the referee is dictator. On a daily newspaper, in the twenty-four-hour rush to do the impossible, the editor's word is supreme. In all of these cases, we know that there *is* an institutional limitation on the authority, outside the immediate situation, whether this limitation be set democratically or bureaucratically.

---

* I cite an excellent remark by that profeminist socialist pioneer, James Morrison, in 1834:

> They [women] have been abundantly bantered and stigmatised for their talents and ambition for petticoat control, their curtain lecturing, and all the other dictatorships of the political economy of home; but all this has been mere twaddle on the part of the male, who whenever woman pretends to dictate to, or even to advise, her robust helpmate, brands the presumption by the name of petticoat rule.[17]

6. The Spectrum of 'Dictatorship'   81

The newspaper example brings up the case of Marx, for he edited a daily newspaper for months under the most hectic circumstances known—a revolution—with inadequate financial resources. Writing thirty-six years later about the *Neue Rheinische Zeitung (NRZ)* of Cologne, Engels remarked:

> The editorial setup was simply dictatorship by Marx. A big daily paper, which must be finished by a given hour, cannot maintain a consistent attitude with any other setup. But in this case, besides, Marx's dictatorship was a matter of course, undisputed, and willingly accepted by all of us. It was first and foremost his clear vision and his steady attitude that made this paper the most famous German newspaper of the revolutionary years.[21]

In the case of the ordinary newspaper, the dictatorship of the editor in chief is limited only by the authority of the owner. In the case of the *NRZ* the supervisory authority was a democratic one: the articles of the joint-stock company that had been set up to own the paper made provision for shareholder control, plus a Supervisory Board of seven; in day-to-day operation there was the editorial board.[22] But in practice there was only one case (as far as Marx remembered) where the editor's decision was challenged on the spot and taken up by the board during the daily operation. "I allowed this as an exception," Marx related afterward, "at the same time declaring that in a newspaper office it is dictatorship that must hold sway."[23] Perhaps it was this incident that stirred Engels' memory when he wrote his article later.

This type of situation, of course, has really nothing to do with 'dictatorship' as a governmental term. It is essentially the problem excellently discussed in Engels' polemic against anarchism, "On Authority," where he discussed how running a railway on time required "a dominant will that settles all subordinate questions," that is, a management with real power to get the job done.[24] Jargonized by journalists, it produces the American term 'baseball czar' for an employee of the baseball team owners.

Still another band in the spectrum should be disposed of here. There is a common usage, found in Marx and Engels more than once, in which a dominant influence—say, in international politics—is called a dictator. After 1830, Engels related, the "petty states" of Germany "completely passed under the dictatorship of the Diet, that is, of Austria and Prussia."[25] In 1859 Marx remarked that the Berlin government submitted to "the Franco-Russian dictatorship," or (in the next paragraph) to "the joint despotism of Russia and France."[26] In 1870, Marx and Engels argued that to "emancipate Europe from the Muscovite dictatorship," Germany had to make an honorable peace with France.[27] Although this usage seems at first blush to have a political content, examination shows that it is really metaphorical in nature.

The main point in laying out the preceding part of the 'dictatorship' spectrum is to enable us to ignore it. These usages have nothing to do with

82   Part II: The Term 'Dictatorship' in Marx and Engels

what we are concerned with here, notwithstanding the fascination of some marxologists with any and every use of 'dictatorship' in Marx.

3. MILITARY DICTATORS AND DICTATORSHIPS

Let us now make a jump to the opposite end of the spectrum, to the type of dictatorship that was most unanimously so designated, the type that was shadowed by the least ambiguity. This was the military dictatorship, in which open armed force imposed or shored up a government with bayonets with a minimum of hypocrisy. The term 'military dictator (ship)' seems to have offered difficulties to no one, certainly not to Marx. As far as I know, he and Engels never used this term for any regime toward which they felt kindly.

For both of them, the "slave states" of the American South, in the Civil War, were under "military dictatorship."[28] Engels, as the military expert of the partnership, had more occasion to discuss military dictatorships. When the Spanish general, Francisco Serrano y Domínguez, was placed at the head of the government by a coup in 1874, Engels commented that he "Anally made himself dictator of Spain."[29] In 1890 Engels had this to say about the illusion that Kaiser Wilhelm was pro-working-class:

> Since little Wilhelm's friendliness to the workers is complicated by hankerings for military dictatorship (you see how the whole pack of princes nowadays becomes Bonapartist *nolens volens),* and he wants to have everyone shot out of hand at the slightest resistance, we have to take care that he gets no opportunity to do this.[30]

There were other dictatorships that, without ceasing to be military-based, took on broader political dimensions, either in time or in intentions. The one that Marx attacked most ardently was the dictatorship of Louis Napoleon Bonaparte.

Now as Napoleon III, Bonaparte was called emperor, and his regime received a multiplicity of imperial appellations, many of them pronounced only with grinding teeth. 'Despot', 'tyrant', and other pleasantries were standard. And 'dictator' was only one of this family. References to Bonaparte's regime as a dictatorship are scattered over Marx's and Engels' writings, but the term was never their consistent label for the Second Empire.

Engels called Bonaparte's regime a "military dictatorship" in the 1850s more than once.[31] In mid-1851 Marx predicted that the French bourgeoisie "would prefer an Empire or a Dictatorship of Napoleon, to a Democratic and Social Republic, and would, therefore, come to terms" with him.[32] In the late 1850s he saw Bonaparte "playing the dictator of Europe" (in an article which

6. The Spectrum of 'Dictatorship' 83

also referred to "his system of domestic terrorism" and "the reign of terror" in the country).[33] In the name of fighting "anarchy" Bonaparte was responsible for "overturning the republican Government by military force, crushing out all freedom of the press, and driving into exile or shipping off to Cayenne all opposers of his sole dictatorship."[34]

While Marx's critical analysis of the regime of Napoleon I was different, the first Napoleon was also a dictator in Marx's language. He linked the two when he wrote in 1858 that, since Louis Bonaparte's alliance with England made him look like "the arbiter of Europe," he was called on to show "that, like a real Napoleon, he holds the dictature of Europe."[35] Engels referred to Napoleon Bonaparte as a dictator (quite incidentally, to be sure) at least twice: the French Revolution, worn out and exhausted, and the Republic it had produced, "brought forth its own dictator—a Napoleon"; this had been made inevitable by the exhaustion of the republic by warfare.[36]

There was the would-be dictator General Georges Boulanger in the late 1880s: 'dictator' is the word that instantly comes to modern lips. But in the long correspondence between Engels and Paul Lafargue (the latter tending to an accommodation with Boulangism), 'dictatorship' and 'dictator' are not the words that came to Engels' pen. This illustrates an important point that should be made around this time: our present enterprise of tracing the use of the word 'dictatorship' is distorting; it tends to skew our view of the real politics of the situation. The word that for Engels most commonly described Boulanger's ism (aside from 'Boulangism') was 'Bonapartism'.

Again and again, trying to straighten out Lafargue's soft-on-Boulanger line, Engels argued that what the general represented in French politics was the current of Bonapartism, and chauvinistic Bonapartism at that.[37] In addition, he characterized Boulanger's aim as "personal government" counterposed to "parliamentary government."[38] In his earlier letters to Engels on the subject, Lafargue did use the word 'dictator(ship)', which was doubtless common enough around Paris; but then his bad politics overtook him. The last time he associated the term with Boulanger was in a letter that scorned the "insane fear of dictatorship" evinced by Boulanger's opponents.[39]

To keep the record straight, Engels did refer to the general as a (would-be) "dictator" in at least one letter, in which he warned Lafargue that Boulanger's victory would mean the crushing of the socialist movement and the imminent danger of war.[40] (Lafargue was the forerunner of the "revolutionary" cretins who in the 1930s trumpeted "After Hitler we come!") 'Dictator' brought to mind the danger of the destruction of the bourgeois-democratic arena; but 'Bonapartist', we must now recall, evoked all of that and much more. It is likely enough that Engels used 'dictator' in letters not now extant, but we must not impose the expectations of twentieth-century language on a previous century.

For the most frequent occurrence of 'dictator' and 'dictatorship' in an article by Marx or Engels, one must go to Marx's article on Simon Bolívar, the South American "Liberator," whom Marx viewed as a Bonapartist dictator whose aspirations for personal "arbitrary power" harmed the anticolonial revolution on his continent.[41] To be sure, Bolívar used the terms officially, and Marx found them plentifully in his sources; but besides the mere terms, Marx emphasized again and again that this Bonapartist general had a "propensity for arbitrary power," proclaimed himself dictator over and over again, and used "martial law and the union of all powers in his single person." "What he really aimed at," wrote Marx, "was the erection of the whole of South America into one federative republic, with himself as its dictator."[42]

Marx's views on Bolívar as dictator are the subject of an article of mine which is of interest in this connection: see the reference to it in the Foreword, Section 4.

Plainly there was no terminological problem here. It is with the cases to be reviewed next that we get a closer look at some problematical uses of 'dictator' and 'dictatorship'.

4. SOME NONDICTATORIAL DICTATORS

So far the individuals whom Marx or Engels called dictators would be so labeled in our current language. But they used the term in a much wider fashion, as we should expect.

(a) *The case of Prince Regent Wilhelm.* In 1858, the Prussian king having been adjudged insane, Prince Regent Wilhelm (later King Wilhelm I) took over the power. In the *New York Daily Tribune* Marx explained that the prince made a display of liberalism by holding an election—with carefully restricted voting, to be sure—which the bourgeoisie took advantage of to assert its influence, though with some trembling and fawning.

> ººThe electors sending back from below the tune played from above, the Ministers became a party Ministry and the Prince became a middle-class Dictator.[43]

The change was in the direction opposite to what we would now call dictatorship. The prince's "dictatorship" is *counterposed* to the absolutism of the king. This "bourgeois dictator" (Marx used 'middle-class' for 'bourgeois' when writing in English) was consolidating an insecure and temporary position by leaning on the bourgeoisie through parliamentary forms, while his power base was still the monarchy. But it would be an idle enterprise to try to deduce a definition of 'dictatorship' from such a usage; one can only get a feeling for how the word was being used.

6. The Spectrum of 'Dictatorship'   85

(b) *The case of Parnell.* In the general election of 1885, the Home Rule party, led by Parnell, won 86 seats out of 580. Engels, writing to a friend, thought it very important that Parnell's tendency would hold the parliamentary balance of power in the new House. They "are in a position here like the Center in the Reichstag: they can make any government impossible." At the end of the letter he threw in a sententious remark: "Parnell will almost certainly become dictator of Great Britain and Ireland."[44]

Portentous news if true! But in fact all Engels was saying was that Parnell would now be able to "dictate" terms to the Liberals and Tories. A few decades later, few would use the "fearful word" in this context.

(c) *The case of Bismarck.* In 1875 Marx casually referred to Bismarck as "dictator of the German-Liberal bourgeoisie."[45] This involves no controversy about Bismarck's political position or power; it is only a matter of the terminology used for it. The Bismarckian state was a compromise with bourgeois political power, with the chancellor holding the whip; and more than once Engels used the term 'semidictatorship' to describe the situation.

If, again, we try to get a feeling for how the word was used, an excellent specimen is provided by a passage written by Engels, which is well-known for other reasons. In a letter to Marx, Engels tossed up the idea that "Bonapartism is indeed the real religion of the modern bourgeoisie." Incompetent to rule directly, in England it turned over the management of the state to an "oligarchy" for "good pay." Hence "a Bonapartist semidictatorship is the normal form" accompanying bourgeois economic power.

> ... it carries out the big material interests of the bourgeoisie even against the bourgeoisie, but deprives the bourgeoisie of any share in the ruling power itself. On the other hand, this dictatorship is itself, in turn, compelled to reluctantly adopt these material interests of the bourgeoisie.[46]

This conjecture was not touched off by some specially "dictatorial" action by Bismarck but by the opposite: he had just enacted universal suffrage for the North German Reichstag elections—"Bismarck's universal-suffrage coup," Engels called it. Indeed, if Bismarck had (say) suppressed the Reichstag out of hand, Engels would not have termed it 'dictatorship'—words like 'despotism', 'absolutism', 'tyranny', and such would more likely have been called into play.

For the most extensive discussion of Bismarck as "dictator," one should turn to Engels' *Role of Force in History.* Here Engels again discussed the German bourgeoisie's inability to gain full political power. It was in a dilemma: on the one hand, a real struggle would mean a long period of internal weakness. "On the other hand, it demanded a revolutionary reorganization of Germany, which could be effected only by force, that is, by a factual dictatorship."[47]

Engels was referring here to the bourgeoisie's achievement of a *democratic* state—by force, that is, by Bismarck's dictatorship. Plainly, dictatorship was not counterposed here to democratic government; it referred to the bourgeoisie's willingness to suspend the old legality and introduce a new one (a more democratic one) without recourse to legal or existing constitutional forms. In another passage he made the same point using not the word 'dictatorship' but the word that Donoso had called even more "fearful," namely, 'revolutionary'.[48]

Engels' analysis of Bismarckism is not itself our subject, but we must mention that—as Engels explained—Bismarck realized that his own class, the Junkers, was not a viable one; that the bourgeoisie was the only propertied class with a future; and that he therefore had to orient toward a modern bourgeois state.

> An immediate transition to a parliamentary government with the decisive power vested in the Reichstag (as in the British House of Commons) was neither possible nor even advisable at the moment; Bismarck's dictatorship in parliamentary forms must have seemed to him as being still necessary for the time being; and we do not in the least blame him for allowing it to exist for the time, we only ask to what purpose it was being used.[49]

Engels would have raised the same question about any other governmental form, of course. In any case, there was no question here of a despot trampling over the people's right with hobnailed boots, or any other modern vision of dictatorship. It was a question of reflecting the power of classes with improvised governmental forms.

(d) *The case of Palmerston.* We have seen that, discussing Bismarckism, Engels made both a comparison and a contrast with the British situation; but neither had much to do with Marx's propensity for calling Lord Palmerston a "dictator."

The background fact is that Marx objected fervently to Palmerston's foreign policy as "Russophile," and even denounced him as a tool of czarist intrigue. While the lengths to which Marx's denunciation went have been hard to explain, it is perhaps even harder to discover why he persistently proclaimed in the public prints that Palmerston exercised a "dictatorship" in England. After all, there was nothing that this long-time parliamentarian did that was outside the forms of British politics in the least degree.

Marx began referring in articles to "Palmerston's dictatorship" in 1855. At first it sounded as if he were merely saying that Palmerston totally dominated his cabinet: "whereas before it was a weak Whig ministry it is now the strong dictatorship of a single man . . ."[50] In 1857 and 1858 he repeatedly made the charge in his *New York Daily Tribune* articles.[51]

What did he mean by it? There is something of a clue in a letter to Engels in

6. The Spectrum of 'Dictatorship'   87

March 1857. The "decomposition of the old parties" which had previously been expressed in a coalition cabinet was now expressed in "Pam's dictatorship," and was likely to lead to "a very intense agitation, perhaps to a revolution." Palmerston, who "helped to draft the 6 gagging acts, will not be bothered in the least."

> *Mutatis mutandis* Pam's dictatorship has the same relation to a coalition cabinet as the domination of the royalist coalition in the last French Assembly has to the domination of Bonaparte. Things will finally be pushed in England to an acute point.[52]

Marx evidently had an overheated notion of the state of Britain, and erroneously viewed Palmerston's course as directed outside the parliamentary framework. In an article of about the same time, he told readers:

> Palmerston's administration was not that of an ordinary Cabinet. It was a dictatorship. Since the commencement of the war with Russia, Parliament had almost abdicated its constitutional functions; nor had it, after the conclusion of peace, ever dared to reassert them.[53]

We know of a succession of prime ministers, presidents, premiers and other governmental executive heads who have dominated their cabinets and legislatures, or have been taxed with doing so, and in the course have been called "dictators" and worse; no one was more often so labeled than Franklin D. Roosevelt. The use of war-crisis powers by a strong executive has usually intensified the charges, even when all constitutional forms have been rigorously observed. Marx's attacks on Palmerston sometimes sounded like this usage. But he also sounded as if he wanted to make more of it than that.

In another article of the same month, he discussed the consequences of a Palmerston victory in the election:

> . . . Palmerston's dictatorship, till now silently suffered, would be openly proclaimed. The new Parliamentary majority would owe their existence to the explicit profession of passive obedience to the Minister. A coup d'état might then, in due course of time, follow Palmerston's appeal from the Parliament to the people, as it followed Bonaparte's appeal from the *Assemblée Nationale* to the nation. That same people might then learn to their damage that Palmerston is the old colleague of the Castlereagh-Sidmouth Cabinet, who gagged the press, suppressed public meetings, suspended the Habeas Corpus Act, made it legal for the Cabinet to imprison and expulse at pleasure, and lastly butchered the people at Manchester for protesting against the Corn Laws.[54]

This certainly sounds more "dictatorial"! But it is a fantasy about the future, not a justification in the present; and Palmerston, who indeed won a big victory in the election, did not execute a coup d'état or otherwise cooperate.

Unquestionably Marx wanted to show that Palmerston was more than a strong executive who ran roughshod over parliamentarians and politicians. In an article the next week, Marx made an extended analogy between Palmerston's course and Bonaparte's in an attempt to prove that the former was on the same road; but there was no substance behind it. In fact, his strongest case was made by lengthily quoting Richard Cobden, who in an oration against Palmerston called him a "despot" who used "the sham appearance of a representative form of government."[55]

Marx's denunciations of Palmerston's "dictatorship" went on into at least 1858,[56] but there was no comparable attempt made subsequently to give it verisimilitude. It is easy enough to show the hollowness of Marx's effort to prove that Palmerston was a "dictator," but the significant thing—for our present purposes—is the way he went about it. He argued that Palmerston was headed toward a Bonapartist extraparliamentary course as his solution for the crisis of government. This was, or rather would be, "Palmerston's dictatorship."

5. THE "DICTATORS" OF THE DEMOCRACY

We now come to more serious candidates for dictatorship—at any rate, would-be dictators. We have seen that Louis Blanc, not only in the heat of 1848 but in postrevolutionary writings, avowed that he looked to a dictatorship, albeit the dictatorship of the democratic elements. At a time when the authoritative dictionaries gave "the dictatorship of the National Convention" as the model of the word's meaning,[57] this did not get him expelled from the democratic club. In the same decade, by the way, an article by Marx in the *New York Daily Tribune* also casually referred to "a revolutionary, dictatorial assembly like the French National Convention of 1793."[58]

Marx was just as willing to apply the term 'dictatorship' to another legislative body—with a proviso. Writing to Engels on the morrow of Bonaparte's coup d'état in December 1851, Marx tried to cheer himself up for a moment with the thought that it might be "easier to deal with Bonaparte than it would have been with the National Assembly and its generals." He added: "And the dictatorship of the National Assembly was standing at the gate."[59] This means: the National Assembly would wield a "dictatorship" if it succeeded in taking all power to itself and away from Bonaparte. *All power to the National Assembly:* this equaled the *dictatorship* of the Assembly, of the representative body of the parliamentary democracy. Again we encounter, in as clear a form as in 1848, the concept of *the dictatorship of the Democracy.*

In the circles of constitutional-democratic liberals who planned and plotted

6. The Spectrum of 'Dictatorship'   89

in exile with an eye to their restoration to power in their respective countries, Blanc and Heinzen and Kossuth and their similars had no inhibitions about avowing the need for a dictatorship—a *democratic* dictatorship, of course. Kossuth was known all over Europe as the democratic dictator of Hungary, now fallen from power.

Garibaldi, a man for whom Marx had much more respect, unabashedly aimed at a democratic dictatorship. When in 1860 articles Marx referred to Garibaldi as "the popular Dictator," he was not attacking him.[60] Garibaldi's best-known statements on this point came later, in 1871, in a letter that was printed in the Paris Commune's *Journal Officiel:*

> The Democracy naturally has an aversion to dictatorship, and rightly so, if one thinks of dictators like Caesar and Sulla; but when one is lucky enough to find a Cincinnatus or a Washington, the honest *temporary* dictatorship is much more preferable to the byzantinism of the 500.
>
> Spain is at a low point because it does not have a man to lead it in its great revolution. France is suffering a misfortune today for the same reason.[61]

In November another letter by him avowed that "I am still in favor of honest Dictatorship, which I consider the only antidote for eradicating the cancers of this corrupt society."[62]

Engels started off his *Revolution and Counterrevolution in Germany* with a jocular salute to "the more or less popular rulers of a day, provisional governors, triumvirs, dictators [etc.] ... thrown upon foreign shores ... there to form new governments '*inpartibus infidelium,*' European committees, central committees, national committees..."[63] The Central Committee of the European Democracy provided a center for the would-be rulers. Marx and his circle referred to these personages quite routinely as the "dictators." In a gossipy letter by Marx's close coworker Schramm, the latter casually referred to Heinzen and Struve as "these two dictators."[64] In a letter to Engels about the latest antics of the same personages, in a similar gossipy vein, Marx reported:

> But Kossuth, for his part, fancies that he is supported on the one side by the dictator of Germany, Kinkel; on the other side, by the dictator of Italy, Mazzini; and that he has, safely covering the rear, his ally the dictator of France, Ledru-Rollin. The poor devil has sunk low.[65]

Of course, this talk partly reflected mockery of these leaders' high pretensions, in part recognition of their real aspiration to become the democratic dictators of their countries.

Another of Marx's coworkers, Eccarius, wrote the following in Ernest Jones' Chartist organ in connection with a demonstration of English workers on behalf of Kossuth, held November 3, 1851:

> They went to admire and worship the leader of a bourgeois revolution,

under whose administration sweeping reforms were introduced—who, as dictator of his country, carried on a bloody war against the legitimate king, and finally caused him and his heirs to be deposed for ever.[66]

Eccarius' article stressed that he did not "find fault with Kossuth because he is a middle-class revolutionist. Far from it." Still less was he finding fault with the detail that Kossuth was called a dictator.

Marx's and Engels' *Great Men of the Emigration* was their most personal review of the political types that populated the Central Committee of the European Democracy, and it fulfills the expectation that the subjects' hopes for dictatorship would be suitably mocked. Heinzen, we are told satirically, "called for two million heads so that he could be a dictator and wade up to the ankles in blood—shed by others." The same paladin of the Democracy

> demanded that during the "revolutionary transition period" there should be a single dictator who should moreover be a Prussian and, to preclude all misunderstandings, he added: "No soldier can be appointed dictator."[67]

Another German member of the Central Committee, Harro Harring, "was co-dictator of Europe *in partibus";* Goegg, who had been a member of the provisional Baden government in 1849, admitted that "he could do nothing against Brentano [the government leader] and in all modesty he assumed the title of Dictator."[68] This was small talk, to be sure, but it was in fact the way people talked.

In this same period—mainly the fifties, when the democratic emigration was still active, and the early sixties—the appellation of 'dictator' came up regularly. It must not be supposed that it came up for discussion; it came up mainly as a mode of language.

There was the Spanish general, Espartero. Writing in 1854, Marx related that in 1840.

> Espartero assumed . . . the supreme authority within the limits of parliamentary government. He surrounded himself with a sort of camarilla, and affected the airs of a military dictator .... During his three years' dictatorship, the revolutionary spirit was broken step by step, through endless compromises...

Espartero was overthrown by General Narváez, and Marx referred to "the ten years of reaction Spain had suffered under the brutal dictatorship of Narváez."[69]

There was James Fazy, the Swiss Radical leader, whose behavior during the 1848 revolution disabused notions that he was of revolutionary mettle. In his work *Herr Vogt*, Marx repeatedly referred to him as the "dictator of Geneva" with virulent hostility. There was no analysis given, except for a

6. The Spectrum of 'Dictatorship'   91

remark that the rule of this "local Bonaparte" was "based on a four-year coalition between the so-called Radical party and the ultramontane party."[70]
There was the Polish nationalist leader, Kościuszko. In a sketch of the Polish national struggle, Marx's chronology listed: "April 17. General insurrection at Warsaw. *Kosciuszko* dictator."[71] This was simply a statement of fact.
There was Ledru-Rollin, compared with whom Louis Blanc was a revolutionist. As late as 1869, when Ledru-Rollin issued a call to the voters of France, Marx (in a letter to Engels) harked back to 1848 and the period of democratic emigration:

> What scares me about the French is the cursed confusion in their heads. Ledru-Rollin's epistle is quite that of a Pretender. He really seems to take seriously the dictatorship over France conferred on him by Heinzen.

Engels agreed that "Monsieur Ledru-Rollin is surely counting on nothing else but dictatorship."[72] They were probably giving him too much credit for political daring.

Finally, there was the collectivity not infrequently called "the dictators of September 4." This referred to 1870 when, with French armies crumbling under the German attack, the Second Empire toppled into the dust. A parliamentary rump, without any constitutional niceties, set itself up as the Provisional Government of the republic it proclaimed. The existing legality was ignored, utilizing the swell of the revolutionary tide among the people— whom they then hastened to head off. If any one man had taken power then, he would have been the very model of the democratic dictator of the contemporaneous language. This eventuality was avoided by the fact that the government was a collectivity of mediocrities. Hence the plural: the *dictators* of September 4.

We find this expression plentifully in the pages of the Paris Commune's official organ, the *Journal Officiel*. It was, no doubt, a commonplace of the time. It is not to be wondered at, then, that it was used by-the-way by Marx in writing one of the drafts of his *Civil War in France*. In fact, he was reporting a news event: a chairman had been named to head the investigating commission into the "doings of the dictators of 4 September."[73]

The preceding list, while incomplete,[74] may give more detail than necessary, but detail is needed to convey the linguistic habits of another day. After all, we are living in times when a social-democratic spokesman can write in all seriousness that Marx

> committed a rhetorical sin which history has not forgiven and which many a totalitarian has celebrated: he used the word 'dictatorship' to describe democracy.[75]

It was all his fault, you see.

In the year 1850, when Marx first used the phrase 'dictatorship of the proletariat', there were all kinds of dictatorships and dictators around in the public consciousness. But we have left for last a type specially important for our enterprise.

7 | SOME DICTATORS OVER THE PROLETARIAT

If we look for those occasions when Marx or Engels spoke of dictatorship *in* the socialist or workers' movement, we will be no more successful than before in finding perfect consistency, but the first thing to be noted is that in this context any form of the term ('dictator', 'dictatorship', etc.) was pejorative. This was true whether they were speaking of enemies or friends, opponents or colleagues; in the former case, it was a denunciation, in the latter case a criticism. Of course, the situation was clearest in the case of opponents; but I know of no case where they used the term as a mere cuss-word, without a certain substance behind it.

The second point to be emphasized is that in none of the cases to be reported was the term 'dictatorship' linked in their minds with that other term 'dictatorship of the proletariat'. These were two separate items of vocabulary.

In Marx's view—and, I think, quite accurately—the worst case of "workers' dictator" among his associates and colleagues was Ferdinand Lassalle; among his enemies, Bakunin.

1. BAKUNIN AND THE "SECRET DICTATORSHIP" OF ANARCHY

We have already seen the first stage (1848) of Bakunin's theory of dictatorship. His later adoption of an anarchist ideology gave this theory additional roots.

What many people do not understand about anarchism is that it denounces the most ideally democratic forms of decision-making as "authoritarian" and evil; for the will of the sovereign individual must not bow before any outside demand. What then do you do when people disagree, in any organized society where individuals have to live in concert? Anarchism has no answer. In words, it rejects both despotism and democracy as "authoritarian," and gropes for a third alternative. But none is found: only elocution about Freedom. The real choice before real anarchists has been this: the safety of highminded but impotent and meaningless rhetoric, or else resort to special forms of elitist despotism alleged to be antistatist in some way. This is Kropotkin vs. Bakunin. Bakunin inaugurated anarchism as a movement on the basis of the second type of solution.

The first work that put forward essentially this understanding of Bakuninism was the First International's brochure of 1873, written by Engels and Lafargue (with Marx collaborating on the conclusion), titled *The Alliance of the Socialist Democracy and the International Working Men's Association* (the first-named organization being Bakunin's front). The evidence contained in this pamphlet, directed to exposing the nature of the Bakunin bore-from-within operation in the International, was hastily assembled. But in all essentials it was correct. The denigration that has long been directed against it stems in good part from the dishonest treatment by that overrated historian Franz Mehring, in his vastly overrated biography of Marx. But later documentation has verified every important charge in the pamphlet, and much besides.*

For present purposes, let us look at two documents in which Bakunin set forth his aim of a dictatorship. Both stem from 1870 when he was just putting together his rule-or-ruin drive in the International; both were unknown to Marx. The first is the only *public* document in which he expressed himself candidly. It was sent to Albert Richard of Lyons, then a friend and disciple, as a message, or manifesto, to be read to a mass meeting, in lieu of Bakunin's coming to speak in person. Richard published its text twenty-six years later. The message called on the audience to "proclaim the liquidation of the State and of bourgeois society, anarchy ... "

> And in order to save the revolution, to lead it to a successful conclusion in the very midst of this anarchy, [there is need of] the action of a collective dictatorship of all the revolutionists who are not invested with any official power whatever, and [are] all the more effective...[1]

Bakunin was the enemy of all 'official" dictatorship; he wanted an "unofficial" dictatorship. In letters to Richard, he explained that the goal was "revolutionary anarchy led on all points by an invisible collective power, the only dictatorship that I accept . . ." He stressed repeatedly that he was for this "collective dictatorship" by his "invisible" secret band of conspirators who imposed their hidden control over an anarchic revolution, without any open political structure (which would be the hated "state"). He explained that "the partisans of open dictatorship" will want to reconstitute the state; but we, having created "anarchy,"

---

* The story of Mehring's operation, just before World War I, will be told in sufficient detail in the next volume of KMTR, which will also deal more thoroughly than here with Bakunin's theory of the "secret dictatorship." For this reason, the present chapter is limited to some highlights.

7. Some Dictators over the Proletariat   95

as invisible pilots amidst the proletarian tempest, we must direct it, not by an open power but by the collective dictatorship of the *Alliés* [Alliance members]: a dictatorship without any badges of office, without titles, without official rights, and all the stronger in that it will have none of the appearances of power. That is the only dictatorship that I accept.

You must not support "official, open dictatorship," he warned; that way lies failure. Bakunin was very repetitious on this idea, and the reader must excuse us for omitting the repeated versions of the "secret dictatorship." Suffice to report that he finally assured friend Richard that he had no ambitious hankerings for fame like Garibaldi. His "whole ambition," he averred, was simply "the desire to help you form that invisible collective force which alone can save and direct the revolution." Nothing grandiose, you see: just the aspiration to be the "real power" controlling the world while anarchy swirls over all..,[2]

Bakunin's letter of June 2, 1870 to Sergei Nechayev was discovered and published only in 1966. It revealed far more about the would-be anarchist dictator's politics than his scheme of "secret dictatorship," but that is the part we are interested in. In this letter Bakunin repeated the whole plan for secret dictatorship in even greater detail, but it would be very repetitious to quote these passages. However, it is much more explicit than before on the organizational end of the scheme. The "invisible force" is now described as "the collective dictatorship of our organization," the "secret organization" of the invisible controllers, whom Bakunin had previously called the "invisible legion" or the "invisible network."

Imagine yourself in a successful revolution, Bakunin invited.

> But imagine, in the midst of this general anarchy, a secret organization which has scattered its members in small groups over the whole territory ... firmly united... an organization which acts everywhere according to a common plan. These small groups, unknown by anybody as such, have no officially recognized power but they are strong in their ideal... strong also in their clearly realized purpose among a mass of people struggling without purpose or plan.

In this wet-dream of invisible power, Bakunin's key idea was not merely the described organization but *monopoly of organization*, for the function of "anarchy" was to destroy everybody else's organization, which was by definition "authoritarian." Again and again Bakunin explained that the "secret collective dictatorship" would hold the real reins of power. He calculated that fifty or sixty, at most seventy, bravos could control a whole continent through the device of "anarchy" plus the secret, invisible "brotherhood." If you took the conception held by a particularly ignorant village constable of the "dictatorship of the party" exercised by Red Subversive Bolsheviki, and stripped it of most rational elements, you would get—Bakunin's orgasmic dream of his Secret Dictatorship.[3]

This was the dream that Bakunin was trying to realize in the International, in order to throw out the "authoritarians" and turn it into the organizational base of the Invisible Brotherhood. The fact that a good part of his scheme existed only in his fantasy did not save the International from being smashed up.

2. MARX ON BAKUNIN'S DICTATORSHIP

As mentioned, Marx and everyone else in the International's leadership were unaware of the documents described above and many others of similar import. There were plentiful suspicions based on experience. In 1869, as Bakunin's operation got under way, Marx remarked in a letter to Engels: "This Russian evidently wants to become dictator of the European working-class movement. He had better have a care. Else he will be officially excommunicated."[4] Marx's mistake was in ignoring this completely correct prevision and, instead, favoring the admission of Bakunin's organization into the International when it pretended to dissolve its parallel structure. Marx was taken in.

I will take up the tale of Bakunin's operation in the International in another work; here we are interested only in one corner of the story, namely, the role played by 'dictatorship'. On the surface, it was a charge flung back and forth. As we have seen, Bakunin had worked out a rationale which permitted him to thunder against "dictatorship" with freedom-loving ardor, keeping his fingers crossed as he told his acolytes that this rhetoric meant only "official dictatorship." On the other side, his opponents gathered only gradually that this paladin of Liberty was building an organization (which called itself the Alliance, for short) that aimed to impose its unfettered domination on the movement.

Writing to the Belgian International leader Cesar de Paepe at just about the same time that Bakunin was baring his scheme to Richard, Marx spoke of the efforts of the Swiss Federal Council "to emancipate itself from the dictatorship of the Alliance."[5] De Paepe, long a dupe of Bakunin, probably thought this usage was metaphorical. A little later the General Council sent out a circular to the sections about the Bakunin operation: in Geneva its opponents had "denied him any 'dictatorial' influence in the movement"; Bakunin's aim was to get the seat of the General Council transferred to Geneva, where "the International would fall under the dictatorship of B."[6] In a long programmatic letter to Lafargue, analyzing Bakunin's campaign in the International, Marx

7. Some Dictators over the Proletariat 97

three times referred to "Bakunin's [would-be] dictatorship over the International association" and to the "intrigues of the Alliance and its Muscovite dictator."[7]

The Bakuninists, of course, systematically accused the General Council of "dictatorship" over the organization, on the basic ground that any leading committee that was more than a mailing address was an authoritarian monster by definition (except naturally for the invisible dictators of the Bakuninist organization). There were no charges whose substance repays examination, but a thick miasmic cloud of accusation was industriously spread. One reply appeared in the International's Zurich organ *Tagwacht*, and Engels sent it on to Lafargue as an example. It said, for example:

> A dictatorship always presupposes that the dictator wields material power enabling him to have his dictatorial orders executed. Now, we should be much obliged to all these journalists if they would kindly tell us where the General Council has its arsenal of bayonets and guns.

More to the present point, it went on to detail the very limited powers of the General Council, the wide-ranging democracy of its organization, the broad range of opinions inside it, and so on.[8] In a circular to sections written by Engels, the members were told that, while the Bakuninists charged the General Council with authoritarian acts without specifying a single one, "these very same men, in practice, constitute themselves as a secret society with a hierarchical organization, and under a, not merely authoritative [i.e., authoritarian], but absolutely dictatorial leadership..."[9]

As the last citation shows, by this time in 1872, the International's leaders had gained a working knowledge of the secret organization and hidden plans of the Bakuninist conspiracy, published in 1873 in the aforementioned brochure, *The Alliance of the Socialist Democracy and the International Working Men's Association*. An article by Engels, who had worked with Lafargue on collecting the dossier, summarized its import: it dealt with "the organization of a secret society with the sole aim of subjecting the European worker's movement to the secret dictatorship of a few adventurers who, to this end, especially through Nechayev in Russia, perpetrated infamies..."[10]

Since those days, the charge that the General Council exercised some sort of dictatorial or "authoritarian" control over the International has been copied from tome to tome, with the same lack of specificity, even though the practices tolerated by the General Council without turning a hair would bring instant expulsion from any social-democratic party in the world. Some of the dirt flung freely about by the "invisible network" was gratefully accepted by the reactionary press. For example, the French government's unofficial London "police sheet" (Marx's term) carried an article headed: "The Universal Dictatorship." This referred to the International, whose overflowing moneybags, it seems, were financing the current strike wave in France. Marx sent the item on to Engels as a curiosity.[11]

3. LASSALLE AS "WORKERS' DICTATOR"

Contrary to the myth that Marx's hostility to Lassalle was personal in origin, the facts show that *up to 1865* Marx was the only one of Lassalle's communist associates who liked him personally and trusted him. For example, when in 1850 or 1851 Marx (from London) proposed to the local Düsseldorf branch of the Communist League that Lassalle be admitted to membership, even Marx's prestige and influence could not prevent the branch from rejecting him, unanimously and repeatedly. For several years Marx and Lassalle corresponded as warm friends.

The turning point came in 1856, when the Rhenish communists sent an emissary, Gustav Lewy, to London with two assignments, one of which was to open Marx's eyes about Lassalle. For a week Lewy talked to Marx about the Rhineland situation and the case of Lassalle. At the end of the week Marx reported to Engels in a letter explaining at some length how deeply shaken he was on the Lassalle side of the visit. There had been several previous attempts by Rhenish comrades to disillusion Marx about Lassalle (by letter) but they had been unsuccessful. Again, we confine ourselves here to one aspect only.[12]

Wonderingly, Marx informed Engels what Lewy had told him:

> ... in Lewy's presence he [Lassalle] constantly expressed his "hankering to be a dictator" (he seems to look upon himself quite differently from how we look on him; he considers himself world-conquering because he was ruthless in a personal intrigue ...) [i.e., in the Hatzfeldt case, which made him a rich man].[13]

This was the first such report Marx received, but not the last. We now know that Lassalle had been quite candid about his overweening ambitions since early youth. Lewy was not retailing gossip. Lassalle had hidden this side of his character in his intercourse with Marx but not in other relations, that is, not in relations with his natural inferiors.

In the next years Lassalle's publications were instrumental in convincing Marx that they were poles apart, agreeing "on nothing except some far-distant ultimate ends" (as Marx told him to his face one day).[14] Then in 1862, when Lassalle visited London, there was intense personal friction, but since we are still concentrating on one aspect we mention only the following. Lassalle told Marx and his wife how "he advised Garibaldi ... to go after Naples and there set himself up as dictator," how he acted as the "presiding genius" over other great events of the day.

7. Some Dictators over the Proletariat   99

Lassalle was very furious at me and my wife [Marx related to Engels] because we made merry about his plans, chaffed him as an "enlightened Bonapartist," etc.

Lassalle sneered at Americans as having no "ideas":

Individual liberty is only a "negative idea," etc., and more of this old, decaying speculative rubbish.[15]

In 1863 Lassalle sent Marx a copy of the pamphlet in which he made his bid for leadership of the German workers' movement, usually tagged the *Open Reply*. Marx read it and saw the essential point, telling Engels:

He behaves... altogether as if he were the future workers' dictator.... the workers must agitate for *universal suffrage* and then send people like him "armed with the unsheathed sword of science" into the Chamber of Deputies.[16]

In the next few months he received reports from Germany that Lassalle was openly talking about his dictatorial perspective (as was his wont). Wilhelm Liebknecht wrote: "Things are in ferment in the Lassallean workers' association. If Lassalle does not give up his 'dictatorial ways' and his 'flirting with reaction,' there will be a scandal."[17] Lassalle had actually openly talked about making an alliance with the monarchy against the liberal bourgeoisie.

In point of fact, as early as June 8,1863, Lassalle had sent a secret letter to Bismarck, crowing over the dictatorial powers he had been given as president of the Lassallean association, just founded—over

the constitution of *my* empire, which perhaps you'd have to envy me! But this miniature picture will plainly convince you how true it is that the working class feels instinctively inclined to dictatorship if it can first be rightfully convinced that it will be exercised in its interests, and how very much it would therefore be inclined, as I recently told you, in spite of all republican sentiments—or perhaps on those very grounds—to see in the Crown the natural bearer of the social dictatorship, in contrast to the egoism of bourgeois society, if the Crown for its part could ever decide on the (to be sure, very improbable) step of taking a really revolutionary and national direction and transforming itself from a kingdom of the privileged classes into a social and revolutionary People's Kingdom![18]

Lassalle was saved from the ditch into which he was steering by two events: Bismarck's rejection of his overtures and Lassalle's death a few months later.

It is hard to see why the myth of Marx's "personal" hatred had to be invented to account for his hostility to a man with such politics. As Marx summed up later about Lassalle's latter-day course:

As soon as he had convinced himself, in London (end of 1862), that he could not play his games *with* me, he decided to come out as the "workers' dictator"*against* me and the old party.[19]

Marx's reiterated label on Lassalle, as the would-be "workers'"dictator," was not a mere accusation, but a self-accepted description. As far as labels go, more often than not Engels' tag for Lassalle was 'Bonapartist', but the content was the same.[20]

Toward the end of his life, Engels carried out his aim of getting the truth about Lassalle's politics written down to educate the ranks of the Social-Democracy about their hero. The job was done under his direction by Eduard Bernstein, then still a revolutionary leftist; it was translated into English (by Eleanor Marx) as *Ferdinand Lassalle as a Social Reformer.* It was one of the best Marxist studies of a political line ever written. Still concentrating on our own subject, we cite only one aspect of this work.

Besides 'dictatorship' and 'Bonapartism', another common term of the day denoting the same family of politics was 'Caesarism' or 'social Caesarism'. In one of his speeches, Lassalle had come out openly as an advocate of the "social monarchy" allied with the People against the bourgeoisie—a monarchy, he said, "leaning upon the hilt of the sword." There was no mistaking this language. "This," said the Bernstein/Engels book, "is the language of Caesarism." It enlarged on the subject of dictatorship:

> The action of the masses does not, by a long way, mean personal dictatorship; indeed, where the masses abdicate their will, they are already on the road to become, from a revolutionary factor, a reactionary one. In the struggles of modern society, personal dictatorship has invariably been the sheet-anchor of the reactionary classes, seeing their existence imperiled. . . . The classes that feel themselves incapable of self-government do that which Lassalle is here imputing to the workers: they abdicate their own will in favor of a single person, and condemn every attempt to oppose any private interests of this person as "restless, malcontent individualism."

The example of Bonapartism is given: the French bourgeoisie attacked its own "malcontents" in this spirit—

> until Napoleon [Louis Bonaparte] was strong enough to proclaim himself dictator *against* the bourgeoisie, instead of contenting himself with the role of mere maintainer of law and order/or the bourgeoisie.... He [Lassalle] needed the dictatorship in order to be sure of the workers whenever he should require them for his actual ends, and he needed the endorsement of his dictatorship to appear to those in higher circles as a power to be treated with.

Those who would not follow this line were purged from the organization by Lassalle. "It is doubly a pronunciamento of Caesarism—Caesarism within

7. *Some Dictators over the Proletariat* 101

the ranks of the party, and Caesarism in the politics of the party."[21] A policy looking to the imposition of a dictatorship over the proletariat in society required the imposition of a dictatorship within the party.

4. THE APPRENTICE DICTATORS

Bakunin and Lassalle, as anarchist and state-socialist respectively, were superficially opposites, in the sense that you can reach the antipodes by going east or west. Both trained a movement that learned from their example how to run an organization—into the ground. Bakunin's lieutenant in the International-smashing operation had been the Swiss schoolmaster James Guillaume, who on the outbreak of the world war was going to publish some of the most violent social-chauvinist and anti-Semitic fulminations in the literature (e.g., *Karl Marx, Pangermaniste*). But when Bakunin died in 1876, Guillaume succeeded him as organizational chief in the anarchist International for a couple of years (before abandoning leftist activity in 1878 and moving from Switzerland to Paris).

Marx and Engels knew his modus operandi very well. In 1877 Engels suggested to his friend that they should keep an eye on "the world government in Neufchâtel," where Guillaume resided. "We have to know, after all, what anathemas the universal dictator and administrator of the Holy See promulgates."[22] Of course, both 'dictator' and (by implication) 'pope' referred to aspirations, not realities.

Less visible to socialist history has been another phenomenon: that of the apprentices who continued the organizational m.o. after the politics had eroded out. (The present-day analogue would be the Stalinists who continued their organizational habits long after shifting allegiance from Moscow to Washington.) One of the most prominent examples of this unappreciated type was the Bakuninist who became the leader of the reformist ("Possibilist") wing of French socialism, Paul Brousse. Engels pinned him up for socialist history with the following vignette:

> Brousse is just about the most helpless muddlehead I have ever seen. From anarchism he has dropped the anarchy, i.e., the fight against political activity and elections, but on the other hand he has maintained all other phrases and in particular the tactics of anarchism. Thus he is now fantasizing in *Le Prolétaire* in tedious articles aimed at Guesde (without naming him) on the insoluble question of how to establish an organization that excludes the possibility of a dictatorship (Guesde's!!).[23]

If I may be allowed a personal remark, which could be made by anyone who has spent time in the socialist movement: the type here described is notoriously eternal and ubiquitous. I have known more than one Brousse, including an obnoxiously bureaucratic type whose main interest was in working out party statutes to end bureaucratism for all time by complex procedures that would create a bureaucrat's paradise.

Engels added another brush stroke to Brousse's portrait:

> *Egalité* will appear one of these days; Brousse, as heretofore, will slander on the quiet, attack in *Le Prolftaire,* without naming names, and the others [the Guesdists] will be impatient enough to fall into the trap, first attacking with naming of names, and then be yelled at as disturbers of the peace, sectarians, splitters, and incipient dictators.[24]

Types like this were ink drops in a teacup when the movement was small and struggling, but became ink drops in an ocean when a class movement succeeded the period of sects.

Lassalle, too, had his epigones, who inherited the dictatorial powers of president of the Lassallean party; but only one of them proved capable of establishing himself as the new party dictator in his own right. This was J. B. von Schweitzer, a Jesuit-educated lawyer, who edited the movement's organ for a number of years, and became president in 1867. His Bismarckian orientation a la Lassalle made it necessary for Marx and Engels to make a public break with the "Royal Prussian government socialism" of the Lassalleans.[25] In addition his top-down dictatorial regime in the party generated a series of faction fights and splits. A superadded problem, especially important in Marx's eyes, was the fact that the Lassalleans also believed in, and implemented, the dictatorship of their party over "their" trade unions. In fact, the only place they saw for trade unions at all was as tools of the party, a view embodied in their own statutes.[26]

Marx kept in touch with dissidents and trade-unionists who tried to fight the Schweitzer steamroller. In September 1868 the Lassallean congress met in Berlin to plan the founding of party trade unions under the presidential control of Schweitzer, statutory dictator. Sending Engels a report received from a participant, Marx commented:

> ... in place of his dictatorship over the GGWA [his party organization] Schweitzer thinks he can put a dictatorship over the German working class in a much simpler fashion. This is being very naive.[27]

Engels replied that he had read in Schweitzer's paper "that he wanted to carry over the 'tight organization' [of the party] into the trades unions," but did not think it would be possible. "Trades [union] business is money business, and here dictatorship comes to an end of itself." (This aphorism, to be sure, referred to an outside party dictatorship for aims alien to trade-union interests.) And he suggested to Marx that he should write directly to the Lassallean boss, to "point out a few things to Schweitzer about his claim to dictatorship."[28]

7. Some Dictators over the Proletariat   103

And in fact Marx did so. This was a very important statement on sectism in the political movement and bureaucratism in the trade-union movement, but, as before, we cannot follow these leads here. Suffice it to say that Marx's direct reference to Schweitzer's dictatorship echoed Engels' suggestion: the trade-union movement "revolves largely around money questions, and you will soon discover that here all dictatorship comes to an end."[29] *

The following year, the anti-dictatorial opposition in the organization was stronger, as the General German Workers' Association held a congress in March. Some of the president's dictatorial executive powers were cut. Engels thought this was "an enormous defeat for Schweitzer." In this connection, he used another locution for dictatorship: "Schweitzer's campaign for the kingship of the tailors," referring to the regime of John of Leyden in the Anabaptist community of Minister—an analogy we have already met.[30] He added sententiously: *"N'est pas dictateur qui veut"* (Wanting to be a dictator doesn't make you one).

Schweitzer was thrown out of office and out of the movement by 1872; three years later, the Lassalleans merged with the Bebel forces (Eisenachers) in the new Social-Democratic Party. Schweitzerism became a historical incident. Marx and Engels recalled it for a moment in 1879 when they prepared a blast against a new and different menace, a move to turn the new party into a middle-class reform group. Drafting their statement, they wrote that while Schweitzer had emphasized the revolutionary class struggle, "he may thereby also have concocted a pretext for himself to cast suspicion on persons dangerous to his dictatorship."[31] Then they struck this passage out of the document, no doubt as irrelevant to the matter at hand. Schweitzer remained in their minds as the very model of the intraparty dictator. Over a decade later, Engels was discussing the bad attitudes of the German party leadership toward minority dissent:

> The largest party in the Reich [he warned, meaning the Social-Democrats] cannot exist without all shades within it being articulated to the full, and even the *appearance* of a dictatorship à la Schweitzer must be avoided.[32]

Not accidentally, the "appearance" came up the following year, in still another quarter. The occasion this time was the uproar that greeted Engels' 1891 publication in the *Neue Zeit* of Marx's suppressed *Critique of the Gotha*

---

* As a point of curiosity, let us mention that Marx did not use the ordinary German word for dictatorship' *(Diktatur)* but rather *Diktatortum,* which more or less corresponds to 'dictatordom'. Indeed, in a previously cited passage Marx had used *Diktatorschaft,* which likewise cannot be found in a German dictionary; it sounds modeled after the English word. In the case of both neologisms, the stem is *Diktator,* thereby emphasizing the person of the dictator rather than the office.

Program of 1875, an uproar led by Liebknecht and swelled by the entire right wing of the party. Proposals came from the Reichstag (parliamentary) fraction that the *Neue Zeit* should be "placed under censorship," Engels wrote in a letter, shocked. This sort of talk by the Reichstag fraction had a history. During the period of illegality under the Anti-Socialist Law of 1878-1890 only the Reichstag deputies were permitted to function for the party, and so the fraction became the *de facto* leading committee inside Germany. Engels made a bitter comparison with the proposal to censor the *Neue Zeit:*

> Is this the ghost of the Fraction's dictatorship during the Anti-Socialist Law (which was certainly necessary and excellently carried out), or is it a reminiscence of Schweitzer's erstwhile tight organization? It's a brilliant idea indeed to put German socialist science, after its liberation from Bismarck's Socialist Law, under a new Socialist Law to be devised and carried out by the Social-Democratic party authorities themselves.[33]

During the period of the Anti-Socialist Law, accusations of 'dictatorship' had been traded on all sides. In 1882, when the tug-of-war between the rightward-leaning Fraction majority and the illegally published organ *Sozialdemokrat* was at a peak, Bebel rebuked the Fraction for wanting to play dictator in the party. Bernstein, the editor, attacked the "censorship" by the Fraction (same thing). On the other hand, Wilhelm Hasenclever, under attack by Bebel for wanting a deal with the conservatives, charged Bebel with "again playing party dictator." Liebknecht, then supporting the Fraction in his muddleheaded fashion, had to deny "that I strive for dictatorship." But in 1896 *he* was denounced by his editorial associates on *Vorwärts* for his "dictatorial" conduct. The following year Liebknecht accused Bebel of trying to establish a dictatorship within the party—by allegedly moving to ignore a congress decision.[34]

I mention these incidents only for their illustrative value; they were a sort of obbligato accompaniment to the strains and tensions of party life. The problem of inner-party democracy had a long history, in which the term 'dictatorship' figured as only one element.

5. A CLUTCH OF DICTATORS

In connection with whom else did Marx or Engels speak of dictatorship? Let us review some miscellaneous cases.

There was the movement founded by Auguste Comte, which called itself Positivist. It was not a working-class movement, certainly, but it sought a working-class membership or clientele—for example, during the period of the International's activity. In fact, a Positivist workers' club had sought affiliation

7. Some Dictators over the Proletariat   105

in France, and had been accepted on condition that it not use its sect appellation. English Comtists were friendly to the International (Professor Beesly had chaired the founding meeting in 1864), but the French variety was much more alien to the workers' movement.

In his first draft for the address on the Paris Commune, the *Civil War in France,* Marx included a passage designed to separate the International from Comte:

> Comte is known to the Parisian workmen as the prophet in politics of Imperialism (of personal *Dictatorship*), of capitalist rule in political economy, of hierarchy in all spheres of human action, even in the sphere of science, and as author of a new catechism with a new pope and new saints in place of the old ones.[35]

But this was left out of the final version, no doubt in the interests of good relations with the English Comtists. (The word 'Imperialism' meant the regime of Bonaparte's Second Empire; it should be taken as a synonym for 'Bonapartism'.)

In England, Engels had a Schweitzer-model party dictator right at hand in the person of H. M. Hyndman, leader of the Social Democratic Federation, which claimed to be a Marxist group. Hyndman's dictatorial conduct of the organization was notorious, and was a major reason for the split (December 1884) that produced the Socialist League under William Morris. A few months before this, Engels had informed Kautsky that Hyndman had alienated his friends and associates by his character as a leader, in particular by "his impatience to play the dictator."[36]

Although Engels greeted the formation of the Independent Labour Party, and apparently even took out membership in it, he was not an admirer of Keir Hardie, the Scottish labor leader who was instrumental in bringing it into existence. Engels seems to have suspected Hardie of dictatorial ambitions; some believe that he was prejudiced against the Scotsman by Aveling. For example, soon after the party was founded at its Bradford conference Engels wrote Bebel as follows:

> From Aveling's oral accounts, a suspicion I had earlier has been strengthened, namely, that K. Hardie cherishes the unspoken wish to lead the new party in a dictatorial way, as Parnell led the Irish, and that besides his sympathies tend more toward the Conservative than toward the Liberal opposition party.[37]

To understand the last point in the indictment, one must keep the Lassalle pattern in mind; Marx's criticism did not imply sympathy with the Liberals. For a socialist to have *more* sympathy for the reactionary wing of politics than for the bourgeois liberal wing raised the specter of "social monarchy" politics in German terms and of "Tory socialism" in British terms. This species of socialist *was* historically inclined toward dictatorial solutions in order to dragoon the working class into an uncongenial course. None of this gainsays the view that Engel's suspicions of Hardie were unjust.

The man whose *drift* toward dictatorship most saddened Marx was his friend Ernest Jones, who outlasted Harney as a left-wing leader of the Chartist movement. Jones was accused of dictatorial aspirations in the movement as early as 1852, and in particular by none other than Harney.* At the end of 1851 Jones had been elected to the Executive of the National Charter Association at the head of the poll, but he resigned immediately on the ground that he could not sit on an Executive so constituted. This paralyzed the Executive, and resulted in a number of accusations of dictatorial methods and desires. Harney published a bitter attack in his *Friend of the People* (April 24, 1852), likewise repeating the charge that Jones was a would-be dictator.

By 1855 Jones was becoming increasingly impatient of internal criticism. In "A Call to Action" in the *People's Paper* early the next year, he proposed that power in the organization be concentrated in the hands of his associate James Finlen and himself:

> If you so confide the movement to our hands, you must expect no explanations, and no long-worded programmes from us. If we say "organise," you must organise—"assemble," you must assemble; obeying implicitly.... Distrust all those that declaim against leadership. ... A thousand times sooner give me the worst Dictatorship; than the blabbing squabbles of contending factions in our ranks.[39]

These were words of despair and disorientation, not hope and militancy. Another difference was that, whereas in 1852 Jones' fight was against the politics of coalition with middle-class politicians, now he had come to favor an alliance with the reformers. He wanted a dictatorship to put through a policy opposite to that which had once gained him the confidence of Chartist militants. He was given his dictatorship at the Chartist Conference of February 1858: the majority voted for a one-man Executive, and he was named the one man.[40]

On both counts, Jones' move to the right and his demand for a dictatorship, Marx repudiated Jones' new views. After the "Call to Action," he wrote Engels: "You probably know that Jones, with Finlen as his shadow, has proclaimed himself dictator of Chartism and has set up a new organization

---

* To be sure, this was not the first outcry against "dictatorship" inside the Chartist movement. The older target had been Feargus O'Connor, leader of the so-called "physical-force Chartists" on the left wing of the movement. In 1889, writing to a Danish socialist who had been expelled from the party by its right wing, Engels attacked other cases in which a party leadership had expelled oppositionists. His first example was "the secret societies of 1840-51," in particular "the dictatorship of O'Connor" among the physical-force Chartists.[38]

which indeed is in process of growing, but on the other hand has also provoked a big storm of indignation against him."[41]

In various letters to Engels, as he watched the development with disgust, he lashed at Jones' "stupidity." Jones was an ass for getting himself into a situation where on the one hand he advocated collaboration with the bourgeois reformers and lost the respect of the left, while on the other hand he himself did not enjoy the confidence of the reformers; he was being knocked on both sides of the head. "That old ass" John Frost, whom Jones had made president, was now knifing him: "Who authorized him [Jones] to designate Frost president and to play the dictator himself, etc.?"[42]

Jones' "dictatorship" solution was simply the specific form in which the movement cut its own throat. But it was an ignoble way to die.

There is a sad epilogue to this sad story. Harney, who in 1852 was storming against Jones' aspirations for a dictatorship to control the movement from within, had the misfortune to grow old and eviscerated. By the latter 1880s he was again corresponding with Engels as an old friend, but the life had gone out of him. In one letter he wrote:

> What Ireland needs, and England, too, is a Cromwell, who should begin by hanging Parnell and his gang, and Gladstone and Morley along with them; and then—having executed *justice on* these ragamuffins, set about doing *justice to*—not only the "farmers"—but the labourers, and others.[43]

"Wanted," he wrote later, "a Dictator with the heart and conscience of Ruskin and the hand and brain of Cromwell."[44] It was perfectly clear that this pathetic faith in dictatorship was the positive side of something that had rotted away: "I have not the least confidence or belief," he wrote, "in the class toward whose political and social emancipation I gave the best years of my life." But the rot was not merely in his view of the working class: speaking of the 1848 revolution, he said that he "then believed what, alas! to my bitterest sorrow, I cannot believe now—believed in the 'sovereign people.' "[45] But he could now believe in the sovereign dictator...*

---

* In an article "Harney and Engels," much referred-to because of its information on the correspondence between these two men, Peter Cadogan came out with the following assertion:

> [Ernest] Jones was the first man (at least in England) to accept Marx's theory of the dictatorship of the proletariat as a working basis for an organization.[45]

Interesting if true! But it was an invention. In an article otherwise outfitted with scholarly references, there was no note on this claim or other explanation of what it was based on. We must guess that Cadogan meant Jones's outreach for a personal dictatorship *over* the Chartist organization—which Marx condemned, which heralded Jones's evolution *away* from proletarian politics, and which in any case had not the least connection in Jones's mind with Marx's[1] 'dictatorship of the proletariat' (which Jones

Surely it is one of the great tragedies in the history of thought when a good man spits on his own past in order to revile everything that made him worth our acquaintance in the first place.

We now have to return to a very different man, Karl Marx, who has been accused of aspirations for dictatorship more often than anyone else. He once commented on this fact, as he described to Engels the gloomy picture of his financial problems and intolerable living conditions:

> You will admit that all this shit is not very pleasant, and that I am stuck in petty-bourgeois crap up to the ears. And besides, they have me exploiting the workers! and striving for a dictatorship! *Quelle horreur.*[47]

In Part III we will see—*quelle horreur!*—what 'dictatorship' it was Marx was striving for.

---

never discussed as far as is known). Cadogan was even more unfortunate: on the next page he specifically counterposed the Freedom-loving Harney to Jones's mythical acceptance of the 'dictatorship of the proletariat'—without any comment on Harney's latter-day acceptance of dictatorship in the very correspondence he was quoting. This is the way that myths get launched.

III | PRELIMINARIES: THE "MARX-BLANQUIST" MYTH

8 | INTRODUCTION TO THE INVESTIGATION

Before we take up Marx's use of the term 'dictatorship of the proletariat' itself, there are a few preliminaries to be set forth.

I. PERIODIZATION

Marx first used the wingèd words 'dictatorship of the proletariat' in 1850. Why? Under what circumstances?

It has been plentifully pointed out, quite justly, that this phrase appeared only infrequently in the writings of Marx and Engels, though we will find that the number of appearances is rather greater than is often claimed. Still, there is no doubt that it was used only at times. Well, at *what* times?

Marx's customary term for the same idea, we have explained, was 'rule of the proletariat', or the like. Yet 'dictatorship of the proletariat' did keep cropping up, as a reformulation, even in Marx's mature years, and also in Engels' last years. Was there a pattern?

It will help to orient our thinking *on* this question if we anticipate one important result of the investigation that follows. *Marx's and Engels' use of the term 'dictatorship of the proletariat' clustered in three periods, and the term was notably absent in between.* These three periods were the following:

Period I: *1850 to 1852*, that is, the postrevolutionary period after the great upheaval of 1848-1849.

Period II: *1871 to 1875,* that is, the postrevolutionary period after the Paris Commune.

Period III: *1890 to 1891*. This period, of course, involved Engels only. We will see that it was a sort of echo from 1875.

This periodization, we will find, is also a major clue to the aforementioned pattern.

2. THE 'RULE OF THE PROLETARIAT'

Marx's customary term, 'rule of the proletariat', represented the view he had come to, probably by 1844, that to achieve communism the proletariat had to conquer political power. The 'conquest of political *(or* state) power', 'rule of the proletariat': this was not only Marx's usual terminology, it was the terminology common in the movement.

One of Marx's first statements of the idea was written into the *German Ideology* (1845-1846), but the term is often obscured by English translations in a typical fashion. *Herrschaft*—variously translated as 'rule', 'domination', 'mastery', 'sway', 'ascendancy', etc.—was Marx's usual term, but here, for example, is how one version of the passage comes out:

> ... every class which is struggling for mastery *[Herrschaft]*, even when its domination *[Herrschaft]*, as is the case with the proletariat, postulates the abolition of the old form of society in its entirety and of mastery *[Herrschaft]* itself, must first conquer for itself political power in order to represent its interest in turn as the general interest...[1]

This sort of translation makes for literary variety but it blurs the fact that Marx used a fairly standard term for a very definite idea: 'rule of the proletariat'.

Looking back very much later, after Marx's death, Engels was going to write:

> ∞... we have always held, that in order to arrive at this [disappearance of the state] and the other, far more important ends of the social revolution of the future, the proletarian class will first have to possess itself of the organised political force of the State and with this aid stamp out the resistance of the Capitalist class and re-organise society. This is stated already in the Communist Manifesto of 1847 *[sic]*, end of Chapter II.[2]

As we have seen, this view went back earlier than the Manifesto. In the year before publication of the Manifesto, Engels explained in a newspaper article that communists wanted to act, as Democrats, together with the Democrats in all practical affairs:

> In all civilized countries the necessary consequence of Democracy is the political rule of the proletariat, and the political rule of the proletariat is the first presupposition of all communist measures.[3]

"The establishment of the rule of the proletariat" was incorporated into the rules of the Communist League, as the aim of the league, that same year.[4]

The very earliest communists, Babeuf's comrades, had been alive to the importance of the revolutionary provisional government, or transitional regime, that was to follow the revolutionary act; by the 1840s this concern was virtually automatic. Everyone had to have an answer to the question. In his draft for the Manifesto, called *Principles of Communism,* Engels described the course of the revolution in a way we have already seen, as the rule of the Democracy.[5]

> First of all, it will establish a *democratic constitution* and thereby, directly or indirectly, the political rule of the proletariat. Directly in England, where the proletarians are already a majority of the people. Indirectly in France and Germany, where the majority of the people consists not of proletarians alone but also of small peasants and petty-bourgeois who are in the process of falling into the proletariat .... Perhaps this will cost a second struggle, but the outcome can only be the victory of the proletariat.[6]

The rule of the Democracy, then, would be the prelude to the rule of the proletariat.

The Manifesto, whose final draft was without doubt due to Marx's pen alone, had nothing to say about the Democratic stage, but reiterated the aim of the *rule of the proletariat.* For a number of reasons, including Marx's own later link-up with the 'dictatorship of the proletariat', it is important to set out what the Manifesto had to say about "rule."[7]

> All previous movements were movements of minorities or in the interest of minorities. The proletarian movement is the independent movement of the immense majority in the interest of the immense majority. The proletariat, the lowest stratum of present-day society, cannot raise itself up, cannot stand erect, without bursting asunder the whole superstructure of strata that make up official society.

This does not say that the proletariat is the majority of society by itself; it is the movement led by the proletariat that represents the "immense majority." The perspective of proletarian "rule" was tied to a vanguard view of the class's role.

> The immediate aim of the Communists is the same as that of all the other proletarian parties: constitution of the proletariat into a class, overthrow of bourgeois rule, conquest of political power by the proletariat.

It is vital to note that this view was explicitly presented as *not* distinctive of the Communists, but common to "all the other proletarian parties."

When the Manifesto took up a direct discussion of the transitional regime and its program, it repeated that "the first step in the workers' revolution is the elevation of the proletariat to the ruling class, the winning of democracy."*

---

* The Engels-Moore translation blurred this last phrase into "win the battle of democracy," giving rise to numerous misunderstandings; but further discussion of this would be digressive.

The next paragraph stated that "The proletariat will use its political rule" to carry through a transitional program which, "by means of despotic encroachments on the right of property," will gradually put production "in the hands of the state, i.e., of the proletariat organized as ruling class." It then went on to say:

> When in the course of development class distinctions have disappeared and all production is concentrated in the hands of associated individuals, the public power loses its political character. Political power in its proper sense is the organized power of one class for the oppression of another. When in the struggle against the bourgeoisie the proletariat necessarily unifies itself as a class, makes itself the ruling class through a revolution, and as ruling class forcibly abolishes the old relations of production, then along with these relations of production it abolishes the preconditions of existence of class antagonism and of classes in general, and therewith its own rule as a class.

We are going to see that Marx himself believed that these passages of the Manifesto already said what there was to say about the 'dictatorship of the proletariat'.[8] When the Manifesto stated that "all the other proletarian parties" stood for the rule of the proletariat, it undoubtedly had the Chartists in mind high up the list. Ernest Jones wrote: "If we make our power tell, we can dictate our own terms, and force every other class to the recognition of our sovereign rights." He put forward the slogan, "Political power—the sovereignty of the People!" George Julian Harney proclaimed: "For the working classes there is but one way of righting their wrongs, that of obtaining mastery of the state."[9]

The labor historian Max Beer commented that the Chartist movement grasped "its immediate aim—the conquest of political power . . . with unmistakable distinctness and energy." So did its enemies: in 1842 the liberal historian and parliamentarian Macaulay, speaking on the presentation of the Charter, told the House that universal suffrage was incompatible with government, with the existence of an aristocracy, and with civilization itself. "Therefore, we can never, without absolute danger, entrust the supreme government of the country to any class" which would make inroads on property. The Charter petitioners, if successful, "will become the sovereign body of the State" because they will have a majority of the people's representatives. "The petitioners ask for supreme power"; capital and property "is to be placed absolutely at the foot of labour." Macaulay had no doubt that military despotism would be the result.[10]

This fear was not simply of the "dictatorship of the Democracy." Theoreticians of liberalism like Macaulay were certain that universal suffrage and the rule of the majority of the people would mean a dictatorship, certainly a dictatorship of the Democracy but even more specifically a dictatorship of the pr— No, the words were not spoken.

3. THE CONCEPT OF CLASS RULE

Macaulay understood a question that baffled a modern marxologist. Bertram D. Wolfe, in his *Marxism, One Hundred Years* [etc.], raised "the question of the very possibility of the dictatorship of an entire class, or for that matter, how and to what extent an entire class can ever rule in a complex government."

> Has the political history of modern times ever known a party which embraces a whole class? Can this be said even of the British Labour Party with its trade-union affiliation and its local clubs, a party which comes nearer to being that of a class than any other?*... Does the entire proletariat, more or less, enter the party, pay dues, select officers [etc.]...? How does an entire class dictate? rule? exercise its *Herrschaft*?[12]

Wolfe implied here that the concept of 'class rule' of the proletariat raises unanswerable questions; he at least offered no answers. But Macaulay *inter alia*, we saw, had no doubt about the answer, which was simple enough: the class rule of the proletariat would be expressed through control of the "sovereign body of the state" by a majority of the people's representatives under universal suffrage. Or, to generalize: proletarian *class* rule would be expressed through the democratic institutions of a government which is set up to maximize control from below. (In contrast, bourgeois democracy is set up, through the forms of universal suffrage and parliamentarism, to keep control from below to a minimum.) Macaulay, it turns out, was in complete agreement with what Engels wrote in his draft for the *Communist Manifesto*: a "democratic

---

* With his flair for swingeing statements offered without a note or reference in factual support, Wolfe added here digressively: "It was precisely this 'class party' [the Labour Party] that Marx and Engels treated with contempt." This is one of Wolfe's many off-the-cuff inventions: it would have been *very* difficult for them to treat the Labour Party with contempt since Engels died a few years before the party was founded. But it is not only over the calendar that Wolfe stumbled. In an anticipatory way, the Labour Party was what Marx and Engels had been calling on British labor to organize. And when the Independent Labour Party was formed in 1893 Engels hailed it with enthusiasm and urged all socialists to join it, even though he was disappointed by its subsequent development.[11]

For Marx's views urging the formation of a broad, class labor party not only in Britain but in America and elsewhere, see a 1934 John Day pamphlet titled *Marx and America*— by Bertram D. Wolfe. *This* pamphlet presented Marx's and Engels' writings on the issue in some detail; having subsequently become an Authority, Wolfe asserted the exact opposite without a syllable of documentation.

constitution" meant "directly or indirectly, the political rule of the proletariat"—directly in England because there the proletariat formed a majority of the people.[13]

The class rule of the proletariat, then, is defined by the institutions of democracy in a workers' state. Wolfe devoted a passage to explaining that no answer to his stumper is to be found in Marx, because poor Marx was "not very sophisticated politically." The sophisticated marxologist, in other words, was ignorant of the fact that his question had been asked in the 1870s—and answered by Marx.

In an 1873 book Bakunin had directed precisely this question to Marx: "What does it mean—'the proletariat organized as ruling class'?"—"Will perhaps the whole proletariat stand at the head of the government?"—"The Germans number about 40 million. Will all 40 million, for example, be members of the government?"

Marx's answers to these Wolfian conundrums were, of course, conditioned by the fact that for Bakunin they were supposed to be arguments for anarchism. Marx's jottings* assumed the existence of a democratic proletarian state (a "Commune," as he puts it here), but he understood that for Bakunin a democratic state was even worse than a despotism. At first he scribbled this, for example:

> For example, in a trade union does the whole union form its executive committee? ... And in the Bakuninist structure "from below to above," will everyone be "above"? Then there is no "below." Will all the members of the Commune likewise administer the common interests of the Region? In this case, no difference between Commune and Region.

We see that, against Bakunin, he had to argue the basic idea of *representative* democracy. Replying to the stumper about the "40 million Germans," he stated the point in an unexpected way:

> °Certainly!° Since the thing begins with the self-government of the Commune.[14]

The "40 million" will be "members of the government" in a new sense which "the self-government of the Commune" makes possible for the first time: so plainly went Marx's train of thought. The entire class (indeed, the entire people) will be *involved* in ruling themselves . . . And at this point the sophisticated marxologists will treat Marx's "illusions" with the usual scorn reserved for the belief that democratic control from below is possible. But at any rate the question has now changed: it is no longer the alleged impossibility

---

* Marx's comments were not formal replies, let alone analyses, but simply remarks jotted down in passing in the course of making his conspectus of Bakunin's book. They were made as reminders to himself, not as expositions for a reader.

of defining 'class rule'; it is the far more basic question of the alleged impossibility of real *democracy*—which, to be sure, is another subject.

For Marx, the 'class rule of the proletariat' was equivalent to the complete and thoroughgoing democratization of society; yet it also meant the 'dictatorship' of the proletariat. This is what we are investigating.

4. THE WORD IN 1850: CABET AGAIN

We saw in Part I that 'dictatorship' was plentifully used by the 1850s in the writings of reactionaries, conservatives, liberals, radicals, revolutionaries, anarchists and statists. Not yet mentioned is a case that is of special interest to introduce Marx's first use of 'dictatorship of the proletariat' in 1850.

Cabet, as we saw in Chapter 3, had advocated an Icarian dictatorship in his description of his Utopia, but by the 1840s had grown milder and more circumspect. Having fled to America on the eve of the 1848 revolution, he witnessed the upheaval from afar; but one effect it all had on him was evidently to reinvigorate his views on dictatorship.

At just about the same time that Marx was writing his *Class Struggles in France,* Cabet was drafting an article in which he gave his prescription for new revolutionary tactics in France looking to a new outbreak. It was published under the title "France.—What Must Be Done After a New Revolution." That it appeared in Cabet's name is interesting, but even more interesting is the fact that it was published in the left Chartist organ put out by George Julian Harney, the *Democratic Review,* which at this time also carried articles by Engels and other members of Marx's circle, as well as supporters of Louis Blanc and other social-democrats.

Cabet was well-acquainted with the English left, for he had lived in exile in England from 1834 to 1839. In the 1840s his ideas had some success among the members of the League of the Just, the group that in 1847 amalgamated with Marx and Engels to form the Communist League. But in 1847 Cabet's proposal to go off to America to found his Icaria met with great resistance from his followers everywhere; in London the Communist League people held a week-long discussion on the issue and condemned Cabet's plan. At a banquet on September 20 held jointly with the Société Démocratique Française (which was the French analogue of the German refugee-worker group), Karl Schapper gave the League's reasons. The case against Cabet was further written up in an article published in the Communist League organ that came out the same month, *Kommunistische Zeitschrift,* titled "Citizen Cabet's Emigration Plan." Harney was present at the banquet, among other English leftists like Ernest Jones.[15] This episode of 1847 was followed by the general dissolution of the

Cabetist tendency in Europe; and so in 1850 Cabet had little influence among the readers of the *Democratic Review*. Still, they knew his name.

Cabet's article on France, undated, was datelined from Nauvoo, Illinois, the site of the Icarian colony; it was published in the September 1850 issue of the magazine.* His prescription for France was unequivocal: establish the next postrevolutionary government as a dictatorship.

Cabet was quite clear that this was not to be a dictatorship *of* the people. For example, he argued that one reason it was needed was so that "the People be brought to be moderate, patient" etc.; to "order and discipline" them. How the dictator or dictators got selected was left in darkness; they were certainly not the product of elections, for after saving the nation, "the dictatorship will call upon the People to elect a National Representation." It "must be temporarily a dictatorship, in the hands of one or a very few individuals," but Cabet did not reveal their provenance.

What was certain was that only a dictatorship could prevent "disorder" and "anarchy"; "it must be revolutionary, energetic, resolute, democratic, popular, devoted, active, rapid in execution." It "should begin by dismissing all office-holders," and replace them by devoted citizens; reorganize the National Guard to include all the People, who should elect their own officers. It should *not* favor any "system of social organisation," that is, it should not take any anticapitalist steps, but leave this future open to decision later.[18]

No doubt Cabet's willingness to advocate a dictatorship—again—had been influenced by Louis Blanc's example: not merely what Blanc had said in 1848 but what he repeated in the postrevolutionary period. Cabet had no doubt that *he* would have gone for dictatorship. A few years later Cabet related that, when he had returned to France to face the lawsuits, he explained his political position to the court. He reminded the judge that his proclamation of February 25, 1848 had urged "moderation and generosity" on the people, but he added

> that if... he had wished to enter into the Provisional Government, he would have done so, and that, in all later events, in March, April, May, his name would always have been written, unknown to him, among the members of a new Government or as a Dictator.[19]

---

* C. J. Johnson's authoritative study of Cabet states that he left Nauvoo to face Paris lawsuits brought by disgruntled emigrants to Icaria, and that he arrived in France "in 1850" (month unstated). [16] Cabet himself, in a history of the American Icaria published in the early 1850s, stated that this trip took place in 1851: he left America on May 15 for "London and Paris," and traveled for 23 days.[17] This would mean he was in London by about June 1851. But if Johnson (who examined the judicial records) had the year right, then Cabet may really have been in London in June of *1850*. Perhaps he saw Harney about putting his article into the magazine; but this becomes speculative. Unfortunately Johnson mentions neither the *Democratic Review* article nor the history of Icaria by Cabet.

Cabet, of course, meant to be Icar himself, a one-man dictator. Louis Blanc, on the other hand, had talked of the dictatorship of a collective ministry. There was, and had been, rampant talk about the 'dictatorship' of a representative assembly. All Marx did was add another variant to this list: the conception of the 'dictatorship' of a class.

* * *

The preliminary investigation to be made next is due to the insistent effort by a century of marxologists to link Marx's use of 'dictatorship of the proletariat' with his alleged adoption of Blanquist views. The next two chapters are devoted to this question.

9 | MARX AND BLANQUI

We have to undertake the following survey, as a necessary preliminary to locus 1 (especially 1c) and locus 2, because of the sheer quantity of marxological claims linking the 'dictatorship of the proletariat' with Blanqui. In Chapter 2 we covered the claim that Blanqui had originated the term; but although this assertion is false, we are going to see that there *is* a connection between Marx's 'dictatorship of the proletariat' and his relations with the Blanquist tendency. To be sure, this relationship is, if anything, the reverse of the one commonly alleged.

The key periods for Marx's relations with Blanquists are considered in separate chapters: Chapters 11-12 (1850) and Chapters 17-18 (1870s). In addition, Special Note B examines published argumentation for the myth that in the 1840-50s Marx held Blanquist views or "was a Blanquist." In this and the next chapter we cover the groundwork, particularly the question of Marx's relations with Blanqui himself.

Since Blanquism issued from the Babouvist tradition, and since the Marx-Blanquist fable is accompanied by the Marx-Babouvist fabulation, we have to begin with Babeuf and Buonarroti. I must warn that the results of this investigation are not exciting, being largely negative.

1. MARX AND BABOUVISM

Since Babeuf's name stands historically at the beginning of the socialist or communist movement, anyone who refers back to the origin and development of socialism is bound to run into his name constantly. And this is how the name is met in the early writings of Marx and Engels—though not constantly.

Their very first references to him were hardly admiring, though they sought to give him due credit for pioneering. In a pre-Marxist article for the English Owenites (1843), Engels explained that the Babouvist "Conspiracy of the Equals" failed "because the then Communism itself was of a very rough and superficial kind; and because, on the other hand, the public mind was not yet far enough advanced."[1] In the *Holy Family,* in a section tracing the history not of communism but of materialism, Marx opined that "the Babouvists were crude, uncivilized [uncultivated] materialists," and on another page pointed out that Babeuf was not "a partisan of *freedom*" but of equality.[2] In this work, too, is a passage of great importance for showing Marx's capsulized view of the main political currents of the French Revolution:

> The revolutionary movement which in 1789 began in the *Cercle Social,* which in the middle of its course had *Leclerc* and *Roux* as its chief representatives, and which in the end succumbed for a short time with *Babeuf's* conspiracy, had given rise to the *communist* idea, which Babeuf's friend Buonarroti again introduced in France after the revolution of 1830.[3]

The surprising thing about this thumbnail sketch of the origins of the movement, based on Marx's period of intensive reading and study on the French Revolution, is that it completely left out the entire Jacobin spectrum—not only Robespierre and Saint-Just, but Hébert and Marat—in favor of two tendencies then little known: the social-Girondins around the Cercle Social and Abbé Fauchet, and the revolutionary left wing of the upheaval (slandered by establishment history as the "Enragés") who rejected Jacobinism and its dictatorship *from the left* and from the standpoint of the then working classes (Leclerc, Jacques Roux). This is especially interesting because Babeuf and Buonarroti thought of themselves as Jacobin-Robespierrists; but in Marx's eyes their communism was a *graft* upon Jacobin ideas. This, indeed, is the sense with which I use the term 'Jacobin-communism' to describe the Babouvist-Blanquist tradition.

In the *German Ideology,* outside of some passing unsubstantive mentions of Babeuf's name, there is only one passage where Marx's attitude shows. When Max Stirner refers to Babeuf's views, Marx writes scornfully: "the idea ... of regarding him [Babeuf] as the theoretical representative of Communism could only occur to a Berlin schoolmaster."[4] This hardly sounds as if Marx regarded himself as a disciple of Babouvism, except in the broad sense (which should certainly never be forgotten) in which *all* socialists are descendants of the first socialist/communist movement in history.

In this period, the view of the Jacobin wing of the French Revolution that was taken by Engels was much more conventional than Marx's. In an article written at the end of 1845, Engels viewed "Babeuf's conspiracy for equality" as revealing "the final consequences of the democracy of '93 [1793]"—hence *"Democracy nowadays is communism"—and* the "iron characters" that came to his mind were "Marat and Danton, Saint-Just and Babeuf." Indeed, his article offered a long speech by Harney in which the Chartist leader praised

"Robespierre and his friends," in particular Saint-Just and Marat, as well as Babeuf and Buonarroti.[5]

This view was the orthodoxy of the European left, including the socialist Chartists: it was not a shockingly "Jacobin" effusion. *It was Marx that was out of step.* After all, Buonarroti's book, which functioned for a couple of decades literally as the textbook of Jacobin-communism, was translated into English by the leading Chartist Bronterre O'Brien, and published in 1836 by another prominent Chartist, Henry Hetherington, editor of the *Poor Man's Guardian.* Yet these estimable Chartists were not known as revolutionary fire-eaters, and have not been transmogrified into the "Babouvist-Blanquist" wing of Chartism by enterprising historians. On the other hand, if a letter were found in which Marx one day urged the reading of Buonarroti's book (a reasonable suggestion since it is interesting and important), I predict the publication of fifteen journal articles, two books, and eight dissertations using this incontrovertible evidence to prove conclusively that Marx was a Babouvist-Blanquist-Jacobin.

As a matter of fact, around this time (spring 1845) Marx and Engels did plan to publish writings by Babeuf and Buonarroti—but only as part of a very ambitious project for an extensive "Library of the Best Foreign [non-German] Socialist Writers," which in turn was momentarily thought of in connection with a "History of Socialism and Communism in France and England from the Eighteenth Century On."[6] Hess was supposed to translate Buonarroti. But nothing came of it. The incident confirms, of course, what scarcely needs to be proved—that Marx and Engels were well acquainted with these writings.* There is other evidence that Buonarroti's book was a part of Marx's personal library[7]—as it would be in the case of anyone interested in social questions.

By 1847 Marx's and Engels' writings show no references to the Babouvists with a significant content, the nearest approach being a purely historical observation on how the "social question" and the first communists emerged out of the bourgeois revolution and republicanism.[8] How this merges into the treatment of Babouvism in the *Communist Manifesto* is discussed elsewhere.[9]

Overwhelmingly, then, in their formative years Marx's and Engels' references to Babeuf and Buonarroti were simply historical, quite critical, and "distanced"—that is, they reflected no close rapport with these forerunners. And afterwards? Mention of Babeuf disappeared from Marx's writings; and

---

* Marx's plan for this series of publications bears out what was said above about his omission of the Jacobin leaders. The figures whom he listed as representatives of the Revolution were: "Cercle Social; Hébert; Jac. Roux; Leclerc." (The left-wing Jacobin Hébert has been added.) Why not Robespierre or Saint-Just? Because they were not really communists? But neither were Hébert, Holbach, Helvétius, and others on this list where Bentham figures along with Godwin.

as for Engels—aside from a rockbottom minimum mention in the historical part of *Anti-Dühring* (hence *Socialism, Utopian and Scientific* as well), there was only a comment in the preparatory notes for *Anti-Dühring* which was the most hostile of all: a certain strategy, he wrote, would be "politically as mad as Babeuf's attempt to make a leap from the Directory directly into communism ..."[10]

As for their correspondence over all the years from the forties to the nineties, the situation is even more extreme. In all of Marx's correspondence, there is *one* mention—and that a mere quip. In Engels', two mentions—one a brief historical mention, and another a reply to an inquiry from the man who was destined to invent the "Marx-Blanquist" myth, Bernstein.[11]

There is, then, very little material available for the purpose of manufacturing a myth. It would have been nice if the young Marx had met old Buonarroti one day, or even been spotted in the same city with him—but Marx was going to the University of Berlin when the old revolutionist died. An Italian authority on Buonarroti, Galante Garrone, has tried to discover some overlap between circles frequented by the two, with only tenuous and scanty results. It would be necessary to screw this procedure up one notch, that is, ferret out circles common to the common circles frequented by those who did the overlapping— a methodology that would prove anyone's "influence" on anyone else, just as we are all related in Adam. Another authority found that Buonarroti was active in Brussels at one time, and that one of the young Belgians who knew him, Jottrand, was in 1847 the president of the Democratic Association of which Marx was vice-president...[12] It's a small world.

One of the authorities whose contribution on this score has beclouded the scene was Harold J. Laski, who, in his *Socialist Tradition in the French Revolution*, stated magisterially of Babeuf and Marx that "The line of affiliation, indeed, is a direct one; for Buonarroti was the master of that generation whose words and acts were the basis of Marxian strategy." He then listed half of the socialist doctrines that most of the movement held for a half-century, to show the "line of affiliation," but the only stab at a "direct" affiliation came at the end: "and it is worth remembering the part that the League of the Just played as an instrument of early Marxism."[13] Laski forgot that, far from being an "instrument of early Marxism," the League of the Just had to be scuttled before Marx and Engels agreed to form a new organization, the Communist League, with its leaders.

But Laski had a real fact to work with. He was thinking of the essay "On the History of the Communist League" published by Engels in 1885, in particular a passage that will also serve us as an introduction to the next section. Engels explained the Babouvist-Blanquist *past* of the German workingmen who were moving to Marxism in 1847, or to as much of it as they had grasped by that time:

Originally it was a German offshoot of the French worker-communism linked to Babouvist reminiscences, which took shape in Paris at about the same time; community of goods was demanded as a necessary consequence of "equality." The aims were those of the contemporaneous Paris secret societies: half propaganda group, half conspiracy, with Paris however always figuring as the center point of revolutionary action, though the preparation of occasional putsches in Germany was by no means excluded. But since Paris remained the decisive battleground, the League was at that time actually not much more than the German branch of the French secret societies, particularly the Société des Saisons led by Blanqui and Barbès, with which it maintained a close connection. The French struck on May 12, 1839; the sections of the League marched with them and thus were involved in the common defeat.[14]

This is the past that these German workingmen had to *overcome* in order to arrive at a merger with Marx and Engels. Somehow this passage gets cited as if it proves that Marx and Engels were tainted with Babouvism—for, you see, they associated with ex-Babouvists (or ex-semi-hemi-demi-Babouvists, at least). Lucky for Marx it was not he who glorified Babeuf as his "master," founder "not only of the socialist doctrine but above all of socialist politics." (It was that master of reformism, Jean Jaurès.[15]) We will return to the Just in the next chapter.

We see that this survey is not very rewarding in itself. The reader's consolation is that, while I have taken some pages to summarize the facts, whole forests have been cut down to provide the paper on which marxologists have claimed that Marx and Engels were originally "Babouvists" in some meaningful sense. When we get to Blanquism, the plot thickens.

2. THE BLANQUIST TENDENCY

Revolutionary secret societies, with ideologies ranging from left republicanism with thoroughly bourgeois views to primitive communist ideas, proliferated after the revolution of 1830 in France. Buonarroti's bible of Babouvism, which had been published in 1828, played an important role in persuading the left wing of this movement that it was communist and in explaining what it meant by communism; and Buonarroti himself was active in creating and training groups here and there. But, without begrudging deserved admiration for the dedication and energy of this "first professional revolutionist," it must not be thought that the movement was an emanation of Buonarroti or of Babouvism.

It was a movement of elemental rebellion that cast about for an ideology. Instead of ideas, it found a leader.

Buonarroti may possibly have known young Auguste Blanqui:[16] it makes little difference, except to underline that Blanqui did not create the "Blanquist" movement. (Blanqui's aphorism was: "On ne crée pas un mouvement, on le dérive."[17]) He rose through its ranks to recognized leadership by virtue of his admirable personal qualities, which few even of his enemies failed to respect. These qualities did not include much competence in the theoretical analysis of social and political problems. Blanqui was typical of his movement in being primarily an activist—the generalissimo of activists. He was militantly opposed to wasting time on general problems of social analysis and revolutionary policy ("theory"). Along with his troops he accepted what seemed obvious: since the mass of people were hopelessly corrupted by the social order, they had to be saved despite themselves—saved by the Good Guys, who would *make* a revolution by the time-honored method of a *coup de main* (putsch) engineered by a gang of honest revolutionists, led by a Virtuous Chief acting in the interests of the People. The Good Guys (in sociological slang, the revolutionary elite) would then institute a new revolutionary regime, which would train the masses up to the point when (some day) they could govern democratically. This, as we have seen, was the Educational Dictatorship.

What was needed for such a seizure of power was the skillful and well-organized use of force, as blueprinted (for example) in Blanqui's famous *Instructions pour une Prise d'Armes,* which gave the exact dimensions for building a proper barricade.

To the world at large and to the people of the left in particular, the Blanquist movement seemed to have two outstanding characteristics—yet both of these have to be heavily qualified.

In the first place, the Blanquist tendency seemed to be thoroughly *revolutionary.* All good Blanquists trumpeted this quality, in all sincerity. And who could have any doubt about it after comparing Blanqui with, say, Louis Blanc's parliamentary state-socialism or Victor Considérant's pink modulation of Fourierism? Only time was going to show how easily Blanquism, so revolutionary under despotic regimes, turned into arrant social-reformism as it began to operate under a democratic republic, and how wildly national-chauvinist it became in the challenge of wartime. But this demonstration was reserved for the future.[18]

The Blanquists also seemed to be, and were usually described as, a "proletarian" movement. Along with everyone else, Marx accepted this standard view that Blanquism, with all its defects, represented what there was of French "proletarian (revolutionary) communism." Even if he had wanted to, he could not have done research on the Blanquists' social composition. Modern investigations of this question, while useful for the history of socialism, are not very relevant to evaluating Marx's relation with the Blanquists. In any case the question is still clouded even after a century of research; but some points may be of interest here.

Part of the trouble is terminological: if 'proletarian' is taken to refer to the modern proletariat of factory wage-workers, there is no doubt that there were few proletarians in Blanquist ranks—or among the Proudhonists, or in the Communist League, or anywhere else. It is well known that Blanqui used 'proletarian' in the usual sense of his day, describing all those who earned a living primarily by their own labor—artisanal craftsmen, even workshop masters, shopkeepers, naturally peasants, etc. In Marxian terminology these constituted the various *working classes,* then overwhelmingly petty-bourgeois in composition in France or Germany. (Marx himself, in journalistic and other popular contexts, not infrequently used 'proletarian' in the same "un-Marxist" way as everyone else.) Instead of 'proletarians', we should read 'workingpeople' in the most general sense.

Once this emendation is made, the composition of the Blanquist tendency can be stated with some confidence at least approximately. Spitzer's summary, I think, is accurate: after conceding the well-known fact that the leaders were "primarily although not exclusively" recruited from the middle class, he says:

> It is, however, probably incorrect to observe with Mason and others that "the Blanquist party itself was composed principally of members of the bourgeoisie, radical students of the schools of Paris, young advocates, and journalists." Although evidence of this nature cannot be absolutely validated, contemporary descriptions of the Blanquists during the three periods (1836-39, 1848, and the 1860s) when they actually constituted a formal organization seem to indicate that Blanqui's following contained more proletarians than any group but the Proudhonists, and that the majority of his organization was drawn from the working class.[19]

One of the best sources of hard data on the rank-and-file comes (via Da Costa) from the Paris police files. On November 7, 1866, a Paris membership meeting was held in the Cafe de la Renaissance under circumstances that assured very full attendance; it was raided by the police, with only a handful evading the net. The police list, giving the occupation of each one arrested, was reproduced by Da Costa and was clearly taken to be reliable.

Of the 41 arrested, the largest single class bloc consisted of 16 artisanal workers (one listed as a "*master*joiner"). Of these 16 the woodworkers (joiners, cabinetmakers, etc.) were easily the largest trade category (6). In addition to the 16 artisans, there were six workers in commercial occupations. One, listed as a *marchand mercier,* was probably a shop owner; the rest were employees, that is, workingmen. These two categories (16 plus 6) constituted a bare majority.

The next bloc comprised 13 students, including six medical and four law students. Then there were five professionals (one lawyer, one "man of letters," the others journalists), and one "rentier." As a result of the mass trial that ensued, Da Costa says, the workers' contingent grew considerably.[20] Many questions remain open, for example, the composition at different periods and in different cities; but it is the Paris picture that would be Marx's ruling consideration, especially for the next two years when Blanquist membership in Paris grew to over two thousand. The other side of the dubieties is this certainty: those marxologists who unqualifiedly assert the middle-class composition of the Blanquist movement are basing themselves on their polemical needs, not hard facts.

The conspiratorial putschism characteristic of the Blanquist-type tendencies (whether associated with Blanqui or not) should not be thought of as some bizarre or irrational vagary of "wild men," as tends to be the view of philistine historians bemused by respectability. Blanquism was a simple version of primitive revolutionism, so simple that any child could understand it. If you and your friends didn't like the status quo, why, you set out to overthrow it, by the same means that it probably came into being, by force of arms. Any complicating notions were just "theory." How easy and commonsensical this notion is! It is constantly being rediscovered, and proclaimed as a new theory to replace "outlived Marxism," right up to our own day. It represents the infantile malady of the revolutionary movement, one of the reasons why, in much of the world, socialism is still a giant in diapers.

3. MARX AND BLANQUI: THE REVOLUTIONARY

There are four points to be made about Marx's attitude to Blanqui before we take up his political views on Blanquism.

The first has already been suggested, whatever Marx's disagreements with Blanquism, he viewed it as the proletarian, revolutionary, communist current of the French movement. He could not have failed to be aware of how amorphous the Blanquists' kind of communism was: as Engels wrote much later about the Blanquists of the Paris Commune, "The great majority of the Blanquists were at that *time* socialists only by revolutionary, proletarian instinct . . ."[21] But this would be reason to stay in contact with them, not grounds on which to dismiss them. This consideration will become clearer in connection with the fourth point (Section 6).

The character of the Blanquists as the revolutionary wing of the London emigration in the 1850s can be seen from another angle: their role as the existing alternative on the left to the "official" leadership of the emigration, the Social-Democratic tendency led by Louis Blanc as the French head of the

"European Democracy." This role of the Blanquists, and the extent to which Marx valued it, was acted out in 1851 in what was known as the affair of Blanqui's Toast.

Marx's connection can be understood only if *two* scandals, not one, are related. On February 24, 1851 the anniversary of the February Revolution of 1848 was celebrated in London by a "Banquet of the Equals." This very Babouvist appellation covered the very non-Blanquist Social-Democrat, Louis Blanc, and a number of London Blanquist refugees plus the Willich-Schapper group (Marx's bitterest enemies). The last two categories had just been affronted by Marx when he dropped SUCR down the drain (as recounted below in Chapter 12). Two of Marx's friends, Schramm and Pieper, attended; egged on by Willichites shouting "Spy!" a large part of the crowd attacked Marx's friends and beat them up badly, while the representatives of peace and democracy, with Willich presiding, looked on—"mouthing their fraternal phrases," commented Marx with understandable bitterness. Marx and Engels decided not to involve the law, and in fact found themselves with no recourse.[22]

Three days after this scandalous affair, the French right-wing press broke a different public scandal, and chortled with glee. The "Banquet of the Equals" had had Blanqui's name blazoned on the wall with others; toasts were offered to Marat, Robespierre—and Blanqui; yet Louis Blanc had not turned a hair. It was now disclosed that the organizing committee had asked Blanqui to send a toast along with the others. From his cell in Belle-Ile, Blanqui had obliged; and his toast, "Avis au Peuple" (Warning to the People) curled Louis Blanc's hair. It was a sweeping political denunciation, by name, of the Social-Democrats and republicans who had ruined the revolution, especially Blanc; warned against giving them power again; and called for the arming of the workers as the only guarantee of socialism. The Banquet committee—Blanc and Willich-Schapper included—voted to suppress the toast. When the "Avis" was printed in the press, they lied like gentlemen claiming they had never seen it, let alone suppressed it—till a couple of the Blanquist committee members broke down and confessed.[23]

Here was an opportunity for Marx to strike back at the left hooligans who had countenanced the beating up of Schramm and Pieper—strike back not in kind, or by calling the cops, but *politically*. Marx and Engels wrote a short prefatory note for Blanqui's "Avis" and had it printed up in 30,000 copies of a flyer for distribution in German (with a certain success in Germany) and in English (with no success in getting into the English press).[24] Marx told the story in an (obscure) polemic against Willich and in the (unpublished) *Great Men of the Emigration.*[25]

It is rather amazing that nowhere in the marxological annals of the "Marx-Blanquist" myth is anything made of the indubitable fact that here we have

Marx publishing and distributing an indubitable writing by Blanqui putting forward an indubitable brand of Blanquism. One reason may be the date: according to the usual myth, this was getting toward the time when Marx was supposed to be *giving up* his "Blanquist aberration"; this episode doesn't fit. For another thing: Marx did not express approval of Blanqui's sentiments, nor was his name attached; he was making available a suppressed document of definite interest—which incidentally also dished his enemies. In the prefatory note to the flyer, Blanqui was referred to by his chief mark of distinction: "the noble martyr of revolutionary communism."[26]

We should add that Blanqui's statement was not unalloyed Blanquism. (This raises an aspect of Blanqui that is important but cannot be taken up here.) On its positive side it called for two steps, comes the revolution: "(1) the general disarming of the bourgeois guards; (2) the arming and military organization of *all* the workers." (Italics added.) True, there was a typically Blanquist glorification of "arms and organization" as sufficient and decisive; but Marx was not voting for it as a congress resolution. When Blanqui concluded, "France bristling with workers in arms, that is the coming of socialism," Marx could recognize common ground. Anyway, its emphasis pointed in the right direction with revolutionary spirit—and pointed *against* the right people.

It is certainly beyond question that Marx regarded Blanqui as "the head and the heart of the proletarian party in France," as he wrote in 1861.[27] True, he wrote this in a letter to a close friend and supporter of Blanqui, Dr. Louis Watteau; but he had expressed the same opinion quite publicly since 1850. In his *Class Struggles in France*, this was stated not in the noted passage referring to the revolutionary socialism or communism "for which the bourgeoisie itself has invented the name of Blanqui," but on the next page, quite casually, when he referred to Deflotte (i.e., Paul de Flotte), "a friend of Blanqui," as "the representative of the revolutionary proletariat" in the elections.[28] In another article of the same year—the same book review in which (we will see) he dissected Blanqui*ism* with a sharp knife—he likewise took it for granted that his readers would accept his characterization of "the proletarian revolutionaries such as Blanqui."[29]

The affair of Blanqui's Toast took place in 1851. In 1852 Marx's *Eighteenth Brumaire of Louis Bonaparte* referred to "Blanqui and his comrades, that is, the real leaders of the proletarian party, the revolutionary communists," and in its last section recalled that "*Blanqui* had made the disbanding of the bourgeois guards the first demand on the revolution"[30]—perhaps a direct echo of Blanqui's "Avis au People." Early that year, Engels wrote to Marx that he was optimistic about Bonaparte's imminent downfall: "One can do no better than this ass [Bonaparte] to prepare the way for a Blanqui government."[31] In

Part III: Preliminaries: The "Marx-Blanquist" Myth

1854 Marx inserted a note in a *New York Daily Tribune* article pointing out that Bonaparte's release of Barbès, but not Blanqui, from prison settled the long-standing feud between the two revolutionaries and their supporters: it "decides the question as to who is the man of the Revolution and who not." Up to now, wrote Marx, "Barbès and Blanqui have long shared the real supremacy of revolutionary France."[32] In 1856, in his "Speech at the Anniversary of the *People's Paper*," Marx remarked that modern technological advances "were revolutionists of a rather more dangerous character than even citizens Barbès, Raspail and Blanqui."[33]* Here the three names simply functioned as paradigmatic synonyms for 'revolutionist'—and Blanqui's name did not head the list.

In 1861 Marx was deeply involved in the defense of Blanqui against prison maltreatment (detailed in the next section), and, in the course, he repeatedly expressed his view of Blanqui as a revolutionary ally. In a letter to Engels, he remarked that "I consider it very good that we again have direct connections with the firmly [*entschieden*, decidedly, decisively] revolutionary party in France."[35] A few months later, he wrote the letter to Dr. Watteau quoted above. In 1863, in a letter to Engels, Marx was again hopeful about the situation in France. He remarked, apparently reflecting the report made by his wife after a visit to Paris: "In Paris party spirit and cohesion are still dominant in the *parti socialist* [i.e., socialist movement]. Even fellows like Carnot and Goudchaux [bourgeois republicans] declare that Blanqui has to be put in the forefront in the next movement."[36]

The "next movement" came in 1870. Early that year (before it came) Engels had told Marx about a newspaper piece by Hess which said that Flourens and other "new forces" were displacing old Blanqui in the leadership. Engels scouted the report as laughable, quite rightly. The Marx family knew Flourens well; this hot-blooded young scientist and revolutionary, who was destined to die in the defense of the Paris Commune, was a loyal follower of Blanqui.

First came the collapse of the Bonaparte Empire. A couple of weeks before, Engels wrote (in a letter) that everything might come unglued in a week or two: "The worst thing is—who is to take the lead in case of a really revolutionary movement in Paris? . . . Blanqui seems forgotten."[37] But Blanqui was not forgotten; yet he could not give leadership to the Paris Commune, for he was arrested exactly one day before the revolt startled friends and foes.

* Readers of Dommanget's valuable book *Us Idées Politiques et Sociales d'Auguste Blanqui* should note that (perhaps through some mixup of translation into French via German) this passage comes out referring to "the *bourgeois* Barbès, Raspail and Blanqui" (italics added).[34] And then Dommanget "explains" why Marx called them "bourgeois"! It is a disconcerting proof of the capacity of tendentious interpretation to explain anything, including mistranslations.

In his *Civil War in France,* Marx noted that the Versailles government had rejected the Commune's efforts to obtain Blanqui's release in exchange for an archbishop: for Thiers "knew that with Blanqui he would give to the Commune a head..."[38]

The "Marx-Blanquist" myth had started before this address was published, indeed before the Paris Commune was more than a few days old. Paris and London papers published the revelation that the revolt had been masterminded in London by Marx and Blanqui in secret conclave with A. A. Assi and others. Marx's denial was printed on April 4;[39] but the flood of lies merely swelled. To most of these defenders of Morality and Civilization, it was irrelevant that Marx's communist views were entirely different from Blanqui's: for they were on the same side of the barricades. This continued to be the "Marx-Blanquist" crime.

4. MARX AND BLANQUI: THE DEFENSE MOVEMENT

The second element in Marx's view of Blanqui concerned the defense of the revolutionist against government persecution.

Marx's personal view of Blanqui was that of a devoted and honest revolutionist of great moral integrity (called 'purity' or 'virtue' in the Blanquists' own jargon). This view of Blanqui was, of course, very common and not limited to supporters: for this was a man of principle, incorruptible and faithful to his convictions. Instead of spending over thirty-three years in prison,[40] he could have enjoyed lucrative posts by yielding to the men of power; and so he was a "fanatic" to those who did. More than merely a martyr, he was a model of revolutionary morality. Marx admired Blanqui in this personal sense. He undoubtedly agreed with Engels' distinction between Blanqui the individual and the Blanquists as a political tendency. Engels wrote in 1874:

> One wants above all to play the role of Blanqui, "man of action." But here little is to be accomplished [simply] by good will; not everyone happens to have Blanqui's revolutionary instinct or his swift decisiveness; and however much Hamlet may talk about energetic action, he still remains Hamlet.[41]

We have already mentioned that in the feud between Barbès and Blanqui, Marx favored the latter.[43] But this was not a question of ideology; Barbès had pressed charges impugning Blanqui's revolutionary integrity, and Marx believed Blanqui's defenders. Also, in 1852, a shady ex-Blanquist or quasi-

Blanquist named Emmanuel Barthélemy (one of the paladins who had suppressed Blanqui's Toast and broken with the revolutionist over it) circulated an alleged compromising letter by Blanqui. Marx reacted with the opinion that it was all a "lie" by Barthélemy.[43] Some years later, Marx's Comtist friend E. S. Beesly asked him naively if Blanqui was a dishonorable man of the Bradlaugh type. Marx laughed to himself at this typical John Bullish estimation of a revolutionary character (so he told the Lafargues in a letter), and sent Beesly a portrait of Blanqui to cure him of his prejudices against the revolutionist.[44]

Defending Blanqui against slander *within* the movement was one thing; defending him against the constant persecution of the Bonapartist despotism was a foregone conclusion. Writing to Engels in 1859, Marx reported that "In Paris, at any rate, the workers are furious over the vileness of Blanqui's deportation to Cayenne."[45] Blanqui's ten-year sentence handed down in 1849 had expired in April, but instead of freeing him, the government planned to deport him to the transatlantic penal colony and in any case kept him interned.

Then in 1861, when Blanqui was shut up in the Mazas prison in Paris, reports started coming out about his physical maltreatment by the prison administration, allegedly on orders from above. Besides, Blanqui's trial and conviction had been a judicial farce.

Marx threw himself wholeheartedly into the Blanqui defense movement launched by the prisoner's friends, particularly Dr. Louis Watteau (pseudonym Denonville). This physician had done time in Belle-Ile as an enemy of Bonaparte, and now lived in Brussels. Marx kept in touch with him, and set about raising money for a Blanqui defense fund to publish a brochure about the case and publicize the issues in general. For this purpose he turned to Lassalle and the Countess Sophie von Hatzfeldt, who differed from most of Marx's friends in having a good deal of the needful.

On May 8 Marx informed Lassalle about Blanqui's prison conditions and about defense activities. His letter shows how thoroughly he was involved:

> Blanqui is still in the prison of Mazas (Paris), where he is *physically* maltreated by gendarmes, etc. on *orders from the juged'instruction*. He had traveled from here [London] to Paris—without any conspiratorial plans—as a businessman's agent, making use of the general amnesty. The dirty press in England as in the rest of Europe 'tries to burk the whole affair.' I have agreed on a get-together for next Saturday with Simon Bernard, who knows the details on the affair, and at that time we will discuss the subject at length. We intend, perhaps together with Ernest Jones, to hold a public meeting on this monstrous business. As soon as I have talked with Bernard and have better information, I will render a report to madame the Countess [Hatzfeldt]. But right now I beg you to get notices about this *guet-apens* [felonious attack] into Brussels papers through any channels whatever.[46]

He also wrote to Hatzfeldt with information on "Bonaparte's infamous conduct in respect to Blanqui," made proposals for articles to get into the press, and asked for her financial support for the brochure on the Blanqui trial.[47] Hatzfeldt did get pieces into the press, and responded positively on June 14. A few days later Marx sent Engels a letter we have already quoted in part:

> It is a question first of all of money to print a pamphlet by D[enonville] on the (infamous) Blanqui trial. (Arguments etc. and analysis thereof.) Blanqui himself, through D[enonville], has very warmly sent thanks to me and the German proletarian party (*in partibus*) for our sympathy. I consider it very good that we again have direct connections with the firmly revolutionary party in France.[48]

Marx was apparently citing a letter from Watteau (Denonville) of June 4, which said that Blanqui was deeply moved by the concern shown by the German proletariat for his fate.[49]

On July 22, after learning that Blanqui's four-year sentence had been upheld, Marx wrote Lassalle: "You have seen that the sentence against Blanqui—one of the most shameful ever—has been confirmed on appeal. I am now curious to see what his Brussels friend will write me."[50] The Brussels friend, Dr. Watteau, did write to him, but this letter is one of a number of letters in the Marx-Watteau correspondence that are not extant. Marx's letter to Watteau of November 10 is extant, and we have already partly quoted it:

> Be assured that no one could be more interested than myself in the fate of a man whom I have always considered to be the head and the heart of the proletarian party of France.[51]

Through all this, to what extent was Blanqui aware of the activity on his behalf by Marx and his friends? We really don't know, though it is customary to quote Watteau's statements as if they settled the matter. It will be observed that Blanqui's thankful and appreciative sentiments came not from Blanqui but from the organizer of his defense fund writing to a valued contributor; and without faulting Watteau at all we should not be naive about these formalities. Other questions of this sort becloud our next section too. Luckily, from a reasonable standpoint, none of this has much to do with the question of Marx's *political* attitude toward Blanquism.

5. MARX AND BLANQUI: PERSONAL RELATIONS

For the third lement in Marx-Blanqui relations, we must summarize the facts about personal links.

Great efforts have been expended on the task of finding some points of personal contact between Marx and Blanqui or at least Blanquists. The first fact to be noted about Marx-Blanqui personal relations is similar to Sherlock Holmes' famous observation on the dog's barking: there wasn't any. The two men never met, despite opportunities to do so. This seems to have been due chiefly to Blanqui's disinclination. However, the story shows a great amount of coolness on both sides.

When Marx first came to live in Paris in October 1843, Blanqui was a prisoner in Mont St-Michel. He had been in one prison or another continuously for four years and was going to remain a prisoner until the February Revolution of 1848 released him. There was no possibility of a meeting.

But did Marx meet Blanquists in the Paris workers' circles he began to frequent and about which he wrote so enthusiastically? Quite probably; but he never mentioned it, at the time or later. In the course of 1844-1845 Marx wrote three times about the workers' clubs he was getting acquainted with, each time with great admiration and respect.[52] But not a word in these three passages reflected any contact with Blanquists.

Much later he related: "During my first stay in Paris, I maintained personal relations with the leaders of the League [of the Just] there, as well as with the leaders of most of the French secret workers' societies, without however joining any of these societies."[53] These secret societies were, of course, rife with Jacobin-Communist types, who can be called "Blanquists" with equanimity; among them were undoubtedly conscious followers of Blanqui himself. The real question is not whether Marx met "Blanquists" but whether he met them *as* Blanquists in any meaningful sense. Paris was a melting pot of leftist ideologies and currents, and no doubt the newcomer from the German hinterland was eager to meet all kinds, and did.

The most definite link we know of is not with any French group but with the League of the Just; for this group of German émigré workers (mainly artisanal workers) cooperated with the Society of the Seasons and other groups modeled on classic conspiratorial lines. We have already quoted what Engels wrote about the Just's participation in the Blanquist putsch of May 1839.[54] Other Germans among the tens of thousands of émigré artisans in Paris were associated with other secret societies; and it is reported that there were Blanquist groups with special German sections.[55] In these circles, some sort of Jacobin-communism was the leading orthodoxy. Not only did Marx not join any of these groups but we will see evidence that he rejected their characteristic politics from the start.[56]

During his Brussels sojourn (1845 to early 1848) Marx was far from any Blanquist group, even geographically. But Dommanget, doggedly pursuing his ambition of merging Marx and Blanqui in morganatic marriage, comes up with the information that the eminent Polish historian Joachim Lelewel, in exile in Belgium, was "an old acquaintance of Blanqui's."[57] Marx was a friend and admirer of Lelewel and his historical work; Lelewel was a friend and admirer of Blanqui. I hesitate to mention that Marx did not become a Lelewelite, Lelewel did not become a Marxist, not every acquaintance of Blanqui's was a Blanquist, and I wish we could drop this sort of thing.

But not yet. Just as we have heard of Jottrand's link to Buonarroti,[58] so too Nicolaievsky has made a "Blanquist" out of Jacques Imbert, one of Marx's colleagues in the leadership of the Brussels Democratic Association. Dommanget says this information is incorrect,[59] but more important is the fact that it is irrelevant.

The first time that Marx and Blanqui were simultaneously in the same city was in early 1848. Marx, expelled from Belgium, came to Paris in the first week of March, and remained until about April 6. Blanqui had been released on February 24 and managed to stay out of jail until May 15. He founded the Central Republican Club as his organizational center. Marx, leading the Communist League in Paris, helped to found a German workers' club as the Communist League "front." Scores of other clubs were formed in the big French cities.

According to the "Marx-Blanquist" myth, Marx should have rushed to join Blanqui's club, which was one of the major political centers. But in fact *if* he participated in any of the French clubs, it was the Society of the Rights of Man; at any rate, a Marx was recorded speaking at its meetings, though it was probably not the Marx we are interested in.* Even Dommanget concedes that in this period Marx's orientation and activity were as far as possible from that of the Blanquists.[61] Besides mentioning Marx's membership in the non-Blanquist club (which he accepts as a fact), Dommanget rightly points to two considerations: (1) Marx's vigorous opposition to the German Legion project organized by the German émigré Democrats in Paris (Herwegh, Bornstedt, et al.)—an adventuristic bit of revolutionism that was quite in line with Blanqui's coeval enthusiasm for "revolutionary war" by the new French republic, but alien to Marx's perspective; and (2) Marx's and Engels' cordial relations with and beneficent attitude toward the left wing of the Provisional Government (Ledru-Rollin and Flocon more than Louis Blanc).[62]

In any case there is no question about the fact that Marx and Blanqui did not meet and had no personal contact whatever.

Marx was next in Paris in 1849, after the defeat of the revolution in Germany. He stayed there from the first week of June until August 24;

---

* The historian Samuel Bernstein found a member named "Marx" speaking at the Society of the Rights of Man during the approximate period when Karl Marx was in Paris; and he insisted, on the basis of slim evidence, that it was Karl Marx himself. P. Amann, re-examining the record, erected a convincing case to show that it could not have been Karl Marx. In his book *AugusteBlanqui* Bernstein dismissed Amann in a note that indicated he had no rebuttal to offer.[60] Bernstein's claim gets repeated, but no one has impugned Amann's case, which in my opinion has given the story its quietus.

expelled by the French government, he arrived in London a couple of days later. During this period Blanqui was in prison in Doullens. Soon after his arrival in Paris, Marx informed Engels: "I consort with the whole of the revolutionary party and in a few days' time I shall have *all* the revolutionary journals at my disposal."[63] This optimistic note was not followed, in Marx's letters of this period, by any further references to contacts with the French movement; one must surmise that such contact was minimal, especially when the government started cracking down on him with a view to his expulsion from the country. As for "*all* the revolutionary journals": Marx could scarcely have been referring to Blanquist organs since there was none at this point; *Les Veillées du Peuple* was not published until November. There is no evidence that the "revolutionary party" meant Blanquists specifically, any more than "revolutionary journals" meant Blanquist ones. Everything we know of Marx suggests that the label had a much wider significance for him. But we really don't know what he was referring to.

The London Blanquists of 1850 and the SUCR episode are reserved for chapters of their own.

Where was Blanqui himself in the decade of the 1850s? In prison until the 1859 amnesty: at Doullens until October 1850, then from November of that year until November of 1857 at Belle-Ile. During this long stint at Belle-Ile he was completely blocked from getting books, and so could not have become acquainted with Marx's publications even if he had wanted to. Freed by the amnesty of 1859 he lived abroad until the beginning of 1861, when he returned to Paris, to be arrested in March and sentenced in June to four years. At least in January 1860 and for an unknown period of time, Blanqui sojourned in London. This, then, was the second time that he was in the same city as Marx. In 1924 Dommanget exercised his ingenuity to suggest that there may have been a meeting at that time; in 1929 Ryazanov did the same; but the speculations came to nothing, and Dommanget later admitted that a meeting could not have taken place.[64]

In connection with the defense movement we have seen the mutual expressions of appreciation in the 1861 period. There were echoes of this feeling near the end of that decade. As we will see in Chapter 18, the Blanquists did not participate constructively in the International before the Paris Commune, and there is nothing to report for most of the 1860s, and little after that. In December 1868, writing to his friend Kugelmann about the antics of the so-called "French Branch" and its leading pseudorevolutionist Félix Pyat, Marx mentioned that he was gratified to see that "Blanqui through one of his friends" had had an article published ridiculing Pyat's pretensions.[65] Actually the article had been published by Tridon in a weekly sympathetic to Pyat; but I have seen no reason to explain why Marx thought that Blanqui had brought it off from prison. I suppose London Blanquist acquaintances told him that, and he was certainly content to believe it.

A few months later, Paul Lafargue, who had married Laura Marx in 1868, began to play the role that Dommanget later played literarily: that is, as marriage broker between Marx and Blanqui. Lafargue, who besides everything else had the proper temperament for the Blanquist tendency, was an admirer of Le Vieux, for understandable reasons. He had returned to France in order to get a French medical degree (besides his British M.D.) by taking examinations, but his father was worried lest he get carried away by political activity and fail to get the degree, hence be unable to set up shop as a physician. Old Lafargue in turn put pressure on Marx to keep Paul's attention on the exams, and in any case Marx was concerned about his daughter's future.

About February 1869 Lafargue started writing Marx about a political weekly that was being founded by a group of Blanquists and republicans. Its name was to be *La Renaissance*, and Paul was involved as a collaborator. He sent Marx the prospectus, along with a piece of news about his book *The Poverty of Philosophy*, guaranteed to scratch Marx's back: "Blanqui," wrote Paul, "has a copy of it and lends it to all his friends. Thus Tridon has read it and was happy to see in what fashion *il Moro* [Marx] trounced Proudhon. Blanqui has the greatest esteem for you . . ."[66] This news about Blanqui's distribution of literature may have been hung on a ribbon of truth, or so one hopes; no such report ever came from any other source. We will come back to the periodical project.

In March, writing to Engels in connection with an inconsequential news note, Marx mentioned that Blanqui *"is now in Paris"* (underlined) and that Lafargue is apparently in touch with him. However, Marx's letter made no comment on this information, except to report a wisecrack by Blanqui about a crackpot named Moilin. In the same letter Marx remarked apprehensively that Lafargue might be getting too deeply absorbed in politics to take his exams successfully. This, he added, "can become bothersome, for his friends [of the *Renaissance* project] are nothing but Blanquists. I will warn him. He should take his exams first."[67] Marx was obviously none too happy about Lafargue's "coterie," as he called it; but, as explained, there were two clashing motives at work. Whatever Marx may have written to Lafargue as the warning, all we have is a letter of June 2 in which Marx merely stated disagreement with Blanqui (as reported by Lafargue) on a minor point.[68] In a letter of the same day to his daughter Jenny (who, remember, was married to a left-republican admirer of Blanqui, Longuet, who had used to visit Blanqui at the Hôpital Necker when the old man was jailed there in 1864-1865), Marx explained why he was reluctant to accept the invitation to collaborate with *La Renaissance*:

"As to Lafargue's paper, I feel rather uneasy. On the one hand, I should like to oblige Blanqui. On the other hand, my other occupations will not allow me to do much for them, but, above all things, I fear lest *old* Lafargue should suspect me to push his son to premature political action and make him neglect his professional duties.[69]

In July Marx went to Paris, apparently at the request of old Lafargue, to ensure Paul's medical career. Writing from Paris, he informed Engels that Blanqui had left the capital—and just as well.

[Blanqui] has left Paris . . . and gone to Brussels, and under the circumstances his absence was by no means unwelcome to me. Also, the paper [*La Renaissance*] has been "postponed" for the same reason.[70]

Marx meant, I suppose, that if he had actually met Blanqui, it would have been harder to extricate Paul from involvement with the periodical. Thus, when Marx was *almost* in the same city at the same time as Blanqui, the situation was entirely beclouded by the extraneous problem around Lafargue's medical future.

In March 1870 the following query occurred in a letter sent by Marx to the Lafargues: "what does one hear of Blanqui? Is he in Paris?"[71] And that was all.

The last mention of Blanqui's name in Marx's and Engels' correspondence can be viewed as symbolic. In Marx's case the last epistolary reference was in connection with the Assi "plot" already mentioned: Marx sent a letter to Assi's lawyer affirming that he had had no connection with Assi nor with the imaginary Blanqui conspiracy in London.[72] Engels' last mention of Blanqui in a letter was in response to Liebknecht's request for a Blanqui photograph: no, he had no photo.[73] *No connection,* wrote Marx; *no photo,* wrote Engels; and then for the remaining near-quarter century there was no mention of the old revolutionist in any letter by either one.[74]

But there was an epilogue, carried out by the *shadchan,* that is, Lafargue. The wise Jewish *shadchan,* literature tells us, engineers a marriage by telling each party how mightily in love the other is, besides extolling each one's virtues. We have seen at least one case in which Lafargue had told Marx of Blanqui's admiration and interest. In 1879 we get a glimpse of the other side of that operation. Two days after Blanqui was released from prison in June 1879, Lafargue sent him a letter. The founding of an independent workers' party in France was on the agenda, and Lafargue proposed to Blanqui that he carry its banner. The letter was rather extravagantly full of compliments (but every *shadchan* knows how easily any bride or groom will believe the attribution of beauty to an otherwise unassuming countenance). At the end Lafargue suggested that Blanqui might want to come to London to rest up; and his last words were: "Marx, who has followed your whole political career with so much interest, would be happy to make your acquaintance."[75]

I have no doubt that Paul asked his father-in-law: "Didn't I hear you say once that you'd like to make the acquaintance of old Blanqui?"—"Mais certainement!" says the father-in-law. And so the writer adds this thoroughly veracious statement to his own letter. There is no difficulty about that. What gets sticky are the conclusions drawn by historians and biographers.*

There is no record of a response to Lafargue's letter by Blanqui. Even if we assume that he sent a thanks-for-your-best-wishes reply, this lack of responsiveness to Marx's interest was consistently true of Blanqui in every case not mediated by someone else (like Watteau). Chief among the people who would have been astonished to learn that Marx was a Blanquist was— Blanqui. Nowhere in his published material, correspondence or personal papers did Blanqui ever mention the *Communist Manifesto*. There is no indication that Blanqui ever read *Capital* or was acquainted with it, though Dommanget says he "saw" the French edition of that work in 1872. Although Blanqui's name figures in *The Civil War in France*, which scandalized the respectable world in 1871, there is no mention of this document by Blanqui (who, to be sure, was in prison when it came out).[77]

There is every reason, then, to believe a report made by Gabriel Deville, one of the leaders of the Guesdist (so-called Marxist) party in France for many years. In 1879 Deville was a young man newly recruited to Marxist views. During the harsh winter bringing that year to a close, Blanqui, who had been released from prison the preceding June, frequented Deville's lodgings every Monday morning. In the course of their conversations, the young man did not fail to bring up his Marxist ideas. He had the impression of being at loggerheads with the old man, and, in a statement written down later, declared that Blanqui did not like Marx and "did not seek to get acquainted with Marx's work."[78]

It boils down to this: Marx was just "Blanquist" enough to be as sincerely

---

* This is a blood-chilling case. On the basis of this last sentence in Lafargue's letter, plus the fact that Marx's other son-in-law Longuet had written Blanqui in similarly complimentary terms (thus proving the unanimity of sons-in-law), Dommanget asserts positively that Marx *did not* agree with the judgment on Blanqui given in Engels' article "The Program of the Blanquist Refugees" (locus 8). He cites the opinion of the socialist historian Zévaès who concluded that Lafargue's letter expressed Marx's opinion not simply on a desire to meet Blanqui but "on the activity and work of Blanqui." Samuel Bernstein, in his *Auguste Blanqui*, suddenly breaks out of his accustomed dullness and turns inventive novelist: Marx and Engels (both) "concluded" that Blanqui was the man to head the coming French workers' party, and selected Lafargue as the logical choice to make the proposal. Unlike Dommanget, Bernstein gives no argument at all for reaching this conclusion.[76] This is, so to speak, putschism applied to historiography.

interested in meeting the old revolutionist as you would be, dear reader; and Blanqui was not even interested in saying hello. The rest is fiction: falsifiction.

6. MARX AND BLANQUI: THE UNITED FRONT

The fourth element in Marx-Blanqui or Marx-Blanquist relations concerns the united-front problem.

The term 'united front', of course, came in after Marx's time, but I use it here because its modern history sets one feature in sharp relief: the united-front problem arises because two or more political tendencies *disagree*. The question is, to what extent and within what limits can they collaborate *despite* the fact that they are different or even hostile.

Only the term is modern; the idea is not, because the problem is old. The same notion was adumbrated in Sections II and IV of the *Communist Manifesto*. As previously mentioned, the Manifesto stated that "In France the Communists ally themselves with the Social-Democrats,"[79] and for Germany it spoke of "fight[ing] with the bourgeoisie" under suitable conditions.[80] Whether we call it an 'alliance', 'coalition', 'joint struggle', or whatever, we are talking about the united-front problem in one form or another.

It is seldom realized that Marx was a pioneer in working out the conception of the united front in practice. In his case it was not linked with doctrinal vagueness, as is sometimes the case, but rather with his antipathy to sects and sectism. Against the sect Marx counterposed the concept of a *broad class party*, a movement embracing a wide variety of working-class elements, its "cement" being participation in the class struggle rather than ideological uniformity. This was Marx's concept of the International, which was, as it were, a united front in the form of an all-in organization.[81] In contrast, the problems raised in the Manifesto's Section IV involved united fronts (or "alliances") linking existing organizations that held antagonistic or competitive political programs.

Traditional sectists believe that anyone who rejects their particular brand of socialism is an enemy, and it follows that they can work only with people they agree with—viz., with themselves. Uncannily, we will find that this is also the standpoint of the marxologists who "prove" that Marx was a Blanquist merely by the fact that he entered into a united front that included Blanquists among others. (The projected united front called SUCR will be the subject of Chapter 12.)

The very first organizational structure devised by Marx—the Communist Correspondence Committee he established in Brussels—was a format designed to provide an umbrella over *different* ideological tendencies within the framework of what he simultaneously called a movement of "Democratic

Communists."[82] The manifesto that Marx finished in early 1848 was not called the manifesto of the Communist League (an organization) but the manifesto of the Communist tendency as a whole ("party"), which did not exist in fixed organizational form. From the beginning Marx's outreach was toward an organizational format that allowed for the coexistence of different (hence potentially antagonistic) programmatic policies within the framework of what was roughly considered "communism," or, even more broadly, within the framework of "proletarian" or "proletarian-revolutionary" politics.

Moreover, the very first organizational forms that Marx tried to work out were essentially *international* in scope. The Brussels CCC was, of course, intended to cover Europe at least. Though the Communist League was largely German in membership (the big limitation was set by the language used in meetings), it too was "universal" in principle, and in fact included a scattering of Scandinavian and other non-German affiliates. Perhaps the earliest organization of the socialist-communist left that was specifically international was the Fraternal Democrats, founded in September 1845 in London by the left Chartist G.J. Harney. Marx and his Brussels CCC were close supporters, as was the League of the Just in London. The Fraternal Democrats, which still had over twenty chapters in England as late as 1850, had members from several European nationalities. *Most of the Frenchmen who lined up with it were no doubt Blanauist;* yet no confused historian has turned up claiming that Harney thereby became a "Blanquist."

To understand the united front of 1850, whose consideration lies ahead, we should try to get an insight into Marx's thinking on the subject of united fronts.* It happens that Marx put his views into a letter in connection with a little-known problem which has to be explained before we can see what Marx was saying.

David Urquhart, whose experience in the British diplomatic service in Turkey had made him Britain's leading Russophobe and Turkophile, had

---

* A special sort of united front is discussed in Marx's and Engels' "Address to the Communist League" of March 1850—special because it is a question of policy in the midst of revolution. The subject here is not the united front of specific organizations but of broad class strata and political currents, "the relation of the revolutionary workers' party to the petty-bourgeois Democrats." The general formula is of wide applicability: "it marches together with them against the faction which it aims at overthrowing, it opposes them in everything by which they seek to consolidate their position in their own interests." Further on, the Address notes a serious difficulty: the bourgeois democrats do not contemplate an alliance with the workers' movement in which the latter have "equal power and equal rights"; yet the workers must be "independently organized"; this does not bode well for a united, front between equal independent powers. But in the course of battle, their interests coincide and a momentary alliance (a battlefield alliance, as it were) may come about of itself.[83] However, we leave these problems of revolution aside for present purposes.

developed the view that Lord Palmerston was really an agent of Russian interests. He organized a movement of "Urquhartite" groups, called Foreign Affairs Committees, with influence in all English circles from the Tories to the Chartists. Marx recognized one point of agreement with Urquhart—opposition to Palmerston's foreign policy as pro-Russian; otherwise he regarded Urquhart as a crazy, crackpot, medievalizing, pro-Turk idealizer of Islam. Marx met him only once, and reported to Engels that he was a "complete monomaniac," thought revolutionists were all Russian agents, and had fits when contradicted. Marx, moreover, made his opinion of Urquhart's general politics quite public, in the *New York Daily Tribune's* columns. Nor was Urquhart himself under any illusion: "he knows, since I have told him so," Marx wrote to Engels, "that I agree with him in *nothing* save the matter of Palmerston."[84]

So Marx published a number of pieces on foreign policy in the Urquhartite press. This was the extent of the "united front."

The question came up sharply when Lassalle wrote Marx about a German Urquhartite named Fischel: this lawyer's domestic politics were bad—why did Marx associate himself with such people in England? This elicited Marx's thoughts about limited political alliances. His reply explained the extent of his collaboration with the Urquhartites, which he called a "cartel relationship." He emphasized that he had "never exchanged a word on domestic politics" with Urquhart "ever since I told him once for all that I am a revolutionist, and he told me just as openly that all revolutionists are agents or dupes of the Petersburg cabinet."

Marx's argumentation went as follows. True, Urquhart is a reactionary in ideology, "metaphysically" speaking.* But in foreign policy his movement is "objectively revolutionary." His motivations are a matter of indifference, just as they would be if, in a progressive war, the man next to you was shooting at the same enemy out of patriotic or revolutionary motives. "Urquhart is a *power*, feared by Russia. He is the sole *official* person in England who has the courage and honesty to stand up against public opinion." We are carrying on a "war," Marx says, "together with the Urquhartites, against Russia, Palmerston and Bonaparte," one in which persons of various political views take part, including Fischel. He indicates that the alliance with the Urquhartites is viable only so long as there is no revolutionary situation: "If we in Germany entered a *revolutionary* epoch," then all this "diplomacy" with

---

* At the end of this letter, however, Marx makes clear the peculiar form of Urquhart's "reactionary" metaphysics:

> . . .this Urquhartite romanticism is extremely liberal in spite of its fanatical hatred of the French Revolution and everything "universal." The freedom of the individual is his last word, only in a very complex fashion. To bring this freedom about, to be sure, he masquerades the "individual" in all kinds of antique costumes.

the Urquhartites would "naturally come to an end"—*naturally* because of the Urquhartites' antirevolutionary position. "No *revolutionary* party presently exists in Germany," however.

In this connection Marx states another basic proviso. In this "diplomacy," he stresses, "neither side gives up anything to the slightest extent nor makes any pretenses." He goes on to dot the i's on this principle of *freedom of mutual criticism*:

> We revolutionaries have to make use of them [the Urquhartites] as long as they are needed. This does not prevent us from hitting them squarely over the head when they become an obstacle in domestic politics. The Urquhartites never took it amiss that I used my own name to write simultaneously in the Chartist paper which they hate like poison, Ernest Jones's *People's Paper,* as long as it existed. E. Jones laughed at Urquhart's crotchets, made fun of them in his paper, and yet in the same paper publicly acknowledged his extraordinary value in the field of foreign policy.[85]

This, then, was an essential aspect of a united front (temporary and limited alliance) in Marx's eyes: reciprocal freedom of all participants to publicly express their political views without "any pretenses," everything in the open and aboveboard. Incidentally, Engels later used the term 'cartel' to describe their pre-1848 collaboration with the Democratic movement in Brussels and the *Réforme* group in France—alliances which likewise assumed the mutual right of criticism without question.[86]

Now, it would take some doing to make an "Urquhartite" out of Marx on the basis of these facts.* Yet Marx's "cartel" with Urquhart was different from his united front with the Blanquists in this respect: Marx had no hope whatever of affecting Urquhart's own views through the association. He knew that this monomaniac was personally immovable, and winning over the Urquhartite rank and file was not a practicable goal; the target of the "cartel" was public opinion. With the Blanquists the situation was altogether different.

Figure to yourself: here in the London French emigration was a loose political tendency—made up largely of young, inexperienced people; without a single leading figure on the spot who possessed any force or prestige; their real leader, the imprisoned Blanqui, only a name and a legend to many or most of them; without an organization of their own, hardly possessing a developed political ideology of their own ... Why, this was a tendency that was almost up for grabs!

---

* Only Isaiah Berlin is equal to the challenge. His biography of Marx states quite flatly that "Marx became an official Urquhartite"—*official,* mind you.[87] Of course, Berlin did not waste space by mentioning Marx's views on Urquhart or any other inconvenient facts.

Yet the annals of marxology are full of the astonishing notion that whenever Marx—who had just gone through a revolution under extreme pressure—had something to do with these émigrés, he (Marx) became a "Blanquist"! That is, he accepted *their* blurry ideas!

To be sure, this fable was fabricated by Eduard Bernstein (as detailed in Special Note B), but it became a fixture of much marxological mythology. The myth-makers have not claimed to present facts about the awesome power of these London Blanquists to impose their views on everyone within range of their vibes. The marxological story simply relies on osmosis: put anyone next to a live Blanquist and the victim starts making putsches ... This is a close analogue of another famous theory about arcane influences: the traditional FBI view that anyone who has a Communist relative, or who has osmotically rubbed shoulders in an organization with Communists real or alleged, is thereby tainted for life. Or perhaps the real parallel is the Dracula myth: once embraced by the pointy-toothed vampire prince, the victim himself becomes—bloodthirsty.

The sane alternative is the view that Marx, looking on the Blanquists as revolutionists with whom he had serious disagreements, was open to the policy of making united fronts with them *while at the same time seeking to win them away from their false ideas.* This, we will find, was indeed the overall pattern of Marx's relations with the London Blanquists. It is hardly surprising to find that Marx strove to convert temporary Blanquist allies away from their infantile-putschist notions. Far from having to swallow the bizarre theory that Marx was convinced by mere contact with relatively idea-less Blanquists, we know on the contrary that the relationship moved in the opposite direction.

10 | MARX VERSUS BLANQUISM

We have sufficiently emphasized that Marx never struck the sectist attitude that said, "We, the Pure, can have nothing to do with Blanquists because we disagree with their views ... " The other side of this picture is that Marx did vigorously reject Blanquist (Jacobin-communist) putschism and conspiratorialism. He did so, moreover, from his earliest known political writings to his last, with unusual consistency. On this score as on others, the "Marx-Blanquist" myth is peculiarly unlucky.

The most important dissection of Blanquism, for our purposes, was published by Engels in 1874, and we will come back to it in locus 8, "The Program of the Blanquist Refugees of the Commune." Blanqui, Engels explained, believed "that a small well-organized minority, attempting a revolutionary *coup de main* at the right moment, can carry the mass of people with them by a couple of initial successes and thus make a victorious revolution." The instrument was a conspiratorial group. Its principles were "that in general revolutions do not make themselves but are made; that they are made by a relatively small minority and in accordance with a plan worked out in advance; and finally, that at any moment it will 'come off soon.'"[1]

But that was written after some decades of experience. What about young Marx?

1. EARLY YEARS

A full thirty years before, Marx had attacked the putschist revolutionism of the Jacobin left just as vigorously.

He had been in Paris for less than a year, a new-fledged socialist or communist. Reacting to one of the earliest violent outbreaks of the workers' class struggle in Germany, the revolt of the Silesian weavers, he had no doubt that "*socialism* cannot be realized without *revolution*," as he wrote in an article published August 1844.[2] But he did not omit to put forward his criticism of mere violence-mongering. His language was not yet fully "Marxist," of course, but the viewpoint was clear:

> The more developed and universal the *political* understanding of a people [this being counterposed to *social* understanding], the more does the *proletariat*—at any rate at the beginning of the movement—squander its forces in senseless, useless revolts, which are drowned in blood. Because it thinks in the framework of politics [alone], the proletariat sees the cause of all evils in the *will,* and all means of remedy in *violence* and in the *overthrow* of a *particular* form of state. The proof: the first uprisings of the *French* proletariat.[3]

We note that this first statement already associated the propensity for putschist revolts with what philosophical jargon calls voluntarism, the exaltation of the will, the belief that a revolution can be pulled off at any time regardless of socioeconomic and political conditions. The same article contained another passage attacking the politics of voluntarism, which we cite elsewhere in connection with Robespierre.[4]

By this time, as we have seen,[5] Marx was already acquainted with the League of the Just elements in Paris (who had been under Blanquist influence) and with the London branch of the Just formed by Karl Schapper and his associates after they fled from France in the aftermath of the May 1839 putsch. Engels later related how he and Marx contributed to the re-education of the Just *without* joining their organization:

> ... we not only kept up our continuous correspondence with the Londoners but remained on still closer terms with... the leader of the Paris branches. Without concerning ourselves with the League's internal affairs, we learned nevertheless of everything significant that went on. On the other hand, we influenced the theoretical views of the most important League members by word of mouth, by letters, and through the press. For this we also made use of various lithographed circulars which we sent to our friends and correspondents around the world on special occasions involving internal affairs of the communist party [movement] that was being formed. In these the League itself was sometimes involved.[Engels then referred to the "Circular Against Kriege."][6]

We know the outcome. As against the myth that Marx was somehow tainted with Blanquism through associating with these Blanquist-tainted characters, it was the Just (Schapper and his comrades) who changed. To see what part of their evolution was ascribable to Marx and Engels, let us see what happened.

Our information is based on the minutes of discussions held in 1845 in London between the leading people of the League, especially Schapper, and the duo constituted by Wilhelm Weitling and his disciple Hermann Kriege. Weitling voiced the politics of the autonomous will as starkly as anyone ever expressed it, while Schapper argued that society was not yet ripe for communism and that a whole period of education and propaganda was first necessary. Weitling responded:

> If the opinion expressed by [Schapper et al.] meets with general support, all our work is for naught. It means eternally postponing things from today to tomorrow, from tomorrow to the day after... In my opinion, everybody is ripe for communism, even the criminals; they have their genesis precisely in the present social system and would no longer exist under community [of goods, i.e., communism]. Humanity is necessarily always ripe or never will be.[7]

Nobody could put it more flatfootedly than that. Kriege backed up Weitling with the intimidating argument that only "police officers and philistines" ever said that society was not ripe for communism. Pfander supported Schapper: "Kriege wants to force people to adopt his views. He tells them: Recognize this or I hit you over the head..." At this point Schapper became autobiographical:

> Kriege's talk is a mirror for me. That is just how I talked ten or eight years ago, yes, even six years ago. But now, when so many bitter experiences have cooled me down, now I must entirely agree with what the reactionaries say: "People are not yet ripe" ... A truth is never knocked into heads with rifle butts.[8]

Schapper made this statement in June 1835; the reference to "six years ago" meant he had gone through a big political swing soon after the debacle of May 1839. This indicates that he had begun changing his views *before* getting acquainted with Marx and Engels.

It was not only Blanquist putschism that Schapper turned against: in these 1845 discussions with Weitling he repudiated revolution as such. "The truth," he said, "needs no physical force; it is strong enough in itself. . . No, no revolution!" We have to "warn against revolutions always and everywhere... It is our most sacred duty everywhere to restrain the youth... In Germany we can advance on legal paths.. ."[9] This peaceful perspective meant to him that generations would pass before the time would be "ripe." It was Weitling who argued that "Enlightenment by peaceful roads is an illusion; what we strive for is achieved only in struggle." To be sure, Weitling utilized the discussions also to urge his theory of communist dictatorship: "If we bring about communism through revolutionary means, then we must have a *dictator* who holds sway over all."[10]

In this period, then, through 1845 at least, Schapper was throwing the baby out with the bathwater: abandoning Blanquist revolutionism, he dumped the revolution along with Blanquism. Yet by 1847, when the League merged with

Marx and Engels to form the Communist League, not a word was heard of this variety of peaceful reform: it had been abandoned in turn, but without going back to the Blanquist style of revolution. *It is this rectification which, I think, has to be ascribed to the influence of Marx and Engels,* in whole or in part. What Schapper learned from Marx was how to be a revolutionary of a different sort from Blanqui or Weitling.

This conclusion is admittedly based on circumstantial evidence, but the evidence is strong. In any case, how different the actuality is from the Bernsteinian fable of a Marx who is converted to Blanquism by mere contact with Schapper and his friends!

2. LESSONS OF THE BRUSSELS PERIOD

There are only a few historical flashes of illumination on what happened the ensuing year. Weitling, more and more isolated in London, went to Brussels for a while, and there completed the process of self-discreditment that he had begun in London. There in Brussels, in March 1846, took place the noted confrontation between Marx and Weitling, which I have discussed elsewhere.[11] A useful light is thrown on this meeting in Brussels when we see it as a continuation of the debates in London during 1845; it was not a quarrel out of the blue, as often represented. It is very likely that some of the issues discussed in the London talks were covered during this evening, but the account of the discussion given, a third of a century later, by a Russian tourist named P. V. Annenkov said little about the actual political content, which may well have been over Annenkov's head. On hearing about the blowup at this meeting, the London people commiserated with Marx: Weitling's behavior, they told him, was to have been expected; Weitling "can get along with no one except those who blindly obey his orders"; "Just the way it went with you, so too here"; and they added a long paragraph on Weitling's pattern of intolerance.[12] (None of this, of course, was known to or understood by Annenkov as part of the prehistory of the confrontation.)

Weitling's disciple Kriege had been operating in America since 1845, carrying on an agitation that was discrediting to the German communism he claimed to represent.[13] In their "Circular Against Kriege" Marx and Engels commented on the Weitlingian talk of "overthrowing" Mammon from his throne through supernal Love: "This idol [Mammon] is overthrown—how we do not learn; the revolutionary movement of the proletariat of all countries shrinks down to an uprising..."[14] The reduction of revolution to an uprising was precisely the view of revolution that separated Marx from Blanquism.

The "we" who accomplish the overthrow (Marx went on to say) then want to "teach" the proletarians what to do, in the manner of "prophets"[15]—in the manner, indeed, of the Blanquist "Educational Dictatorship."

A year after Schapper had insisted "No, no revolution!" in the London discussions, the League's leading committee wrote to Marx in Brussels in connection with the ongoing efforts to achieve collaboration. In this letter, signed by nine people though probably drafted by Schapper, it was clear that the antirevolutionary position had been overcome:

> As for conspiratorial plans, we have long been done with such stupidities; up to now conspiracy has been no good for anyone but our enemies, and we have seen with pleasure that you hold the same opinion.— To be sure, we are convinced that it will not and cannot work out without a good *[tüchtige]* revolution, but wanting to carry out such a revolution by conspiracies and stupid proclamations à la Weitling is ridiculous.[16]

Exactly a year later, in June 1847, the Communist League was founded at a congress in London. Engels' draft for a communist programmatic credo was submitted to this congress. It contained a substantial passage (Question 16) on the use of "peaceful methods," with the main emphasis on revolutionary action, but it included a warning against revolution-making:

> The Communists ... know only too well that revolutions are not made deliberately and arbitrarily, but that everywhere and at all times they have been the necessary outcome of circumstances entirely independent of the will and the leadership of particular parties and entire classes.[17]

In September the first number of a League organ was published. The programmatic leading article, probably written by Schapper, took pains to repudiate both the "peaceful" perspective and conspiratorialism in the same paragraph:

> We are not communists who preach everlasting peace now while our opponents everywhere gird themselves for battle. We know very well that nowhere—with the possible exception of England and the North American free states—will we be able to enter the better world unless we have first won our political rights by force. Now if there are people who condemn us for this and denounce us as revolutionaries, that is of little consequence to us... —We are not conspirators who want to start a revolution on a predetermined day or assassinate princes; but neither are we patient sheep who bear their cross without grumbling.[18]

The formulation about revolutionary force was quite moderate, much more so than the *Communist Manifesto* was going to be.

In November 1847 Engels introduced a new element into the analysis of

150 Part III: Preliminaries: The "Marx-Blanquist" Myth

putschism, one with great importance for the future. His article on France in the Chartist press raised the question *of revolutionary self-restraint*. We have seen that Schapper in 1845 had counseled restraint in the usual context, that is, as part of an antirevolutionary policy: but how does restraint figure in the opposite sort of perspective?

The French government, Engels explained, is afraid of the workingpeople. "They are afraid," he said, "because the people have entirely given up all attempts at insurrection and rioting." A paradox, a most ingenious paradox! But the idea was really very simple:

> The government desire a riot, they provoke it by every means. The police . . . make the most brutal attacks upon the people, in order to provoke them to riot and violence. Tens of thousands ... were on the very brink of repelling force by force; but they held out and no pretext for more gagging laws are to be forced from them. And think, what a tacit understanding, what a common feeling of what was to be done, at the moment, must have prevailed; what an effort it must have cost to the people of Paris, to submit to such infamous treatment rather than try a hopeless insurrection. What an enormous progress this forbearance proves in those very same working men of Paris...

This does not mean that "the revolutionary ardour of the people is decreasing"; the necessity for a thoroughgoing revolution is more widely felt than ever; but the people realize they need a thought-out social program, not "mere fighting." Revolution is taken for granted, by general agreement; they are waiting only for the right moment—

> . . . and when the moment will have arrived, at which a collision between the people and the government will be inevitable, down they will be in the streets and squares at a moment's notice, tearing up the pavement ... barricading every alley (etc.].[19]

This advanced analysis showed that a putsch was not merely ineffective but a positive danger to the real possibility of revolution. As 1847 drew to a close, the political atmosphere was heating up. What had previously been closet discussions among revolutionists was now being acted out on the Continental scale.

3. THE QUESTION OF ALLIES IN THE MANIFESTO

The *Communist Manifesto*, off the press as the revolution was getting under way, had nothing directly to say about putschism—or about any other problems of revolutionary tactics; even the references to forceful revolution were incidental. Still, there were three passages relevant to the subject. The preamble repudiated conspiratorial organization, for one thing. Near the end of Section I, there was the well-known statement that "The proletarian movement is the independent movement of the immense majority, in the interest of the immense majority." And Section III assumed that the proletarian goal could not be attained in an "undeveloped state of the proletariat," in "the absence of the material conditions for its emancipation, which are indeed only the product of the bourgeois epoch."[20]

These passages, to be sure, bore upon the theory of Blanquism, but more important was the policy set forth in Section IV, which said nothing about put schism—and yet excluded it totally. The question taken up was: *Which political tendencies do we look to as allies in the coming revolution?*

The Manifesto, as we have seen,[21] had said very emphatically that *all* the "proletarian parties" (read: proletarian political tendencies) stood for the same "immediate aim" as the Communists, including the overthrow of bourgeois rule and the conquest of political power by the proletariat. So Marx thought on the eve of the revolution. Section IV of the Manifesto made clear that the "working-class party" in England was the Chartists (by which Marx really meant the left wing). *And who constituted the working-class party in France?*

"In France," said the Manifesto, "the Communists ally themselves with the Social-Democrats," that is, with the political current represented by *La Réforme*, comprising Ledru-Rollin on its parliamentary right wing and Louis Blanc on its socialistic left.[22] The "Marx-Blanquist" mythologists have never explained why, in the Manifesto, Marx turned an entirely cold shoulder to the Blanquist tendency in France. Not only did the Manifesto *not* extend a politico-organizational hand to the Blanquists, it embraced their enemies among the rival socialistic tendencies.

While Marx was writing this as he drafted the Manifesto in Brussels, Engels was in Paris. He had moved there in August 1846, at first with the aim of forming a branch of the Communist Correspondence Committee (Marx's political base in Brussels); later he sought to establish the new Communist League. From his arrival in Paris to the outbreak of the 1848 revolution, we have seventeen letters or reports which he sent to Brussels, describing his political activities. Of course, most of his attention was devoted to the German émigré groups he was trying to win over. Aside from this, *which French political tendencies did he contact?* With what sectors of the French left did he aim at a rapprochement?

The first one, right off in August 1846, was the chief of the "Icarian communists," Cabet, whom he wanted to involve in correspondence with the Brussels Communist Correspondence Committee, without success.[23] His early letters also referred to Pierre Leroux and Buchez's *Atelier* (Christian socialist), but there was little rapport there; later there was passing mention of Dézamy's communist group. And over a period of a year and a half, *there was not so much as a bare mention of Blanqui or any Blanquist tendency whatever.*

The Engels-vs.-Marx myth will not operate here: Engels was not acting on his own but as Marx's direct agent. In fact, while Engels was back in Brussels from July to October 1847, he evidently came to a decision with Marx to make overtures to the Social-Democratic group around *La Réforme* for a political alliance. In his first report back to Marx, he began: "it was only today that I managed to see little Louis Blanc..."[24]

Engels enthusiastically described his efforts to "win over" Blanc and Flocon; mentioned plans or tentative relations with Cabet and the *Atelier* people; shortly afterwards, observed that collaboration with *Le National* (the *right-wing* republican current!) was probably not obtainable; by January, recorded disillusionment with Louis Blanc but happier relations with Flocon.[25] ... And in the course of all this, *there was not a single word reflecting even the existence of Blanqui and the Blanquists.*

Then, when Marx was expelled from Belgium after the outbreak of the revolution, he came to Paris and immediately wrote for *La Réforme* and became friendly with Flocon. In short: right up to his return to Cologne to launch the *Neue Rheinische Zeitung,* Marx, with Engels at first as his agent, acted out the Manifesto's view that the Communists' ally in France was the Social-Democracy. For the three to four years during which this line was implemented, until the defeat of the revolution, there are two facts to be set down for the benefit of all who have read the mass of marxological assertions that Marx was a "Blanquist" from at least 1847 to 1851-1852:

- In all of Marx's and Engels' correspondence from the year 1 up to 1850, there is not a single reference to Blanqui or the Blanquist tendency or to Blanquists as such.
- In all of Marx's and Engels' complete writings up to 1850—published, written, or scribbled, comprising well over five thousand pages—there is not a single reference to the same.[26]

This, remember, includes the entire period of the revolution and a vast quantity of writings by Marx and Engels in their Cologne paper. It is rather an extreme case; for if Marx had happened to refer to Blanqui *once* in some stray article or letter, this would hardly convince us he was a "Blanquist." What bad luck for this whole phalanx of marxologists to have picked, as their nominee for Marx's mentor, precisely the one party leader for whom not a *single* mention can be found during the revolutionary years!

The consolation is that the historical truth of the matter becomes all the more obvious. The course of the revolution had completely disillusioned Marx about the revolutionary bona fides of the Social-Democrats; it is from this postrevolutionary period that the term 'Social-Democracy' became a dirty word in his vocabulary.[27] To whom *now* could Marx look as he gazed across the Channel to descry a "revolutionary proletarian party" to work with? What political tendency was *left* in France—in both senses of the word?

The whole socialistic wing of the Provisional Government was discredited; the Cabetists (Icarian communists) had sailed off to their Nauvoo never-never land and virtually vanished from the French scene; there was no Proudhonist movement in existence even to oppose, let alone ally with. And in the London microcosm of the French left, where the refugees of revolution still carried on internecine struggle, there was now only one revolutionary current: the Blanquists, or what was left of them.

What a difference from 1847!—when Engels was groping his way through the thickets of the French left, trying to find out what currents the German communists could collaborate with. The revolution had cleared all the underbrush away with its blast. From Marx's standpoint, there was now no choice whatever: only the Blanquists remained as a possible French contingent in the coming European revolution.

The marxologists who fabricate reasons for a "Marxist-Blanquist alliance" not only have the wrong answer, they do not know what the question was. The question before Marx was not "Do we agree or disagree with Blanquism?" It was: "Is the Blanquist group among those revolutionary currents we can work with despite differences?"

Marx's answer to this question was *yes*.

4. REVOLUTION AND RESTRAINT

The test of revolutionary policy is—revolution. In revolution one finds out not only whether one's policies are effective but what those policies really are. In the course of the revolution of 1848-49 Marx established many "firsts," and among them was one that E. H. Carr stated a little onesidedly in writing the following:

> Marx was the first revolutionary in history who consistently sought to restrain his followers. Again and again he preached the supreme folly of rash and premature adventures.[28]

What Marx did was "restrain his followers" from making a putsch instead of a revolution, from resorting to the final arbitrament of armed force under conditions that would have meant ruinous defeat. We have called this "revolutionary restraint." The key is revolutionary *generalship:* a general who always and unconditionally urged his troops to attack under any circumstances would be a disaster. The very concept of generalship in revolution implies a revolutionary strategy that in practice excludes putschism.

It is true that Blanqui himself had a notion about the need for thought-out tactics in insurrection; but strategic generalship goes beyond this. It is also true that Blanqui on occasion *wanted* to restrain his band on strategic grounds, being an intelligent man, but it was precisely here that putschism showed its nature: he failed to do so because of the outlook instilled into his followers, who "led the leader" into battle against his better judgment. Engels noted this relationship in his 1874 analysis of Blanquism:

> . . .what happened was what usually happens with conspiracies: the people involved, tired of being continually put off with empty promises that the thing will come off soon, finally lost all patience and became rebellious; and so there remained only the alternatives of letting the conspiracy fall apart or of striking without any externally visible occasion.[29]

The first problem of generalship in 1848 came up during the Paris prelude to participation in the German revolution (already mentioned in Chapter 9).[30] Expelled from Belgium, Marx reorganized the Communist League branches in Paris. In the course, he confronted a typical proposal of adventuristic revolutionism: a scheme to form a "German Legion" with the help of the French government and thus import the revolution into the home country on foreign-financed muskets. The sponsors in this case were not "wild" leftists but the liberal émigrés of the German Democratic Association in Paris, led by the poet Georg Herwegh and the journalist Bornstedt.

"We opposed this playing with revolution in the most decisive fashion," recounted Engels later. To carry out such an invasion "into the midst of the ferment then going on in Germany meant to undermine the revolution in Germany itself.. ."[31] It negated the conception that "Germany had to make her revolution herself."[32] And these activities "have already aroused in a part of the German nation the old national and reactionary prejudices against the French people."[33]

We may remark here that the same issue of "importing the revolution" on foreign bayonets came to Marx's attention in 1870, in the midst of the Franco-Prussian War, when he learned that Arnold Huge was counting on the Prussian army to "proclaim the French republic in Paris." He informed Engels of this with a great guffaw and a blast of ridicule against Ruge.[34] It has since turned out, historically, to be a more widespread conception than Marx apparently thought.

The French Blanquists would have been enthusiastically in favor of the German Legion enterprise (and of the other national "legions," like the Polish, being prepared in Paris); for the Blanquists reflected the old Jacobin

10. Marx Versus Blanquim 155

ardor for launching a revolutionary war across the French borders. Nicolaievsky has made this point, probably with justice.*

Instead of the glory-road theatricals of the German Legion—which turned out to be both a farce and a small disaster, as predicted by Marx—Marx's associates moved back into Germany individually and in small batches, while conducting a two-month organizational campaign to found a chain of workers' associations in the main centers.[36] The largest concentration, as already discussed in Chapter 4,[37] was in Cologne with Marx and Engels themselves and their organ, the *Neue Rheinische Zeitung*. In Cologne, here only, Marx led the left wing of the revolutionary movement, and thus confronted the problems of revolutionary generalship in a day-to-day sense.

The Cologne movement, under the leadership of Marx's *NRZ* group, was the boldest wing of the revolution in Germany, with its tax-refusal campaign, peasant-organizing drives, frequent mass meetings, and a series of challenges to the state authority in what was, after all, the fortress center of Rhenish Prussia.† This fact also defined the danger: the danger of getting too far ahead of the rest of the revolutionary scene and thus making it possible for the government to cut it down. The reader's picture of the events may be distorted if we detail only the policy of restraint, not the audacity of the challenge.

Most of the *NRZ's* warnings to the Cologne movement were written by Engels. The first warning came during the first two weeks of the paper's existence. The government was feverishly arming the Cologne forts, in such a manner (as Engels showed technically) that the measures were pointed against the city itself. "The reaction is preparing a big coup," without the least provocation by the calm population. The rumor was spread that an uprising would take place on a given day: "They will try to provoke a small row so as to call the troops out immediately..."

We warn the workers of Cologne not to fall into this trap set for them by the reactionaries. We urgently plead with them *not to give* the

─────────

* However, I think Nicolaievsky overreaches when he goes on to portray the situation as if Marx was denounced chiefly by "hyper-revolutionaries" because he "had opposed the blind, desperate enthusiasm, the reckless, plunging spirit of the insurgents."[35] Nicolaievsky seems to be trying to make the German Legion out to be a Blanquist enterprise in its auspices. There is no evidence for this, and no other corroboration. The proponents of the German Legion were not "hyper-revolutionaries" but liberals in a state of exaltation.

† This aspect of Marx's year of revolution is very inadequately represented in biographies. One should read, at least, Oscar Hammen's *Red '48ers* (Part 3), preferably Gerhard Becker's relation to the Cologne working-class movement is so common that it is found even in David McLellan.[37] I mention this because the mythical version of Marx's policy makes it difficult to understand why it was so important to exercise restraint at crucial points.

old-Prussian party *the slightest pretext* for placing Cologne under the despotism of martial law...

But if the reaction really dares to unloose its assault, then the people of Cologne will not hesitate to defend the revolution "with their blood and lives"—so ended the article.[39] In this situation, a published warning of this sort was itself part of the obligations of generalship, especially in circumstances where one couldn't really know what the government's intentions were.

In July two local leaders of the Workers' Association were arrested. A *NRZ* editorial warned again: "The workers will be smart enough not to let themselves be drawn into a brawl by any provocation."[40]

There was a near-blowoff in the so-called September crisis. With the fate of the revolution coming to a critical stage in Berlin, the Cologne movement stepped up revolutionary agitation. We read in the historian Oscar Hammen (whose accurate presentation of the facts is all the more impressive since he plainly understands little of Marx's politics):

> ... the Communists were evident everywhere. They appeared to be in command, almost like a party, or at least an overwhelming presence. Newspapers commented on the fact that the editorial staff of the *New Rheinische Zeitung* occupied the public platform, gave many speeches, and initiated motions.

The *NRZ* group organized demonstrative mass meetings through the Democratic Association and the Workers Association. A popular paper for workers, peasants, and soldiers was started in Cologne to supplement the *NRZ*. The "Red Company" of the militia, staffed by friends of the *NRZ*, became more active. A "Committee of Public Safety" was established at a mass meeting, as the first step toward a dual power. A gigantic meeting was held in nearby Worringen, involving the regional peasantry. At the same time, the soldiers of the army garrison (mainly recruited from backward areas of east Prussia) multiplied clashes and brawls with civilians.

Then, outside Cologne, the revolution came to a boil with a revolt in Frankfurt, September 17 to 20—a serious uprising against the government that was put down by troops with some difficulty. The revolutionary situation passed its zenith. In Cologne the government made plans to suppress the explosion it saw coming, by arresting the Cologne leaders, including Schapper and Engels. On September 25, when the second congress of the Rhenish Democratic Associations was scheduled, a number of arrests were made.

That afternoon, Marx had to assess the situation: the movement in Berlin and Frankfurt had been suppressed for now; Cologne had its collective neck stuck out, with the government planning to cut it off. Speaking at a Workers Association meeting, Marx warned against police provocations and explained that this was *not* the moment for an armed uprising by an isolated Cologne. In

10. Marx Versus Blanquim   157

this exposed salient of the battle line, the movement had to pull back. Nevertheless barricades began arising around the city. The *NRZ* group worked indefatigably to restrain action; during the night the barricades were abandoned, while the Prussian commander* waited for daylight to start the assault. Although the reaction was triumphing all over Prussia, the Cologne movement was at least preserved, even though the *NRZ* was banned for a short while, Engels and others had to flee arrest, and other consequences weakened its activity.[42]

In short, Marx's problem of revolutionary generalship was how to keep the movement in Cologne ready for a national revolutionary outburst—and contributory as a vanguard—without forging so far ahead of the national movement as to precipitate an all-or-nothing armed struggle which could only drown the Cologne movement in blood. In this situation the Blanquist mentality would have been a mortal danger.

"Revolutionary restraint" had to be called on again more than once before the period ended. But there were other strategies too. In November 1848 the *NRZ* turned to the pseudolegal campaign of "No more taxes!" The National Assembly, whose decisions on tax-refusal had given this demand its juridical cover, had called for "passive resistance" only. At this point Marx's editorial agitation in the *NRZ* suggested that more was needed; officials who rejected the Assembly's tax-refusal position should be replaced by "committees of public safety":

> Where counterrevolutionary authorities have a mind to obstruct the formation and official activity of these committees of public safety, *force must be counterposed to any kind of force.* Passive resistance must have *active resistance* as its foundation. *Otherwise it is like the struggles of a calf against its slaughterer.*[43]

But here again the national movement was determining: the tax-refusal campaign was stifled outside of Cologne, therefore could not be screwed to a revolutionary pitch inside Cologne.

By 1849 the revolutionary temperature of the whole country was declining. Marx was concerned lest desperation and frustration lead to an adventuristic disaster, which indeed the government desired. By May the end was near. On May 1 Engels published an article exposing the government's plan "to provoke the Berlin people into street fighting" and then follow the bloody pattern set by Cavaignac the preceding June. But: "The calm behavior of the people despite all provocation upset the calculations of the counter-

---

* By one of those freakish coincidences that no novelist would dare invent, the name of the colonel who commanded the Cologne garrison was—Friedrich Engels (in full Karl Friedrich Gottfried Engels).[41]

revolutionaries."[44] On May 4 another article by Engels made an educational presentation that could well go into a textbook on revolutionary strategy:

> The government is trying *at all costs* to provoke a conflict ... By their calm behavior, by unshakable stolidity in the face of the soldiers' provocations, the Cologne workers can deprive the government of any excuse for acts of violence.
>
> Decisive events are at hand. Vienna, Bohemia, South Germany, Berlin are in ferment and await the right moment. Cologne can play its part, play a very powerful part, but it cannot *begin* any decisive blow.
>
> ...[The government provocations] aim only at causing an outburst of *such* a kind as will occur *at a moment unfavorable for us but favorable for the government.*
>
> Only by great events can revolutions be carried through; but if one accepts the provocations of the government, the most that can result is a riot.[45]

Engels repeated the warning a couple of days later, in an article entitled "Hankering for a State of Siege."[46] Then came the end of the line, and the *NRZ* printed its last issue on May 19 in red ink. Marx's final words "To the Workers of Cologne" gave the last warning of revolutionary restraint:

> We warn you, in conclusion, against any putsch* in Cologne. In Cologne's military situation, you would be irretrievably lost.... A state of siege in Cologne would demoralize the whole Rhine province, and a state of siege would be the necessary consequence of any uprising on your part at this moment.[48]

The Cologne period was over; but before the year ended, Marx and Engels participated (politically and militarily respectively) in the armed insurrection that had broken out in Baden and the Palatinate. It was a revolution, though a badly conducted one.

5. RETROSPECTION IN THE FIFTIES

Since this section surveys the views expressed by Marx in the 1850s on putschism and related Blanquist notions, we have to inform the reader that it is precisely the year 1850 (sometimes 1850-52) which, according to the "Marx-Blanquist" myth, is the zenith of Marx's alleged Blanquist aberration.

* This, I think, was the first time the word 'Putsch' was used by Marx; it was still relatively new. Ladendorf says that it came into German (from a Swiss dialect form) at the beginning of the 1840s, but the example he gives is from 1849; by this time, he adds, the usage was already current.[47] For a comment on the MECW mistranslation of 'Putsch', see Special Note D, Section 8.

The wraithlike evidence that has been adduced to give this popular story a semblance of verisimilitude is considered in Special Note B, and will not concern us here.

Marx's article series on the failed revolution in France, later published under the tide *The Class Struggles in France*, is the main subject of the next chapter, because it inaugurates the phrase 'dictatorship of the proletariat'. We will see what it says about 'dictatorship' in general and we will throw some light on its notable reference to Blanqui. At this point we only ask what if anything it said about putschism and allied subjects. The short answer is: not much; for, contrary to the myth, Marx was not particularly interested in that issue nor was the issue itself demanding to be discussed at length. Unfortunately Marx himself did not know that he was going to be charged with "Blanquism."

But there were passing references. In Section (or article) III, about a page after the famous passage on permanent revolution and dictatorship of the proletariat (locus 1c), Marx mentioned the royalists' challenge to the left "to betake themselves to the streets, and his declaration that the government was ready to receive them." His comment was that

> The proletariat did not allow itself to be provoked into a *riot*, since it was looking to make a *revolution.*[49]

We have seen him make this point more than once before; nothing has changed in his thinking on this score.

In Section II, a passage (incidental, to be sure) offered an interesting treatment of the attempt by the liberal monarchist Barrot to close the Assembly. Marx makes a parallel in which this move is equated, or at any rate paired, with Blanqui's putsch of May 15 against the same Assembly.

> On May 15 Blanqui, Barbès, Raspail, etc. had attempted to break up the Constituent Assembly by forcing an entrance into its hall of session at the head of the Paris proletariat. Barrot prepared a moral May 15 for the same Assembly when he wanted to dictate its self-dissolution and close the hall.

Barrot's antidemocratic attempt was the "moral" equivalent of the *attentat* against the same Assembly in the name of the proletariat; and, says Marx, Barrot appeared before the Assembly "as a royalist Blanqui."[50] On the next page it is Barrot who is quoted by Marx as saying, "Legality is killing us."

The prime evidence adduced by marxologists for Marx's alleged "Blanquist aberration" is the "Address to the Communist League" of March 1850, a circular letter to members.* Like most of the *Class Struggles in France*, it was wntten while Marx still considered the European revolution to be on the boil,

---

* Why the Address has been the target for marxological mythopoesis is explained in KMTR 2, in a chapter that expounds the actual political content of the document; here our aim is much narrower.[51]

waiting only for a new blowoff. In late summer he decided that, the economic depression having ended, the revolutionary situation in Europe was over for the nonce. It is this conclusion, by the way, that is used by the "Marx-Blanquist" mythologists to claim that Marx revised all his basic ideas of revolution. In point of fact, Marx changed nothing whatever about his views, only how those views were to be immediately implemented.

But, as we said, the March Address was written while Marx still thought there was an ongoing revolutionary situation in Europe. Even so, however, in this circular Marx specifically rejected the notion that a communist revolution could be carried out in an outburst. The revolutionary crisis to which he looked would mean that "the Democrats will come to power with the next movement," and *then there would start the process of opposition to this government*, a process that would eventually bring the proletarian revolutionary wing to power at the head of a leftward-moving coalition. (The very notion of a Democratic revolution as the first stage was quite alien to Blanquism, as has been explained elsewhere.[52])

The period of revolutionary opposition to the new government of the Democracy is the period *par excellence* of "permanent revolution," as put forward in the Address. How long this period might be is, of course, the sort of question that Marx refused to answer; but the Address itself spoke of it as a "lengthy" one *in Germany*. The penultimate paragraph of the Address struck exactly the same note as would be sounded by Marx during the September 1850 split (in a speech, which we will come to, that the mythologists claim to be the very opposite of the Address). In the March circular, it was put this way:

> If the German workers are not able to attain power and achieve their own class interests without completely going through a lengthy revolutionary development, they at least know for a certainty this time that the first act of this approaching revolutionary drama will coincide with the direct victory of their own class in France and will be very much accelerated by it.[53]

As for France, it should go without saying that what Marx expected was an overwhelming rising of the workers as in the massive insurrection of June 1848, not a wretched putsch.

6. MARX'S 1850 ATTACK ON BLANQUISM

The SUCR episode, which is taken up in Chapter 12, will show us that Marx and Engels were involved in the spring of 1850 with a projected alliance

10. Marx Versus Blanquim 161

of communists of different countries, an alliance in which the French contingent was the Blanquist émigré group in London. This fact—their association with genuine Blanquists—is the hard core of the "Marx-Blanquist" myth.

The SUCR agreement was signed in mid-April. Just before this date or at the same time, Marx and Engels* wrote an article on the secret societies of France, and Marx published it in his London magazine, which we call the *NRZ Revue* for short. This article was a devastating critique of the world of the secret societies characteristic of the Blanquist movement.

The article was in the form of a book review of two recent publications—the longest book review in the run of the magazine.[54] The books under review were: *Les Conspirateurs* by A. Chenu, a police agent who operated in the pre-1848 secret societies and in the police administration of the Provisional Government in 1848; and *La Naissance de la République* by L. de la Hodde, who, through a different route, also pursued the career of a professional secret-society conspirator while acting as a police spy.

Let it be said at once that nowhere did Marx's review mention Blanquism and Blanquists as such. We have to keep in mind that it was only afterwards that historians began using these labels for the Jacobin-communist style of the conspiratorial secret societies in general. The book review dealt with what is called Blanquism today, not then. Secondly, at a couple of points the review left an *out* for the Blanquist allies of 1850: it discussed the "professional conspirators" as virtually an excrescence on the "revolutionary party." But when the revolutionary communist "party" was mentioned specifically, it turned out to specify the Cabetist (Icarian communist) movement.[55] At one point the review hastened to exempt Albert (Alexandre Martin) from the general strictures on personal grounds, thus keeping the indictment all the more impersonal.[56] The article was not written as an attack on sincere conspirators ("Blanquists") themselves, including the allies in SUCR, but as a demolition job on the ideology and organization of what is now called Blanquism.

All through Marx's review the emphasis is on the basic distinction: between a revolution on the one hand and a putsch *(coup de main, émeute)* on the other.†

---

* All six of the book-review articles in the *NRZ Revue* were unsigned, hence ascribed to the joint authorship or Marx and Engels. But the question is: who drafted which? For the article under consideration, there is no information; answers are speculative. I lean to the guess that, unlike some of the other reviews, this one was really a collaborative product, with Marx establishing the final form (which he would be likely to do as editor anyway). It is not an important problem since Marx necessarily took overall responsibility for the publication. Below I refer to Marx as the author simply as a matter of convenience.

† The reader is warned that this distinction is badly blurred in the MECW translation of this book review. The problem is discussed in Special Note D, Section 8.

Chenu's book, it says, "demonstrates that a real revolution is just the opposite of the notions held by the *mouchard* [police spy], who, in agreement with the 'men of action,' sees in every revolution the work of a small coterie." But "all movements provoked more or less arbitrarily by coteries remained mere *émeutes* [riotous outbreaks]."[57] Tracing the growing predominance of working-class elements in the conspiratorial societies after 1830, Marx wrote: "These conspiracies naturally never embraced the great mass of the Paris proletariat. They were limited to a relatively small and continually fluctuating number of members, consisting partly of old, unchanging conspirators regularly handed down by every secret society to its successor, partly of newly recruited workers."[58]

In a striking passage Marx describes the "class" or stratum of professional conspirators as a part of the lumpen-bohème of society; the "sinister conspirator" is shown as a pub-crawling boozer. (I have cited this passage elsewhere.[59]) He is daring, yes—

> The desperate recklessness that shows up in every Paris insurrection is injected precisely by these old professional conspirators, the *hommes de coups de main* [the *coup de main* men, putschists]. It is they who set up the first barricades and command them, who organize the resistance, take the lead in plundering weapon shops and seizing arms and ammunitions from houses, and in the midst of the uprising carry out those daring *coups de main* that so often throw the government side into confusion. In short, they are the officers of the insurrection.[60]

This leads into the best-known passage of the article, on the political nature of "these conspirators" as a stratum:

> Their business consists precisely in forestalling the process of revolutionary development, pushing it artificially to crisis, making a revolution impromptu, without the preconditions for a revolution. The sole precondition of revolution, for them, is the adequate organization of their conspiracy. They are the alchemists of the revolution, and they entirely share the earlier alchemists' disorder of ideas and narrow-mindedness in fixed conceptions.

The "alchemist" analogy, the most frequently quoted phrase of this article, deserves its popularity; for the alchemists had a limited positive role to play for a while. Marx develops the analogy a bit:

> They leap at inventions that are said to perform revolutionary miracles: incendiary bombs, demolition devices with magical action, *émeutes* that are supposed to have astounding miracle-working effects all the more the less they have a rational basis. Preoccupied with such scheming, they have no aim other than the immediate one of overthrowing the existing government, and they look with the profoundest contempt on

the more theoretical enlightenment of the workers on their class interests. Hence their irritation, not proletarian but plebeian, at the *habits noirs* [frock coats], the more or less educated people who represent this side of the movement—people, however, from whom, as the official representatives of the party, they can never make themselves entirely independent.[61]

Finally, there is the symbiotic relationship with the police. The conspirators battle the police, and the police have a use for the conspiracies: "They tolerate them as centers easy to keep an eye on, where the most violent revolutionary elements of the society get together, as foundries *of émeutes,* which in France have become a government instrument just as necessary as the police themselves, and finally as a recruiting place for their own political *mouchards.*"[62] Cops and conspirators (like cops and crooks) exchange places; suspicion is endemic; double roles blur reality.

The conspiracies encountered serious competition from the "proletarian secret societies which had as goal not an immediate insurrection but the organized development of the proletariat." In the pre-1848 period some of the conspirators were impelled into the proletarian movement proper. The development proved that "only the proletariat as a whole can carry out [the revolution]."[63]

Q.E.D. The conclusion came around, like much of Marx's writing, co the basic principle of the self-emancipation of the proletariat. Blanquism was the "left" way to reject this self-emancipation.

The two men who published this annihilatory dissection of Blanquist conspiratorialism are the same men who are portrayed as Blanquists in the marxological myth. This is so embarrassing that fantasmagorical explanations have been devised, including a remarkable claim that the article shows "Marx did not take the Blanquists seriously."[64]

7. THE REST OF 1850

Let us continue our account of Marx's attitude toward Blanquism through 1850, the crucial year. We are interested here only in the expression of views on the issues involved, not in the questions about Marx-Blanqui relations set forth in Chapter 9. As mentioned before, these issues cropped up only infrequently, and can be listed handily.

(1) In 1850 the left-wing Chartist Harney was collaborating closely with Marx, and his magazine *Democratic Review* was open to contributions by Marx's friends. During the year, from January to August, the magazine

carried a series of eight articles under the rubric "Letter from France." It is probable that these articles were written by some member of Marx's circle (not Engels[65]). True, this does not necessarily mean they were even read by Marx before publication, but they have a certain interest in reflecting views held by Marx's associates.

For what it is worth, then, we can record that the July "Letter from France"—written and published in the midst of the SUCR episode—took a far from flattering view of Blanqui. It said that the French people, so often deceived, have "a deep distrust towards all men who ever have acted as their leaders—not excepting even Barbes or Blanqui..."[66] On the other hand, Ernst Dronke, one of Marx's associates, had written to Engels from the Continent that Blanqui's standing with the French workers was rising.*

(2) Engels' *Peasant War in Germany,* written in the summer of 1850, was not produced simply as an exercise in history. It was bracketed fore and aft by passages tying it to the lessons of the revolution just ended. Its sixth chapter began with one of these lessons, on the plight of "the leader of an extreme party" who is "compelled to assume power" prematurely. The premature seizure of power regardless of social conditions may appear to be connected with Blanquist strategies, but here we see it has another side.

> To prevent action, Munzer was compelled to act as a moderator [on the revolutionary impatience of his supporters], but his disciple, Pfeifer, who held the reins of the movement there [in Mühlhausen] had committed himself so greatly that he could not hold back the outbreak, and as early as March 17, 1525, before the general uprising in South Germany, Mühlhausen made its revolution.[68]

Engels links this, not to Blanquist-type putsches, but to a quite different issue that had appeared in 1848: "the position in the last French Provisional Government of the representatives of the proletariat" such as Louis Blanc,

---

* If, as MECW mistakenly claims, it was Engels who wrote the "Letters from France," he certainly put no faith in Dronke's opinion. Dronke had reported on February 21 (from Paris) that the social-democratic "chatterboxes" and the "pure anarchist" fools like Proudhon were finished, but that "Blanqui's support among the workers has become enormous." About May 7 he wrote (from Frankfurt) that in the next Paris outbreak Blanqui would come to the helm. The outbreak that Dronke expected was to come "after the vote on the new electoral law." As it happened, a few days after Dronke's letter, Lassalle wrote Marx (from Düsseldorf) that he was "firmly convinced" there would be an insurrection in Paris on the same occasion. Clearly, expectation of a blowoff in Paris was widespread; Marx's acceptance of this expectation was no idiosyncratic opinion of his, but doubtless was the orthodoxy of the left at the moment—an orthodoxy with which Marx broke in late summer.—Dronke's report on the Blanquists in France was reiterated in his letter of December 1 (from Geneva): "In Paris, despite all the efforts of Louis Blanc and Ledru(-Rollin], the Blanquists are the only *real* party."[67]

10. Marx Versus Blanquim   165

that is, the policy of socialist participation in bourgeois-dominated coalition governments.[69] Coalitionism (what a half century later was going to be tagged Millerandism) would appear to be the opposite of Blanquism, the former a reformist deviation, the latter ultraleftist in repute; but we have here another way of seeing the reformist side of Blanquism itself.[70] (Symbol: the later leader of the Blanquist tendency, Vaillant, was going to wind up his career in 1915 as a member of a coalition government engaged in an imperialist war, sitting alongside his fellow social-democrats.)

(3) Until late summer 1850 Marx held the opinion that the revolutionary situation was continuing in Europe, but of course this did not mean to him that communism could be introduced by a coup any day. If more evidence is needed, it is provided by the testimony of Peter Roser, one of the leaders of the Communist League in Cologne, who remained in that city after the collapse of the revolution.* According to the account given by Roser, about the end of July 1850 he received a letter from Marx, via courier—a letter which will also concern us later in connection with Willich. The letter referred to the period of the winter of 1849-1850, and so we take it up at this point. Roser related that Marx's letter

> gave vent to his anger at Willich & Company and said it was a great pity that Schapper should have attached himself to this bunch of frauds. He said that during the winter of 1849/50 he had lectured to the London Workers' Society [GWEA] on the Manifesto and had explained that communism could only be introduced after a number of years, that it would have to go through several phases and that generally its introduction could only be effected by a process of education and gradual development, but that Willich had violently opposed him with his rubbish—as Marx called it—saying that it would be introduced in the next revolution, if only by the might of the guillotine, that the hostility between them was already great and he [Marx] feared it would lead to a split in the League, General Willich having got it firmly into his head that, come the next revolution, he and his brave men from the Palatinate would introduce communism on their own and against the will of everyone in Germany.[71]

For the period here described, on no evidence at all, the "Marx-Blanquist"

---

* This testimony by Roser was given to the Prussian authorities after his conviction in the Cologne Communist trial of 1852 and during his subsequent imprisonment, specifically in the period from December 1853 to the following February. The fact that Roser broke and "sang" has been used to impugn not only his character (which is understandable) but also his truthfulness. However, I agree with those like Nicolaievsky who have argued that Roser was honestly trying to tell what he knew, though he might have been inaccurate on details; his attempt to recollect the contents of letters was obviously subject to error.

mythologists portray Marx as a fire-eating Blanquist, who changed over to a well-behaved social-democrat all of a sudden in September 1850 when the split actually took place. This tale is simply falsification. The "process of education and gradual development" was not an alternative to revolution but represented the period in which the proletariat was to become capable of revolution.

(4) When Marx came to the conclusion, in the late summer of 1850, that the European revolutionary situation was over, and that the period lying ahead had to be given over to preparatory propaganda and education of a working-class movement not yet ready for power, the differences in outlook inside the Communist League came to a head.[72] Schapper and Willich wanted the League to act as if the revolution was on the order of the day. True, neither Schapper nor Willich was a "Blanquist," but Willich in particular was a military martinet type turned communist relatively recently, whose understanding of the issues was primitive. It was Schapper, not Marx, who was going through a period of Jacobin aberration, as he himself came to see a few years later.

At a meeting of the CL Central Committee held on September 15, 1850, the question of policy was debated, leading to a split forced by the Willich-Schapper group. Marx formulated the issue in a speech that is frequently quoted:

> In place of the critical outlook the Minority substitutes a dogmatic one; in place of the materialist, an idealist one. Instead of the actual conditions, *pure will* becomes the drive-wheel of the revolution for them. Whereas we tell the workers: "You have fifteen, twenty, fifty years of civil wars and people's struggles to go through, not only to change the conditions but in order to change yourselves and make yourselves fit for political rule," you say on the contrary: "We must come to prower right away, or else we might as well go to sleep."[73]

This attack on the politics of voluntarism was a position that we have seen Marx take more than once. It was no new departure. The claim that it somehow represented a repudiation of the March "Address to the Communist League" rests on sheer assertion repeated so assiduously that no evidence has been considered necessary. The continuity of Marx's thought is shown by the fact that, in the September 15 session itself, it was he that defended (indeed flaunted) the March Address as his own programmatic position *against* the Willich-Schapper group.[74]

(5) The account by Peter Roser, cited above in point 3, included some recollections about the September split, or rather about the reports on it that came to the Cologne branch of the Communist League. These recollections are therefore second- or thirdhand, but essentially they reflect Marx's viewpoint in good part, if not his formulations. Thus, a CL member named Haupt

reported to Cologne that the split had taken place because the Willich-Schapper group maintained that Marx and Engels did not believe it would be "possible to introduce communism already in the next revolution."

> Schapper-Willich [said Röser's deposition] propose to introduce communism on the basis of the present state of education, if necessary in the next revolution and by force of arms. Marx considers it to be feasible only by a process of education and gradual development and, in a letter to us, cites four phases through which it must pass before it is introduced.[75]

Leaving aside details of formulation, like the division into four phases, the difference between Marx and the Willichites is fairly clear. Marx's own summary of the Willich-Schapper tendency can be read in Chapter 6 of his *Revelations Concerning the Communist Trial in Cologne.*[76]

(6) Shortly after the September split, Marx wrote a long article reviewing the period from May to October, for the last issue of the *NRZ Revue*, published November 29. This review devoted space to a depreciation of the political emigre center called the European Central Committee (Mazzini, Ledru-Rollin, Ruge for Germany, etc.)—the liberal Democratic camp. These people were far from Blanquist, naturally, but we see again the pattern noted in point 2 above. Marx gave considerable attention to criticizing these Democrats' view of the "revolution" they preached: a shallow view of revolution as a quick grab for power, rather than a serious social struggle. In fact, the conceptions of the gentlemen of the European Central Committee (if not their actions) constituted a sort of reformist version of Blanquist putschism:

> Their conceptions about social organizations are expressed very strikingly: a crowd gathered in the street, a brawl, a hand clasp, and all's over and done. For them the revolution consists on the whole simply in the overthrow of the existing government; when this goal is attained, "*the* victory" has been won. Movement, development, struggle—these then come to an end, and under the aegis of the European Central Committee then in power there begins the golden age of the European republic and of the sleepyheads declared in permanence.

The last phrase is a satirical version of the "revolution in permanence." Marx went on to say that these people detested theory; in their view the people should empty their minds of all ideas: "when the day of decision dawns, it will be electrified by mere contact, and the riddle of the future will be solved by a miracle."[77] (The "electrification" metaphor had a great future before it in the twentieth century.)

I repeat: Marx was not writing this about Blanquists but rather about Democratic reformists who were setting themselves up as "revolutionaries" against the existing despotic regimes. *A leftist did not have to be a Blanquist to possess these notions in a crude form;* they were the common property of primitive radicals, doing and saying "what came natural." The marxologists' theory that voluntaris tic Jacobinism was the very *definition* of Blanquism is at variance with an elementary knowledge of the history of the movement.[78]

8. THROUGH THE FIFTIES

For the rest of the 1850s, the story can be briefly summarized as: more of the same.

(1) October 1851: a couple of months before Bonaparte's coup d'état, the question of universal suffrage was being used as a political ploy. Marx wrote to Engels:

> In any case the "revolution"—in the sense of a |mere| outburst—has been conjured away. With universal suffrage it's not to be thought of.[79]

"Outburst" here is *Losgehn* (a breaking loose). The contrast is with a real revolution: it is a contrast, or counterposition, alien to Blanquist thinking.

(2) In 1852 there was an indication that Marx had no high opinion of the London Blanquist emigre's, or some of them. In a letter to Engels, mentioning a February Revolution anniversary held by "the French" (the French emigre community in London), he remarked: "Only the lowest dregs of the emigration were there, most of whom style themselves Blanquists."[80] True, this was a passing sideswipe that does not work vice-versa, that is, it did not mean that the real Blanquists were the "lowest dregs"; but it reminds us that there was a sharp distinction made between Marx's view of Blanqui himself and of the people who at any given time were calling themselves (or being called) Blanquists.

(3) In a followup article to the series on "Revolution and Counterrevolution in Germany" in the *New York Daily Tribune*—drafted by Engels but published by Marx under his own name—there was a careful line drawn between Marx's views and Blanquism. The names were not used, of course; the counterposition was between the "advanced Communist party in Germany" (meaning the Marxist tendency) and the communists of the secret societies and conspiracies. Not for the first time, Engels explained the distinction between conspiratorialwm and mere secrecy as a legal necessity. If there is no legal alternative, " he is a coward that under certain circumstances would not conspire" (that is, carry on secret work) "just as he is a fool who, under other circumstances, would do s o..." There were "numerous secret societies which

10. Marx Versus Blanquim   169

have, ever since 1849, one after another been discovered by the police and prosecuted as conspiracies," but on the other hand there were other societies "formed with a wider and more elevated purpose, which knew that the upsetting of an existing Government was but a passing stage in the great impending struggle," and which prepared for the final combat against capital. The latter, the "advanced Communist party,"

> never imagined itself capable of producing, at any time and at its pleasure, that revolution which was to carry its ideas into practice.

These "advanced" Communists looked ahead to overthrowing, not the present governments, but rather those that would succeed them in the next revolution. Since the reference was not to the Blanquist movement itself but to the Willich-Schapper group, the article referred to the split in the Communist League, obliquely and inaccurately:

> So well was this foundation of the society [League] understood by the majority of its members, that when the place-hunting ambition of some tried to turn it into a conspiracy for making an *ex tempore* revolution, they were speedily turned out.[81]

(4) Every now and then the issues involved in the difference between Marxism and Blanquism came up in Marx's journalistic work. Marx was always ready to admire and even celebrate struggles for freedom however hopeless, but it does not follow that he had to view them as models. In 1853 a Mazzinist outbreak in Milan was crushed by General Joseph Radetzky's Austrian troops. Marx pointed out to the discredit of the Austrian authorities that they mulcted fines from the people even while admitting "that the bulk of the population took no part whatever." To *New York Daily Tribune* readers, this served also to reveal that the affair was not a revolution but a putsch; but in the *NYDT*'s columns Marx did not want to simply condemn the whole thing. First he stated the positive side:

> The Milan insurrection is significant as a symptom of the approaching revolutionary crisis on the whole European continent. As the heroic act of some few proletarians... proletarians who, armed only with knives, marched to attack the citadel of a garrison and surrounding army of forty thousand of the finest troops in Europe, it is admirable.

That much said, he stated what was wrong with it:

> But as the finale of Mazzini's eternal conspiracy, of his bombastic proclamations and his arrogant capucinades against the French people, it is a very poor result. Let us hope that henceforth there will be an end *of révolutions improvisées,* as the French call them. Has anyone ever heard of great improvisators being also great poets? They are the same in

politics as in poetry. Revolutions are never made to order. After the terrible experience of '46 and '49, it needs something more than paper summonses from distant leaders to evoke national revolutions.[82]

Still, he went back to the positive side: "That the revolution is victorious even in its failures, one may see from the terrors the Milan *échauffourée* [affray] has thrown in the very heart of continental potentates."[83]

In a followup article Marx took note of Mazzini's explanation that the Milan insurrection was forced on his followers by circumstances beyond their control. On this Marx made the same comment as he had done on the Bianquists:

> But, on one side, it belongs to the *very* nature of conspiracies to be driven to a premature outbreak, either by treason or by accidents. On the other side, if you cry, during three years, *action, action, action*—if your entire revolutionary vocabulary be exhausted by the one word "Insurrection," you cannot expect to hold sufficient authority for dictating, at any given moment: *there shall be no insurrection.*[84]

The modern reader, especially the modern marxologist, should take note of the fact that, in this period, conspiratorialism was epidemic not on the adventurist left (tagged Bianquism) but on the desperate right: Mazzini, for example, was as bourgeois an anticommunist as the authorities he wanted to overthrow. *When the Willich-Schapper group, having split with Marx, adopted the perspective characteristics of the Blanquist, they actually moved to an alliance with the reform-Democratic putchists.*

"The immediate practical reason for the split," wrote Marx in 1860, "was *Willich's* efforts to involve the League in the playing at revolution by the German Democratic emigration."[85] This was also the crux of Marx's political analysis of the Willich-Schapper group in his *Revelations Concerning the Communist Trial in Cologne*. Granting that the Communist League had to be a "secret society" in Germany because of the repressive laws of that land, Marx made a basic distinction: it "was no conspiratorial society, but a society which secretly strove to create an organized proletarian party... Such a society can only be said to conspire against the status quo in the sense that steam and electricity conspire against it." The League "aims at forming not the *government party of the future* but the *opposition party of the future*" and therefore has little attraction for people who "wished to satisfy their narrowminded ambition on the day of the next revolution,... to snatch their share of the proceeds of demagogy and to find a welcome among the quacks and charlatans of democracy." The individuals who strutted about "in the theatrical cloak of the conspirator"— who "demanded, if not real conspiracies, at any rate the *appearance* of conspiracies"—longed for quick results in terms of state power, "and

10. Marx Versus Blanquim 171

accordingly called for a direct alliance with the Democratic heroes of the hour
... "Therefore it was typical of the Willich-Schapper group that "Willich was, together with *Kinkel*, one of the entrepreneurs in the business of the German-American revolutionary loan [fund]."[86]

This was the bridge that linked superficial ultraleftism with practical opportunism.

This, not Blanquist conspiratorialism, was Marx's chief concern of the fifties. A remark to the same effect can be found also in the unpublished manuscript of *Great Men of the Emigration* that Marx and Engels wrote in the spring of 1852. They waxed sarcastic about the "fear" that the Democratic conspirators thought they were inspiring in the breasts of the "tyrants" while their followers "retired from the putschist swindles *[Putschschwindelei]*"[87] While they were working on this manuscript, their correspondence reflected the same thinking. Marx informed his friend that the Kossuth-Mazzini forces were planning a new putsch:

> If these gentlemen don't suffer defeats and get a beating twice every year, they feel uncomfortable. That world history unfolds without their help, without their intervention, indeed without official intervention—this they cannot concede.[88]

Engels replied in the same vein:

> This Carbonari-style, self-important, pseudo-activist, order-of-the-day-ish approach betrays how much these gentlemen delude themselves again about their alleged organized forces. To aim at a putsch now is a stupid thing and a mean trick. But of course "Something has to happen! something has to be got going!" It makes you wish that the leaders who are supposed to direct the thing all get themselves caught and shot; but naturally the great men will take care of themselves...[89]

The Carbonari, to whom Engels referred, represented a common source of conspiratorialism on both the right and the left; Blanqui had roots in this movement, like Mazzini. The two flowering stems that rose from this root, twining left and right, also did some intertwining: the next sentence in Engels' letter was about Willich's connection with the Democratic putschists, through Gottfried Kinkel. The modern marxologist's obsessive belief that 'putschism' was spelled 'Blanquism' is, as mentioned, a matter of ignorance. *All through the fifties, Marx's consistent opposition to putschism and conspiratorial adventurism was pointed not simply against the left (or ultraleft) but against the reformist Democrats-in-a-frenzy.*

These preliminaries understood, we can now see what, and under what circumstances, Marx wrote about the 'dictatorship of the proletariat'. (Our account of Marx's views on Blanquist politics will be continued in Chapter 17.)

IV 'DICTATORSHIP OF THE PROLETARIAT' IN MARX AND ENGELS

11 | MARX'S CLASS STRUGGLES IN FRANCE

Marx's first use of the term 'dictatorship of the proletariat' came in 1850, in a series of articles later republished in book form with the title *The Class Struggles in France 1848-1850*.

In London in 1850, Marx began publishing a theoretical journal that took its name from the newspaper he had put out in Cologne during the revolution. The new title was *Neue Rheinische Zeitung, politisch-ökonomische Revue* (for short, *NRZ Revue*). Marx's article series comprised three articles, each containing a reference in some form to the 'dictatorship of the proletariat'. (The fourth chapter of this work in book form was added by Engels from the "Review, May to October" which appeared in the last issue of the magazine.)

1. 'DICTATORSHIP' TIMES FIVE

Since Marx used 'dictatorship of the proletariat' in this work for the first time, let us examine his use of the word 'dictatorship' by itself in other parts of this article series. The survey is rewarding, for we find that, at one point or another, it was applied in passing to *four* different periods or regimes. Then there was a fifth that was discussed in his *Eighteenth Brumaire of Louis Bonaparte* (1852).

(1) *The Cavaignac dictatorship.* As explained in Chapter 3, the conferral of a dictatorship on Louis Eugene Cavaignac to suppress the June uprising was a turning point. Marx called it a "bourgeois dictatorship recognized officially" (strict accuracy would say "semiofficially"). Marx also wrote of "the military dictatorship and the state of siege," in reference to Cavaignac. He made an important distinction:

> But Cavaignac was not the dictatorship of the saber over bourgeois society; he was the dictatorship of the bourgeoisie by the saber.[1]

First of all, we have here the dictatorship of a *class*, a dictatorship moreover

175

nominally instituted under a democratic government. This usage is not a great leap from previous references to the dictatorship of a democratic collectivity, but it is suggestive—it *was* suggestive. Secondly, we have the first differentiation of a *dictatorship over* a class from a *dictatorship of* a class. This is a distinction not always carefully represented by the little word *of,* which has to be watched like a malefactor.

Alongside Cavaignac's "commissioned dictatorship" (Rossiter's term) there was the parliamentary republic and its sovereign National Assembly, based on universal suffrage at least in form. In reality, Marx wrote, the bourgeoisie held power "only by the suspension of all formulas, by force *sans phrase,* by the state of siege."[2]

"The bourgeois dictatorship," Marx later wrote in his *Eighteenth Brumaire,* was "set aside on December 10 by the election of Bonaparte as president." In this work, the former regime was called both "the dictatorship of Cavaignac" and the "dictatorship of the pure bourgeois-republicans."[3]

We see that Marx did *not* use the term 'dictatorship' to differentiate between the Cavaignac operation and the regime that had created it. He used it for the class reality behind both, regardless of the state form.

(2) *The dictatorship of the party of Order.* The election of Bonaparte as president of the republic led to "the legislative dictatorship of the united royalists," that is, of the so-called "party of Order," exercised through a joint majority of the two royalist factions in the Assembly. In the next paragraph this was also called "its parliamentary despotism."[4]

In his *Eighteenth Brumaire* Marx called it "the parliamentary dictatorship of the party of Order" and the "parliamentary dictatorship of the bourgeoisie."[5] In the *Class Struggles in France* this regime was also called a "bourgeois dictatorship." Marx commented on its eventual scrapping of universal suffrage:

> By repudiating universal suffrage with which it had hitherto draped itself and from which it sucked its omnipotence, the bourgeoisie openly confesses,"*Our dictatorship has hitherto existed by the will of the people; it must now be consolidated against the will of the people.*"[6]

It is hard to see how this passage has so thoroughly escaped comment by marxological expositors. It clearly referred to a class dictatorship based on universal suffrage reflecting "the will of the people," even if one adds the necessary qualifications that Marx would have added to *how* it reflected the will of the people. And Marx wrote this without any evident consciousness of innovation.

(3) *Bonaparte's imperial regime.* Marx wrote the *Class Struggles* before Louis Bonaparte's coup d'etat. His *Eighteenth Brumaire,* dealing with this event, did not usually apply the label 'dictatorship' to the regime of the Second Empire; there were several terms currently common. But he did use 'dictatorship' in one summary passage in his *Eighteenth Brumaire,* in which he referred to "the

downfall of its [the bourgeoisie's] own rule, the dictatorship of Bonaparte."[7] For other cases in which Marx or Engels called Bonaparte's regime a 'dictatorship', see Chapter 6.[8]

Thus the word 'dictatorship' was applied, sporadically, to each of the three periods that France went through from the June days of 1848 to 1852.

(4) *Dictatorship of tin social democracy.* In the *Class Struggles in France* Marx also referred to a regime that did not come to life: a possible government of the petty-bourgeois left, the forces that in February 1849 united "the social and the democradc party, the party of the workers and that of the petty-bourgeoisie ... to form the *Social-Democratic party*, i.e., the *Red* party." The redness of this contemporaneous terminology is misleading for modern readers: the "reds" were then the timid democrats of the Mountain plus the pink "socialist doctrinaires," Louis Blanc, Ledru-Rollin, and their friends—a tendency that "represented a mass hovering between the bourgeoisie and the proletariat, a mass whose material interests demanded democratic institutions"—a tendency combining "the half conservative, half revolutionary and wholly Utopian reformers of this order."[9] Before the revolution Marx or Engels would have usually called this tendency the Democracy. It was discredited now, but had a "redder" label, the Social Democracy.

In a passage discussing the plight of the peasantry, Marx described how things looked to that class:

> Only the fall of capital can raise the peasant; only an anticapitalist, a proletarian government can break his economic misery, his social degradation. The *constitutional republic* is the dictatorship of his united explorers; the *social-democratic*, the *Red* Republic, is the dictatorship of his allies.[10]

The government of the Social Democracy would, then, also be a 'dictatorship'. Indeed, remember, Louis Blanc had been even more specific about the dictatorship he wanted. For this social-democrat, the notion of a 'dictatorship' had been associated with the postponement of the election, with the rule of a government *not* elected by the people. There was no such connection made in Marx's *Class Struggles in France* with regard to any of the dictatorships discussed.

(5) Finally, this Social-Democratic dictatorship was clearly distinguished in Marx's work from what he was going to call the 'dictatorship of the proletariat' in the same work. We will quote this passage more fully below, as locus 1 b; suffice to note now that in it Marx said that the proletariat,

> not yet enabled through the development of the remaining classes to seize the revolutionary dictatorship, had to throw itself into the arms of the doctrinaires of its emancipation, the founders of socialist sects...[11]

In other words, the proletariat itself could not rule, because it had not yet gained the support of the "remaining classes" (meaning the other working classes in this case), and so it supported the Social Democracy.

Here, then, were the five 'dictatorships' that appeared in Marx's survey of the revolution of 1848-1849, *of which the 'dictatorship of the proletariat' was only one.* The word 'dictatorship', from a historical term about a Roman institution, had now become a political term flung around the popular newspapers.

2. LOCUS 1: THREE PASSAGES

Heavy emphasis on *class* dictatorship is characteristic of the first locus.

The first article of Marx's series was written in January, and was published in the first number of the journal, which was dated "January 1850" but came out in early March. The French proletariat, said Marx, went into the June 1848 uprising with the illusion that they could gain immediate demands within the bourgeois system, but—

[Locus 1a]
... only its defeat convinced it of the truth that the slightest improvement in its position remains a *Utopia within* the bourgeois republic, a Utopia that becomes a crime as soon as it wants to become a reality. In place of its demands, exuberant in form, but petty and even bourgeois still in content, the concession of which it wanted to wring from the February republic, there appeared the bold slogan of revolutionary struggle: *Overthrow of the bourgeoisie! Dictatorship of the working class!*[12]

There is an obvious problem posed here. Marx wrote that "the bold slogan" appeared, "Overthrow of the bourgeoisie!" No doubt it appeared. But this slogan was immediately followed (in Marx's article) with the slogan of the "dictatorship of the working class." Was Marx saying that this slogan also "appeared" among the revolutionary workers?

There is no record whatsoever that it did appear. Marx himself had not been in France at the time and could not be writing from personal knowledge. Perhaps Louis Blanc's remarks about dictatorship filtered down. After all, we have already seen that Lorenz von Stein reported, at about the same time, that "Social dictatorship became the slogan of the proletariat," and it is likely he was thinking of Louis Blanc.[13]

But there is a much likelier possibility. It is reasonable to believe that Marx was not literally claiming that this hitherto unknown slogan "appeared," but rather that he was explaining, in apposition, the meaning of this "bold slogan" (which is in the singular, not plural)—in the first place, its meaning to him, Marx. In other words, he was really proposing the slogan himself,

11. Marx's Class Struggle in France   179

putting words to the inchoate working-class aspiration expressed in the revolution. In my opinion, this is how the passage should be read.

In April, George Julian Harney's magazine *Democratic Review* began a series of articles, "Two Years *of a* Revolution," which presented Marx's *Class Struggles in France* in summaries, paraphrases and quotations. The third installment, in June, reached locus   (no other installments were published). For the first time, English-speaking readers read of "the daring, revolutionary battle-cry: *Down with the bourgeoisie! Dictatorship of the Working Class!*"[14] (It is unlikely that these article-paraphrases were written by Engels, to whom they have been erroneously attributed.*)

Incidentally, both in Marx's magazine (the original) and in Harney's (the paraphrase), the paragraph comprising locus 1a was followed by a paragraph that freely used "bourgeois terrorism and "bourgeois dictatorship" interchangeably with bourgeois "rule" as a description of the 'bourgeois republic" established by the revolution. (For the meaning of 'terrorism', see Special NoteC).

The second article of the series, which Marx finished writing on March 4, was published in the second number of the magazine (dated "February 1850") about March 20. We have already mentioned its relevant passage, which did not actually use the term 'dictatorship of the proletariat'. It spoke of the proletariat's seizing the "revolutionary dictatorship."

[Locus 1b]
... the Montagne, the parliamentary champion of the democratic petty-bourgeoisie, was forced to unite with the socialist doctrinaires of the proletariat—the proletariat, forced by the terrible material defeat of June to raise itself up again through intellectual victories and not yet enabled through the development of the remaining classes to seize the

---

* For the first time, Volume 10 of MECW ascribed to Engels three series of contributions to Harney's *Democratic Review:* "*Two* Years of a Revolution"(an unfinished condensation of Marx's *Class Struggles in France),* a series of "Letters from Germany," and a like series of Letters tan France." This attribution, without adducing any evidence, was originally suggested by A.R. Schoyen—with a qualification: "probably the work of Engels."[15] All this material is now included in MECW under Engels' name as if positively identified, on the basis of no acceptable argument. An editorial note on "Two Years of a Revolution"[16] cites reasons to believe that the author must have been close to Marx's circle (as would be obvious anyway) but adduces not a single reason why the author had to be Engels rather than, say, J.G. Eccarius or someone else. (The situation is similar with regard to the "Letters" but they are not our present concern.) On the other hand, we have Marx's clear statement, in a letter to Joseph Weydemeyer (not mentioned by the MECW note), that it was Harney himself who translated (i.e., paraphrased in English) the *Class Struggles in France* in his *Democratic Review.*[17] There are other indications that the person who did this chore could not have been Engels.

revolutionary dictatorship, had to throw itself into the arms of the doctrinaires of its emancipation, the founders of socialist sects...[18]

In explaining that the proletariat could not establish its own "revolutionary dictatorship" as long as it lacked the support of the other working classes, Marx was excluding the idea of establishing it through a band of Blanquist-style conspirators; he was excluding the dictatorship even by the proletariat as long as it did not have the support of the majority of the people.

This thought had already been expressed in the first article of the series, as follows:

> The French workers could not take a step forward, could not touch a hair of the bourgeois order, until the course of the revolution had aroused the mass of the nation, peasants and petty-bourgeois, standing between the proletariat and the bourgeoisie, against this order, against the rule of capital, and had forced them to attach themselves to the proletarians as their protagonists. The workers could buy this victory only through the tremendous defeat in June.[19]

The possibility of the dictatorship of the proletariat was here firmly linked to majority support, whether or not this was registered in an election.

The third use of the term in this work is the most interesting in many respects. It appeared in the third article, which was written March 5-15, and was published in issue No. 3 of the magazine, dated "March 1850" but issued in mid-April.

This passage discussed, as had the *Communist Manifesto,* the trends of "bourgeois socialism" and "petty-bourgeois socialism" in the country. The latter, the socialism of Louis Blanc, was dissected at greatest length as "doctrinaire socialism." As against these currents, wrote Marx,

[Locus 1c]

the *proletariat* increasingly organizes itself around *revolutionary socialism,* around *communism,* for which the bourgeoisie itself has invented the name of *Blanqui.* This socialism is the *declaration of the permanence of the revolution,* the *class dictatorship* of the proletariat as the necessary transit point to the *abolition of class distinctions generally,* to the abolition of all the relations of production on which they rest, to the abolition of all the social relations that correspond to these relations of production, to the revolutionizing of all the ideas that result from these social relations.

The scope of this exposition does not permit of developing the subject further.[20]

It is rarely observed that, with all the typographical emphasis that goes on in this passage, it is *not* the 'dictatorship of the proletariat' that is underlined as a term: it is *'class dictatorship'*.

Here at last we have a connection between Blanqui and the term 'dictatorship of the proletariat'—and the 'permanent revolution' to boot—but it has not usually been used in the long campaign to ascribe 'dictatorship of the proletariat' to Blanqui. With good reason: for, of course, Marx was *not* saying that it was Blanqui's slogan. The bourgeoisie itself had attached Blanqui's name to revolutionary ideas—had "invented" Blanqui's name for them.*

We know this is true, for, as mentioned, "Blanquism" was "invented" as a generic term for a whole current of the socialist and communist movement. Marx had no desire to repudiate Blanqui in this passage, but he was saying quite clearly that Blanqui's name had been fastened onto revolutionary socialism by its enemies. Just about a half century later, this ploy became Eduard Bernstein's main device for discrediting Marx's revolutionary views.

This interpretation is powerfully corroborated when we know that Marx's words applied specifically to an important episode in 1848, when the figure of Blanqui was brandished by the bourgeoisie as a bogeyman. The following account is based on Louis Blanc's narrative published ten years later.

3. BLANQUI AS BOGEY

On March 17, 1848, an immense and majestic workers' demonstration threw a major fright into the class-conscious bourgeois majority of the Provisional Government, led by Lamartine, Marrast and Marie. Lamartine (like the Girondins before him) started trying to mobilize armed forces from outside Paris to overawe the workers of the capital. Then another workers' demonstration was announced for April 16, to prod the government on reform measures. The right wing resolved to frustrate its intended effect. This (Blanc believed) was the starting point of the active bourgeois counterrevolution, recovering its balance after the February upheaval.

> The surest way to achieve this [wrote Blanc] was to make the bourgeoisie believe that the intended procession of the operatives [workers] was connected with a communist conspiracy, and more especially with M. Blanqui, to whom the kind of mystery with which it was his study to envelop himself imparted the proportions of an enormous scarecrow.

Marrast busily circulated the story that the demonstration intended to overthrow the government in favor of communism, led by Cabet and Blanqui. Louis Blanc then triumphantly proved that Cabet's position was just the opposite:

---

* For garbled versions of locus 1c and mistranslations which have served to obscure the plain meaning of the passage, see Special Note D, Section 5.

So much for the Communist conspiracy. As to the part so cleverly assigned to M. Blanqui, the better to frighten the bourgeoisie, it is necessary to know that there never was anything in common between the delegates of the Luxembourg [Blanc's political center] and M. Blanqui.

It was at this time, also, that an attempt was made to smear and discredit Blanqui through the famous "Taschereau letter."

On the eve of the April 16 demonstration, Ledru-Rollin, as minister of the interior, was persuaded to issue a call for the mobilization of the National Guard against the alleged communist plot. This was accomplished "by a number of persons ... by dint of talking to him about the supposed projects of M. Blanqui, making use of that person's name as a sort of bugbear, and also by frightening him at the increased ascendancy of the Luxembourg..." And so on April 16 the peaceful, if vast, workers' demonstration was surrounded by armed men harassing and intimidating. The rumor was circulated that a Committee of Public Safety was being prepared "and Blanqui had been named ..." Besides the armed National Guard, there was a paid corps of anonymous men who circulated through the crowd crying "Death to the communists!"[21]

Louis Blanc's account, which we have been following, agrees in essentials with Marx's short reference, in the *Class Struggles in France,* to the April 16 demonstration. It was an engineered "misunderstanding," says Marx, engineered by the Provisional Government and the bourgeoisie.

> Suddenly throughout Paris, from one end to the other, a rumor spread as quick as lightning, to the effect that the workers had met armed in the Field of Mars, under the leadership of Louis Blanc, Blanqui, Cabet and Raspail, in order to march thence on the Hotel de Ville, overthrow the Provisional Government and proclaim a communist government.

Armed men occupied all points—

> ... the cry "Down with the Communists! Down with Louis Blanc, with Blanqui, with Raspail, with Cabet!" thunders throughout Paris.

This "sham battle" "furnished the excuse *for recalling the army to Paris.*" Louis Blanc's history put *more* emphasis on Blanqui than Marx did, not less.

In the sequence of events, the social-democratic wing ot the Provisional Government *was* undermined, and the drive to counterrevolution accelerated. The "invention" of the Blanqui bogey was a great success. When Marx referred to it with a few words, it was still freshly bitter recent history.

In all of this, Blanqui himself played the part of an uncomprehending dupe. When the chief plotter, Lamartine, invited him to come to the government

11. *Marx's* Class Struggle in France   183

offices for a talk, very prominently, he came, and talked, and smiled, and shook hands, and clearly did not know what was going on. Blanqui himself was an irrelevancy; it was his bogey that the plotters needed. It was still the bogey that was operative when Bernstein made a "Blanquist" out of Marx.

12 | THE SUCR EPISODE

About the same time that the third issue of the *NRZ Revue* appeared, containing locus 1c, the term 'dictatorship of the proletariat' (or a near equivalent) was written into another document, the second to bear this distinction. Mid-April is the date usually assigned to it.

The document in question was a sheet of paper, headed "Société Universelle des Communistes Révolutionnaires," offering the *règlement* (statutes or bylaws) of this projected society, in six articles. Since, like locus 1c, this discovery involved the Bianquists, at least the London Blanquist émigré group, it quickly became the chief exhibit of the mythologists of the "Marx-Blanquist" school, and indeed we have already had occasion to mention it in this role.

Let us examine all the facts about the society whose name thus came to light. This is not hard to do since the above-mentioned *règlement* is the only document that mentions SUGR by name, and there are only a couple of others that refer to it in any way. Given such a paucity of facts, the inevitable result has been a plethora of free-form fantasizing.

1. LOCUS 2: THE SUCR STATUTES AND THE SIGNERS

The document was found in seven copies, all on the same thin, smooth paper. They are evidently fair copies written down in the same hand, which is thought to be Willich's. Slight differences among the seven copies do not go beyond normal slips. Signatures were all written by the signers themselves.[1]

The heading is the society's name alone; the term "Statutes" *(Règlement)* which may be found as the title is actually derived from the text itself. The text is in French; no English version was found. Here it is.

[Locus 2]
INTERNATIONAL SOCIETY OF REVOLUTIONARY COMMUNISTS

Art. 1.— The aim of the association is the downfall of all the privileged classes, to subject these classes to the dictatorship of the proletarians, maintaining the revolution in permanence until the realization of communism, which is [or has] to be the last form for constituting the human family.

Art. 2.— To contribute to the realization of this aim, the association will form ties of solidarity among all sections of the revolutionary communist party, bringing about the disappearance of nationality divisions in accordance with the principle of republican fraternity.

Art. 3. —The founding committee of the association is constituted as the central committee; wherever there is a need for the accomplishment of the work, it will establish committees which will correspond with the central committee.

Art. 4. —The number of members of the association is unlimited, but no member can be admitted unless he has gotten a unanimous vote. In no case can the election take place by secret ballot.

Art. 5. —All the members of the association are bound by oath to keep the first article of the present statutes absolutely in the same terms. A modification that can have the consequence of weakening the intentions expressed in Article 1 releases the members of the association from their agreement.

Art. 6. —All the decisions of the society are taken by a two-thirds majority of those voting.

    Adam   J. Vidil   Ch. Marx
    Auguste Willich   F. Engels   G.Julian Harney[2]

The following details may be noted about this text.

(1) *Name of the society.* The name can be, and has been, englished as "World Society..." or "Universal Society...," but these renderings may give, sometimes intentionally, an impression of grandiloquence which was no necessary part of the original. *Universel* was in common use in French to mean 'worldwide' with no undue flourish. For example, the title *of* Ledru-Rollin's émigré monthly was *Le Proscrit; Journal de la République Universelle,* but there was no implication that the republic would reach beyond the solar system.*

(2) *Locus 2.* The first article looked to "la dictature des prolétaires"—"the dictatorship of the proletarians," not the 'dictatorship of the proletariat'. In hindsight (which is a great educational force) there is a distinct difference

---

* Gustav Mayer's prestigious biography of Engels gave the society's name in German as "Weltbund der Revolutionären Sozialisten," rendered in the English edition as "World League of Revolutionary *Socialists.*"[3] This is one of the many errors that have dogged this question.

introduced by this formulation, for it de-emphasizes precisely that aspect so heavily stressed in *The Class Struggles in France*, viz., the *class* dictatorship. When we discuss who may have written this draft, I will argue that this formulation points away from Marx himself.

Since attention is inevitably focused on the document's use of the term in question, it is unfortunate that one of the early reprints of the document embodied an erroneous text, precisely at this point; this source has been widely quoted from, and the mistake is still going strong to this day. The French Communist Party's theoretical organ *Cahiers du Bolchévisme* published the text in 1933 with two errors.[4] In Article 1, it erroneously replaced "dictature des prolétaires" with the normal form, "dictature du prolétairiat" (dictatorship of the proletariat); and among the signatures, "J. Vidil" became "G. Vidal."

(3) *Translation.* The *MECW* English translation is seriously defective in blurring the fact that Article 1 contains the phrase "the revolution in permanence." Its version reads: "keeping the revolution in continual progress ... " (which is not even a good paraphrase).

(4) *Signatures.* For what it is worth, we point out, in passing, that the signatures, like the text, are given in French form, in the case of both "Ch. [for Charles] Marx" and "Auguste Willich." The New Mega text prints all the signatures in a single line; we have, above, followed the same order but in two lines.

Who were the signatories? Of the six signers, the three Germans—Marx, Engels, Willich—were recognized leaders of the Communist League. Schapper's name was missing; while it will be justly argued that the inclusion of four Germans would be unbalancing, why Willich rather than Schapper? We will come back to this question.

The lone Englishman, Harney, is usually called, in this connection, the representative of the left-wing Chartists. This he was, indeed; but was he *representing* the left wing of the Chartist movement as such, and if so in what capacity? There was no organized left wing for him to represent. But Harney was also the initiator and leader of the Fraternal Democrats, itself an international society in principle though its membership was largely British. It can be argued that the Fraternal Democrats functioned in practice as a Chartist left-wing organization. In any case, there is good reason to consider that unofficially Harney signed the SUCR statutes with his Fraternal Democrats hat on.[5]

The two Frenchmen were refugees. The organization in which they were active was the Société des Proscrits Démocrates-Socialistes; this refugee group organized the left wing of the current French emigration in London while the right was comprised in a society led by Ledru-Rollin and Louis Blanc. The SPDS was dominated by the Blanquists in its ranks.

12. The SUCR Episode 187

Adam and Vidil were Blanquists in the proper narrow sense, that is, they were followers of Blanqui himself. They were not prominent figures either in their own right or as Blanquist leaders (but then, neither was any other person in the émigré group). Adam is such a shadowy personage that his name is not known; "Adam" may have been his given name, his surname, or neither, a *nom de guerre*. He has been described as a worker-craftsman, either a leather worker (tanner or leather blocker) or a woodworker (camberer). He had been a member of revolutionary secret societies under the July monarchy of Louis Philippe. In February 1848 he was on the staff of the communistic journal *La Fraternité*; in June he ran in the election as a socialist candidate. There is no trace of him after 1856.

Jules Vidil (not to be confused with François Vidal, a more prominent person but no Blanquist) had originally been a captain of hussars in the French army. (Engels described him in a letter as an ex-captain of dragoons, perhaps meaning the same.[6]) Dommanget, studying Vidil's letters to Blanqui, judged that

> he retained the energy and inflexibility of the professional military man. Trusting above all in the use of force, he affected disdain for phrasemaking. His objective, on the morrow of a revolution, was to hurl the proletariat into a "second June 24" [outbreak of the 1848 June insurrection] and, in case the working class gave no proof of radicalism, to force it into [an insurrection] by bayonet thrusts. His temperament led him to see the social question as above all a question of character and to consider the men of the Mountain [social-democracy] as "good-for-nothings," to use his favorite expression.[7]

Adam and Vidil were active in the Blanquist fraction within SPDS, though we do not know if they held any leading post. (But then we don't know if there was any post to be held.) Samuel Bernstein has referred to these men, in connection with SUCR, as "two agents of Blanqui,"[8] but this *is* a deplorable example *of* putting the "fix" on history. Calling them "agents" of Blanqui gives the impression of a close link between Blanqui and SUCR, and therefore, in another step, between Blanqui and Marx; but Blanqui had nothing to do with SUCR and (as we will see) may not even have known of it.

On the other hand, to describe Adam and Vidil as "leading Blanquists" in the London emigration is doubtless justified; but what it meant to lead Blanquists must be examined by looking more closely at the Blanquist scene.

2. THE BLANQUIST REFUGEES AND THE "ALLIANCE"

In 1850 London was a center for French and German émigrés who had fled after the defeat of the revolution. Switzerland was another gathering place for émigrés who were still oriented toward promoting revolution in the homeland; America received German emigrants who had largely given up this personal perspective—a fact to be kept in mind in considering what happened to the American movement. In London the different revolutionary currents still existed and still fought, mostly among themselves; emigration produces new reasons for old hostilities, and lines of friendship and cooperation undergo shifts and strains.

Blanqui was in prison—again, or as usual—and tried to keep in touch with affairs by correspondence. There was no Blanquist organization functioning in France. The London Blanquists were not a branch-in-exile of a movement; they *were* the movement, or what there was of it. It wasn't much: a small number of disparate individuals. Arthur Rosenberg has accurately explained one aspect:

> The socialistic French workers no longer wanted to have anything to do with Ledru-Rollin and his friends. On the other hand the imprisoned Blanqui exercised a great moral authority over the French workers. They had subsequently recognized that in 1848 he had been the only one who had opposed the prevailing illusions and who had warned the workers. At that time there was indeed no actually flourishing Blanquist organization either in France or in England, but the great name of Blanqui had its effect and was a symbol for the fighting French proletariat. Consequently the French socialist exiles who wanted to differentiate themselves from the bourgeois democrats usually called themselves Blanquist.[9]

Rosenberg's reference to "no actually flourishing Blanquist organization" needs tightening. *There was no Blanquist organization as such in London.* The organization we mentioned above, the SPDS, was *not* established as a Blanquist group but as a refugee organization; it became "Blanquist" only insofar as it was controlled by the Blanquists within it, who were the activists.

This distinction—between a Blanquist party organization and a Blanquist-controlled organization of more general character—is one that unfortunately tends to dim out in the eyes of historians who have little appreciation for the internal relations of the socialist movement. But it is very important. (Since the International was at first dominated by the Proudhonists in France, was the International a "Proudhonist organization"?) This consideration may be of importance especially to other tendencies dealing with this sort of organi-

12. The SUCR Episode   189

zation, in particular when the organization as established had an objective reason for existence apart from political struggles. The simplest case is a trade union, which may be dominated by a given tendency but has to be dealt with as an "economic" organization. This consideration applied to refugee organizations, even though they notoriously tended to split up along political lines, as misguided zealots sought to politicalize them.

The notion that SUCR was some sort of united front of organizations comes up against the problem that there was *no* Blanquist political organization on the scene, any more than there was a "left Chartist" organization to be "represented" by Harney.

There is another problem with the common marxological picture of SUCR as "Marx's alliance with the Blanquists." *This Blanquist handful was itself split two or three ways during 1850.*

Our information on this vital aspect comes from Norman Plotkin's "Les Alliances des Blanquistes dans la Proscrition," which is still the chief attempt to work out some facts from a study of the Blanqui papers, in particular, letters written to the Old Man from his London friends. "From the beginning of 1850," Plotkin writes, Blanqui's friend Flotte (whom we have already met[16]) "understood that the various elements united by their common exile could not constitute a solid party; in this, it is evident, Flotte shared Blanqui's opinions. . . Writing in a letter to Blanqui in February 1850 on the refugee circles, he foresaw the rupture..."

Flotte himself (acccording to Plotkin) wanted to abandon the central characteristic of Blanquism, its conspiratorial organization: "No secret societies now, no conciliabules. We are going to govern. It is necessary to drop the habits of struggle and take on those of calm and forcefulness." Flotte, evidently, wanted to drop more than conspiratorial forms; and this trend was doubtless an element of tension.

In the same letter Flotte reported on the degree to which the Blanquists dominated the leading committee of the refugee society, the SPDS. But by July the split had taken place. Plotkin, trying to follow events through the Blanqui correspondence, reports the highlights, none too clearly perforce. Some of the Blanquists (Cazavant and Dupont are mentioned) went over to a new refugee society founded together with Louis Blanc and Caussidière, that is, moved to the right. "Insofar as it was only a matter of aid[-to-refugee] questions, everybody had been in agreement," wrote Barthélemy to Blanqui on July 4. "But the discussions had been extended to principles; a split took place; and we were immediately divided into two camps..." The dissidents created a refugee organization of their own. "At the same time," Barthélemy added, "I took part with Adam in another society composed of workers only, which had been formed in London after the February Revolution."

Barthélemy's idea was to use this society's members to enter into the SPDS and take it over; this in turn raised a fight inside Barthélemy's own group.

One of the difficulties here is that Dommanget portrays this Barthélemy as a noisome scoundrel; "diabolical character," "brutal ferocious tyrant," slanderer, center of constant disturbance—these are some of his characterizations.[11] So it is with some hesitancy we report that, according to Barthélemy (whose letters to Blanqui were naturally self-serving), "The ideas of the [Paris Blanquist] central society are little regarded here," being held by only six or seven (Vidil included).

Blanqui sought confirmation from other London émigrés. Vidil, writing July 19, confirmed the split and the hostility of the two camps, but was optimistic. The SPDS, he said, is "essentially communist," and "its most energetic section" is Blanquist. However, he indicated there was a third party to the split: "a small party, placed between us and the Mountain . . . communist, but still bourgeois..." He gave four names as the membership of this "party," including Pardigon (whom we will meet).[12]

All of this splitting up, already foreshadowed in February, apparently took place in June and July. If Marx was "allied" with "the Blanquists" at this time, what "Blanquists" are meant, and what does an "alliance" mean under the circumstances?

I regret burdening readers with the sorry goings-on of tenth-rate conspirators in exile; but I must remind that, according to the "Marx-Blanquist" myth, these are the people—these muddleheaded, pygmy-size factionalism—who were supposed to have won Marx over to *their* murky views ... If this myth made any sense we would have to ask: who among these people is supposed to have influenced Marx? Both in Marx's and their correspondence, there is no indication of anything but the most distant relations. With one exception: a poet, Louis Ménard, whose poem on the June days was in fact printed in Marx's magazine,[13] did frequent Marx's circle; but—alas for the myth—Ménard was inactive in the Blanquist milieu.[14] I have no doubt that Marx was working on Ménard to de-Blanquify *him,* and that the poet had no ambition to de-Marxify Marx. (Even myths should be distinguished from fantasies.)

In Part II and Special Note B, comments have been made on the marxological habit of treating SUCR as simply a "Marx-Blanquist alliance." It was particularly pointed out that, even in terms of the signers, there was another political current represented, Harney's left Chartists. Now let us go over this question more fully.

One of the defects of the "Blanquist alliance" myth is that it makes impossible an understanding of Marx's organizational concerns and motives. In order to see this episode in the context of Marx's course before and after

SUCR, we have to return to the standpoint already emphasized in Chapter 9.[15] Every organizational structure with which Marx experimented, from his Brussels days on, was aimed at establishing *an international framework for the coexistence of different political tendencies.*

What changed in the course of time was the scope of the framework. The first experiment, the Communist Corresponding Committee, established "communist" views as the scope, but, as we have explained,[16] this appellation was a very wide and flexible one. The Communist League, developing out of roots in German emigre sectism, was turned toward international membership and all-inclusiveness *within* the "communist" area. During the revolution, in Cologne, the "Communist" framework was operationally shelved, if not abandoned, for the more flexible boundaries of the *NRZ* "party." The "Communist" frame was resumed in London in 1849, and was operating again when the SUCR episode came up. When the Communist League came to an end in 1852, Marx was going to insist with great emphasis on cutting all organizational connections, waiting for the opportunity to build not a communist sect, even a broad one, but a class movement, an opportunity which he seized in 1864 to build the International.

To be sure, in 1850, where we are situated now, Marx still viewed the "communist" boundary as the necessary frame for the inclusive international movement to be founded. But even so, it will be useful *to* keep an eye on the type of organization that the International was going to be. First of all, it is the *international character of the* project that needs emphasis.

It cannot be overstressed that in 1864 the International was founded as a virtual three-nationality united front, *just like SUCR:* an English contingent (certain trade unions primarily), a French contingent, and a couple of Germans.* In 1864 the French contingent was Proudhonist to a dominating extent, just as in 1850 it was Blanquist. It goes without saying that to call the International a "Marx-Proudhonist alliance" would be a sad example of galloping sciolism; the case is just as sad when SUCR is called a "Marx-Blanquist alliance."

The three-nationality alliance around SUCR could only have been viewed by Marx as a starting point, just as in 1864. The Communist League tried to gain contact with other nationality groups or representatives. Two groups in particular were mentioned in the "Address to the Communist League" of June (the second address).

---

* In the leading committee set up by the founding meeting in St. Martin's Hall, the only other nationality represented was Italian. The committee included two Mazzinists; but they played no positive role and dropped out entirely in a few months, leaving nothing behind. The development of an Italian section owed nothing to them.

192   *Part IV: 'Dictatorship of the Proletariat' in Marx and Engels*

• *Swiss migration.* There was a group of German Imigrls in Switzerland, with its Central Committee in Zurich, called the Revolutionfire Zentralisadon (Revolutionary Centralization). Headed by a lawyer and parliamentarian named Tzschirner, with little or no working-class membership and indeterminate politics, it proposed amalgamation to the CL, which refused. The RZ also proposed a sort of united front in which the CL would preoccupy itself with the workers and the RZ with the rest of the universe; but this modest proposal was also turned down, after discussions with the RZ's representative in London, Techow. The group disintegrated by the end of 1850 as Switzerland expelled the refugees.[17]

• *Hungarians.* About May, Marx came into contact with Hungarian leftist emigres whom he might well have considered suitable for an international revolutionary organization. The June Address reported contacts with "the resolutely revolutionary parties among the French, English and Hungarians," said Hungarians described as "the most progressive party of the Hungarian refugees," important because it has "a number of excellent military leaders whose services would be available to the League in a revolution."[18] This optimistic report may have had in mind J&nos (or Johann) Bangya and Istvan (or Stefan) Tiirr, whom Marx mentioned in his *Herr Vogt.* [19] (Bangya later turned out to be a police spy).

• *Belgians.* The Address's reference to the Brussels situation indicated that the Belgian government had successfully purged the country of Imigre' revolutionaries for the nonce at least. It systematically harassed French and German refugees of '48-49 who wanted to settle in Brussels, so as to speed them on their way to London.[20]

• *Poles.* It is rather surprising that the June Address said nothing about contact with Polish emigre groups, which must have existed on the London scene.

It was not an encouraging situation, to be sure, but that is not the point. The point is that these were the conditions which had to be reckoned with in the lull of revolution; and *one* of the conditions was the fact that the indicated French contingent was Blanquist-dominated.

And so you had to deal with Adam and Vidil and the like. SUCR was not planned (one must conclude) because Marx wanted a "Blanquist alliance." The Blanquist connection came along with the conditions, just as the Proudhonist complication did in 1864, and all you could do was accept the position—in order to change it by re-educating the Blanquists to the extent possible.

3. WHY THE SUCR PROJECT COLLAPSED

One of Marx's and Engels' main activities in the postrevolutionary period was refugee-aid work; and the German refugee-aid societies had to cooperate with the French, Hungarian, and others. This was an immediate mode of international collaboration in the London emigration. There were good relations with the French SPDS at the beginning of the year.

For example, in January, when the Marx group was planning to send Conrad Schramm on a fund-raising trip to America, both the Chartists and the French refugee group were involved in the project too; Schramm was charged with missions to be performed on their behalf as well as on behalf of the CL.[21]

On February 25, the SPDS sponsored an international banquet to celebrate the anniversary of the February Revolution. "Everybody" was there; attendance at the Bayswater Tavern was variously estimated at 200-400; the guests included several European nationalities, particularly Poles, Hungarians, and Spaniards, besides the French, English, and Germans. Marx, Engels, and Ferdinand ("Red") Wolff attended as representatives of the London GWEA and the Communist League. (They were the only ex-editors of the Cologne *NRZ* in London at that time.) Toasts were offered by Engels and Wolff (Marx rarely gave a public talk). Engels' toast was to "The insurrection of June 1848!" after a short talk that elicited "immense applause" (according to a newspaper report). Wolff's was to "The Revolution *sans phrase!*"[22]

The French SPDS representatives who ran the banquet were Adam, Barthélemy, Pardigon, and Vidil,[23] whom we have already met as Blanquist activists in the group. (One wonders if they were the only activists.)

On April 5, the Fraternal Democrats sponsored a "social supper" to celebrate Robespierre's birthday (which actually fell on the next day). Harney presided over the assembly of nearly seventy, and toasted the memory of Robespierre, seconded by Bronterre O'Brien (who defended Marat and Saint-Just in particular) and G. W. M. Reynolds (who explained the Reign of Terror). In general, the Chartist left-wingers tended to be rabidly pro-Jacobin, probably in reaction to the tendency of English public opinion to view the Jacobins as bogeymen.

The German Communists of Marx's circle had two speakers in the series of toasts, Engels and Conrad Schramm. Marx attended, nonspeaking as usual. Though two Frenchmen sang songs and other French émigrés attended, the newspaper accounts reported no French speakers among the lot: a singular fact. Engels' toast was to "The proletarians of England!" and his talk "pointed out that a party of Levelers had already existed at the time of the English Revolution."[24]*

Schramm's speech is of first importance for our story. Conrad (or Konrad) Schramm was then personally quite close to Marx and the Marx family. He was the business manager of the *NRZ Revue,* an invaluable aide. He contributed articles to many German papers, and wrote articles for Harney's left Chartist publications; later he became active on the island of Jersey as a correspondent for American papers.[25] When the year 1850 opened, Schramm had taken part, with Marx, Engels, and Willich, in a New Years Eve affair put on by the Fraternal Democrats.[26] Now, at the Fraternal Democrats affair on April 5, he chose to talk about—the dictatorship of the proletariat.

What we know about Schramm's talk comes from a German newspaper report written by a CL member:

> C. Schramm spoke on the necessity of the dictatorship of the workers over all other classes of society until the complete destruction and elimination of the relations conditioning the same. He ended with a cheer for Aug. Blanqui, the most progressive representative of the French proletariat.[27]

According to a briefer report in Harney's magazine, Schramm eulogized Marat, and his concluding toast was to "Citizen Blanqui and the extinction of classes!"[28]

It was doubtless not accidental that Schramm covered both Blanqui and the "dictatorship of the workers" (which term, allowing for translation, was the SUCR formulation "dictature des prolétaires"). If the customary dating of the SUCR agreement, mid-April, is accurate, then it must have been under discussion at the time this "social supper" was held. Indeed, I do not know of any hard reason why the SUCR agreement should not be dated in the first week of April.

Nothing is known about the actual signing of the SUCR agreement, other than what can be derived from the document itself. That it was signed some time in April is indicated by a letter written in December by one of Marx's and Engels' associates, Pieper, which we will have occasion to quote later.[29]

Since we know so little about the affair, we can hardly expect to have firm answers to the question: why was SUCR abrogated so quickly? Explanations of how the SUCR project ended are as speculative as theories about how it began. However, let us set down some facts that have given rise to speculation.

---

* Engels' toast was the only one (judging from the newspaper reports) that turned away from French Revolutionary leaders to other revolutionary traditions; and in celebrating the English Revolution it pointed not to Cromwell but to the little-known Levelers. In this connection the reader is referred to Marx's and Engels' views on Robespierrism, partially dealt with in Special Note C, Section I.

12. The SUCR Episode 195

A point of tension between the CL and the SPDS Blanquists arose before a month was up. People who are used to thinking of Blanquists simply as ultraleftasts or "wild men" may be surprised to find that the cause of this tension, from Marx's standpoint, was their rightwinging opportunism.[30] On May 6, Marx and Engels wrote a letter to Pardigon, clearly addressing him as a representative of the SPDS. Following is the letter, from the draft written in Engels' hand:

> My dear Pardigon,
> We have learned this very moment that your society has the intention of submitting your program to the German society on Greek Street and asking it if it does or does not give it its support.
> We do not believe this, after our conversation of Saturday; but if you or your society denounced an individual, or any batch of individuals whatever, to us as being nothing but a bad lot, we would very simply show them the door, without asking if they were willing to support our program.
> We have denounced the leaders of this society to you as charlatans and swindlers. Swindlers and charlatans sign anything. They might well have signed our manifesto if we had wanted to accept their reiterated proposals of union and concord.
> You understand that if a similar proposal were adopted by your society, our honor would impel us to immediately break off any connection with the members of Rathb[one] Place.
>
> Greetings and faternity,
> F. Engels
> Ch. Marx[31]

The first thing to be said about this letter is that there is no direct reference to SUCR in it. The reference to *"your* program" cannot mean the SUCR statutes; it must mean the program of SPDS itself, just as the reference to "our manifesto" must mean the CL's. (It doubtless means the *Communist Manifesto,* though no one "signed" that document; the act of "signing" must be meant metaphorically.)

What then were Marx and Engels objecting to? They were warning that the relations between the CL and SPDS would be harmed, hence perhaps broken, if SPDS cozied up politically to the CL's right-wing enemies in the German emigration.

The "German society on Greek Street" was the German Democratic Association formed in November 1849 by one Kallenberg. It was joined by some right-wing elements excluded from GWEA, such as Louis (or Ludwig) Bauer. Dr. Bauer, Friedrich Bobzin and Gustav Struve then formed their own refugee-aid committee, rivaling the one established by Marx's friends in GWEA, in order to channel aid to refugees of their own political coloration.

The preceding December Engels had told a friend what he thought of these people:

> Struve and Heinzen are intriguing with all and sundry against the Worker's Society [GWEA] and ourselves, but without success. They, together with some wailers of moderate persuasion who have been thrown out of our society, form a select club at which Heinzen airs his grievances about the noxious doctrines of the communists.[32]

The analogous grouping in the French emigration was the Société Démocratique Française run by Ledru-Rollin and Blanc; and although the reference to "Rathbone Place" has not been identified, my guess is that it was the address of this French society.

The warning to Pardigon, then, can be spelled out as follows: *You people of SPDS, who want to be our allies in a revolutionary struggle, should not seek to ally yourselves—over our heads, not to speak of behind our backs—with the enemies of revolution in the German emigration; just as we would not seek an alliance with the antirevolutionary right wing of the French emigration, as identified by you.*

The implied threat, we suppose, is this: *If this goes on, the SUCR project will become unviable.* One of the dark references in the letter is to the conversation *(entretien)* on Saturday, May 1; since nothing is known about it, one is free to speculate that it involved a discussion of SUCR's future, and apparently went satisfactorily.

We must mention here, looking ahead down the historical road, that the trend which the letter to Pardigon tried to nip was characteristic of the ambiguous politics of the so-called ultraleftists. After the end of SUCR and the split in the CL, the apparently ultraleft Willich-Schapper group that broke with Marx allied itself with people like Adam and Vidil to—make a bloc precisely with the Heinzen-type right democrats of the grandiloquently named "Central Committee of the European Democracy." We will return to this pattern, but we mention this now to confirm the fact that there was a deep-seated cause for political tension showing itself early.

Exactly how this tension developed after May 6 is quite unknown, and the details can be filled in only by guesswork (or fantasizing). We have to mention, of course, that the book review about the conspiratorial secret societies[33] appeared in the fourth number of the *NRZ Revue* on May 19 or 20, and no doubt failed to make Adam and Vidil happy; but there is no record of their reaction. There is a gap in the account until September.

The next relevant event was the split in the Communist League, beginning September 15, after which Willich and Schapper formed their own league and went into business for themselves. The subsequent close reladons between Willich-Schapper and Adam, Vidil & Co. indicate, with little room for doubt, that in this split the Blanquists (or their core) lined up with the enemies of the

Marx group. To be sure, we do not know how this tied in with the various splits among the Blanquists themselves; but no matter.

The CL split was itself conditioned by Marx's reorientation, in late summer, away from expecting an immediate outburst of the revolutionary volcano on the Continent. His estimation that the revolutionary situation was over for the period changed nothing in his political thinking, but it naturally demanded a change of current tactics, with emphasis on long-term propaganda and education. Just as this readjustment alienated the Willich-Schapper group, so too it no doubt displeased the Blanquist types who were lining up with Willich-Schapper. One trouble with this line of thought—which has even been suggested onesidedly as *the* cause of SUGR's breakdown—is that in early October, three weeks after the CL split—it was the Blanquists who pressed Marx to take steps to develop SUCR.

Here is the letter they sent to "Citizens Marx and Engels" on October 7:

> We have the honor to inform you that we must have a meeting in the course of this week in order to take up affairs of the association we have formed. We have already informed Citizen Willich. We await your letting us know the place and the day you choose, these two points being of no importance for us.
> We have the honor to greet you.
> Barthélemy
Adam
J. Vidil[34]

The following comments on this letter are in order.

(1) There can be no doubt that "the association we have formed" was SUCR, even though it was not named.

(2) When the three signers wrote that they had "already informed Citizen Willich," it might be more accurate to suppose they meant: "We have cooked this *démarche* up with Willich."

(3) It appears that Barthélemy had taken over at the Blanquist end. Although he was not a signatory to the agreement, he now signed first, as if in charge.

(4) The tone of the letter is obviously stiff, though "correct," like a note from a second arranging for a duel—"Name the time and place, Messieurs!" Perhaps the three regarded it as a mere formality, or (my own supposition) were prepared to make demands that would blow the agreement up.

Marx and Engels, however, were in no mood to fence with these people. On October 9, they sent back the following game-ending reply (in English):

> Messrs Adam, Barthélemy and Vidil
> Gentlemen,
> We have the honour of informing you that we have, long since,

considered the association you speak of as dissolved by fact. The only thing remaining to be done would be the destruction of the fundamental contract. Perhaps Mr Adam or Mr Vidil will have the kindness to call, on Sunday next October 13th at noon, on Mr Engels at Nr 6, Macclesfield street Soho, in order to witness the burning of the same.

We have the honor to be, Gentlemen,

Your most obedient servants,
Engels, Marx, Harney[35]

The copies of the "fundamental contract" were in fact not burned, but retained in Marx's archives. If the Blanquists had their own copies of the agreement, also unburnt, these have not shown up.

An interesting fact that does not appear in the above text of the letter indicates the state of hostilities. Not only did the Marx-Engels-Harney letter address the Blanquists as "Messrs" and "Gentlemen," but the manuscript (Engels' draft) shows that in both cases the appellation "Citizens" (equivalent of modern "Comrades") was crossed out and replaced.[36] The message was: *You people are no comrades of ours.*

Two words in the letter are especially important: "long since." Marx and Engels had, they say, considered SUCR as dissolved *defacto* long ago... How long ago? The answer is purely speculative, but the two words speak against the idea, which has been suggested, that the break was due to the September 15 split in the CL. That was not "long since." The break must have matured earlier, between May and September, without coming to a formal explosion. It is quite possible to agree that the September 15 split made the final breakup of SUCR inevitable. But a more accurate formulation may be this: during that summer, the development of Marx's political thinking and of the Blanquists' political opportunism, moving away from each other, made inevitable *both* the SUCR breakup and the CL split.

In summary, why did the SUCR project founder? Let us hazard a guess (properly so labeled). My best guess would go back to the letter to Pardigon as the main clue. From Marx's standpoint: the putative revolutionary allies on the French side were showing that they were not firm revolutionaries but uncertain opportunists, ready to ally themselves with the very political elements whom Marx had pointed to as the enemy—in the March "Address to the Communist League."

In order to appreciate this motive, one must be free of the illusion already mentioned, namely, that the views expressed in the March Address reflected *Willich's* politics. I have elsewhere shown that there is documentary evidence to contravene this idea.[37] Now we find that the SUCR episode and its ending can be understood only if we realize how far the Willich-Schapper politics veered from the line of the March Address; indeed, how essentially opportunistic

12. The SUCR Episode 199

was the apparently ultraleftist notion that a revolution had to be "made" to order no matter what. This was why bitter anticommunists like Heinzen and Kinkel remained conspiratorial putschists in the 1850s, at least in theory, though they were quite incapable of bringing it off—and why Willich-Schapper flanked by Adam and Vidil joined with these anticommunists rather than with Marx.

This interpenetration of ultraleftism and opportunism, though notorious and often crystal-clear inside the revolutionary movement, is one of the most difficult concepts for outside historians to grasp, despite its simplicity. But this, in so many words, was how Marx explained the CL split, at the very September 15 session where the matter was thrashed out. Marx explained that the Willich-Schapper line was not an ultraleft mistake but a reflection of "petty-bourgeois" politics (his usual designation for socialist reformism), a position that "could at best be described as social-democratic."[38] This, Marx's own interpretation of the situation, is the very opposite of the view embodied in the marxological myth. It is also the interpretation that best explains why SUCR had no chance of getting off the ground.

4. THE TROUBLE WITH NICOLAIEVSKY'S FABULATION

What sort of organization was SUCR supposed to be?

To repeat: there is no information on this except the SUCR statutes themselves. Yet numerous writers have stated very confidently exactly what the type of organization was. All of these statements are based, with or without credit, on Nicolaievsky's biography of Marx.

Nicolaievsky (as we have had occasion to point out more than once[39]) was not a man to be intimidated by lack of facts. With nothing but the statements in the SUCR statutes to guide him, he was able to state with magisterial certainty what no one else knew:

> It was necessary to create an association of secret societies for simultaneous action in the revolution which might break out any day. [So] ... an international militant alliance was formed in April.[40]

He expounds the "organizational structure":

> The rank and file of the secret societies did not themselves become members of this secret society, which was restricted to their leaders. Thus it was a secret society of higher degree. An essential feature of this organization was that it should not come into the open.[41]

Nicolaievsky then refers to the June "Address to the Communist League," expatiates on the Blanquist pattern of conspiratorialism, and asserts that Marx accepted all this and brought his associates "to join a Blanquist group"—a fantasy which is discussed in Special Note B.[42] Nicolaievsky concludes, on the "organizational structure":

> It should be observed, however, that the rules of the super-secret society assured the existence of the Communist League and—a highly important consideration in Marx's eyes—preserved it from the danger of being outvoted by the other organizations.[43]

This description of the organization is mostly sheer invention, at best speculation.

(1) SUCR, asserts Nicolaievsky, was "an association of secret societies." The first thing this implies is that the six founders signed as representatives of their organizations only: the Germans for the CL, Harney for the left-wing Chartists, Adam and Vidil for "the Blanquists" or, more knowledgeably, for the SPDS. This assumes that these individuals were able to, and did in fact, *commit their organizations.* If this were true, it is remarkable that the committed organizations were not even mentioned. The names of the signers were not even accompanied by an organizational identification.

If the commitment hypothesis were accepted, it would mean that the organizations themselves had previously discussed and approved the plan. There is not the slightest evidence that this was so, nor trace of any attempt to bring it up—in any one of the three political circles concerned.

(2) Nicolaievsky's most imaginative contribution is his unexamined assumption that SUCR was an *organization of organizations*—some sort of federation or coalition of organized groups as such. Even as speculation, this notion has no basis whatever in the SUCR statutes.

If we go back and read the six articles (page 185), we find that there is no provision for, or reference to, any sort of organizational affiliation to SUCR; the only membership envisaged in the statutes is individual membership. The reference (Article 2) to forming "ties of solidarity among all sections of the revolutionary communist party" is immediately interpreted in the rest of the same sentence as linking different *nationalities.* To be sure, the founders naturally expected the membership to come from a variety of organized tendencies, thereby forming "ties of solidarity" across tendency lines—this is not in question—but the *organizational structure* for attaining this end was based on individual membership only, not a system for getting existing organizations affiliated to SUCR.

There is not the slightest sign of a provision whereby (for example) the Communist League as such would become an affiliated part of SUCR; likewise the French SPDS. As for the third nationality: we have already asked what organization Harney was supposed to be representing.[44] Nicolaievsky,

12. The SUCR Episode   201

like others, says that Harney was "representing the Chartists." But it is impossible to believe that anyone expected to ask "the Chartists" to affiliate to SUCR. If, more accurately, Harney is taken as a representative of *left* Chartists, what organization of that tendency was there to be affiliated? What remains is the notion that the affiliation of the Fraternal Democrats was in question; but (1) no one has ever suggested this; (2) the FD was never mentioned in such context; and (3) for Harney to have tried to get the FD to vote affiliation to SUCR would have wrecked the organization in a trice, and to imagine he intended to try is to assume he was a fool.

To believe that SUCR could be a coalition of organizations, without a word being said in the statutes by way of provision for this structure, is to be ignorant of organizational realities. Did affiliated organizations have a vote? Only one vote each regardless of size? What was the relationship between affiliated organizations and individual members? Was SUCR open to individual members who were not members of other organizations, and if so ... The questions can be multiplied by anyone who has ever tried to write bylaws for a school association.

No: the SUCR statutes, on the face of them, were written for an individual-membership organization of some kind.

(3) The next prominent element in Nicolaievsky's story-line is *secrecy.* After four uses of the word 'secret' in his description, he wound up with the climactic assertion that SUCR was a "super-secret society." *That* is the thirteenth bong of the clock. As if multiplying assertions to make up for the lack of facts, he then wrote down that "An essential feature of this organization was that it should not come out into the open."

This is fiction: falsifiction. There is not a word in the statutes about secrecy. Nicolaievsky's fabrication was devised to give a faint blush of verisimilitude to his inventions about Marx's Blanquism, as aforementioned.

Of course, for Marx, as for everyone, the question of secrecy was a practical matter: this is what distinguished his attitude from conspiratorialism. In England the CL functioned as an open, legal, nonsecret organization; in Germany its branches and members had to practice secrecy, or else practice in prison. The Blanquist SPDS was not a secret society—in London. Harney belonged to no secret organization whatever. The idea of SUCR's being a secret organization in England was nonsense; the idea of its *not* being a secret organization in Germany was inane. As for "super-secret" organizations, not even Nicolaievsky knew what this sensational term might mean.

(4) Although Nicolaievsky claimed to expound the "organizational structure," one of the curious things about the six articles was the *lack* of attention to organizational structure. The six founders were established as the (first) central committee, but nothing was said about how the central committee was to be elected, re-elected, replaced or renewed. Nothing was said about the

basic organizational question of branch and lower-echelon structure, encountered in any set of bylaws known to the signers—except that the central committee established *corresponding* committees, presumably in localities. The very existence of local organizations raises a number of structural questions, none of which is mentioned in the statutes.

Instead, the statutes show concern for such unusual details as unanimous admission of members and two-thirds voting on *everything* (not merely on resolutions, as Nicolaievsky says). We will come back to this anomaly; but the general comment can be made—contrary to the spirit of the Nicolaievskian description of SUCR—that this is *a very unfinished organizational foundation*. The statutes do not yet provide for a finished organization; they are like a memo to initiate talks on the subject.

(5) To tie up a loose end, let us mention specifically one more of Nicolaievsky's fictional assertions. He simply invented the provision about "the rank and file of the secret societies . . ." and in so doing represented Harney to be a secret-society man like Adam or Vidil. But he went beyond this: this rank and file, said Nicolaievsky, "did not themselves become members of this secret society [SUCR], which was restricted to their leaders." This falsification is concocted out of thin air.

The wide uncritical acceptance of Nicolaievsky's fabulation in the literature of marxology is one of the saddest commentaries on a sorry scene. Some examples: (a) It was soon followed by Arthur Lehning's description of SUCR as a " *'Dachorganisation'* of the national secret organizations."[45] A *Dachorganisation* (lit., roof organization), or "umbrella organization," means the same sort of "organization of organizations" that Nicolaievsky dreamed up. No more than Nicolaievsky did Lehning say what word, phrase, or mark of punctuation in the documents allowed for such an organizational structure, let alone mandated it. (b) An otherwise valuable work by Ernst Schraepler on early German working-class organization repeated Nicolaievsky's story that SUCR admitted only "the leaders of the various associations, not their members," and that it was "strictly secret." (No documentation offered, not even a note crediting Nicolaievsky.)[46] (c) Richard Hunt, usually a more careful writer, repeated exactly the same two inventions—referring them to Nicolaievsky and Schraepler.[47] This is the sort of snowballing effect that establishes an invention as an accepted fact through a concatenation of footnotes.

Among the many oddities of the SUCR episode is the fact that there is not a single mention of this organization by name, and very few mentions of the episode in any fashion or form, in a whole series of places where one would expect to find it.

The first place that demands listing is the report that was sent out by Marx and Engels to the membership of the Communist League in June 1850, right

12. The SUCR Episode 203

in the middle of the period of SUCR's alleged existence. This "Address [Circular] to the Communist League" of June, unlike the March Address, was an organizational accounting: "to report on the present state of the League."[48] One of its chief concerns was to report on contacts with other groups and tendencies. It tells the members *inter alia* about the Revolutionäre Zentralisation group in Switzerland at some length, as already mentioned.[49]

But there is no mention of the existence of SUCR, let alone a report on it, in the June Address.

It is typical of the marxological situation that the opposite statement is frequently set down. The apparent contradiction will lead us to the heart of the matter. Nicolaievsky's statement is, in this case, circumspect: he refers only to "what appears to be an allusion to it [SUCR]."[50] The "allusion" was a report, not given under the rubric of "France" or "Germany," let alone the world, but under the head of activities of the Central Committee in England. Under the rubric "England," the third and fourth paragraphs, sandwiched between other matters, reported on relations with the Blanquists and the Chartists. But instead of reporting some sort of agreement with these tendencies, or even the establishment of a world organization, the Address went as follows.

Of the French revolutionaries the really proletarian party in particular, whose head is Blanqui, has joined forces with us. The delegates of the Blanquist secret societies are in regular and official contact *[Verbindung,* connection, tie-up] with the delegates of the [Communist] League, to whom they have turned over important tasks preparatory to the next French revolution.

The heads of the revolutionary Chartist party are likewise in regular close contact with the delegates of the Central Committee. Their journals are at our disposal. The break between this revolutionary independent workers' party and the section led by O'Connor which is more inclined to conciliation was substantially hastened by the delegates *of* the League.[51]

If this is taken as an "allusion" to SUCR, one has to fabricate a story about why the mere existence of that organization could not be communicated to the membership in a confidential internal organizational report. To tell of "joined forces" and "official contact," etc. is a far cry from reporting the establishment of the world organization that is to lead the next revolution. What was reported here about both the London Blanquists and Harney's Chartists is what could have been written back in February, *before* SUCR was a gleam in its founders' eyes.

If the very existence of SUCR could not be communicated, how could the policy be approved? It would be necessary to fabricate the fable that the CL, the Fraternal Democrats and the Blanquist group were all simply bureaucratic dictatorships, like (say) the Democratic Party's National Committee or the AFL-CIO's executive board. SUCR must have been so "super-secret" as to destroy the whole democratic character of the CL and all the other groups—and at the same time so unimportant that nowhere else was it taken notice of. This would make great material for one of Robert Payne's novels, like the one entitled *Marx;* but if this sort of historical methodology were generalized, the history of society would be a shambles.

Not only is nothing like SUCR mentioned in connection with the Blanquists, but, besides, there is not a hint that anything exists involving *both* the Blanquists and the left Chartists, who are reported on as separately as any other two items. Two minor bits of news about Chartist relations are presented—but not the big news that the revolutionary instrument for the next upheaval has been created! Either the explanation is very strange or it is very simple—and I am going to suggest a simple one.

First, a subsidiary question that has been raised with great concern, which will lead us to another example of the oddity that surrounds the accepted view of SUCR. What were the "important tasks preparatory to the next French revolution" that were turned over to CL representatives by the Blanquist group?*

The main proposal for an answer to this question comes from the aforementioned article by Norman Plotkin, important not only because of its valuable research content but also because it has been so widely cited for many years. After writing about the alleged formation of SUCR as an international revolutionary alliance, Plotkin asserts that "Blanqui was informed of this alliance [SUCR] by Barthélemy in his letter of July 4, 1850." Very interesting, if true! The trouble is that Plotkin then cites the letter to Blanqui (which is also found in Dommanget, more fully)—*and there is not the least mention of SUCR in it.* Moreover, Plotkin repeats this singular performance: he asserts that a letter to Blanqui on July 19 by Vidil "sent Blanqui the same information." He cites Vidil's letter (as does Dommanget)—and, again, *there is not a word in it about SUCR.*

Since this may be hard to believe, I hereby put both letters in evidence, especially since they give useful information, if not about SUCR. First, Barthélemy's letter:

> We have begun, together with the German communists, to draw up a revolutionary Manual, containing in numerical order all the measures

---

* Bertram Wolfe's *Marxism* turns this passage on its head and interprets it to mean that Marx "was using Blanquist conspirators as emissaries to the branches or the Communist League."[52] This is simply a blooper, but, for what it is worth, it is discussed in Special Note B.[53] This Special Note also takes up Nicolaievsky's response to the same passage, irrelevant at this juncture.

that the People will have to take immediately after the revolution in order to ensure its results and avoid a repetition of what happened in February. Our intention is to make this Manual into a litde book that we will distribute among the workers so that everyone knows what he has to do to ensure the victory of the People. We will also print this Manual in the form of proclamations to be posted up in the streets of Paris. Let us know if we can get our manuscript to you without any problem about it so that you can put the finishing touches on it. When you read it you will see what our intentions are, and I do not doubt for my part that you will approve them.

It is difficult to confuse the collaboration of a few people on a "little book" with the establishment of a world organization. And here is Vidil's letter:

Barthélemy promises you to send you a bit of work we have done here; you will get it at the first opportunity. This work contains what the People must demand on the morrow of a revolution.[54]

Vidil continues with his description of the "little manual," and winds up: "This book will displease our Montagnards, who call us men of disorder"— and that's all.

The astonishing thing about these letters is precisely the opposite of Plotkin's empty claim: if SUCR was really in existence, how can one possibly explain the failure of both Barthelemy and Vidil (both involved with SUCR, we know) to mention this important international demarche to Blanqui? In all of the correspondence to Blanqui, there is no other letter that Plotkin finds to mention in this connection.

We have, then, the French counterpart of the puzzle: an organization of "universal" importance is formed, allegedly, but the CL ignores it in its June report and the Blanqust leaders refrain from mentioning it to Blanqui. That leaves Harney, who is the clearest case of all: every month his magazine, which contains work by the German and French signatories, fails to report a world-shaking revolutionary formation, while it tells its readers about tavern affairs!

The accepted—or Nicolaievskian—version of the SUCR story makes no sense.

As for the joint work on a "revolutionary Manual" between some Blanquists and "German communists," let us leave it hanging on a hook for the moment. It may or may not be the "important tasks" mentioned in the June Address, but there is no other information.

No connection can be established between Blanqui and SUCR. Here again the acid test is Dommanget, who looks behind every punctuation mark to find a reason for announcing a Marx-Blanqui link. But he has to write of SUCR: "Blanqui, still in prison, no doubt had nothing to do with this operation." As usual, he finds a silver lining: "at any rate," he adds with what appears to be a straight face, Blanqui "did not disavow it," nor break relations with the London Blanquists involved![55] This would have been difficult to do if he did not even know that SUCR existed—as appears probable from Dommanget's own account. In any case, there was no reason for him to "disavow" it.

5. THE SIMPLE SOLUTION

I suggest a solution to the mysteries surrounding SUCR—a solution so simple that it will not appeal to the fable fabricators, but that is at least compatible with all the known facts:

The organization named SUCR never really came into existence at all. What happened in April was a preliminary agreement to undertake the working out of such an organizational project; but that was as far as it went.

Here is an alleged "international alliance of struggle"[56] that is never again mentioned in either Marx's or Engels' correspondence, at this time or later; never mentioned in any of their writings current or subsequent, including Engels' later articles on CL history, Blanquism, etc.; never mentioned in the archives of Blanqui or the London Blanquists; never mentioned in the contemporaneous English, French, or German press; never mentioned in any reminiscences or memoirs by contemporaries...What accounts for all these negatives?

More than that: even aside from the Marx-Engels correspondence and the Blanqui papers, we now have in publication a considerable number of letters of the period, written by and to members of the Communist League, sent from and to London and the Continent. In (say) April-May 1850 the news of the formation of SUCR to lead the world revolution should have been momentous, in the eyes of all these correspondents. Yet what do we find? For these two months, one group of letters has appeared in New Mega, another in a CL document collection.[57] Yet not a single letter mentions the name of SUCR; and exactly one letter refers to the episode in any form. Judging by a statement in the editorial apparatus of New Mega, there are altogether only two letters known to the Institute of Marxism-Leninism that at any time mentioned the SUCR episode even indirectly![58]

These two letters deserve a close look.

First letter. During April-May, Conrad Schramm, one of Marx's closest associates in London, was corresponding with Karl Bruhn (or von Bruhn), who was then in the Hamburg area. We do hot have Schramm's letters, but a reply by Bruhn on May 2 shows that Schramm must have told him about the signing of the SUCR accord. In a longish letter Bruhn devoted one sentence to his favorable reaction: "Your information regarding the agreement [*Verständigung*] with the French is very glad tidings."[59]

That's all. The word *Verständigung* means a coming to an understanding, an arrangement. It does not sound as if he had just learned that the leadership of the world revolution had been assumed by a hew society.

Second letter. Writing from Middlesex on December 16, after SUCR was all over, in a rather gossipy sort of letter, Wilhelm Pieper told Engels:

> The Messrs. Adam-Schapper-Willich have fired off a second manifesto, in which they have taken up the points agreed on last April between you and the French society, but in such a silly and defective fashion that it does no harm.[60]

Which manifesto is meant is unclear, doubtless one or another of the manifestos signed by the Willich-Schapper group (which still called itself Communist League) together with their erstwhile SUCR partners of the Blanquist group (Adam, Vidil, Barthélemy, et al.) together with the German Democratic Association moderates and other emigres. If it was the manifesto of November 16, it was the one that Marx considered "champion drivel." Its text can be read in Marx's letter to Engels of December 2.[61] Here there is nothing that corresponds to "the points agreed on last April," certainly not to the point on "la dictature des prolétaires."

I would spotlight one phrase in the Pieper letter just quoted: he does not refer to an organization, or the program of an organization—only to "points agreed on." If we take this at face value, we can conclude: what happened in April was merely the preliminary step of agreeing on a number of "points" which an alliance *might* be based on. The next steps would require discussion of many other points before the establishment of a real organization could become a reality. For the reasons previously discussed, these implementing discussions—such as the May 1 *entretien*, perhaps—did not achieve any definite results before political tensions quashed the whole project.

This hypothesis is compelling because it squares with the two big known facts: the existence of the sheets of paper headed with a name that never was seen again, and the nonexistence of any mentions of SUCR in so many places where they would be expected. The hypothesis means that no organization like SUCR ever operated in fact; it was an idea that got to first base, and died there.

There can be little doubt that the main problem was the political differences between Marx's circle and the Blanquists. In this sense, it is accurate to say that the problem was Marx-Blanquist *agreement*, though if such an agreement had been achieved the result would have been much more than a "Marx-Blanquist alliance," as we have argued. Pieper naturally referred to "the points agreed on" as being between "you and the French society." On one of the four copies of the SUCR document held in Moscow, there is a note by Engels on the verso: "Document on the *affaire* with the Blanquists and Harney."[62] Of course, there is no telling how long after 1850 this note was written.

We may remark, also, that the odd phrase "fundamental contract"—used for the agreement in the Marx-Engels-Harney letter of October 9, drafted by Engels—may now be more understandable. Engels, a good businessman, knew that a "contract" only initiated a project.

If SUCR never actually came into existence as a real organization, some of the appreciations of its significance that have been published require some second thoughts. Plotkin, whose contribudon was to study the contents of the Blanqui papers, where he found *nothing* on SUCR, nevertheless found it possible to write the highly quotable opinion that SUCR "achieved the unity of the European parties of the left after the revolution of 1848" and "marked the first step toward a durable international revolutionary organization."[63] This is simple puffery. David McLellan echoed this homage with the statement that SUCR "achieve[d] a temporary unification of the European left wing after 1848 and as such was a forerunner of the First International."[64] For a nonexistent organization that no one ever heard of, this *is* good going. For people who think that history records what happened, it is disconcerting.

We can now pose the last question, which brings us back to the "dictatorship of the proletarians": who actually wrote these words—and the rest of the SUCR document?

Let us stipulate at the outset, at the risk of repeating ourselves, that there is no information on this. But informed speculation is possible; there is a hypothesis worth mentioning.

Ernst Schraepler, followed by Richard N. Hunt, raised the question in another form: whose was the "initiative" for the planned alliance? Who was "the prime mover in bringing the group together"? Marx or Harney, Schraepler thought; Hunt's candidate was Harney[65]—certainly reasonable speculations. As we have mentioned, Harney showed consistent interest in international organization, evidenced by the Fraternal Democrats. As for Marx, we have mentioned that all of his organizational initiatives were in the direction of international organization.

The trouble with the question as posed is this: an orientation toward international organization was not as unique or advanced as many historians seem to think, hence does not require special explanation.* The idea of

---

* The prime example of this misapprehension is the commonly repeated claim that Flora Tristan pioneered the idea of international workers' organization, a claim based on a footnote in her *Union Ouvrière*. This belief has no factual basis. The Saint-Simonians

international organization—at least across French, English, German, and other European boundaries—arose virtually simultaneously with the socialist movement itself. Not only can we cite almost any of the first socialist currents, but we must remember that there was an active and continuous migration across national borders by hundreds of thousands of artisanal workers, among whom indeed the first German revolutionary groups struck root (e.g., Weitling's tendency). The entire membership of the Communist League was international-oriented by their very conditions of existence; London Blanquists were national transplants, forced to be cosmopolitan if not truly internationalist. The material basis for early socialist internationalism involved other factors too.

The problem, then, is not to account for the idea of a "universal" revolutionary society, which needs no accounting for. The question is more specific—and more difficult: who might have been the practical initiator of this particular episode?

The fact that the SUCR agreements were found to be written in Willich's hand has been a sort of "double bluff" by history: it was easy to point out that this fact proves nothing about authorship, for Willich might simply have been the one to write out fair copies of an agreed-on text. Perfectly true; but a number of other indications, taken together, keep pointing the finger at Willich. There is no single piece of evidence that stands out as decisive, but I would adduce three signposts.

(1) The indications are that Willich was the *trait d'union*, or go-between, in CL-Blanquist relations in a personal sense. A nonintellectual, elbow-crooking bar-companion, hearty-man-to-man type with a man-of-action background and reputation, Willich was personally congenial to the French Blanquist elements. If we look back to Dommanget's portrayal of Vidil, an ex-military man like Willich in career and character,[66] we will find Willich's French counterpart; and there is no doubt that the two were personally friendly. As for Barthélemy: he and Willich were even "confidants" (according to Willich himself); they acted as seconds for each other in duels fought in 1850; when Willich infamously forced a duel on Conrad Schramm, Willich was flanked by Barthélemy and Vidil.[67] These facts help to explain why Barthélemy took over SUCR relations for the Blanquists. After the CL split it became even more obvious how personally involved Willich was with the Adam-Barthélemy-Vidil current of the Blanquists.[68]

---

were sending out international proselytizing "missions"—to Belgium and Germany, for example—before Tristan wrote her book; Fourier wrote much about international organization; Buonarroti was an international organizer; a European-wide (if not "universal") perspective was commonplace very early. The belief that such internationalism had to be pioneered by someone is due to the *later* deformation of the movement by national chauvinism.

There is no such evidence of personal closeness to the Blanquists on the part of Karl Schapper, Willich's factional partner. I would suggest that this indicates the reason why Willich, not Schapper, was the signer of the SUCR agreement, despite the fact that Schapper was the CL leader with by far the longest standing and Willich was a comparative Johnny-come-lately. This anomalous fact would require no explanation if Willich was in fact the initiator and linchpin of the project.

(2) In terms of personal relations, all of these considerations point to Willich as the man most likely to have been the "prime mover" in the affair. The easiest question of all is why Willich himself would have been specially eager to see the formation of a supranational bloc, swallowing up the German group where Marx's politics dominated.

It is a classic calculation: in a coalition or bloc of this sort, it is the *trait d'union*—the person who constitutes the bridge—that holds the balance. Instead of being a newcomer to the CL with personal popularity but little political weight, with unity Willich would have become the one man who could have a special relationship to both the Marxist and the Blanquist camps, the indispensable linchpin. (From Willich's standpoint, it follows, the basic deal was between the CL and the French, with Harney an added starter.)

(3) The most elusive consideration is the text of the SUCR statutes—the matter of style and formulation. The extant text was no doubt the outcome of some preliminary discussion, but may not have been regarded as final—only as a basis for further negotiation; the text we have may therefore not be, in all respects, the text originally drafted by the "prime mover." Taking all the uncertainties into consideration, I feel that the wording does not point to either Marx or Engels as the actual author. My candidate would be Willich.

Such an impression is by nature impossible to prove but I can point. I have already pointed to the difference introduced by changing 'proletariat' to 'proletarians'.[69] On a different level I would point to such formulations as those about the "human family" and "republican fraternity." One is reminded that Marx himself later (1852) commented on Willich's characteristic style: citing a communication signed "The Revolutionary Committee," Marx remarked that

> the references to "civic virtues" and the way in which they are "definitely counting on" this military "instruction being carried out" seem to reflect the imagination of a Willich.[70]

The writer's concern with such gimmicks as unanimous admission and the two-thirds rule, with the special proviso in Article 5 for the inviolability of Article 1—all these being carefully detailed though no attention is paid to obviously basic structural provisions: this sort of thing is unlike Marx's and

Engels' practices before and after this episode. There is no hard-and-fast reason why Marx might have held out against these elements, at least to start the *entretien* off, but I do not see Marx going about it this way on his own.*

On the other hand, it is precisely the lopsided emphases in these statutes that remind one of people inexperienced in the organized socialist movement, trotting out their favorite hobbyhorses.

Finally, I would urge the view that the signatures attached to the six statutes should not necessarily be interpreted in the same way as signatures attached to a finished public document. This document was neither public nor finished, and we simply do not know what the signatures were supposed to signify. Perhaps they merely represented an interim agreement, e.g., to use the draft as a basis for further discussion.

6. OUR CENTRAL THESIS

If in fact Willich did draft the six statutes, there is no mystery about why he included the phrases "dictatorship of the proletarians" and "revolution in permanence" in the sacrosanct Article 1. These phrases, or something like them, had just prominently appeared in Marx's writings, the former in his magazine and the latter in an official CL document. And they sounded very r-r-revolutionary to him and to his similars among the Blanquists. So much so that after reverently writing them into Article 1—with a little distortion since he did not really understand them—he enshrined them in Article 5 as inviolable.

The attractive appeal of these terms to Blanquist types who did not understand their content suggests my hypothesis on why, and under what

---

* *In* notes added to the 1973 edition of Nicolaievsky's biography, there is an exceedingly confused remark on the question of authorship:

> It has been suggested that they [the SUCR statutes] were written by Willich (MEW), but it is no less probable that Marx had a hand in them; note the phrase "permanent revolution," which appears in a different context in the *Jewish Question*.[71]

(1) What MEW reports is not that Willich drafted, or authored, the statutes, but merely that the copies were written down by his hand. (2) To counterpose the observation that "Marx had a hand in them" is muddling, since it is quite certain that Marx "had a hand" insofar as he signed the statutes. (3) The reference to "permanent revolution" (which does *not* appear in the statutes in this form) as something in Marx's essay "On the Jewish Question" is an irrelevancy in view of the fact that Marx had just prominently used that term twice in 1850.[71] This congeries of confusions is typical of treatments of SUCH when they go beyond copying from Nicolaievsky.

circumstances, Marx occasionally employed the new term 'dictatorship of the proletariat'. I explained it as follows in my 1962 essay:

> We can now suggest why the term 'dictatorship of the proletariat' makes its appearance *in connection with* the Blanquists but not *by* the Blanquists. Ordinarily Marx's expression for this idea would be, as it was in the *Communist Manifesto,* such a term as 'political power of the working class' or 'rule of the proletariat.' When, however, it is a question of counterposing this class concept to the Blanquist-type dictatorship, it is dressed in the formula 'class dictatorship.' Class dictatorship is then counterposed to Blanquist dictatorship, to make the contrast.
>
> In "united fronts" with the Blanquists, it was only such a formulation that could be acceptable to Marx.... The united front, then, was based on a formulation which preserved the class character that was basic for Marx, while at the same time making the Blanquists happy, no doubt, with its revolutionary flavor.[73]

During the years since this hypothesis was published, I have seen no reason to doubt that it was the operative motive. I would add only that the motive applied not only to Blanquists outside of the Communist League but also to the sort of elements inside the League who needed the same approach. We have seen that the Blanquists accepted a conception of dictatorship as a necessary part of a revolutionary program; and after 1850 we will find that Willich (as a leader of the Willich-Schapper league) was prolific in concocting schemes for dictatorship. The problem was how to educate them to a new conception about 'dictatorship'.

The reader must forget about the modern aura that makes 'dictatorship' a dirty word for us; this aura did not yet exist. How do you counteract the primitive-Babouvist notion of dictatorship that was so common precisely among the people who wanted to be good revolutionists? You tell them: *Yes, dictatorship—that means rule—we want the rule of the proletariat; but that does not mean the rule of a man or a clique or a band or a party—the 'rule of the proletariat' means the rule of a class.* Class rule means *class* dictatorship.

Thus the term came from Marx's pen in 1850—as much an instrument in the "re-education" of the Blanquist and Jacobin-revolutionary currents in and out of the CL as was Marx's anti-conspiratorialist book review in his magazine. The marxological myth which had 'dictatorship of the proletariat' pegged as a Blanquist notion had history turned upside-down. 'Dictatorship of the proletariat' came into existence as an attempt to show Blanquists and other Jacobin-left currents that there was another way of being revolutionary, Marx's way.

If this is true, as I believe it is, we can now state our main thesis on the meaning *to Marx* of the term 'dictatorship of the proletariat', together with a

12. The SUCR Episode 213

claim which the reader will be able to put to the test as we go along. Namely: *For Marx and Engels, from beginning to end of their careers and without any exception, 'dictatorship of the proletariat' meant nothing more and nothing less than 'rule of the proletariat', the 'conquest of political power' by the working class, the establishment of a workers' state in the first postrevolutionary period.*

Nothing more: Whatever Marx believed would be, or might be, characteristic of the postrevolutionary period, it was not *this* term that dealt with such problems of a workers' state. 'Dictatorship of the proletariat' did not refer to particular characteristics, methods, or institutions of proletarian rule—it meant the proletarian rule itself, and nothing more. Contrary to a frequent assertion, Marx had a good deal to say about the problems of a workers' state, but it was not this term that said it. Those problems, and Marx's views on them, have to be studied, of course, but there is no short cut to them via this terminology.

Nothing less: The 'dictatorship of the proletariat' did not merely mean proletarian "ascendancy" in some sense short of the definitive conquest of state power by the proletariat. In this sense the term is inextricably linked to Marx's basic theory of social revolution as against notions of gradual socialistic permeation of capitalist society without a transformation of the state power.

The chapters to follow will present proof after proof of this thesis, while at the same time we will find no evidence to gainsay it: this is the claim to be tested in the light of the facts.

13 | REVERBERATIONS IN 1850: THE *NDZ EXCHANGE*

While the reference to proletarian dictatorship in the SUCR statutes was unknown to most contemporaries, the loci in Marx's *Class Struggles in France* had reverberations. But not because the term itself excited special perturbation. At the time, the equation of 'dictatorship' with 'rule of the proletariat' was commonly accepted.

1. "PROLETARIAN ASCENDANCY"

This equation, as we have said, was in the first place accepted by Marx and Engels themselves. Let us begin with a special illustration of this fact.

The month of March 1850 saw the publication of the first two passages containing a version of 'dictatorship of the proletariat', in the first installments of Marx's *Class Struggles in France* (loci 1a and 1b), and also witnessed the circulation of the "Address to the Communist League" among the League membership. The same month saw the publication of a notable article by Engels, which concluded with a rousing call for the conquest of political power by the proletariat—and which saw this victory coming about in England through the utilization of universal suffrage.

Let us stipulate that later Engels' view of the relationship between suffrage and revolution would become more sophisticated; but this is not our present subject. Right now we are concerned with discovering what 'dictatorship (or rule) of the proletariat' meant to Marx in 1850; and while it is not enough to cite Engels, his coeval writings are certainly indicative.

In an article on "The Ten Hours' Question" for Harney's *Democratic Review*, Engels was intent on arguing, with a view to educating backward Englishmen, that reforms were not enough, though useful. The "working classes," now the "fourth estate," must become the first estate; lasting benefit will not be conferred on them by others—*"they must obtain it themselves by conquering, first of all, political power."*

... *under no circumstances have they any guarantee for bettering their social position unless by Universal Suffrage*, which would enable them to seat a *Majority of Working Men* in the House of Commons.[1]

This was only one of a series of statements by both Marx and Engels, throughout their lives, acknowledging the possibility that in England workers' political power might be *initiated* through a parliamentary majority. (But remember that, according to the marxological myth, at this time in 1850 Marx and Engels were supposed to be "Blanquist" wild men pullulating with putschist proclivities...)

Engels' article did not stop at the vision of a parliamentary majority. He went on to explain (in very simplistic terms) that inexorable economic crises meant that "a *revolution* [was] made inevitable," and this revolution, "uprooting society far deeper than 1793 and 1848 ever did, will speedily lead to the political and social ascendancy of the proletarians."

The word 'ascendancy' in this context was a well-accepted Chartist term. No doubt the corresponding German term in Engels' mind was *Herrschaft*. He was translating *Herrschaft des Proletariats* not only into English but into Chartist language. With this train of thought, he went on to counterpose "the ascendancy of the manufacturing capitalists" (as Marx would later counterpose the dictatorship of the bourgeoisie to the dictatorship of the proletariat). The accumulation of economic contradictions would mean that

> there is *an end to mill-lord ascendancy*. And *what next?* "Universal ruin and chaos," say the free-traders. *Social revolution and proletarian ascendancy*, say we.

He concluded with an exhortation "to work out your own salvation"—"boldly and at once struggle for *that political and social ascendancy of the proletarian class which will enable you to protect your labour yourselves*"[2]

Thus the last page of the article offered the word 'ascendancy' six times.

When this article appeared in the *Democratic Review*, Engels was writing a German version for the *NRZ Revue*, and it was published in the issue after the one containing locus 1c. In this German article there was less attention paid to pressing the question of proletarian rule—which had already been much emphasized in the magazine—but the meaning of universal suffrage was, if anything, brought out even more strongly:

> ... universal franchise in an England two-thirds of whose inhabitants are industrial proletarians means the exclusive political rule of the working class with all the revolutionary changes in social conditions which are inseparable from it.'

Instead of the exhortation that closed the English article, there was an unadorned statement that the solution "lies in the *proletarian revolution*."

In neither article did the term 'dictatorship of the proletariat' appear, though it might have. (This lack was "corrected" by an English translation which illustrates a clear and ever-present danger in Marx studies: see Special Note D, Section 1.)

2. OTTO LÜNING AND THE *NDZ*

At the end of Chapter 12 we argued that the term 'dictatorship of the proletariat' was intended to help re-educate the Jacobin-communist elements inside and outside of the Communist League. If this was so, it may also be supposed that it elicited adverse reactions from the other side of the political spectrum, from reform-socialistic elements to the right of the League. If the Blanquists or Willich types thought it was gratifyingly "revolutionary" in tone, the others may have found it correspondingly disturbing to moderate souls.

It has been asserted that the censorious reaction to 'dictatorship of the proletariat' was exemplified by the episode of the *NDZ* exchange, in which we will meet locus 3. Schraepler's history of early German working-class organization states:

> ... Otto Lüning, who was now publishing the *Neue Deutsche Zettung* in Frankfurt am Main, protested against the concept 'dictatorship of the proletariat."[4]

According to this, Lüning would have the honor of a world-historic "first"— the first attack on the idea of the dictatorship of the proletariat or at least on the term. But the claim is not true; the episode illustrated a different pattern, equally important.

One of Marx's earliest followers in Germany, Joseph Weydemeyer, had remained in the country after the revolution instead of emigrating. We will introduce him in more detail in Chapter 15, where he will play a prominent part; suffice to mention here that he had joined the Communist League in 1847, was active in the Rhineland, and, after the outbreak of the revolution, joined forces with Otto Lüning on a left-democratic daily in Darmstadt, the *Neue Deutsche Zeitung*.

Weydemeyer was Lüning's brother-in-law as well as his associate editor— he had recently (October 1847) married Louise Lüning—but it was Lüning who ran the daily. Weydemeyer, to be sure, tried to influence Lüning and the paper's policy in the direction of Marx's politics, with occasional successes in terms of opening the paper to CL material. But Lüning was no communist, though he had briefly been a member of the CL.[5]

13. Reverberations in 1850: The NDZ Exchange

Heinrich Otto Lüning, born the same year as Engels, was a physician by profession, turned journalist in the mid- 1840s. He published the *Weserdampfboot* in 1844—the same year that the pre-Marxist Engels told the English Owenites that Dr. Lüning was one of the leading socialist writers in Germany[6]—and then, in 1845-48, the *Westphälische Dampfboot;* finally the *NDZ.* The *Neue Deutsche Zeitung,* subtitled "Organ of the Democracy" just as the *NRZ* was in Cologne, began in Darmstadt on July 1,1848, and stayed in that city through the following March. On April 1,1849 it began publishing in Frankfurt, the seat of the National Assembly; and in September the paper dubbed itself "Organ of the German National Assembly," setting up an editorial commission of five Left deputies. The following month it merged with Frankfurt's *Deutsche Reichszeitung,* which Robert Blum had founded, and took on its editor J. Georg Günther in addition to Weydemeyer. The *NDZ* was going to come to an end in December 1850 as a result of the government's harassment of its editors. Lüning later (1859) joined the Nationalverein and, after 1866, the National Liberals. He died in 1868.

Lüning's socialism was the hazy, sentimental sort that the *Communist Manifesto* had immortalized under the name of "True Socialism," originally shaped by Moses Hess and best represented by Karl Grün's writings. Above all, in a movement of "hards" and "softs," Lüning was a doughy "soft."

Marx, Engels, and Weydemeyer had had cause to know this characteristic of Lüning while he was still publishing the *Westphalische Dampfboot* in Bielefeld and Paderborn. Weydemeyer, who participated in the editorial work, was already trying to win Lüning and the paper over to CL politics,[7] and in the summer of 1846 Lüning went so far as to publish Marx's and Engels' "Circular Against Kriege," their critique of the CL-discrediting "communism" being preached by Weitling's disciple in America.[8] But Lüning made changes in the text to soften it, added some meditations of his own, introduced it with a misty foreword, and sanitized it with a concluding afterword, ruefully allowing that in publishing the Circular the paper was indulging in self-criticism.[9]

Engels groaned over Lüning's performance in a letter to Marx, once more giving the marxologists proof of how "intolerant" he and his friend were of hopeless muddleheads: "... Lüning's rubbish above all is splendiferous stuff. One can see the fellow in the flesh before the mind's eye, as he ventures to shit in his pants like a good philistine." Engels then quoted the last two lines of a famous epigram by Goethe:

> A cavalier noble in mind and breast
> Is everywhere welcomed and fêted;
> There's many a girl with wit and a jest
> He's totally captivated;
> But if he lacks force and fists in a brawl,

> What then can protect him a bit?
> And if he has no behind at all,
> On what can this noble chap sit?[10]

A question of fundaments and fundamentals, in Engels' opinion: Lüning seems to be noticing that he too has no "material basis" on which to seat his communism.[11]

In the early part of 1847 Engels worked on a supplement to the *German Ideology* dealing with "True Socialism"—unfinished and unpublished. It began with a section devoted to Lüning's *Westphälische Dampfboot,* not omitting the lines from Goethe, mostly concerned with politico-literary banter. The *Dampfboot*'s "True Socialism" was mainly a matter of shedding "bitter tears over the misery of suffering humanity"... It has a "soft nature" like milky rice pudding; it prefers "merciful and loving reviewers rather than ... heartless, cold severity of judgment..." And so on.[12]

The rice pudding should certainly be kept in mind when we come, later the same year, to Marx's dealings with Lüning on a contribution to the paper. With Weydemeyer's support Marx tried to get Lüning to publish his critique of Grün.[13] Now a number of writers[14] have published the statement that Lüning protested to Marx that his own views were "close" to Marx's; but now New Mega has published the source of this information, namely, Lüning's letter to Marx of July 16, 1847, in connection with the piece on Grün. It turns out that Lüning's protestation—"I believe that not only W[eydemeyer]'s but also my own writings are not far from your standpoint"—was a prelude to demonstrating its own inaccuracy. For, after this vague claim of agreement, Lüning proceeded to his real business: upbraiding Marx at length for being so "bitter and antagonistic" in criticizing people like Kriege and Grün. He "approved" of the criticism of Kriege's "extravagant tomfoolery" but it should have been milder; he agreed that Grün's writing was "empty phraseology," but this empty phraseology should not be "treated so roughly" (nor in fact revealed to be empty phraseology); and so on.[15]

This letter is the proper prelude to the *NDZ* exchange of 1850. A historical note must be attached. There is no logical reason why a person could not have really agreed politically with Marx's critique and at the same time *really* disapproved only of a too harsh tone. Unquestionably there is room to take a position in the space between content and form. We can even grant that such a person may have existed, though no name comes readily to mind. (For one thing, such persons would be more likely to express their opinion privately, rather than in the form of a public attack, since their aim, by the terms of the hypothesis, would *really* be to help Marx.) In any case, it will not do for marxologists to assume that anyone who denounces Marx's harshness in criticism is himself a seraph of sweetness and light whose objection is *really* not based on disagreement with the content of Marx's thought. Indeed, the opposite has to be assumed till proved otherwise, for this is what history and experience teaches.

3. LÜNING LIFTS A LANCE

When the first three issues of Marx's London magazine *NRZ Revue* came out in March and April, the contents were dominated by Marx's article series on *The Class Struggles in France.* Weydemeyer naturally wanted to get publicity for the magazine in the *NDZ* by running a review of Marx's publication. His intention was to write such a review himself, but Lüning informed him he was going to do the job and in fact had already started on it. But by June nothing had appeared.[16]

Meanwhile Marx was becoming impatient. Not only Marx but others in his circle who knew Lüning had a low expectation of the Westphalian. Ernst Dronke, who traveled on the Continent for a commercial firm, wrote Engels in February and May, from Paris and Frankfurt respectively, that his experiences as a contributor to Lüning's *NDZ* had been discouraging: "that fat beer-swiller Lüning has become the worst sort of bourgeois... Weydemeyer, as you know yourself, is entirely the will-less wage-worker in his brother-in-law's shop."[17] Later he referred to Lüning similarly as a *Bierphilister*.[18]

On June 8 Marx complained to Weydemeyer that "your paper seems to have joined the rest to form a *conspiration du silence* in regard to our Revue."[19] Weydemeyer replied by explaining the circumstances already mentioned. Lüning's plan to write a review was dragging on because he was waiting to receive the fourth number of the *NRZ Revue* (which, as a matter of fact, had come off the press about May 19). Besides, his personal relations with the chief editor were on a bad footing and so he could not press.[20]

On hearing that it was Lüning who planned to write the review, Marx sent up a storm signal. It was his wife Jenny who actually wrote to Weydemeyer about it (as she did when it was necessary to take over his correspondence now and then). Marx wants to tell you, wrote Jenny,

> that it would really not be desirable for Lüning to do a criticism, a strong attack would do, only no approbation. Also, my husband has never expected a profound criticism, but rather the simple thing such as all papers do for magazines and brochures, what your paper does too when you want to publicize and propagate writings. In this case you give suitable short extracts. This requires little work.[21]

This request for an attack rather than approval is surely the most vivid way

Marx could express his opinion of what might be expected from Lüning; and he was not disappointed. Lüning wrote a four-part article on the *NRZ Revue*, mainly on Marx's writing.[22] After Marx had seen the first two installments, he commented in a letter to Weydemeyer: "L[üning]'s criticism—I have seen 1 and 2—shows that he does not understand what he would like to criticize. Perhaps I will give him some elucidations in our *Revue*."[23] But only one issue of the *NRZ Revue* was published after this, and Marx did not include a comment on Lüning. Instead, he sent a comment to Lüning himself for publication in the *NDZ*. (It will be presented in the next section.)

As we might expect, Dronke was also disgusted by Lüning's criticism. Unlike Engels, he was moved to think not of Goethe's but of Heine's verse:

> As for Atta-Troll Lüning and his article against Marx in the feuilleton of his *Scheissblatt* [shitty sheet], I would like to send an article right away from Geneva, in which it will accompany the verse "Manchmal auch gestunken habend"* with *proofs* of his bourgeois venality and venal bourgeois-ness.[24]

Finally, to anticipate a little, let us record the effect of Lüning's anti-Marx article on his associate editor and brother-in-law Weydemeyer. About a week after the last installment, and just as the *NDZ was* printing Marx's statement, he told Marx:

> I had asked to have my name stricken from the list of editors beginning July 1 and thenceforth figure only as a contributor, a position which is in fact the only one I hold now. L[üning] did not want to accede to this; and to get out entirely is under present conditions a desperate business which would have to be thought over many times.[25]

There was good reason for the sharp reaction by Dronke and Weydemeyer. To see this, we have to do justice to Lüning and his article.

4. LOCUS 3: LÜNING VERSUS MARX

Otto Lüning's four-part article criticizing Marx's *Class Struggles in France* is, or rather should be, a historic document in the history of anti-Marxism, which after all is part of the history of Marxism. It has been ignored, for one thing, because it is thoroughly unavailable, never having been anywhere reprinted

---

* "Atta Troll," Heine's fable about a performing bear, had been published in book form only three years before this. Chapter 24 closes with an epitaph for this "primitive sans-culotte of the forest": bear with a cause . . . bad dancer, but with strong opinions...and (the line cited) "Sometimes also *gestunken* . . ."

13. Reverberations in 1850: The NDZ Exchange   221

or summarized.* Yet it has a right to be called the first presentation of the Bernstein-revisionist viewpoint in print: Bernsteinian before Bernsteinism.

Not that Lüning's views were innovative: on the contrary, his line of thought was run-of-the-mill "petty-bourgeois socialism" (to use the classificatory system of the *Communist Manifesto*). Its pioneering aspect was this: it was the first time (as far as I know) that the aforesaid run-of-the-mill reformist ideas were *counterposed* to Marx's in a critique of Marx's basic sociopolitical theory of the class struggle.

This is the task that Lüning undertook, in fact began with. Like many others who have denounced Marx for being "intolerant" of disagreement—said intolerance being manifested by his otherwise unexplainable determination to defend his point of view—Lüning showed *his* benign tolerance by devoting the entire first installment of his review to an attack on Marx's basic theory before telling his readers more than two words about what the writing under review was about.

In the present volume we cannot digress to discuss Lüning's views in general; but let us summarize his first part enough to provide the context for the passage which, we will find, elicited Marx's reply.

After high praise of Marx's style, Lüning set up the target to shoot at:

> The red thread that winds through Herr Marx's whole world and conception of history is the cleavage of present-day society into different *classes,* whose interests at almost all points are so mutually contradictory that the triumph of one entails the destruction of the other. The struggles of these classes are the motivating factors in the life of peoples and states; they form the crux of all historical events.

Such a class-struggle theory of history, therefore of politics, was anathema to Lüning, of course. He went on to explain that, for Marx, the bourgeoisie had triumphed over the feudal aristocracy and must now yield to the proletariat. "The future belongs to this class," according to Marx. He then represented Marx as believing that *only* the proletarian struggle against capital had significance: here his summary of Marx's thought went awry, but it was his prelude to the key passage, which went as follows:

> Any revolutionary movement of the present day that has a content different from this struggle of proletariat versus bourgeoisie is without significance; but all more or less take on this character. And the aim and the final end of all revolutionary movements of the present day is the *revolutionary rule, the dictatorship of the working class.*

---
* It is cited here from photocopies kindly supplied me, in 1960-61, by the Institute of Marxism-Leninism of Moscow. I am grateful for this assistance, even though since this notable case of cooperation the Institute has steadfastly refused to acknowledge my letters, let alone answer them.

This is what Lüning is exercised about—but which is it, "rule" or "dictatorship"? Let us continue and see.

There is a great deal of truth in these views of Marx, he goes on to say: there *are* struggles between classes in history (he next calls them "castes of society," speaking in his own voice); there *are* "harsh contradictions in social life"; the "knife and fork" question" (bread-and-butter question) can*not* be ignored; labor *is* the "slave" of capital; all this is an "unnatural state of affairs" and cannot last. All of these concessions naturally lead up to the main indictment of Marx's viewpoint:

> The result of the present revolutionary movements will in the end be what Marx denotes as *"rule" of* the working class. It is probable that a dictatorship instituted by the revolutionary party, predominantly through the weight of the working class, will direct the transition from the old to the new society, no matter how angry the gods of the Stirnerian Olympus in the Berlin *Abendpost* get over this limitation on personal freedom.[26]

To interrupt for a comment: it is clear that Lüning's target is the "rule" of the working class—he stresses that word himself. He concedes what his own social-democratic party leaders have already made clear—that the transition will entail a "dictatorship." It is important to note that the dictatorship he *accepts* is one instituted by the leading party, and the relationship to the working class which he envisages is that the dictatorship of the party will be based on the "weight" of the working class. The implication is that the working class is there to be used as a "weight," as an instrument. (The modern reader should not think of Stalin but—Louis Blanc!)

Let us now continue with the passage, for he has just gotten to the point of unsheathing the knife. The target is "rule":

> But class rule is always an immoral and irrational condition; and though we regard the rule of the working class as a hundred times more moral and rational than the rule of the classes of Junkers and stock-exchange wolves—because the former comprises useful members of society and the latter useless ones—yet we can (at the risk of being thrown in among the "petty-bourgeois democrats") find the aim and the goal of the present-day revolutionary movements not in the *transference of rule from one class to another* but in the *destruction of class differences.*

There it is: the specific point he chooses to attack on. (In other parts of the article he is going to snipe away at Marx's concept of class, for his own view of society is essentially based on the dichotomy of good and bad people.) Let us continue this passage for a few lines to let him wind down:

> And if the basic evil of present-day society, the *legalized* exploitation of labor by capital is eliminated, then the most hateful class differences

disappear by themselves, namely, that a person who contributes nothing toward fulfilling the purpose of society can idly carouse and live in luxury, while another who toils in drudgery for the service of and in the interest of society and devotes all his strength and abilities to it [like a newspaper editor] must live in want and hunger.

It is only in the middle of his second installment that Lüning starts telling his readers about the content of Marx's work. In this connection one should recall the point that Jenny Marx had made in her letter to Weydemeyer: namely, that the customary content of such a review article was a presentation of the writing, with "short extracts"—enough to make the publication known and promote it: certainly not a polemic on social theory. The heading over Lüning's article suggested the simple, standard approach: it was merely the name of Marx's magazine plus "by Karl Marx." *And this critique was not signed*—not at the beginning or the end.

Lüning was, in fact, treating Marx's work not in the simple, standard way but as the work of a political opponent. This after a couple of years of protestation that the trouble with Marx was that he was so hard on people who disagreed with him!

There was another example of this pattern, which we can cover here only in part. This was Lüning's treatment of Engels' contribution to the *NRZ Revue* on "The German Campaign for a Reich Constitution."[27] Lüning took swipes at Engels' piece in the first paragraph of his first installment and in the last part of his last, pretending great scorn, in a virulent tone that can only be accounted for if we assume that he was allowing himself to write in Engels' case the way he would have liked to have done in Marx's.

As we have seen, Marx first entertained the idea of taking up Lüning's political attack in his own magazine, in which case he would no doubt have discussed its theoretical content. As it was, Marx's response to Bernsteinism-*avant-la-lettre* had to wait till 1879.[28] For whatever reason (there is no record of his thinking on the matter) he plainly decided to limit himself to a very brief, indeed curt, letter to the editor on one point which *(he)* felt) needed no theoretical argumentation.

We have to quote the whole of Marx's letter in order to show what is *not* in it as well as to elucidate its several references.

[Locus 3]
STATEMENT

To the Editor of the *New Deutsche Zeitung:*
In your paper's feuilleton of June 22, this year, you taxed me with advocating the *rule and the dictatorship of the working class,* while as against me you put forward the *abolition of class differences altogether.* I do not understand this correction.

You knew very well that the *Manifesto of the Communist Party* (published before the February Revolution in 1848), p. 16, says: "When in the struggle against the bourgeoisie the proletariat necessarily unifies itself as a class, makes itself the ruling class through a revolution, and as ruling class forcibly abolishes the old relations of production, then along with these relations of production it abolishes the preconditions of existence of class antagonism* and of classes in general, and therewith its own rule as a class."

You know that I advocated the same view in the *Misère de la Philosophie* against Proudhon, before February 1848.

Finally, the very article you criticize, p. 32, Number 3 of the *N.R.Z.* [*Revue*], says: "This socialism" (i.e., communism) ["] is the declaration of the permanence of the revolution, the class dictatorship of the proletariat as the necessary transit point to the abolition of class distinctions generally, to the abolition of all the relations of production on which they rest, to the abolition of all the social relations that correspond to these relations of production, to the revolutionizing of all the ideas that result from these social relations. ["]

K. Marx, June 1850

Engels also had a short statement published, on a point which does not concern us now.[30]

5. MARX'S EQUATION

The phrase 'dictatorship of the proletariat' had occurred in Lüning's article and it was echoed in Marx's statement, but the first point to be made is that neither piece was *about* this term. Neither Lüning nor Marx saw any special point, to be explained or defended, in the use of 'dictatorship' rather than 'rule'. *This was not the problem.*

For Marx the passage in the *Class Struggles in France*, which is our locus 1c,[31] was assimilated in his own mind with the two other passages he cited.

The first is from the Manifesto: we have already seen this passage and its context in Chapter 8.[32] That Marx cited it as an equivalent of locus 1c tends to confirm the often-expressed view that the Manifesto's formulation "rule of the proletariat" was equated in *his* mind with 'dictatorship of the proletariat'.

---

* Since this translation follows the first edition of the Manifesto, we must note that, in citing the Manifesto here, Marx took the opportunity to correct a typographical error in the first edition, which, at the point shown by the asterisk, had omitted a comma. How this was treated in subsequent editions is a complicated story, but involves no substantive point. The difference involved was between abolishing *classes* in general or abolishing "the preconditions of existence" for them.[29]

13. Reverberations in 1850: The NDZ Exchange   225

The second passage adduced by Marx was the especially strong statement at the end of his *Poverty of Philosophy:*

> Does this mean that after the fall of the old society there will be a new class domination culminating in a new political power? No.
> The condition for the emancipation of the working class is the abolition of all classes, just as the condition for the emancipation of the third estate, of the bourgeois order, was the abolition of all estates and all orders.
> The working class, in the course of its development, will substitute for the old civil society an association which will exclude classes and their antagonism, and there will be no more political power properly so-called, since political power is precisely the official expression of antagonism in civil society.[33]

There is still another invocation of the abolition of all classes in the very last paragraph. Truly, the emphasis here was overwhelmingly not on the "rule" but on the abolition of classes.

The third citation, from the very article Lüning was reviewing, was the game-winning point. That this *NDZ* exchange was not at all centered around 'dictatorship' of any sort, but squarely around the basic concept of 'class rule' in any form, was fully confirmed by Lüning's rejoinder to Marx's statement:

> As regards the correction by Herr Marx, I am glad I can admit that it is well-founded. The remark about the abolition of class differences is found, to be sure, even in one of the articles under discussion; but it comes in so incidentally that surely many people have overlooked it, as I did. Therefore I am not even very sorry I made the error. For Herr Marx himself, and even more his supporters, constantly put the accent on the *rule* of the class, the *abolition* of which they let peep out only reluctantly as a later concession. In contrast I wished to place the abolition in the foreground, as the goal and aim of the movement.[34]

Unlike his article, which had been printed without a by-line, Lüning appended his name to this rejoinder. Weydemeyer claimed credit for pressing Lüning into coming out behind the screen of anonymity.[35]

In his rejoinder Lüning made out that the "remark about the abolition" was concealed in some other part of Marx's article, hard to find and hence easy to overlook, when in fact it was before his eyes in the very same sentence about the "rule" and the "dictatorship." In this, Lüning was pioneering the system that was going to dominate the whole first era of Bernsteinian Revisionism—namely, the pretense that the difference was not a basic clash of political position but rather a secondary matter of emphasis, in which mistakes by Marx were to be cleaned up to produce a better version of Marxism. Lüning struck the posture of advocating the "rule" but merely wishing to spotlight the "abolition": an odd choice, this, for a practical reformist to concentrate attention on a dim future rather than an immediate political goal. In fact, of course, what Lüning rejected was the very idea of the conquest of political power by a class movement of the proletariat. Where Bernstein was going to get the idea of denouncing this as "Blanquism," Lüning resorted to a feint about "emphasis."

Speaking of emphasis, the passage (locus lc) as cited here by Marx was stripped of its typographical emphasis in the *NDZ*, though there is no way to know whether this omission was due to Marx's letter or Lüning's editing.

That Lüning was uneasy about any working-class "rule," whether it was in the background or foreground, was further illustrated in his rejoinder to Engels' statement. Here he intimated that it was illegitimate to talk about the proletariat itself (let alone its rule) since "the sharply defined classes in his [Engels'] sense is a result of his schematism, which I do not find in life." Although Lüning had begun by acknowledging the existence of classes in historical struggles (though they quickly turned into "castes"), he showed that Marx's analysis of the recent class struggles in France was perturbing to his own sense of classlessness. So it transpired that this honest burgher's disagreement with Marx—far from having anything to do with the 'dictatorship of the proletariat'—was not even limited to the "rule" of the same, but was in fact over the class basis of political power in general, not to speak of the very existence of a "proletariat."

Finally, there was Lüning's interesting side-blow against those "supporters" of Marx who "constantly put the accent on the *rule* of the class." Lüning, who had briefly been a member of the Communist League, no doubt knew a number of Marx's supporters, but he may well have had specially in mind the particular Marx supporter who was his own associate editor and brother-in-law, Weydemeyer. Given Lüning's own "accent," this may or may not tell us something about Weydemeyer, but we may bear it in mind when we return to the latter for locus 4.

The main conclusion from this account is this: for Marx's opponent as well as for Marx, 'rule of the proletariat' and 'dictatorship of the proletariat' were equated one to the other. This equation will remain our guide throughout.

14 | MORE REVERBERATIONS

This chapter brings together some peripheral developments that cropped up in the train of loci 1 and 2. None of these is central to our story, but they have this in common: they illustrate how others, not Marx, reacted to talk about proletarian dictatorship.

1. MIQUEL'S "DICTATORSHIP"

In 1830 the future statesman Johannes Miquel was a 22-year-old law student who had been won over to communism by Wilhelm Pieper. He had taken part in the revolution, and joined the Communist League in the late 1840s. Then in his own person he acted out part of the history of German liberalism.

From an initial radicalism, he moved rightward during the 1850s, as a lawyer in Göttingen, and by 1859 helped found the Nationalverein. He was mayor of Osnabrück for many years, a leader of the National Liberals from 1867 on, a director of the Discontogesellschaft banking enterprise in 1870-1873, mayor of Frankfurt in 1879. Entering the Reichstag in 1887, he helped reorganize the National Liberals, became minister of finance during the 1890s, and in 1897 received the crowning honor of ennoblement, henceforth known as "von Miquel." In his last years he moved beyond liberalism to Bismarckian conservatism. The perfect mirror of German bourgeois politics, he was an eminent man in the last part of the nineteenth century. We may add, as a contribution to curiosa, that Miquel continued to supply "inside" political information to Marx for some years after abandoning revolutionary politics, apparently under duress (fear of exposure of his political past).

Some time in the summer of 1850* Miquel wrote his first letter to Marx, "to enter into closer relations."[1] By this time he had no doubt read Marx's *Class*

---

* On the dating of Miquel's letter, see Special Note D, Section 6.

Struggles in France and very likely also the exchange in the *Neue Deutsche Zeitung*. In his letter Miquel began with a short political autobiography, ending with his current position as Communist organizer in Göttingen. Politically—

> [I] assure you that your aims are mine. Communist and atheist, I, like you, want the dictatorship of the working class.

We note that Miquel ascribes this idea to Marx; Blanqui is nowhere mentioned. The myth that 'dictatorship of the proletariat' was a term affected by the Blanquists was at any rate unknown to Miquel.

But this revolutionary student likewise knew little about Marx's aims, nor had he ever seen Marx couple "communist" and "atheist" as a political program in this typical Jacobin-leftist way. Miquel had absorbed his leftist ideas (judging from his own letter) from Karl Blind and Pieper; and as we read his letter we can have no doubt about the course he will take when the CL split between Marx and Willich-Schapper forced him to choose.

> I choose my means solely and exclusively according to expediency. But I separate myself from you in this respect: I am firmly convinced that the *next* revolution will bring the petty-bourgeoisie to the helm ...

This alleged difference is confused, since Marx would have agreed with the last statement, but we will not try to sort it out. Miquel's own program (he went on to explain) called for opposing any constituent assembly. He was in favor of "terrorism" in particular cases (whatever that meant to him) and "local anarchy"—these in order to "make up for what we lack on a larger scale."

> Class-consciousness is altogether lacking in most German workers; we must exploit the personal hatred, the desire for revenge by the peasant against the usurer, the embitterment of the day-laborer against the "master"; in every individual locality (since we do not yet have a center) we must terrorize quickly and intensively ... We must not let the petty-bourgeois take a breathing-spell; we must drive the revolutionary fury to its peak through the petty-bourgeois's own methods—then perhaps for a short time we will succeed in carrying through the dictatorship of our party.

This line of thought was familiar: *since* the workers are not class-conscious, we approach them on a more primitive level—in fact with the same political methods that Marx (unbeknown to Miquel) was seeking to combat. There was more of this in his letter:

> But how do this without a common plan, without a supreme command, without a common will of the leaders—this is what I have been asking myself for a year now .... I saw that I was dependent on myself alone, and with my closest friends began to set up a league whose

ultimate aim was communism, whose first principle was "the end sanctifies the means," and whose first law was "unconditional obedience."

Thus Miquel explained his home-brewed rediscovery of what the Jacobin left had been doing for about a half century. To say that Miquel's view of dictatorship was "Blanquist" would be to mistake the part for the whole: he had absorbed the general notion of dictatorship that permeated the Jacobin left, of which the Blanquists represented a sector. His letter breathed the spirit of crude "revolutionism" characteristic of all who were disgusted with the pink social-democrats and aspired to be revolutionaries. We should note in particular that, like Lüning if from a different standpoint, he automatically associated dictatorship with "dictatorship of our party." This was the left-socialistic orthodoxy of the day, not some future deformation.

What Miquel did not yet grasp at all was that Marx was trying to move the idea of dictatorship into a different context, to transform this protean notion of dictatorship into a more specific political idea: *class* dictatorship. When Miquel found out the difference between Marx and Willich, he opted for Willich's political line, though retaining membership in the CL.

Miquel's biographer Wilhelm Mommsen explains that Miquel never understood Marx's ideas and was never even really interested in them primarily; that his temporary flirtation with communism was due to the yearning of "hotblooded youth" for political activism, plus "a certain incapability of clear political thinking."[2]

There is no record of a reply by Marx to this letter of Miquel's.

2. ENTER HOOLIGAN, RAVING

Around September 1850 a pamphlet was published in Cologne with the title *Vorgeschmack in die künftige deutsche Diktatur von Marx und Engels* (Foretaste of the Future German Dictatorship by Marx and Engels), signed "Tellering."[3] One might think that this sensational title would excite marxological admiration for its author's prescience, and perhaps this would have been the glorious destiny of the Tellering pamphlet—if a reading did not make instantly clear that this was gutter literature.

The inquirer into socialist history quickly finds out that a certain number of charges flung around in political disputes were automatic reflexes. The two leading types of knee-jerk denunciations involved *(A)* financial exploitation and embezzlement, and *(B)* dictatorship or bureaucratic domination of some sort. If Smith falls out with Jones over the fate of a revolution or the destiny of the world, Jones will be immediately accused of robbing some organization or seeking to run it as his barony, preferably both, but in that order. The fact that these charges were sometimes true was only one reason for the pattern, which has been more important in wrecking socialist organization than all counterrevolutionary government measures taken together. There is an additional historical principle at work here: the chances are very good that the main danger of dictatorship came from the one making the charge, not its target.

Marx was on the receiving end of this system no more than was his fair share.[4] Acutely aware of the pattern, he bankrupted himself (at the end of the *NRZ* period in 1849) in order to leave no room for the charge that he had "enriched himself at the expense of the workers" (the standard form of denunciation)—without however avoiding the attention of the hooligans who in every period have befouled the socialist movement. But at this point we are concerned with knee-jerk *B*.

The first opponent of Marx, as far as I know, who knee-jerked into this pattern was Karl Heinzen. Back in 1847 Heinzen had launched a campaign against communism in the Brussels left-democratic press, no doubt in response to the fact that the Communist circle around Marx was becoming too influential on the left.[5] His stridently anticommunist articles were rebutted by Engels, then by Marx in an essay "Moralizing Criticism and Critical Morality."[6] In September 1847, Karl Schapper took a very conciliatory tone in an unsigned statement for the Communist League, urging the need for unity between communists and other democrats on that part of a progressive program they agreed on, such as a democratic republic.[7]

Heinzen spurned such overtures with principled anticommunist fury. In 1848 he published a pamphlet titled *Die Helden des teutschen Kommunismus* (The Heroes of German Communism), "dedicated" to Marx. Here he rejected any unity with the Communists because

> what the Communists understand by republic [is] nothing but an institution in which a German Blanqui is to get a base prepared for the communist dictatorship.[8]

It must not be supposed that this meant Heinzen opposed dictatorship on democratic principle. He was entirely sympathetic to Kossuth's, Blanc's, and others' conception of a good dictatorship by good democrats, and there is no reason to suppose him averse to trying his own hand, if Humanity were to call him into service.

The pamphlet by Tellering was as clinical a case of knee-jerk denunciation as any known. Eduard von Müller-Tellering was originally a lawyer in Coblenz; he held a post in the judiciary system until 1846, then quit, and set out on travels. In Vienna during the 1848 revolution, he became the local correspondent for Marx's *Neue Rheinische Zeitung* by late July, without having ever met Marx, who visited Vienna only in August-September. Tellering's articles from Vienna against the brutal reaction that smashed the revolution were fiery and full of revolutionary fervor—"violently revolutionary to an extravagant extent," Engels said later.[9] Expelled from Vienna at the year's end, Tellering came to Cologne to edit Hermann Becker's *Westdeutsche Zeitung;* and before long he published a denunciatory pamphlet against Becker.

In reply to an inquiry near the end of his life, Engels recalled what he knew about Tellering:

> Our Vienna correspondent was a certain Müller-Tellering from Coblenz, fanatical like all Coblenzers and a first-class brawler. After his return to Germany, he came first to Cologne at the end of '49 and started a brawl with Red Becker. Then he came to London; on account of some unimportant personal business (which, given somewhat less perversity on his part, would have been straightened out in two minutes of conversation) he immediately started a brawl with us too, and right off launched a pamphlet... Then he went to America, tried to raise a stink against us, but faded away very soon.[10]

The "personal business" over which Tellering exploded like a firecracker was (hard to believe, but Tellering says so) something about tickets to a GWEA ball which Engels refused to help him get free.[11] If one declines to believe him, then the alternative explanation is that he was a mental case (which many believed anyway) or that the whole thing was a pretext, which hypothesis is not inconsistent with any other. Certainly, Tellering had already shown that he was lining up politically with the right-wing German Democratic wing of the emigration and against Marx's friends.[12] By April, we find, Tellering was operating as part of the anti-Marx clique in the emigration (with Struve, R. Schramm, Dr. Bauer, etc.) and was helping to spread the rumor (knee-jerk *A*) that the refugee-aid committee supported by Marx was pocketing the funds it collected.[13]

Such were the circumstances under which this "first-class brawler" announced Marx's future dictatorship. Even so, Tellering's pamphlet is deeply disappointing to all of us who want to find out what dictatorial crimes Marx had committed; for this information never appears. The writing is often incoherent; one never finds out exactly what he is complaining, or ranting, about—outside of the fact that GWEA, or the CL, expelled him on the basis of a commission headed by *Willich* (who was already Marx's opponent in the League, not his ally).

Above all, the pamphlet is filled with the coarsest anti-Semitic epithets of the raving kind. To call this pamphlet anti-Semitic may be misleading, for that label has been somewhat devalued by misuse. An article, which tells far more than anyone wants to know about Tellering and his pamphlet, rightly says that its anti-Semitic gibberish "recalls the Nazi *Stürmer*" This article deplores the fact that other opponents of Marx, such as "Heinzen, Ruge, R. Schramm, Struve, Willich, etc." took up Tellering as if he were a respectable person, and that Arnold Ruge even sought to "exalt" Tellering at Marx's expense in a piece in the Bremen press.[14] The writer was apparently unaware of the unwritten law of anti-Marxism, which is that anyone who attacks Marx is a pure and moral person interested only in Truth and Justice.

This disappointing pamphlet with the sensational title does nothing with its 'dictatorship' theme, either. 'Dictator', 'dictatorship', 'dictatorial' are used a few times, as when Tellering exclaims: "Marx, the future German dictator, is a Jew . . ."[15] But there is no reference to the term or idea 'dictatorship of the proletariat' in any form, and, although Tellering has clearly read Marx's *Class Struggles in France* (for he refers to it), he does not mention its passages on any relevant matter.

After Tellering took his half-cracked brain to America in 1852, Marx occasionally heard echoes of his anticommunist imprecations floating back across the Atlantic. It seems that Marx "had something" on Tellering that would "demolish him, not only in the eyes of *our* party but in the eyes of *all* parties."[16] But he was reluctant to use it: "To launch a public scandal with such a crackbrain would do him too much honor, and that is the whole aim of his maneuver."[17]

But 'Telleringesque' *(Telleringsche)* entered Marx's private vocabulary as a word to describe a vile slanderer. This is a kind of immortality.

3. WILLICH'S "DICTATORSHIP"

We can observe by now—long before 1874 when Engels will comment on it explicitly—that while Marx persists in *speaking of class* dictatorship, everyone else thinks of dictatorship in the traditional terms. This is scarcely surprising, to be sure, for it takes time and experience for a new idea to sink in.

Now we have to see how this pattern—reversion to traditional dictatorship—was true even of that section of the Communist League that split with Marx in 1850: the Willich-Schapper group, which continued to use the League's name.

The traditional approach was already indicated in the debate that took place when the Central Committee split on September 15, 1850. After Marx's exposition of the Willich-Schapperite position,[18] Schapper replied in a speech that included the following:

The issue is whether at the outset we ourselves do the head-chopping or get our heads chopped off. . . . When we get in, we can take such measures as assure the proletariat of rule. I am fanatical about this view. But the Central Committee has favored the opposite.[19]

It must be noticed that in Schapper's perspective—not argued but taken for granted—the Communists' conquest of power does not establish the rule of the proletariat: it makes possible the (subsequent) taking of measures to "assure" the rule of the proletariat. If there is a substantial interval between the rule (dictatorship) of the party and the rule (dictatorship) of the proletariat, Schapper would not be surprised. *The immediate goal is assumed to be the dictatorship of the victorious party,* or at least of its Central Committee. This was not a "Blanquist" deviation; it was the standard leftist view, which the Blanquists proper naturally shared.

This view of the matter was confirmed by the line of the Willich-Schapper league after it tore free of the Marx tendency and went off on its own. The Willichized league reverted to the conspiratorial pattern that Marx had so sharply limned in his book review only a few months before,[20] and thus it made it easy for the German government to stage the Cologne Communist trial of 1852 on the basis of agent-provoked "plots," as Marx explained in his pamphlet on the trial.[21] Part of the government's case was based on real documents seized in house searches—documents produced by the Willich-Schapper group to define their own politics. In the summer of 1851 the group's Paris congress adopted a programmatic statement of directives in case of revolution, titled "Instructions for the League Before, During and After the Revolution." This and other documents, including a list of "Demands of the People," were published by the government as part of the indictment. *

These Willich-Schapper documents contain no formulation resembling 'dictatorship of the proletariat'.

The "Demands of the People" is actually a list of measures to be taken by the victorious revolution. The first point would have been treated by Marx with simple hilarity: "At the moment the revolution breaks out, all existing governmental authorities cease to exist"—would it were so! The second point gets down to Willichite reality: the "armed people" elect revolutionary committees "which take all power into their hands" and send delegates to a central committee; and "The Central Committee has dictatorial power."

The judiciary is replaced by "tribunals that will be decided on by the

---

* Both documents are cited here from a curious pamphlet published in 1920 by a Social-Democratic official explaining his conversion to the Communist Party: Ernst Drahn's *Karl Marx und Friedrich Engels ueber die Diktatur des Proletariats*. He cites the documents from an old compilation by the German police chiefs Wermuth and Stieber (see Bibliography). Drahn assumes that Marx must have agreed with them, for he has not the least idea of the relation of the Willich-Schapper group to Marx.[22]

revolutionary committees, and will be assigned to commissars appointed by the Central Committee."[23]

The dictatorship of the Central Committee is reiterated in the "Instructions," which offers a somewhat more detailed scenario in its Section B. Not only has the "dictatorship of the proletariat" disappeared: the proletariat itself has vanished, its place being taken by something called the "fourth estate." The revolution puts all power in the hands of the People's Army, which is "under the control of the representatives of the fourth estate" (though there is no provision for the election of these "representatives"). As before, the "insurrectionary committees" elect a Central Committee. "This Central Committee has dictatorial power," states the program laconically as before.

All government subdivisions are replaced by corresponding "committees":

At the head of each stands a government commissar. At the disposal of each commissar is a detachment of the revolutionary People's Army.

The socioeconomic program calls for a thoroughgoing militarization of labor.* The new state, which will be the "societal capitalist" *(Gesellschaftskapitalist)*, guarantees a job to every citizen.

Those who are employed in this way are state workers *[Staatsarbeiter]*, and their existence is inseparably bound up with that of the new state. Where the workers are revolutionary, the election of foremen will be left to them; where they are not, the latter will be decided by the commissars.

The last sentence is my favorite: its contemplation is recommended.

The program then provides for the gradual fusion of People's Army and statified labor force, and for the complete statification of all children. Near the end, looking to the future, there is finally a provision for the eventual introduction of universal suffrage.[25]

Elaborations of such plans for party dictatorships were a dime-a-dozen in this period, and Willich's fantasy should not be considered specially interesting—except in one respect: the people who adopted this document at their congress were, in effect, counterposing it to the political statements previously written for the Communist League by Marx. The Willich-Schapper

* This is the *opposite* of the conception of an "industrial army" pioneered by Charles Fourier, adopted by Weitling and Théodore Dézamy, very popular in the early socialist movement, also mentioned in the *Communist Manifesto*. This idea looked to the industrialization of the military, not the militarization of industry, that is, the transformation of the army into a framework for useful labor. It merged with another leftist proposal, for putting standing armies to productive use instead of having them simply draining off resources. Marx associated the military like regimentation of labor with the organization of labor in the modern factory, as described very early in the Manifesto and Engels' *Condition of the Working Class in England*, and most vividly in *Capital*.[24]

statements do not contain the least echo of the political thinking found in (say) the March "Address to the Communist League."

Marx and his friends did not have to wait for the discovery of these documents to get acquainted with Willich's yearning for a military dictatorship; this was already a by-word. In the fall of 1850 Conrad Schramm set out to get documentary evidence by means of a trick or hoax. He wrote a letter to Willich in the name of Hermann Becker of Cologne, offering Willich a "military dictatorship," specifying the complete suppression of the press, etc. "That ass" Willich fell into the trap, "bombarded" Becker with letters about this coming glory, and "readied an emissary for immediate dispatch." (So Marx summarized the ploy in 1851.)

> ... [Willich] has already adopted the lordly ways of a Cromwell II, has grown irritable, no longer tolerates any contradiction, and has assigned Becker the task of making a revolution in Cologne, after which he declares himself ready to take over the supreme command.[26]

The letters sent by this "communist Cromwell" (Marx's term)[27] apparently laid out Willich's dictatorial conceptions in some detail.[28] Engels chortled over Schramm's trick to smoke out Willich's real ambitions: Willich was a "muttonhead" for not having seen through the offer of dictatorship—"But the opportunity for a military dictatorship in the Rhine province, without any press that could bother him, *sapristi*, this naturally must have turned the head of this woodenheaded duffer. Typical master-at-arms and drill-sergeant type!"[29] It seems that, according to Willich's epistolary revelations, "all 'literary elements' were to be eradicated root and branch and the dictatorship of the mobilized Eifel peasants proclaimed."[30]

Later, when Willich was publishing scurrilous attacks on Marx in America, Marx returned to this episode in his reply, quoting a statement by Wilhelm Steffen, who had seen Willich's letters to Becker—

> [letters, wrote Steffen] in which the great Field Marshal and social Messiah sends out from England the order to capture Cologne, to confiscate private property, to establish an artificially contrived military dictatorship, to introduce a military-social code of laws, to ban all newspapers except *one,* which would have to publish daily orders about the prescribed mode of thought and behavior, and a quantity of further details.[31]

In his *Hen Vogt* (1860) Marx printed another appreciation of Willich as a "despot."[32] In his 1885 sketch of the history of the Communist League, Engels included a vignette of Willich:

> . . . entirely the prophet, convinced of his personal mission as the predestined liberator of the German proletariat and as such a direct

claimant as much to political as to military dictatorship. Thus, to the primitive Christian communism previously preached by Weitling was added a kind of communist Islam.[33]

In 1851, Willich's "dictatorship" was still prominent in their minds when Marx and Engels ran into another case: Techow's.

4. TECHOW'S "DICTATORSHIP"

On September 23, 1851, when he began writing a letter to Engels, Marx had just read about the publication of the Willichite document "Instructions &c." in the French and German press and about police efforts to attribute it to the "Marx party." A "stupid business," he grumbled. What he really wanted to discuss in the letter, however, was not Willich's jape, which he dismissed with a few lines, but an essay he had just read in *the New-Yorker Staatszeitung* on revolution and war by Gustav Techow. Only—it led him back to Willich, we will see.

Gustav Techow, whom we have already met in connection with the Revolutionäre Zentralisation group in Switzerland,[34] was an ex-lieutenant in the Prussian army, who had taken part in the storming of the Berlin arsenal at the outset of the revolution. In 1849 he became chief of staff of the Palatinate revolutionary army. After its defeat, he emigrated to London, where he discussed RZ unity with the Communist League. In 1852 he was going to remove himself from our scene by going to Australia.

Techow's long essay, titled "Outline of the Coming War,"[35] envisaged a revolution combined with the inevitable war that would determine if Europe would be "republican or Cossack." Besides discussing some technical-military aspects of Techow's article (Engels' bailiwick), Marx picked out and stated what would be his target: Techow's basic "political tendency" as expressed in his presentation.

This was the thesis that a revolution had to be organized as a military dictatorship in order to prevent the expression of political differences within the ranks of the revolution until after the victory has been won. This was also the real issue behind Willich's fantasy-dictatorship, and would continue to be a basic line of division in the socialist movement. This is of such great significance that it is remarkable that this letter has been so thoroughly ignored.

First of all, Marx summarized Techow's viewpoint in such a way as to make the choices obvious. Here the formulation of the question is almost enough to express the viewpoint. Marx presents Techow's "lessons" with the main targets underlined:

Constituent assemblies of a country are not capable of organizing for a war. *They always waste their time on questions of internal politics,* while the *time* for their *solution* comes only *after victory.*
... Organization for a war, in the republican camp just as much as in the royalist, can be based only on compulsion [not on "political enthusiasm," Techow says]... Even more than in the internal organization of a country, democratic principles can be applied in armies only after the victory of the revolution.[36]

Still summarizing Techow's view, he ties it up with Cavaignac's dictatorship and Willich:

[Techow believes] No revolution breaks out, i.e., no party struggle, no civil war, no class discord, until after the *ending of the war* and the fall of Russia. But in order to organize these armies for this war, *force* is needed. And where is *this force to come from?* From General Cavaignac or a similar military dictator in France who has his generals in Germany and northern Italy. *Voilà la solution,* which is not very far removed from Willich's ideas.

Marx argues that this conception is false:

World war, i.e., in the thinking of the revolutionary Prussian lieutenant, [means] the rule of the military over the civil sector at least provisionally. But how any general whatever—even if the old Napoleon himself rose from the grave—is to get not only the means but also this influence without preceding and simultaneous *internal* struggles, without the damned "internal politics"—on this the oracle is silent.

This desire for revolution without "internal politics," without a democratic arena of "discord," is, Marx suggests, the aspiration of Democratic liberals, for it is they who pretend that politics is "classless":

At least "the pious wish" of the future world-warriors, which finds its suitable political expression precisely in the classless politicians and Democrats as such, has been clearly expressed.[37]

Thus, by a principle well known to Hegel, the bourgeois and petty-bourgeois Democrats, who objected so piously to "communist dictatorship," found internal revolutionary democracy a terrible inconvenience and turned to their own *good* dictatorship—as we have seen.

Writing to Engels, Marx of course did not have to spell out the whole argument. Engels' reply spelled out some more of it, with respect to the military aspect that most insistently demands dictatorship according to the Techow types: *discipline.*

... aside from the well-intentioned plan of suppressing the bothersome "internal politics," hence the actual revolution, by a military dictator as yet undiscovered (despite Cavaignac and Willich), and aside from this very characteristic political formulation of the view taken by these gentlemen on the revolution, one should note, militarily speaking:

(1) Iron discipline, which alone can secure victory, is exactly the reverse of the "shelving of internal politics" and of military dictatorship. Where is this discipline to come from? ... It is an obvious fact that disorganization of the army and thoroughgoing loosening of discipline have up to now been both a precondition and result of every victorious revolution.[38]

For Marx and Engels, the discipline of a revolutionary army had to arise precisely out of its "internal politics"; for Techow and the Willich types, discipline was imposed by the ordinary hierarchic military structure, which always finds dissent disturbing and disorganizing.

It must not be supposed that either Techow or Willich represented some unusually dictatorial point of view: every military structure they knew was a dictatorship, and if the revolution was to be militarily effective, they instinctively felt that it had to be a dictatorship too. On the basis of this thinking, a 'dictatorship of the proletariat' made no sense. From Marx's standpoint, they represented new "Cromwells" and "Cavaignacs" at the levers of the old military and state structures.

5. ECCARIUS, THE "VRAI PEUPLE," AND A NEAR-LOCUS

Since the key to the term 'dictatorship of the proletariat' is the concept of *class dictatorship,* this concept is of interest to us whenever we meet it.

We meet it, for example, in an article by Marx's friend and associate J. G. Eccarius, in January 1851, published in Harney's *Friend of the People AS* "The Last Stage of Bourgeois Society." Eccarius, a tailor who was trying to become a political writer, was getting eager help from Marx at this time, and there can be little doubt that Marx at least previewed the manuscript.[39]

Eccarius' main theme was the revolutionary basis for supporting bourgeois reforms—but, he emphasized, not as friends but as foes of the bourgeois reform movement. At the very end of the four-part essay, he formulated the basic thesis of the March "Address to the Communist League." If we help them as foes, with independent class organization, "we can drive them farther than they wish to go themselves" and eventually defeat them. But if we cooperate with them as friends, we will be thrown into confusion whenever they choose to halt the revolution.

14. *More Reverberations* 239

If we cooperate with them, we give all command of the course to be pursued into their hands, we submit to their dictatorship...[40]

Eccarius, of course, had read more than one passage in which Marx had viewed the rule of the bourgeois democracy as a class dictatorship; there is no need to comment on this usage.

Also of interest is an exchange of letters between Marx and Engels a few months later, in December 1851, right after Bonaparte's coup. Marx's first momentary reaction to the coup was "bewilderment,"[41] to such an extent that he uncharacteristically fell into the syndrome of "the worse the better": Bonaparte's seizure of power may offer better possibilities of revolution than "the National Assembly and its generals" (like Cavaignac). He added: "And the dictatorship of the National Assembly was standing at the gate."[42]

The "dictatorship of the National Assembly" would simply have meant the assumption of all power by the representative assembly of the democracy, power taken away from Bonaparte. We have met this usage, too, in Marx before.

Engels' letter, the next day, expected Bonaparte to rule as a "military dictator," basing himself primarily on the army.[43] Then, the day after, he continued the discussion on the impact of Bonaparte's coup with an excursus to Proudhon's latest book, which he had just read. The book was *Idée Générale de la Révolution;* Proudhon's introduction was addressed "To the Bourgeoisie." Contrary to myths about the Father of Anarchism, it was a straightforward call to the bourgeoisie to kindly make the revolution from above. Since it involved a conception of dictatorship, let us devote a word to the nostrum he was temporarily flogging, just as he was shortly going to appeal to Bonaparte himself to make the revolution which the bourgeoisie neglected.

Proudhon appealed to the bourgeoisie, which *alone* (he stressed) "proclaimed all the revolutionary ideas" and alone "put forward the principles and laid the foundations of the Revolution of the nineteenth century—"You, bourgeois of France: yours is the initiative in the progress of humanity." In 1793, continued Proudhon, the bourgeoisie had been temporarily ousted by "the sans-culotte people," the "tribunes of the people"—"presumptuous...chatterboxes." All the latter could do was continue the bourgeoisie's work. Unfortunately the bourgeoisie, feeling hurt, "seemed" to turn to reaction. Proudhon appealed to the bourgeoisie for "reconciliation with the proletariat"[44]—the same proletariat the bourgeoisie had recently subjected to the bloodiest counter-revolutionary massacre that had been seen up to that day.

In this appeal to the bourgeoisie, Proudhon argued that, in 1848 as in 1793, the power was in the hands of men who "were not *of the* people" (my emphasis added).[45] Writing to Marx, Engels filled out Proudhon's thought with the phrase "the true people" *(vrai peuple).* As in many letters between Marx and Engels, the line of argument is rather telescoped, or syncopated. (My bracketed interpolations are guesses.)

> See Proudhon: *Appel à la Bourgeoisie,* page 2. And what reasoning! If the insurgents [of June 1848?] were beaten, this is due to the fact that they were not the *vrai peuple;* the *vrai peuple* cannot be beaten; and if the *vrai peuple* did not fight [against Bonaparte's coup?], this is due to the fact that it did not want to fight for the National Assembly; to be sure, it may be objected here that the *vrai peuple,* once victorious, would have been dictator itself, but it was unable to think of this, being taken by surprise; and then too, it has been duped so often![46]

It is clear that Engels' statement, "the *vrai peuple,* once victorious, would have been dictator itself," is formulated from Engels' standpoint, not Proudhon's.

It would be unfruitful to try to pin down Proudhon's thought about the revolutionary leaders who were not "of the [true] people" —given that he was celebrating the leaders of the bourgeoisie and its intellectuals as the representatives of the People *par excellence.* When Proudhon attacks the people of 1793 for "dictatorship," the present-day reader may fail to understand that he is charging them with the sin of being extreme democrats. Later in his book, he characteristically denounces "direct government" —meaning here government directly by an Assembly that chooses and controls the Executive. This "direct government" was the "stairway to dictatorship" and the "anteroom to despotism."[47] In point of fact, insofar as Robespierre gained dictatorial power, it was by reversing this relationship; but do not send to ask of Proudhon why the control of an Executive by a democratic assembly is a step to dictatorship.

No one should think that Proudhon's appeal to the bourgeoisie to make the revolution was simply meant as a trick of some sort. In his journal, jotted down when he began to think about this book, he wrote down this germinal thought: "It is the bourgeoisie that will save us. They want liberty."[48]

In 1852, when the bourgeoisie had not yet saved France, Engels wrote up his explanation of a question he had been working on since December. Ernest Jones's *Notes to the People* gave his article a long explanatory title: "Real Causes Why the French Proletarians Remained Comparatively Inactive in December Last," that is, why there had been little resistance in France to Bonaparte's coup. Looking ahead, Engels wrote:

> ∞How long it may be ere both the working and the capitalist-classes may have regained strength and self-reliance enough to come out and openly claim, each for themselves, the dictatorship of France, of course nobody can tell...[49]

This is a good example of the coordinate counterposition of proletarian and bourgeois dictatorship. In fact, it may reasonably be argued that this passage qualifies as an independent locus for the use of 'dictatorship of the proletariat' in content if not in form (similar to locus 1b).

Like all such cases, the counterposition of dictatorships makes clear that what is involved is the *class content* of the regime and not the form of government or type of political institutions.

15 | FROM WEYDEMEYER TO VOGT

We now come to one of the two loci most frequently cited, the only one that occurs in a personal letter by Marx. We will see that it too is a reverberation from 1850. Explaining why it came to Marx's pen at this point will throw some light on what he meant by it.

This locus revolves around the figure of Joseph Weydemeyer. It occurred in a letter by Marx *to* Weydemeyer, but by putting some facts together we will see that Weydemeyer was not so much the recipient as the begetter.

1. INTRODUCING WEYDEMEYER

Joseph Weydemeyer was born the same year as Marx, 1818, the son of a Prussian government official in the Westphalian city of Münster. Educated in a Berlin military academy, he entered on a career in the army. As a 24-year-old artillery lieutenant in Minden, in 1842, he became acquainted with the circle around the Cologne *Rheinische Zeitung*. Marx was one of the contributors and supporters of the paper from the beginning of the year, and in October became editor. Weydemeyer discussed social questions with the *Rheinische Zeitung* people and in a study circle with fellow officers, some of whom likewise became communists (Willich, Anneke, Korff, Beust, for example). Having been imbued with socialist-communist ideas, Weydemeyer quit the army after six years as a professional officer, and went over to journalism.

In 1844 he joined the staff of the *Trier'sche Zeitung*, which was then influenced by Karl Grün's 'True Socialism." He read *The Holy Family* and Engels' *Condition of the Working Class in England*, visited Marx in Paris, and in short by 1845 became an enthusiastic supporter of Marx's new ideas. In 1845 he entered into a journalistic partnership with Otto Lüning, as an associate editor of the *Westphälische Dampfboot.* Visiting Marx in Brussels in 1846, he was definitively converted to Marx's communism, and took part in the work of the

242

15. From Weydemeyer to Vogt 243

Communist Correspondence Committee in Brussels. In 1847 he joined the Communist League along with Marx, and became an organizational as well as literary colleague of Marx's, and also a warm personal friend. With the outbreak of the 1848 revolution, he became active in Hamm, which he represented at the first Democratic Congress. In July he went along with Lüning again to help edit the *Neue Deutsche Zeitung*, first in Darmstadt and then in Frankfurt: here we met him in Chapter 13.[1]

Weydemeyer remained on as an associate editor of the *NDZ* until government harassment made continued publication of the paper impossible, so that it ceased appearing in December 1850. He fled in good time to Switzerland, remained active in the CL and in touch with Marx, but, unable to find work, finally decided to emigrate to the United States.

Soon after arriving in New York in November 1851, he launched the journal *Die Revolution*, of which two issues appeared. During the 1850s he helped form the Proletarian League of New York along lines influenced by his conception of Marx's approach, was active in the German-American labor movement (especially in a New York strike wave in 1853), helped establish *Die Reform* until it died in April 1854, did free-lance writing and lecturing. Then moving to Milwaukee for a job as notary and surveyor, he worked in the socialist and labor movement there and in Chicago. Returning to New York, he continued his trade-union work, and in 1857 joined the Communist Club of New York.

The Civil War impelled him into the Union army, where he rose to colonel (1865). After the war he worked as a county surveyor in St. Louis, still writing for the German-American press. Throughout, up to his death in a cholera epidemic in 1866, he remained a correspondent and disciple of Marx, according to his lights.[2]

A word is necessary on the label "disciple of Marx." There is a tendency in works on socialist history to pin the tag 'Marxist' on anyone who was influenced by Marx's ideas in any way or to any degree. How valid the label may be can only be discussed in terms of cases, but a general caution must be issued: Marx should not be held responsible for all the acts and words of everyone who was indebted to him for some degree of insight into social problems. The 'Marxist' label has been carried to absurd lengths—as when Laurence Gronlund is called a Marxist—but even in a legitimate case like Weydemeyer, it should not be supposed that all of the ideas he expressed came from Marx. How was he supposed to have come by a reasonably adequate acquaintance with Marx's complex of socioeconomic and political views—by merely reading the Manifesto? by reading *The Holy Family?* by correspondence? by sympathetic vibrations? And this aside from the question of whether Marx was a 'Marxist' in 1845 when Weydemeyer consorted with him in Brussels. The fact is that, even for most of Marx's associates, their 'Marxism' was a fairly thin layer superimposed on the mass of common socialist-communist ideas which Marxism was eventually going to replace.

In actuality, what we are going to see is Weydemeyer trying to express the ideas of the *Communist Manifesto,* and doing the best he could. In this sense he was writing as a Marxist.

2. WEYDEMEYER'S ARTICLE ON "DICTATORSHIP"

Immediately after his arrival in New York on November 7, 1851, Weydemeyer began writing for the radical German-American press. He wrote his first article for what he considered the best of the local socialist publications, the *Turn-Zeitung* of New York, a semimonthly that had been only recently founded by the Turnerbund. Weydemeyer's article appeared in the third number, dated January 1, 1852, which also included the first installment of Engels' *Peasant War in Germany* (reprinted from the *NRZ Revue)* as well as Weydemeyer's announcement of his own forthcoming weekly.

The title of Weydemeyer's article was "Die Diktatur des Proletariats" (The Dictatorship of the Proletariat). This was no doubt the only article with a title of this sort until the twentieth century.

Yet, except glancingly in the last paragraph, the article had nothing to say about the 'dictatorship' of the proletariat. It was about the *rule* of the proletariat as the aim expounded in the *Communist Manifesto.* Most of the article is a condensation of a good part of the Manifesto.

There was a specific reason why an exposition of the Manifesto would have been on Weydemeyer's mind. Shortly before he sailed into New York harbor, the Manifesto had appeared for the first time in an American publication, even if in unfinished form. Weitling's *Republik der Arbeiter* had started running installments on October 11, and cut them off in mid-course on November 8 (the day after Weydemeyer's arrival). Since Weitling was furiously anti-Marx and had printed attacks on Marx only weeks before, this was a surprising development; but what had actually happened was that Weitling's departure from New York on a cross-country propaganda trip was utilized by the substitute editor (who has not been identified). The Manifesto installments stopped abruptly when Weitling got back.[3]

This was not the only evidence of interest in the Manifesto. Eduard Ignaz Koch, an ex-priest who had taken part in the revolution in Germany, emigrated in 1850, and turned to journalism in New York, had recently written Marx asking for a bundle of copies of the Manifesto. Marx sent him a batch of twenty, plus the Macfarlane English translation of 1850, suggesting that he publish the translation in pamphlet form. Then—no word from Koch. Even while Weydemeyer was still on the high seas, Marx shot him a letter with some urgent publishing proposals, including the suggestion that Weydemeyer rescue the Macfarlane translation from Koch and carry out the pamphlet publication plan.[4] Weydemeyer found this letter awaiting him in New York. On December 1 he wrote back that he would try to get the English Manifesto edition published through *New York Daily Tribune* editor Charles A. Dana; but in fact nothing ever came of the project.[5]

Weydemeyer must have started writing his *Turn-Zeitung* article about the same time he was trying to accomplish this plan. As mentioned, he expounded much of the Manifesto—with some trimmings of his own: development of capitalism, modern industry, class struggle, role of the petty-bourgeoisie and other classes, etc.*

In view of this background, one aspect of his article is puzzling. The article quotes two passages, complete with quote marks, from the *Communist Manifesto*, but attaches no ascription or identification. Indeed, Marx's name is nowhere mentioned. Yet in that issue of the *Turn-Zeitung* Weydemeyer had an announcement of his own forthcoming magazine *Die Revolution* featuring "the collaboration of the editors of the former *Neue Rheinische Zeitung*, Karl Marx, Friedrich Engels, Ferdinand Freiligrath, etc." Why then was Marx's name suppressed in the article? Regrettably, the only hypothesis that occurs to me is the Eccarius syndrome.[6]

The statement about "dictatorship" in Weydemeyer's last paragraph was entirely his own. Failing to find any passage in the Manifesto or elsewhere in Marx to explain 'dictatorship', he had to get the answer out of his own head. It came out as follows:

> If a revolution is to be victoriously carried through, it will require a concentrated power, a dictatorship at its head. Cromwell's dictatorship was necessary in order to establish the supremacy of the English bourgeoisie; the terrorism of the [first] Paris Commune and of the Committee of Public Safety alone succeeded in breaking the resistance of the feudal lords on French soil. Without the dictatorship of the proletariat which is concentrated in the big cities, the bourgeois reaction will not be done away with.

Contrary to the impression given by translation, the article (outside of the title) does not offer the term *Diktatur des Proletariats*. It speaks, in the above-cited paragraph, of "*die Diktatur des in den grossen Städten konzentrirten Proletariats*": that is, the words "concentrated in the big cities" are inserted as a restrictive qualifier limiting the meaning of "proletariat." (An awkward translation would be: "the dictatorship of the urban-

---

* Regarding the text of "Weydemeyer's article, see the Foreword, Section 4.

concentrated proletariat.") Now, this means that Weydemeyer has wrenched the concept back to the old formula which in France meant the *dictatorship of Paris* over the rest of the country—a popular formula typical of the Blanquists but by no means restricted to them, as we saw in the case of Louis Blanc.[7] One can be sure Weydemeyer was quite unaware that Marx and Engels rejected and ridiculed this notion.

A second characteristic of Weydemeyer's formulation is indicated by the first sentence of the paragraph. If the "revolution," i.e., the revolutionary regime, has "a concentrated power, a dictatorship at its *head*," it cannot itself *be* that dictatorship. Weydemeyer's formulation is clearly conditioned by the idea, familiar to him before he ever read the *Communist Manifesto*, of a dictatorship *over* the revolution, the prospect of a "concentrated power" dominating the proletariat. Weydemeyer too did not grasp the point about *class* dictatorship, despite the fact that he had seen it repeatedly emphasized by Marx.

There was no obvious need for Weydemeyer to have given this title to the article, no compelling reason why he made 'dictatorship of the proletariat' the focus, at least terminologically, and for this reason had to invent an explanation of his own for the term 'dictatorship'. The psychological reason must have been the impact made upon him by the *NDZ* exchange of 1850. Outside of Lüning, he was the one man whom that exchange involved personally, and it can scarcely be considered accidental that this same man made 'dictatorship of the proletariat' a central term eighteen months later. That Weydemeyer's relations with Lüning grew tenser around the episode of the *NDZ* exchange is a known fact, not a speculation, and so it is not very speculative to believe that there must have been some lively argumentation going on, between the brothers-in-law, over the points in dispute between Lüning and Marx. One has a right to presume that the term 'dictatorship of the proletariat' was thus driven deeper into Weydemeyer's consciousness.

The next link in the chain produced locus 4.

3. LOCUS 4: MARX'S LETTER

Weydemeyer must have sent Marx and Engels a copy of his *Turn-Zeitung* article, of course; we know he sent other articles. Unfortunately it does not show up in the extant correspondence.

After receiving a letter from Weydemeyer dated January 5, 1852, Marx and Engels grumbled about not hearing further from their friend for about a month. Finally, Weydemeyer's letter of February 6 arrived at Marx's on February 18 or so (the date Marx sent it on to Engels). The separate replies sent back by Marx and Engels did not mention the *Turn-Zeitung* article. Weydemeyer wrote again on February 9, to Engels (who replied on February 27); and he may well have written again to Marx by, say, February 21.[8]

The point is this: when Marx wrote to Weydemeyer on March 5, he must have seen the *Turn-Zeitung* article by then—even though he did not mention it. He did make a comment for Weydemeyer's edification on "your article against Heinzen," and from there on, his letter discussed a series of points involved in current or possible polemics with Heinzen. After a train of thought that takes about three printed pages, he added: "From the preceding notes, take whatever you think good."[9]

This indicates that what Marx was doing, in most of this letter, was making suggestions to Weydemeyer for material to be used in subsequent articles, especially against Heinzen, whose name continued to dominate the letter.

This is the context of the famous passage which is our locus 4. The polemic is against Heinzen's "silly" refusal to recognize classes in society. American capitalism, writes Marx, is too immature to have developed a sense of the class antagonisms in its society; for example, its top economist, Carey, denounces Ricardo as a fomenter of class struggle and accuses all the leading European economists of tearing society apart.

> As for myself now, no credit is due to me for having discovered the existence of classes in modern society or the struggle among them. Bourgeois historians had, long before me, described the historical development of this struggle of classes and bourgeois economists [had described] their economic anatomy.

This statement, by the way, will not entirely stand up: it is a "polemical exaggeration" in reverse—a polemical minimization. To discuss this further would be digressive, but it is enough to say that its function in this line of thought is to emphasize the newness of the claim that follows:

[Locus 4]
What I did that was new was (1) to show that the *existence of classes* is simply bound up with *certain historical phases of the development of production;* (2) that the class struggle necessarily leads to the *dictatorship of the proletariat;* (3) that this dictatorship itself only constitutes the transition to the *abolition of all classes* and to a *classless society.*[10]

This striking statement was immediately followed by another blow against "ignorant louts like Heinzen" who deny not only the class struggle but even the existence of classes, and this in turn led to the aforementioned invitation to Weydemeyer to use these notes (or glosses, *Glossen*) for further articles. They *were* used in this way, the following year, by Weydemeyer's colleague Cluss, with whom he shared Marx's letters,[11] but Cluss's adaptations made no use of locus 4, which must have appeared to him as a personal digression or footnote.

In context, Marx was emphasizing that—though not the discoverer of classes and class struggle—he had shown why class struggle leads *to proletarian revolution*. Ordinarily, no doubt, he would have worded this in terms of 'rule of the proletariat', 'conquest of political power by the proletariat', or another of the formulations he customarily used. In substituting 'dictatorship of the proletariat' he was echoing the title of the article just published by Weydemeyer, who himself was echoing the recent *NDZ* exchange between Marx and Lüning, Marx was throwing in a phrase that had special associations for his correspondent; there was an "understood" background behind this usage in a private letter.

This is the sense in which Weydemeyer not merely received this notable passage in the mail but was effectively its initiator.

4. ECHO IN *HERR VOGT*

For about the next twenty years, between 1852 and 1871, there was no occurrence of any term like 'dictatorship of the proletariat' in any of Marx's and Engels' writings or letters.

In the context of our periodization[12] and of our central thesis,[13] we must point out that, during this lull between the storms of 1848-49 and 1870-71, Marx virtually cut all organizational ties and hence dropped all organizational problems, including any problem of relations with the Blanquists proper or with the Blanquist types in the movement.

But reverberations from the preceding period continued. An echo of sorts is encountered in Marx's work *Herr Vogt*, written and published in 1860. The events leading up to the writing of *Herr Vogt* are extremely complicated, like all scandalous episodes, but the details are essentially irrelevant to our present purposes.[14] The following summary will do.

Karl (or Carl) Vogt was a prominent public figure both as a scientist-naturalist and a political leader. His main reputation was as a Darwinian scientist, a professor at Giessen and later Geneva, who wrote works of popular science and advocated a crude form of mechanical materialism. In 1848 he was a member of the Frankfurt National Assembly, and in June 1849 was named one of the five Reich regents. His main political work, *Studien zur gegenwärtigen Lage Europas*, was published in 1859; it caught Marx's (and others') interest because of its advocacy of pro-Bonapartist policies. The later revelation by the Paris Commune in 1871 that he was actually paid by the

Bonaparte government—"almost beyond doubt," as McLellan says[15]—has tended unwarrantably to obscure the fact that, paid or not, this noted liberal was a Bonapartist propagandist.

Through a series of events in which Marx was at first only peripherally involved, Vogt was publicly denounced in 1859 as a pro-Bonapartist. Vogt, mistakenly believing that Marx had organized the entire campaign against him, answered in the Swiss press with an attack on Marx that was a tissue of scandalous fabrications. It is enough to mention that Vogt concocted a detailed story purporting to prove that Marx was the criminal leader of a gang of blackmailers and desperadoes, called the *Schwefelbande* ("Brimstone Gang") in the Geneva area in 1848-49. This story was embellished with phantasmagoria) touches so outlandish that no one could possibly believe that a respectable scientist and political figure had fabricated the tale not out of the whole cloth but out of noisome rags. Then, still in 1859, Vogt published these concoctions in a book, *Mein Prozess Gegen die Altgemeine Zeitung.*

Marx decided that, ridiculous though they were, Vogt's charges had to be publicly exposed as fabrications. And so, sad to relate, he had to suspend work on his economic opus and spend most of 1860 gathering the crushing mass of evidence which he presented in *Herr Vogt.* To be sure, there are passages in this book that are valuable for history and biography; and for modern readers a chapter dealing with Vogt's Bonapartist book (Chapter 8) is more interesting and useful than the exposure of this grand-daddy of anti-Marxist liars.

As far as our own subject is concerned, we must report that 'dictatorship of the proletariat' occurs in *Herr Vogt* several times; yet we have not listed a locus for it. The reason is that, with one partial exception of a sort, all the occurrences are in the course of quotations from other people.

Vogt's *Mein Prozess* had made repeated references to the term. His first one, for example, was in his preface:

> The Communist party with its "dictatorship of the proletariat," with the "destruction of every opposing personality," with "poison and dagger, robbery and pillage," was always the paralyzing Medusa-head ...[16]

At the very beginning of *Herr Vogt,* Marx quoted two other passages by Vogt that happened to contain references to the term; but he quoted them not *because* of this fact but in order to present the *Schwefelbande* fable. Vogt, as cited by Marx, wrote that the gang

> gradually got together in London and there revered Herr *Marx* as their visible chief. The political principle of these fellows was the dictatorship of the proletariat, etc.[17]

The original passage in Vogt did not end with "etc." but continued on, after "dictatorship of the proletariat," with the following: "and with this illusion they at first deceived many of the best people to be found among the refugees . . ."[18] This same passage occurred a second time in *Hen Vogt*, much further on, this time as part of a passage quoted from the editor of the Berlin *National-Zeitung,* which reprinted Vogt's slanders.[19]

The next passage cited by Marx, still about the *Schwefelbande,* included the following:

> Their chief is *Marx* . . . their watchword "Social Republic, Workers' Dictatorship"—their occupation, hatching leagues and conspiracies.[20]

In a couple of other passages, the term occurred in the course of letters printed by Marx as part of his evidence against Vogt. His friend Viktor Schily had sent him a letter about the real *Schwefelbande,* a group of free-spirited youth who had no connection with Marx, crime, or politics:

> They would have given a bad reception to anyone who would have wanted to spoil their siesta with Marx's political economy, with workers' dictatorship, etc.[21]

Here the term occurs as an echo of Vogt, and exactly the same is true when we come to the aforementioned exception—the passage which is not a quote from someone else but written by Marx. Vogt claims (says Marx) that Bonaparte has the support of the Paris workers and is "ruining the bourgeoisie"—

> Thus Louis Bonaparte is a *workers' dictator,* and as workers' dictator he is puffed up to the German workers in Switzerland by the same Vogt who, in his [book *Mein Prozess*], foams over with bourgeois indignation at the mere phrase "workers' dictatorship"![22]

Note that it is not Marx who is saying that Bonaparte is a "workers' dictator"; he is ascribing this puffery to Vogt, and by implication ridiculing it.

In none of these passages is there any special comment of any kind on "dictatorship of the proletariat," "workers' dictator," etc. The first passage we quoted, from Vogt's preface, lumped "dictatorship of the proletariat" with several unpleasant inventions of a nonpolitical nature. In the second passage, Vogt seemed to consider "dictatorship of the proletariat" an "illusion" attractive to the "best people among the refugees" but bad because unreal. In the third passage from Vogt, "Social Republic" and "Workers' Dictatorship" are perfectly coordinate—both, to be sure, reprehensible to any anticommunist but equally so. And when Marx finally uses the term himself, it is only to let Vogt confute himself, without making a substantive statement of his own about it.

In his own book Vogt himself made no comment about "dictatorship of the proletariat." He simply threw it in and exhibited it, along with various scurrilous mendacities of his own fabrication. It is true that, in the last passage cited, Marx said that Vogt foamed with indignation over the phrase, but this must have been a deduction from Vogt's way of exhibiting the phrase, not supported by a more specific attack. It seems to "sound bad" to him.

Thus from both sides, Vogt and Marx, no special content was ascribed to the term, nor any recognition that it *had* a special content that needed explanation.

5. MORE ECHOES

It remains to add that Vogt's practice in this respect was continued by his son. William Vogt's reverential biography of his father in 1896 simply repeated the original slanders, copied from *Mein Prozess,* in the course of which he followed the paternal pattern of mentioning "dictatorship of the proletariat" in passing. He did this twice in the section devoted to his father's anti-Marx campaign.[23]

The question may be raised where Vogt got the term in 1859. In the absence of any facts about this, the conjecture must be this: as a leading figure in the Frankfurt National Assembly, which Marx flayed in his *Neue Rheinische Zeitung,* it is quite possible that Vogt subsequently read Marx's *NRZ Revue* in 1850 with its articles on *The Class Struggles in France,* and even the exchange with Lüning in the *NDZ* (which, remember, had styled itself the organ of the Frankfurt National Assembly). When he started looking around in 1859 for some mud to throw at Marx, he either remembered this material or had it recalled to him by someone else. His evocation of the term in 1859 was therefore a belated echo from 1850: this is a reasonable presumption.

The fact that he picked up *this* term, rather than another, to go along with poison, pillage, poniards, and other pleasantries, *is* an indication that *the term had a rather high visibility.* We have already seen this in the way it was picked up by Lüning, Miquel, and Weydemeyer, each in his own way.

There had been a similar case in mid-1859. At this time Marx was helping the editorial work *of Das Volk,* the London GWEA's organ, and contributing to its columns. Together with editor Elard Biskamp, Marx wrote a series of satirical critiques of the democratic leader Gottfried Kinkel and his organ *Hermann,* under the title "Gatherings from the Press." In the last of these, a passage from Kinkel was quoted, ridiculing among others people who discuss "the great problem of whether in the next revolution the millennial regime of the journeymen tailors will dawn under the title *workers' dictatorship.*"[24]

Why the term occurred to Kinkel at this time is probably related to the Vogt affair, but I am not sure how the dates jibe. Vogt's slanders, in the great tradition, went echoing on into the future. When another democratic anticommunist of note, Heinzen, published his autobiographical *Erlebtes* in 1874, his venomous outpourings on Marx did not neglect Vogt's inventions about the *Schwefelbande*, as well as some of his very own.[25]

16 | THE MANY DICTATORSHIPS OF MOSES HESS

The figure of Moses Hess appears at this chronological point because we will be mainly interested in his operations of the 1860s, when they involved Marx peripherally. But in this chapter Marx himself will be on the sidelines. His 'dictatorship of the proletariat' will be conspicuous by its absence, or, to put it differently, the subject of the chapter is that it does not appear. The interest of the Hess story is that it plays the spotlight on what some *other* people meant by 'workers' dictatorship'.

Moses Hess's name is encountered down many of the byways of the first half century of socialist history, despite the fact that he founded no lasting school of socialism, made no theoretical contribution that is still remembered, and fathered no socialist organization. Ideologically, he did not stand still long enough to do any of these things. Few figures in this history have leaped with such volatile inconstancy from ism to ism, thus covering a good part of the territory: early communism, Proudhonism, anarchism, solipsism, "True Socialism," Marxism, Bonapartism, Bismarckism, Lassalleanism, Zionism, and some others for which suitable isms would have to be invented.

For this reason it is disgraceful that no book in English that is worth reading has been published on his career, and that the very valuable study by Silberner has not been translated. Silberner's virulently anti-Marx point of view would certainly not stand in the way of publication; at the same time Silberner's scholarship is incontestable. Much of the present chapter is based on his work.

1. INTRODUCING HESS

Six years before Marx, Hess was born to a well-to-do Jewish merchant of the Rhineland, and received a Jewish upbringing. With virtually no exposure to university education, he early became a journalist and began to write books. He made the acquaintance of socialism in Paris in the late 1830s, and became one of the first socialists (or communists) in Germany. In 1837, aged 25, he published a book that ambitiously offered a bird's-eye view of history, *Die heilige Geschichte der Menschheit* (The Sacred History of Humanity); four years later, a work on world politics, *Die europäische Triarchie* (The European Triarchy). At the same time he helped to found the new organ of left democracy in the Rhineland, the Cologne *Rheinische Zeitung,* of which Marx became editor in October 1842. Hess was a contributor and correspondent. In 1842 (he claimed) he converted Engels to communism, or to what he then called by that name. He wrote for the *Deutsch-Französische Jahrbücher* when Marx and Ruge got out its one double number; also in parallel to Marx, he wrote for the Paris *Vorwärts!* in 1844. He edited the Elberfeld *Gesellschaftsspiegel,* which Engels originally helped found but did not stay with.

In the following period Hess was the progenitor of "True Socialism." Engels attached Karl Grün's name to this school of socialism in a note to the *Communist Manifesto,* but it owed most to Hess. Auguste Cornu opines that this viewpoint was a retrogression for Hess,[1] but it was more like a zigzag. From about 1846, the inventor of "True Socialism" made the zag to go with the zig: as the revolutionary atmosphere heated up, he was more and more influenced by Marx's viewpoint, becoming about two-thirds Marxist and, for once in his life, a bit of a revolutionary. But this state of exaltation passed with the revolutionary crisis itself. By 1850 Hess lined up with the Willich-Schapper group against Marx; for a while he acted as secretary of the Willichite league.

In the lull of the fifties, Hess devoted himself largely to natural-science studies in Paris. Politically, his views shifted over to that substitute for revolution named Louis Bonaparte. His Bonapartism lasted well into the 1860s. In 1863 he joined up with Lassalle and indeed became a patriotic Lassallean, as well as an advocate along with his mentor of the Bismarckian revolution-from-above. By 1867 he broke with the Lassallean movement, now led by Schweitzer, and in 1868 joined the International, which he had sneered at previously.

It must be added that, in the course, he developed one of the most consciously thought-through theories of social-reformism then to be found, and might well have been the world-historic founder of a pre-Bernstein Bernsteinian-Revisionism if he had worked at it. Around the same period he struck off another germinal spark with his book *Rom und Jerusalem* (1862), which heralded Zionism. He died in 1875.

This sketch suggests that Hess discovered more than one dictator to make the revolution for him. The first was Louis Bonaparte, Emperor of the French. Hess was only one of the many leftists who saw Bonaparte as the enemy of capitalism and friend of the workers,[2] with the added advantage that Bonaparte was not one of the "generals without an army" of communism: *he* had power.

Like Lassalle [writes Silberner] Hess was also convinced that Napoleon III might be a despot personally, but that the principles on which he based his rule, and which he was forced to proclaim again and again, were democratic: the will of the people, universal suffrage, improvement of the condition of the working classes.[3]

On behalf of a group of émigré democrats in Paris, in March 1859, Hess drafted a confidential communication to Bonaparte suggesting that he make the revolution *s'il vous plaît*. The Emperor was for popular freedom, peace, and the repudiation of conquest—the "liberator of the peoples"; there are only three truly modern civilized societies in the world: the United States, Russia, and France.[4] This inclusion of the czarist autocracy along with the Bonapartist dictatorship means that Hess swallowed most of the contemporary fraud of the Revolution from Above.[5]

Marx heard about Hess's Bonapartist euphoria from his friend Schily, who reported that Hess was "so Bonapartist that even *a Frenchman* broke off relations with him."[6] (So Marx informed Engels.) But Marx, who was working on *Herr Vogt* at the time, may not have known what an extreme case this principled social-reformist had become by this time.

"We need," wrote Hess, "soldiers and generals, dictators, Emperors. To put down the counterrevolution we need Napoleons."[7] Bonaparte (thought Hess) is leading the revolution consciously and willingly; he is no longer savior of the monarchy but rather the "Dictator of the revolution, tomorrow perhaps Tribune of the People."[8] As late as 1863 Hess was calling Bonaparte "the testamentary executor of the French Revolution in Europe."[9]

Hess's Bonapartist views were similar to Karl Vogt's. Especially since Hess was much occupied with studies in natural science, Vogt's field, he became an admirer of Vogt as one of the "coryphees" of German popular-scientific literature. He does not seem to have been in touch with Vogt personally[10] (most likely, I think, because Vogt's anticommunism would have made him hostile to Hess). But Hess must have been sympathetic to Vogt's *Studien* of 1859, the book that first alerted Marx to Vogt's role as a Bonapartist propagandist.

By 1863, when Lassalle founded the General German Workers Association (GGWA), Hess was able to combine his enthusiasm for two dictators. At the GGWA founding congress in May 1863 Hess re-entered active socialist work by accepting Lassalle's appointment as the organization's representative in Cologne.

That summer, Hess published a pamphlet which showed that his enthusiasm for the Bonapartist dictatorship was not being replaced, just extended. The pamphlet *Rechte der Arbeit* argued that the French people preferred the dictatorship of Napoleon III, who represented their desire for the Right to Work, to the dictatorship of a bourgeoisie which fought this right. The Emperor must carry out the workers' demand or lose his basis of power; but in the long run he could not carry the demand through without transforming the whole mode of production.

> Sooner or later [Silberner summarizes Hess] he will come to just this hard step, by which his whole governmental system would be transformed from the ground up, or else would be forced into the renunciation of his dictatorship by the French people.[11]

In the same pamphlet Hess made clear his principled social-reformist and antirevolutionary point of view. Everything in society changes only gradually, he maintained.

> Revolutions [wrote Hess] can only bring to political recognition that which had gradually grown into existence. *Social* revolutions in the sense conferred on them by communist fanatics are fantasies that belong in the lunatic asylum.[12]

He would propose state intervention, he wrote, only in those cases where this step would satisfy the needs of "*all* productive classes," not the interests of one class only.[13] That is, state intervention would have to be in the interests of the bourgeoisie and of the economy itself, not of the proletariat alone.

It is indubitable that Hess has never been given his proper recognition as pioneer of the social-democracy of the future. At the same time, this pioneer was, in his day, one of the clearest proponents of a revolutionary dictatorship over the people, his current candidate for "workers' dictator" being the Emperor.

2. LASSALLE AS HESS'S DICTATOR

This, of course, explains his lack of objection to a similar course taken by his new leader, Lassalle. "Lassalle's lordly character," writes Silberner, "his dictatorial tendencies in the General German Workers Association, his vainglorious posturing and excessive self-serving personal drive seem not to have disturbed Hess." (If Hess was not repelled by Bonaparte's character, it is hard to see why he should find Lassalle's harder to take.) Nor was Hess bothered by the reports of Lassalle's personal dealings with Bismarck, dealings that were already hotly rumored and undenied by mid-1863.* An old friend of Hess

---

* For Lassalle's dictatorial operations and relations with Bismarck, see Chapter 7, Section 3.

16. The Many Dictatorships of Moses Hess 257

fervently warned him against links with these sinister political figures, to no avail.[14]

Hess's ardor for Lassalle rested on the two legs of his standpoint: reformism and dictatorship. In a pamphlet published toward the end of 1863, Hess's line was that the program of the Lassallean organization was the road to peaceful and gradual change.

> Perhaps, says Hess [in Silberner's summary], there are still other means which lead to the same end, as for example the revolutionary, direct legislation by the people, or the temporary, limited dictatorship of an individual to whom the people entrust the carrying-out of social reforms.

But as far as we see now (Hess thought) it is the Lassallean way of the GGWA that is best.[15] In this context Hess *counterposed* the Lassallean course to "the temporary, limited dictatorship of an individual" charged with carrying out social reforms; but at the same time he accepted with equanimity the form of dictatorship embodied in Lassalleanism itself.

Back in Paris in 1864, Hess began contributing to a financial weekly, *Journal des Actionnaires*, for which he undertook to review Lassalle's economic polemic against Schulze-Delitzsch. This article was (in Silberner's words) a "hymn of praise" for Lassalle, in the course of which Hess wrote that, if a revolution broke out in Germany, the GGWA leader might perhaps undertake the role of dictator.[16] Lassalle had this eulogy reprinted in Germany. Not long afterward, the future dictator was shot in a duel and died at the end of August.

Before his death, the Maximum Leader of the GGWA had written a testamentary statement bequeathing the presidency of the organization to Bernhard Becker. Since Becker was an incompetent nonentity, there was much opposition, but Hess steadfastly supported his presidency. Soon the presidency was taken over by J.B. von Schweitzer, editor of the GGWA organ *Social-Demokrat*. Schweitzer was a more open supporter of the Bismarck regime (the Prussian form of Bonapartism) than Lassalle had been publicly; and, as we have seen,[17] Marx and Engels made a formal break with Schweitzer's "Royal Prussian government socialism." Hess published a statement in the German press attacking "this ridiculous demonstration" by the "gentleman from London" (Marx) with "his secretary [Engels] and general staff without an army." And Hess continued printing bitter attacks on Marx and Engels, all in defense of Schweitzer (with whom he himself was going to break two years later).[18]

When J. P. Becker made a proposal to democratize the GGWA presidency structurally and to eliminate the presidential dictatorship established by Lassalle, Hess opposed the change and defended the institution of presidential rule.[19] J. P. Becker's reply accused Hess of supporting an "enslaving dictatorship."*

It is clear, in all this, that Hess supported the Lassalle line of pro-Bismarckism. At least for a while, pro-Bismarckism ran concurrently with pro-Bonapartism in his mind: the difficulty in this combination was not political but national. Around the turn of the year 1864 into 1865, Hess had a conversation with Schily, in which he still maintained that Bonaparte would bring democracy and socialism. Hess, Schily concluded, was a "Bonapartist Democrat and Socialist in good faith." There was similar testimony by others.[21] In fact, there was no open break by Hess with his publicly expressed pro-Bonapartist position, but from 1865 on he was simply not recorded any more as speaking of the Emperor as the executor of the revolution.[22] At this stage, apparently, Hess's view of the revolutionary dictatorship from above crystallized around the pro-Bismarckian form of this faith.

Nothing was more predictable. Back in 1859, when the Italian War broke out, a friend of Hess—another Bonapartist German émigré living in France, named Semmig—had written to Hess fearful that Germany might interfere with France's "liberation" of Italy. "In the end," wrote Semmig, "these Germans will yet have to be *forced* to become free men." He meant: forced by Bonaparte. Hess replied in agreement: "The Germans—as you say, and indeed I say it without joking—must be *forced* to set up a free, national confederation, like the Italians."[23]

Lassalle's pamphlet on *The Italian War* (1859) impressed Hess as a "masterpiece of common sense" in its support of the Bismarckian policy. In turn, Hess thought, Bismarck executed Lassalle's program: "he [Bismarck] is, in fact, in general politics, the disciple and executor of the Lassallean ideas."[24]

Bismarck did force his unity on the Germans: in 1866, with his military triumph over Austria, a wave of Prussian chauvinism swept over the liberal left. Hess joined in the pro-Prussian euphoria, which he expressed in an article in July.[25] Soon after, however, says Silberner, he drew back from this advanced position. For many years now, Hess had been one of the most extreme Francophiles to be found east of the Rhine, and when he reacted against Prussian chauvinism (and against its Lassallean representative) from 1867 on, we can be sure that his deeply imbued Francophilism was operative.

---

* J. P. Becker (still according to Silberner) had his own ideas about dictatorship. In his reply to Hess, there was an excursus

> on the "liberating dictatorship" which J. P. Becker counterposed to "enslaving dictatorship," indeed on the basis of the personal experiences that he had accumulated during the revolution of 1848 in the defence force "Hilf Dir," a group of men organized by him, which had unanimously chosen him as President with dictatorial authority. Becker, it seems, wanted to show that Hess, "an armchair book man," understood nothing about "true dictatorship."[20]

3. MESSIANIC INTERLUDE

In the early 1860s, still inspired with the great mission of France and its imperial dictator to liberate the world, Hess thought to unleash this emancipatory force upon the Middle East to solve the Jewish question. Hess's pioneer Zionism is not part of our subject, but one element in it is. This element was a combination of Messianic dictatorship with imperialist domination, as set forth in Hess's germinal book *Rome and Jerusalem* in 1862.

Hess's type of Zionism can fairly be called Messianic. His book is peppered with references to the "Messianic kingdom," which is spoken of in the same way as elsewhere he does of the socialist future. The great Rabbis, he wrote, "never separated the idea of a future world from the conception of the Messianic reign."[26] When he was "actively engaged on behalf of the European proletariat," he wrote, "my Messianic belief was, at that time, the same that I profess at present..." Every Jew is potentially a Messiah; we will all carry "the yoke of the 'Kingdom of Heaven' until the end."[27]

This deliberate equation of his socialist career with his new Messianism can only be a conscious reference to his support of that other Messianic kingdom, the Second Empire of Napoleon III, messiah of the peoples.

Alongside the Messianic theme is that of the subordination of the individual to the mystic power above. (Again we must keep in mind that the earthly ism representing the real power subjugating the individual for his own good was—Bonapartism.) "Nothing is more foreign to the spirit of Judaism than the idea of the salvation of the individual..." "The point of view of our sacred history ... never separated the individual from the race ... " "Judaism does not allow either spiritualistic or materialistic sects to exist in its midst. Jewish life... is undivided..."[28] Admittedly, I am picking these scraps of ideas out of his book like raisins out of a cake, but they are suggestive of the book's train of thought and feeling. The overwhelmingly dominant theme of the book is the concept of blood-racism, a relation in which the individual is swamped. *

The Messianic-racial-tribal conception is linked by Hess with his faith in the Bonapartist dictatorship. The Emperor is "true to his revolutionary descent," and therefore the French people "submits at present to the iron dictatorship of kinghood." As in the Middle Ages, France has "sent its brave

---

* This theme as such is also out of our purview, but its meaning has to he exhibited.

(1) Jews will "always remain strangers among the nations"; they cannot assimilate among or be accepted by the peoples with whom they live, whose "racial antagonism" to the Jews is "inborn."[29]

(2) The race question "must be solved before attempting the solution of the political and social problems." The "race war" must be fought out before social and humane ideas can be accepted. It is race that "forms life." "The race struggle is the primal one, and the class struggle is secondary.. ."[30]

soldiers to Syria" and prepared the way of the Lord in the desert.[31] When "the Jewish tribes return to their fatherland"[32] in Palestine, the Bonaparte regime will help establish a Jewish state because

> It is to the interest of France to see that the road leading to India and China should be settled by a people which will be loyal to the cause of France to the end . . . But is there any other nation more adapted to carry out this mission than Israel...?[33]

"The French can rule the world," and world Jewry is predestined to aid this great cause, "under the protection of the European powers." France's mission to civilize and annex the orient was recognized by Napoleon I and the Saint-Simonian group, "one of which is at present at the head of the Suez enterprise." The Suez Canal once completed, "the interests of world commerce will undoubtedly demand the establishment of depots and settlements along the road to India and China..."[34]

A neat scheme: the same Bonapartist dictatorship that is bringing the social revolution to the French people, as they grovel in gratitude, is also ready to bestow the same beneficent sway on the world, beginning with the East, using a Jewish state in Palestine as the base of its rule ... Few forms of the Zionist idea have been more frankly based on imperialist dictatorship at home and abroad.

After publishing *Rome and Jerusalem,* Hess moved to Paris, where he tried to found a Zionist journal with a banker named Lévy-Bing, without success. In subsequent years he tried to implement plans for Palestine colonization by wealthy finance-capitalist circles close to the French imperial court. But by the end of the 1860s Hess was disillusioned with the work accomplished by the rich Jewish financiers with whom he was trying to make the international racial revolution, and in 1870 he bitterly attacked their role in Jewish work.[35]

The Messiah, it seems, was just another dictator who did not pan out according to Hess's plans.

4. HESS IN THE INTERNATIONAL

Let us now return to where we dropped Hess at the end of Section 2. Developments had left him without any continuing faith in a crowned "workers' dictator." His break with the Lassalleans meant that he was organizationally homeless. In this sadly dictatorless situation, he turned for the first time to the International.

Since the foundation of the International in 1864, Hess had distinguished himself mainly as a sniping enemy. Back in 1865, as Paris correspondent for

16. The Many Dictatorships of Moses Hess 261

Schweitzer's *Social-Demokrat,* he had twice published articles slandering the French section of the International as pro-Bonapartist, with suspicious connections with the "Palais Royal." The French section, being dominated by Tolain's Proudhonists, was peculiarly vulnerable to such insinuations. When Hess's first such article was published, Marx protested to Schweitzer against his printing Hess's lies or lying rumors; Schweitzer temporarily mollified him. The second time, Marx almost broke off relations with the Lassalleans over it, but was dissuaded from breaking over this kind of issue rather than over Schweitzer's "Royal Prussian government socialism."[36]

Now, at the very time that Hess was seeking to discredit the International's French section for being pro-Bonapartist, and attacking the General Council for having relations with these people, he himself, Moses Hess, was still an enthusiastic Bonapartist admirer and propagandist, as we have seen. No comment is necessary.

In November of 1865 Hess was still attacking the idea of the International as "premature"; he remained hostile to the Geneva Congress of 1866. He was kinder to the Lausanne Congress of 1867; and that year also greeted Marx's *Capital* with approval. He probably joined the International by the summer of 1868. At the Brussels Congress in that year, he showed up as a delegate of J. P. Becker's German Swiss center.[37]

He approved the proceedings of the congress as having "not in the least a communist-dictatorial [spirit] à la Schweitzer." The statutes of the International are a bulwark against "such dictatorial or Caesarist tendencies," he wrote, apparently repudiating his Lassallean past.

> The whole of the younger generation of workers [wrote Hess] is completely cured of the theory of workers' dictatorship, which necessarily always turns into that of a personal dictator; even in the former party chiefs of this tendency a salutary reaction has taken place.[38]

Silberner is undoubtedly correct in believing that *Hess* was referring here to the Lassalle-Schweitzer theory and practice of "workers' dictatorship." His talk of a "cure" can also be considered autobiographical.

By 1869 Hess was supporting the Bebel-Liebknecht tendency against Schweitzer's GGWA; he approved the establishment of the "Eisenacher party" in August because it countered "all dictatorial hankerings." He probably thought the Eisenachers represented a reformist development, for in coeval writings he was spelling out his fully formed reformist conception of socialism and politics.[39]

At the Basel Congress of 1869, Hess was a delegate from Berlin. In a speech (known from his own draft) he aimed a blow at "an imperial or any other dictator." The Bonaparte government itself is laying the ax to its dictatorship, in order to save as much of its regime as possible; the emancipation of the workers must be the aim, through the "necessary social reforms" or by "free workers' associations" of all kinds.

A third road [said Hess], that of carrying out social reforms through the dictatorship of a class, is today closed to all classes, including the working class.[40]

This may have been a reference to Marx's view; but he went on to say that "the dictatorial tendency of the revolutionary workers" had been embodied in Louis Bonaparte in 1849. Today the dictatorial form of government was discredited "so that it had called forth a countercurrent, which today made impossible any dictatorship in France, even the most revolutionary." What he counterposed to this, as "full freedom," was his own reform program.

His remarks about revolutionary dictatorship may also have been aimed at Bakunin, for at the congress he vigorously supported the General Council against the Russian. (This was of dubious value to Marx, for Hess thus helped to tie up anti-Bakuninism with extreme reformism, in the minds of delegates who wanted to be revolutionaries.) In a passage of his draft speech which was stricken in manuscript, he remarked that Marx would today perhaps see that even the workers' dictatorship which was still justified in 1848 for introducing radical socialist reforms is no longer possible and no longer necessary.

He did say, in this speech, that a workers' dictatorship was superfluous now "since we can count on the free assent of all productive classes [meaning the bourgeoisie in particular] to the reforms we request, if we know how to bring these reforms, which are in their interest, nearer to their comprehension." He defied "dictatorial, authoritarian socialism," represented by Prussians and Russians (meaning Schweitzer and Bakunin), to charge him with deserting communist principles.[41]

It is important to understand the angle from which he was now repudiating the *need* for a "workers' dictatorship" by anyone. In the manuscript of an unpublished pamphlet written 1871-73, he counted "revolutionary dictatorship" out only because reform-socialism was in. He saw France on the very road to socialism or communism:

> France is today attaining, by the legal and peaceful road of universal suffrage, all the social reforms that will finish by abolishing the proletariat.... All the violent roads are exhausted in France today. There is no place any more for reactionary dictatorship or for revolutionary dictatorship. The conservatives must resign themselves, like the revolutionaries, to accepting the verdict of universal suffrage.[42]

This explains Hess's zigzags on "workers' dictatorship." They are difficult

16. The Many Dictatorships of Moses Hess   263

to understand only if we think that it was the "dictatorship" he was exercised about, even at the end.

We have seen, more than once now, that he tied the question up with the fact that the bourgeoisie itself must assent to the changes in society that are styled socialistic; that socialism must never mean the rule of one class (meaning the proletariat). It was not dictatorship *per se* that he attacked—how could he, with his record? It was the *rule of the proletariat* in any form that he rejected.

Others may have held a point of view that said *"Rule* of the proletariat, yes; dictatorship, no." Hess's guiding position was the reverse: *"Dictatorship, yes; rule of the proletariat, never!"* Insofar as he ever directly confronted Marx's 'dictatorship of the proletariat', he would have to say that what he objected to was *the fact that it was the equivalent of 'rule of the proletariat'*.

17 | THE SECOND PERIOD OF THE 'DICTATORSHIP OF THE PROLETARIAT'

To recapitulate:

The first period during which 'dictatorship of the proletariat' occurred in Marx was 1850-52, that is, the period following the revolution of 1848-49, a period of stock-taking and analysis. In this period Marx confronted the Blanquist tendency and similar tendencies of Jacobin-communism within the ranks of the Communist League; and, we have seen, as against their ideas of the revolutionary dictatorship of the party or communist band, he counterposed the conception of a class dictatorship. The dictatorship *of* the proletariat was his alternative to the dictatorship of the party *over* the proletariat.

This confrontation was accompanied by Marx's and Engels' consistent critique of Blanquism and Blanquist politics. We traced this through the 1850s in Chapter 10. Now, as introduction to the Second Period, let us continue this presentation through the 1860s and beyond.

Warning: the results are exactly the same as before, and the hurried reader has our permission to skip this section.

1. MARX VERSUS BLANQUISM—CONTINUED

The aim of this summary sketch is not to show that Marx opposed putschism—that is breaking in an open door—but to illustrate the issues and approaches involved. Here are a dozen examples.

During the 1850s and 1860s, when revolutionary spirits were barely warmed on the back burner, putschism was not a live option, and Marx scarcely had occasion to take it up. There was one incident in 1860.

(1) *Lewy's mission*. A representative of the Rhenish Communists, Gustav Lewy, visited Marx in London in February 1860 with two missions, one of which interests us now. He "offered me right on a silver platter a factory workers' insurrection in Iserlohn, Solingen, etc. I expressed my opinion bluntly against such useless and dangerous *foolishness.*"[1]

264

17. The Second Period of the 'Dictatorship of the Proletariat'   265

But more such problems were ushered in by the revolutionary upheavals of 1870-71.

(2) *Blanquists in "The Civil War in France."* Marx's references in this Address to the Blanquist role were inhibited by the fact that this document had to be adopted by the General Council of the International and had to speak for all sections of the movement. There was no possibility of Marx's expressing his full opinion. The Address took note of the role of Blanqui in a couple of well-known clashes with the government and of the government's refusal to exchange the imprisoned Blanqui for an archbishop held hostage.[2] (The information which we will take up below, in Section 3, was not yet known, of course.)

But in the third section of the Address, the "theoretical section," Marx did insert a passage about two types of Jacobin elements, described anonymously:

> In every revolution there intrude, at the side of its true agents, men of a different stamp; some of them survivors of and devotees to past revolutions, without insight into the present movement, but preserving popular influence by their known honesty and courage, or by the sheer force of tradition; others mere bawlers, who, by dint of repeating year after year the same set of stereotyped declamations against the Government of the day, have sneaked into the reputation of revolutionists of the first water. After the 18th of March, some such men did also turn up, and in some cases contrived to play pre-eminent parts. As far as their power went, they hampered the real action of the working class, exactly as men of that sort have hampered the full development of every previous revolution. They are an unavoidable evil: with time they are shaken off; but time was not allowed to the Commune.[3]

This was only in part a description of the Blanquists as such; it was more about the less reputable elements among the Jacobin types generally, such as the sinister scoundrel Félix Pyat.

In view of the inhibition, let us look ahead to Engels' later statement about the Blanquist majority of the Commune, in his 1891 introduction to Marx's Address:

> The great majority of the Blanquists were at that time socialists only by revolutionary, proletarian instinct; only a few had attained greater clarity on principles, through Vaillant, who was familiar with German scientific socialism.[4]

Engels, discussing the Commune's mistakes, noted that the Blanquists had to be held responsible for the political errors, as the Proudhonists for the economic. Further:

> Brought up in the school of conspiracy, and held together by the strict discipline which went with it, they started out from the viewpoint that a

relatively small number of resolute, well-organized men would be able, at a given favorable moment, not only to seize the helm of state, but also by a display of great, ruthless energy, to maintain power until they succeeded in sweeping the mass of the people into the revolution and ranging them round the small band of leaders. This involved, above all, the strictest, dictatorial centralization of all power in the hands of the new revolutionary government.[5]

In the Commune, he explained, the Blanquists acted contrary to these predispositions (in part, I would add).

(3) *Bakunin's putsch in Lyons.* On September 28, 1870, Bakunin and a band of his cronies went through a farcical charade in which they "abolished," not the capitalist state, but the revolutionary government established in the city on September 4. "The Hôtel de Ville was seized—for a short time—and most foolish decrees on the *abolition de l'état* and similar nonsense were issued," Marx informed a friend.[6] Farce it was, to be sure, but, as Utin told the Hague Congress commission, this "revolutionary" disruption turned the Lyons workers against the International for a whole period.[7]

(4) *General strike as substitute revolution.* In his essay on "The Bakuninists at Work" (1873), Engels discussed the anarchist notion of the general strike as a "miraculous" device for bypassing the need for a revolutionary movement. A real general strike "required a well-formed organization of the working class and plentiful funds"; when the Bakuninists asked the workers "to oppose the armed government force not with arms in thier hands, but with a general strike," the workers rightly thought it ridiculous.[8]

(5) *Engels on the Blanquist refugees.* The 1874 article on "The Program of the Blanquist Refugees of the Commune" is very important in this account; it figures as our locus 8 in Chapter 19.

(6) *Polemic against Tkachev.* In 1875 Engels' article on "Social Questions in Russia" took up Peter Tkachev's Narodnik-Blanquist views. Like Bakunin, Tkachev's idea of revolution involved the utilization of robber bands, incendiarism, and the unleashing of an outburst of elemental hate. Engels commented:

> It is impossible to conceive of a revolution on easier and more pleasant terms. One starts shooting, at three or four places simultaneously, and the "instinctive revolutionist," "practical necessity," and the "instinct of self-preservation" [Tkachev's phrases] do the rest "of themselves." Being so dead easy, it is simply incomprehensible why the revolution has not long ago been made....[9]

This is a "childish" conception of revolution, said Engels, and referred back to his exposé of the "Bakuninists at Work" for illustration of its consequences. He concluded: a Russian revolution is surely approaching but—

> Only two events could still delay it: a successful war against Turkey or

17. The Second Period of the 'Dictatorship of the Proletariat' 267

Austria . . . or—a premature attempt at insurrection, which would drive the possessing classes back into the arms of the government.[10]

(7) *Government provocation.* From about the late seventies on, Engels became increasingly concerned about an old counterrevolutionary pattern he saw developing with new force, especially in Germany, and about which he wrote again and again. One example: in a letter to a comrade in 1878, Engels pointed to Bismarck's hope of stopping revolutionary development: "what he longs for above all" is "an attempt at a putsch, whereupon he can start *shooting.*"[11] The police, of course, could get provocateurs to do this service, but what was more dangerous was the number of righteous "revolutionaries" who were eager to do the job with the best intentions.

The year 1878 was also the beginning of the Anti-Socialist Law, under which the Social-Democratic Party was banned, and which had been jammed through by Bismarck on the pretext of a couple of assassination attempts on the kaiser by nonsocialists. This background conditioned the entire issue for a long time.

(8) *Marx on Bismarck.* About the same time as Engels' letter, Marx made a similar point in a newspaper interview, about the expulsion of forty-eight socialist leaders from Berlin. According to the interviewer (who reprocessed Marx's words), Marx said:

> ∞Once those leaders were gone, he [Bismarck] was confident that the mob would rise, and that would be the cue for a carnival of slaughter. The screws would then be put upon the whole German Empire; his pet theory of blood and iron would then have full sway, and taxation could be levied to any extent. So far no emeute [riotous outburst] has occurred . . .[12]

(9) *Against "overnight revolution."* In a letter to Bernstein, Engels argued against the view that "the revolution is something that can be made overnight." His target was not the Blanquists but some immaturely impatient elements in the Social-Democratic Party.

> In fact, it [the revolution] is a process of development of the masses over several years under accelerative conditions. Any revolution that was brought off overnight merely got rid of a reaction that was already hopeless from the start (1830) or led directly to the opposite of what was striven for (1848 in France).[13]

(10) *Putsches and phrases.* In France in 1884 Engels was looking forward to a steady leftward movement in politics under the pressure of revolutionary workers. He hoped it would not be interrupted by premature revolutionism: "I am glad that our people are not yet strong enough in Paris . . . to be led astray into making putsches through the might of the revolutionary phrase."[14]

(11) *The danger of impatience.* Writing to Lafargue in 1891, Engels emphasized tactical restraint in given situations, as Marx had done so many times:

> The danger in countries with a revolutionary past is that any new district invaded by socialism is tempted to make a revolution in 24 hours. There's not the slightest need to urge them on, quite the contrary, one has to hold them back. In particular the Walloons understand only riots [l'émeute], in which they are almost always beaten. Look at the struggles of the Belgian miners; organization nil or well-nigh, irrepressible impatience, hence certain defeat.[15]

(12) *The bourgeois trap.* In a letter of 1892 to Laura (Marx) Lafargue, Engels again warned about the government's hopes in the stupid use of revolutionary violence:

> ∞The idea that the 1st of May is to be a day of rows and riots is a mere trap set by the bourgeois and we have no interest whatever to fall into that trap. We want to show our strength, that's all; as to when we are to use that strength, that's our business, not that of our opponents, if we can help it.[16]

This question raises another which is on the agenda of a different volume, namely, the myth that Engels in old age softened into an advocate of peaceful tactics only. Nothing of the sort is involved. It was then, as always, a question of the evaluation of suitable tactics for different situations and periods. The repudiation of Blanquist notions about revolutionary force is only one side of revolutionary policy, though it is the side we are concerned with at the moment.

Few of the remarks cited above were directed against actual Blanquists; and indeed the Blanquist tendency itself became more and more assimilated to the general movement. "Blanquism" was only one historical form of the problem. Marx had taken this historical view of the phenomenon by 1860, when he looked back on his organizational experiences in the movement of 1849-52:

> The [Communist] League, like the Société des Saisons in Paris, like a hundred other societies, was only an episode in the history of the party, which is everywhere constituting itself in a natural process out of the soil of modern society.[17]

Marx then amended the reference to the "party" to make clear that he meant only "the party in the great historical sense,"[18] that is, the movement rather than a specific organization. The Society of the Seasons was the very archetype of the Blanquist conspiratorial group, and Marx had had nothing to do with it himself; yet he threw it into the same historical bag as the Communist League.

17. The Second Period of the 'Dictatorship of the Proletariat' 269

He was looking on Blanquism not simply as an error but as a moment in the historical pattern of the maturation of the movement.

The last historical episode in which the Blanquists as such played a distinctive role was the Paris Commune. It is this that gave rise to our Second Period.

2. THE PARIS COMMUNE

If our line of analysis has been well-founded, it was no accident that the two decades before the Paris Commune produced no cases of Marx's use of 'dictatorship of the proletariat'. During this interval, Marx referred, as he usually did, to the 'rule of the proletariat' or 'conquest of political power' to carry the same fundamental idea. For the same reason, the term 'dictatorship of the proletariat' did not appear in *The Civil War in France*. Our thesis will be tested again when we find the term reappearing.

To be sure, we know now that Marx had no compunction about applying the term to the Paris Commune (see locus 5). For a long time it was frequently argued that, since only Engels had actually used the term for the Commune, this represented his peculiar opinion. (According to the Engels-vs.-Marx myth, anything that Engels wrote that was not notarized by Marx was an Engelsian deviation.) It is a sad commentary that this notion has been scotched only by the discovery of a suitable Marx-quote.

The question should not be whether Marx actually happened to apply the term (which he used sparingly anyway) but whether the Commune *in Marx's analysis* answered to the conception. This may be problematical if one thinks that the 'dictatorship of the proletariat' is a particular form of governmental structure or set of political methods or institutions. It is not problematical if we adopt the only meaning of the term that corresponds to the way Marx actually used it: a 'dictatorship of the proletariat' is a state in which the proletariat exercises dominant political power—a 'workers' state', the 'rule of the proletariat'. No more, no less.

In this connection there are three important points to be made about Marx's view of the Commune.

(1) *Workers' state.* In Marx's opinion, the Paris Commune—shortlived and precarious though it was, and therefore more difficult to analyze than a political entity that has worked itself out in experience—represented the political ascendancy, or "rule," of the proletariat. Marx presented the Commune as a workers' government, as the political form of the transition to a new social order.

Two cautions should be added, to avoid misunderstanding. (1) As we have pointed out, the term 'proletariat' is narrower than 'working class(es)'; and Marx's statement about the Commune as a "working-class government" should be read with the looser meaning. (2) A "working-class government" that lasted only 72 days can hardly be expected to clearly exhibit the expected historical characteristics of a workers' state. This was an incipient workers' state—a workers' state viewed a-borning. Discussions of Marx's view not infrequently ignore this obvious fact.

Marx's view of the Commune as a 'workers' state' is all over the "theoretical" section, Section 3, but the following brief excerpts will be sufficient illustration:

- The cry of "Social Republic"... did but express a vague aspiration after a Republic that was not only to supersede the monarchial form of class-rule, but class-rule itself. The Commune was the positive form of that Republic.
- It was essentialy a working-class government... the political form at last discovered under which to work out the economical emancipation of Labour.
- The Commune was, therefore, to serve as a lever for uprooting the economical foundations upon which rests the existence of classes, and therefore of class rule.[19]

These formulations are so sweeping that a government so described must be, for Marx, what he elsewhere called a dictatorship of the proletariat. It represented the *rule* of the proletariat.

Now this statement is often confused with two others.

(a) To say that this was Marx's view is not yet to prove that the Commune *was* a workers' state. But our present subject is *Marx's* view. An analysis of the Commune's class character, that is, a testing of Marx's view, will be of importance for another volume.

(b) Marx's view that the Commune was a workers' state or "working-class government" is often counterposed to Marx's later-expressed opinion that "the majority of the Commune was in no wise socialist, nor could it be."[20] This counterposition assumes that "workers' state" and "socialist government" are synonymous. But they are not; this is an important error. The former describes a *class content,* the other a *political program.* To be sure, a workers' state that is not yet socialist in its majority or in its measures will be in a precarious condition, which must end in one change or the other. But the Commune was given no time to work out this element of tension. There had always been the possibility that a conquest of political power by a working-class movement might *precede* that movement's political maturation; and in fact it was precisely this sort of situation that Marx and Engels had long feared.[21] There can be no doubt that the Commune made this possibility a reality: it broke out completely unprepared ("spontaneously") and without any political leadership except what could be supplied *ad hoc.*

Besides, how socialistic the Commune's majority was depends entirely on whether one uses that term with greater or less hospitality. Even the men of the Jacobin majority, who are usually counterposed to the socialist minority (and with good reason), considered themselves socialistic in some sense for the most part; 'socialist' was a very acceptable designation. What Marx meant by a socialist majority was unexplained, but it is an exaggeration to speak of the socialist tendencies as "unconscious" only. There was a good deal of conscious consideration of and demand for socialistic measures, as a perusal of the Commune's *Journal Officiel* will show. If it mostly remained talk, it is hardly necessary to explain that there was no time for the Commune to do much else.

To sum up: just how socialistic the Commune could get in its few weeks of existence is one question; it is not the same as the question of the class character of the political power.

In Marx's view, then, the Paris Commune was a workers' state or working-class government. Therefore we must expect him to view it also as a 'dictatorship of the proletariat' whenever that term became relevant.*

(2) *Hegemony of the proletariat.* Another widespread element of confusion about Marx's view of the Paris Commune is the assumption that a workers' state automatically means a working-class majority in society or government. But this assumption is a false one, as we have emphasized elsewhere more than once.[23] Marx usually saw the proletarian revolution as *led* by the working class, not limited to the working class.

Marx was very conscious of the fact that a majority of the French people were not proletarian, and this was precisely the reason for his unusual emphasis on the peasantry in *The Civil War in France.*[24] What determined the class character of the Commune, for Marx, was the *hegemony of the proletariat* in the revolution; that is, the fact that the other class elements in the revolution looked to it as the vanguard and leader. This view goes all the way back in Marx; witness the passages we have previously cited from his *Class Struggles in France* and the *Communist Manifesto.*[25]

In the Address on the Commune, he made this point so many times that it is very difficult to overlook. For example:

* In her book *On Revolution,* Hannah Arendt asserts that after writing his *Civil War in France,* Marx "soon became aware to what extent this political form contradicted all notions of a 'dictatorship of the proletariat' . . ." And she quotes something Marx allegedly wrote "only two years later," i.e., presumably in 1873. This is a rather embarrassing blunder. The lines she quotes actually come, unbeknown to her, from the "Address to the Communist League" of March 1850, and naturally have nothing to do with the Paris Commune; nor do they bear on the 'dictatorship of the proletariat'.[22]

• ... this was the first revolution in which the working class was openly acknowledged as the only class capable of social initiative, even by the great bulk of the Paris middle class—shopkeepers, tradesmen, merchants—the wealthy capitalists alone excepted.

• If the Commune was thus the true representative of all the healthy elements of French society, and therefore the truly national Government, it was, at the same time, as a working men's Government, as the bold champion of the emancipation of labour, emphatically international.

• The majority of its members were naturally working men, or acknowledged representatives of the working class.

• ... the Communal Constitution brought the rural producers under the intellectual lead of the central towns of their districts, and these secured to them, in the working men, the natural trustees of their interests.[26]

In Marx's First Draft for the Address, there are several strong passages along the same lines: "the actual 'social' character of their Republic consists only in this, that workers govern the Paris Commune."[27] Here Marx immediately added: "As to their measures, they must, by the nature of things, be principally confined to the military defence of Paris and its approvisionment!"—which is precisely the distinction we have made between class character and socialist measures.

There are other passages in Marx's two drafts which show how important the concept was to Marx.[28] In one, he remarks that *"It was only the working class that could* formulate ... this new aspiration" through the Commune.[29]

Now it is true—again—that Marx's view of the working-class hegemony in the Commune can be disputed, but, as before, this otherwise interesting question is not to the point now. It was the view itself which meant that Marx naturally looked upon the Commune as the temporary rule (or 'dictatorship') of the proletariat.*

* For an educational example of inability to grasp Marx's approach, George Lichtheim comes to hand. The Paris Commune, he argues, "could not well be described as a 'proletarian dictatorship,' for not only had it been duly elected, but its political composition ran all the way from middle-class republicans to socialists of the most varied hues."[30] Lichtheim, then, believes that for Marx a dictatorship of the proletariat (1) precludes elections, (2) demands a "political composition" of certified proletarian purity, uncontaminated by middle-class elements, and (3) excludes even socialists if their hues are too varied. Needless to say, he offers no wisp of evidence for this bizarre version of Marx's thought. He adds that, but for the panic flight of the propertied, the Paris government *might* have had a "bourgeois-republican majority" (but it didn't), and that the Commune army "included considerable numbers" representing "the traditional republicanism of the French middle class"—a compendium of irrelevancies. In these few lines we have a sort of anthology of marxological blunders. One way to break out of this sort of thing is to ask how these alleged criteria would apply, in Marx's view, to the present 'dictatorship of the bourgeoisie' in a democratic capitalist state.

17. The Second Period of the 'Dictatorship of the Proletariat' 273

(3) *Commune democracy.* Those who assume that 'dictatorship of the proletariat' means dictatorship in the twentieth-century sense are understandably confused by Marx's paeans of praise to the extreme democracy of the Commune government. The confusion, however, is not in Marx.

Well-known and lengthy sections of *The Civil War in France* point in glowing and approving colors to the characteristics of the Commune that differentiated it from the bourgeois democracies. These passages[31] are too extensive to cite here in detail, and in any case it is not the detail that is relevant to the present subject. It will suffice to mention these highlights in illustration:

- Election of all Commune members by unlimited universal suffrage—"nothing could be more foreign to the spirit of the Commune than to supersede universal suffrage by hierarchic investiture"[32];
- All officials "responsible and revocable at short terms";
- Workmen's wages for all officials;
- Depoliticalization of the police, under Communal control;
- Separation of church and state;
- All judges elective, responsible, and revocable;
- Local municipal liberty;
- The Commune "to be a working, not a parliamentary, body, executive and legislative at the same time";
- Abolition of the standing army and "state functionarism," etc.

Marx summed up by saying that the Commune "supplied the Republic with the basis of really democratic institutions" and that its measures "could but betoken the tendency of a government of the people by the people."[33]

The First Draft had another passage ending with a version of Lincoln's famous words, in somewhat shaky English:

°°The glorious British penny-a-liner has made the splendid discovery that this is not what *we* use to understand by self government. Of course, it is not. It is not the self-administration of the towns by turtle-soup guzzling aldermen, jobbing vestries, and ferocious workhouse guardians. It is not the self-administration of the counties by the holders of broad acres, long purses and empty heads. It is not the judicial abomination of "the Great Unpaid." It is not political self-government of the country through the means of an oligarchic club and the reading of the *Times* newspaper. It is the people acting for itself by itself.[34]

A selection of other relevant passages would deal with democracy in the armed forces (National Guard) and with Marx's attack on the antidemocratic character of the Versaillese National Assembly, *inter alia.*[35]

It should scarcely be surprising that, to Marx, a workers' state meant "bursting asunder the whole superstructure of strata that make up official society,"³⁶ and inaugurating a political system of democratic control from below. That is what he thought the dictatorship of the proletariat was supposed to do.

3. BLANQUISTS IN THE COMMUNE

The French Blanquists, one of the major political tendencies among the Communards, had an entirely different conception of the Commune and of what it should do.

In the period that led from the Franco-Prussian War to the Commune revolt, this group had played a role that does not jibe with the historical myth about its fearsome revolutionary character. Let us exhibit this in two acts.

Act One. Three weeks before the Second Empire was going to be pulled down by the elemental rising of the people, the revolution of September 4, 1870 which installed the Second Republic, the Blanquists became impatient for "the revolution." Right after the first reverses in the war, Blanqui had begun scheming for a surprise attack on the fort of Vincennes; arms were accumulated in General Eudes' lodgings; but "the revolution" had to be postponed because Blanqui could not move from Belgium to Paris soon enough, before the Vincennes garrison was strengthened. Eudes chafed; Blanqui reluctantly agreed to an attempt on the barracks of La Villette.* So on August 16, a sunny Sunday, the Blanquist band assembled on the Boulevard de la Villette, and mingled with the strolling crowd. A signal from the leader—the men moved on the barracks—there was an exchange of fire. Now let the Blanquist historian Da Costa tell it:

> The Blanquists were masters of the field. With Blanqui, Eudes and Granger at their head, they went toward Belleville by the exterior boulevard, crying "Vive la République! Death to the Prussians! To arms!"
> Unfortunately, no one followed. The crowd seemed literally dumbfounded. Seeing that this attempt at an uprising of the crowd that they had hoped for had completely failed, the three leaders gave orders to the column to disperse...³⁸

* This is a fine example of why Engels wrote in 1874:
> Of course, under Louis Philippe he [Blanqui] could organize such a nucleus only as a secret society, and then what happened was what usually happens with conspiracies: the people involved, tired of being continually put off with empty promises that the thing will come off soon, finally lost all patience and became rebellious; and so there remained only the alternatives of letting the conspiracy fall apart or of striking without any externally visible occasion. They struck (May 12, 1839) and were suppressed in a trice.³⁷

Eudes wound up in a cafe on the Boulevard Saint-Michel, with another comrade. The butt of his revolver peeping from his pocket was spotted by a stander-by, who told the police. They were arrested, and would have been executed—except that the *real* revolution broke out in time to save their necks.

Act Two. When the real revolution (which they had nothing to do with) changed the political face of France, Blanqui and his faithful band met and decided to publish a paper *La Patrie en Danger.* Their political declaration, issued on September 6, told the revolutionary workers of Paris to forget about revolution and to drop all political struggle—because the one and only enemy was the Prussian foe: "no more parties or shadings... The government that has emerged ... represents the thinking of the people and national defence. That is enough. All opposition, all contradiction must disappear before the common welfare."[39]

In the succeeding months, leading to the Commune revolution, this pre-1914 appeal for *Union Sacrée* was ignored by the people. In the intensifying revolutionary situation, our "revolutionists" were nonentities. Da Costa himself says: "The formidable insurrection of March 18 broke out without warning. The Blanquist party was more or less scattered and it had the greatest difficulty in reconstituting itself on the spot, on the battlefield, one might say." A couple of Blanquists hurried to cash in by taking over the police prefecture and the war ministry.[40]

If the Blanquist group was a zero in the prerevolutionary situation, it was no bargain in the Commune itself. G. D. H. Cole's *History of Socialist Thought* summarizes their role as follows:

> The Blanquists saw the Paris Commune as a working model of the revolutionary elite in action, and blamed the Internationalists for having spoilt it by insisting on democratic notions quite inappropriate during a period of revolutionary dictatorship. For the Blanquists the interest of the Commune lay not in its electoral system or its notion of the responsibility of the delegates to the electors, nor in the basis of Trade Union organization on which it partly rested, but in the dictatorial character enforced on it by the exigencies of civil war.[41]

Maurice Dommanget, the Blanquists' laureate among historians, is more specific:

> As soon as the Commune of 1871 was established, the Blanquist members planned to introduce a resolution which would suspend all democratic forms, appoint a committee of public safety and militarize the Commune, until the government of France had been overcome.

E. S. Mason, repeating this information, adds: "They desisted only because of the realization that there was no hope of carrying the measure through the Commune assembly itself."[42]

Their common source was the work by the Blanquist historian of the Commune, Gaston Da Costa (brother of the Charles Da Costa previously quoted), who had been Raoul Rigault's lieutenant in the police prefecture of the Commune. Gaston's *La Commune Vécue* insists that "the Paris assembly had to be a revolutionary and military dictatorship" with military victory as its "sole mission," postponing "all democratic and social reforms." The Blanquist group even drafted a measure and "thought of making a proposal of this kind, from March 29 on," but did not follow through because they were convinced that they could not get a majority vote for it. The author consoles himself with applying the label "dictatorship of the Central Committee" of the National Guard to the short period between the revolt and the first Commune election. But it was a "good-natured dictatorship," he explains. He pays little attention to the Majority-Minority split that came in May, because, he says in disgust, the Commune lacked "conscious dictators" anyway.[43]

There could hardly be a sharper contrast than between this Blanquist program and Marx's. The Blanquists wanted *dictatorial forms* of government as against the democratic measures of the Commune. The conception of a *class* dictatorship meant nothing to them; they looked to the institution of a dictatorial power within, and hence over, the Commune itself.

The Blanquist perspective of dictatorship took a new lease on life as the situation of the Commune worsened, and a sense of desperation grew. On April 28 the old Jacobin Miot reintroduced the proposal. In form, the motion was for the setting up of a five-man executive, actually a controlling commission to take over the nine commissions (government departments). And it was to be called—the Committee of Public Safety. On the surface, it was a historical reminiscence; just below, a hankering to turn responsibility over in despair to a dictatorial authority.

The word "dictatorship" was not made official, of course, but it was not denied or concealed; the three-day debate was for or against the dictatorship. The word had not yet acquired its modern meaning, remember; it was only three-quarters of the way through the nineteenth century; both sides denied any despotic or authoritarian intentions; the dictatorship would simply—get things done. A majority of 45 voted for the dictatorship of the Committee of Public Safety, against a minority of 23.

Some of the less prominent members of he Majority were more brash in calling for dictatorship. One wanted a stiffer rule, wielded by only three, not five; another demanded that the Committee of Public Safety "be endowed with full powers which may even be used against members of the Commune."[44] Even the anarchist Elie Reclus was inclined to go along with the dictatorship solution; the historian Koechlin, who writes as an anarchist sympathizer, laments over others, but is consoled by the case of Lefrançais, who supported the minority side.[43]

17. The Second Period of the 'Dictatorship of the Proletariat' 277

The Minority formed itself into an opposition on what it considered a fundamental abandonment of the very reason for existence of the Commune; the Majority, it felt, was discrediting the ideal of democratic freedom. *We fought for liberty under Bonaparte's Empire*, they said—*in power ourselves, we will not deny it.*[46] A first Minority Declaration after the vote denounced the decision because it "will have the essential effect of creating a dictatorial power that will in no way contribute to the strength of the Commune;... the creation of a dictatorship by the Commune would be a veritable usurpation of the sovereign rights of the people..."[47]

The Minority was further exasperated when the Majority dismissed some of its most capable men from their posts—Varlin, Vermorel, Longuet, and others. The suppression of newspapers by the "dictators" roused new displays of passion. On May 15 the Minority issued a declaration, beginning:

> ... the Commune has abdicated its power into the hands of a dictatorship, to which has been given the name of Committee of Public Safety. The Majority has declared itself irresponsible by its vote. The Minority, on the contrary, affirms that the Commune owes it to the revolutionary movement to accept all responsibilities. As to ourselves, we claim the right of being alone answerable for our acts without screening ourselves behind a supreme dictatorship.[48]

And the Minority announced that its members were withdrawing from participation in the Commune's councils and would devote themselves to their arrondissements.

It was too late for anybody and anything. Just about as the Commune split between Majority and Minority, the Versaillese started their final military assault on the Commune. The political meaning of the split was never further developed, as the Commune had to fight for its life. The "dictators" were impotent from the start; if they had been worth much to begin with, the dictatorship would not have appeared so attractive, even as a dodge.

It is clear that while the line between Majority and Minority did not neatly follow the lines of political tendencies, the core group of the Blanquist and Jacobin tendency was the core of the pro-dictatorship Majority, and the bulk of the Minority was formed by members of the International and the Proudhonists. The most prominent crossover was the leading Blanquist, Tridon, who went over to the minority by May 15.

There was another clear correlation. There were a few men in the leadership who had a relationship of sorts with Marx or were close to his views. Closest was Serraillier, who had in fact been sent into the situation by the International's General Council and by Marx personally. Serraillier was with the Minority steadfastly from the start. Frankel was the Commune leader who had written to Marx for advice on socialization (he was going to be a founder of the Hungarian movement and close to Marx in the emigration). Frankel supported the Minority. Of all the Proudhonists, Varlin is sometimes described as a semi-Marxist, not because of any connection with Marx himself but because his political thinking was most advanced. Varlin was with the Minority. Longuet has been mentioned. The summary statement that the best and most advanced socialists in the Commune supported the Minority is by and large true, despite room to cavil.

With this background it is surprising that no substantive comment on the Majority-Minority split can be found in Marx's or Engels' extant writings or correspondence.* Perhaps there was a reluctance on all sides, in the post-revolutionary emigration, to rediscuss the question and reawaken hostilities. Yet there must have been talk: the mentioned members of the Minority (save Varlin, who was killed fighting) were close to Marx in the General Council; Vaillant, who emerged as Blanquist leader in the emigration, was also active in the GC. It is a pity we do not know how the postmortems went.

And so as the Commune went down in bloody defeat at the hands of the Versaillese state, it was split down the middle over the issue of dictatorship. The issue was not the dictatorship of the Commune, but of a *dictatorship within and over the Commune.*

The Minority had not come out against 'dictatorship' in general; it denounced *this* dictatorship. If the antagonistic sides, reassembled in emigration, were to get along, it would help to emphasize this common ground. The circumstances were new, but again there was a special reason to counterpose Marx's specific conception of *class* dictatorship against the Blanquist-Jacobin conception of a dictatorship over the revolution itself.

Marx wrote his defense of the Commune, *The Civil War in France,* while the Commune's forces were still fighting. It could not be, and was not, merely an attempt at historical summation; it was a blow in the social struggle that was opening up around the great upheaval. When he wrote the Address, he still had had no contact with the Blanquist tendency for two decades; this contact was established when Commune refugees began flowing into London.

---

* Marx's notebook of press excerpts for April-May included a quote from the Commune paper *Le Cri du Peuple* (May 17) on the Minority Declaration of May 15. Marx copied the beginning of the statement, including the reference to "dictatorship."[49]

18 | MARX AND THE BLANQUISTS AFTER THE COMMUNE

From the middle of 1871 on, Communard refugees flowed into London, including many Blanquists. For the first time a number of them came into continuous contact with Marx and his circle of cothinkers and with the General Council of the International.

1. THE BLANQUISTS AND THE INTERNATIONAL

Before the Commune, the Blanquist group had kept apart from the International in France, since it was dominated from the start by the Proudhonists. When the first congress of the International was scheduled for Geneva in September 1866, the Blanquists decided to send a delegation—"with the mission," says Da Costa, "of denouncing this attenuation of socialism and of preventing the majority of the workers from falling into the trap."[1] In other words, as a hostile and disruptive visitation.

The Blanquist delegation was headed by Protot, a lawyer. Tridon, Blanqui's chief lieutenant, also went to Geneva, but at the last moment he brought an order from Blanqui to abstain from taking part in the congress. Protot protested vigorously, and declared that he had committed himself to Paris supporters whom he represented; he insisted on participating.* To be sure, he participated as disruptively as planned. The Blanquists remained hostile to the International for the next several years.

Marx had made attempts, before this, to find a *modus vivendi* for the coexistence of the Proudhonists and the Blanquists in the French International. Such a development would not only enormously strengthen the International

---

* Da Costa notes that this was the first case in which Blanqui's orders had not only been questioned but disobeyed; there was a violent reaction in Paris. A meeting was called to get Protot thrown out for violation of "discipline," with Tridon leading the hunt. It was this meeting that was raided by the police (see Chapter 9).[2]

but also supply a counterpoise to the Proudhonists. On April 22, 1866 Paul Lafargue wrote to Blanqui via Dr. Watteau (who told Blanqui that, in his opinion, the move was inspired by Marx).[3] Despite the failure at Geneva, Marx tried again in 1867, with no greater success in changing Blanqui's mind.[4]

There was, apparently, some hope that the Brussels Congress of 1868, which saw the defeat of the Proudhonists on the issue of collectivization, would make the Blanquists more favorable. Writing to Engels, Marx noted that "Blanqui was constantly present during the Brussels Congress,"[5] but this report does not seem to have been true. Despite the fact that, at that point, the International in France was growing rapidly under conditions of vicious governmental persecution, Blanqui rejected any relationship to a working-class mass movement as such—on the ground that it was not revolutionary enough.[6] Thus he condemned his group to be an increasingly irrelevant sect.

These events were, perhaps, reflected in a couple of changes Marx made in the text of his *Eighteenth Brumaire* when this work appeared in a second edition in 1869. Section 1 had referred to "Blanqui and his comrades" as "the real leaders of the proletarian party, the revolutionary communists"; but the second edition deleted "the revolutionary communists." In Section 7 two substantial paragraphs were left out of the new edition, containing a reference to Blanqui that seemed to echo the Toast of 1851; but of course this reference may not have been part of the reason for the omission.[7]

Marx's preface to the second edition explained that he had revised the text only by "striking out allusions now no longer intelligible,"[8] but the first change in particular seemed to reflect a feeling of greater political distance from the Blanquists.

2. MARX AND THE ÉMIGRÉS

The Blanquist refugees regrouped in London. Among the leading people mentioned in Da Costa's listing were Vaillant, Eudes, and Granger, plus Gois, Edmond Levraud, Ranvier, and Dr. Regnard. A background fact was brought out by Engels in his 1874 article:

> These Blanquists are so called not as a group founded by Blanqui—only a couple of the 33 signers of this program [the Blanquist 1874 pamphlet] have probably ever spoken with Blanqui—but because they want to be active in his spirit and according to his tradition.[9]

Political life in London made a considerable impact on the Blanquist émigrés in a number of ways.

(1) Marx's *Civil War in France* was met with great denunciation by respectable England and thus had a sort of *succès de scandale;* to the same extent it was recognized by the Communards as the most powerful literary blow struck in defense of the Commune. Marx was their champion in the eyes of the world.

(2) For months, much of Marx's work consisted of massive relief work on behalf of the refugees streaming across the Channel; he worked with an aid committee to provide money, jobs, and succor of any sort. Refugees of all shades came to his house in need.[10]

It can be assumed that this work not only engendered good will but also led to political discussions with the émigrés; we will see some examples.

(3) The General Council co-opted a number of Blanquist Communards to its own ranks, including Edouard Vaillant, Gabriel Ranvier, Antoine Arnaud, Frédéric Cournet, and Jules Johannard. On the General Council, of course, they worked closely with Marx. Other Blanquists, while not GC members, also became acquainted with Marx: Constant Martin, Eudes, Regnard, and others.[11]

Of all these, Vaillant eventually emerged as the leading figure. Tridon was dying in Belgium; Blanqui himself was in prison as usual (during 1871-72 he was held successively at Cahors, the Château du Taureau in Morlaix, Versailles prison, and Clairvaux). Eudes was next in command, but he was much less competent than Vaillant, who however was a comparative newcomer. A big difference was the fact that Vaillant, who had been educated in Germany, was tinged with Marx's socialist ideas.*

In his 1891 introduction to *The Civil War in France,* Engels was going to remark that "only a few [of the Blanquists] had attained greater clarity on principles, through Vaillant, who was familiar with German scientific socialism."[13]

(4) The Blanquists on the General Council were, at this point, lined up with Marx against the Bakuninist faction and its campaign to take over the International. (This alliance lasted only until the Hague Congress.) In this struggle the Blanquists, who had traditionally scorned theoretical questions, inevitably had to follow Marx's political lead and line of argumentation, learning in the process.

(5) Marx's two French sons-in-law, Charles Longuet and Paul Lafargue, were both acquainted with Blanqui and the Blanquists and had worked with them on good terms. Lafargue was not a Blanquist (or ex-Blanquist) but

---

* Dommanget says that Vaillant made 'dictatorship of the proletariat' "more precise" with the formulation "impersonal dictatorship of the proletariat."[12] By giving no source or date for this information, Dommanget allows the imagination to date it at will, but in fact Vaillant could not have used this expression until after his contact with Marx. It is not in either of the Blanquist declarations discussed in this chapter.

rather an admirer of the Old Man.[14] Longuet, despite his lack of revolutionary fire, had a warm feeling for Blanqui, especially since his talks with the Old Man in the Necker hospital in 1865,[15] and also regarded Vaillant as a friend.[16] Both Lafargue and Longuet were in a position to act as go-betweens.

3. THE BLANQUIST SPLIT

In 1872 the International broke under *two* stresses. The main pressure, which is also best known, came from the battle against the Bakuninist takeover bid; the Blanquist delegates worked with the General Council against the Bakuninist plotters. But the Blanquists were by no means behindhand in proclaiming that they wanted to make the International the "revolutionary organization" it should have been from the beginning, that is, to remold it into a Blanquist sect.

Marx's proposal to move the General Council's seat from London to New York was motivated (there can be little doubt) by the desire to keep it out of the Blanquists' hands now that the Bakuninists had been beaten back. If the Bakuninists had schemed in secret to take over the International by infiltration, the Blanquists were no less intent on taking it over in plain sight. Of course, it is not at all certain that they could have succeeded against the old GC coalition led by Marx, but what loomed before Marx's eyes, at the best, was a second wracking internal war that was sure to leave the organization in tatters if it left anything at all. The transfer to New York was an attempt to save *something* of the International from the Blanquists.

This was how the Blanquists saw it too. They reacted a few days after the Hague Congress, with a manifesto, *Internationale et Révolution*,[17] announcing their withdrawal from the International because of its insufficiently revolutionary character. During the following year they sought to renew relations with Blanquist fragments in France, and looked to reconstitute a group of their own. In June 1874, under the name of the Commune Révolutionnaire, they issued a propaganda pamphlet presenting a declaration of Blanquist principles: *Aux Communeux*.[18]

In both of these programmatic statements there were references to the "dictatorship of the proletariat."

What this shows is not that the Blanquist group had become Marxist, but only that their very meager theoretical equipment had become tinged with some ideas of Marx's. More than once, publicly and privately, Engels stated in this period that the new Blanquist programmatic statements had been dressed up in Marxist ideas. He wrote Sorge about the first pamphlet:

> Blanquists. Have put out a pamphlet, *Internationale et Révolution*... Explain their exit from the International, which is said to have killed itself by the deportation of the General Council to New York. Will establish a society of their own and are already extensively cliquing up in France . . . [The "Pure," as they call themselves,] are playing at *Commune Révolutionnaire* quite in the old fashion. You will have fun reading the little brochure in which Vaillant quite seriously explains all our economic and political principles as Blanquist discoveries. . . . Harmless though they be, they must nevertheless not be given the means of starting more quarrels. . .[19]

In the following year, in his *Housing Question,* he included a remark on the new Blanquist program. We will quote this passage below, more fully, as locus 7a. Suffice to mention that the Blanquists "adopted, and almost literally at that, the views of German scientific socialism on the necessity of political action by the proletariat and of its dictatorship as the transition to the abolition of classes and with them of the state."[20]

This says in so many words that among the London Blanquists' borrowings from Marxism was the view about proletarian dictatorship. (This is of special interest for those people, like Postgate, who took these pamphlets as proofs of Blanquist responsibility for 'dictatorship of the proletariat'.[21])

In his 1874 article "Program of the Blanquist Refugees of the Commune" Engels explained the extent to which the Blanquists had been "Marxified" while making clear that their essential Blanquist politics were unchanged. After criticizing the first point in their program, strident atheism, he says:

> The second point of the program is communism. Here we are already in more familiar waters, for the ship on which we sail here is called the "Manifesto of the Communist Party," published in February 1848. The five Blanquists who left the International in the autumn of 1872 already espoused a socialist program which in all essential points was that of present-day German communism, and based their exit only on the fact that the International refused to play at revolution in the manner of these five. Now the council of the thirty-three adopts this program together with its whole materialist view of history, even if its transmogrification into Blanquist French leaves much to be desired, insofar as they have not stuck to the Manifesto pretty much verbatim...

A number of criticisms follow; then—

> Enough. Through all of the refugee foolishness and all of the attempts verging on the comic to... look fearsome, this program is a substantial step forward not to be ignored. It is the first manifesto in which *French workers espouse present-day German communism* .... To have brought them to this point is the indisputable service of *Vaillant,* who was one of the signers and who is known to be thoroughly familiar with the German

language and German socialist literature. Anyway, the German socialist workers... can regard it as a good sign if French workers adopt correct theoretical principles even though they come from Germany.[22]

I think Engels was here exaggerating the degree of clarity to be seen in the Blanquist pamphlets, for obvious reasons.

4. THE NEW BLANQUIST FORMULATIONS

The Blanquists' adoption of 'dictatorship of the proletariat' was one of the new features of their program. That this was a *new* view of the Blanquists was virtually stated by themselves in the passage on "dictatorship of the proletariat" in *International et Révolution*. The proletariat, says the pamphlet, must form a "party of proletarians" for a

> struggle without mercy or truce, one which will end only when, by the conquest of political power and by its dictatorship, the proletariat breaks the old society and creates the elements of a new one.

At this point a footnote is appended, as follows:

> In formulating this truth, which has become axiomatic since the 18th of March [Commune uprising in 1871], that the conquest of political power by force was a necessity for the proletariat for the realization of the social revolution, we did not expect that our thought would be misinterpreted.

(This introduces a passage directed against the Bakuninists.) Dating this "axiomatic" truth to the 18th of March has, of course, meaning only for the Blanquists, since Marx and the International had formulated it long before. As Engels had said in his letter, the Blanquists now merely proclaimed this as their own discovery.

In the same footnote the Blanquists had a longer statement on the dictatorship' formulation:

> But to achieve this emancipation of the workers, this abolition of class, goal of the social revolution, it is necessary that the bourgeoisie be dispossessed of its political privilege, by means of which it maintains all the others. The proletariat must, in a period of revolutionary dictatorship, use that power for its own liberation which up to now has been directed against itself; it must turn against its adversaries those same weapons which up to now have held it in oppression. And only then when it has made a clean sweep of these institutions, these privileges which constitute present-day society will this dictatorship of the proletariat cease, no longer having an object, the abolition of all classes

making one-class government pass away by itself. Then groups like individuals will be autonomous; then will be realized that federation—the result and not the means of victory—that *anarchy* which victory will produce, and which during the struggle is disorganization and failure when it is not treason or folly.[23]

The appendix of this pamphlet reprints the resolution presented by the Blanquist leaders to the Hague Congress on September 5, 1872, proposing their own program. Incidental to the language of the resolution is the following:

> Considering... that abstention from political action is the negation of the first duty of the working class: the conquest of political power having as its goal making a clean sweep of the old society and creating the elements of the new by the dictatorship of the Proletariat...

At the same Hague Congress, Vaillant used the phrase in a speech, saying that "it is necessary to hold down *[courber]* the owning classes under the dictatorship of the proletariat."[24]

In the 1874 programmatic pamphlet *Aux Communeux*, the term occurred in the section explaining why "we are revolutionaries" and have to overthrow the system by force:

> Because we recognize that it is necessary to conquer that political power which the bourgeoisie jealously guards for the maintenance of its privileges. Because, in a revolutionary period when the institutions of present-day society must be destroyed, the dictatorship of the Proletariat must be established and maintained until, in the emancipated world, there are no longer any but equal citizens in the new society.
>
> As a movement toward the new world of justice and equality, the Revolution is itself the bearer of its own law, and everything which stands in the way of its triumph must be crushed.
>
> We are revolutionaries; we want the Commune; for in the future Commune, as in the Commune of 1793 and 1871, we see not the selfish endeavor of one city, but the Revolution triumphant in the whole country: the communal Republic. For the Commune is the revolutionary Proletariat armed with dictatorship, for the destruction of privilege, the crushing of the bourgeoisie.[25]

Although the foregoing passage testifies to Vaillant's new influence by its apparent repudiation of the dictatorship of Paris over the country, the Blanquist program retains the idea of *minority* dictatorship. Further on, we get a blast against "the fraud of universal suffrage" and the argument that by no means must "the revolutionary minority abdicate before the average, distorted opinion of majorities that have been subjected to all of the influences of ignorance and privilege."

The retention of the Blanquist minority dictatorship was even more evident in the 1872 *Internationale et Révolution* where, in addition to the modest proposal that the International should become something very like a Blanquist band, we read that

> The revolutionary minority of the proletariat of the cities must, then, count only on itself; it is up to it to compensate for its numerical inferiority by its organization and its energy. At this price only can it produce the revolution, and while waiting to win them over, paralyze that inert and hostile mass ...[26]

The Blanquists' adoption of the term 'dictatorship of the proletariat' did not cause others to forget that these people had always advocated a party dictatorship over the people. One of the replies to the Blanquists' 1872 pamphlet came from Cluseret, a leftist military man who had fought with Garibaldi, the Union army in America, and the Irish Fenians before his participation in the Commune, where he had briefly and ingloriously headed the war department.

In a long article "L'Internationale et la Dictature," in the Geneva *Egalité* in December 1872, Cluseret attacked the Blanquists' pose as International leaders. He pointed out that they had been co-opted as GC members only as Commune symbols or representatives. They complained that the International "could not become the powerful lever that we desired": you see, they want to use the International only as their own "lever" or tool. "Children of authority, these gentlemen understand only dictatorship." Here, he said scornfully, are men who have no past except defeat and incompetency but who yet demand our confidence... His polemic against dictatorship assumed that it meant the traditional Jacobin dictatorship. The new formulation was not mentioned.[27]

5. DELAHAYE'S FORMULATION

There is an interesting indication of how far the term 'dictatorship of the proletariat' traveled in this period, at least in the London émigré circles of the Communards. In 1874 it cropped up not only in the Blanquists' manifesto but also in a programmatic pamphlet issued by a quite different wing of the French emigration, whose most prominent member was Victor Alfred Delahaye.*

---

* This man is incorrectly named Pierre Louis Delahaye in a number of works, including MEW. The information in this section is mostly based on the entry for V. A. Delahaye in Maitron's *Dictionnaire Biographique du Mouvement Ouvrier Francois*. Delahaye's correct name has recently been confirmed in the New Mega."

18. Marx and the Blanquists After the Commune   287

Twenty years younger than Marx, Delahaye was a mechanic, active in the French movement since about the late 1850s. When the Commune revolt broke out, he was president of the mechanics' union, which adopted a statement advocating a socialist reorganization of production; he also worked on Commune commissions. In London emigration, he became a member of the International's General Council. There he tended to the right—at any rate, in May 1872 Marx mentioned that Delahaye supported Hales's faction, with the comment that the other Communard members of theGC had a low opinion of him.[29]

In August 1872 Delahaye took a leading part in the formation of a new group in emigration: Comite Revolutionnaire du Proletariat. Two years later, in October 1874, this group published a program *A la Classe Ouurierè*.[30]

The group clearly had in mind the formation of a mass "workers' socialist party," unalloyed with Blanquist secret-society-ism. The nine signers all identified themselves as workers (craftsmen). The organization would be "federated nationally and internationally" and conduct "electoral political action for working-class candidates"; its "principal means of agitation" would be "elections, strikes, and antireligious propaganda." The pamphlet specified what would happen upon the conquest of power:

> As to the form of government, although in principle we are federalists, we believe that the dictatorship of the working class is indispensable, at least during the period of transformation, in order to establish a society based on social equality. We are convinced that the means which serves the bourgeois minority so well in order to oppress us could with greater reason serve the working-class majority to emancipate itself.[31]

Though this formulation assumed a working-class majority, in opposition to the Blanquists, it is likely that by "dictatorship" this group meant dictatorial deviations from democratic forms and methods. However, there is no clarification one way or the other. Further along, the program for the revolution in power called for the following actions *inter alia* to implement a program of immediate "abolition of individual and private property":

> Organize the army of the revolution, finances, police, education; crush the clerico-bourgeois reaction at home;
> Prepare to defeat the foreign coalition abroad.
> When the ground is cleared, when the destruction of the bourgeoisie and its institutions is complete, the form of government will evidently be no more than a detail, a simple administrative question.[32]

The group apparently did not last long. Delahaye returned to France after the amnesty, became a Radical (i.e., nonsocialist) municipal councillor in Saint-Ouen in 1883-88, a member of the government's Labor Commission, and in 1890 a government delegate to the International Labor Conference in

Berlin; then he was decorated with the Legion of Honor. I mention this sad end because it was already implicit in his politics when Marx found him voting with Hales, and just before he came out for "the dictatorship of the working class."

Delahaye was trying to work out a reformist solution to the problems of the movement, and the dictatorial forms he envisioned must have seemed to him mainly a convenience. (Dictatorship has greater affinity to a desire for efficiency or efficacy than to a hankering for absolute power.) His 1874 program testified mainly to the spread of the 'dictatorship of the proletariat' formuladon in the Communard ranks in this period.

19 | MARX AND ENGELS IN THE SECOND PERIOD

The preceding chapter has shown how the 'dictatorship of the proletariat', at least as a phrase if not a concept, made its way in the London emigration of the Communards. Once again, very much as in the period following the defeat of the 1848-49 revolution, Marx had to discuss political issues with revolutionaries and would-be revolutionaries who started from the traditional Jacobin notion of dictatorship.

Once again—this is my hypothesis—Marx found it most educational to counterpose his own version of 'dictatorship', rather than to flatly reject the word; to argue for the dictatorship of a *class* in terms which equated this dictatorship with the generally accepted goal of the conquest of political power by the proletariat. In this period we will find Engels setting down in so many words the distinction between Marx's view of 'dictatorship' and the Blanquist idea.

As a result, in the Second Period, 'dictatorship of the proletariat' crops up five times in Marx's and Engels' productions—three times by Marx, twice by Engels.

1. THE CASE OF VERMERSCH

First: an incident which is too dubious to count as a locus. This is a secondhand reference to Marx's thinking that comes to us via Eugene Vermersch, who had been the editor of *Le Pire Duchene* during the Commune period.

An émigré in London after the defeat, Vermersch had one talk with Marx—probably in mid-September of 1871.[1] Vermersch told of this conversation two years later in a letter to Maxime Vuillaume, who published it just before World War I. Vermersch's letter quotes Marx as telling him that "Society is historically obliged to pass through the working-class dictatorship."[2]

This reported formulation raises no particular problem, of course; Marx might well have said something of the sort to any of the Communard visitors. But the source is so tainted that it has to be treated with reserve.

Vermersch was notorious as editor of a "filthy sheet" (so commonly called) which achieved a large circulation in Paris as a yellow-journal type of sensational rag of the worst sort, yelling wildly for bloodletting and mass guillotining. Its language was marked by the routine use of "fuckin'(this or that)" as an expletive in every other sentence or several times in one. Its main approach to politics was uninhibited slander.

In London Vermersch launched another sheet, *Qui Vive!* When it died, Engels, informing Liebknecht that it had "choked in its own filth," observed that "If the editor Vermersch was not a stoolpigeon, he at least wrote in such a way that the French police could not wish anything better."[3] Of the few scoundrelly elements that came along with the Communard influx, Engels wrote, Vermersch was the "arch-scoundrel."[4] When this habitual liar got into a row with the Blanquists, Engels referred to him publicly as

> one of the most disreputable people of the Paris yellow press, a certain Vermersch, who under the Commune published the *Phi Duchene,* a wretched caricature of Hebert's paper of 1793. This gentleman answered their moral indignation with a pamphlet... and poured a rare flood of scatalogical invective over their heads ...[5]

Vermersch's reputation crossed party lines: not only the Blanquists but also the Bakuninist faction leader Guillaume held him in bad odor.[6]

Not only is this wretch a dubious source in general, but the letter in question is a brew of poisonous hatred, the longest section being a racist hymn of hatred against Germans in a fulsome vaunting of French chauvinism. This follows another quotation ascribed to Marx, against the "Latin races," which is simply absurd. Even Vuillaume, his old ally, in a footnote separated himself from Vermersch's racist ranting against Marx as a "pan-Germanist"—an exercise in which this blackguard repeated the similar racist ravings that Bakunin was sending around about this time in his assault on the International.

It is questionable whether anything in this letter is trustworthy for any purpose, but it provides the following vignette. Vermersch's letter bitterly informs his friend that "after the Commune, the City Hall rascals [i.e., the Commune leaders], or those who passed for such, had gathered around Karl Marx," whom he calls a pope. When he, Vermersch, arrived in London and saw "X," the latter took him to Marx's house. Marx, he boasts rather naively, was very affable and spent much time talking to him; but (he soon adds) he resented being pumped of information or grilled like a prisoner in the dock. In the course of this conversation we get the reference to the remark on "working-class dictatorship." Vermersch was never in Marx's house again, he says.

It is likely that Vermersch omitted from this account, for understandable reasons, any report on what really was discussed by Marx under the head of 'dictatorship'—namely, Vermersch's own views on the subject. These were made plentifully clear in the next two years (probably before, too, but I find no record). Vermersch was an assiduous proponent of a kind of dictatorship, and his talk with Marx did not change his style.

In February 1872 he published a letter to a French deputy in which he explained that before the people can govern there must be a dictatorship.[7] The following year, in the second of a series of little pamphlets, this one titled *La Dictature,* Vermersch elaborated on what he meant. His starting point was of course similar to the Blanquists': the mass of people is not "capable of directing public affairs" ... "when it comes to power, the People turns stupid, because, being uneducated—hence no logicians—it is naturally goodhearted ... because from the viewpoint of real politics each generation of workers is no more advanced than the preceding one, the People gets the cruel but just punishment for its ignorance and presumption." The People must have the good sense "to understand that the task which it was not up to accomplishing by itself should be handed over to a well-tested agent... who will assure its safety." Therefore "for the revolutionary people there is only one means of safety, that is, the establishment of a dictatorship."[9]

He repeatedly stressed the theme of the incapacity of the people to govern, almost as often as he quoted Machiavelli. His original contribution was a proposal for a two-phase dictatorship. The first dictator, whose task was to repress counterrevolution with bloody violence, would inevitably become "too odious" in the eyes of the people; the "second part of the dictatorial mission," construction of the new order, required a "second dictatorship," ergo a second dictator to take over. Take over how? This depended on circumstances, but Vermersch was certain that Marat's idea *of electing* a dictator was wrong ("the political capacity of the people" being lacking, as before, etc.). The dictatorship, then, would be the "prize of force." That is, to interpret in Vermerschian terms, the most bloody-ruthless jungle killer would prove himself fit to wield power.[9]

Though Vermersch started from the traditional Jacobin notion of dictatorship, he soon steered in the direction of Bakuninist concepts. In the last of his pamphlet series, *La Société Secrète,* he polemized against the idea of a secret society by glorifying a vague notion of revolutionary mass spontaneity, which he counterposed to any organized leadership. This pamphlet wound up with a vicious (or Vermerschian) attack, solely slanderous, on the anti-Bakuninist exposé which the International published in mid-1873, written mosdy by Engels and Lafargue.[10] It seems apparent that Vermersch was speculating on taking over Bakunin's clientele. We have mentioned Vermersch's repetition of Bakunin's anti-German racist agitation, which was a very important element

292   *Part IV: 'Dictatorship of the Proletariat' in Marx and Engels*

in the Russian's propaganda leading up to the Hague Congress. In another of his pamphlets Vermersch took over the Bakuninist notion of "revolutionary" brigandage: "Let [the people] pillage, let them steal, let them kill—... you [the bourgeois] have made them beasts of prey!"[11]

This exponent of revolutionary cretinism operated, to be sure, in a corner of what passed for the workers' movement, but it was not without all effect on the muddle of ideas pullulating in the emigration.

2. LOCUS 5: MARX'S BANQUET SPEECH

Did Marx regard the Paris Commune as a 'dictatorship of the proletariat'?

This question was long considered moot; for, while it was well known that Engels had attached the label (in locus 11), it was long believed that Marx had refrained from doing so. Behind this issue was the interpretation of the term itself. If, in Marx's view, it meant a workers' state or the 'rule of the proletariat', no more and no less, then obviously Marx would have called the Commune by one or the other term interchangeably. If however it meant some special form of workers' state, or only one that takes some specific "dictatorial" steps, then the Paris Commune could be called a 'dictatorship of the proletariat' only by some process of argumentation, or not so called at all because it was "too democratic"...

My thesis in this book has been the first of these two opinions. It was also the thesis of my 1962 essay. Shortly after its publication, Volume 17 of the Marx-Engels *Werke* appeared, calling attention to a hitherto obscure report of a speech by Marx. For anyone who needed a Marx-quote to settle the matter, here it was.*

Right after the end of the September 1871 Conference of the International, held in London because the scheduled congress had had to be postponed, a banquet was held as usual. It was billed as the seventh anniversary celebration of the International's founding, but it was also the London Conference's wind-up social affair. The detailed account we have is an unsigned article that appeared in the *New York World*, headed "The Reds in Session . . . [etc.]," datelined from London.[12]

It was a convivial affair, at which Marx was voted into the chair by

---

* A quicker way to settle the matter was taken by Iring Fetscher in a 1976 book: he quoted Marx's *Civil War in France* as stating flatly that the Commune was "the *dictatorship of the proletariat*"—between quote marks, too. This aberration is discussed in Special Note D, Section 2.

acclamation. In the only other extant notice of the banquet, Marx's daughter Jenny told friends in Germany:

> °°Mohr [Marx] was made to preside on the occasion (much against his will, as you may imagine), and he had the honour of having on his right hand the heroic Polish general Wroblewski. On the other side sat the brother of Dombrowski. A great many members of the Commune were present.[13]

The *World* dispatch said that the banquet was held "by the members of the general council and a select company of friends, most of them members and officers of the Paris Commune." Marx's short speech as chairman was reported in some detail, not between quotation marks but in paraphrase. The passage that concerns us, on the Commune, went as follows:

> [Locus 5]
> The last movement was the Commune, the greatest that has yet been made, and there could not be two opinions about it—the Commune was the conquest of the political power of the working classes. There was much misunderstanding about the Commune. The Commune could not found a new form of class government. In destroying the existing conditions of oppression by transferring all the means of labor to the productive laborer, and thereby compelling evey able-bodied individual to work for a living, the only base for class rule and oppression would be removed. But before such a change could be effected a proletarian dictature would become necessary, and the first condition of that was a proletarian army. The working classes would have to conquer the right to emancipate themselves on the battlefield. The task of the International was to organize and combine the forces of labor for the coming struggle.[14]

Thus Marx's first recorded use of the term since 1852 took place in a setting heavily conditioned by an audience that was Blanquist in good part. There were many little speeches and toasts, said the *World,* "but the name that set the whole assembly in motion like an electric shock was Blanqui's."

I submit that to find Marx reviving, or reusing, the term after two decades in *this* context tends to confirm the thesis that Marx's term 'rule of the proletariat' was reformulated as 'dictatorship of the proletariat' *when Marx had to confront the Blanquist mind.*

There are four circumstances to note about this affair.

(1) Marx's formulation here was "proletarian dictature": the Gallicized form of 'dictatorship' may have been due to the fact that Marx was speaking, at least at this point, in the type of macaronic English that is so common in his

letters; or perhaps he was even speaking in French, in whole or part. Besides, the form 'dictature' is met with in English writers at this time.*

(2) There can be no doubt that Marx was applying "proletarian dictature" to the Commune. This passage began with the reiteration of the proposition that "the Commune was the conquest of the political power of the working classes," and it continued with an exposition of that idea.

(3) The *World* paraphrase had Marx saying, contradictorily, both that the Commune represented "the political power of the working classes" and that it "could not found a new form of class government." Of course, Marx must have been making his customary point that the working-class *state* or government had the task of inaugurating a classless *society*. As usual, he presented the "proletarian dictature" as a transitional stage toward the abolition of all class rule: "before such a change could be effected ... "

(4) Because of the interest attaching to this banquet speech, it is unfortunate that its exact date has been muddled. It is usually dated September 25, because the *World* article, datelined September 26, said that the celebration took place "last night." But the aforementioned letter by Jenny (who was at the banquet table, according to the *World)* gave the date as September 24. To be sure, Jenny might have made a mistake; on the other hand, editors have been known to change (for example) "two nights ago" to "last night" in order to make a piece look more current. I think Jenny's date is more likely for two reasons: (a) The Conference sessions ended on September 23, and the pattern was to hold the banquet the next day; (2) the 24th was a Sunday; the 25th, a Monday.

Outside of Marx, it is difficult to find anyone who raised the question of the relationship of the Paris Commune to the common formulations about "revolutionary dictatorship," "dictatorship of the people," or any other favored dictatorship. According to Venturi, the Russian revolutionist Lavrov was "one of the first in Europe ... to define the Commune as an instrument of power of the proletariat," as a "government of the workers"—this in an article published shortly after the Commune revolt broke out. Then he went to London, became well acquainted with Marx and Engels (with whom he corresponded for many years) and with the General Council, and participated in discussions on the Commune. (He must have chatted with Marx about 'dictatorship'.) Some years later, in 1879, he summarized his views in a long

---

* Under the impress of the Commune, in his 1875 poem "Aristophanes' Apology," Robert Browning advocated

    Choosing the rule of few, but wise and good,
    Rather than mob-dictature, tools and knaves ...

Thus Browning praises what we would be inclined to call an oligarchic dictatorship as he rejects what he calls mob-dictatorship, i.e., popular rule.

pamphlet, *The Paris Commune of the 18th of March 1871*, and here he mentioned that

> Only Millière, in Nos. 23, 29 and 30 of the *Marseillaise*, had described a plan to organize the "revolutionary dictatorship of the people."[15]

This report is secondhand and rather vague, but it is all I can find.

3. LOCUS 6: MARX ON POLITICAL INDIFFERENCE

Marx's next use of the term came in an article written for the Italian socialist press: Enrico Bignami's annual *Almanacco Repubblicano per l'Anno 1874*, published in Lodi in December 1873. Marx had written it about a year before, in December-January around the turn of the year 1872 into 1873. Bignami was the editor of *La Plebe* and an opponent of the Bakuninists (though on the reformist side), a valued ally of the General Council.

Marx's article was an attack on the antipoliticalism of Proudhonism, an important target at the time since it was Proudhon's theoretical writings (certainly not Bakunin's) that fed the anarchoid ideology of Bakunin's Italian clientele. The article was entitled "L'Indifferenza in Materia Politica" (Indifference to Political Affairs), a title probably conferred by Bignami, who also did the Italian translation. (Marx's own manuscript, probably in French, is not extant.)

Since this passage was one of those cited by Lenin in *State and Revolution*, it has often been referred to and reproduced, but usually without an explanation of its peculiar context. Out of context, it must be puzzling.

The article begins abruptly with a long section, all in quotation marks, which purports to set forth what an antipolitical Proudhonist-anarchist would say *if he* wrote down his views frankly and bluntly. In other words, this part is a fictitious speech, *purporting to represent not Marx's views but those of his target*. The 'dictatorship' phrase occurs in the course of this fictitious speech; for the speaker is shown attacking the idea of the 'dictatorship of the proletariat' in the same way as any idea of political action or power. It is quite clear if you read the entire article, but if you are only served up the cited paragraph you have to remember that the formulations are being put in the opponent's mouth by Marx.

[Locus 6]

" If the political struggle of the working class assumes violent forms, if the workers substitute their revolutionary dictatorship for the dictatorship of the bourgeois class, they commit the terrible crime of violating principle;* because, in order to satisfy their wretched, profane everyday needs, in order to crush the resistance of the bourgeois class, instead of laying down arms and abolishing the state they give it a revolutionary and transitional form."[16]

The idea is being alluded to only in passing. The fictitious speaker is using the 'dictatorship' phrase only as another formulation for workers' political power.

This is underlined by the direct counterposition of the two *class* dictatorships, one the alternative to the other, thereby putting the accent on the social basis of the power rather than on the political forms or methods of a regime. Here the "dictatorship of the bourgeois class" is clearly used as a general formulation for the bourgeois state, any bourgeois state, just as the "[workers'] revolutionary dictatorship" is being used as a general formulation for a workers' state.

Here we very clearly find Marx using the "dictatorship of the bourgeoisie" as a term *coordinate with* the "dictatorship of the proletariat," one counterposed to the other. Earlier, in 1850 for example, Marx's *Class Struggles in France* had referred to Cavaignac's rule as a "bourgeois dictatorship recognized officially" and "the dictatorship of the bourgeoisie by the saber";[17] but in those cases the generalized meaning of "bourgeois dictatorship" was only latent.

This use of "bourgeois dictatorship" was certainly not unknown in socialist circles, where *tu quoque* arguments were common enough. At the 1866 congress of the International in Geneva, a report by Dupont and Eccarius had argued that cooperatives could "transform the wage system and destroy the capitalist dictatorship, which was deliberately hostile to cooperatives."[18] At the same congress, the report on trade-unionism incidentally remarked that unions could be "organs of transformation of the system of wage-labor and of capitalist dictatorship."[19]

Such a general counterposition of "dictatorship of the bourgeoisie" to "dictatorship of the proletariat" implicitly defines the latter in terms of the class nature of the political power rather than special governmental forms.

4. LOCUS 7: ENGELS ON THE HOUSING QUESTION

Hard on the heels of Marx's Italian article, the term was next used by Engels in Part III of his work *The Housing Question*. This is the first time that it occurred in Engels' writing (unless we count Engels' signature on the SUCR document, locus 2).

* Lit., "crime *of leso-principio,*" on the analogy *of leso-maestà*, i.e., lèse-majesté.

This work was originally published as a series of articles in the Leipzig *Volksstaat*, mostly in 1872, but the installments constituting Part III were written in January 1873 and published in the course of February. The term occurred in two passages of Part III.

The first one, dealing with the Blanquists, has already been mentioned.[20] The reason why the term occurred to Engels in this connection is contained right in the passage itself, namely, the reference to the Blanquist manifesto *Internationale et Révolution*, which had been published in 1872. Here is the passage:

[Locus 7a]

... when the so-called Blanquists made an attempt to transform themselves from mere political revolutionists into a socialist workers' group with a definite program—as was done by the Blanquist refugees in London in their manifesto *Internationale et Révolution*—they... adopted, and almost literally at that, the views of German scientific socialism on the necessity of political action by the proletariat and of its dictatorship as the transition to the abolition of classes and with them of the state—views such as had already been expressed in the *Communist Manifesto* and since then on innumerable occasions.[21]

Obviously Engels was not saying that the 'dictatorship' phrase appeared in the Manifesto nor that it had been expressed "on innumerable occasions." These statements applied directly only to the rest of the formulation about "political action by the proletariat." What is striking is that Engels treated it all as a single integrated idea. In this sense he *was* dating the 'proletarian dictatorship' idea back to the Manifesto, where the term does not appear.

The second passage is interesting for a similar reason. Here Engels was polemizing against a Proudhonist, whom he has just quoted:

[Locus 7b]

Friend Mülberger thus makes the following points here:
1. "We" do not pursue any "class policy" and do not strive for any "class rule." But the German Social-Democratic Workers Party, just *because* it is a *workers' party*, does necessarily pursue a "class policy," the policy of the working class. Since every political party sets out to establish its rule in the state, so the German Social-Democratic Workers Party is necessarily striving for *its* rule, the rule of the working class, hence a "class rule." Moreover, *every* real proletarian party, from the English Chartists onward, has always put forward a class policy, the organization of the proletariat as an independent political party, as the first condition of the struggle, and the dictatorship of the proletariat as the immediate aim of the struggle. By declaring this to be "ridiculous," Mülberger places himself outside the proletarian movement and inside the ranks of petty-bourgeois socialism.[22]

What leaps to the eye is Engels' assumption that "dictatorship of the proletariat" has no *special* meaning whatever other than the establishment of the "rule" of the working class. This is put beyond doubt by the direct statement, underlined by Engels, that *every* real proletarian party necessarily stands for it, including the Chartists, and has *always** put it forward. The reference to the Chartists is sufficiently explained in Chapter 8.[23]

This statement by itself speaks volumes about Engels' conception of the 'dictatorship of the proletariat' and singlehandedly refutes a good deal of what has been written about it. It can make no sense to anyone who believes that there is some special "theory of proletarian dictatorship" in Marx and Engels, some "theory" beyond that of the workers' state as the embodiment of the political power of the proletariat. At such points, the Engels-versus-Marx myth becomes very handy.

Incidentally, in this same work we find that Engels considered it a tactical matter of indifference whether the proletariat in power

> will simply take possession of the instruments of production, raw materials and means of subsistence by force, or whether it will pay compensation for them immediately or whether it will redeem the property involved there by slow installment payments.[24]

It does not sound very "dictatorial." But, as is well known, Marx agreed with this relaxed view of the compensation-confiscation issue. The point is that the character of a workers' state as a 'dictatorship of the proletariat' has nothing to do with tactics of this sort.

5. MARX'S NOTES ON BAKUNIN'S BOOK

The two preceding loci were directed against Proudhonist lines of thought, involving not anarchism so much as general antipoliticalism. In response Marx and Engels were led to emphasize the necessity for the conquest of political power, the transitional 'rule of the proletariat'.

While Marx had brought out the formulation 'dictatorship of the proletariat' as a counterpoise to the Blanquists, we are now at an interesting point where he obtrusively *refrained* from using the term. This negative fact is relevant to our inquiry.

The case concerns Bakunin's book *Statism and Anarchy*,[25] published in 1873. Marx made his way through this work—partly for his Russian language study—during 1874 and early 1875, writing out a detailed summation, in

---

* Unaccountably, the translation in MESW and allied works omits the word 'always'.

quotations and paraphrase.[26] It was mainly toward the end of these notes (which take over forty printed pages) that he began to interpolate some comments of his own. Even so it must not be thought that he wrote up a systematic refutation; the scribbled comments tend to be expletive, exclamatory, telegraphic, and ungrammatical.

The background issue is Bakunin's principled attack on democracy (as we explained in Chapter 7)[27]–not simply his criticism of universal suffrage but his rejection of democratic control of authority as an aim; any limitation on the sovereignty of the ego is "authoritarian"; representation is an unalloyed evil; the more thoroughly democratic, the worse. While Bakunin sometimes gave the impression he was only complaining about the *defects* of democracy, *Statism and Anarchy* as usual excludes any possibility of democratic representation:

> Both the theory of the state and the theory of the so-called revolutionary dictatorship in equal measure are based on this fiction of the pseudo-representation of the people and on the real fact that the popular masses are governed by a handful of privileged people elected–or indeed not even elected—by mobs voting under constraint and ignorant of whom they're voting for, on this abstract and fictional expression of what is represented to be the people's will and thought, of which the real, living people do not have the least idea.[28]

So it must be understood that Bakunin's objection to "revolutionary dictatorship" is essentially the same as his objection to any *democratic* state. He attacks Marx from the same direction that he attacks the very idea of representative institutions:

> By a people's government the Marxists understand the government of the people by means of a small number of representatives elected by the people by universal suffrage. The election by the whole of the nation of the self-styled representatives of the people and leaders of the state—this is the last word of the Marxists as well as of the democratic school—is a lie that conceals the despotism of the governing minority, a lie all the *more* dangerous in that it is presented as the expression of the alleged will of the people.[29]

There are always two possibilities about such attacks on democracy: (1) they criticize democratic forms for not being democratic enough, for not really effecting democratic control by the people; or (2) they utilize the widespread cynicism about elections solely for the purpose of discrediting democracy itself. In general, anarchism takes the second road. Bakunin continually denounces the "Marxists" *because* they favor universal suffrage.

It is interesting that at no point in his book does Bakunin refer to the 'dictatorship, of the proletariat'—or to any 'dictatorship' really advocated or discussed by Marx. Instead, by a juggle equating Marx and Lassalle, he ascribes to Marx the notion of a "dictatorship by savants" and whips himself to a fury of denunciation against this mythical Marx's idea of "the despotic government of the proletarian masses by a new and very small aristocracy of real or alleged savants." Since such a dictatorship is the worst of all, says Bakunin, the Marxists "console themselves with the idea that this dictatorship will be temporary and short-lived."[30]

Marx scribbles a note on this: *"Non, mon cher!* [We console ourselves, rather, with the thought] that the *class rule* of the workers over the old world's strata they have been fighting can last only as long as the economic basis of the existence of classes is not destroyed."[31] We see that Marx underlines "*class rule*" here, as if demonstratively refusing to follow Bakunin in using the word 'dictatorship'; he substitutes *Klassenherrchaft*.* The concoction about the "government of the savants" he dismisses with a scornful "*Quelle rêverie!*"

If Marx refuses to take the term 'dictatorship' from Bakunin, it is no doubt because he knows well enough what meaning was attached to it by our "libertarian," especially with respect to the various dictatorships he planned for himself.

Among Marx's interpolated notes are other remarks bearing on his customary description of the 'rule' or 'dictatorship' of the proletariat. In one passage Bakunin poses what he doubtlessly considered a very clever stumper:

> If the proletariat becomes the ruling class, one asks, whom will it rule? There will, then, remain still a class subjected to this new ruling class, to this new state...[32]

(In Marx's paraphrase-summary, this reads: "there will still remain another proletariat...")

In his comment on this, Marx does not bother to make the elementary point that the proletariat as ruling class has to "rule" (in the first place) the old defeated ruling class which seeks to regain power. He does make a general point:

> This means: as long as other classes, especially the capitalist class, still exist, as long as the proletariat fights against them (for upon its taking governmental power its enemies and the old organizations of society do not yet disappear), it must employ *forcible* means, hence governmental means; it is itself still a class, and the economic conditions on which the class struggle is based along with the existence of classes have not yet disappeared and must be forcibly cleared out of the way or transformed, and their process of transformation forcibly hastened.[33]

---

* Though Marx declined to use 'dictatorship' here and made it "class rule" the Sorbonne sociologist Georges Gurvitch felt the need to "correct" him. See Special Note D, Section 3.

19. Marx and Engels in the Second Period   301

(The style leaves something to be desired, but Marx did not intend these notes for any eyes but his own.)

Bakunin asks, about a passage in the *Communist Manifesto:* "What does it mean, 'the proletariat organized as the ruling class'?" Marx scribbles:

> It means that the proletariat, instead of struggling as individuals against the economically privileged classes, has gained enough strength and organization to employ general means of coercion in the struggle against them; but it can only employ economic means that abolish its own character as a *salariat* [body of wage-earners] and hence as a class; therefore, with its complete victory its own rule is ended too, since its class character has disappeared.[34]

The "dialogue" of paraphrase and scribbled comment goes on for a bit:

> [Bakunin] *"Will perhaps the whole proletariat stand at the head of the government?"*
>
> [Marx] For example, in a °trade union° does the whole union form its executive committee? Will all division of labor in the factory cease, also the various functions which arise from it? And in Bakunin's formation "from below to above," will everyone be "above"? Then indeed there's no "below." Will all members of the commune likewise administer the common interests of the region? In that case, there's no difference between commune and region.
>
> [Bakunin] *"The Germans number about 40 million. Will, for ex., all 40 million be members of the government?"*
>
> [Marx] °Certainly!° Since the whole thing begins with the self-government of the Commune.[35]

The last remark is unexpected: what, all forty million will be "members" of the government? This is how it is summed up in Marx's notes, but the original wording by Bakunin provides a more explanatory context:

> What does it mean, the proletariat organized as ruling class? Is this to say that the proletariat will be, all together, in control of public affairs? The Germans number about forty million. Can it be that these forty million will form part of the government and, with the entire people governing, there will no longer be any governed?...[36]

To this Marx answered "Certainly!"

Bakunin's challenging question might just as well have been: *What does it mean, the "dictatorship of the proletariat"?* Or, equally, substitute *"workers' state."*

6. LOCUS 8: ENGELS ON THE BLANQUIST REFUGEES

The most important expository statement on the 'dictatorship of the proletariat' came in 1874 in an article by Engels. In terms of our thesis on the genesis of the term, we should not be surprised to find that this article was an overall sketch of the Blanquist group in London and its political ideology.

That year, Engels started writing a series of articles for the *Volksstaat* on "Refugee Literature"; the second of these took up the "Program of the Blanquist Refugees of the Commune," a review of the Blanquists' pamphlet *Aux Communeux*.[37] We have already cited several passages from this article, especially to describe the Blanquist group.[38] But this article is one of the most important presentations of political views to be found in Marx and Engels: I would urge the reader to study it in one piece and as a whole. Unfortunately, it is typical of the situation that this important article appeared in English for virtually the first time[39] in *MESW*, that is, in 1969, and that it has been included in none of the "selected writings" collections that have come out since.

Engels writes of Blanqui himself:

> Blanqui is essentially a political revolutionary, a socialist only by sentiment,* sympathizing with the sufferings of the people, but he has neither a socialist theory nor definite practical proposals for social remedies. In his political activity he was essentially the "man of action," believing that a small well-organized minority, attempting a revolutionary *coup de main* at the right moment, can carry the mass of people with them by a couple of initial successes and thus make a victorious revolution.[40]

In this article Engels pinpoints the meaning of 'dictatorship of the proletariat' as against the Blanquist dictatorship:

[Locus 8]
> From the fact that Blanqui conceives of every revolution as the *coup de main* of a small revolutionary minority, what follows of itself is the necessity of dictatorship after its success—the dictatorship, please note, not of the entire revolutionary class, the proletariat, but of the small number of those who made the *coup de main* and who themselves are organized beforehand under the dictatorship of one person or a few.
>
> One can see that Blanqui is a revolutionary of the previous generation.[41]

---

* Dommanget, French communism's attorney for Blanqui, objects to this characterization of Blanqui as a "socialist by sentiment," and claims that Marx did not agree. For his argument, see Special Note D, Section 7.

There could be no clearer differentiation between Marx's conception of the 'dictatorship of the proletariat' as a class dictatorship and the traditional conception: the dictatorship of the party as the anteroom to popular-democratic government, hence excluding the latter at least as first, hence entailing the dictatorship of the party *over* the proletariat.

7. LOCUS 9: MARX ON THE GOTHA PROGRAM

The confrontation with the Blanquists, which led directly to loci 5 and 8, had produced several contexts for the 'dictatorship of the proletariat' during the first half of the 1870s. The term was around, and this no doubt accounts for the fact that it was used by Marx in an important document in 1875.

The two German socialist parties—the "Eisenachers" of Bebel and Liebknecht and the Lassalleans—were preparing to unite at a congress in Gotha. The draft program was filled with concessions to the Lassalleans; Marx was incensed. He sent a letter of critical analysis to some of the Eisenacher leaders, attacking the Lassallean formulations and ideas. This document, usually called his "Critique of the Gotha Program," was neither a personal letter nor a public article, but a restricted circular of political discussion.

The passage referring to 'dictatorship of the proletariat' here is one of the two most often-quoted loci, but also one of the barest. It came in the course of Marx's discussion of the "democratic section" of the program, that is, the section on democratic demands and planks.

Marx aimed his shafts, for one thing, at the Lassallean term, the "free state." He wanted to show how imprecise and misleading it is to call a state "free." One should keep in mind that Marx insisted on differentiating scientifically between the term 'state'—meaning the organized machinery of suppression of one class by another in the course of enforcing its political power—and other terms such as 'government', 'society', 'country'.

> Free state—what is this?
> It is by no means the aim of workers who have rid themselves of the narrow mentality of subjects to make the state "free." In the German Empire the "state" is almost as "free" as in Russia. Freedom consists in transforming the state from an organ set above society into one thoroughly subordinated to it, and today too the state forms are more free or less free to the extent that they restrict the "freedom of the state."[42]

In emphasizing that, for real freedom, the state must be transformed "from an organ set above society into one thoroughly subordinated to it," Marx was, of course, hitting at Lassalle's fetishism of the state, the theoretical side of his pervasive authoritarianism. As Marx wrote, a little further on, "the whole program, for all its democratic ring, is contaminated through and through with the Lassallean sect's servile belief in the state."[43]

Marx went on to argue that the state is based on existing society and is not "an independent entity that possesses its own *'intellectual, moral and freedom-related bases.'* "[44] He objected to the terminological confusion involved in the program between "present-day state" and "present-day society." Present-day society is capitalist society: there are different present-day states, yet what they have in common is their social basis. Then:

[Locus 9]
In this sense one can speak of "the present-day state," in contrast with the future, in which its present root, bourgeois society, has died off.

The question comes up, then: what transformation will the state undergo in a communist society? In other words, what societal functions will remain there that are analogous to the present state functions? This question can be answered only scientifically, and you don't get a flea-hop nearer the problem by juxtaposing the words 'people' and 'state' a thousand times.

Between the capitalist and the communist society lies the period of the revolutionary transformation of the one into the other. To this there corresponds a political transition period whose state can be nothing but *the revolutionary dictatorship of the proletariat*.[45]

Marx adds: "Now the program has nothing to do either with the latter [i.e., the dictatorship of the proletariat] or with the future state of communist society." And in fact he does not discuss the matter any further.

Another passage is relevant. Marx wrote that in the transition period the *state* would be the dictatorship of the proletariat; and on the next page he injects a sharp reminder that when he says 'state' he does not mean the *government machinery*.

This came up because he objected to the program's formulation that the party "demands *as the economic basis of the state:* a single progressive income tax," etc. No, Marx insisted, taxes are not the economic basis of the *state:* "Taxes are the economic basis of the government machinery and nothing else." He put the finger on the terminological confusion in the program: "by 'state' is meant the government machine," which really means "the state [only] insofar as it forms an organism separated from society through division of labor."[46] Perhaps this objection struck Marx's correspondents as terminological quibbling, but it is today that this "quibble" takes on a vital meaning.

Do not confuse the nature of a *state* with government *forms*, Marx warned. This has to be applied to the preceding statement that the *state* in the transition period will be a dictatorship of the proletariat. For Marx, this is a statement about the societal content of the state, the class character of the political power. It is not a statement about the forms of the government machine or other matters of government structure or policies.

Marx's statement that "the program has nothing to do either with this [the dictatorship of the proletariat] or with the future state of communist society" has been subjected to some scrutiny. The preceding is a literal translation of Marx's words, which has also been translated more freely as follows: "Now the program does not deal with this...."[47] The result is that Marx's statement has been interpreted as a *complaint* that the draft program did not deal with this question.

Even if we leave aside the meaning of Marx's words (the translation issue), it is very difficult to believe that Marx was urging the party to include 'dictatorship of the proletariat' in its program. There is not the slightest ground in the next paragraphs to leave this open. On the contrary! In the next paragraph Marx objects to the inadequacy of the "democratic" section of the program, and he points out that "one thing has been forgotten." It is not, of course, the 'dictatorship of the proletariat', but rather the demand for the *democratic republic:*

> ... the main thing, namely, that all those nice little things are based on the recognition of the so-called sovereignty of the people and that hence there is room for them only in a *democratic republic.*[48]

And even with repect to the 'democratic republic' demand, he immediately agrees that it is wiser for the program to omit it, simply out of "prudence" before the threat of government persecution.

Not before the "Critique of the Gotha Program" and not after it did Marx ever indicate that the party program should include the 'dictatorship of the proletariat', or any formulation involving the word 'dictatorship'. He did not do so when the program of the French Guesdist party was drafted in his London study in 1880. It was enough for a program to call for the conquest of political power by the proletariat. And if the 'dictatorship' formulation was only a special form of this plank, why *should* he have brought it up? The opposite view is based entirely on the belief that 'dictatorship of the proletariat' was a formula with special properties—properties that were evidently entirely alien to Marx's own view.

Though the statement about the 'dictatorship of the proletariat' is quite undetailed, it does say enough to quash one common misinterpretation. In the later socialist and communist movement, it was quite frequently said or implied that a workers' state might *or might not* be the 'dictatorship of the proletariat' depending on what it did—by which, one supposes, some staunchly "dictatorial" measures were expected. But in this locus Marx wrote very clearly that the transition period can be "nothing but" the dictatorship of the proletariat. He was plainly *not* thinking that the 'dictatorship of the proletariat' was only one kind of a transitional state, other workers' states being "non-dictatorial"... Once again, we find, Marx refutes in advance the conception of a "theory of the dictatorship of the proletariat" which is any thing other than the theory of the workers' state.

Marx did not change his mind: the passage in the "Critique of the Gotha Program" was the last appearance of the 'dictatorship of the proletariat' during his lifetime.

20 | THE THIRD PERIOD OF THE 'DICTATORSHIP OF THE PROLETARIAT'

The 'dictatorship of the proletariat' was Marx's terminological contribution, not Engels': this is beyond doubt. It was only in the 1870s that Engels adopted it in his own writings. When Marx died, the term had not surfaced for eight years; and another seven years passed before it appeared again from Engels' pen.

During this fifteen-year hiatus, of course, the old Blanquist problem that had originally elicited the term had completely changed. As the 1880s wore on, the tendency on the French left that was still reminiscently called Blanquist was rapidly moving toward social-democratic normalization, though it still preened itself on being "revolutionary." The era of secret-society conspiratorialism and putschism was buried under Vaillant's leadership; our previous discussion of the Blanquism of the fifties would be irrelevant now—except for our analysis of the reformist essence of Blanquist politics.

The term might never have re-emerged, conceivably, except for the reappearance of Marx's "Critique of the Gotha Program," as related in Section 3 below. But first, a couple of preliminaries.

1. LAFARGUE'S LANDMARK

In 1888 there took place what can be considered a landmark event in the history of the term, as far as the movement was concerned. It prefigured what was going to happen after Engels' death.

Emile Bottigelli's introduction to the *Correspondence* between Engels and the Lafargues claims that Paul Lafargue "was one of the few members of the [French Workers, or Guesdist] Party to affirm the necessity for the dictatorship of the proletariat..."[1] What this says or implies was not true: rather, Lafargue was one of the first to *utilize* the reverberations of the term to apologize for politics that can be called dictatorial in the modern sense.

The article in which Lafargue performed his alleged service was written for

307

the *Sotsial-Demokrat* published by the Russian Social-Democrats in Geneva. Its title was "Parliamentarism and Boulangism." In "Boulangism" lies the tale. The background fact is that Lafargue was, at this time, one of the few people in the leadership of the French Guesdists ("Marxists") who leaned toward critical support of the would-be military dictator General Boulanger. To give him the benefit of the doubt: he was "soft" on Boulangism. To put it more accurately: he wanted the movement to ride on the Boulangist wave in order to get a piece of the action, thus appearing as left-Boulangists.

There *were* leftists galore who were taking this line; and Boulanger had a substantial socialist-republican wing for a while, led by Henri de Rochefort, editor of *L'Intransigeant*. The Blanquist group split on the issue: a wing under Granger, breaking with Vaillant, formed its own "Boulangeo-Blanquist" organization and ran candidates as supporters of the Man on Horseback. Lafargue tended to push his own party into a similar position, but not as boldly.

Lafargue's position emerges from the correspondence at the time between him and Engels, who was trying to straighten him out on the issue.* There was no doubt at all, in the mind of anyone in France over four, that General Boulanger aimed to install a military dictatorship. The left-Boulangists could only dream that, in such a dictatorial regime, they could grab their share of power—naturally, in order to Do Good Things and eventually elbow the bumbling Boulanger out. *What was at stake was the destruction of France's democratic-republican institutions in favor of a military dictatorship.* this was the little **game** that Lafargue was inclined to play.

It would be anachronistic, of course, to call Boulanger a fascist flat-out, but it would be not at all invalid to investigate the many similarities between the Boulangist movement, short-lived as it was, and the fascism of the twentieth century. And the politics of "Boulangeo-Blanquism" and of left-Boulangism can only be clarified by this analogy. For one thing, part of the support for Boulanger from both right and left came from a general disillusionment and disgust with "parliamentarism," which in practice meant: with bourgeois-democratic institutions. Boulanger was going to rid France of its "parliamentary" paralysis and Get Things Done ...

In the middle of this situation, our Boulangeo-Marxist-on-the-half-shell, Lafargue, faced with the task of justifying his flirtation with the military

* Bottigelli's description of Lafargue's position on Boulanger glosses over the reality.[2] However, the facts are in the *Correspondence* collection which he edited. The exchange of letters between Engels and the Lafargues (Laura Marx Lafargue shows herself more competent politically than her husband) winds from the end of Volume 1 through the next two volumes, and can best be followed by using the index for 'Boulanger'. The next volume of KMTR will present a section on the politics of the Engels-Lafargue difference on Boulangism.

20. The Third Period of the 'Dictatorship of the Proletariat' 309

dictator, remembered something: hadn't Marx himself talked about "dictatorship" somewhere? or was it Engels? . . . Lafargue might not have known as yet of Marx's "Critique of the Gotha Program," but Engels' polemic against the Blanquists (locus 8) would be familiar. That was fourteen years ago...
The foregoing line of thought is speculative, to be sure. What is certain is that in his article on "Parliamentarism and Boulangism," Lafargue wrote:

> When the proletariat . . . takes possession of the state, it will have to organize a revolutionary authority and rule society dictatorially until the bourgeoisie has disappeared as a class, i.e., until there has been completed the nationalization of the means of production...[3]

There is no conception here of a *class* dictatorship, and it is doubtful that Lafargue understood this to be Marx's meaning. If he did, he would have known that "when the proletariat takes possession of the state," this possession already *is* the 'dictatorship of the proletariat'. Instead, he has the "proletariat" undertaking to "rule society dictatorially . . ." But a class cannot, as such, "rule dictatorially" in this sense; what Lafargue implicitly meant was that the representatives of the class, real or alleged, would "rule dictatorially."

There can be no question about what Lafargue's words would have meant in 1888 to any French reader. Indeed, Lafargue did not leave it entirely to speculation, for in the same article he referred to a number of dictators into whose arms the French people had thrown themselves: Cavaignac, Louis Bonaparte, Thiers in 1871—he does not quite apply the term to Boulanger.[4]

So, at precisely the time when a mass movement was being attracted to a military dictator, Lafargue found it opportune to mention that, after all, "we" too want to "rule dictatorially. . ."

2. LOCUS 10: ENGELS' LETTER TO SCHMIDT

The first time we meet the term again, after the fifteen-year hiatus, was in a private letter by Engels written in October 1890. The only evident reason why the term might have reoccurred to Engels at this point is that he was already looking at the old manuscript of Marx's "Critique of the Gotha Program," in preparation for making it public the first time (see next section). In mid-December he was already telling Karl Kautsky confidentially that a clear copy of the manuscript had been produced.[5] And so there is good reason to suppose that in October he had just dug it out of the archive.

The letter he wrote to Conrad Schmidt on October 27, 1890 was one of the group on the materialist conception of history which constitutes a basic source on the meaning of Marx's theory. In this letter Engels explained that historical materialism does *not* say that only economic factors are operative in history. He was discussing a book by Paul Barth:

[Locus 10]
If, then, Barth thinks that we deny any and every reaction by the political etc. reflections of the economic movement on this movement itself, he is simply tilting at windmills. He need only look at the *Eighteenth Brumaire* by Marx, which almost exclusively concerns itself with the *special* role that political struggles and events play, naturally within the framework of their *general* dependence on economic conditions. Or *Capital*, e.g., the section on the working day, where legislation, which after all is a political act, operates so incisively. Or the section on the history of the bourgeoisie (Chapter 24 [26-32 in English]). Or why then do we fight for the political dictatorship of the proletariat, if political power is economically powerless? Force (i.e., state power) is also an economic power![6]

The great significance of this locus is the extreme casualness with which 'dictatorship of the proletariat' is tossed in, as a mere synonym for the conquest of political power by the proletariat. It plays no other role, can be explained in no other way. As soon as the term is assigned a narrower or more specialized meaning in this context, Engels' statement ceases to make sense.

3. SECOND ROUND ON THE GOTHA PROGRAM

When Engels was writing to Schmidt, the German party was preparing to adopt a program to replace the one on which unification had been effected at the Gotha Congress in 1875. The new program was going to emerge from the Erfurt Congress in 1891 as a more Marxist-sounding document than the earlier one.

In the pre-congress period, Engels was determined to make known to the movement what the party leaders had been doing their best to suppress, namely, Marx's views on Lassalle and Lassalleanism. Besides, the party was supposed to discuss the Gotha Program in order to replace it, and so more than ever Marx's 1875 critique of that program was in order.

As we have seen, Engels disinterred the old document from the archive and moved to get it published for the first time. Getting it into the party organ *Vorwärts* would be difficult, for its editor was Liebknecht, who had the greatest interest of all in suppressing it again, as he had done in 1875, when he had kept it from Bebel's knowledge.[7] The alternative was the *Neue Zeit*, less widely read, of course. Engels twisted arms a bit: he threatened editor Kautsky that he would otherwise send the document for publication in the Vienna party press.

20. The Third Period of the 'Dictatorship of the Proletariat' 311

In any case Kautsky went along, and got the "Critique" into print before the party executive could order it killed.

Engels warned Sorge in advance that Marx's suppressed document would raise a storm:

> A bombshell is coming in No. 17 of the *Neue Zeit:* Marx's critique of the draft program of 1875. You will be delighted, but there will be anger and indignation from many in Germany.[8]

This prediction came true in spades. Engels' target was not only the shards of Lassalleanism in the program but also the rapidly developing opportunist trends among the party leaders and ranks in Germany, now that the pressure of the Anti-Socialist Law had been removed.

The most violent reaction came from the parliamentary group (Reichstag Fraction) of the party, where the right-wing power was concentrated. After the bombshell had detonated, Engels wrote Kautsky:

> You say Bebel writes you that the treatment of Lassalle by Marx has caused bad blood among the old Lassalleans. That may be. These people, indeed, do not know the real story, and it seems besides that nothing has happened to enlighten them about it....
>
> A very nice thing, that voices have been heard in the [Reichstag] Fraction saying that the *Neue Zeit* should be placed under censorship. Are we still haunted by the ghost of the Fraction's dictatorship during the Anti-Socialist Law (which was necessary, to be sure, and well carried out), or is it a matter of reminiscences of Schweitzer's old tight organization?[9]

The reference to the Reichstag Fraction's "dictatorship" was to the recourse the party had been forced into when Bismarck outlawed it in Germany: the Reichstag deputies, who still operated legally, became the equivalent of the party executive inside the country, while the elected party leadership worked out of Zurich, in exile. Even around that time Marx had commented, in a letter to Sorge, that the reformist-corrupted Social-Democratic deputies "are already so much affected by parliamentary idiotism that they think they stand *above criticism* and condemn criticism as a crime of lèse-majesté..."[10]

The situation was worse in 1891. Engels told Lafargue:

> Marx's article has excited great anger in the Central Committee of the Party and much praise in the Party itself. There was an attempt to suppress that whole edition *of Neue Zeit,* but it was too late, so they put a good face on it and boldly reprinted the article in the official organ [*Vorwärts*]... In the meantime I am not receiving news of them directly, they boycott me a bit.[11]

In fact, the irate leadership sent Engels to Coventry for a considerable period, for his effrontery in forcing Marx's "Critique" into the open.

The center of the party hubbub was Marx's uninhibited attack on the Lassalle fetish in the party. The other element that got involved was the fact that the document used the term 'dictatorship of the proletariat' (locus 9). This led to a confrontation in the Reichstag.

4. RUMPUS IN THE REICHSTAG

In the Reichstag, as might be expected, the uproar in the socialist camp was utilized for antisocialist purposes. Dr. von Bennigsen arose on February 28 to bait the Social-Democratic deputy Karl Grillenberger about Marx's document. Let us quote Bennigsen's speech on this point so as to get an idea of the reverberations in the country:

> He [Grillenberger] has stressed that his position and that of his friends provide no basis for the charge that they intend a violent overthrow or revolutionary acts; and this is certainly very gladdening to hear. But I want to point out here that Herr Grillenberger, one of the leaders of the German Social-Democratic Party, thereby puts himself in open contradiction with the program of the intellectual head of the German and European Social-Democracy, Herr Marx, which was published not long ago by Herr Engels.
>
> Herr Marx said there, with a clarity that leaves nothing to be desired, that, between the present state of the bourgeois economy and state institutions and the social-democratic economic and political order to follow, an in-between state of affairs must necessarily intervene; this is to be the state of affairs [called] the dictatorship of the proletariat. *[Hear, hear!* on the right.] Is there anyone here in the House who thinks such a "dictatorship of the proletariat" possible on the path of reform, to be carried out in a gradual transition, *[Mirth]* instead of only on the path of a victorious revolution of the Social-Democracy? Even Herr Grillenberger will maintain the contrary with difficulty; in any case he will not believe it.[12]

Herr Dr. von Bennigsen, of course, knew well enough that Herr Grillenberger was furious at the publication of the Marx document; he wanted to get the Social-Democratic spokesman to repudiate Marx in public—and he succeeded handsomely. Grillenberger took the floor again, and toward the end of the speech, confronted the challenge:

> Herr Dr. von Bennigsen has . . . said that it seems we are not so serious about our reforming activity because the most prominent savant *[Gelehrte]* whom the Social-Democracy has to show, the late Carl Marx, stated, in the letter that recently was made public, that as a transitional

20. The Third Period of the 'Dictatorship of the Proletariat' 313

stage from the present-day capitalist to the social-democratic society, a dictatorship of the revolutionary proletariat must come to pass. But Herr Dr. von Bennigsen has forgotten to add that the Social-Democratic Party *did not acquiesce* to this programmatic proposal by Marx. Marx was, indeed, indignant that the Social-Democracy made its programmatic decisions just as it felt was right for German conditions, and that in consequence for us there was never any question of a revolutionary dictatorship of the proletariat. Precisely that which we ought to get some appreciation for, the fact that we don't jump up and salute when somebody from outside expects us to adopt an unacceptable program, this is brought up here *against* us![13]

Grillenberger and the party had, of course, the right to separate themselves from Marx's statement—if the party made a decision to that effect, as it had *not* done; but Grillenberger, no doubt carried away by rage at the parliamentary difficulties Marx was erecting for him, went much further in this speech. "Marx was indignant," he told his chortling audience, because the party insisted on making its own decisions, without being ordered around "from outside"... This was simple slander.

It should be noted, too, that Grillenberger assumed that Marx was proposing 'dictatorship of the proletariat' for inclusion in the program. It is doubtful that he could read Marx's words clearly through the red haze that obscured his vision. When the worthy burgher repudiated the "revolutionary dictatorship of the proletariat," he certainly shuddered less over "dictatorship" than the word before it: after all, the Social-Democrats knew as well as anyone how often 'dictatorship' had been on the lips of their hero Lassalle, and with an entirely familiar meaning.

About two months later, Liebknecht took the floor to treat the question in a different way. On the floor was a bill attacking the workers' right to organize. If you destroy the right to organize, Liebknecht warned, the development of the workers' movement "in peaceful, legal ways" would be negated; those who advocated "forcible means" would be encouraged. He then veered off to discuss the recent to-do about the dictatorship of the proletariat. After this he came back to his main subject in a passage which needs quoting in order to provide the context. He said:

By giving the workers full possession of their political rights, and especially the right to organize, by protecting them from the predominant economic power of capital—by doing this you can moderate the struggle, and bring it about that, as has been the case *in* England up to now, the sociopolitical movement in Germany will get into the bed of peaceful, legal development, and any possibility of a solution by force and violence, a *social revolution,* and indeed a *bloody social revolution* such as the police and the bourgeoisie imagine, will be precluded ... The assured right to organize guarantees—as much as possible—the social peace that you, the Conservatives and National Liberals, have on your lips...[14]

This, coming from a party leader, constituted a promise of "social peace" and opposition to revolution in return for dropping the bill; it should be kept in mind when interpreting Liebknecht's role in 1895 of bowdlerizing Engels' introduction to Marx's *Class Struggles in France*. At any rate, it will help to dispel the notion that Liebknecht was following the line of revolutionary parliamentarism. It was in this context that Liebknecht formulated his remarks on the 'dictatorship of the proletariat'. Essentially, his tactic was to take the *tu quoque* line:

In your press you have been throwing at our heads the phrase *dictatorship of the proletariat* used by Marx;—by the way, it is 30 or 40 years since Marx used it. At your heads I throw the *dictatorship of the bourgeoisie,* or rather let's say, the *dictatorship of capitalism.* What have you done in this Reichstag since 1878 other than dictatorially take care of capital's business affairs by means of the *instrument of legislation,* by the grain tariffs, by the whole of the so-called economic policies? Haven't you systematically shaped the economic conditions to your class advantage, and furthermore politically suppressed the class and the party that came out against you, that stood in your way, by an *Anti-Socialist Law?* Can dictatorship be exercised in sharper, more brutal fashion than it is by the united German capitalist class, to which the Messrs. Junkers over there belong as surely as do the Messrs. National-Liberals, and in part also the members of the Center Party? Can one imagine dictatorship more sharply pronounced? When you take away from the workers the right and possibility of carrying out their demands in legal ways, then you simply prepare the way for the revolution and make the dictatorship of the proletariat a *necessity.*[15]

This was a cleverer effort than Grillenberger's attempt to appease the right by slandering Marx. In effect, Liebknecht was arguing that a dictatorship of the proletariat would be the bourgeoisie's punishment for abolishing the right to organize. He was probably unaware that he was giving a thoroughly false interpretation to the term: in his explanation, 'dictatorship of the proletariat' became necessary only if the workers had to take power in a forcible revolution. The implication was that in the latter case some specially dictatorial measures or institutions would have to be adopted. But at any rate he avoided a repudiation of Marx.*

---

* A recent biography of Liebknecht by R. H. Dominick states that "For him, the manipulative dictatorship of the proletariat always remained an embarrassing and incongruous part of Marxism. He flatly and publicly denied that his party subscribed

The Reichstag ruckus helped to give a certain public notoriety to the publication of Marx's "Critique of the Gotha Program" and to the term 'dictatorship of the proletariat'. And the frightened reaction of the Social-Democratic targets made the term seem, in comparison, the very embodiment of a revolutionary orientation.

5. LOCUS 11: ENGELS ON THE PARIS COMMUNE

In between the speeches made by Grillenberger and Liebknecht in the Reichstag, Engels finished his introduction to a new edition of Marx's *Civil War in France,* adding the dateline: "London, on the twentieth anniversary of the Paris Commune, March 18, 1891." The last words of this piece were: "dictatorship of the proletariat."

Let us follow the line of thought developed by Engels in leading up to this climax. We start with a passage in the middle which also speaks of dictatorship, specifically of Blanquist dictatorship. Engels was here using a good deal of the material he had put into his article "Program of the Blanquist Refugees of the Commune," which at this time had not yet been reprinted from its original periodical form.

Engels made the point that, although the Commune was composed largely of Proudhonists and Blanquists, yet, "in both cases the irony of history willed—as is usual when doctrinaires come to the helm—that both did the opposite of what the doctrines of their school prescribed."[18] In the case of the Blanquists, this meant the following:

> Brought up in the school of conspiracy, and held together by the strict discipline which went with it, they started out from the viewpoint that a relatively small number of resolute, well-organized men would be able, at a given favorable moment, not only to seize the helm of state, but also by a display of great, ruthless energy, to maintain power until they succeeded in sweeping the mass of the people into the revolution and ranging them round the small band of leaders. This involved, above all, the strictest, dictatorial centralization of all power in the hands of the

---

to it."[16] This statement is reference-noted to the Reichstag speech quoted here, obviously incorrectly. It *would* apply, however, to Grillenberger.

In 1899 (beyond our time frame) Liebknecht wrote his well-known essay *No Compromise* [etc.] in which he denounced the "allegation" that "the aim of Social-Democracy is *the dictatorship of the proletariat"* without so much as a mention of Marx. He wound up with an overt repudiation: "Not the establishment of a dictatorship of the proletariat, but *the destruction of the dictatorship of the bourgeoisie* is the object of the political power which Social-Democracy wants to attain..."[17]

new revolutionary government. And what did the Commune, with its majority of these same Blanquists, actually do?[19]

Here again, as in the 1874 article, Engels was pointing to the connection between the Blanquist conception of revolution and the Blanquist conception of dictatorship. Yet the Blanquists (Engels went on to say) found themselves acting in a different way.

Firstly: instead of their oft-proclaimed "dictatorship of Paris," the Commune came out for a "free federation of all French Communes with Paris, a national organization which for the first time was really to be created by the nation itself."[20] Here, Engels was echoing Marx's views, as described in Chapter 2.[21]

Secondly: instead of "the strictest dictatorship, and centralization of all power in the hands of the new revolutionary government," a whole series of democratic measures was taken against the old centralization and against the old type of repressive state machinery.

In this connection Engels resurveyed the Commune's expansion of democracy, as had Marx before.[22] The working class had *to* "safeguard itself against its own deputies and officials, by declaring them all, without exception, subject to recall at any moment." The old state organs had

> transformed themselves from the servants of society into the masters of society. This can be seen, for example, not only in the hereditary monarchy, but equally so in the democratic republic ... It is precisely in America that we see best how there takes place this process of the state power making itself independent in relation to society, whose mere instrument it was orginally intended to be.

The Commune went in the opposite direction:

> Against this transformation of the state and the organs of the state from servants of society into masters of society—an inevitable transformation in all previous states—the Commune made use of two infallible means. In the first place, it filled all posts—administrative, judicial and educational—by election on the basis of universal suffrage of all concerned, subject to the right of recall at any time by the same electors. And in the second place, all officials, high or low, were paid only the wages received by other workers.[23]

Engels explained that he was repeating this (as Marx had done)

> because in Germany particularly the supersitious belief in the state has been carried over from philosophy into the general consciousness of the bourgeoisie and even to many workers.[24]

This "superstitious reverence for the state and everything connected with it"

20. The Third Period of the 'Dictatorship of the Proletariat' 317

leads people to think that even a democratic republic would be a very bold step. But the state, as a machine of class oppression, is

> at best an evil inherited by the proletariat after its victorious struggle for class supremacy, whose worst sides the victorious proletariat, just like the Commune, cannot avoid having to lop off at once as much as possible until such time as a generation reared in new, free social conditions is able to throw the entire lumber of the state on the scrap heap.[25]

It was after this line of thought that Engels had his say on the recent party uproar over Marx's critique:

[Locus 11]
> Of late, the Social-Democratic philistine has once more been filled with wholesome terror at the phrase: dictatorship of the proletariat. Well and good, gentlemen, do you want to know what this dictatorship looks like? Look at the Paris Commune. That was the dictatorship of the proletariat.[26]

The Social-Democratic philistines who infested the party office had the last word in one respect: they changed the reference to "Social-Democratic philistines" to "German philistines" when the introduction was printed. (This little bowdlerization was a warm-up for the big bowdlerization to come, the one that sanitized Engels' introduction to Marx's *Class Struggles in France* in 1895.)

But they did not dare change Engels' essential idea: the Paris Commune was, in the view of Marx and Engels, the fearsome 'dictatorship of the proletariat' that had the Reichstag Fraction trembling with fury. In calling the Commune a 'dictatorship of the proletariat' Engels was repeating Marx's banquet speech of 1871.

6. LOCUS 12: ENGELS ON THE ERFURT PROGRAM

Three months later, Engels had another bombshell ready for the "Social-Democratic philistines": a critique of the new draft program of the party which was to be taken up at the coming Erfurt Congress. He had written it, between June 18 and 29, for the edification of the party leadership involved in drafting the program.

In this critique, as he wrote Kautsky on June 29, 1891, he

> took the occasion to strike out at the peaceable opportunism of the

Vorwärts and at the *frisch-fromm-fröhlich-freie** "growth" of the dirty old business "into socialist society."[27]

Engels' critique of the draft program was directed head-on against the trend toward reformist adaptation to the German imperial state. In the course, he sharply raised the question of including a demand for the democratic republic as one of the "democratic" planks, and argued that a peaceful assumption of power was not possible in Germany:

> One can fancy that the old society could peacefully grow into the new in countries where the people's representation concentrates all power in its own hands, where you can constitutionally do what you will as soon as you have the majority of the people behind you: in democratic republics like France and America, in monarchies like England where the imminent buy-out of the dynasty is spoken of day after day in the press and where this dynasty is powerless against the people's will. But in Germany, where the government is almost all-powerful and the Reichstag and all other representative bodies have no real power—to proclaim something like this in Germany, and without any necessity at that, means to take the figleaf off absolutism and cover one's own nakedness by tying it on oneself.[28]

To forget the big essential considerations because of the transitory interests of the day is opportunism, he explained.

[Locus 12]
Now which are these ticklish but very essential points?

Firstly. If anything is established, it is that our party and the working class can come to power only under the form of the democratic republic. This is even the specific form for the dictatorship of the proletariat, as the great French revolution has already shown. It is after all unthinkable that our best people should become ministers of state, as Miquel did.[29]

He immediately added that it *might* be inadvisable for legal reasons to include the demand for a democratic republic in the program, but if so, this fact itself showed "how colossal is the illusion that a republic could be instituted there [in Germany] in a goodnatured-peaceful way, and not only a republic but communist society."

It is easy to understand why the reference to the 'dictatorship of the proletariat' came to Engels' pen: there was not only a party but a public to-do

---

* This alliterative phrase (lit., brisk, pious, cheerful, free) is untranslatable because its significance is that it was the watchword of the chauvinist-nationalist Turner movement (sports and gymnastics) founded by the patrioteering F. L. Jahn ("Father Jahn"). *Vorwärts* was the party paper, edited by Licbknecht. Here, the "dirty old business" means present-day capitalist society.

20. The Third Period of the 'Dictatorship of the Proletariat' 319

over the term. There are two other problems about this passage that have led to a great deal of confused discussion.

(1) What "great French revolution" was Engels referring to? The assumption has been common that this combination of words meant the Great French Revolution inaugurated in 1789; and in fact English translations tend to add the capitalization (which is *not* in Engels' German text, incidentally). This assumption has been made from various standpoints, from Jean Jaurès[30] to Lenin. Thus the historian Daniel Guérin supposes that Engels was stretching the term 'dictatorship of the proletariat' to cover "the dictatorship of the sans-culottes in arms, democratically organized in their clubs and in the Commune."[31] Not only does this fail to square with everything else that either Marx or Engels wrote about the Jacobin dictatorship[32] but it would require a rather tortuous interpretation to justify. I think it is next to impossible to believe that Engels thought a dictatorship of the *proletariat* existed in, say, 1793.

There is a very simple alternative to this impossible interpretation. At least in the nineteenth century, it was not uncommon to refer to recent French revolutions—1848 and 1871—as "the French revolution," or even to call them "great." Two such cases can be found in the minutes of the General Council of the International in 1872, referring of course to the Commune.[33] Marx called the 1848 revolution "the French Revolution" in the letter which gave us locus 4.[34] In a letter to Marx in 1851, Engels referred to the Great French Revolution of 1789 as "the first French Revolution."[35] There is actually no problem at all in assuming that Engels was using "French revolution" to refer to the Revolution of March 18 (as it was long called) and that he was describing it as "great." Only three months previously, he had already described the Commune as a "dictatorship of the proletariat": this new allusion to the same thought would require no special explanation, especially since the document was not being addressed to the broad public but to the party leadership.

(2) The second problem is the meaning of Engels' statement that the democratic republic is "even the specific form for the dictatorship of the proletariat, as the [Paris Commune] has already shown."*

This statement raises no problem for me: plainly Engels was thinking that the dictatorship of the proletariat would exist *in the form of* a democratic republic. The 'dictatorship' term describes the class content of the state; the term 'democratic republic' describes the governmental form. Not only is there

---

* The question has been further muddied by a frequently seen but erroneous English translation of this sentence: "specific form *of* the dictatorship of the proletariat." (The same erroneous translation appeared in French, e.g., in Jaurès, also later in Guérin.[36]

no incompatibility between the two concepts: they necessarily complement each other.

It presents a problem for those who (as was common in the Second International) regarded a 'dictatorship of the proletariat' as a *special* form of state outfitted with some *special* dictatorial methods or institutions not to be found in an "ordinary" workers' state. This was why Lenin, in his *State and Revolution,* implicitly offered a reinterpretation of Engels' words when he wrote that they meant merely "that the democratic republic is the *nearest approach to* the dictatorship of the proletariat."[37] (My emphasis added.) Lenin avoided repeating Engels' actual statement, that the democratic republic was "the specific form for the dictatorship of the proletariat," even though he had just quoted those words.*

Let us try to disentangle some lines of thought which have led many into the same difficulty.

For one thing, there seems to exist a belief in some Marxist circles that the term "democratic republic" means *only* "bourgeois-democratic republic," and that it is forbidden to apply it to a workers' state. The exegetical basis of this superstition may lie in a musclebound reading of Marx's "Critique of the Gotha Program," which criticized

> vulgar democracy, which sees the millennium in the democratic republic and has no suspicion that it is precisely in this last state form of bourgeois society that the class struggle has to be definitively fought out ...[39]

Now this idea, that the "democratic republic" (meaning the "bourgeois-democratic republic")† is the "last state form of bourgeois society," also appeared in Engels' 1891 document, but it did not exclude the added thought that this state form, no longer bourgeois in content, was also characteristic of

---

* Yet only a couple of years before, in 1915, Lenin had completely accepted and echoed Engels' own formulation. He wrote then that "The political form of a society wherein the proletariat is victorious in overthrowing the bourgeoisie will be a democratic republic," and in the very next sentence, continuing the thought, referred to the dictatorship of the proletariat.[38] Here the two concepts, far from being incompatible, were properly used as complements: the "democratic republic" is specifically called the "political form" of the new proletarian state. It is the latter-day Marxist (and Leninist) theoreticians that muddled this simple question, not Engels.

† "Bourgeois republic" was the formulation when Engels referred to Marx's views on this point in 1894, in the Italian press:

> And the bourgeois republic, Marx said, is the only political form in which the struggle between proletariat and bourgeoisie can be decided.[40]

Marx did not make a precise use of these terms—bourgeois republic or democratic republic or bourgeois-democratic republic—with mathematical exactness, as if writing a thesis; you have to follow his train of thought.

20. The Third Period of the 'Dictatorship of the Proletariat' 321

the workers' state. This was equally the combined thought in a polemical piece by Engels in the Italian press in 1892:

> For forty years Marx and I have repeated to the point of satiety that for us the democratic republic is the only political form in which the struggle between the working class and the capitalist class can be first universalized and then reach its conclusion with the decisive victory of the proletariat.[41]

Now even a musclebound interpretation of Marx's words in the "Critique of the Gotha Program" can hardly maintain that the democratic republic *must* be the "last" state form of bourgeois society, since both Marx and Engels thought it quite possible that the embattled bourgeoisie might as a last resort institute a dictatorial regime against the threatening working class. This sort of exegetical rigidity makes nonsense of a fairly simple idea. That a workers' state would be a *republic was* unquestioned in the socialist movement; that this republic would be *democratic*—well, this too was unquestionable *unless one counterposed dictatorship (of the proletariat) to democracy.* Since the latter notion was incompatible with Engels' 1891 critique, Engels had to be thrown into the discard.

For another angle on this question, let us recur to the fact that Engels was alluding to the Paris Commune as the "dictatorship of the proletariat." In the eyes of Marx and Engels, the Paris Commune was not the "nearest approach" to a dictatorship of the proletariat: it *was* a dictatorship of the proletariat. (Lenin's interpretation was bedeviled by the assumption that Engels was referring to 1793.)

For still another slant, we can come back to Engels' remark about "ministers . . . like Miquel." It is unthinkable that our leaders should enter the cabinet *under a kaiser,* Engels said; and obviously he was saying this because it was not unthinkable that they should become ministers *in a democratic republic which is the specific form for the dictatorship of the proletariat,* that is, a democratic republic clothing a workers' state.

Why then did Lenin (and many others) boggle at what is, after all, the simplest interpretation of Engels' words, and one which is in no way at odds with the views expounded in *State and Revolution?* The answer may lie in the aforementioned common assumption *that the word 'democratic' meant only and exclusively 'bourgeois-democratic'.*

This terminological custom, sometimes found in Marx and Engels, became far more widespread in the period of the Second International, especially in political formulas. Compare Lenin's famous political formula 'democratic dictatorship of the proletariat and peasantry', whose meaning is decipherable only if you understand that 'democratic' here stands for 'bourgeois-democratic' and specifies the *class* content of the regime. Or we can think of the pattern—most common, I suspect, in the Russian movement—of distinguishing between the 'democratic revolution' and the 'socialist revolution', without implying that the latter is undemocratic: the 'democratic revolution' is simply a short form for 'bourgeois-democratic revolution', a form which eventually took on a life of its own.

In short, part of the difficulty with later interpreters, including Lenin, is that they assumed anachronistically that Engels was using the later terminological pattern. Therefore Lenin could not understand how Engels could say that a (bourgeois-)democratic republic could also be a dictatorship of the proletariat.

However, the question must now be brought around to its beginning. The exegetical difficulty we have been discussing would likely have been overcome except for the more important misunderstanding behind it: the assumption that a 'dictatorship of the proletariat' *had* to be something more than a democratic workers' state, that it *had* to be a workers' state with special dictatorial attributes. This, at bottom, is the conception that makes it difficult for its holders to accept Engels' statement in locus 12.

Once again, then—with apologies for the repetition—we see what the distinction is: the dictatorship of the proletariat, formula for the *class* character of the political power in the transitional workers' state, is clothed in the democratic republic as *the form of its governmental structure* (or state form). The first labels a type of state in class terms; the second, a form of government.*

In this "Critique of the Erfurt Program," Engels pressed the demand for the democratic republic on the gentlemen of the party's Reichstag Fraction who were so appalled by the idea of revolutionary dictatorship. He agreed that legally the program could not openly come out so boldly, but insisted that ways had to be found to express the same idea:

---

* In a valuable essay on Marx and the Paris Commune, Monty Johnstone, referring to this view as expressed in my 1962 article, noted that "Draper appears to have modified this subsequently. More recently he has written that for Marx and Engels 'the idea of the Commune state, any genuine workers' state, is not merely a state with a different class rule but *a new type of state* altogether.' "[42] I do not understand why Johnstone sees a modification. A workers' state, "any genuine workers' state," *is* a new type of state altogether, in Marx's view. A reminder of this well-known fact has nothing to do with the thesis that for Marx the term 'dictatorship of the proletariat' did *not* denote special governmental forms but only the workers' state as such. Elsewhere in his essay Johnstone states his own opinion: my thesis applies to Marx up to the Paris Commune, but "after the experience of the Paris Commune, he added a general indication of the type of state and the forms of government" that he looked to. Yes, Marx added these "indications," but—after the Commune as before—not once did he ever attach these "indications" *to the term 'dictatorship of the proletariat'*. And that is the whole point.

20. The Third Period of the 'Dictatorship of the Proletariat'   323

Still, one can possibly get around the question of the republic. But in my opinion what should go in and can go in is the demand for the *concentration of all political power in the hands of the people's representation.* And this would suffice for the time being if one cannot go any further.[43]

So: "concentration of all political power in the hands of the people's representation" stands for the illegal "democratic republic," and this in turn is "the specific form for the dictatorship of the proletariat." Engels, the advocate of that revolutionary dictatorship which so perturbed the "Social-Democratic philistines," was arguing with them that they should at least hint at their goal of a democratic republic instead of adapting themselves to the legality of the kaiser's regime.

7. ENGELS' TALK WITH VODEN ON PLEKHAVOV

By a coincidence that was not entirely fortuitous, the last echo of 'dictatorship of the proletariat' to be recorded during Engels' lifetime, and involving him, points straight ahead to the next period, in which the term parted company with Marx and Engels.

Alexei Mikhailovich Voden was a young man of 23, a Russian Social-Democratic émigré living in Switzerland, when he came to London on a visit in 1893. Plekhanov gave him letters of recommendation to a number of people in England, including Engels, whom Voden was naturally eager to meet. A third of a century later, Voden wrote up his memoirs; we are interested in his account of "Talks with Engels."[44]

The 'dictatorship of the proletariat' came up in one of these conversations. Just why it came up is not clear from Voden's account; the two were discussing the relations between Narodniks and Social-Democrats in the Russian movement, including Plekhanov's attitude to the Narodniks. The following passage occurs *in* Voden's memoirs without even a paragraph break to introduce it:

> Engels asked how Plekhanov himself stood on the question of the dictatorship of the proletariat. I was forced to admit that G. V. Plekhanov had repeatedly expressed his conviction to me that when "we" come to power, of course "we" would allow freedom to no one but "ourselves" .... However, in response to my question who exactly should be taken to be the monopolists of freedom, Plekhanov answered: the working class headed by comrades who correctly understand Marx's teachings and who draw the correct conclusions from those teachings. And in response to my question on what comprises the objective criteria for a correct understanding of Marx's teachings and the correct practical conclusions

flowing therefrom, G. V. Plekhanov limited himself to the statement that it was all laid out "clearly enough, it seems" in his (Plekhanov's) works. After inquiring whether I personally on the other hand was satisfied with such an objective criterion, Engels expressed the opinion that the application of that sort of criterion would either lead to the Russian Social-Democracy's turning into a sect with its unavoidable and always undesirable practical consequences, or it would give rise in the Russian Social-Democracy—at least among the émigré Russian Social-Democrats—to a series of splits from which Plekhanov himself would not benefit.[45]

Engels also remarked that Plekhanov seemed to him a Russian analogue of H. M. Hyndman (leader of the "Marxist" sect in Britain). Voden footnoted that Plekhanov took this as a compliment. A Russian analogue of Hyndman would not know any better, naturally.

It goes without saying that the complete accuracy of Voden's 1927 recollections cannot be guaranteed; but if they are at least approximately valid, we have a prototype and archetype of what the 'dictatorship of the proletariat' was going to mean in the period of the Second International. We have already emphasized the general characteristic: the 'dictatorship of the proletariat' would be a *special* kind of workers' state or pos revolutionary regime, one with special dictatorial attributes. In Plekhanov's interpretation, specifically, there would be two attributes in particular: withdrawal of democratic rights ("freedom") from some portion of the population; exercise of the dictatorship by the revolutionary party ("we") or by its leadership (those who "correctly understood").

Now we have seen that others had given a similarly "dictatorial" interpretation to the term, but this was the first time that either Marx or Engels was confronted with it and commented on it. Engels' comment to Voden went far beyond mere disagreement: in his view, such a perspective by the party would wreck the movement, either by a split or (what amounts to the same thing) sectification.

In a few years, the Russian Social-Democratic Workers Party was going to become the first socialist organization in the world to include the 'dictatorship of the proletariat' in its program—though Marx and Engels had refused to propose such a step. The term was written into the party program by Plekhanov, who by that time was perhaps the most prestigious theoretician of Marxism outside of Germany.

Thus the new era of the 'dictatorship of the proletariat' was launched on its way—not by Lenin (as the usual myth has it) but by the future leader and theoretician of Menshevism, G. V. Plekhanov. The latter's antidemocratic

20. The Third Period of the 'Dictatorship of the Proletariat' 325

interpretation of the idea, though repudiated by Engels as soon as it was reported to him, was going to blossom in the Second International and particularly in the Russian movement.

But that is another story.

SPECIAL NOTES

SPECIAL
NOTE
A | MARXOLOGISTS AT WORK

Various writings have been mentioned in the course of this work, but special bibliographical attention should be paid to those publications that purported to provide surveys of Marx's, or Marx's and Engels', uses of the term 'dictatorship of the proletariat'.

1. SURVEYS

The first substantial effort to bring together Marx's and Engels' statements about the 'dictatorship of the proletariat' was Lenin's *State and Revolution*—a work that has rarely been given credit for its innovation simply in the field of scholarship.[1] As originally published in early 1918, the first edition mentioned only four loci in Marx and Engels: the loci here numbered 6, 7a, 9, and 12 (two by Marx and two by Engels); that is, nothing earlier than 1873. That Lenin was unaware of any earlier use was indicated by his statement, after quoting some passages from the *Communist Manifesto*, that these concerned "the idea of the 'dictatorship of the proletariat' (as Marx and Engels began to call it after the Paris Commune)..."[2]

In his *Anti-Kautsky*,[3] written in the fall of 1918 and published toward the end of that year, Lenin charged that Kautsky

> *must know* that both Marx and Engels, in their letters as well as in their published works, *repeatedly* spoke about the dictatorship of the proletariat, before and especially after the Paris Commune.

He added that Marx and Engels spoke about the idea "*for forty years*, between 1852 and 1891."[4] The reference to 1852 showed that Lenin was now aware of Marx's letter to Weydemeyer (locus 4); but it was not actually mentioned in this pamphlet. It was, however, covered in a new section (Section 3 of Chapter 2) added in the second edition of *State and Revolution*, written December 1918 and published in early 1919.

329

Although Lenin had written about the 'dictatorship of the proletariat' concept before the war, he had never published a survey of Marx's use of the term (nor had anyone else). In his important pamphlet of 1905, *Two Tactics of Social-Democracy in the Democratic Revolution,* he had a closing section on "The Vulgar Bourgeois and the Marxist Views on Dictatorship,"[5] but here he discussed material he had found in the volumes edited by Mehring, *Aus dem literarischen Nachlass [etc.],* namely, Marx's *Neue Rheinische Zeitung* articles of 1848-1849 about 'dictatorship' in revolution.[6]

Kautsky's brochure *The Dictatorship of the Proletariat* (1918) gave only Marx's locus 9 (*Critique of the Gotha Program*) as if this were Marx's only use of the term; it also referred, without quoting, to Engels' locus 11 (about the Paris Commune). Kautsky alluded disparagingly to "the little phrase, 'thedictatorship of the proletariat', which Marx used in a letter in 1875."[7] Even in his later work *Social Democracy Versus Communism,* Kautsky added only Engels' locus 12 (on the Erfurt Program), even though much had been published on the subject by this time.[8]

The first serious attempt at a work entirely devoted to our subject was Ernst Drahn's *Karl Marx und Friedrich Engels ueberdie Diktaturdes Proletariats* (1920), a pamphlet. Drahn, whose letter of resignation from the Social-Democratic Party was reprinted in the pamphlet, signed himself "ex-archivist of the SDP." The work is rather rambling; and though he could already have read Lenin's *State and Revolution,* Drahn knew only of loci 4, 9, and 11—omitting three that Lenin had already cited, and adding only one new one (locus 11).

The next contribution was made by the German-born historian of British and international socialism, Max Beer, in a three-part essay, "An Inquiry into Dictatorship," published in the pro-Communist *Labour Monthly* (London) in 1922. As the title indicated, its scope was wide, and indeed Beer posed the question of the historical development of the word 'dictatorship'; and while his answers were inadequate, he deserves great credit for suggesting an approach that no one else picked up. In the third installment Beer mentioned Marx's loci 1 a and 1 c as well as 4,6, and 9—hence he was the first to bring up Marx's initial mention of the term in *The Class Struggles in France.* He mentioned nothing by Engels, not even the two loci already offered in *State and Revolution.* It is hard to see why he did not, but in all the cases we are listing, the reasons for inclusions and exclusions are very dark. (The answer may be something simple, like *Schlamperei.*)

The preceding publications were sympathetic to the new Third International; but Social-Democrats other than Kautsky also took a hand—for example, Cunow and Hillquit.[9] Another right-winger weighed in, in 1924, with a brochure on *Die Diktatur des Proletariats und das Rätesystem* (second edition) which cited more loci than anyone else had done: while locus la was paraphrased only, Diehl gave loci 1c, 6, 7a, 9, 11, and 12. These were all the passages so far pointed out, with the exception of locus 4 (the letter to Weydemeyer). Diehl remarked in passing that "There are perhaps only a half dozen places in all of Marx's and Engels' writings where the expression 'dictatorship of the proletariat' is used" (though he himself had pointed to seven) "and at that mostly in letters or small political articles, but not in the major fundamental works."[10] Presumably he demoted *The Class Struggles in France* from the list of major works. In terms of interpretation, Diehl's essay was a rather standard argument in favor of Bernsteinian Revisionism. But he had no idea what Marx meant by 'dictatorship': he thought that for Marx a dictatorship was necessary "wherever generally speaking there is no democratic constitutional situation yet available."[11]

For the next survey We jump to 1931. Sherman H. M. Chang was a young Chinese scholar, a follower of Sun Yat-sen, who came to the University of Pennsylvania to study political science and wound up writing "the first scholarly book on the Marxian Theory of the State" (as John R. Commons said in the introduction). Chang's *The Marxian Theory of the State* expounded the viewpoint of Lenin's *State and Revolution*. His two chapters on the 'dictatorship of the proletariat' (Chapters 5-6) easily constituted the most thorough analysis seen up to that point.

Chang noted loci 1a, 1c, 4,6, 7a, 9, and 11, thus doing slightly better than Diehl, and better than anything else up to the 1960s. Yet Chang cited no loci that had not already been pointed to by Lenin, Drahn, or Beer; in fact, he omitted one that Lenin had given, locus 12 (once again, difficult to understand since he quoted other passages from the same work by Engels).

In 1945 a French periodical *Economic et Humanisme* published a survey by Charles-Fr. Hubert, en tided "Note Chronologique sur l'Idée Marxiste de Dictature du Prolétariat." It looked like an attempt to trace all usages, but actually, in the midst of a standard exposition of Leninist-Stalinist state theory, it offered only five loci: 4,6, and 9 by Marx; 11 and 12 by Engels.

If, up to the 1960s, Chang did best, the opposite record was held by Stanley W. Moore, whose *Critique of Capitalist Democracy* (1957) offered an "introduction to the theory *of* the state in Marx, Engels and Lenin." It is the only book devoted to this subject that fails to mention that the term was used at all by Marx and Engels, even though the book is structurally a collection of citations.

My essay "Marx and the Dictatorship of the Proletariat" was published in 1962. Two books by others based one or more chapters directly on its material, with due acknowledgment: Bertram D. Wolfe's *Marxism* (1965), Chapters 10-11, and Richard N. Hunt's *The Political Ideas of Marx and Engels*, Volume 1 (1974), Chapter 9. As far as I know, there has been no other independent inquiry into the subject since Chang's 1931 study.

There are a number of books whose titles *look* as if the main subject was Marx's 'dictatorship of the proletariat' but which are actually concerned with Russian Bolshevism and Stalinism, not with Marx. Here are three examples:

- Tasin, N. [pseud. of N. Y. Kagan], *La Dictadura del Proletarido según Marx, Engels, Kautsky, Bernstein, Axelrod, Lenin, Trotzky y Bauer*, Madrid, 1920.
- Priklmajer-Tomanović, Zorica, "Contemporary Socialist Thought: The Discussion on Democracy and the Dictatorship of the Proletariat in the West-European Communist Movement," in *Review of International Affairs* (Belgrade), Vol. 17, No. 394-97, Sept. 5-Oct. 20,1966—A four-part essay in a Titoist theoretical-propaganda organ.
- Radjavi, Kazem, *La Dictature du Prolétariat et le Dépérissement de l'État de Mar àLénine*, Paris, 1975.

This listing does not mean that these works lack interest on subjects other than our own.*

2. MARXOLOGICAL MENTIONS

General works on Marx customarily have a mention of the 'dictatorship of the proletariat', but, as we have said elsewhere, it is rather surprising to find what a high proportion of simple factual errors are to be found in these mentions. We are concerned here not with books on general subjects that happen to mention Marx, but only with substantial works on Marx many of which are considered authoritative. For convenience, the authors are listed in alphabetical order, with a brief note on what they do. Full bibliographical information is given in the Bibliography.

Avineri, Shlomo. *The Social and Political Thought of Karl Marx*. Marx, says Avineri, "does not use the term more than two or three times in his life, and then always in what is basically a private communication."[12] He lists only loci 4, 5, and 9. Aside from the oddity of thinking that a speech at a banquet, reported in a daily paper, is a "private communication," it is (as usual) hard to understand why Avineri does not know about the three passages in *The*

---

* Other publications with relevant titles came out in connection with the Lenin-Kautsky debate: for example, L. Kamenev, *The Dictatorship of the Proletariat* (1920); Ka Radek, *Proletarian Dictatorship and Terrorism* (1920); N. Bukharin, "The Theory of th Dictatorship of the Proletariat," published in 1919 in a collection. I will discuss these i another work (see Foreword).

Class Struggles in France, or any one of them; also, locus 6 was quite a public article.

Berlin, Isaiah. *Karl Marx.* This biography mentions no loci, but offers one of the most singular interpretations, highlighted by the belief that the 'permanent revolution' is "brought about" (or "dominated") by the 'dictatorship of the proletariat'.[13] Berlin seems to have no idea of how Marx uses either term.

Calvez, J.-Y. *La Pensée de Karl Marx.* Its section on the term devotes much space to the *Communist Manifesto* but thinks the term was first used in locus 4; also mentioned is locus 9.[14]

Carr, E. H. *The Bolshevik Revolution 1917-1923,* Volume 1. "In 1849 [he means 1850, locus 1c] Marx described Blanqui's 'revolutionary socialism' as 'a class dictatorship of the proletariat' ... " We have explained that this is a very common misquotation. Carr adds: "in 1852 [locus 4] he adopted the term himself." Elsewhere Carr makes clear he knows only locus 9 in addition.[15] Since much of Carr's discussion is on Lenin's *State and Revolution,* it is especially odd that he does not utilize the facts in this study. In his biography of Marx, which cited no loci, Carr thought the idea of the 'dictatorship of the proletariat' was an "incidental after-thought, which is devoid of any theoretical basis...."[16]

Caute, David. Introduction and notes to *Essential Writings of Karl Marx.* Caute mentions that Marx first used the term in 1850, without further reference, and among his excerpts, cites locus 9. He opines that to Marx the term "implied a harsher, post-revolutionary concentration of power than mere working-class rule." He also thinks that Engels "rashly" described the Paris Commune as the dictatorship of the proletariat.[17]

Cole, G. D. H. *History of Socialist Thought.* In Volume 1, Cole retailed the Marx-Blanquist myth, as discussed elsewhere.[18] In Volume 2, where Marx's views are expounded, Cole quotes only locus 9.[19]

Duncan, Graeme. *Marx and Mill.* Duncan asserts that for Marx and Engels the proletarian dictatorship "requires a centralised, autocratic structure of power," some pages after he has cited loci 4, 9, and 11; but he makes no effort at a tie-up.[20]

Fetscher, Iring, hrsg. *Grundbegriffe des Marxismus.* Subtitled "A Lexicographical Introduction" to the concepts of Marxism, Fetscher's book has a section on "The dictatorship of the proletariat and its political form" which is, however, despite the title not mainly concerned with the 'dictatorship of the proletariat'. He cites only loci 9 and 12. His peculiar treatment is discussed elsewhere.[21]

Gay, Peter. *The Dilemma of Democratic Socialism.* Gay claims that Marx's "call" for a dictatorship of the proletariat was "made only in one or two places of his work."[22]

Harrington, Michael. *Socialism.* Author of the theory of Marx's "rhetorical sin" (mentioned elsewhere[23]), Harrington claims that Marx used 'dictatorship of the proletariat' during his "ultra-Leftist period" of 1848-1850, and, it seems, "recovered from that tragic error within a matter of months," so that "in the 1850s Marx became the first Marxian revisionist." Where Marx "revised" the dictatorship of the proletariat is not revealed. Harrington cites locus 2, gives locus 8 incompletely, and alludes to locus 11.

Hook, Sidney. *Marx and the Marxists.* Hook says that "The phrase...was not used in any major published work of Marx and only twice in his correspondence."[24] In this popular game of minimization, Hook must argue that Marx's *Class Struggles in France* was not a "major" work, and that one of Marx's political documents on the list of loci was simply "correspondence," that is, a personal letter. He implies that there were only three Marx loci.

Hunt, R. N. Carew. *Marxism: Past and Present.* Hunt quotes loci 7b and 9, alludes to locus 4 and one passage in locus 1, and asserts that "Marx only uses the expression ... on the three occasions noted" (that is, loci 1, 4, and 9).[25] In his *Theory and Practice of Communism* Hunt knew only of loci 1 and 9, plus Engels' 11 and 12.[26]

Jászi, Oscar. Article "Socialism" in *Encyclopaedia of the Social Sciences*. In a passage on the 'dictatorship of the proletariat', we learn that "It was not only in his youth that Marx entertained such an opinion; as late as 1875..."—and he quotes locus 9. We do not find out anything more about Marx's youth in this connection, or about any other loci.[27]

Landauer, Carl. *European Socialism.* Landauer asserts, as a fact so well known as to need no evidence, that "Marx accepted the idea" from Blanqui that a "convinced minority must establish its own dictatorial rule," and that the 'dictatorship of the proletariat' means "depriving the persons of the enemy class of political and personal liberties."[28] Apart from this, he cites locus 1c (mistranslated[29]) plus loci 4 and 9, also Engels' 11 and 12.

Leff, Gordon. *The Tyranny of Concepts.* Leff states that "It was in 1875 that Marx in his *Critique of the Gotha Programme* first publicly spoke of the 'dictatorship of the proletariat.' "[30] A footnote refers to the 1852 Weydemeyer letter (locus 4) as a nonpublic case. But Marx's three passages of 1850 (locus 1) were exceedingly public, and in 1875 Marx's *Critique* document was not yet public at all (it became known in 1891). It would be difficult to pack more misinformation into one sentence.

Lichtheim, George. *Marxism.* This work is unusual in its refusal to cite a single passage about the 'dictatorship of the proletariat', or even allude to a locus apart from a footnoted allusion to locus 9. The sole reference to a work that is supposed to present the term is to the *Address to the Communist League* (which however is innocent of the term). Nevertheless Lichtheim twice calls the term "quasi-Jacobin."[31] For a reference to the Paris Commune, see Chapter 17, Section 9

McLellan, David. *The Thought of Karl Marx.* Mentioning loci 4 and 9, even McLellan falls into the usual error: "This expression was seldom used by Marx and never in documents for publication."[32] (See the comment on published loci at the end of this section.)

Sanderson, J. B. *An Interpretation of the Political Ideas of Marx and Engels.* Though this book is specifically devoted to Marx's political theory and has separate chapters on the state, revolution, and future society, there are two bare mentions of the term: no loci are quoted or even alluded to; not two words are devoted to explaining what the term means.[33] I think Sanderson walks away with the prize.

Schapiro, Leonard. *The Communist Party of the Soviet Union.* This work, of course, is not primarily about Marx, but it is piquant to quote an authority who knows all about Lenin's *State and Revolution:* "... the idea of the 'dictatorship of the proletariat,' which Marx on one sole occasion had asserted would intervene between the conquest of power by the proletariat and the establishment of socialism."[34] This telltale case shows, I think, how many Authorities simply looked it up in Kautsky's *Dictatorship of the Proletariat* and took the word as gospel.

The preceding is not intended to be a complete list—far from it—but only to record some prominent examples. A rollcall of howlers could go on endlessly, but do bear with me while I present my personal favorite. It is from *Time* magazine's 1948 "celebration" of the hundredth anniversary of the *Communist Manifesto,* which (with Marx on the cover) summarized Marx's life and ideas, communism, etc. It said:

> Toward the end of his life he wrote the words "dictatorship of the proletariat"... That phrase had always been buried in Marx's thought; he had in fact used it in conversation. Written down, it was to become an extension of his own tyrannical political methods... [etc.][35]

If *Time's* writers are scorned as politically illiterate, one cannot claim that all socialist theoreticians are necessarily more knowledgeable. The Socialist Labor Party issued an edition of Marx's *Critique of the Gotha Program,* in which the publisher's preface averred that "So far as we know, it contains Marx's only direct reference to and authority for the phrase, 'the dictatorship of the proletariat.'"[36]

As I have mentioned before, I do not understand why so many well-intentioned authorities have remained ignorant of the fact that the 'dictatorship of the proletariat' appeared in Marx's *Class Struggles in France* in 1850, three times moreover. It is not an obscure work. When it was first published in book form in 1895, under Engels' editorship, it made a great splash—not because of Marx's brilliant analyses, to be sure, but because of the bowdlerization of Engels' preface. Indeed, perhaps this controversy kicked up so much dust that no one paid any attention to Marx's writing. But whatever happened in 1895, this peculiar situation obtains to this day, as the above cases show. It would be breaking in an open door to point out that few of our Authorities are much interested in finding out "what Marx really said."

In part because of the fact that *The Class Struggles in France* is commonly ignored, the above list shows how often the assertion is encountered that Marx never "published" any reference to the dictatorship of the proletariat or that he never stated it "publicly." Yet of Marx's seven loci, *all* but one were either immediately published or were written with a view to present or future publication. The obvious exception was Marx's 1852 letter to Weydemeyer (locus 4). Locus 1 was immediately published, in three different installments of Marx's essay; loci 3 and 6 were written for periodical publication and published more or less promptly. Locus 2 (the SUCR statement) was written for publication—some sort of eventual publication; it remained unknown only because the society never came to life. Locus 9 was written immediately for a considerable group of people, the party leadership collectively, and undoubtedly with a view to greater publicity in the future. That leaves locus 5, the banquet speech, which was "published" (made public) to a substantial audience, and printed in a daily paper. Whatever the circumstances, not one of these six loci was a "personal" or "private" communication in any sense. Yet the myth hangs on and repeats itself with all the tenacity of the other myth that Marx got the whole thing from Blanqui.

Finally, let us look at the opposite end of the spectrum: those writers who have explained the 'dictatorship of the proletariat' with at least a basic amount of knowledge and understanding. Before the 1960s this was quite rare; all the more reason to say a good word for J. K. Turner's *Challenge to Karl Marx*, H. B. Mayo's *Democracy and Marxism* (later revised to *Introduction to Marxist Theory*), and M. M. Bober's *Karl Marx's Interpretation of History*, quite apart from their difficulty in understanding other aspects of Marx's theory. As for later books—leaving aside works that are discussed elsewhere in these pages—attention should be called to the useful section on our subject in Michael Evans' *Karl Marx*.

SPECIAL
NOTE
B | FABRICATION OF A FABLE:
THE "MARX-BLANQUIST" MYTH

The substantive content of the Marx-Blanquist myth is taken up in several sections of this volume,[1] describing the real relationship between Marx and Blanqui or Blanquism. But a word is necessary on the myth itself, which lies leadenly over all the products of the marxological industry. In the usual way (repeated from one book to another, by one eminent authority after another) it has by now been established as a rockribbed article of marxological faith that Marx's revolutionary views were "Blanquist" at least in his early years.

The starting point of this phenomenon is well known: it was the book by Eduard Bernstein that presented his "Revisionist" version of Marx, that is, his successful effort to found a systematic social-democratic reformist doctrine that pretended (in its first period) to be a "new and improved" form of Marxism. This approach was necessary in Germany because by the time of Engels' death the Social-Democratic movement in that country had solidly accepted Marxism as its theory; in contrast, essentially the same reformism could be established in England by the Fabians (Bernstein's mentors) without any obeisances to Marx's image.

The history of Bernsteinian "Revisionism," then, began with the pretense that this neosocialist reformism was simply a better kind of Marxism, purged of revolutionary foolishness and all that. Later, Bernstein more or less dropped the pose when it was no longer useful.* But back in 1896 when, with Engels safely dead, he began cobbling up a sham-Marxism, Bernstein had to explain away in some fashion the revolutionary ideas that every Social-Democratic recruit was familiar with from the *Communist Manifesto*. He solved this problem

---

* For example, in mid-1929 Bernstein "cheerfully admitted" to a visitor that he was a "methodological reactionary" who was really "an eighteenth-century rationalist."

> Towards the close of the conversation when I asked him whether he regarded this method to be the method of Marx, he lowered his voic and in confidential tones, as if afraid of being overheard, said, "The Bolsheviks are not unjustified in claiming Marx as their own. Do you know? Marx had a strong Bolshevik streak in him!"

The visitor who reported this open secret in 1933 was Sidney Hook.[2]

337

handily in his basic work of Revisionist theory, *Die Voraussetzungen des Sozialismus und die Aufgaben der Sozialdemokratie* (1899). It was translated into English in 1909 as *Evolutionary Socialism.*

With this a curve ball breaks into the picture. The *Voraussetzungen* had done the job in its Chapter 2, "Marxism and the Hegelian Dialectic," which in its Section 1 exposed "The Snares and Pitfalls of the Hegelian-Dialectical Method," and in Section 2 went to work on "Marxism and Blanquism." (The link was the thesis that Hegel's dialectic is the real devil of the plot, but we skip this aspect.) It was in Section 2 that Bernstein set out the story that Marx had really been a "Blanquist," and that all his revolutionism was really due to the pernicious influence of Blanqui.

But the English version, *Evolutionary Socialism,* simply omitted all of Chapter 2, without a word to the hapless reader.

Not only in its first edition of 1909. For some reason, the information that the English version is seriously incomplete has never been brought to readers' attention by those from whom we would expect this service. I know of no bibliographical reference to the book that mentions it. Not only was it kept mum by the publisher in 1909, but a new edition published in 1961 likewise forbore from letting it out—even in the special introduction contributed by none other than Sidney Hook.[3] The chief English-language biographer of Bernstein, Peter Gay, found no call to mention the omission even in his bibliography.[4]

The result is that the very source of the "Marx-Blanquist" myth is scarcely known in English-speaking circles, both Marxist and marxological.

1. BERNSTEIN'S CASE

Since Bernstein's argumentation on "Marxism and Blanquism" has never appeared in English, let us review it: what were those powerful arguments, those cogent items of evidence, in Bernstein's treatment that were so irrefutable that they convinced everyone who was eager to be convinced?

(1) Bernstein's section begins briskly by putting the finger on precisely that early article by Marx from which everything went wrong. It was (says Bernstein) his "Critique of Hegel's Philosophy of Right: Introduction," published in 1844.[5] In this article, we are told, Marx "idealized" the modern proletariat, exaggerated "its capacities and propensities," and came out for a proletarian revolution. (It was, in fact, the very first article in which Marx identified the proletariat as the revolutionary class.) "This essay," writes Bernstein, "led directly to Blanquism."

This is a very clear statement, yet all the more puzzling. The offenses

B. Fabrication of a Fable: The "Marx-Blanquist" Myth

committed by the article, as listed, were undoubtedly serious from the standpoint of Revisionism—but how did *these* sins lead to Blanquism, moreover "directly"? Perhaps Blanqui also exaggerated and idealized the "modern proletariat"? This is the reverse of historical truth,* to be sure—in fact, falsifiction. But we need not argue this point because Bernstein does not even raise it.

What! he asserts that this article of Marx's "led directly to Blanquism" and does not say what it had in common with Blanqui?

Right: he does not; not a word. The assertion stands by itself.

(2) Having refrained from boring us with evidence for the first assertion, Bernstein goes on to a second. What *defines* Blanquism, he states, is not its "method" (putschism, etc.) but rather its theory of the "boundlessly creative power of revolutionary political force," its apotheosis of pure Will as the revolutionary drive.[7] In fact, Blanqui's putschism, he finds, is partly defensible—"not so irrational as Germans think"—and besides Blanqui had some "important temporary successes."†

Now unquestionably Blanquist conspiratorial putschism (the "method") was indeed based on an extreme-voluntaristic view of politics. (As explained in Chapter 10, voluntarism is characteristic of Blanquism but is not its definition.) Bernstein uses the ploy of *counterposing* voluntarism to putschism, instead of linking them as a unity; for he has to get around the fact that Marx was a virulent opponent of putschism. Yes, Bernstein keeps telling us, Marx did oppose putschism but—he was a Blanquist because, like Blanqui, "Marx and Engels... made *'pure-and-simple will* the driving force of revolution.'"

---

* This has already been touched on in Chapter 2; see page 38. Whatever the terms he used, for, Blanqui the social struggle ("class" struggle) was primarily between rich and poor, plebeian mass and aristocratic elite. Even insofar as the Blanquist group comprised workingmen, they tended to be not of the "modern proletariat" but of the traditional artisanal crafts. Spitzer writes that Blanqui's "conception of a revolutionary elite was always focused on the Paris of artisans and intellectuals," though he appreciated the promise in the small Lyons proletariat. In Blanqui's primitive economic theory, the main villain was not capital but interest on capital; anyone who held this ancient theory looked primarily not to the modern proletariat but rather to the working-class pettybourgeois elements—"the peasant proprietors, petty functionaries, shopkeepers, and self-employed artisans," in Spitzer's summary.[6] To print the claim that Blanqui "idealized" the modern proletariat would make the toughest paper curl in despair. To be sure, it cannot be said that Bernstein actually makes this claim; but if he does not, what on earth is he talking about in this connection?

† This is not true. Bernstein alleges that the proclamation of the republic in both 1848 and 1870 was "to a great extent owing to the intervention of the Blanquist social revolutionaries."[8] In fact, both times the Blanquist activists were virtually on the shelf, admits the Blanquist historian of Blanquism, Charles Da Costa, in *Les Blanquistes*. But it would be pointless to argue this question, since it is thrown in by Bernstein in order to shift the spotlight from conspiratorial putschism as the reality of Blanquism, and focus attention in another direction. It is falsifiction.

What! Bernstein claims this of Marx? *But his very quotation about "pure-ana-simple will" is from Marx's blistering ATTACK on this notion!* What does he cite in evidence for this startling claim?

Nothing whatever. This cannot be proven by citation because there is nothing to cite. "Nothing," writes Bernstein, "shows this more clearly than the study of the writings of Marx and Engels deriving from the period of the Communist League."[10] This sounds like a prelude to such a study—but Bernstein does not make it; in fact he makes no pretense of citing a fact to show that Marx and Engels, like Blanqui, made "pure will" the revolutionary driving force. Since Bernstein's chief butt is naturally the Marx-Engels "Address to the Communist League" of March 1850, perhaps he thought the evidence was contained in that document? Unfortunately this address says nothing about the primacy of the will. So Bernstein writes that the Address says "the Communists have to exert themselves to the utmost to make the revolution ' permanent.'" One is supposed to gather that "exerting" oneself (which is not Marx's formulation anyway[11]) = exerting the will = willing the revolution = Blanquism: Q.E.D. Set down in black and white, this looks silly, but that's all there is.

(3) Perhaps more to the point, Bernstein then argues that since a "theoretical understanding" of capitalism shows that socialism was impossible on the Continent at that time, advocacy of revolution *must have been* based only on apotheosis of the Will. Therefore anyone who advocated revolution at a time when it was (in hindsight) impossible *must have been* relying on the power of Will... The logic of this argument will not overwhelm one, but it is nevertheless very significant. For it means that it is *advocacy of revolution* that is "Blanquist." All that logic-chopping about methods and voluntarism and putschism was beside the point: if you advocate a revolution, you are a Blanquist, regardless of anything else. No matter what else might be proven about Marx's views, as long as it is clear that he advocated socialist revolution then it is deducible that he was a "Blanquist." All revolutionaries are "Blanquists" whether they are Blanquist or not: we are dealing with a code word.

Even Bernstein's biographer Peter Gay at this point departs from custom and separates himself from his hero. It is "revolutionary violence," says Gay, that Bernstein characterizes as "Blanquism"; and he argues against "Bernstein's charge . . . that [Marx] overestimated the effectiveness of the creative power of violence." He adds that Bernstein was ill-advised to charge "the advocates of a forcible revolution with being imbued with irrational Blanquism."[12] *

---

* However, Gay errs in putting his emphasis on force: Bernstein would reject any sort of revolutionary approach, regardless of the role of force. He had no difficulty in hailing forcible revolutions—*if they* were and remained bourgeois revolutions. (One need only read his book on the English Revolution, *Cromwell and Communism,* or his work on the 1848 revolution, *Wie eine Revolution zugrunde ging.*)

B. Fabrication of a Fable: The "Marx-Blanquist" Myth 341

(4) But Bernstein cannot do without the obfuscation, since he is not (in 1899) yet willing to put forward the above antirevolutionary conclusion baldly. Instead of trotting out some evidence that Marx's views entailed a Blanquist-type apotheosis of revolutionary will, he brings up a brilliant exploit in dialectics for which he has never been given due credit.

We have mentioned his claim that Marx's and Engels' writings in "the period of the Communist League" (1847-1852) clearly "breathe the Blanquist or Babouvist spirit over and over again." And now he adduces evidence: we hasten to quote it.

> In the *Communist Manifesto*, significantly, of all socialistic literature the writings of Babeuf remain uncriticized. Of them the Manifesto says only that in the great [French] revolution they [Babeufs writings] "expressed the demands of the proletariat"—which is anyhow an anachronistic characterization.[13]

If this statement were true, we would have an extraordinary exploit in forensics. The fact that the Manifesto does *not* criticize Babeuf is *"significantly"* tipped to us as proving that Marx was then a "Babouvist," or breathed the Babouvist "spirit," etc. (Otherwise why bring it up so "significantly"?) The possibilities of this polemical method are endless: it proves, for example, that Marx was also breathing the spirit of Savonarola (who is not repudiated anywhere in the Manifesto), of Moses and Jesus (neither of whom, significantly, is attacked), and of Genghis Khan (who emerges from the Manifesto scot-free) ... If this method becomes generalized, the intellectual history of the world is likely to be revolutionized.

But in point of fact, Bernstein's statement is a fafsifiction. As it happens, the Manifesto did not leave Babeufs writings "uncriticized." The first sentence of this section stated prominently that it would not take up the literature that has "given voice to the demands of the proletariat, such as the writings of Babeuf and others." Thereupon the Manifesto exercised the Ciceronian *praeteritio* (or paraleipsis) and devoted the whole next paragraph to precisely this subject.

Now it seems to me outside the pale of possibilities that Bernstein failed to grasp the fact that this paragraph is about Babeufs movement and its similiars—about "The first direct attempts of the proletariat to attain its own ends," etc. (for this is how the paragraph begins). Only a few years before, Bernstein had himself supplied an Afterword to his own translation of a book about the Babouvist conspiracy by the Guesdist, Gabriel Deville.[14] Whom else did he think the paragraph was about?

But for Bernstein to have brought out this paragraph of the Manifesto (the paragraph whose existence he ignored) would have been peculiarly embarrassing, for this paragraph refutes him. This paragraph on Babouvism concludes:

... these attempts necessarily failed, owing to the then undeveloped state of the proletariat, as well as to the absence of the economic conditions that had yet to be produced, and could be produced by the impending bourgeois epoch alone.[15]

With this, the proof of Marx's original-sin Babouvism would have blown up before the reader's eye left Bernstein's page, since Marx here (as elsewhere) makes it crystal-clear that he entertains no fanciful notion about "making" a revolution while the economic and class conditions for proletarian revolution were absent. The Manifesto's paragraph continues with a stern criticism of Babouvist-type movements:

The revolutionary literature that accompanied these first movements of the proletariat had necessarily a reactionary character. It inculcated universal asceticism and social leveling in its crudest form.[16]

To be sure, even if Marx *had* left mention of Babeuf completely out of the Manifesto, this would hardly prove him a Babouvist. Marx had criticized this "crude communism" before the Manifesto and would do so after it. The indications are that Marx decided at some point not to include sections in the Manifesto on those tendencies that called themselves communist, viz., Cabet, Weitling, Babeuf. A fragment of an early draft outline shows that Marx originally did plan to cover these three[17]; a discussion of the probable reasons for the change would be digressive here. But in any case, the whole business fails to prove that Marx was not only a Babouvist but also a Cabetist and Weitlingite!

(5) Bernstein's section on "Marxism and Blanquism" continues with blatantly unsupported assertions. The next one after the Babeuf bust is, I think, as mind-boggling as any:

The revolutionary program of action of the Manifesto is Blanquist through and through.

This dictum refers to the ten-point transitional program near the end of Section II[18]—a series of measures popular in leftist groups, proposed for the postrevolutionary period, sometimes scorned as being unexpectedly mild. It does not, for example, propose the general socialization of industry. "Blanquist through and through"? *every* plank? The demand for a graduated tax was "Blanquist"? free education was "Blanquist" extremism? This begins to verge on nonsense.

When this fairly moderate program is labeled "Blanquist through and through," one has to suspect that "Blanquist" is a code word: it has to do with the conquest of political power. For Bernstein, the conquest of political power is *ipso facto* "Blanquist"—unless it is done by the bourgeoisie, when it becomes realistic, responsible, respectable reform. For Marx, as the Manifesto itself

B. Fabrication of a Fable: The "Marx-Blanquist" Myth

says, the conquest of proletarian power is the aim of *every* proletarian tendency, including the Chartists. There is the crux.

By this time, Bernsteinian Marxo-teratology begins to suffer some of the difficulties that confronted Senator Joe McCarthy, as he "revealed" that everyone he didn't like was a "Communist." If *personae* who were *non gratae* to Joe McCarthy were all "Communists," then—could Communists really have tails and hooves? And so McCarthyism started turning dialectically into the old business of making Communist dupes. Similarly: if anyone who is not a Bernsteinian-revisionist parliamentary-legalist-constitutional-cretinic reformist is a "Blanquist," then can "Blanquism" be all bad?... But it is a falsification to say that politics divides between Bernstein and Blanqui, that is, between two ways of wrecking revolution.

Two other aspects *of* Bernstein's argument are taken up elsewhere: the social composition of the Blanquist movement, and the meaning of 'terrorism'.[19]

Finally, let us clear up a misapprehension. At the start of his section on "Marxism and Blanquism," Bernstein seems to say that Marx was a "Blanquist" in the period that ended 1852. By the end of that section he was saying something different:

> Marxism has shaken off Blanquism only from one side—in respect to method. But as for the other side, the overestimation of the creative power of revolutionary force for the socialist transformation of modern society, it has never fully got rid of the Blanquist conception.[20]

"Never," says Bernstein now, having screwed himself up to a pitch of undocumented assertiveness: Marx and Engels (he must mean them) "never fully got rid of the Blanquist conception." Their "Blanquism," then, was permanent. Bernstein has still not given a single statement by either Marx or Engels which "overestimates" etc., but we can now recognize the code word. What they "never fully got rid of" was their dedication to socialist revolution. But was it really necessary for this news to come from Bernstein in this peculiar way? Marx had said it for him, writing to a good friend and comrade about the philistine crew that made up the London German societies: ". . . these Germans, young and old, are nothing but all-too-clever, solid, practical-minded men who regard people like you and me as immature fools who have still not been cured of revolutionary fantasies."[21]

2. LICHTHEIM'S PUTSCH AGAINST MARX

For about a half-century, Eduard Bernstein's authority made references to Marx's "Blanquism" a common feature of marxological presentations. Even some of Bernstein's opponents, sharing the common ignorance, assumed that where there was so much smoke there must be fire (neglecting the possibility of smoldering rubbish). There is a piquant example in a 1932 lecture by the Menshevik leader Theodore Dan, writing in *defense* of the Russian party's adoption of the 'dictatorship of the proletariat' into its program in 1903. His argument was that the *mature* Marx was for majority revolution, thereby throwing the young Marx to the Bernsteinian wolves:

> Marx and Engels, in the years of their youth, no doubt pictured the dictatorship of the proletariat in the "Jacobin" form of a seizure of power by a proletarian minority conscious of its revolutionary mission and basing itself on an amorphous social agitation inside the broad proletarian masses. But already in 1845-46 ...[22]

The phrase "no doubt" meant that he knew nothing about it; he was willing to make the concession in order to rescue the mature Marx from Bernstein's clutches. In point of fact, "in the years of their youth" Marx and Engels never mentioned the 'dictatorship of the proletariat' at all.

Dan's comrade Martov did very much the same thing in his essay "Marx and the Dictatorship of the Proletariat."[23]

During this half-century it cannot be said that any new contributions were made to the shoring up of Bernstein's case. But in 1961 George Lichtheim's *Marxism* made a notable effort. We review some of the features of his exposition.

(1) In one respect Lichtheim did not go as far as Bernstein, for he saw Marx's "brief Jacobin-Blanquist aberration" as extending only to 1852. The prize exhibits, of course, are the March 1850 Address and the SUCR episode.

In the March Address, says Lichtheim, is found "the entire compendium of Communist tactics" in 1848, including the establishment of "proletarian dictatorship."[24] (In fact, 'dictatorship of the proletariat' is *not* mentioned in the Address.) But the question is: what's *Blanquist* about all this?

There is no answer in Lichtheim.

(2) Marx, asserts Lichtheim on the same page, "was then under the influence of Blanqui": what is the evidence? There are three erudite footnotes on this page of Lichtheim's, but not a word on this allegation. Lichtheim does not indicate that this is a *deduction* of his (perhaps from what he calls a "hint of terrorism" in the Address, for he does not know what 'terrorism' meant at that time). He states it as a bald fact. Since he is an Authority, a naive reader would assume there is evidence behind the assertion, and would be disappointed to learn that Lichtheim is inventing falsification freehand.

(3) Even in terms of the marxological habit of referring to SUCR as if it were simply a "Marxist-Blanquist alliance,"[25] Lichtheim is one of the slipperiest, for he does not give so much as a mention to the presence of the Chartists in the enterprise. Marx in 1850, says Lichtheim, was

B. Fabrication of a Fable: The "Marx-Blanquist" Myth 345

in a tactical alliance with the Blanquist emigrants in London. The latter even persuaded him to join a super-secret international society...[26]

The Blanquists *persuaded Marx?* Lichtheim, of course, knows nothing of the sort; he is inventing his "facts" with as much originality as any fictioneer. At the risk of boring the reader, I must repeat that he offers not a hint of evidence in text or notes.*

Marx, relates Lichtheim, "never quite repudiated his activities during this period."[28] The aforesaid naive reader would be eager to learn where Marx *almost* repudiated them, if "never quite." Alas, as I have detailed elsewhere,[29] Marx and Engels kept showing their approval of the 1850 Address until the end. When Engels actually had the Address reprinted in 1885, he explained that this 35-year-old Address "is still of interest today," etc.[30] Lichtheim even quotes this, because, he says, "Engels skims over this point, with a brief remark..."[31]

Thus, to support an assertion that Marx "never quite repudiated," and a further assertion on the same page that Marx "tacitly" abandoned the "assumptions" of the Address and Engels did so "explicitly"—to prop up this whole farrago of falsifiction, we find the argument that *although Engels reprinted this "abandoned" and "repudiated" document, he did so with merely a "brief remark"...* in an essay for party education which had already gone through the whole history of the Communist League with general approval.

(4) After quoting Marx's words at the September 1850 split meeting of the CL,[32] Lichtheim winds up with a complaint: in Marx's speech there was "no specific recognition that the day of Blanquist coups might be over for good."[33] The naive reader will think that somewhere in his book Lichtheim has presented some evidence that Marx *ever* approved of "Blanquist coups." But *no:* all Lichtheim has done is refrain from mentioning the several writings in which Marx had been repudiating Blanquist coups for several years already. He left out this material because it might confuse his readers.

---

* In another book, *Short History of Socialism*, Lichtheim again has Marx being "persuaded"—by Blanqui himself! But it is not clear of what he was supposed to be persuaded. The following occurs right after a sentence about Blanqui's anticipation of Bakunin and Lenin on the matter of dictatorship:

> For a while [Lichtheim writes]—between 1847 and 1850 to be precise—he [Blanqui] also persuaded Marx that it was possible to short-circuit the democratic process. Then their ways parted: a circumstance not often noted in later Communist literature.[27]

That last clause must have taken iron nerve to write; for a circumstance "often noted" is the fact that Marx never met Blanqui; it would be very difficult for their "ways" to part. This statement that Blanqui (personally) "persuaded Marx" edges close to something other than falsifiction. Was Lichtheim trying to see what enormities he could get away with?

(5) Lichtheim quotes the passage in the March Address which sees the proletariat as the successor to the bourgeoisie in political power. (I give his translation, with his mistakes and omissions corrected in brackets.)

> Alongside of the new official government[s] they must establish simultaneously their own revolutionary workers' government[s], whether in the form of [municipal committees and] municipal councils, or workers' clubs or workers' committees, *so* that the bourgeois-democratic authorities [governments] . . . from the outset see themselves supervised and threatened by authorities backed by the whole mass of the workers.[34]

Lichtheim then states: "This was the Blanquist strategy in a nutshell."

What! The Blanquists looked to organize "the whole mass of the workers" into workers' committees, etc., as a "dual power" alongside the official state?! What Blanquist ever suggested anything like this?

None whatever; and the naive reader by this time should not be surprised to learn that Lichtheim makes no effort to link this type of revolutionary strategy with any Blanquist he ever heard of. It is just another assertion—diametrically contrary to the entire political character of Blanquism. In fact, the cited passage in the March Address is the first great sketch of an approach to revolutionary power around what later came to be called *workers' councils.*

"This was the Blanquist strategy in a nutshell": our naive reader may wonder why a certain something seems to disappear when Lichtheim is fabricating links between Marx and Blanquism. What disappears is the content of Blanquism as conspiratorial putschism by a small band of bravos. It simply vanishes from Lichtheim's nutshell.

(6) After 1850, says Lichtheim, the German Communists' "actual circumstances" had little to do with Blanquist strategy, and so— We get another exercise in falsifiction:

> As soon as Marx realised this—it did not take him long—he dissolved the League, turned his back upon the Blanquist emissaries (though not upon Blanqui himself), and for the remainder of his life adamantly refused to engage in revolutionary conspiracy.[35]

Every phrase in this sentence is a triumph of creative imagination. There is no record of any moment when Marx realizes, with a start, that his "actual circumstances" have "little to do" with Blanquism, and thereupon hies himself off to dissolve the Communist League. Indeed, we know very well the circumstances under which Marx proposed dissolution of the League: this took place on November 17, 1852, three days after the sentences were handed down in the Cologne Communist show-trial after the smashing of the League organization throughout Germany. Hence it was more than a year after Marx had "turned his back" upon the Blanquists in SUCR. Lichtheim's scenario, we see, has the biographical reliability of a Hollywood script on the life and

B. Fabrication of a Fable: The "Marx-Blanquist" Myth 347

times of Billy the Kid; and he enjoys the same privilege as any director not to let mere facts interfere with his art.

(7) All this, says Lichtheim, amounts to "Marx's tacit renunciation of Blanquism." "Tacit" means that Marx said nothing about "renouncing" Blanquism: how true! This is something of an improvement on the famous question by the fabled prosecutor who asked, "When did you stop beating your wife?" In the up-to-date version, that cross-examination would go somewhat as follows:

—When did you tacitly renounce beating your wife?
—I never said anything about renouncing beating my wife!
—Exactly: that's what I just said—you renounced it *tacitly*...

(8) The rest of Lichtheim's falsifiction is outside our purview, for practical reasons. He claims that in abandoning "Blanquism," Marx also repudiated "Communism" (meaning revolutionary socialism) and "abandoned the entire perspective of a worker-peasant rising" at least in Germany, becoming a respectable social-democrat.[36] Naive readers who are eager to find out where Marx performed these renunciatory feats will find that Lichtheim—is still directing Billy the Kid.

It is such a beautiful story, this tale of the young fire-eater who settles down to be a parliamentary cretin even as you and I ... so touching that it is especially popular among types who have themselves done some heavy repudiating. Ex-Communists, for example, and ex-Marxists. The Ex, or Former Person, knows with what pleasure Lichtheim reports: "it is not too much to say that after 1848-49 he [Marx] became what is nowadays called an ex-Communist."[37]

This is a delightful improvement on all that chortling over Marx's revelation, "I am no Marxist."[38] It turns out that Marx is an ex-Marxist. Just like Lichtheim himself, as it happens. A divine idea: the sky-pilots create God and Marx in their own image.

3. DECRYING WOLFE

Not long after Lichtheim, another ex-Communist went into the lists to make much ado over Marx's alleged period of "Blanquism": Bertram Wolfe. I think there is a connection between their own devolution from communism to anticommunism and the fact that these two have become the outstanding contemporary proponents of the "Marx-Blanquist" myth. These are men who early fell under the spell of a rebellious sort of revolutionism, and then with the onset of age whined about their youthful foolishness: for such unfortunates, all revolutionaries are also misguided dupes of their early illusions. Wolfe writes in his Chapter 9:

> Marx was completely under the spell of the barricade and conspiracy traditions of Paris ... Marx's socialism during this period [1848-1850] was the romantic, equalitarian, street-fighting, barricade, and seizure of public-buildings brand of socialism of the Paris conspirators Babeuf, Buonarroti, and Blanqui.[39]

This is such a phantasmagorical description of Marx's activity in Cologne, as hard-working editor of the most successful revolutionary daily in Germany, that no one can doubt who is sitting for the portrait. It is autobiographical bitterness, typical of ex-Communists who have spent the best years of their lives working for a cause, and then have spent the rest of their years spitting on their former selves. Anyway, out of the several volumes of writings and letters by Marx and Engels during these years, Wolfe cannot find one passage in which the above type of socialism is expressed; he certainly cites none. He is doing the Foxy Grandpa act: *"Ah yes, my children, I too was a revolutionary when I was young and green,"* etc. This goes very well over a cracker barrel, but elsewhere one expects that some evidence will be offered for the flat statement that *"Marx's socialism"* was that of *"the Paris conspirators, Babeuf, Buonarroti, and Blanqui."*

But to avoid repetition, we will now ignore mere assertions in Wolfe's Chapter 9 and look for some argument or documentation, leaving aside some points taken up elsewhere.

(1) Wolfe undertakes to expound the "Blanquist" content of the much-abused Address of March 1850. The question, of course, is not whether the views in the Address are good or bad, but only whether they are Blanquist. Wolfe cites the Address's plan for setting up "their own revolutionary workers' governments in the form of workers' clubs and workers' committees"—the same passage targeted by Lichtheim and quoted above.[40] Well now, what's Blanquist about *that?* Wolfe explains in a parenthesis:

> Here one is reminded of the many clubs Blanqui formed, of the Jacobin clubs of the 1790s which were his model—and no less of his Jacobin centralism and his conviction that Paris should control and decide for all France.[41]

All this just from the mention of clubs! Blanqui formed clubs, the Jacobins formed clubs, Marx wants clubs—aha! *Blanquism!*

I hesitate to mention that everyone formed clubs, republicans left and right, royalists, militant women, society dames, coffeeshop habitués—for to make this point might suggest that this Wolfian nonsense should be taken seriously. But it is perhaps better than boringly repeating that Wolfe shovels in assertions without a pretense of evidence.

B. Fabrication of a Fable: The "Marx-Blanquist" Myth   349

(2) Wolfe cites the injunction in the Address that the Communists should seek to take the lead in militant actions reflecting "the people's revenge against hated individuals or public buildings ..." And he comments:

> In these words echo the storming *of* the Bastille, the clubbings to death with rifle butts, the heads raised on pikes, and rise and fall of the sharp blade of the guillotine.[42]

In Wolfe's mind, the "storming of the Bastille" is assimilated to mob slaughter!

More important, the whole point of Marx's exposition was precisely to replace wild mob passion with organized and rational political action, disciplined struggle, and leadership. But in any invocation of revolution, all Wolfe can hear is the "clubbings to death by rifle butts." Very well—who is clubbing whom? Historically, of course, it is usually the police, gendarmes and soldiery who club demonstrating rebels. Perhaps this is Law and Order, while the reverse is Revolutionary Anarchy? If so, it is not the "clubbings" that exercise Wolfe but the different question of whose noggin gets knocked. The apparently moral revulsion against "clubbings to death" then turns out to represent the opinion that only the revolutionary side should be conscientiously cudgeled.

(3) Wolfe's Chapter 9 is one of the worst cases of those who distort locus 1c into a (mythical) avowal of Blanquism by Marx. (The middling cases are those who at least quote the passage, so that a reader can see what they are doing.) The defeat of the revolution, claims Wolfe (with Marx on the couch),

> had for the moment made Marx into a Blanquist and Blanqui in Marx's eyes into the living incarnation of the movement of "revolutionary socialism or communism."[43]

Notice that Marx is "a Blanquist," squarely, flatfootedly, unqualifiedly. The telltale words in quotes at the end leave no doubt what Wolfe is using for this claim: Marx's words in locus 1c. There Marx refers to "revolutionary socialism," "communism," "for which the bourgeoisie itself has invented the name of Blanqui." In short, Marx writes that Blanqui had become the incarnation (etc.) *in the eyes of the bourgeoisie;* Wolfe alters this to "in Marx's eyes"!

I repeat that I do not think Wolfe is consciously falsifying, no matter how hard it may be to explain this blatant alteration in any other way. I think that in his last incarnation Wolfe could no longer read plain English or plain German as soon as his anticommunist button was touched. A red haze hung over Marx's Address, there was a dull roaring in the ears, and the damnedest things came off the pen. I do not insist on this explanation.

(4) So far, Wolfe's Chapter 9. A strange thing happens in Chapter 10: it presents a point of view according to which everything in Chapter 9 is nonsense.

I have been told by an acquaintance of Wolfe's that he had decided at this point to investigate Marx's use of 'dictatorship of the proletariat', and was delighted to find that it had already been done—in my 1962 essay.[44] He found this essay "thorough and dispassionate" and its "interpretation sound": so he states in Chapter 10, and proceeds to summarize my essay in his next ten pages. True, he leaves out some material that would ruin his "Marx-Blanquist" thesis, but it makes him uneasy.

The puzzling question is why at this point Wolfe did not throw away Chapter 9, if not more of his book. Instead, there is one point in Chapter 10 where he seeks to retrieve some remnant of the "Marx-Blanquist" falsification in Chapter 9. This attempt hinges on the citation of locus 1c, which, we have seen, he previously distorted. Now he does quote it, including the crucial phrase *"for which the bourgeoisie itself has invented the name of Blanqui"*; and he lifts a lance.

> This leads Mr. Draper to conclude that in the cited passage Marx was not defining "Blanquism" but expressing his own views, the "revolutionary socialism or communism" which he himself advocated, and to which the bourgeoisie has given (invented) the name of Blanqui. Obviously, Mr. Draper's "solution" of the enigmatic passage raises as many problems as it solves.[45]

What are these "problems"? Wolfe states four, which I quote in full seriatim:

(a) "For when Marx wrote it, he was entering into his *Association* with the Blanquists;..."

This refers to SUCR, which we have already discussed. Wolfe does not realize that *his* problem is whether Marx became a "Chartist" or a "Blanquist"—since both of these tendencies were supposed to become his allies in SUCR. The first problem is in pretending that SUCR was "a united front *with the Blanquists*"[46]

More important, we have seen that at the same time that Marx entered into this nearly nonexistent front that included the Blanquists as its French wing, he published a scathing dissection of traditional Blanquism. Now the next strange thing about Wolfe is that he discovers this in his *next* chapter, Chapter 11. There Wolfe suddenly reveals that (as I had stressed in my 1962 essay)—

> Marx attempted to "re-educate" the Blanquist emigrés, to induce them to substitute his idea of "the dictatorship of the proletariat," which Marx considered synonymous with the "winning of the battle of democracy," for Blanqui's "revolutionary dictatorship" of an elite, conspirative minority.[47]

To be sure, he does not disclose what Marx actually wrote in 1850 about these

B. Fabrication of a Fable: The "Marx-Blanquist" Myth

Blanquist allies of his (for this would have terribly confused the readers of his Chapter 9). But anyway: why on earth should Marx—described in Chapter 9 as bubbling over with Blanquism, flatly labeled "a Blanquist"—*want* to "re-educate" his fellow Blanquists? What does this Blanquist Marx want to re-educate the other Blanquists *to?*
No answer. In fact, no question.

It is admittedly gratifying that Wolfe has learned, by Chapter 11, that Marx attempted this "re-education" of the Blanquists, and it is good to report that he passes this information on to his readers; and I do not want to seem to demand too much of a marxologist. Yet one must mention that, in the same passage, he quotes Engels' devastating characterization of Blanquism in 1874 (our locus 8), but introduces it with these words: "At least, so Engels has explained the matter." Does he offer any counterexplanation of his own? No. All this, remember, in Chapter 11. When Wolfe, in the preceding chapter, had written as if Marx's "entering into his *Association*" is a "problem" for which he has no explanation, the puzzling thing is why (after getting to Chapter 11) he didn't throw away this part of Chapter 10 into the same round receptacle as Chapter 9.

(b) "... he [Marx] was agreeing to, or more probably he was writing, virtually the same formula into the joint statement of principles [of SUCR]; ..."

We now have a second point (out of four) on SUCR, which Wolfe obviously thinks is the "smoking gun" of Marx's "Blanquism." A minor point: the SUCR statement, as extant, is copied out in a handwriting that is probably Willich's, certainly not Marx's or Engels'; and there is absolutely no information on who drafted it. When Wolfe writes that Marx "probably" wrote it, he is simply inventing a falsifiction.[48] Of course, it makes no difference one way or t'other; but such inventions suggest that mere facts do not quite suffice for the fable under discussion.

The crux of this second Wolfian "problem" is: what is meant by "virtually the same formula"? Same as what? Same as what Marx had written in locus 1 c *(Class Struggles in France)?* In this case, I do not know what the "problem" is. Or—is it possible?—does Wolfe mean "same as *Blanqui's* formula"? But we have shown that Blanqui never had a formula about 'dictatorship of the proletariat' or anything like it.* What, then, is the point of trying to squeeze a second "problem" out of SUCR?

---

* The SUCR statement included reference to "permanent revolution," and it should be mentioned that Wolfe is still, in Chapter 10, under the impression that "Marx had acquired from Blanqui his formula of the 'revolution in permanence'..."[49]—although he handsomely acknowledged his debt to my 1962 essay for disposing of the parallel belief that Blanqui had originated 'dictatorship of the proletariat'.[50] The myth of Blanqui's priority on 'permanent revolution' was disposed of in *KMTR 2.*[51]

(c) "... he was issuing his peculiarly 'Blanquist' *Circular,...*"—that is, the March 1850 Address.

The "problem," obviously, lies with Wolfe's preceding demonstration that the content of the Address was Blanquist—not merely deplorably revolutionary but Blanquist. The reader will remember that on this point we had to discuss clubs and "clubbings to death"; but a repeated examination of Wolfe's two pages on the matter turns up no other effort to make a connection.[52] I suggest there is an element of circularity here: Marx is a Blanquist because we know the Address is Blanquist, and we know the Address must be Blanquist because it is filled with revolutionary talk by a Blanquist...

(d) Finally: "... and he was using Blanquist conspirators as emissaries to the branches of the Communist League."

This refers to Wolfe's deduction from the June 1850 Address, based on a passage discussed in Chapter 12.[53] If I explained that Wolfe's deduction is half-imaginative, the reader might think that the deduction, if valid, has something to do with Wolfe's fourth problem. For present purposes, then, let us assume that Marx really did use "Blanquist conspirators as emissaries" to Communist League branches on the Continent. (I can make this assumption all the more happily since, personally, I hope that Marx did get some use out of these characters.)

Well now, what exactly is Marx's crime?

In the first place: as we have seen, Marx is trying to work on these French Blanquist elements politically (to "re-educate" them); and it is not fanciful to assume that he may have had some impact on two or three. As we have stressed elsewhere, these "Blanquist conspirators" were not hardshelled revolutionary fossils: they were largely young and relatively inexperienced recruits who were "Blanquist" mainly because they admired Blanqui, wanted to be revolutionaries, and had never heard of any other way of being revolutionary.[54] Why doesn't Wolfe ask himself *why* a "Blanquist conspirator" would consent to act as emissary for a rival tendency, German at that, which moreover published sharp critiques of their fellow conspirators?

Wolfe thinks the arrangement shows something awful about Marx; he does not realize that it shows something quite different *about the self-selected "Blanquist conspirators" who agreed to work for the CL.* I think that in Wolfe's mind's-eye there was a different picture: as if some naive liberal were trying to "use" a Communist KGB agent on a mission abroad . . . But the young Blanquist refugees in London had no resemblance to the types who give Wolfe his modern jitters. Many of them were passing through the Blanquist group, which (like most sects) had a turnstile style of turnover in membership.

Let us imagine Wolfe as Marx, in a historical playlet. A Blanquist, who perhaps has been undergoing "re-education," says he is willing to be "used as emissary" for the CL.

B. Fabrication of a Fable: The "Marx-Blanquist" Myth 353

Wolfe-Marx *(handon heart):* No! I cannot permit you to help us. You are a *(hiss)* conspirator!
Blanquist *(astonished):* Why, are you afraid I'll cook up a "conspiracy" with your CL branch?
W-M *(huffily):* No, our Communists know very well to stay away from conspiracy.
B *(reasonablelike):* Don't you agree that our mission has to be kept secret, since the Continental governments will throw me and your people into the pokey if I'm caught?
W-M *(offended):* Yes, I understand the difference between secret work and conspiratorial organization and have explained the difference several times.
B *(wheedling):* Then, please, why can't I do this service for you and your estimable CL?
W-M *(drawing himself up):* Because then the marxologists will be able to prove that I'm a Blanquist.

This "theater of the absurd" suggests a link between the pathos of a kind of marxology and the pathology of a kind of American anti-Communism.

4. TARRADIDDLES AND SCIOLISTS

Up to the 1960s, when Lichtheim and Wolfe published the books we have reviewed, most references to Marx's mythical "Blanquism" were, I think, more or less routine echoes of Bernstein. Thus, in 1912 Simkhovitch quoted the Manifesto's introduction to the ten-point program near the end of Section II, and opined that "Babeuf or Blanqui might have written this passage" because it was in keeping with the viewpoint of "conspiracy or forcible overthrow."[55] It seems that "conspiracy" and "forcible overthrow" fused in his mind like two fogbanks merging in a murk.

Isaiah Berlin's much-praised biography of Marx—which on strictly factual matters is one of the least reliable ever published—has Marx persuaded by "Weitling and Blanqui" in 1847-1848 "that a successful revolution could be made only [really!] by means of a coup d'etat, carried out by a small and resolute body of trained revolutionaries.."[56] In the case of Berlin's biography, to complain of lack of evidence is an irrelevancy; but it is hard to see why he did not refer to 1850, which more knowledgeable writers emphasize. But then, Berlin does not even mention the *existence* of the March Address or SUCR. And if he did, he would be in trouble, for he has not the slightest idea what 'permanent revolution' meant.[57]

Berlin had his rivals in sciolism (one of the major isms of history). Adam

Ulam, for example, repeating the obligatory exposition of Marx's "Blanquism," reveals that he thinks the Blanquists were anarchists, and that Blanqui was a pioneer of syndicalism![58]

Such a survey could go on indefinitely—

> Before each tarradiddle,
> Uncowed by sciolists,
> Robuster persons twiddle
> Tremendously big fists...[59]

but to little avail. However, two other cases have some claim on our attention.

The first is the Marx biography by Nicolaievsky and Maenchen-Helfen, because it has so often been cited on this point as an eminent authority. This work by Nicolaievsky (I use his name as the major author) was partly considered in Chapter 12 under SUCR, but another, more general passage requires notice.

Nicolaievsky's takeoff point is a little odd, for it is *not* the March 1850 Address, the document in which Lichtheim and Wolfe had particularly discerned the imprint of the devil's hoof. By not a word does Nicolaievsky suggest that the March Address is "Blanquist." What shakes his soul is apparently the paragraph about the Blanquists in the June 1850 Address, with its news that Communist League delegates "had been entrusted by the Blanquists with important preparatory work in connection with the next French revolution." (This is the reverse of Wolfe's problem, but the considerations are similar.) Nicolaievsky wonders: who were these delegates and what was this work? He replies that the answer to both questions is "unknown."

> But what the Blanquists were occupied with during the years 1850 and 1851 is known.[60]

He then summarizes the oft-repeated characterization of Blanquist plans for a putsch by a small gang of men. This is followed, without so much as a paragraph break, by this conclusion:

> The fact that Marx accepted this kind of revolutionism, which he condemned so violently both before and afterwards *[note that, please!]*, and was so utterly foreign in every way to the essential nature of the proletarian revolution, *the fact that he formed an alliance with the Blanquists*, proves better than anything else the extent to which his judgement had been affected ... [Italics added.][61]

"*The fact that Marx accepted this kind of revolutionism* ..."—but Nicolaievsky (here we get repetitious) has not adduced a single fact, note, argument, or ground to "prove" (his word) that Marx accepted the Blanquist putsch idea. Worse than that: *five pages later, he gives a substantial passage from the book review by*

B. Fabrication of a Fable: The "Marx-Blanquist" Myth 355

Marx and Engels which dissected conspiratorialism so cuttingly—published at exactly the same time that Marx "accepted this kind of revolutionism." No explanation for this self-refutation; apparently no consciousness of a problem. Was it poor Marx whose mind had been sadly affected?

Moreover, the above-quoted paragraph by Nicolaievsky ascertains a second fact that shows how poor Marx's mind was affected: this is "the fact that he formed an alliance with the Blanquists" at all. We have already said enough about this item of proof, insofar as it pertains to 1850. But Nicolaievsky is in a stranger position than Wolfe or Lichtheim. For him, the Blanquist aberration suddenly descends on Marx's psyche in the midsummer of 1850—nothing like it "before or afterwards," he says—and all on the basis of the "unknown" revolutionary work done by unknown CLers with unknown Blanquists!

Bernstein had seen Marx's "Blanquism" as covering 1848-1852 at least, and Marx's whole life at large; Wolfe and Lichtheim saw it ectoplasmatically enveloping Marx at least through 1850; but Nicolaievsky sees it as a brief moment of midsummer madness unrelated to anything "before or afterwards"— except the poor man's shock (apparently much delayed) at personally losing the revolution...

This approaches utter nonsense on the face of it; but to this baseless fantasy we can counterpose a historical fact not yet brought up. It concerns alliances with the Blanquists: a comparison. In 1850 the so-called united front "with the Blanquists" never got off paper; in 1872 what Wolfe calls another "united front with the Blanquists" never existed at all, since the Blanquists (Commune refugees) entered into the wide-open International. But a little later came the period of *real united fronts* between the French Marxists (that is, Guesdists) and the Blanquist movement in France, especially when the latter was led by Vaillant (who, German-educated, had absorbed a considerable amount of "re-education"). The period of the development of the French socialist movement in the 1880-1890s, leading up to the unification of 1905 (when— *gulp!*—they actually *merged!),* is full of united fronts, alliances, coalitions and collaborations with the Blanquists. Somehow this has never "proved" to any sane person that, say, Guesde (or Jaurès, *sacrebleu)* had become a Blanquist. But when people write about Marx, the simplest laws of logic go through a space warp.

The second case takes us full-circle back to Bernstein, with a difference. Also in the 1960s, Stanley Moore published a curious book, *Three Tactics; the Background in Marx,* with a thesis. He wants to marry Bernsteinism with Stalinism. This is not a strange aspiration in these days when sectors of the Communist movement are thinking of how to create "Eurocommunist" parties that would slough off the revolutionary socialist component and leave them unembarrassed practitioners of parliamentary reformism, to fill the slot being vacated by the Social-Democracies as these slough off any kind of socialism at all. In this context Moore has several pages arguing in favor of Bernstein's thesis about the young "Blanquist" Marx.

Moore's specialty is running Marx-quotes through his interpreting machine, which minces them up and reconstitutes them in the desired form like a sausage. Investigating the contents of these sausages is very space-consuming. Thus, out of quotes by Marx not one of which comes near favoring "minority revolution," he deduces handily (after processing) that Marx proposed minority revolution, just as Bernstein said; and he naturally ignores all the passages where, unminced and unprocessed, Marx stated straight-out that he advocated majority-supported revolution.

When Moore comes out with a whopper, he starts off with "Undeniably..."

> Undeniably Marx and Blanqui shared at that time the doctrines of class struggle, permanent revolution, and proletarian dictatorship.[62]

Let us taste one sausage because it is another case of the distortion of locus 1c. Moore writes as follows:

> The communism of Blanqui, he [Marx] writes in *The Class Struggles in France,* is "the declaration of the permanence of the revolution, the class dictatorship of the proletariat [etc.]..,"[63]

This is a falsifiction, fabricated by joining Moore's own words to the truncated Marx-locus. As we have seen more than once now, Marx really wrote that the bourgeoisie has "invented the name of Blanqui" for revolutionary socialism or communism. The rump-quote used by Moore then occurs in the *next* sentence.

Not all of Moore's falsifictions are as unoriginal as this one. He strikes a new vein with the argument that the very name "Communist League" was Blanquist.

> For the predominantly German-speaking League to call itself communist was to affirm publicly its solidarity with the French followers of Blanqui.[64]

He deduces this, he says, from locus 1c; for he is under the impression that in those days if a German or French worker said "communist" he meant Blanquist. But if our sciolist had looked in any one of several places, he would have found that in the 1840s Marx knew of a whole bushelful of different "communisms."

On a single page of the *German Ideology,* Moore could have learned of four different kinds of communists: Cabetists, who may have been the most prominent, Weitling, "nonrevolutionary Communists," and apparently the Chartists: *no mention of Blanquists.*[65] Another page of the same work lists no less than fourteen English communists alone, past and present, besides Weitling, Cabet, and François de Chastellux; *no mention of Blanquists.*[66] On a single page of the *Holy Family,* Marx mentions the "communists" Owen, Bentham, Cabet,

B. Fabrication of a Fable: The "Marx-Blanquist" Myth

Dézamy, and Gay, besides the Babouvists; *no mention of Blanquists*.[67] In a pre-Marxist article of 1843, written for the English Owenites, Engels surveyed the ranks of French communists, beginning with Babeuf and featuring Cabet's "Icarian communism," together with their differences from English "communism" (meaning Owenism). We learn further that Leroux is a communist, apparently also George Sand, Lemennais and Proudhon. But *Blanqui is not mentioned*, nor any Blanquist.[68] The label 'communist' usually referred to the Cabetists. In 1850 Marx's and Engels' book review on the conspiratorial societies clearly identified the "communists" as the Cabetists only, counterposing them to the professional conspirators.[69] Another interesting case: in March 1848, in Paris, Marx and his CL associates wrote to Cabet, as editor *of Le Populaire,* asking him to publish their protest against the "German Legion" scheme, since such a declaration was "in the interests of the communist party, and it is this," the letter adds, "which makes us count on your compliance."[70] In other words, Cabet was viewed as a fellow communist.

Of course, Marx later narrowed this usage, it goes without saying, but the usage reflected the popular opinion of the time. And that is precisely what Moore is appealing to—the popular image of 'communist'—but he simply does not know that in the 1840s (and later) 'communist' was as amorphous a term as 'socialist'.

It is not Moore's argumentation that is interesting. It is his demonstration of an old pattern from a new direction, the unflagging need among marxologists to stamp Marx's revolutionary socialism as "Blanquism." For the Bernstein-Lichtheim-Wolfe type, the need is to smirch revolutionary socialism with an unsavory label, especially one associated with minority revolutionism. For Moore the need is to legitimize minority revolutionism with Marx's imprimatur, thus using the Bernsteinian component to underpin the Stalinist component. Or, as Samuel Hoffenstein put it—

> The small chameleon has the knack
> Of turning red or pink or black,
> And yet, whatever hue he don,
> He stays a small cham-e-le-on.[71]

5. THE CASE OF ERNST SCHRAEPLER

Since its publication in 1972, Ernst Schraepler's *Handwerkerbünde und Arbeitervereine 1830-1853* has been regarded as an authority on the early history of German workers' organizations. It appears to the naked eye to be well annotated and documented, and for all I know, may be so in general. But the author is not well served by his violent anti-Marx obsession, and where the devil (Marx) shows up on the scene, scholarship goes to the place the devil came from. Especially on SUCR, I have run into several references to the authority of Schraepler's work. Let us look into it, since Schraepler repeats the "Marx-Blanquist" tale.

In the first place, Schraepler has found no hard facts, or soft ones, about SUCR that have not been known for fifty years. This is no fault of his, of course. He had to carpenter his own interpretation of the facts; but instead of doing so, he took an unusual course. He translated Nicolaievsky's old biography—without credit.

In question are some of the same passages by Nicolaievsky that I have discussed in this Special Note. In both Nicolaievsky and Schraepler the spotlight is put on the paragraph in the *June* (not March) "Address to the CL," referring to "Blanquist delegates" associated with CL delegates. The main point is made as follows in both books:

Nicolaievsky	*Schraepler*
Who these delegates were and the nature of their duties is unknown, But what the Blanquists were occupied with during the years 1850 and 1851 is known. They were engaged in preparations for an armed rising, just as they had been before 1848 .. ,[72]	There was nothing said about these delegates and the nature of their duties. But what the Blanquists were occupied with during the years 1850-51 was generally known. They were preparing for an armed rising, as they had done before 1848.. [73]

Taking the passage which we quoted from Nicolaievsky,[74] beginning "The fact that Marx accepted ...," Schraepler transposed a few expressions from other lines, and came out with the following, the crux of his conclusion (and Nicolaievsky's):

> The fact that the leader of the Communist League entered into a close alliance with Blanqui [*sic*], whom he esteemed as a resolute revolutionary though putsch methods were repugnant to him, proves unequivocally that after the breakdown of all revolutionary efforts in Europe Marx had lost above all his previous inner certainty.[75]

Note that Schraepler has added the falsifiction (which was not in his source) that Marx's alliance was with "Blanqui"—the man himself. Not for Schraepler the small beer of charging little alliances with inconsequential Blanquists in London. But outside of this artistic *retouche,* he has copied Nicolaievsky without credit. Why he omitted the customary footnoted acknowledgment (without which this sort of business is called plagiarism) is hard to understand:

B. Fabrication of a Fable: The "Marx-Blanquist" Myth 359

perhaps he wished to conceal the fact that he had nothing of his own to say.

We trust that future footnoters will be saved from committing the *gaffe* of referring their own readers to Schraepler's secondhand version when the original fable can be read in Nicolaievsky.

SPECIAL NOTE C | **THE MEANING OF 'TERROR' AND 'TERRORISM'**

'Dictatorship' has a close competitor in the contest for the nineteenth-century word most abused in marxological writings. The original meaning of 'terror' and 'terrorism' appears to be almost completely forgotten today. Since much conjuring with these words takes place in discussions of Marx's "dictatorial" politics, the question has to be taken up.

Many passages in Marx and Engels make no sense whatever if 'terror' is taken in its current sense; the situation testifies to the prevalent belief that our present-day vocabulary began with Adam.* To be sure, everyone knows that the beginnings of 'terror' as a political term lie in the French Revolution; but this is part of the trouble: for distortions of that historical experience color all our perceptions of what happened in 1793-1794, the period of the "Red Terror." Not only the popular but the lexicographical view of the "Reign of Terror" comes from sources typified by *The Scarlet Pimpernel:* the Terror meant the bloodthirsty massacre of innocent women and children (and a few God-fearing nobles) unless they were saved by Leslie Howard; or, as in certain novels, it meant that the revolutionary masses were depicted as degenerates drooling at the sight of spurting blood.

Now it is no part of our task to investigate "what really happened" in the so-called Reign of Terror, let alone the French Revolution *in toto:* we are only interested in explaining how Marx used the term, that is, what 'terror' meant to *him.* But we must immediately add that it was not a question of his personal

---

* Even Richard N. Hunt, who devotes a long chapter to expounding the contents of my 1962 essay on the 'dictatorship of the proletariat', and who is therefore well aware of the problem, never stops to ask himself the question when he comes to the word 'terror', which chills his social-democratic soul. He thinks that Marx's and Engels' pronouncements on "revolutionary terror" were "bloodthirsty," and that a "systematic policy of terror" meant that "a minority would be imposing its will on the reluctant majority."[1] He does not *argue* this—that is, present evidence—because he apparently assumes it to be as axiomatic as the belief that a pound of iron weighs more than a pound of feathers. If this is true of Hunt, it is hardly necessary to cite the legions of vulgar statements on the same subject.

C. The Meaning of 'Terror' and 'Terrorism' 361

opinion. Marx used 'terror (ism)' in the current fashion of his time. Indeed, the first question for an objective historian would be to inquire into what the "Terrorists" conceived themselves to be doing—what 'terror' meant to them. We will see, then, that a distinction will have to be made between the 'Terror' proper and *the final degeneration of the Terror into a bloody caricature of itself*. We will be especially interested in the first; it is a mistake to confound the first with the second.

Later, the political meaning of 'terror' went through a new transmogrification at the other end of the nineteenth century: this was due to the rise of what was called *individual terrorism,* especially as practiced by anarchists in Western Europe and by the Narodniks and nihilists in Eastern Europe. The term *'individual* terrorism' arose precisely to differentiate this political mode from what the left had previously called 'terrorism'; and from there on, *it tended to take over the ism.* Today the end-product of this process has brought it about that 'terrorism' is mainly a short form of 'individual terrorism'. It has merged in the public consciousness with what was previously the philistine calumniation of leftist violence. The other side of the merger in this century has come from the mindless bomb-thrower, who has adapted himself to what the calumniators told him was the proper way to be a "revolutionary." But this gets us into territory we cannot explore here.

We focus on what 'terror(ism)' meant to Marx, and to political circles in his time.

1. MARX ON THE JACOBIN TERROR

We have already seen one important aspect of Marx's view of the French Revolution: the distinctive emphasis he laid on the social-Girondin current (Cercle Social, etc.) and the "Enrages" (Jacques Roux, Leclerc) as the precursors of communism, with a concomitant devaluation of the Jacobins.[2] Marx and Engels were not "Robespierrists" in historical interpretation: they did not regard Robespierre's political current as the central progressive leadership of the revolution.[*]

[*] This fact has been blurred over in Marxist literature since the dominant interpretation has been heavily influenced by "Robespierrist" historians like Mathiez and political forces like the French Communist Party, including the able historian Soboul. An analogous situation obtains with respect to the English Revolution: parallel to "Robespierrist" historiography is the similar view of Cromwell as against the democratic Levelers (not to speak of the True Levelers or Diggers). "Cromwellism" is the line embodied in Eduard Bernstein's work *Cromwell and Communism.* In general, this approach is characteristic of social-reformism, not only of modern Stalinism. Very early (1844)

Let us begin with an early reference by Marx to *Terrorismus* (the Gallicized form, not *Schrecklichkeit*). This occurred in the very first political article written by Marx (in 1842, published 1843)—hence while he was still a radical democrat but not a communist. It was the first-written of Marx's two powerful polemics in favor of complete freedom of the press.[4] The government's censorship decree permitted suppression for a writing's "tendency," its intentions or point of view; and Marx argued that this creates a police state and "sanctions of lawlessness":

> The writer is thus subjected to the *most frightful terrorism,* the *jurisdiction of suspicion.* Laws about *tendency,* laws that do not provide objective norms, are laws of terrorism, such as were conceived by the state's exigencies under Robespierre and the state's rottenness under the Roman emperors.[5]

Now, obviously the writer who was subjected to this "terrorism" was not about to be guillotined and did not require Leslie Howard's services; blood was not flowing like borscht. What was this "terrorism" which reminded Marx of Robespierre's resort to similar laws?

Before answering this question, let us look at Marx's remarks on the Jacobin terror soon after adopting communist views, in a period of intensive study of the French Revolution. Perhaps he became more favorable to Robespierrism after becoming a communist? The opposite is true, for plainly seen reasons. In an article of the summer of 1844 Marx focused on the neglect of social issues by the Jacobin leadership of the revolution. Robespierre, he wrote, saw the existence of extremes of poverty and wealth "only as an obstacle to *pure democracy*" not as a social issue to be overcome. His solution was "a universal Spartan frugality." His politics were based on the glorification of the will:

> [For Robespierre] The principle of politics is the *will.* The more onesided .... the *political* mind is, the more does it believe in the *omnipotence* of the will, the more is it blind to the *natural* and spiritual *limits* of the will, and the more incapable is it therefore of discovering the source of social ills.[6]

With this line of thought Marx naturally rejected the Jacobin tendency in favor of the revolutionary elements who confronted "the source of social ills." He specified this in his next work, *The Holy Family,* in the passage on Babeuf and the Enrages that we have quoted.[7]

In *The Holy Family,* Marx certainly connected the Terror with the work of the guillotine, like everyone else, but what exactly was the connection?

Engels made the connection: "Cromwell is Robespierre and Napoleon rolled into one ..."[3] Marx's viewpoint is distinct from historical "Robespierrism."

C. The Meaning of 'Terror' and 'Terrorism' 363

Bloodthirstiness? In point of fact, his mentions of the Terror (or *Terrorismus*) were associated with the following: the use of porters by the secret police; the campaign against speculative hoarding; the "terroristic attitude of the French Revolution to religion"; Napoleon as "the last struggle by the *revolutionary Terror* against the bourgeois society...," and a couple more similar associations that did not run with blood, to which we have to add the above-mentioned passage on Babeuf and the Enragés.[8]

If we ask what conception unites all of these usages, the only answer is: the idea of *coercion through intimidation*. This indeed is the original background meaning of *terrorization*. The Oxford English Dictionary's "general" definition of 'terrorism' says:

> A policy intended to strike with terror those against whom it is adopted; the employment of methods of intimidation; the fact of terrorizing or condition of being terrorized.*

Now "intimidation" can be accomplished by various methods and on several planes; and Marx's and Engels' use of the term 'terror' evoked different kinds of cases, from purely psychological intimidation to "bloody" force. But when forceful intimidation of the enemy is carried on by government troops in a war—is this 'terrorism'? It was in Marx's language, speaking of Napoleon's wars.[10] Engels also remarked that Napoleon's "reign of terror" took the shape of war.[11] Internally, Napoleon applied "revolutionary *Terrorismus* to the liberal bourgeoisie[12]—while the Scarlet Pimpernel took a rest. In an 1847 article Marx associated the Reign of Terror with "bloody action," right enough: "the bloody action of the people" (not Robespierre) that cleared away "the remnants of feudalism from French soil with its powerful hammer blows"—a job which "the timidly overcareful bourgeoisie would not have completed in decades."[13] During the revolutionary year of 1848, Engels compared the reactionary Belgian government's prosecution of republicans with the "mock trials" framed up during the Reign of Terror in 1793, though "even the fanatical Fouquier-Tinville" did not conduct a trial with so much barefaced lying as the Belgians.[14] The same year, Marx returned to his

---

* The O.E.D.'s specimen for 1863 was from a work on political economy: "If anyone should disobey the decision of the meeting, he would subject himself. . .to a social terrorism." Its general definition of 'terrorist' is this: "Anyone who attempts to further his views by a system of coercive intimidation" (followed by a reference to the "extreme revolutionary societies in Russia"). As for German lexicography: Ladendorf confirms that *Terrorismus* came into the language as the designation of Robespierre's regime of 1793-94, but it quickly "became a catchword and is now used with the most freely transferred sense." He quotes a 1799 passage from Wieland, in which the wise statesman is advised that governmental management should supplement the usual virtues with "a little terrorism."[9] Clearly not very bloodthirsty.

analysis of the Terror with this seminal observation: *"All French terrorism was nothing but a plebeian way of dealing with the enemies of the bourgeoisie, absolutism, feudalism and philistinism."*[15] By the same token, it was no model: the wielders of this power were doing it for another class element, without political consciousness of what they were really doing. It was neither a horrible aberration of history nor a glorious prototype.

In 1851, reviewing Proudhon's recent book in a letter to Engels, Marx noted its positive or favorable side: its "well-written attacks on Rousseau, Robespierre, the Montagne [Jacobin group], etc."[16] From *The Holy Family*, in which he castigated Robespierre's illusions, Marx's references to Robespierre are only scattered passages, but these are always cool or hostile, whether in connection with the Jacobin's suppression of civil liberties or their antiworking-class legislation.[17]

This view, up to now expressed by both Marx and Engels in brief remarks, was given its sharpest formulation by Engels in discussion with Marx. Writing to Marx as Bonaparte's empire fell in September 1870 amidst a chaotic rising, Engels' thinking made a connection:

> From these perpetual little °panics° of the French—which all arise from fear of the moment when one finally must face the truth—we get a much better idea of the Reign of Terror. We take this to mean the reign [or rule] of people who inspire terror; on the contrary, it is the reign of people who are themselves terrorstricken. *La terreur* is in large part useless cruelties committed by people who are in fear themselves, for their own self-assurance. I am convinced that the blame for the Reign of Terror in '93 lies almost exclusively on the shoulders of the terribly frightened bourgeois behaving like patriots, and on the little philistines who are shitting in their pants, and on the lumpen-mob making a profit out of the *terreur*. These are exactly the classes in the present little *terreur* too.[18]

In this view the Reign of Terror in the narrow sense was regarded as the *terminal stage* of the revolutionary terror already in pathological condition. This distinction of stages was stated again by Engels in a late letter to Kautsky:

> As for the terror, it was essentially a *war measure* as long as it had any sense. The class, or factional group of the class, that alone could ensure the victory of the revolution not only kept itself in control in this way (this was the least of it after the victory over the revolts) but assured itself of freedom of movement, °elbow room,° the possibility of concentrating forces at the decisive point, the frontiers.

By early 1794 (Engels went on to say) the defense against foreign intervention was going well, and Robespierre, who wanted an end to the war, saw the

C. *The Meaning of 'Terror' and 'Terrorism'* 365

revolutionary wing as a danger to his power, especially the Commune led by the Jacobin left:

> The Commune, with its extreme tendency, became superfluous; its propaganda for revolution became a hindrance for Robespierre as well as for Danton, both of whom wanted peace—though each in a different way. In this conflict of three elements Robespierre won out, but *now terror became for him a means of self-preservation* and thereby became absurd...

When the foreign threat seemed to be completely ended, Robespierre became superfluous in turn:

> On June 26 [1794] at Fleurus Jourdan laid all Belgium at the republic's feet; with this, it [the terror] became untenable; on July 27 Robespierre fell, and the bourgeois orgy began.[19]

Where popular history sees only bloodthirsty irrationality in the last, pathological stage of the Terror, this interpretation made a quite different analysis. But our own subject is not the French Revolution, only the meaning of 'terror'. Before summing this up, let us note a last statement by Engels along these lines. It came two years after the letter to Kautsky, but said exactly the same thing:

> ... While the Reign of Terror was now intensified to the point of madness because it was necessary to keep Robespierre in control under the existing internal conditions, it became totally superfluous as a result of the victory at Fleurus . . . , and thereupon Robespierre became superfluous and fell...[20]

In this letter Engels, furthermore, counterposed the peace perspective pursued by Robespierre and the leadership of the Committee of Public Safety *against* the left-wing Commune elements "who wanted the propagandist war and the republicanization of Europe" (that is, who wanted to internationalize the revolution in order to deepen it). It is this issue, measured at the time in the fortunes of war, that Engels saw as the very "heart beat" and central nerve of the whole revolution and of the ups and downs of the plebeian wing "whose energy alone saved the revolution." This wing which pressed the "war for the liberation of the nations" was proved to be in the right, said Engels—but only after Robespierre had beheaded it.[21]

This passage in Engels' letter was preceded by a reference to Marx which indicated his agreement in a general way. But we have already seen that Engels had not developed this analysis by himself.

We see that from Marx's very first political year to Engels' old age, in a continuous and consistent analysis, both men viewed Robespierre and the leading faction of Jacobins with political hostility, as compared with either the

Hébertists or the "Enragés," that is, in terms of the *internal* pattern of the revolutionary forces.*

The apotheosis of Robespierre and his methods came out of the Jacobin-communist (Blanquist) tradition from Babeuf onwards. In line with the principle that it is much easier to imitate great men's flaws than their feats, Blanquists tended to glorify the pathological side of the Terror as well as its necessities. When the Blanquists repeated this pattern with respect to the Paris Commune of 1871, Engels commented (in the article which will produce our locus 8) on the silliness of such an uncritical approach. If (he told the Blanquists) you glorify even the stupidities that are inevitably committed in the course of a mass revolution, if you declare every measure sacred and every step infallible, then—

> Doesn't this mean maintaining that, during that week in May [1871], the people shot exactly those persons it was necessary to shoot, and no more; that they burned down exactly those buildings which had to be burned down, and no more? Doesn't it mean the same as saying of the first French revolution: every single individual beheaded got his just due—first those whom Robespierre got beheaded, and then Robespierre himself? This is the kind of childishness reached when people who are basically quite good-natured give free rein to their desire to seem fearsomely hair-raising.[23]

Marx's and Engels' anti-Robespierrist viewpoint naturally conditioned their view of the Terror. The precondition was their analysis of what the Terror was—the revolutionary terror as such, apart from the pathological distortions engrafted by Robespierrism. *The revolutionary terror was the mobilization of force to intimidate the counterrevolution,* to defend the revolution against its enemies, to "terrorize" the reaction. Since we are not dealing with a scientific term, it tended as usual to sprawl—to include intimidatory action by the central government, by the Commune, or by the plebs from below. But it had nothing whatsoever to do with what today's newspaper headlines or government communiqués call 'terrorism'.

La Terreur, as the organized use of force to repress (terrorize) the counterrevolution, entered into the vocabularies of left and right through the nineteenth

---

* Since this fact does not fit into marxological fables, the opposite is often asserted with great determination and no documentation. For example, Bertram Wolfe's *Marxism:* "The natural authoritarianism of Marx's temperament was reinforced by the deep admiration he and Engels conceived for the Jacobins in the first French Revolution, who had striven to make Paris the ruler of all France."[22] The last clause, tacked on with a relative pronoun, is a special triumph of the historian's art since, as we have seen, Marx and Engels never imitated the social-democrat Louis Blanc and the Jacobin-communists in advocating the dictatorship of Paris. Wolfe's assertion is simply falsifiction.

century, except that the right wing of politics turned it inside-out like a pocket. If the White Terror tended to be systematically brutal and murderous, that fact could be gleaned only from serious histories, while popular literature wept only over the aristocratic victims of popular vengeance for centuries-long crimes.

In the course of the nineteenth century, as we will see in Marx's and Engels' writings, the meaning of 'terror (ism)' broadened out and weakened—like a light beam—until at times the term meant little more than some form of coercion. Since we have been discussing the French Revolution, we have seen 'terror' used for a revolutionary government's strivings to defend itself from counterrevolution, but the meaning did not remain so confined.

2. MARX ON 'REVOLUTIONARY TERRORISM'

It should be clear that 'terrorism' as the use of force or other coercion in social struggle was not a usage peculiar to Marx. The fact that we focus on his writings should not give a false impression; Marx used the term precisely because it was a "catchword," as Ladendorf said. Lorenz Stein, a very clever young man of a declassed noble family, looking over the French scene before and after 1848, found the catchword at hand and fitted it into his own line of thought, like everyone else.

Stein's thought was that the proletariat could never gain power through universal suffrage, contrary to a widespread opinion; only force was open to it. Therefore the "rule of the proletariat" (he used this term freely) would have to be a despotism.

> Like all domination, this despotism is directed against whatever threatens its rule ... The proletariat must use its power to destroy not only the opposing class, but also the social foundation of this class. Here a struggle starts which we call *terrorism,* a bloody and essentially endless struggle.

Since working-class power is an impossibility, terrorism must seek to accomplish its goal by "mass murder"; then the tide is reversed and "the counter-movement begins." Any temporary victory by the proletariat is swept away; the ruling class usually takes "bloody revenge," and may establish a dictatorship (as we saw in Chapter 5).[24]

Stein's use of 'terrorism', then, is almost explicitly class-bound: it is what a *proletarian* revolutionary power has to do for its end of a civil war. What the ruling class does is called police power, law and order, self-defense, etc., even though it may eventuate in a 'dictatorship'. Further on, we find an amendment: terrorism is the inevitable result not only of a *proletarian* bid for power but "the necessary consequence of the situation in which state power was exclusively in the hands of democratic extremists." The function of terrorism is defined as follows: "the use of state power against any differences in society which might lead to differentiation within the state. "[25] Stein understood the relation of state power to wealth and property; he brought 'terrorism' down from thirst for blood to thirst for something else that the ruling class possesses in greater abundance. Note that 'terrorism' is the use of *state power* in a certain way, not the use of bombs against the state power.

Here, then, was one prominent explanation of 'terrorism' published at around the middle of the century. We saw, in Section 1 above, that Marx's very first use of the term spoke of the government's censorship as a form of 'terrorism' against a writer, that is, a form of coercive intimidation. No rumblings about "mass murder" like Stein. He used it again in a few months— during his first year as a radical democrat—in a context that was not even political. In a sally against a right-wing religious paper, he concluded by asking whether half-and-half or lukewarm types "will get on better with the *terrorism of faith* than with the *terrorism of reason*."[26] There is no "terror" really involved here; the term merely means 'coercive pressure'. Bruno Bauer had recently used the term in much the same way in a letter to Marx: a believer in the efficacy of ideas to change the real world, Bauer had referred to "the terrorism of real theory" whose job it was to "clear the ground."[27]

We find no less "soft" a meaning when the term occurs in a letter by Engels to Marx in 1846. The context was self-explanatory, as Engels discussed debates on communism in the Paris branch of the League of the Just: "By dint of a little patience and some terrorism I have emerged victorious..." Let no one think that he cut an opponent's throat while gurgling with glee; it was done with his tongue. He described his "terrorism": his speech was so "intimidating" that an opponent made off; "I lashed him so mercilessly with my tongue that he never showed his face again."[28] Of course, marxologists like to prove that Marx and Engels were mean to opponents (unlike their own sweet and forbearing selves as they heap their falsifictions on Marx's hapless head); but we are only discussing the meaning of 'terrorism'.

In 1815-19, according to an article Engels published in early 1847, there was a "reign of terror" in Germany. These were years when a relative freedom of the press was temporarily permitted in German states, and the press took advantage of it. Engels observed: "finally the Federal Decrees of 1819 put an end to this reign of terror by public opinion."[29] Of course, the remark was jocular—these decrees introduced new press-censorship measures and other illiberal changes—but it implied the meaning of coercive intimidation.

C. The Meaning of 'Terror' and 'Terrorism' 369

Jocularity was difficult as the revolution of 1848-1849 sputtered out in political tragedies and counterrevolutionary massacres. In the *Neue Rheinische Zeitung,* Marx and Engels used the term 'terror(ism)'only a few times, but usually in connection with its basic historical content: coercive intimidation, in this case in the exigencies of civil war. Another part of the context was the practice of mass slaughter by the reactionary governments—mass killings which historians do not habitually call White Terror. Marx and Engels were more evenhanded about the terror of civil war, and in fact the first occurrence of the term in their *NRZ* articles was in such a balanced fashion. It referred to the terrible June Days' fighting in Paris: "After a battle like that of the three June days," wrote Engels, "only *terrorism* is still possible whether it be carried out by one side or the other."[30]

"One side or the other," red terror or white terror, the meaning of 'terrorism' was determined by the reality of civil war, coercion at its maximum. Civil war was also the sign over Marx's formulation in November, after the bloody suppression of the democratic revolution in Vienna. Only equally ruthless warfare could have won for the revolution, wrote Marx:

> The fruitless massacres since the June and October days, the long-drawn-out sacrificial rites since February and March, the cannibalism of the counterrevolution itself will convince the peoples that there is only one way to *shorten,* simplify, and condense the murderous death-agony of the old society and the bloody birth pangs of the new society— only *one way: revolutionary terrorism.*[31]

This "revolutionary terrorism" was no more and no less exactly what the revolution *was* doing in 1848 whenever it really fought back. Of course, Lorenz Stein considered that the shooting of live ammunition in the direction of the counterrevolutionary troops was "mass murder"; we must allow him his class point of view.

Engels greeted this "revolutionary terrorism" in Hungary when he saw, or thought he saw, the Magyar revolutionary movement under Kossuth seizing the situation with ardor. Summarizing the situation of the revolution as 1849 began—"the new Italian movement," "the war against the Magyars," the defeats, etc.—he wrote: "The last act of 1848 passes through *terrorism* into the first act of 1849." (Here it is not a threat of the future but a description of the recent past.)

> For the first time in the revolutionary movement of 1848, for the first time since 1793, a nation surrounded by superior counterrevolutionary forces dares to counter the cowardly counterrevolutionary fury by revolutionary passion, the *terreur blanche* by the *terreur rouge.*[32]

White terror or red terror—this was the choice. With this challenge Engels' article celebrated Kossuth, whose effort to "terrorize" the Whites has not tagged him in history as a Red Terrorist.

There were a couple of other such occurrences of the term in the *NRZ* in 1849, referring to "revolutionary terror" by the Democrats.[33] For an illustrative case, we can look to an article by Engels on the Austrians' defeat of the Italian army lighting under the Piedmontese king, who would be afraid to use the levy en masse as a revolutionary instrument:

> But the uprising en masse, the general insurrection of the people, these are means which a monarchy shrinks from using. These are means that only a republic uses—1793 offers proof of this. These are means whose carrying out presupposes *revolutionary terrorism*, and where has there been a monarch who could resolve to make use of that?

It would mean "a real revolutionary war" and "a national mass uprising," possible "if the conventional strategic war of *armies* had been turned into a *people's* war, like that waged by the French in 1793."

> But, really now! Revolutionary war, mass uprising, and terrorism— the monarchy will never agree to this. It would rather make peace with its bitterest enemy of equal rank than make common cause with the people.[34]

Here "terrorism" and "revolutionary war" are virtually synonymous, especially when the question is raised of the possible adoption of these means by the nationalist monarchy.

Finally, there was Marx's farewell piece in the last issue of the *NRZ*, as the paper bowed out before government harassment. This defiant editorial statement quoted the passage on "revolutionary terrorism" published after the Vienna fighting, and promised merciless revolutionary struggle the next time around:

> *We are merciless; we ask no mercy from you. When our turn comes, we will make no excuses for terrorism.* But the *royal terrorists*, the terrorists by the grace of God and Right, in practice are brutal, contemptible and vile, in theory cowardly, underhanded and deceitful, in both respects *dishonorable.*[35]

The "merciless" tone of this imprecation has been found very dazzling by quoters, for marxologists tend to be violent champions of mercy in civil war except when dealing with the June days of 1848 and the massacre after the Paris Commune—so dazzling that they fail to notice that the view of "terrorism" here is again two-sided. There are the "royal terrorists" (the Prussian monarchy) as well as the revolutionary terrorists, just as there is a White Terror and a Red Terror—in fact, just as there is a dictatorship of the proletariat and a dictatorship of the bourgeoisie—though it does not follow that both sides of the dichotomy are on the same moral plane in terms of social interests. The white terror, the counterrevolutionary violence of the reaction, is always the terrorization of the majority by a minority; the revolutionary terror is the "movement of the immense majority, in the interest of the immense majority" (to paraphrase the Manifesto). *So Marx believed,* at any rate, and that is what we are investigating.

3. 'TERRORISM' AFTER 1848

The period of the revolution concentrated the meaning of 'terrorism' on what was actually happening: civil war. After it, as before, the light-beam effect could again operate, that is, the meaning could broaden out and weaken. Writing about the upheaval in the immediate postrevolutionary period (1850-51), Marx tended to use 'revolutionary terrorism' (when used at all) to mean just about the same thing as revolutionary action in general.

For example, in his *Class Struggles in France* Marx stressed the political heterogeneity of the leftist alliance which the reaction called the "party of anarchy":

> From the smallest reform of the old social disorder to the overthrow of the old social order, from bourgeois liberalism to revolutionary terrorism—as far apart as this lie the extremes that form the starting point and the finishing point of the party of "anarchy."[36]

Now, what the right wing called the "party of anarchy" was, in Marx's language, the Social-Democratic party; and he *counterposed* it to the proletarian party of "revolutionary socialism" or "communism" which stood for the dictatorship of the proletariat (cf. locus 1c, for example). This "coalition of different interests" was, then, not even the left wing of French politics but its left-center; and it was this left-centrist coalition that included the acceptance of "revolutionary terrorism" on its flank. But for Marx this was merely the equivalent of saying that the leftmost wing of the Social-Democracy advocated revolutionary action.

How willing Marx was to ascribe "revolutionary terrorism" to relatively moderate elements was best shown, the same year, in the March 1850 "Address to the Communist League," which is so often ignorantly cited by marxologists as an expression of wild revolutionism. In this document, the "petty-bourgeois Democrats" (the German equivalent of the French Social-Democracy) were expected to take power in the coming revolution; the task of the communists was to press the revolution to the left, "to make the revolution permanent" until the bourgeoisie was ousted from power. This entire section described the various ways by which the proletarian revolutionists would exert pressure on the centrists in power. It was in this context that Marx and Engels wrote the following:

> Above all things, the workers must counteract, as much as is at all possible, during the conflict and immediately after the struggle, the bourgeois endeavors to allay the storm, and must compel the Democrats to carry out their present terrorist phrases.

And a couple of pages later:

> If from the outset the democrats come out resolutely and terroristically against the reactionaries, the influence of the latter in the elections will be destroyed in advance.[37]

It is hardly necessary to add that the terrorist "phrases" being used by the respectable Democrats were not bloodthirsty ones, merely revolutionary-sounding. They were promising to clean out the old regime with energetic forcefulness. The Address challenged these moderates to carry out *their* "terrorist phrases," not Marx's! Yet this plain statement has been denounced as a terrible revelation by Marx of *his* sanguinary proclivities.*

Energetic forcefulness: this accounts for the way the term crops up in a production by Engels of the same year, *The Peasant War in Germany*. Usually, 'terrorism' referred to action against the ruling-class enemy; here it came to Engels' pen in an entirely different context. Recounting the desperate defense of Thomas Münzer's plebeian forces against the princes' troops, he described the last life-or-death struggle in which the revolutionary army was finally duped, defeated, and massacred in the thousands. The princes had promised indulgence to the rebels if they delivered their leader Münzer alive; a knight and a priest spoke in favor of surrender—that is, in favor of beheading both Münzer and the revolution. Münzer had them executed. "This act of terrorist energy, jubilantly received by resolute revolutionaries, instilled a certain order among the troop," the historian related.[39] Others who wanted to surrender no doubt found the prospect intimidating, in fact terrorizing.

In 1851, as part of its preparation of the Cologne witchhunt trial of Communists that took place the next year, the government conducted raids which turned up the text of the "Address to the Communist League." It was published in the press; there was a blast of denunciations; middle-class Democrats who were cooperating with the Communists showed signs of panic. In a letter to Marx, Engels underestimated the possible damage:

> ... this ordinary petty-bourgeois Democracy, though evidently greatly piqued by this document, is itself far too much squeezed and oppressed

---

* Thus Bertram Wolfe, in *Marxism*, cites precisely this passage to show "the streak of terrorism that then possessed him [Marx]."[58]

not to arrive much sooner, together with the big bourgeoisie, at the necessity of *passer par la mer rouge* [going through the red sea—word-play on the Biblical reference]. The fellows will more and more resign themselves to the necessity of a momentary terroristic rule of the proletariat—after all [they will tell themselves] this can't last long, for the positive content of the document is indeed so nonsensical that there can't be any question about permanent rule by such people and eventually carrying out such principles!

The vein here, of course, is ironic; but, besides, the passage itself contains the proof (if needed) that Engels did not suspect anyone would regard the contents of the Address as especially "terroristic" in some unusual sense. After some argumentation he asked: "Why, then, the outcry now about a program that simply sums up in a very calm and particularly quite impersonal way what was printed long ago?" and he pointed out, "Any halfway intelligent Democrat must have known from the first what he had to expect from our party—the document could not have told him much that was new."[40] The document also could not have reeked of bloodthirstiness, as he viewed its language.

'Terror(ism)' occurred infrequently in the subsequent writings of Marx and Engels, especially if we exclude passages in which it is plainly used to mean individual terrorism in the late-century fashion. We can find one case in the large corpus of *New York Daily Tribune* articles: a reference to Bonaparte's "system of domestic terrorism." Bonaparte makes "attempts at playing the dictator of Europe"; but these are failing; he needs to overawe France (that is, intimidate or terrorize it). "Consequently, the reign of terror is progressively extending."[41] The readers of the *NYDT knew* well enough that the guillotine was not being overworked in France.

The term occurred in *Capital* in connection with the "methods of primitive accumulation" that included "the usurpation of feudal and clan property and its transformation into modern private property under circumstances of ruthless terrorism."[42] Very similar was its use by Marx in 1867 in a lecture outline on Ireland, referring to "English terrorism" in that island during the "time of transition" after 1776.[43]

In the *Civil War in France,* it was the bourgeois republic after the June days of 1848—"the *Parliamentary Republic,* with Louis Bonaparte for its President"— that was called "a regime of avowed class terrorism and deliberate insult toward the 'vile multitude.'" In the First Draft, this appeared as "the *terrorism of* class rule." In the Second Draft, it was "the reign of terror of the ruling class," set in virtual apposition with "the *avowed instrument of the civil war."* The state of siege that followed the June days of 1849 also ushered in "a new reign of terror."[44] In these passages, "class terrorism" differed little from "class despotism" and other less terroristic labels.

In the last usage that I can trace, 'terror' appeared as little more than the everyday word. This case underlines very nicely how *'terrorism'* came to be used for the defense of revolutionary power. In his 1873 anti-anarchist polemic "On Authority," Engels argued that the victorious proletariat must be prepared to maintain its state "authority" with armed force, as did the Paris Commune:

> ... and if the victorious party does not want to have fought in vain, it must maintain this rule by means of the terror which its arms inspire in the reactionaries.[45]

Here it is hardly a political term; *col terrore,* in the (Italian) text, might just as well be translated "through the fear..." But in the last analysis there is little more to these usages of the term 'terror (ism)"about which marxologists have raised such a brouhaha. Their unwillingness to investigate the changing meaning of political language is characteristic of the industry.

| SPECIAL NOTE D | GHOSTS, GOBLINS, AND GARBLES |

This Note takes up four ghost-loci and four goblin-garbles. A ghost-locus (on the analogy of a bibliographical ghost) is a locus that isn't there: that is, a quoted passage in which Marx or Engels is erroneously alleged to use the term 'dictatorship' or 'dictatorship of the proletariat'. A goblin—well known to the spirit of research—is a sprite (says Merriam-Webster's) conceived as malicious or mischievous, sometimes sinister. Goblins produce garbles.

Mangled quotations are mischievous indeed, especially when they appear in a book, for then they may reverberate down the marching columns of others' quotations, on and on into the vast stretches of scholarly notes which nobody ever rechecks. For example...

1. GHOST-LOCUS: FEUER OUT OF MAYER

Lewis S. Feuer's *Marx and the Intellectuals* (1969) offers a number of essays which, the author feels, provide an antidote to the "irrationalism and amorality of the new movement" of the 1960s which evinced a quickened interest in Marxism. Striking a sturdy blow against irrationalism, Feuer discovers that Marx suffered from a "lifelong Promethean Complex"; and his essay on this subject offers a number of innovations, including the revelation that the newly detected Promethean Complex was centered in Marx's liver troubles and "determined" his philosophy of history.[1] This liverish lucubration is accompanied by splenetic slips of a factual nature that dot the work.

Among the innovations, I find, is a passage by Engels using the term 'dictatorship of the proletariat' that I had never previously seen. The new locus is given by Feuer as follows (the suspension points are his):

> In 1850, he [Marx] was writing that "the revolution is imminent." Engels was reassuring him that the capitalist system was at the end of its tether: "There are no more new markets to open,... it is obvious that

the domination of the factory-owners has reached its end. What then? ... Social revolution and the dictatorship of the proletariat, say we."[2]

Unfortunately, though there are two other footnotes on the same page, giving source references, there is none for this contribution. On the face of it, it would seem to be from a letter by Engels to Marx ("Engels was reassuring him").

In actuality, Feuer (unbeknown to himself) is quoting this from the English edition of Gustav Mayer's biography of Engels, where a fuller version of the passage is given in its Chapter 13.[3] The words "dictatorship of the proletariat" do appear in this edition.

Mayer's book gives the source accurately: it had nothing to do with "reassuring" Marx, but occurred in Engels' article on "The Ten Hours' Question" in the 1850 *Democratic Review*, which we quoted in our Chapter 13.[4] If we look back to this passage, we find that the phrase "dictatorship of the proletariat" does *not* appear in it; instead, it says: "*Social revolution and proletarian ascendancy, say we.*" (Italics in the original.) The article was in English, and so there would appear to be no problem of translation.

How did "proletarian ascendancy" get transmuted into "dictatorship of the proletariat" between quote marks?

The answer is that there *was* a translation problem: not Feuer's, for he was simply copying without checking. (He could not have been copying directly from the English-language Mayer since the paragraph in question prominently identifies the correct source.) The problem then shifts from Feuer to the English edition of Mayer. What did Mayer actually write?

It was not Mayer's German text that inserted "dictatorship of the proletariat."[5] That was done in the English edition of his book. This edition is *not* really a translation of the work, though it is so labeled: "Translated ... by Gilbert and Helen Highet/The translation edited by R. H. S. Crossman." It is a condensed rewriting of Mayer's book.

It is only a part of Mayer's work, though there is no warning on the book's title page or verso that it is not complete. However, the introduction by G. D. H. Cole states that he, Cole, welcomed "the chance of arranging for my friend Professor Gustav Mayer... to rewrite his classical German biography for the English-speaking public." This implies that Mayer himself, and not the Highets or Crossman, did the abridgment. The result is visible: the two-volume German work has been reduced by substantially more than 50 percent to a single volume, not only by omissions but by rewriting everything.

Whoever is responsible, whether Mayer or another, the result is so inferior to the original as to be a different work. The original work is still the "classical biography" of Engels, unsuperseded; and it remains untranslated. No doubt the existence of the aborted English edition forestalled a real translation.

The introduction of the ghost-locus on 'dictatorship of the proletariat' was, then, only one example of how this book was treated. In a sense, Feuer was one of the victims, out of innocent ignorance.

2. GHOST-LOCUS: IRING FETSCHER

Iring Fetscher's *Grundbegriffe des Marxismus* (Basic Concepts of Marxism), subtitled "A Lexicographical Introduction," presents itself as a reference work. But users had better beware: Fetscher *freely rewrites quotes from Marx and Engels between quote marks* without notice. Such rewrites are put in italics, but italics are also used for two other purposes, so you never know whether the Marx "quotation" you are reading is by Marx or by Fetscher! This remarkable system is revealed to those careful readers who notice a "Technical Remark" following the table of contents.

Fetscher actually does rewrite Marx and Engels to make them say, between quotation marks, what Fetscher thinks they should have said. In his section on "The Dictatorship of the Proletariat and Its Political Form," Fetscher "proves" a difference between Marx and Engels by putting this unique method to work:

> In distinction from Marx, who in 1871 had greeted the Commune as "the political form at last discovered of the *dictatorship of the proletariat*," Engels pointed in his critique of the Erfurt Program (1891) to *parliamentary democracy* as the form for the dictatorship of the proletariat...[6]

In this case the italics indicate rewrites. Two pieces of misinformation are offered:

(1) In *The Civil War in France,* what Marx actually wrote was that the Commune was "the political form at last discovered under which to work out the economical emancipation of labor."[7] Thus what Fetscher claims is that the words "work out the economic emancipation of labor" stand for "dictatorship of the proletariat"—a claim which is distorting even if the reader understands Fetscher's peculiar practice. There *is* evidence (as we have seen) that Marx looked on the Commune as a 'dictatorship of the proletariat', but Fetscher does not mention it.

(2) In Engels' locus 12—which in fact Fetscher then proceeds to quote correctly—it is the "democratic republic," *not "parliamentary democracy,"* that is suggested as the specific form for the dictatorship of the proletariat.[8] In effect, what Fetscher claims, without analysis, is that these two phrases are mere synonyms. This is confusion compounded.

3. GHOST-LOCUS: GEORGES GURVITCH

Discussing "Marx's Notes on Bakunin's Book"[9] we emphasized that at one point Marx *declined to* use 'dictatorship of the proletariat', as he commented on Bakunin's distortion of his views. No use: this did not serve the purpose of the Sorbonne sociologist Georges Gurvitch, in his book *Etudes sur les Classes Sociales*. Gurvitch proceeded—he too—to "correct" Marx by rewriting his words between quote marks. One reads in this book that, in these notes on Bakunin,

> Marx insists: "The dictatorship of the proletariat is the class rule of the workers over the remains of the old world [etc.]..,"[10]

The Gurvitch operation is a little more complicated than a simple insertion of the term 'dictatorship of the proletariat'. He has taken this already rewritten passage and hitched it onto the front end of another passage some pages away—thereby constructing a quotation that satisfied him.

With all that going on, we had better ignore the fact that Gurvitch's word "remains" (in his French, *vestiges*) is a mistranslation of Marx's "strata" *(Schichten);* the mistake blurs the meaning a little but doesn't matter much.

4. GHOST-LOCUS: EASTON-GUDDAT

The Easton and Guddat collection *Writings of the Young Marx on Philosophy and Society* was the first, and is still the most comprehensive, of the anthologies covering Marx's first years in politics; but nobody is perfect. It provides an example of a ghost-locus engendered solely by translation. According to an unwise rendering, the first political article that the young Marx wrote for publication contained a reference to "dictatorship." But it did not.

It is a question of Marx's article "Comments on the Latest Prussian Censorship Instruction," written in January-February 1842 and published in a collection a full year later in Switzerland to escape the German censorship. At one point the Easton-Guddat translation refers to the Prussian state, or a similar government, as a "dictatorship." Actually, Marx labeled it a *Zwangsstaat*, a state based on coercion, "coercive state" in MECW's translation.[11]

This bears on our discussion in the last pages of Chapter 2.[12]

5. THE GOBLINS OF LOCUS 1c

There is a telltale situation around locus 1c, namely, the passage in the third part of Marx's *Class Struggles in France* which speaks of *"communism, for which the bourgeoisie itself has invented the name of Blanqui."* This passage goes on to speak of the 'permanent revolution' watchword and the "class dictatorship of the proletariat."[13]

We have already noted more than one garbled interpretation of this passage, especially the kind brought off by astute paraphrasing. The frequent aim—as we know from our discussions of the "Marx-Blanquist" myth—is to work in Blanqui's name so as to have Marx saying that he, Blanqui, represented communism, Marx's communism. This, we saw, is supposed to make Marx a "Blanquist."[14]

The stumbling block is the fact that Marx's reference to Blanqui is quite clear: the bourgeoisie, he says, has *invented* the name of Blanqui for communism; it is the *bourgeoisie* that has attached Blanqui's name to the thing as a bogey. And we saw in Chapter 11 that this referred to what actually happened in 1848 to "invent" the Blanqui-bogey.[15]

All this offers marxologists a challenge to ingenuity. One simple solution is—mistranslation.

There is no problem about Marx's statement in the original German:

| ...*communism,* for which the bour- geoisie itself has invented the name of *Blanqui.* | ...*Kommunismus,* für den die Bour- geoisie selbst den Namen *Blanqui* erfunden hat.[16] |

The crux is the word 'invented'; the German verb used here *(erfinden)* offers no problem: it is the ordinary, standard, customary word for 'invent'. It may vary slightly in the direction of 'fabricate', 'concoct', but these synonyms only drive the point home more firmly.

Now consider three translations.

(A) Vladimir G. Simkhovitch's *Marxism Versus Socialism* (1912), a work often praised by right-minded anti-Marxists, translates the crucial passage as follows:

> ... communism, which the bourgeoisie has had interpreted to it by Blanqui.[17]

According to this, Marx says that Blanqui became *the* interpreter of communism. The difference is blatant. One must wonder how Simkhovitch convinced himself that *erfinden* means 'interpret'...

(B) Carl Landauer's two-volume history *European Socialism* gives the following translation of the same words:

... communism, which to the bourgeoisie is symbolized by the name Blanqui.[18]

This finds another odd way to avoid saying that the bourgeoisie has *invented* a Blanqui bogey. One still wonders: how did Landauer transmogrify *erfinden* into 'symbolize'?

(C) Robert C. Tucker's *The Marxian Revolutionary Idea* raises a different problem about locus 1c.

My 1962 essay on "Marx and the Dictatorship of the Proletariat" had a footnote warning that a certain edition of Marx's *Class Struggles in France* gave a garbled version of locus 1c. It was the International Publishers edition (Marxist Library, Volume 24) published about 1935.[19] This version inserts six words into the passage, given here in brackets:

> This socialism is the *declaration of the permanence of the revolution,* [the class dictatorship of the revolution,] the *class dictatorship* of the proletariat as the necessary transit point [etc. ...] [20]

The result is that a brand-new phrase has been fabricated and inserted in Marx's name: "the class dictatorship of the revolution." It makes little sense, but this has never been an insuperable obstacle to Marx interpreters. At any rate, Tucker's book came out with precisely this garbled version of the passage. He plainly liked the new nonsense-phrase: after quoting it once, he cited it yet again a few pages later as evidence for the proposition that Marx rejected "democratic protection of the rights of the class minority."[21] He liked it so very much that he cited it a third time.[22] Send not to ask how the new garble was supposed to prove the old myth; Tucker did not explain.

Later, Landauer's citation of locus 1c (partially quoted above) inserted the same garbled formulation—"the class dictatorship of the revolution"—but *his* reference note claimed to be translating from the original German. This was puzzling. I eventually traced the common source of these garbled citations. It was indeed a German edition of Marx's work: that of 1911.[23]

The phrase invented by an errant typesetter, "the class dictatorship of the revolution," will no doubt reverberate down the halls of scholarship from tome to tome as marxologists rediscover it or copy it from Tucker or Landauer.

6. THE MIQUEL GOBLIN

When I started on this inquiry in 1960, the very first mystery encountered was young Miquel's letter to Marx.[24] The invaluable *Karl Marx, Chronik seines Lebens (KMC),* which the Marx-Engels Institute published in 1934, dated

Miquel's letter at February 12, 1850.²⁵ This is what created the mystery, for the letter spoke of the "dictatorship of the working class" as Marx's aim. Where had Miquel seen this phrase? The very first appearance of the term—locus la, in the first installment of Marx's *Class Struggles in France*—did not come off the press until the first week in March, though Marx had written it in January. How could the young law student in Göttingen have known of it? *KMC* gave two sources for its information. (1) E. Bernstein had published the letter in the *Neue Zeit* in 1914.²⁶ But the date he assigned to it was not the one in *KMC:* it was even stranger, viz., "the second half of 1849." At this time not even Marx had yet seen the phrase. (2) The other source did clear up the dating problem, though not the *KMC* mistake: it was Wilhelm Mommsen's biography of Miquel. Mommsen said nothing about the February 12 date, but he pointed out that the letter had been correctly dated by Bebel back in 1893 when he read parts of it to the Reichstag. In addition Mommsen gave more evidence to show that the letter was written in the summer of 1850.²⁷

In 1981 a volume in the New Mega series summarized the dating problem and its answer, without adding new information.²⁸ But part of the mystery remains: where *KMC* and Bernstein got their respective dates.

7. ECTOPLASMIC QUOTES: DOMMANGET

There are a number of quotations ascribed to Marx that float, disembodied, without a local habitation and a name—noted and quoted, but seldom or never pinned down to a source. Since we have focused on Marx's view of Blanqui and the attendant myths, we should not overlook an ectoplasmic Marx-quote used by Dommanget.

Dommanget objected to the derogation of his hero in Engels' article "Program of the Blanquist Refugees of the Commune," and wanted to show that Marx's opinion of Blanqui was higher. He offered evidence with the following statement:

> ... it is known that Marx, as reported by Edouard Vaillant—who frequented him in London after the Commune—not only thought that Blanqui was "the most profoundly socialist of the French and the most revolutionary," but that he had arrived at a "correct *[exacte]* conception of communism."²⁹

His footnote gives sources. The first quote is entirely believable, as we have seen,³⁰ given Marx's opinion of Blanqui's rivals: Blanqui *was* the "most revolutionary" of the French (it is not clear if this is the same as "profoundly socialist"). But Dommanget is citing from an anniversary article of ceremonial recollections published by Vaillant in 1911, where the characterization of Blanqui is put between quote marks without any indications of its source.[31] One can be fairly sure that Vaillant was giving his memory's version of various old statements by Marx which we have already reviewed (for example, in Chapter 9, section 3).

The second quote is a shady thing, befitting a wraith. Dommanget quotes it—with his own "improvements"—from a book by Léon de Seilhac, *Le Monde Socialiste* (1904), which contains a "quick history" of the Blanquist party done by Vaillant, apparently for this volume. Vaillant presents his news in a subordinate clause in a sentence about the convergence of socialism and communism in France:

> If Blanqui had arrived at a correct conception of communism, as Marx recognized, it is evidently one more proof of that necessary progression that has more and more caused socialism and communism to converge ...[32]

We see: (1) There are no quote marks. Vaillant does not claim to be quoting any specific statement by Marx. (2) The reference to Vaillant's association with Marx after the Commune was inserted by Dommanget. This addition gave the impression that Vaillant was relating something Marx might have told him, also the impression that this dated to the post-Commune period. Unlike Dommanget's version, Vaillant's subordinate clause did not sound like a new revelation, but merely a reference to public knowledge. In other words, there was *no* new Marx-quote involved here at all: the ectoplasm dissolves as light is turned on it.

I think it likely that what Vaillant really had in mind was our locus 1c, utilizing the pro-Blanqui interpretation of that passage which was by that time becoming common among anti-Marxists and Bernsteinians. After all, if it was becoming standard anti-Marx dogma that Marx had been a "Blanquist," Vaillant would be quite willing to exploit the story—if only to carpenter a subordinate clause.

In this operation with, or on, Vaillant's remark in Seilhac, one can see Dommanget's predilections—which have been pointed out more than once in these pages. Here is as good a place as any to summarize an understanding of Dommanget, whose work is too valuable to be ignored and too onesided to be accepted naively.

Dommanget, who was associated politically with the French Communists, was capable of excellent scholarly contributions in the handling of historical material, and of extreme tendentiousness in his argumentation and conclusions; but the dividing line was usually clear. He did not twist facts to support his ideological ends; hence the weakness of his line was more apparent. His motivation was the opposite of Bernstein's: he did not want to make Marx a Blanquist so much as he wanted to make Blanqui a Marxist. Still, he was capable of uncritically quoting Bernstein's charge about Marx's "Blanquism" as it this testimony validated his own view."[33] Careening along on his hobbyhorse, Dommanget could go to lengths as fantastic as Bernstein in assuming without evidence what he wanted to prove. For example, he assumed that Marx's French sons-in-law, Lafargue and Longuet, both "strong friends and admirers of Blanqui," *must* have been speaking also for their father-in-law when one or the other wrote something to Blanqui.[34] Given Marx's reiterated low opinion of their political capacities, this takes great determination.

8. QUESTIONS ABOUT MECW TRANSLATIONS

The English translations presented in the Marx-Engels *Collected Works* are bound to be of the greatest importance for Marx studies; their reliability is vital to all work in the field. We are here concerned with a case of tendentiousness in translation which blurs the understanding of Marx's views on a certain subject.

We have devoted a great deal of attention to the "Marx-Blanquist" myth— the claim that at some period Marx underwent a "Blanquist aberration," or indeed "was a Blanquist." This marxological campaign comes mostly from the anti-Marxist (bourgeois or social-democratic) right. In analyzing this claim, it is crucial to distinguish between a *revolution* and a *putsch* in Marx's view. Well, it is precisely this distinction that is systematically obscured and confounded in MECW, at critical points, so that the MECW translations throw a veil over Marx's critique of Blanquism. The articles in which this occurs are discussed in Chapter 10.[35]

The first case in which this occurs (in terms of Chapter 10) has to do with the use of the word 'putsch' (in German *Putsch*) in the final warning "To the Workers of Cologne" published in the last issue of Marx's *Neue Rheinische Zeitung* in May 1849.[36] As noted on page 158, this was the first time that this word occurred in Marx, for it was still quite new. But amazingly enough, the MECW translation refused to use 'putsch' in the English, substituting the word 'revolt'. This word has no pejorative force, in terms of Marx's views, and is broad enough to cover both revolutionary uprisings and almost any kind of outburst. The significance of its use in the translation is that Marx is not seen as condemning putsches.

MECW had to go out of its way to insert this translation. An English translation of the farewell warning had appeared in a previous collection of Marx-Engels writings put out under the same auspices, published jointly by Progress Publishers of Moscow and International Publishers of New York:

The Revolution of 1848-49 (1972). There, on page 266, *Putsch* was translated 'putsch'. The translation was by S. Ryazanskaya, "edited by Bernard Isaacs." In MECW 9, five years later, the translator was the same Ryazanskaya. But *putsch* had now been pursed of its content and transmogrified into 'revolt'

This incident might be considered an aberration; but the hypothesis will not hold when we come to Marx's crucial attack on Blanquist conspiratorialism and putschism in 1850, namely, the book review of A. Chenu and L. de la Hodde, which is the subject of Chapter 10, Section 6. Here there are several cases, not one, of the same tendentious mode of translation with the same effect: blurring of the distinction between putschism and revolution, through the use of English words chosen to avoid the 'putschist' connotation.

Example 1. Where Marx (or Marx and Engels) wrote that movements provoked by small coteries remained mere "émeutes" (using *Emeuten* in the German), MECW makes the word 'insurgency'.[37] Now the French word *émeute* is not an obscure term, being fairly common even in English. It means a riot, or riotous outbreak, or a disturbance. To render it as 'insurgency' takes a deal of strenuous reaching.

Example 2. Where Marx called the Blanqui-Barbès putsch of May 1839 an 'émeute', MECW makes it 'revolt'.[38] Since we are dealing here with an actual event, we can say that 'revolt' is downright unhistorical, as well as erroneous translation. There are other loci where MECW uses 'revolt' to translate *émeute* (or Marx's German form, *Emeuten*).[39]

Example 3. This is the most striking case of all. It is a question of the French term *coup de main*, which is not as common in English as its related *coup d'etat*. A *coup de main* is as close as need be to the word 'putsch'. The German literal translation *of coup de main* (which means a 'blow of the hand') is *Handstreich*. Well now: where Marx referred to "coups de main," an editorial footnote in MECW translated it as (are we ready for this?)—"daring raids." In the same passage Marx referred to "daring *Handstreiche*"; and the MECW translation makes this "daring raids" as well![40] "Raids" indeed—the *coup de main* has been "vanished" out of sight, as magicians say.

There is a party line operating here to conceal the strength of Marx's attack on adventurist politics and putschism, hence to distort Marx's views. For some reason this has become the line of the Institute of Marxism-Leninism (Moscow and Berlin).

The upshot is that, more than ever, Marx's attitude toward Blanquism becomes a football, as Marxism has been for a century—a football kicked around, from several directions, to achieve various goals alien to Marx himself. It is particularly interesting that an objective united front on the question is established between the Stalinist professoriat and the bourgeois marxologists.

SPECIAL NOTE E | MARX-ENGELS LOCI: SUMMARY LIST

The (W) column gives the date of writing; the (P) column, the date of first publication, with brackets for dates of posthumous publication. The last column gives the page number on which the locus is quoted in this volume. A brief citation from the locus, just enough for reminder or identification, is placed in the third column, in italics (with emphasis removed).

Loc.		Writing / Source	(W)	(P)	Pg
1a	M	Article series: Class Struggles in France, Ch. 1. *"... there appeared the bold slogan..."*	Jan. 1850	Mar. 1850	178
1b	M	Ditto, Ch. 2. *"... to seize the revolutionary dictatorship..."*	Mar. 4 1850	Mar. 20 1850	179
1c	M	Ditto, Ch. 3. *"... communism, for which the bourgeoisie itself has invented the name of Blanqui..."*	Mar. 5-15	Apr.	180
2	M–E	SUCR Statutes. *"... the dictatorship of the proletarians..."*	Apr. 1850	[1926]	185
3	M	Statement to Neue Deutsche Zeitung. *"...you taxed me with advocating the rule and the dictatorship of the working class..."*	June	July 4	223
4	M	Letter to Weydemeyer. *"... the class struggle necessarily leads to the dictatorship of the proletariat..."*	Mar. 5 1852	[1906-07]	247

385

Special Notes

5	M	Banquet speech at the 7th Anniversary Celebration of the International. "... *a proletarian dictature would become necessary...*"	Sep. 24 or 25, 1871	Oct. 15 1871	293
6	M	Article, "Indifference to Political Affairs." "... *workers substitute their revolutionary dictatorship for the dictatorship of the bourgeois class...*"	Dec. 1872 to Jan. 1873	Dec. 1784	295
7a	E	Article series: The Housing Question, III. "... *the proletariat... its dictatorship as the transition to...*"	Jan. 1873	Feb. 1873	297
7b	E	Ditto. "... *every real proletarian party ...has always put forward ...the dictatorship of the proletariat.*"	Ditto.	Ditto.	297
8	E	Article, "Program of the Blanquist Refugees of the Commune." "... *the dictatorship... of the entire revolutionary class, the proletariat... [not] of one person or a few.*"	June 1874	June 26 1874	302
9	M	Circular to party leaders: "Critique of the Gotha Program. "... *a political transition period whose state can be nothing but...*"	Apr.-May 1875	[Jan. 1891]	304
10	E	Letter to Conrad Schmidt. "... *we fight for the political dictatorship of the proletariat...*"	Oct. 27 1890		310
11	E	Introduction to Marx's Civil War in France. "...*the Paris Commune. That was the dictatorship of the proletariat...*"	Mar. 1891	Mar. 1891	317
12	E	Circular to party leaders: "Critique of the Erfurt Program." "... *the democratic republic [is] the specific form for the dictatorship of the proletariat.*"	June 1891	[1901]	318

REFERENCE NOTES

Titles are given in abbreviated form; full titles and publication data are provided in the Bibliography. Book and article titles are not distinguished in form. Where only the author's name is given, there is only a single entry in the Bibliography. Page numbers apply to the edition cited in the Bibliography. Volume and page are usually separated by a colon: for example, 3:148 means Volume 3, page 148.

A Marx/Engels source is sometimes followed by a bracketed reference. In this case, the first source given is the one actually used; the bracketed reference cites an extant translation if the first one is to the original, or vice versa. This bracketed reference is for the reader's convenience only, in case a further check is desired.

To identify initials, see the Index. Some frequently used abbreviations are:
DBZ = Deutsche-Brusseler-Zeitung (Brussels).
E = Engels
ed = editor, editorial
GCFI = General Council of the First International [see Biblio.]
IISH = International Institute for Social History (Amsterdam)
IML = Institute of Marxism-Leninism
IRSH = International Review of Social History (Amsterdam)
KMTR as Karl Marx's Theory of Revolution [see under Draper, Hal]
Ltr • Letter
M = Marx
ME = Marx and Engels
M/E = Marx or Engels
MECW = ME: Collected Works
MEGA = ME: Gesamtausgabe [the old edition]
MESW = ME: Selected works in Three Volumes [this ed. only]
MEW=ME:Werke
New Mega = ME: Gesamtausgabe [new edition]
NOZ = Neue Oder-Zeitung (Breslau)
NRZ = Neue Rheinische Zeitung (Cologne, 1848-49)

NRZ Revue • Neue Rheinische Zeitung, politisch-ökonomische Revue (London, 1850)
NYDT = New York Daily Tribune
Rev. after = Revised after [original text]
Rev. from = Revised from [an extant translation]
qu. = quoted, quotation
tr = translation, translated in
For full bibliographical data on above titles, see the Bibliography.

1. FROM ROME TO ROBESPIERRE

1. Spencer: Dictatorship, in *Encyclopaedia of the Social Sciences*, Vol. 5.
2. Lenin: The Victory or the Cadets [etc.], in his *Coll. Wks.* 10:245.
3. Cobban: Dictatorship, 135; this is the source of all figures cited on the invocation of Article 48.
4. Rosenberg: History of the German Republic, 306.
5. Rossiter: Constitutional Dictatorship; the three passages cited are from page vii, 14, and the last page of the book.
6. Rossiter: Marxism, 187.
7. Ibid., 107.
8. Merriam: The New Democracy and the New Despotism, 221.
9. MacIver: Leviathan, 105.
10. Halévy: Era of Tyrannies, 266 fn. This is from an essay that Halévy originally published in 1936. He repeats this idea in other parts of his book, e.g., 306, 308.
11. On Halévy, see below, Chap. 2, Sec. 3, p. 35.
12. Columbia Encyclopedia, p. 1220.
13. E: British Disaster in the Crimea, in *NYDT*, Jan. 22, 1855 (MECW 13:569). When Marx revised this article for publication in *NOZ* as "On the English Military System," this passage did not appear; therefore MEW, which carries the *NOZ* version only, does not contain this passage.
14. Machiavelli: Discourses on the First Decade of Titus Livius, Chap. 34; in his *Chief Works* 1:267.
15. Ibid., 269.
16. Spinoza: Tractatus Politicus, Chap. X, 1.
17. Marx was using a German translation of Spinoza: Theologisch-politischer Tractat; see MEGA I, 1.2:104, 108-09. Cf. also Rubel: Cahiers de Lecture de K. M., 396.
18. Milton: Paradise Regained, Book 1.
19. Sidney: Discourses Concerning Government, Chap. 2, Sec. 13; in his *Works*, 126.
20. Furetière: Dictionnaire Universel... (1691).
21. Académie Française: Dictionnaire ... (1694).
22. Dictionnaire Universel François et Latin [commonly called Dictionnaire de Trevoux] (1734).
23. [Diderot, Denis, ed.:] Encyclopédie ou Dictionnaire Raisonné..., Tome 4; article "Dictateur," by Chevalier de Jaucourt.
24. Rousseau: Social Contract, Book 4, Chap. 6, p. 125.
25. Federalist Papers, No. 70, p. 423.
26. Qu. in Levy: Jefferson and Civil Liberties, 18.

27. For example: ibid., 90f.
28. Bax: Last Episode of the French Revolution, 16.
29. M: Eighteenth Brumaire, in MESW 1:398.
30. Ibid., 399.
31. E: Intro, to Marx's *Class Struggles in France,* in MESW 1:189.
32. Cobban: Dictatorship, 63.
33. Culver: Brissotin-Robespierrist Struggle [etc.], 144f.
34. Ibid., 101.
35. Ibid., 114.
36. Ibid., 106,112.
37. Ibid., 154f.
38. Ibid., 187,194.
39. Wollstonecraft: French Revolution, 267f.
40. M: From the Memoires de R. Levasseur, in MECW 3:364, 369; see also 3:608 n. 127.
41. Cobban, 67.
42. Encyclopaedia Britannica, 11 th ed., "Marat" by Robert Anchel, 17:669.
43. Gottschalk: Marat, 110 (re Rousseau), 114,137.
44. In Marat's *Appel à la Nation,* qu. in Bougeart, 2:47.
45. *Journal de la République,* No. 1, in Bougeart, 2:56. The italics, here and elsewhere, are possibly added by Bougeart.
46. *L'Ami du Peuple,* No. 177, in Bougeart, 2:56f.
47. *Journal de la République,* No. 41, in Bougeart, 2:57.
48. Bougeart: Marat, 2:119-23. The quotes from Marat's speech that follow are in 2:126-28.
49. Mathiez: French Revolution, 240. This sentence is not in Bougeart's citation.
50. Bougeart: Marat, 2:221,267.
51. Article "Despotism," in *Dictionary of the History of Ideas,* 2:14.
52. Qu. in Laski: Socialist Tradition in the Fr. Revolution, 22.
53. Kropotkin: Great Fr. Revolution, 161.
54. Lefebvre: French Revolution, 1:209.
55. Robespierre: Discours et Rapports, 395.
56. Ltr, M to E, Dec. 2,1856, in MEW 29:88f.

2. SOCIALISM AND DICTATORSHIP: THE BEGINNING

1. Laveaux: Nouveau Dictionnaire de la Langue Fr. (1820).
2. Philipon de La Madelaine: Dictionnaire de la Langue Fr., abrégé du Dict, de l'Académie(1823).
3. Littré: Dictionnaire de la Langue Fr. (1863).
4. Larousse: Grand Dictionnaire Universel du XIXe Siecle, Tome 6 (1870).
5. Heard over KQED-TV (PBS, San Francisco), June 20,1974.
6. Bulwer-Lytton: Rienzi, 22,140f, 317.
7. Buonarroti: Conspiration pour l'Egalité dite de Babeuf, 1:109f; the cited passage is on 110.
8. Ibid., 111.
9. Ibid., 112f.
10. Ibid., 113f.
11. Ibid., 209f.

12. Eisenstein: First Professional Revolutionist, 130, 127, 129.
13. From a Buonarroti ms. qu. by Eisenstein. ibid., 92.
14. From a Buonarroti notebook, ibid., 40.
15. Eisenstein, 40, 135. The reference to Marcuse is particularly to his essay "Repressive Tolerance " in *A Critique of Pure Tolerance* by R. P. Wolff et al.; see especially p. 106, 109f. See also Marcuse's essay on Babeuf (listed in Bibliography), but it is more opaque.
16. Bourguin: Le Socialisme Français de 1789 a 1848; qu. in Martov: State and Socialist Revolution, 29.
17. For Bernstein's contribution to the myth, see the beginning of Special Note B.
18. Cole: Hist, of Socialist Thought, 1:165; see also 164,17,21.
19. Berlin: Karl Marx, 14.
20. Halévy: Era of Tyrannies, 279f.
21. Sombart: Socialism and the Social Movement, 118. Lorwin: Blanqui, in *Encyclopaedia of the Social Sciences*, 2:585. The first sentence of Blanqui's "Instructions pour une Prise d'Armes" (omitted from abridged versions) should be especially noted.
22. Spitzer, 176.
23. Dommanget: Idées Polit. et Soc, 171; see also 378.
24. Postgate: Out of the Past, 54; see also 60f, 70.
25. Ibid., 61.
26. Leroy: Histoire des Idées Sociales, 2:414.
27. Qu. in Mason: Blanqui and Communism.
28. Blanqui: Critique Sociale, 1:219, qu. in Mason, ibid., 508; cf. also S. Bernstein: Beginnings of Marxian Socialism in France, 13. Another interpretation is offered by Spitzer, 164.
29. Spitzer, 96-98, 102. This point is also made by Rosenberg: Democracy and Socialism, 31. The ambiguity of Blanqui's attitude toward the class struggle has often been noted; e.g., see Landauer: European Socialism, 1:1040,1045, 291, and Cole: Hist, of Socialist Thought, 1:307.
30. Dommanget: Idées Polit. et Soc., 173.
31. Ltr, E to M, July 6,1869, in MEW 32:336.
32. M: Notebook on the Paris Commune, 35.
33. M: Civil War in France, in MESW 2:221-23. See also its First Draft, in ME: Writ, on Paris Com., 166, and Engels' Intro, to Marx's *Civil War in France*, in MESW 2:187.
34. Qu. in Max Beer: An Inquiry into Dictatorship, Art. III, in *Labour Monthly*, Aug. 1922. For Marx's and Engels' opinion of Girardin, see their review of a book of his, in MECW 10:326.
35. Qu. in Kautsky: Dictatorship of the Proletariat, 20.
36. Nomad: Apostles of Revolution, 29.
37. Qu. in Morton: Life and Ideas of Robert Owen, 171. Morton thinks that remarks like this were Owen's "eccentricities"; not a bit.
38. For 1830, see Charléty: Hist, du S.-Simonisme, 106; also Butler: S.-Simonian Relig. in Ger., 13.—For 1832, sec Saint-Simon: Oeuvres de S-S et d'Enfantin, Vol. 47, p. 552 (article undated here; not necessarily by Enfantin).
39. Cabet: Voyage en Icarie; the quoted passages are on pages 39,217f, 262f, 269,308, 337- 46, 349, 353, 358,499.
40. Ibid., 440,443.
41. Johnson: Utopian Communism in France, 59,63,112, 136.
42. Dézamy: Le Jésuitisme Vaincu et Anéanti, par le Socialisme, 9, 132.
43. Beer: Hist, of British Socialism, 1:340.

44. E: Condition of England—2. The English Constitution, in MEW 1:571 [MECW 3:491f]. For a word on Engels in this period, see *KMTR* 1:216-18.
45. ME: German Ideology, in MECW 5:461 [MEW 3:448).

3. DICTATORSHIP IN 1848

1. Blanc: 1848; Historical Revelations, 296; the enlarged French version of this book, which Blanc published in 1859, has the same passage on p. 320. The expression "dictatorial authority" comes from the earlier (1850) book by Blanc, *Pages d'Histoires* [etc.], 79. An English-language abridgment of this latter book was published in Harney's magazine *Democratic Review*, July 1850; the quote is on p. 70.
2. Louberê: Louis Blanc, 95.
3. Ibid.
4. Ibid., 96.
5. This is cited from the abridged version in the *Democratic Review*, 70 (see note 1 above).
6. Blanc: Pages d'Histoire, 80; the same idea is in his *1848; Historical Revelations*, 297 (or 321 in the French edition).
7. Ibid., 97,71.
8. Same as note 6 above.
9. Qu. in Larousse [etc.] du XIXe Siècle, 13:1112, under "Revolution."
10. Blanc: Pages d'Histoire, 19.
11. Ibid.,29.
12. *Le Moniteur Universel,* Mar. 8, 1848, qu. in S. Bernstein: Blanqui, 148.
13. Blanc: Pages d'Histoire, 96.
14. See Chap. 1, p. 11.,
15. M: Class Struggles in France, in MESW 1:224—this passage in particular, but all of Chap. 1 is relevant.
16. Jean Vidalenc, in an article published in 1948, as quoted by De Luna, 152.
17. Garnier-Pagès, 106.
18. Pierre, 383; see also De Luna, 138. Girardin republished the piece in his book *Questions de Mon Temps* in 1858.
19. This account follows Gamier-Pages, 106-08, supplemented by De Luna, 138.
20. Garnier-Pagès, 270.
21. The account of this session follows Garnier-Pagès, 271-75; *Journal des Débats, June 25, 1848.* Also see Pierre, 385.
22. Robertson: Revolutions of 1848, 97.
23. For example: Robertson, 96; Langer, 421; Duveau, 157.
24. De Luna, 175; the quote gives Cavaignac's own words from the official report of the session.
25. Duveau, 155f.
26. De Luna, 200-04; Lougee, 99-101.
27. DeLuna, 174.
28. Ibid., 210f.
29. Ibid., 212.
30. Rossiter: Constitutional Dictatorship, 81.
31. E: Intro, to Marx's Class Struggles in France, in MESW l:202f (MEW 22:526].
32. See Chap. 2, p. 39f.
33. Kühn: Derjunge Hermann Becker, 1:107, qu. in Bund d. Kom., 1:1121.

34. MECW 7:650 n. 346.
35. *Wächter am Rhein,* Aug. 23, 1848, qu. in Bund d. Kom., 1:827, 1122; in the latter work, the editors separate the quote into two parts, the less reliable second part being relegated to the end notes.
36. For Marx's views on this question, see KMTR 2, Chap. 7.
37. Wittke: Utopian Communist, 259. For the Communia episode, see ibid., Chap. 13, especially pp. 250,259,269.
38. Ltr, M to E, Jan. 29, 1853, in MEW 28:209. Cf. the discussion of this in KMTR 2:640f.
39. Wittke, 136. For a note on some other aspects of Weitling, see KMTR 2:654-59.
40. Intro. by Orton in Bakunin: Confession, especially 19-26; Carr: M. Bakunin, 222-26.
41. Bakunin: Confession, 91.
42. Ibid.,98f.
43. Ibid.,96.
44. Ibid., 112,118f.

4. THE DICTATORSHIP OF THE DEMOCRACY: MARX IN 1848

1. Draper: A Note on the Father of Anarchism (see Biblio.).
2. Proudhon: Carnets, 3:235, written ca. July/Aug. 1849.
3. Ibid., 192; written June 13 or 14, 1849.
4. Ibid., 248; written Sept. 20, 1849.
5. Ibid., 300; written Apr. 23,1850. Ibid., 249, Sept. 20, 1849.
6. Ibid., 20; written ca. Mar. 2,1848.
7. Ibid., 39f; written Apr. 1, 1848.
8. For the term, see KMTR 2:176f, 193,211f,212n,254.
9. This briefly summarizes KMTR 2, Chap. 7.
10. Ditto, Chaps. 8-9 and part of 10.
11. Vidal: Second American Revolution? (see Biblio.).
12. Webb: What Happened in 1931, p. 3.
13. E: Assembly at Frankfurt, in *NRZ,* June 1, 1848, in MEW 5:14 [MECW 7:16].
14. M: Camphausen's Statement, *NRZ,* June 3, 1848, in MEW 5:26f [MECW 7:311]. The quotes given here are from Camphausen's speech, reported in Marx's article.
15. E: Programs of the Radical-Dem. Party and the Left at Frankfurt, *NRZ,* June 7, 1848, in MEW 5:40 [MECW 7:49].
16. Ibid., MEW 5:41 [MECW 7:50].
17. E: Berlin Debate on the Rev., *NRZ,* June 16, 1848, in MEW 5:71 [MECW 7:80].
18. ME: Valdenaire's Arrest, *NRZ,* June 19, 1848, in MEW 5:84 [MECW 7:95]; ME: Marrast and Thiers, *NRZ,* July 3, 1848, in MEW 5:157 [MECW 7:168].
19. E: Conciliationist Session of July 4, *NRZ,* July 11, 1848, in MEW 5:195 [MECW 7:205].
20. M: Crisis and the Counterrevolution, Article 3, *NRZ,* Sept. 14, 1848, in MEW 5:401-03 [MECW 7:430-32].
21. Ibid., MEW 5:403f [MECW 7:432fl].
22. E: Rev. and Counterrev. in Ger., Chap. 7, in MESW 1:336.
23. Mehring: Intro, to *Aus dem literarischen Nachlass* [etc.], 3:53f. Mchring did not name

the source of the attack. His citations from Waldeck and Bucher were without quote marks.
24. E: Rev. and Counterrev. in Ger., in MECW 11:40. The other two passages mentioned are on 86, 92. For mentions of the word 'dictators', etc., see 5, 22, 41.
25. Ibid., 86, 92, 41.
26. M: Crisis and the Counterrevolution, Art. 2, *NRZ*, Sept. 13, 1848, in MEW 5:400 [MECW 7:429].
27. The curious investigator will find these passages in MECW 9:102, 357, 441, 444.
28. The passages cited are found on the following pages of MEW 5 [bracketed page numbers correspond to MECW 7]: 116 [128], 120 [132], 376 [402], 123-25 [134-36], 148 [160].

5. THE "DICTATORSHIP OF THE PEOPLE":|
CONSERVATIVE VERSION

1. Holcombe: Government in a Planned Democracy, 171.
2. M: Manteuffel's Speech, [etc.], *NYDT*, Dec. 12, 1853, in MECW 12:512f.
3. M: Czar's Views [etc.], *NYDT*, Feb. 11, 1854, in MECW 12:592.
4. Tocqueville: Old Regime and the Fr. Rev., 167, 208f; cf. KMTR 1:639n.
5. M: Critique of Hegel's Philosophy of Right (Ms.), in MEW 1:223 [MECW 3:22].
6. Guizot's book was quickly published in English. In the English edition, *Democracy in France*, the passages referred to are found on p. 10f, 51, 58, 60, 65; but other parts of the book are relevant too.
7. Graham: Donoso C., 40; see also 41f.
8. Donoso Cortés: Obras, 3:255.
9. Ibid., 256f.
10. Besides the preceding references, see Graham: Donoso C., 147, on the speech.
11. Donoso Cortés: Obras, 3:274.
12. Stein's 1850 edition was titled *Geschichte der sozialen Bewegung in Frankreich von 1789 bis auf unsere Tag;* for previous editions see the Biblio. A one-volume abridgment in English was published as *The History of the Social Movement in France, 1789-1850,* ed., & tr. by K. Mengelberg. In my opinion the translator took unwise liberties with Stein's political terms, and the result is sometimes misleading, especially for our purposes; hence the English edition, though used here, has had to be checked against the German original at times.
13. Stein: History ..., 90.
14. Ibid., 89.
15. Ibid., 89 f.
16. Ibid., 90.
17. Ibid., 192.
18. Ibid., 193.
19. Stein: Geschichte..., 3:213.
20. Stein: History ..., 398.
21. Ibid., 400, bit revised after the German, 3:289.
22. Stein: History ..., 400.
23. Ibid., 400f.

6. THE SPECTRUM OF DICTATORSHIP

1. See Chap. 1, p. 25, Chap. 5, p. 69.
2. For accounts of the word 'despotism', see the article by M. Richter in the *Dictionary of the History of Ideas*, Vol. 2, or the study by Koebner (see Biblio.). Their conclusions do not always follow from their facts. Richter knows Marx's usage only in the term 'Oriental despotism'; and his account ends about the time ours has to begin.
3. M: Class Struggles in France, in MECW 10: 102, 107.
4. ME: Communist Manifesto, in MECW 6:491, 504.
5. M: Eighteenth Brumaire, in MECW 11:111.
6. Ibid.. 185
7. This view held by Marx is explained in KMTR 1, Chap. 18.
8. M: Civil War in France, in MESW 2:218.
9. M: First Draft, in ME: Writ. on Par. Com., 127f.
10. Ibid., 160; for another similar formulation, 127.
11. Ibid., 128.
12. Ibid., 211.
13. See, for ex., ibid., 198, 210.
14. Ibid., 198.
15. Ltr, M to Fontaine, Apr. 15, 1865, in ME: Corr. (Fr.), 8:165 [MEW 31:473].
16. Lafargue & Liebknecht: K.M., His Life and Work, 51; Remin. M. & E., 117; and cf. McLellan: K.M., 271 (but McLellan's reference is mistaken).
17. Morrison, in *The Pioneer*, Apr. 26, 1834, in what was probably the first feminist "Woman's Page" in journalistic history. (The fact that this innovation appeared in a socialist trade-union organ does not jibe with the myths of bourgeois feminist history.)
18. E: Dialectics of Nature (Notes, etc.), in MEW 20:312, 464.
19. Ltr, M to Sorge, Nov. 5, 1880, in MEW 34:477.
20. M: Contrib. to Critique of Political Economy, in MEW 13:76 fn.
21. E: Marx & *NRZ*, in MEW 21:19 [MESW 3:167].
22. For the articles of the *NRZ* Company as a business, see MECW 7:543-53.
23. Ltr, M to Lassalle, Sept. 15, 1860, in MEW 30:565.
24. For Engels' article "On Authority," see MESW 2:376.
25. E: Revolution and Counterrevolution in Germany, in MECW 11:22.
26. M: Erfurt Echoes in 1859, in MEW 13:415f [MECW 16:405f].
27. ME: Letter to the Brunswick Comm., in MEW 17:269.
28. For Marx, see his article "The Civil War in the U.S.," *Die Presse*, Nov. 7, 1861, in MEW 15:343f. For Engels, see ltr, E to Weydemeyer, Nov. 24, 1864, in MEW 31:425.
29. E: Refugee Lit., III, *Volksstaat*, Oct. 1874, in MEW 18:539.
30. Ltr, E to Sorge, Apr. 12, 1890, in MEW 37:381.
31. E: England, Jan. 1852, in MECW 11:198 [MEW 8:208]. E: Prosecution of Montalembert, Nov. 24, 1858, in MECW 16:91. See also ltr, E to M, Dec. 10, 1851 (a few days after Bonaparte's coup), in MEW 27:385 [MECW 38:509].
32. M: Constitution of the Fr. Republic, in MECW 10:580.
33. M: Bonaparte's Present Position, *NYDT*, Apr. 1, 1858 (not yet in MECW).
34. M: Fair Professions, in MECW 16:309. See also ltr, M to E, June 16, 1860, in MEW 30:64.
35. M: Pelissier's Mission to England, in *NYDT*, Apr. 15, 1858 (not yet in MECW).
36. E: Foreign Policy of Russian Czarism, as published in *Time* (London), Apr. 1890, p. 365. The German version (in MEW 22:25) says "a ruler, a Napoleon"; but the

English version in *Time*, which was overseen by Engels himself, had the formulation given in my text. The second locus mentioned here is the letter, E to Borgius, Jan. 25, 1894, in MEW 39:206.
37. Engels' discussion of Boulangism is contained in the collection, the Engels-Lafargue *Correspondence*, especially Vol. 2. It is obvious that a number of Engels' letters to Paul Lafargue, critical of the later, somehow did not survive the period during which they were held by the Lafargue family heirs. For Engels' references to Boulanger's politics as Bonapartism, see Vol. 2, p. 131, 165, 193, 209, 302, 371.
38. Ltr, E to Laura Lafargue, June 3, 1888, ibid., 2:131; and see also 2:109.
39. Ltr, Lafargue to E, July 25, 1888, ibid., 2:147.
40. Ltr, E to Lafargue, May 7, 1889, ibid., 2:238.
41. For the article, written for the *New American Cyclopaedia*, see MECW 18:219; for a comment, see KMTR 1:438.
42. See especially the passages at MECW 18:230, 225, 231, 221f.
43. M: Affairs in Prussia (conferred title), in *NYDT*, Dec. 27, 1858, in MECW 16:126.
44. Ltr, E to Liebknecht, Dec. 1, 1885, in MEW 36:398.
45. M: Afterword to his pamphlet on the Cologne Communist trial, in MEW 18:570.
46. Ltr, E to M, Apr. 13, 1866, in MEW 31:208. For discussion of Engels' view as expressed in this letter, see KMTR 1:413 and Chap. 16 as a whole.
47. E: Role of Force in History, in MESW 3:398.
48. Ibid., 400.
49. Ibid., 419. For minor loci, see also 415, 416.
50. M: Palmerston, *NOZ*, Mar. 3, 1855, in MECW 14:50 [MEW 11:92]. The first such statement I know was in the same paper, Jan. 30, 1855, in MECW 13:607f [MEW 11:11]. See also another article in *NOZ*, June 18, in MECW 14:275 [MEW 11:299].
51. The first such statement was in M: New English Budget, *NYDT*, Mar. 9, 1857. For one of Marx's more extreme assertions, see the beginning of his article in *NYDT* of Mar. 15, 1858, "The Derby Cabinet [etc.]." All of the *NYDT* articles mentioned in notes 52-56 below have not yet appeared in MECW, since Vol. 15 is still unpublished.
52. Ltr, M to E, Mar. 18, 1857, in MEW 29:111f.
53. M: Defeat of the Palmerston Ministry, *NYDT*, Mar. 25, 1857; the same paragraph twice more referred to Palmerston's "dictatorship."
54. M: Coming Election in England, *NYDT*, Mar. 31, 1857.
55. M: English Election, *NYDT*, Apr. 6, 1857.
56. See the following articles:—M: Defeat of Cobden, Bright and Gibson, *NYDT*, Apr. 17, 1857; M: untitled article, *NYDT*, Mar. 15, 1858; M: untitled article, *NYDT*, June 24, 1858; M: India Bill, *NYDT*, July 24, 1858.
57. See Chap. 2, p. 28.
58. M: Fall of the Aberdeen Ministry, *NYDT*, Feb. 17, 1855, in MECW 13:631.
59. Ltr, M to E, Dec. 9, 1851, in MEW 27:384 [MECW 38:508]. For the context, see Chap. 14, Sec. 5, p. 239.
60. M: Interesting from Sicily, *NYDT*, Aug. 8, 1860, in MECW 17:421; see also 423, 424. E: Garibaldi's Progress, *NYDT*, Sept. 21, 1860, in MECW 17:472.
61. Ltr, Garibaldi to Bignami, Apr. 4, 1871, published in *Journal Officiel de la République Française* (organ of the Paris Commune), previously published by Bignami in *La Plebe* (Lodi).
62. Qu. in Hostetter, 217.
63. E: Revolution and Counterrevolution in Germany, in MESW 1:300.
64. Ltr, Schramm to Weydemeyer, Jan. 8, 1850, in MEW 27:605.
65. Ltr, M to E, Feb. 4, 1852, in MEW 28:20.
66. J. G. Eccarius: Legality and Demagoguism, Chap. 1, in *Notes to the People* (London),

Mar. 1852, II:45. In its Chap. 2, by the way, it was incidentally mentioned that Cavaignac "was made dictator" in France, but this was not taken as a matter for comment. For a routine reference to Kossuth as dictator, in the *NRZ* of 1849, see MECW 8:299 (not in MEW).
67. ME: Great Men of the Emigration, in MECW 11:279, 280.
68. Ibid., 287, 309; see also 310.
69. M: Espartero, *NYDT*, Aug. 19, 1854, in MECW 13:342f.
70. M: Herr Vogt, in MEW 14:584 [MECW 17:228]; for other references to Fazy as "dictator," see MEW 14:544, 548, 656 [MECW 17:187, 192, 229, 302].
71. M: Poland, Prussia and Russia (a manuscript), in M: Manuskripte über die polnische Frage, 134.
72. Ltr, M to E, Nov. 12, 1869, in MEW 32:388; and E to M, Nov. 17, 1869, ibid., 390.
73. M: Civil War in France—First Draft, in ME: Writ. on Par. Com., 143.
74. Some usages are obscure. Thus, in the letter E to M, Feb. 11, 1853, in MEW 28:212, there is a reference to "these great dictators, quite à la Seiler," but it is not clear what this mention of Sebastian Seiler implies about the man.
75. Harrington: Socialism, 62.

7. SOME DICTATORS OVER THE PROLETARIAT

1. Richard: Bakounine et l'Internationale, 139.
2. Ibid., 129-33.
3. Bakunin's letter to Nechayev was published in full by its discoverer, in its original Russian, in *Cahiers du Monde Russe et Soviétique*, 1966; in French, in his book *Violence dans la Violence*, 106-49. An English translation was published in *Encounter* (London), July & Aug. 1972. No excerpts can do justice to this document; it must be read in full.
4. Ltr, M to E, July 27, 1869, in MEW 32:351.
5. Ltr, M to De Paepe, Jan. 24, 1870, in MEW 32:645.
6. M: Confidential Communication of March 1870, in MEW 16:409, 412.
7. Ltr, M to the Lafargues, Apr. 19, 1870, in MEW 32:673-77; original French in M: Lettres et Doc., 173-76.
8. Ltr, E to Lafargue, Jan. 19, 1872, in E & Lafargues: Corr., 1:40.
9. E: GC to All the Members [etc.] (Aug. 1872), in GCFI 5:440.
10. E: Refugee Lit., III, *Volksstaat*, Oct. 1874, in MEW 18:539; see also 540.
11. Ltr, M to E, Aug. 10, 1869. The publication was *L'International*, published in London with French government subventions—not to be confused with *L'Internationale* of Brussels.
12. Marx's relations with, and views on, Lassalle will be covered in the next volume of KMTR. For present purposes I suggest two available works on the background: David Footman's biography of Lassalle, and the study of Lassalle's politics written by E. Bernstein under Engels' eye in London, translated into English under the title *Ferdinand Lassalle as a Social Reformer*.
13. Ltr, M to E, Mar. 5, 1856, in MEW 29:28.
14. Marx reported this in a letter to Engels, Aug. 7, 1862 (MEW 30:270), after Lassalle's London visit.
15. The citations are from Marx's letter to Engels, July 30, 1862 (MEW 30:257f), giving an account of Lassalle's sojourn in London.
16. Ltr, M to E, Apr. 9, 1863, in MEW 30:340.

17. Ltr, Liebknecht to Marx, June 12, 1864, in Liebknecht: Briefwechsel mit M & E, 37.
18. G. Mayer: Bismarck und Lassalle, 60f, where this letter was first published in 1928.
19. Ltr, M to Kugelmann, Feb. 23, 1865, in MEW 31:451.
20. For Engels, see: ltr, E to Kautsky, Feb. 23, 1891, in MEW 38:40; and E: Role of Force in History, in MESW 3:418f. Marx used it also: cf. ltr, M to E, July 30, 1862, in MEW 30:258.
21. Bernstein: F. Lassalle as a Social Reformer, 172, 176, 178f.
22. Ltr, E to M, Feb. 23, 1877, in MEW 34:30f.
23. Ltr, E to Bernstein, Oct. 25, 1881, in MEW 35:230f.
24. Ltr, E to Bernstein, Nov. 30, 1881, in MEW 35:238.
25. Ltr, ME to Edit. Board of *Social-Demokrat*, Feb. 23, 1865, in MEW 16:79.
26. For a closeup look at how the Lassallean dictatorship over trade unions operated in practice, see the case described in KMTR 2, Special Note B; also the discussion at p. 133-35.
27. Ltr, M to E, Sept. 29, 1868, in MEW 32:169.
28. Ltr, E to M, Sept. 30, 1868, in MEW 32:170f.
29. Ltr, M to Schweitzer, Oct. 13, 1868, in MEW 32:571.
30. See above, Chap. 3, p. 55, re Weitling.
31. ME: Circular Letter to Bebel et al., Sept. 1879, in MEW 34:402n; this stricken passage is not in any English editions of this document so far published.
32. Ltr, E to Sorge, Aug. 9, 1890, in MEW 37:440.
33. Ltr, E to Kautsky, Feb. 23, 1891, in MEW 38:41.
34. Dominick: Liebknecht, 303, 304, 308, 316, 323, 351, 370, 396.
35. M: Civil War in France—First Draft, in ME: Writ. on Par. Com., 161. This passage distinguishes between the French and British Comtists.
36. Ltr, E to Kautsky, July 19, 1884, in MEW 36:177.
37. Ltr, E to Bebel, Jan. 24, 1893, in MEW 39:13.
38. Ltr, E to G. Trier, Dec. 18, 1889, in MEW 37:327f.
39. *People's Paper*, Jan. 26, 1856, qu. in Saville's intro. to his collection *Ernest Jones, Chartist*, 61.
40. This account follows Saville, ibid., especially p. 48f, 61, 68.
41. Ltr, M to E, Apr. 10, 1856, in MEW 29:38.
42. Ltr, M to E, Nov. 24, 1857, in MEW 29:218.
43. Ltr, Harney to E, Feb. 19, 1886, in Harney: Harney Papers, 308.
44. Ltr, Harney to E, Feb. 21, 1892, ibid., 330.
45. Ltrs, Harney to E, July 21, 1893 and Feb. 23, 1894, ibid., 350, 355.
46. Cadogan: Harney and Engels, 79.
47. Ltr, M to E, Mar. 31, 1851, in MEW 27:227.

8. INTRODUCTION TO THE INVESTIGATION

1. This appeared in the first good English translation: The German Ideology (Parts I & III), Marxist Lib., Vol. 6 (1939), p. 23. The version in MESW 1:35 is a bit better, that in MECW 5:47 more so; for the original, see MEW 3:34.
2. Ltr, E to Van Patten, Apr. 18, 1883, in ME: Sel. Corr., 362.
3. E: Communists and K. Heinzen, in MEW 4:317 [MECW 6:299].
4. Text of the rules, in MEW 4:596 [MECW 6:633].
5. See above, Chap. 4, p. 59f.

6. E: Principles of Communism, in MEW 4:372f.
7. The following four passages are translated from the 1848 text of the Manifesto: MEW 4:473, 474, 481, 482. For the standard English (Moore-Engels) version of these passages, see MECW 6:495, 498,504,505f.
8. See, for example, Chap. 13, Sec. 5.
9. Jones: To the Chartists, in *Northern Star,* July 1, 1848, repr. in *Anthol. Chartist Lit.,* 358. Saville: Intro., Ernest Jones, Chartist, 192. Schoyen: Chartist Challenge, 207.
10. For both Beer and Macaulay, see Beer: Hist, of British Socialism, 2:281,135f.
11. Engels' views were expressed by him at a London meeting reported in the *Workman's Times,* Mar. 25,1893.
12. Wolfe: Marxism, 208.
13. See note 6 above.
14. M: Conspectus of Bakunin's book *Statism and Anarchy,* in MEW 18:634.
15. Johnson: Utopian Communism in France, 247.
16. Ibid., 288, 290.
17. Cabet: History of... Icaria, 229.
18. Cabet: France [etc.], in *Democratic Review,* Sept. 1850, 136-39.
19. Cabet: History of... Icaria, 230. Cabet writes of himself in the third person.

9. MARX AND BLANQUI

1. E: Progress of Social Reform on the Continent, in MECW 3:393f.
2. ME: Holy Family, in MECW 4:131, 47 [MEW 2:139,49].
3. Ibid., MEW 2:126 [MECW 4:119].
4. ME: German Ideology, in MECW 5:210 [MEW 3:191]; cf. also MEW 3:207,308, 448.
5. E: Festival of Nations, in MECW 6:5f [MEW 2:612,614].
6. For the "Library" plan, see MECW 4:667; cf. also *Karl Marx Chronik,* 28, and ltr, E to M, Mar. 7 and 17,1845, in MECW 38:25,27f.
7. Rubel: Cahiers de Lecture de K.M., 419.
8. M: Moralizing Criticism [etc.], in MECW 6:321f (MEW 4:341). Cf. also MECW 5:552f (MEW 4:260,262).
9. See Special Note B, p. 341f.
10. E: Anti-Dühring—Preparatory Writings, in MEW 20:587.
11. In the order mentioned: M to E, Sept. 23, 1852, in MEW 28:143; E to Kautsky, Feb. 20, 1889, in MEW 37:156; E to Bernstein, May 5, 1887, in MEW 36:650.
12. Eisenstein: First Professional Revolutionist, 154 (re Garrone), 86 (re Jottrand).
13. Laski: Socialist Tradition in the Fr. Rev., 31 f.
14. E: On the History of the CL, in MEW 21:207 [MESW 3:174].
15. Auclair: Vie de Jean Jaurès, 273.
16. Lehning: Buonarroti's Ideas on Communism and Dictatorship, 282f, argues that he did know Blanqui; see also Spitzer, 126f.
17. Qu. in Jaurès: Etudes Socialistes, xxviii.
18. For an example, see Chap. 17, Sec. 3, p. 275.
19. Spitzer, 165.
20. Da Costa: Les Blanquistes, 21f, 25.
21. E: Intro, to Marx's Class Struggles in France, in MESW 2:186.
22. See the letters in MEW 27:198-213 passim and 545-47 (MECW 38:297-312 passim).
23. See the letters in MEW 27:214-22 passim (MECW 38:313-19 passim).

24. ME: Introductory Note to Blanqui's Toast, in MECW 10:537f [MEW 7:568f].
25. M: Knight of the Noble Consciousness, in MEW 9:515f (MECW 12:505-07); ME: Great Men of the Emig., in MEW 8:302f (MECW 11:295f).
26. ME: Introductory Note [to Blanqui's Toast], in MEW 7:568.
27. Ltr, M to Watteau, Nov. 10, 1861, in ME: Corr. (Fr.), 6:371 [MEW 30:617].
28. M: Class Struggles in France, in MECW 10:128 [MEW 7:91].
29. ME: [Review of] "Les Conspirateurs [etc.]," in MECW 10:322 [MEW 7:278]. The next sentence is also relevant.
30. M: Eighteenth Brumaire, in MECW 11:110,183. I cite these passages in accordance with the first (1852) edition; both passages were changed in the second edition of 1869; this revision and its meaning will be discussed in Chap. 18, Sec. 1.
31. Ltr, E to M, Jan. 22, 1852, in MEW 28:11 [MECW 39:13].
32. ME: Sevastopol Hoax, *NYDT*, Oct. 21, 1854, in MECW 13:491.
33. M: Speech at Anniversary of *PP*, in MECW 14:655.
34. Dommanget: Idées Polit. et Soc., 381.
35. Ltr, M to E, June 19, 1861, in MEW 30:176.
36. Ltr, M to E, Jan. 2, 1863, in MEW 30:306.
37. Ltr, E to Mrs. M, Aug. 15, 1870, in MEW 33:137.
38. M: Civil War in France, in MESW 2:239. The First Draft of this work had a critical reference to Blanqui: see ME: Writ, on Paris Com., 144f.
39. M: Letter in *Times* (London), Apr. 4, 1870, in M: On First International (ed. Padover), 280f [MEW 17:302f].
40. For a tabular summary of Blanqui's prison terms, see the table "Blanqui Enchainé" in Dommanget: Idees Polit. et Soc., 404-07.
41. E: Program of the Blanquist Ref., in MEW 18:530 [MESW 2:382].
42. See above, Sec. 3, p. 130.
43. Ltr, M to E, Sept. 28, 1852, in MEW 28:147f.
44. Ltr, M to Lafargues, Feb. 15, 1869, in MEW 32:592 (original in English).
45. Ltr, M to E, Apr. 22, 1859, in MEW 29:426.
46. Ltr, M to Lassalle, May 8, 1861, in MEW 30:603.
47. This letter is not extant; but see MEW 30:758 n. 599; also ltr, M to Lassalle, May 29, 1861, in MEW 30:605.
48. See note 35 above.
49. Based on the ed note, MEW 30:759 n. 602, which does not give a direct quote from Watteau.
50. Ltr, M to Lassalle, July 22, 1861, in MEW 30:615.
51. See note 27 above.
52. These three passages are quoted in KMTR 1:137f, from the following sources:— M: Econ. & Phllos. Mss., in MEW Eb.l:553f; ltr, M to Feuerbach, Aug. 11, 1844, in MEW 27:426; ME: Holy Family, in MEW 2:89.
53. M: Herr Vogt, in MEW 14:439.
54. Cf. this chapter, Sec. 1, p. 124. Marx also referred to the Blanquist-related past of the League of the Just in a foreword he drafted in 1880 for the publication of the French edition of *Socialism, Utopian and Scientific*; text in ME: Lettres et Doc, 206 [MEW 19:181].
55. Nicolaievsky & M.-H.: Karl Marx, 75.
56. See Chap. 10, Sec. 1.
57. Dommanget: Idees Polit. et Soc, 376.
58. Cf. this chapter, Sec. 1, p. 123.
59. The claim was made in Nicolaievsky & M.-H.: Karl Marx, 132; rejected in Dommanget: Idées Polit. et Soc, 376.
60. The case for Marx's participation in the French club was made by Samuel

Bernstein: "Marx in Paris, 1848," *Science & Society,* 1939, III, 323-55, and 1940, IV, 211-17. The argument against it was made by P. Amann, "Karl Marx, 'quarante-huitard français'?" in *IRSH,* 1961, VI, 249-55. Bernstein had an opportunity to rebut in his book *Auguste Blanqui,* 144f, 153 n.32.
61. The reason for saying *"Even* Dommanget" is given in Special Note D, Sec. 7, p. 382f.
62. Dommanget: Idées Polit. et Soc., 377 refers for support to the passage in Nicolaievsky & M.-H.: Karl Marx, 152. For Engels' high opinion at this point of Ledru-Rollin and Flocon, see his two letters to his brother-in-law E. Blank, Mar. 26 and 28,1848, in MECW 38:166,168f.
63. Ltr, M to E. June 7,1849, in MECW 38:199 [MEW 27:137].
64. Dommanget: Ideés Polit. et Soc, 386-89.
65. Ltr, M to Kugelmann, Dec. 5, 1868, in MEW 32:580f.
66. Lafargue's letter to Marx was quoted in: ltr, M to E, Mar. 1,1869, in MEW 32:264. Engels commented Mar. 3, in MEW 32:270.
67. Ltr, M to E, Mar. 1, 1869, in MEW 32:264.
68. Ltr, M to Lafargue, June 2, 1869, in MEW 32:608-10.
69. Ltr, M to daughter Jenny (Mrs. Longuet), June 2, 1869, English original, in M: Lettres et Doc, 168 [MEW 32:611]
70. Ltr, M to E, July 14,1869, in MEW 32:337.
71. Ltr, M to Lafargues, Mar. 5,1870, in MEW 32:656 (retrans., original in English).
72. Ltr, M to L. Bigot, July 11, 1871, in MEW 33:244 (retrans., original in French). The "plot" was the one mentioned above in Sec 3, p, 131.
73. Ltr, E to Liebknecht, Apr. 23, 1872, in MEW 33:451.
74. Aside from letters, Marx mentioned Blanqui's name in 1875 in a speech on Poland (see MEW 18:575) and in the 1880 foreword referred to in note 54 above.
75. Ltr, Lafargue to Blanqui, June 12, 1879, unpublished, extant among Blanqui's posthumous papers and mss. A combination of quotes and summaries is presented by Dommanget: Idées Polit. et Soc, 395f, and S. Bernstein: Blanqui, 346-49.
76. Dommanget: Idées Polit. et Soc, 396 (he gives no source for his quote from Zévaés); S. Bernstein: Blanqui, 346-48.
77. Dommanget: Idées Polit. et Soc, 377, 390,392.
78. Deville's testimony is related, with heavy heart, by Dommanget, ibid., 397, giving the following as source: "Statement by Gabriel Deville.—See *Blanqui sous la IIIe Ripublique* (manuscript), Chap. IV."
79. See Chap. 10, Sec. 3, p. 151.
80. See Sec. 4 of the Manifesto, in MECW 6:518f.
81. This concept of the International is portrayed in detail in Collins & Abramsky: K.M. and the British Labour Movement.
82. The term 'Democratic Communists' appeared over the communication sent from Brussels to the Chartist leader O'Connor; see MEW 4:24 (MECW 6:58). For the Brussels CCC, see McLellan: K.M., 154f; for its activity, see Förder, Chap. 3.
83. ME: Address to the CL, in MECW 10:280,282 [MEW 7:246f, 249].
84. For Marx's opinion of Urquhart in his correspondence, see the letters at MECW 39:284f, 395, 440, 455, and the piece by Cluss based on a letter from Marx, in MECW 12:477. For Marx's meeting with Urquhart, see ltr, M to E, Feb. 9,1854, in MEW 28:324 (MECW 39:4120- For Marx's published critiques of Urquhart, see his untitled *NYDT* articles published Apr. 19, 1853 (in MECW 12:22, drafted by Engels); Oct. 4, 1853 (in MECW 12:309); Jan. 28, 1854 (in MECW 12:559); June 9,1854 (in MECW 13:227). For the last statement ("agree in *nothing"),* see ltr, M to E, Apr. 22,1854, in MECW 39:440 [MEW 28:348].

85. Ltr, M to Lassalle, Juneca.2,1860, in MEW 30:549; the discussion of Fischel is on 547-49.
86. E: On Hist. of the CL, in MEW 21:213 (MESW 3:179).
87. Berlin: Karl Marx, 190; see also 263.

10. MARX VERSUS BLANQUISM

1. E: Program of the Blanquist Ref., in MEW 18:529f [MESW 2:381].
2. M: Crit. Notes on "The King of Prussia ...," in MECW 3:206 [MEW 1:409].
3. Ibid., MECW 3:204 [MEW 1:407].
4. See Special Note C, Sec. 1, p. 362.
5. See Chap. 9, pp. 124,134.
6. E: On Hist. of CL, in MEW 21:213 [MESW 3:179f].
7. Diskussionen im Kommunistischen Arbeiterbildungsverein in London, in Bund d. Kom. 1:217f.
8. Ibid., 220.
9. Ibid., 220f, 226f; the citations are from the discussions of June 23 and July 6, but there is much more of the same throughout.
10. Ibid., 223 (peaceful roads), 231 (dictatorship), Schapper mentioned Cabet's advocacy of a dictator, 229. For Weitling's advocacy of dictatorship, see Chap. 3, Sec. 4, pp. 53-55.
11. See KMTR 2, Spec. Note I.
12. Ltr, London CCC to M, June 6, 1846, in Bund d. Kom. 1:348.
13. On Kriege's agitation and M's criticism, see KMTR 2:154,419-22.
14. ME: Circular Against Kriege, in MEW 4:14 [MECW 6:47].
15. For this passage, see KMTR 2:154.
16. Ltr, London CCC to M, June 6, 1846, in Bund d. Kom., 1:347.
17. E: Principles of Communism, in MECW 6:349.
18. *Kommunistische Zeitschrift*, Sept. 1847, in Bund d. Kom., 1:505.
19. E: Reform Movement in France, *Northern Star*, Nov. 20,1847, in MECW 6:380f.
20. These three passages are cited from the original text of the Manifesto, not the standard (Moore-Engels) translation: in MEW 4:461, 473, 489 [MECW 6:481, 495,514].
21. See above, Chap. 8, p. 113.
22. ME: Com. Manifesto, in MECW 6:518. Engels' note on the then meaning of 'Social-Democrats' was published in the English ed. of 1888.
23. Ltr, E to M, Aug. 19,1846, in MECW 38:53.
24. Ltr, E to M, Oct. 25-26,1847, in MECW 38:133.
25. This picture is obtained from E's letters to Marx from Oct. 1847 to Jan. 1848 (see MECW 38:133-57 passim).
26. There was one *NRZ* article by E in which Blanqui's name occurred—in a quotation from a French bourgeois writer, not picked up by E; see MEW 5:143 or MECW 7:155.11 does not qualify as a reference by E himself.
27. Cf. KMTR 2:261, 263. For M's analysis of the Social-Democracy in 1850, see his *Class Struggles in France*, especially MECW 10:125f.
28. Carr: Karl Marx, 78.
29. E: Program of the Blanquist Ref., in MEW 18:529 [MESW 2:381].
30. See Chap. 9, Sec. 5, p. 135.
31. E: On Hist, of the CL, in MESW 3:184 [MEW 21:218].
32. E: Karl Marx, in MESW 2:158.

402 Notes to Pages 154-164

33. ME et al.: Ltr to Cabet, Mar. 1848, in Bund d. Kom., 1:748 [MECW 7:8; MEW 5:6].
34. Ltr, M to E, Aug. 8, 1870, in MEW 33:33.
35. Nicolaievsky & M.-H.: Karl Marx, 150, 154, 153.
36. This little-known campaign is sketched in KMTR 2, Spec. Note J.
37. See Chap. 4, Sec. 3-4.
38. The criticism refers to McLellan: Karl Marx, 201 f; for an antidote, see KMTR 2:211-19.
39. E: Cologne in Danger, *NRZ*, June 11,1848, in MECW 7:69-71; the extract is from 71.
40. M/E: Arrests, *NRZ*, July 4, 1848, in MEW 5:165 [MECW 7:176].
41. See New Mega III, 3:1485; the colonel is called "Friedrich Engels" by the editors; for ex., see 3:13-17.
42. This summary is mainly based on Hammen's chapter on "The September Crisis," p. 272 on; see especially p. 307f, 349,389, 397.
43. M: Decree of Eichmann's, *NRZ*, Nov. 19,1848, in MEW 6:32 [MECW 8:38].
44. E: Counterrevolutionary Plans in Berlin, *NRZ*, May 1, 1849, in MECW 9:371 [MEW6:452fl.
45. E: Rhenish Congress of Municipalities, *NRZ*, May 4, 1849, in MECW 9:392f rev. after MEW 6:468.
46. E: Hankering for a State of Seige, *NRZ*, May 6, 1849, in MEW 6:471 [MECW 9:402].
47. Ladendorf: Hist. Schlagwb., 257.
48. M/E: To the Workers of Cologne, *NRZ*, May 19, 1849, in MEW 6:519 [MECW 9:467]. For Engels' back-reference in 1884, see E: Marx & the *NRZ*, in MESW 3:171 [MEW 21:23].
49. M: Class Struggles in France, in MEW 7:91; for the mistranslation in MECW 10:128, see Special Note D, Sec. 8.
50. M: Class Struggles in France, in MECW 10:88 [MEW 7:52].
51. See KMTR 2:259-65 for an exposition of the Address; note the footnote on p. 259. In addition, Special Note E of that volume surveys the claim that Marx later repudiated the Address.
52. See KMTR 2:208f.
53. ME: Address to the CL, in MECW 10:286f [MEW 7:2531].
54. ME: [Review of] "Les Conspirateurs [etc.]," in the magazine's No.4, in MEW 7:266 +[MECW 10:311 +].
55. Ibid., MEW 7:275 [MECW 10:320].
56. Ibid.
57. Ibid., MEW 7:269 [MECW 10:314].
58. Ibid., MEW 7:271[MECW 10:316].
59. See KMTR 2:463, in connection with the lumpenproletariat. The passage itself is in MEW 7:272 [MECW 10:317].
60. ME: op. cit. (note 54 above), in MEW 7:273 [MECW 10:318].
61. Ibid., MEW 7:273f [MECW 10:318].
62. Ibid., MEW 7:274 [MECW 10:319].
63. Ibid., MEW 7:275f [MECW 10:320f].
64. D. Felix: Marx as Politician, 96; but this comes from the bottom of the marxological barrel.
65. On this problem, see below, Chap. 11, Sec. 2, p. 179n.
66. Ascribed to E: Letter from France, VII, in MECW 10:35.
67. For Dronke's letters, see New Mega III, 3:486, 541f, 684. For Lassalle's letter (May 16,1850), ibid., 548.

68. E: Peasant War in Germany, in MECW 10:469 [MEW 7:400].
69. Ibid., MEW 7:400f [MECW 10:469f].
70. See the reference to this aspect in Chap. 9, Sec. 2, p. 125.
71. Röser: From P. Röser's Evidence, in MECW 38:551.
72. This situation was touched on in Sec. 5 above, p. 160; for the background, see KMTR 2:78.
73. M: Revelations Conc. the Com. Trial, in MEW 8:412 [MECW 11:402f]. This is how Marx quoted himself "verbatim" in an account written two years later. The minutes of the CC meeting give the passage with essentially the same content but with slightly different wording; see the text in MEW 8:598 [MECW 10:626]; cf. KMTR 2:78 fn.
74. This is documented in some detail in KMTR 2:604-06.
75. Röser: From P. Röser's Evidence, in MECW 38:552, 554.
76. M: Revelations Conc. the Com. Trial, in MECW 11:445.
77. ME: Review, May to Oct., in MEW 7:461 [MECW 10:530f].
78. About the invention of this definition of Blanquism by E. Bernstein, see Special Note B, Sec. 1.
79. Ltr, M to E, Oct. 19, 1851, in MEW 27:365 [MECW 38:484].
80. Ltr, M to E, Feb. 27, 1852, in MECW 39:50 [MEW 28:30].
81. E: Late Trial at Cologne, *NYDT*, Dec. 22, 1852, in MECW 11:389f. This article was included by Eleanor Marx in *Revolution and Counterrevolution in Germany* when it was first published in book form, but it was not part of that series in the *NYDT*.
82. M: Attack on Francis Joseph [etc.], *NYDT*, Mar. 8, 1853, in MECW 11:513f.
83. Ibid., 515.
84. M: untitled art. [Kossuth and Mazzini etc.], *NYDT*, Apr. 4, 1853, in MECW 11:536.
85. M: Herr Vogt, in MEW 14:440 [MECW 17:81].
86. M: Revelations Conc. the Com. Trial, in MECW 11:446, 449.
87. ME: Great Men of the Emig., in MECW 11:287 [MEW 8:295].
88. Ltr, M to E, May 6, 1852, in MEW 28:68 [MECW 39:101].
89. Ltr, E to M, May 7, 1852, in MEW 28:70 [MECW 39:103].

11. MARX'S *CLASS STRUGGLES IN FRANCE*

1. M: Class Struggles in France, in MECW 10:69, 72, 76.
2. Ibid., 77.
3. M: Eighteenth Brumaire, in MECW 11:119, 180.
4. M: Class Struggles in France, in MECW 10:107.
5. M: Eighteenth Brumaire, in MECW 11:181, 124n. The second citation is in a passage omitted after the first edition.
6. M: Class Struggles in France, in MECW 10:131.
7. M: Eighteenth Brumaire, in MECW 11:179.
8. See Chap. 6, p. 82f, with ref. notes 31-34.
9. M: Class Struggles in France, in MECW 10:97, 98, 99.
10. Ibid., 122.
11. Ibid., 98.
12. Ibid., 69.
13. See Chap. 5, p. 74, with ref. note 21.
14. The three-part series "Two Years of a Revolution" was published unsigned in the *Democratic Review* for April to June 1850, covering Sec. 1 (only) of Marx's work. The

passage discussed was published in the June issue (Vol. II, p. 23). The whole has now been reprinted in MECW 10 (see 10:368 for the passage), with an unsupported attribution to Engels.
15. Schoyen: Chartist Challenge, 204.
16. Ed note, MECW 10:680 n.260.
17. Ltr, M to Weydemeyer, Mar. 5, 1852, in MEW 28:504 [MECW 38:61].
18. M: Class Struggles in France, in MECW 10:98.
19. Ibid., 57.
20. Ibid., 127.
21. Blanc: 1848; Hist. Revelations, Chap. 14, p. 318-42 passim. Blanc wrote this English-language account a year before his French version, which was expanded as a whole but not in respect to this episode, which is told in virtually the same way in the French (Vol. 2, Chap. 16).

12. THE SUCR EPISODE

1. For information on the physical appearance of the document, see New Mega I, 10:1080f. Of the seven copies, four are held by the Moscow IML, three by the Amsterdam IISH. The New Mega description, which we are following here, does not state flatly that the handwriting is Willich's but qualifies with *vermutlich*.
2. My translation has been made from the original French text in New Mega I, 10:568. (Cf. MECW 10:614f; MEW 7:553f.) This original text can also be found in *Unter dem Banner des Marxismus*, Jg.II, Heft 1/2 (4/5), March 1928, p. 141f, and in *Revue Marxiste* (Paris), No. 4, May 1929. It was first published, by Ryazanov, in the Russian *Bulletin* of the Marx-Engels Institute, Moscow-Leningrad, 1926, No. 1, p. 5-11. A facsimile of the original document was published in *Das Kommunistische Manifest*, an edition edited by Hermann Duncker (Berlin: VIVA, 1927), p. 73.
3. Mayer: F.E., Eine Biographie, 2:9; English edition, 135.
4. "Marx-Engels et le Blanquisme," in *Cahiers du Bolchévisme* (Paris), Numéro Spécial, March 14, 1933, p. 451f. This erroneous text was quoted by Dommanget (see note 7 below), 379, and by Plotkin in the otherwise valuable article cited here (see note 12 below), 120; then quoted from Plotkin in McLellan's *Karl Marx*, 235. Nicolaievsky & M.-H.: Karl Marx, 209, is odd in that it quotes the French original correctly but mistranslates into English.
5. On Harney and the Fraternal Democrats, see also Chap. 9, p. 141.
6. Ltr, E to Dronke, July 9, 1851, in MEW 27:561.
7. Dommanget: Idées Polit. et Soc., 381; supplemented by information from Maitron's DBMOF.
8. S. Bernstein: Review of Jellinek, in *Science & Society*, Summer, 1938, p. 426.
9. Rosenberg: Democracy and Socialism, 140f.
10. For the mention of Paul de Flotte, see Chap. 9, Sec. 3, p. 129.
11. Dommanget: Idées Polit. et Soc., 382f.
12. Plotkin: Alliances des Blanquistes..., 116-19.
13. For Ménard, see MECW 10:289; New Mega I, 10:264, 872-75.
14. Dommanget: Idées Polit. et Soc., 382.
15. See Chap. 9, Sec. 6, p. 141.
16. See Chap. 2, Sec. 4, p. 40, and especially Special Note B, Sec. 4, p. 356f.
17. ME: Address to the CL in June 1850, in MECW 10:371f; M: Herr Vogt, in MEW 14:435, 453f [MECW 17:75, 94f]. See also the notes in MECW 10:682 n. 271 and 17:546 n. 72.

18. ME: Address to the CL in June 1850, in MECW 10:376f.
19. M: Herr Vogt, in MECW 17:219. The old *Karl Marx Chronik,* 89, refers also to two sources inaccessible to me: *Norddeutsche Freie Presse,* Apr. 19, 1850, and the Vienna governmental archives, "H.P.-Akten ex 1850. Hamb. 26 IV."
20. Bertrand: Histoire ..., Vol. 2, Chap. 3.
21. Ltr, M to Freiligrath, Jan. 11, 1850, in MECW 38:225 [MEW 27:521, letter dated Jan. 10].
22. New Mega I, 10:562, 1073; see also last note on 1072. Cf. MECW 10:607, 706 n.430.
23. These four are named in the note, New Mega I, 10:1073.
24. New Mega I, 10:566, 1077; MECW 10:611, 706 n. 431.
25. Rumyantseva: Konrad Schramm, in Kandel, ed.: M&E und die ersten prol. Rev., 408f.
26. Ibid., 411.
27. Written by Sebastian Seiler; published in *Die Hornisse* (Cassel), Apr. 17, 1850; qu. in New Mega I, 10:1076. Cf. the paraphrase in MEW 7:642 which inserts the words "Marx's idea of..."; but these words are not in the newspaper report.
28. *Democratic Review,* May 1850; qu. in New Mega I, 10:1077.
29. See below, Sec. 5, p. 207.
30. On the political nature of the Blanquist tendency, see Chap. 9, Sec. 2, p. 125, and its ref. note 18.
31. Translated from the French original in New Mega III, 3:79, or ME: Corr. (Fr.) 2:59. Cf. also MECW 38:235; MEW 27:532.
32. Ltr, E to Schabelitz, Dec. 22, 1849, in MECW 38:222 [MEW 27:519; New Mega III, 3:56].
33. See Chap. 10, Sec. 6.
34. Ltr, Barthèlemy et al. to ME, Oct. 7, 1850, in New Mega III, 3:654; this is the first publication of the complete French text.
35. New Mega III, 3:89 or (with slight differences) MECW 10:484 [MEW 7:415].
36. The list of such changes is given in New Mega III, 3:874.
37. See KMTR 2:603-06.
38. Minutes of the CC of the CL, session of Sept. 15, 1850, in MECW 10:626f [MEW 8:598f].
39. See KMTR 2:208n, 214n, 592, 602f, 605, 610-12. See also below, Special Note B, Sec. 4.
40. Nicolaievsky & M.-H.: Karl Marx, 208.
41. Ibid., 209.
42. See Special Note B, Sec. 3, p. 352f.
43. Nicolaievsky & M.-H., 210.
44. See above, Sec. 1, p. 186.
45. Lehning: International Association, 199.
46. Schraepler: Handwerkerbünde, 372. On Schraepler, see also Special Note B, Sec. 5.
47. Hunt: Polit. Ideas of M&E, 1:249.
48. ME: Address to the CL in June 1850, in MECW 10:371 [MEW 7:306].
49. See this chapter, Sec. 2, p. 192.
50. Nicolaievsky & M.-H., 209.
51. ME: Address to the CL in June 1850, in MEW 7:312 [MECW 10:377].
52. Wolfe: Marxism, 177, also 153 fn.
53. See Special Note B, Sec. 3, p. 352f.
54. Ltrs, Barthèlemy to Blanqui, July 4, 1850, and Vidil to Blanqui, July 19, 1850: originals in Blanqui papers; qu. in Dommanget: Idèes Polit. et Soc., 383f, and in Plotkin: Alliances, 120. Dommanget's citation, which is fuller, is followed here.

55. Dommanget: Idées Polit. et Soc., 378.
56. This was the formulation in the French edition of the biography by Nicolaievsky & M.-H., clearer than the phrase used in the English edition: "international militant alliance" (p. 208).
57. New Mega III, 3:326-58; Bund d. Kom., 2:155-94.
58. New Mega I, 10:1080.
59. Ltr, Bruhn to Schramm, May 2, 1850, in Bund d. Kom., 2:173.
60. Ltr, W. Pieper, to E, Dec. 16, 1850, in New Mega III, 3:702.
61. Ltr, M to E, Dec. 2, 1850, in MECW 38:246-49.
62. New Mega I, 10:1081.
63. Plotkin: Alliances des Blanquistes, 120.
64. McLellan: Karl Marx, 236.
65. Schraepler: Handwerkerbünde, 372; Hunt: Polit. Ideas, 249.
66. See this chapter, Sec. 1, p. 187.
67. Re confidants, see ltr, Schramm to M, Sept. 9, 1850, New Mega III, 3:633, 1355. Re duels, see M: Knight of the Noble Consc., in MECW 12:492-96. Re Barthélemy as second, see Liebknecht's memoirs, in *Remin. M&E*, 113, or Liebknecht: Biog. Mem., 106f.
68. See Dommanget: Idées Polit. et Soc., 385; see also ltr, M to Becker, Feb. 28, 1851, in MEW 27:546 [MECW 38:310].
69. See this chapter, Sec. 1, p. 185f.
70. M: Revelations Conc. the Com. Trial, in MECW 11:445 [MEW 8:456f].
71. Nicolaievsky & M.-H.: Karl Marx (revised edition), 460 n. 16. (These notes, added to this new edition, are by various hands; individual notes unsigned.)
72. For the use of the term in Marx's "On the Jewish Question," see KMTR 2:594, also 592; for the 1850 usages, see ibid., 253, 263.
73. Draper: M. and the Dict. of the Prol., 34, 36.

13. REVERBERATIONS IN 1850: THE *NDZ* EXCHANGE

1. E: Ten Hours' Question, in MECW 10:275.
2. Ibid., 276.
3. E: English Ten Hours' Bill, in MECW 10:298 [MEW 7:241].
4. Schraepler: Handwerkerbünde, 374.
5. According to New Mega I, 10:1175, date unspecified.
6. E: Rapid Progress of Communism, in MECW 4:232; see also 240.
7. Ltr, Weydemeyer to M, Apr. 30, 1846, in New Mega III, 1:533.
8. On Kriege, see KMTR 2:154, 419-22; see also the mention, above, in Chap. 10, Sec. 1, p. 147, and Sec. 2, p. 148f.
9. See the ed notes in MECW 38:580 n. 94 and New Mega III, 2:643; and see E: True Socialists, in MECW 5:543.
10. Goethe, "Totalität."
11. Ltr, E to M, Sept. 18, 1846, in MEW 27:47f [MECW 38:68 has a bad trans.].
12. E: True Socialists, in MECW 5:541f.
13. The critique of Grün was part of the unpublished ms of the *German Ideology*, Vol. 2, Chap. 4; see MECW 5:484.
14. E.g., Obermann: Joseph Weydemeyer, 77.
15. Ltr, Lüning to M, July 16, 1847, in New Mega III, 2:346f.
16. Ltr, Weydemeyer to M, June 15, 1850, in New Mega III, 3:564.

Notes to Pages 219-231   407

17. Ltr, Dronke to E, Feb. 21, 1850, in New Mega III, 3:485.
18. Ltr, Dronke to E, May ca. 7, 1850, ibid., 541. Cf. also Marx's reference to "philistine Lüning," ltr to Weydemeyer, Apr. 30, 1852, in MECW 39:97 [MEW 28:520].
19. Ltr, M to Weydemeyer, June 8, 1850, in MECW 38:237 [MEW 27:534].
20. See note 16 above.
21. Mrs. Jenny M to Weydemeyer, June ca. 20, 1850, in MEW 27:611 [MECW 38:559f].
22. *Neue Deutsche Zeitung,* June 22, 23, 25, 26, 1850.
23. Ltr, M to Weydemeyer, June 27, 1850, in MEW 27:535 [MECW 38:238].
24. Ltr, Dronke to E, July 3, 1850, in New Mega III, 3:573. See also Dronke's report to the CC/CL, July 3, 1850, ibid., 574.
25. Ltr, Weydemeyer to M, July 3, 1850, in New Mega III, 3:582.
26. On the reference to the *Abendpost,* see MECW 10:694 n. 346.
27. Engels' work is entitled 'The Campaign for the German Imperial Constitution" in MECW 10:147.
28. The reference is to ME: Circular Letter of Sept. 17-18, 1879, section on "The Manifesto of the Three Zurichers," in MEW 34:401.
29. The typographical error is noted in Andréas: Le Manifeste Communiste de M et E, 330, item 196; in the appendix, see facsimile of first edition, p. 16.
30. For E's statement, see MEW 7:324 [MECW 10:388].
31. For locus 1c, see Chap. 11, Sec. 2, p. 180.
32. See Chap. 8, p. 114. For the standard (Moore-Engels) translation of this passage, see MECW 6:505f or MESW 1:127.
33. M: Poverty of Philosophy, in MECW 6:212.
34. Cited from photocopy of *NDZ* (see footnote, p. 221). The rest of Lüning's rejoinder dealt with Engels' statement.
35. Ltr, Weydemeyer to M, July 3, 1850, in New Mega III, 3:582.

14. MORE REVERBERATIONS

1. Ltr, Miquel to M, summer 1850, in New Mega III, 3:592f.
2. Mommsen: J.M., 1:49, 40f, 51.
3. The title page read, after the title: "Von Tellering. Cöln, 1850. Gedruckt auf Kosten und im Selbstverlage des Verfassers" (By Tellering. Cologne, 1850. Self-published by the author at his own expense). There were 32 pages. Only one copy is known to exist, held by the Amsterdam IISH.
4. See, for ex., M: Herr Vogt, in MECW 17:69, 312f.
5. See note, MECW 6:680 n. 124.
6. For E's articles, see MECW 6:291; for M's essay, ibid., 312.
7. Schapper (probable author): Einleitung, in *Kommunistische Zeitschrift,* trial number, Sept. 1847, reprinted in Bund d. Kom., 1:507.
8. Heinzen: Die Helden des teutschen Kommunismus, 98; qu. in Grünberg, ed.: Londoner Kommunistische Zeitschrift [etc.], 44 fn.
9. Ltr, E to V. Adler, Jan 9, 1895, in MEW 39:372.
10. Ibid.
11. Besides Tellering's pamphlet, see ltr, E to Müller-Tellering, Feb. 7, 1850, in MEW 27:522 [MECW 38:227f]; M to same, Mar. 12, 1850, in MEW 27:525f [MECW 38:229f]; see also note, MEW 27:675 n. 407.

12. Ltr, M to Müller-Tellering. Jan. 1, 1850, in MEW 27:520 [MECW 38:223].
13. Ltr, E to Weydemeyer, Apr. 25, 1850, in MEW 27:530f [MECW 38:234].
14. W.B.: Eduard von M.-T., 178.
15. Müller-Tellering: Vorgeschmack, 19.
16. Ltr, M to Weydemeyer, Apr. 30, 1852, in MEW 28:519 [MECW 39:96].
17. Ltr, M to Cluss, mid-May 1852, in MEW 28:521 (MECW 39:105].
18. See above, Chap. 10, p. 166.
19. Minutes of CC/CL, Sept. 15, 1850, in MEW 8:599 [MECW 10:628].
20. See Chap. 10, Sec. 6.
21. M: Revelations Conc. the Com. Trial, especially Chap. 6, in MECW 11:445.
22. Drahn, 27f for the intro. to the documents, which are on p. 28f and 30-34.
23. Forderungen des Volkes (1850-51), in Drahn, 28f.
24. For the Manifesto, see MECW 6:485; E: Condition of the Working Class in England, in MECW 4:468; in M: Capital, Chap. 13.
25. Verhaltungsmassregeln für den Bund vor, während und nach der Revolution, (B) Massregeln beim Ausbruch und während der Revolution; in Drahn, 30-34.
26. Ltr, M to E, Feb. 10, 1851, in MEW 27:183 [MECW 38:284].
27. Ltr, M to E, Mar. 31,1851, in MEW 27:226 [MECW 38:323].
28. On the fate of these letters, see the note in Easton: August Willich, M and Left-Hegelian Socialism, 116 fn.
29. Ltr, E to M, Mar. 19, 1851, in MEW 27:222 [MECW 38:320].
30. Ltr, E to Dronke, July 9, 1851, in MEW 27:561 [MECW 38:382].
31. M: Knight of the Noble Consc., in MECW 12:504 [MEW 9:514]. See also Engels' statement, ibid., 500 [490f].
32. M: Herr Vogt, in MEW 14:443 [MECW 17:83].
33. E: On Hist of the CL, in MESW 3:186.
34. See Chap. 12, Sec. 2, p. 192.
35. Umrisse des kommenden Kriegs; in *New-Yorker Staatszeitung,* Sept. 6, 1851.
36. Ltr, M to E, Sept. 23, 1851, in MEW 27:348 [MECW 38:464].
37. Ibid., 350f[466f].
38. Ltr, E to M, Sept. 26, 1851, in MEW 27:353 [MECW 38:469f].
39. On Eccarius' relations with Marx, see KMTR 2:644-46.
40. Eccarius: The Last Stage of Bourgeois Society, in New Mega I, 10:639.
41. In this connection, see KMTR 1:403f.
42. Ltr, M to E, Dec. 9, 1851, in MEW 27:384 [MECW 38:508]. For a previous reference to this passage, see Chap. 6, Sec. 5, p. 88.
43. Ltr, E to M, Dec. 10, 1851, in MEW 27:385f [MECW 38:509].
44. Proudhon: Idée Générale, page v-vii.
45. Ibid., page vi.
46. Ltr, E to M, Dec. 11, 1851, in MEW 27:387 [MECW 38:511].
47. Proudhon: Idée Générale, 182, repeated on 186f.
48. Proudhon: Carnets, 4:118, dated Dec. 7, 1850.
49. E: Real Causes [etc.], in *Notes to the People,* No. 50 (Vol. 2, p. 977), Apr. 10, 1852. (MECW 11:218 here follows the deplorable practice of silently "correcting" the language of the original.)

15. FROM WEYDEMEYER TO VOGT

1. See Chap. 13, Sec. 2, p. 216.
2. For Weydemeyer's life, see Obermann: Joseph Weydemeyer (which unfortunately reads like a long note in the *Great Soviet Encyclopedia*) and the sketch by Pospelova in Kandel, ed.: M&E u. d. erst. prol. Rev., 261.
3. Andreas: Le Manifeste Communiste [etc.], 30.
4. Ltr, M to Weydemeyer, Oct. 16, 1851, in MECW 38:481 [MEW 27:5811].
5. Andréas: Le Manifeste Communiste [etc.], 31.
6. For the Eccarius syndrome, see KMTR 2:650 fn.
7. See Chap. 3, Sec. 1, p. 46.
8. See MECW 39:25-52 passim, and the notes, ibid., 603-04 n. 55, 66.
9. Ltr, M to Weydemeyer, Mar. 5, 1852, in MEW 28:508 [MECW 39:65].
10. Ibid., 507f[62f].
11. For Cluss's article, see MECW 12:627; cf. notes, MEW 28:701 n. 310 and MECW 39:607 n. 88.
12. See Chap. 8, Sec. 1.
13. See Chap. 12, Sec. 6.
14. For a summary, see Mehring: Karl Marx, 307-09, 312-24, or McLellan: K.M., 310-15.
15. McLellan: Karl Marx, 315.
16. Vogt: Mein Prozess, preface; see also p. 138f, 140, 183.
17. Qu. in M: Herr Vogt, in MEW 14:389 [MECW 17:28].
18. Vogt: Mein Prozess, 136.
19. M: Herr Vogt, in MEW 14:615 [MECW 17:260].
20. Qu. in M: Herr Vogt, in MEW 14:389 [MECW 17:29]; the passage is in Vogt: Mein Prozess, Part 3, p. 31f.
21. Qu. in M: Herr Vogt, in MEW 14:404 [MECW 17:44].
22. M: Herr Vogt, in MEW 14.548 [MECW 17:191].
23. William Vogt: Vied'un Homme, 124, 125.
24. M: Gatherings from the Press, *Das Volk*, July 16, 1859, in MEW 13:654 [MECW 16:634]. Actually, this is part of a quotation inside the quote from Kinkel.
25. Heinzen: Erlebtes, 2:414, 416.

16. THE MANY DICTATORSHIPS OF MOSES HESS

1. Cornu: M.H. et la Gauche Hégélienne, 105.
2. See KMTR 1:440f.
3. Silberner: M.H., 359.
4. Ibid., 363f, 368.
5. Cf. KMTR 1:640.
6. Ltr, M to E, June 2, 1860, in MEW 30:61.
7. Qu. in Hirsch: Denker und Kämpfer, 93f.
8. Silberner, 369.
9. Ibid., 373.
10. Ibid., 335, 345, 367f.
11. Ibid., 451.
12. Ibid., 453.
13. Ibid., 454.

14. Ibid., 447f.
15. Ibid., 466. Hess's pamphlet was titled: Ober sozial-okonomische Reformen.
16. Ibid., 508.
17. See Chap. 7, Sec. 4, p. 102.
18. Silberner, 519, 522.
19. Ibid., 529f.
20. Ibid., 532.
21. Ibid., 520f.
22. Ibid., 538.
23. Ibid., 368.
24. Ibid., 358 fn.
25. Ibid., 542f.
26. Hess: Rome and Jerusalem, 51.
27. Ibid., 75, 45, 164.
28. Ibid., 48, 50f, 84.
29. Ibid., 74, 57, 59, 61, 74.
30. Ibid., 40, 80, 85, 226.
31. Ibid., 68f, 148.
32. Ibid., 159.
33. Ibid., 167f.
34. Ibid., 168, 169, 259f.
35. Silberner: M.H., 476f, 496-98, 505f.
36. Silberner, 514f; ltr, M to Schweitzer, Jan. 16, 1865, in MEW 31:444.
37. Silberner, 571.
38. Article by Hess published Oct. 10, 1868; qu. in Silberner, 576.
39. Silberner, 586, 579-83.
40. Ibid., 590f.
41. Ibid., 595.
42. Ibid., 633.

17. THE SECOND PERIOD OF THE 'DICTATORSHIP OF THE PROLETARIAT'

1. Ltr, M to Freiligrath, Feb. 29, 1860, in MEW 30:489f.
2. M: Civil War in France, in MESW 2:210, 213, 239.
3. Ibid., 228f.
4. E: Intro. to Marx's Civil War in France, in MESW 2:186 [MEW 22:195f],
5. Ibid., 187 [197].
6. Ltr, M to Beesly, Oct. 19, 1870, in ME: Sel. Corr., 250.
7. Molnar: Declin de la Prem. Intle., 218.
8. E: Bakuninists at Work, in MEW 18:480f.
9. E: Social Ques. in Russia, in MESW 2:396 [MEW 18:566].
10. Ibid., 398 [567].
11. Ltr, E to Becker, Dec. 12, 1878, in MEW 34:366.
12. H.: Karl Marx. Interview... (*Chi. Daily Tribune* of Jan. 5, 1879), pamphlet reprint, p. 24.
13. Ltr, E to Bernstein, Aug. 27, 1883, in MEW 36:55.
14. Ltr, E to Bebel, June 6, 1884, in MEW 36:160.
15. Ltr, E to Lafargue, May 19, 1891, in E & Lafargues: Corr. 3:66 (French edition, 3: 54f).

16. Ltr, E to Laura Lafargue, May 3, 1892, ibid., 3:172.
17. Ltr, M to Freiligrath, Feb. 29, 1860, in MEW 30:490.
18. Ibid., 495.
19. M: Civil War in France, in MESW 2:219f, 223.
20. Ltr, M to Domela Nieuwenhuis, Feb. 22, 1881, in MEW 35:160.
21. Look back, for example, to Engels in 1850: see Chap. 10, Sec. 7, p. 164.
22. Arendt: On Revolution, 261 and note on 324. The passage she quotes from Marx can be found at MEW 7:252 [MECW 10:285 or MESW 1:183].
23. This point is emphasized in KMTR 2:38f, 358, and elsewhere; see also above, Chap. 8, p. 113.
24. See KMTR 2:392-95.
25. See Chap. 8, p. 113; Chap. 11, Sec. 2, p. 180.
26. M: Civil War in France, in MESW 2:224, 226, 220, 222.
27. M: First Draft, in ME: Writ. on Par. Com., 162.
28. Ibid., 146, 151, 159f; Second Draft, 190.
29. Ibid. (First Draft), 151.
30. Lichtheim: Marxism, 118f.
31. M: Civil War in France, in MESW 2:219-28 passim.
32. Ibid., 221.
33. Ibid., 223, 227.
34. M: First Draft, in ME: Writ. on Par. Com., 130.
35. Ibid., 147, on National Guard; on Versailles Assembly, see 107, 115-18, 132-36, 145, 186f; on related matters, see also 152-54, 160f.
36. See Chap. 8, p. 113.
37. E: Program of the Blanquist Ref., in MEW 18:529 [MESW 2:381].
38. Da Costa: Les Blanquistes, 33.
39. Ibid., 34.
40. Ibid., 37f.
41. Cole: Hist. of Socialist Thought, 2:166.
42. Dommanget: Blanqui (1924), 27 fn; Mason: Blanqui and Communism, 509.
43. G. Da Costa: La Commune Vécue, 1:312, 326f, 252, 3-37.
44. From the debate in the Commune, as quoted in Edwards: Communards of Paris, 87, 89.
45. Koechlin: Die Pariser Commune, 125f.
46. Lissagaray: Hist. of the Commune, 243.
47. Qu. in Edwards: Communards of Paris, 92.
48. Qu. in Lissagaray, 287; also in Edwards, 93f.
49. M: Notebook on Paris Commune, Press Excerpts, Apr.-May, 150.

18. MARX AND THE BLANQUISTS AFTER THE COMMUNE

1. Da Costa: Les Blanquistes, 17.
2. Ibid., 18f. See above, Chap. 9, Sec. 2, p. 126.
3. S. Bernstein: A. Blanqui, 293.
4. Ibid., 303-05.
5. Ltr, M to E, Sept. 25, 1868, in MEW 32:165.
6. See the summary of Blanqui's views on this point in S. Bernstein: A. Blanqui, 305-07.
7. For these changes, see MECW 11:110n and 183n. Neither MEW nor MESW takes note of the edition changes.

8. M: Preface to Eighteenth Brumaire, in MESW 1:395.
9. E: Program of the Blanquist Ref., in MEW 18:529 [MESW 2:381].
10. For a little-known account of Marx's refugee-aid work, see Czobel & Kahn, Part 2, p. 31 on.
11. Dommanget: Idées Polit. et Soc., 393f.
12. Ibid., 171.
13. E: Intro. to Marx's Civil War in France, in MESW 2:186.
14. See Dommanget: Idées Polit. et Soc., 391, 395f, and editor's Afterword in E & Lafargues: Corr. 3:497.
15. Dommanget: Les Blanquistes dans l'Intle., 142.
16. Longuet: Marx et la Commune, 71.
17. See the Biblio. under title.
18. This pamphlet is given in full in Da Costa: Les Blanquistes, 44-51; also in Louise Michel: La Commune, 413-23, where it is dated.
19. Ltr, E to Sorge, Nov. 16, 1872, in MEW 33:538.
20. See locus 7a, Chap. 19, p. 297.
21. On Postgate, see Chap. 2, Sec. 3, p. 36f.
22. E: Program of the Blanquist Ref., in MEW 18:532, 534f [MESW 2:384, 386].
23. Internationale et Révolution, 5.
24. Qu. in Guillaume: l'Internationale, 2:328.
25. Qu. in Da Costa: Les Blanquistes, 48f.
26. Internationale et Révolution, 11.
27. Cluseret: Intle. et la Dictature, 7-8.
28. Maitron, ed.: Dict. Biog. du M.O.F., Vol. 5; New Mega I, 22:1497 (Index).
29. Ltr, M to Sorge, May 29, 1872, in MEW 33:481.
30. For the full title and data, see Biblio.
31. A la Classe Ouvrière, 11.
32. Ibid., 14.

19. MARX AND ENGELS IN THE SECOND PERIOD

1. Karl Marx, Chronik seines Lebens, 450.
2. Ltr, Vermersch to Vuillaume, Sept. 4, 1873, in Vuillaume, 57f.
3. Ltr, E to Liebknecht, Dec. 15, 1871, in MEW 33:360.
4. Same, Nov. 4, 1871, in MEW 33:306. For more, see also MEW 33:344f, 377, 688.
5. E: Program of the Blanquist Ref., in MEW 18:530 [MESW 2:382].
6. Ltr, Guillaume to Jeanneret, Jan. 17, 1872, in Jeanneret: La Correspondance du Peintre G. Jeanneret (see Biblio.).
7. For this letter, see the article on Vermersch in Maitron's DBMOF, 9:299.
8. Vermersch: La Dictature, especially p. 5, 4, 8.
9. Ibid., especially p. 13, 15f.
10. Vermersch: La Société Secrète, 14f. (Incidentally, Maitron's DBMOF is mistaken in stating that this pamphlet was planned but never published.) For the International's exposé, see ME: Alliance of the Soc. Dem. [etc.].
11. Vermersch: Le Droit au Vol, 16.
12. Citations here are from the English original as reprinted, with my intro., in *New Politics*, summer 1963, 130-32 [MEW 17:432f].
13. Ltr, Jenny Marx (Mrs. Longuet) to Kugelmann, Oct. 3, 1871, repr. in English original in *Labour Monthly*, Mar. 1957, "Marx Family Letters," p. 127 [MEW 33:683].

14. See note 12 above.
15. Venturi: Roots of Revolution, 453f.
16. M: Indifference to Political Affairs, in ME: Scritti Italiani, 99 [MEW 18:300].
17. See Chap. 11, Sec. I, p. 175.
18. Puech: Le Proudhonisme dans l'A.I.T., 139; the quotation is from Puech's paraphrase.
19. Testut: Le Livre Bleu, 225.
20. See Chap. 18, p. 283.
21. E: Housing Question, in MEW 18:266 rev. from MESW 2:355.
22. Ibid., MEW 18:267f rev. from MESW 2:356.
23. On the Chartists, see Chap. 8, Sec. 2, p. 114.
24. E: Housing Question, in MEW 18:282 [MESW 2:370].
25. For the original publication, see *Gosudarstvennost i Anarkhiya* (Biblio.); it is cited here from the *Archives Bakountne* (French version). In the notes below, the pagination of the first edition is given in parentheses after that of the new edition.
26. M: Conspect on Bakunin's Book, in MEW 18:597-642.
27. See Chap. 7, Sec. I, p. 93f.
28. Bakunin: Statism and Anarchy, 312f (215).
29. In Bakunin, op. cit, 346 (279), translated from the French version. In M: Conspect, in MEW 18:635.
30. In Bakunin, op. cit., 347 (280). In M: Conspect, MEW 18:636.
31. M: Conspect, in MEW 18:636.
32. In Bakunin, op. cit., 346 (248). In M: Conspect, MEW 18:630.
33. M: Conspect, in MEW 18:630.
34. Ibid., 634.
35. In Bakunin, op. cit., 346 (2780- In M: Conspect, MEW 18:634. Bakunin's wording is slightly different from the paraphrase but the sense is the same.
36. In Bakunin, op. cit., 346 (2780.
37. On the Blanquist pamphlet, see Chap. 18, Sec. 3, p. 283 and Sec. 4, p. 285f.
38. For passages from the article, see the following end-notes: Chap. 9. note 41; Chap. 10, note 1,29; Chap. 18, note 9,22; Chap. 19, note 5.
39. A defective translation, quite inaccessible, appeared in the "Enlarged Edition" of M's *Civil War in Frame* published by Kerr in 1934.
40. E: Program of the Blanquist Ref., in MEW 18:529 [MESW 2:381].
41. Ibid.
42. M: Critique of the Gotha Program, in MEW 19:27 [MESW 3:25].
43. Ibid., 31 [28].
44. Ibid., 28 [25].
45. Ibid., 28 [26].
46. Ibid.,29f[27].
47. This is the translation in MESW 3:26.
48. M: Critique of the Gotha Program, in MEW 19:29 [MESW 3:27].

20. THE THIRD PERIOD OF THE 'DICTATORSHIP OF THE PROLETARIAT'

1. Bottigelli's intro. to the Engels/Lafargues Correspondence in the French edition (I :xxiii) is here cited from the English edition, 3:503, where it is printed as an Afterword.
2. Ibid., 3:503 (French ed., l:xxii).

3. Lafargue: Parliamentarianism and Boulangism, reprinted in *Labour Monthly*, 375.
4. Ibid., 377.
5. Ltr, E to Kautsky, Dec. 13, 1890, in MEW 37:522; see also ltr, E to Frankel, Dec. 25, 1890, in MEW 37:531.
6. Ltr, E to Schmidt, Oct. 27, 1890, in MEW 37:493 [MESW 3:494j.
7. See, for ex., ltr, E to Kautsky, Feb. 11,1891, in MEW 38:34.
8. Ltr, E to Sorge, Jan. 17,1891, in MEW 38:12.
9. Ltr, E to Kautsky, Feb. 23,1891, in MEW 38:40,41.
10. Ltr, M to Sorge, Sept. 19,1879, in MEW 34:413f.
11. Ltr, E to Lafargue, Feb. 10,1891, in E/Lafargues: Corr. 3:29f.
12. Steno. Berichte/V.d.R., Feb. 28, 1891, p. 1798.
13. Ibid., 1805.
14. Steno. Berichte/V.d.R., Apr. 21,1891, p. 2475f.
15. Ibid., 2475.
16. Dominick: W. Liebknecht, 401; see also similar statement on 243, unreferenced however.
17. W. Liebknecht: No Compromise [etc.], in *On the Political Position of Social-Democracy*, 78f.
18. E: Intro, to M's Class Struggles in France, in MESW 2:186 (MEW 22:196].
19. Ibid., 187 [197].
20. Ibid.
21. See Chap. 2, Sec. 3, p. 39.
22. See Chap. 17, Sec. 2.
23. E: Intro, to Ms Class Struggles in France, in MESW 2:187f [MEW 22:197f).
24. Ibid., 188 [198].
25. Ibid., 189(199).
26. Ibid., 189, slightly revised after MEW 22:199.
27. Ltr, E to Kautsky, June 29,1891, in MEW 38:125.
28. E: Critique of the Erfurt Program, in MEW 22:234 [MESW 3:434].
29. Ibid., 235 [435].
30. Cf. Jaurès: Etudes Socialistes, Preface, p. LXIV.
31. Guerin: Luttes de Classes sous la Prem. Rép, 1:40; see also 1:38–41 and 2:4f, 6f footnote. Guerin repeated the idea in *his Jeunesse du Socialisms Lib.*, 38.
32. See, for ex., Special Note C, Sec. 1.
33. See the minutes of Jan. 23 and June 4,1872, in GCFI 5:87, 215.
34. Ltr, M to Weydemeyer, Mar. 5, 1852, in MEW 28:504.
35. Ltr, E to M, Sept. 26, 1851, in MEW 27:353 or MECW 38:470.
36. Jaures: Etudes Socialistes, page LXIII; Guerin: Jeunesse du Socialisme Lib., 38 fn.
37. Lenin: State and Revolution, in his Coll. Wks., 25:445.
38. Lenin: On the Slogan for a U.S. of Europe, ibid., 21:342.
39. M: Critique of the Gotha Program, in MEW 19:29 [MESW 3:27].
40. E: Reply to G. Bovio, in ME: Corrisp. con Ital., 414 [MEW 22:280].
41. E: Future Ital. Revolution, in ME: Corrisp. con Ital., 519 [MESW 3:455; MEW 22:441].
42. Johnstone, 461. The quotation is from my article, "The Death of the State in M&E," 301.
43. E: Critique of the Erfurt Program, in MEW 22:235 [MESW 3:435].
44. The selections from Voden's "Talks with Engels" in *Reminiscences of M&E*, 325-34, comprise excerpts from Voden's article "At the Dawn of 'Legal Marxism'" published in the journal *Letopisi Marksizma*, No. 4,1927, but they do *not* include the passage quoted here; they are interesting for background.

45. Voden: Na zare "Legalnogo Marksizma," 94f; translation from the Russian by Ernest Haberkern of the Center for Socialist History.

SPECIAL NOTE A.
MARXOLOGISTS AT WORK

1. For my comments on this aspect, see Foreword, KMTR 1:20f.
2. Lenin: State and Revolution, in his Coll. Wks., 25:402.
3. Short title for Lenin's brochure: The Proletarian Revolution and the Renegade Kautsky.
4. Lenin: Proi. Rev. and Reneg. K., in his Coll. Wks., 28:233.
5. Lenin: Two Tactics [etc.], in his Coll. Wks., 9:130-40.
6. For these Marx articles, see Chap. 4, Sec. 3.
7. Kautsky: Diet. of the Proletariat, 42-44,140, trans, slightly revised.
8. Kautsky: Soc. Democracy vs. Com., 38-40.
9. For the writings by these two men, see Biblio. Hillquit's book *From Marx to Lenin* was the most important social-democratic treatment of the question. Both of these contributions will be discussed in another work (see Foreword).
10. Diehl,44.
11. Ibid., 46.
12. Avineri; Soc. & Polit. Thought of K.M., 204.
13. The first reading is given by Berlin's 2d edition, p. 172-74, the second reading by the 4th edition, p. 137-39.
14. Calvez,498f.
15. Carr: Bolshevik Revolution 1917-1923,1:151,235.
16. Carr: Karl Marx, 82 fn.
17. Caute, ed.: Essential Writings of K.M., 217,220.
18. See Chap. 2, Sec. 3.
19. Cole: Hist, of Socialist Thought, 2:250.
20. Duncan: Marx and Mill, 179, 170.
21. Fetscher, ed.: Grundbegriffe [etc.], 105-07; see Special Note D, Sec. 2.
22. Gay: Dilemma of Dem. Socialism, 248.
23. See end of Chap. 6, p. 91.
24. Hook: Marx and the Marxists, 33.
25. R. N. C. Hunt: Marxism, Past and Present, 141-43. Hunt: Guide to Communist Jargon, 62, makes a similar statement but omits Engels.
26. R. N. C. Hunt: Theory and Practice of Com., 72.
27. Encyclopaedia of the Social Sciences, 14:202.
28. Landauer: European Socialism, 1:168; see also 169-72.
29. See Special Note D, Sec. 5, p. 380.
30. Leff: Tyranny of Concepts, 177.
31. Lichtheim: Marxism, 124,87,372; cf. also 125-28.
32. McLellan: Thought of K.M., 202.
33. Sanderson: Interp. of the Polit. Ideas [etc.], 86,98 (these are the bare mentions).
34. Schapiro: CPSU, 205.
35. rime, Feb. 23,1948, p. 32.
36. Marx: The Gotha Program [and] "Did Marx Err?" by De Leon; first printing 1922, by Natl. Exec. Com. of SLP. This statement is on p. 7.

SPECIAL NOTE B.
FABRICATION OF A FABLE:
THE "MARX-BLANQUIST" MYTH

1. See especially Chap. 2, Sec. 3; Chaps. 9-10; Chap. 17,Sec. 1;Chap. 18.
2. Hook: Towards the Und. of K.M., 43 fn.
3. See the Bibliography under Bernstein.
4. Gay: Dilemma of Dem. Socialism, 314 (where the English edition is listed).
5. M: Zur Kritik der Hegelschen Rechtsphilosophie— Einleitung, in MEW 1:378 + or MECW 3.175+.
6. Spitzer, 166,67,102.
7. Bernstein: Voraussetzungen [etc.], 28f.
8. Ibid., 28.
9. 11 is from Marx's speech at the Sept. 15,1850 split meeting of the CC/CL, quoted in Chap. 10, Sec. 7, p. 166.
10. Bernstein: Voraussetzungen [etc.], 29.
11. Marx's formulation: " it is our interest and our task to make the revolution permanent, until..." (MEW 7:247for MECW 10:281).
12. Gay: Dilemma of Dem. Socialism, 223f.
13. Bernstein: Voraussetzungen [etc.], 29.
14. In the Biblio., see Deville: Gracchus Babeuf und die Verschwörung der Gleichen.
15. ME: Com. Manifesto, Sec. III, 2 (MEW 4:489 or MECW 6:514).
16. Ibid.
17. A page of Marx's Draft Plan for Section III is extant; see MECW 6:576.
18. M: Com. Manifesto, Sec. II (MEW 4:481 or MECW 6:505).
19. See Chap. 9, Sec. 2 (for social composition); Special Note C (on terrorism).
20. Bernstein: Voraussetzungen [etc.], 31.
21. Ltr, M to J. P. Becker, Feb. 26, 1862 (MEW 30:619); cf. KMTR 1:13.
22. Dan: Les Socialistes Russes et la D. du P., 10.
23. Martov: Marx and the D. of the P., 63.
24. Lichtheim: Marxism, 124.
25. See Chap. 12, Sec. 2.
26. Lichtheim: Marxism, 125.
27. Lichtheim: Short History of Socialism, 56.
28. Lichtheim: Marxism, 125.
29. See KMTR 2, Spec. Note E, which is specifically about the March Address.
30. For the references and further details, see KMTR 2:610.
31. Lichtheim: Marxism, 125 fn.
32. See note 9 above.
33. Lichtheim: Marxism, 126.
34. For this passage, see MEW 7:250 or MECW 10:283.
35. Lichtheim: Marxism, 127.
36. Re the abandonment of "Communism," see Lichtheim: Origins of Soc, 87, 209; Short Hist, of Soc, 54. Re worker-peasant revolution, see Lichtheim: Origins of Soc, 208.
37. Lichtheim: From Marx to Hegel, 85.
38. For Marx's sally "I am no Marxist," see KMTR 2:5-11.
39. Wolfe: Marxism, 151.
40. See above, Sec. 2, p. 346.
41. Wolfe: Marxism, 153.
42. Ibid., 154.
43. Ibid., 157.

44. Draper: M. and the D. of the P., in *Etudes de Marxologie* (see Biblio.).
45. Wolfe: Marxism, 177.
46. Ibid., 152 (italics added); and cf. also 153, 159, 184; but on 156 Wolfe mentions that Harney was also in SUCR.
47. Ibid., 185.
48. Or perhaps Wolfe picked this falsifiction up from a previous fabricator: I cannot vouch for his priority. The facts involved were laid out in Chap. 12, p. 209f.
49. Wolfe: Marxism, 178.
50. Ibid., 177.
51. SeeKMTR2:591f.
52. The two pages are 153-54.
53. See Chap. 12, Sec. 4, p. 203.
54. See Chap. 12, Sec. 2, p. 188, and Chap. 18, Sec. 2, p. 280f.
55. Simkhovitch: Marxism versus Socialism, 245f.
56. Berlin: Karl Marx, 172.
57. Ibid.
58. Ulam: Unfinished Revolution, 52,157.
59. Branch Cabell: Jurgen (dedication).
60. Nicolaievsky & M. H.: Karl Marx, 209.
61. Ibid., 210.
62. Moore: Three Tactics, 30.
63. Ibid., 29.
64. Ibid., 27.
65. ME: German Ideology, in MEW 3:207 or MECW 5:226.
66. Ibid., MEW 3:448 or MECW 5:461.
67. ME: Holy Family, in MEW 2:139 or MECW 4:131.
68. E: Progress of Social Reform, in MECW 3:396-400. For an example from a later period, see E: On Hist, of Early Christianity, in MEW 22:460.
69. ME: [Review] "Les Conspirateurs [etc.]" in MECW 10:320.
70. ME et al.: Ltr to Cabet (late March 1848), in Bund d. Kom. 1:748 (Frenchoriginal) or M E: Corr. (Fr.) 1:533. (MECW 7:8 is wrong in capitalizing "Communist Party.")— See also ME: Ltr to Cabet, Apr. 5, 1848, in MECW 38:170 or ME: Corr. (Fr.) 1:538.
71. HofTenstein: Poems in Praise of Practically Nothing. From "Songs of Faith in the Year After Next." (Second line has been adapted.)
72. Nicolaievsky & M.-H : Karl Marx, 209.
73. Schraepler: Handwerkerbünde, 373.
74. See above, this Special Note, Sec. 4, p. 354.
75. Schraepler, 373.

SPECIAL NOTE C.
THE MEANING OF'TERROR' AND 'TERRORISM'

1. Hunt: Polit. Ideas of M&E,l:340f.
2. See Chap. 9, Sec. 1,p. 121.
3. E: Cond. of Eng.: 18thCent., in MECW 3:473.
4. For these articles and their views, see KMTR 1:36-59.
5. M: Comments on Latest Pruss. Cens., in MEW 1:14 [MECW 1:119); cf. KMTR 1:45 for context.
6. M: Crit. Notes on Article "King of Prussia [etc. J," in MECW 3:199 [MEW 1:402].

7. Same as note 2 above.
8. ME: Holy Family, in MECW 4:74,95,111,123; and see also 81,119,122,124.
9. Ladendorf: Hist. Schlagwb., 311.
10. ME: Holy Family, in MECW 4:123.
11. E: State of Germany, I, in MECW 6:19.
12. ME: Holy Family, in MECW 4:124.
13. M: Moràlizing Criticism [etc.], in MEW 4:339 [MECW 6:319]. Cf. KMTR 2:184 for context.
14. E: Antwerp Death Sent., *NRZ*, Sept. 3,1848, in MECW 7:405.
15. M: Bourgeoisie and the Counterrevolution, 2d article, *NRZ*, Dec. 15, 1848, in MECW 8:161.
16. Ltr, M to E, Aug. 8,1851, in MECW 38:409; see also Engels' agreement, Aug. 21, ibid., 435.
17. ME: Holy Family, in MECW 4:121f; M: To the Ed. *of People's Paper*, Sept. 4,1853, in MECW 12:291; ltr, M to E, Jan. 30,1865, in MEW 31:48.
18. Ltr, E to M, Sept. 4, 1870, in MEW 33:53.
19. Ltr, E to Kautsky, Feb. 20, 1889, in MEW 37:155f.
20. Ltr, E to V. Adler, Dec. 4,1889, in MEW 37:317.
21. Ibid., 318.
22. Wolfe: Marxism, 20.
23. E: Program of the Blanquist Ref., in MEW 18:534; for context see ME: Writ, on Par. Com., 230.
24. Stein: Hist, of the Social Movement, 90. (For Stein on 'dictatorship', see our Chap. 5, Sec. 3.)
25. Ibid., 146f.
26. M: Rhein- und Mosel-Ztg. as Grand Inquis., *Rh. Ztg.*, Mar. 12, 1843, in MECW 1:372 [MEW 1:433].
27. Ltr, Bauer to M, Mar. 28, 1841, in MEGA I, 1.2:247.
28. Ltr, E to M, Oct. ca. 18,1846, in MECW 38:80; E to CCC, Oct. 23,1846, ibid., 81.
29. E: Ger. Socialism in Verse & Prose, in MECW 6:253 [MEW 4:226].
30. E: The 24th of June, *NRZ*, June 28, 1848, in MECW 7:138 [MEW 5:127].
31. M: Victory of the Counterrevolution in Vienna, *NRZ*, Nov. 7,1848, in MEW 5:457 [MECW 7:5051].
32. E: Magyar Struggle, *NRZ*, Jan. 13,1849, in MECW 8:227.
33. E: Democratic Pan-Slavism, in MECW 8:375, 378 [MEW 6:284,286].
34. E: Defeat of the Piedmontese, *NRZ*, Apr. 1,1849, in MEW 6:389 [MECW 9:173].
35. M: Suppression of the *NRZ*, May 19, 1849, in MEW 6:505 [MECW 9:453].
36. M: Class Struggles in France, in MECW 10:125 [MEW 7:88].
37. ME: Address to the CL, in MECW 10:282,284.
38. Wolfe: Marxism, 154.
39. E: Peasant War in Germany, in MECW 10:472.
40. Ltr, E to M, July ca. 20,1851, in MEW 27:287f [MECW 38:3921]. For the context, see KMTR 2:277,607f.
41. M: Bonaparte's Present Position, *NYDT*, Apr. 1,1858; not yet in MECW.
42. M: Capital (Fowkes' trans.), 1:895 [MEW 23:760f].
43. M: Outline of a Report [etc.] (Dec. 16,1867), MEW 16:449.
44. For M: Civil War in France, see MESW 2:218 or ME: Writ, on Par. Com., 71. For the passages in the drafts, see ME: Writ, on Par. Com., 127, 211,192, and see also 160.
45. E: On Authority, in MESW 2:379 [ME: Scritti Ital., 97; MEW 18:308].

Notes to Pages 375-384   419

SPECIAL NOTE D.
GHOSTS, GOBLINS, AND GARBLES

1. "The Character and Thought of K.M.," in Feuer: Marx and the Intellectuals, 10, 11; see also intro., p. 2.
2. Ibid., 13.
3. Mayer: F.E., A Biography, 159.
4. See Chap. 13, Sec. 1, p. 215.
5. Mayer: F.E., Eine Biographie, 2:68.
6. Fetscher, ed.: Grundbegriffe [etc.], 106.
7. M: Civil War in France, in MESW 2:223, slightly corrected.
8. For this passage (Engels' locus 12), see Chap. 20, Sec. 6.
9. See Chap. 19, Sec. 5, p. 300.
10. Gurvitch: Etudes sur les Classes Sociales, 70f. (Gurvitch's reference is to the *Marx-Engels Arkhiv*, Vol. 4.)
11. M: Writings of the Young Marx, 92. Cf. MECW 1:130; MEW 1:25.
12. See Chap. 2, p. 44 especially.
13. For locus 1c, see Chap. 11, Sec. 2, p. 180; for the text, see MECW 10:127 or MESW 1:282 (English) and MEW 7:89f (German).
14. For ex., see Special Note B, Sec. 3, p. 349; Sec. 4, p. 356.
15. See Chap. 11, Sec. 3.
16. M: Class Struggles in France, in MEW 7:89.
17. Simkhovitch: Marxism vs. Soc, 194 fn.
18. Landauer: European Socialism, 1:168.
19. Draper: M. & the D, of the P.,*Etudes de Marxologie*, 33 fn.
20. M: Class Struggles in France (Marxist Library, Vol. 24, Intl. Pub., n.d. [1935]), 126. For the correct text, see note 13 above.
21. Tucker: Marxian Rev. Idea, 72, 78.
22. Ibid., 79.
23. M: Die Klassenkämpfe in Frankr. (1911), p. 94.—Landauer: European Socialism, 1:168; ref. note on 1:1051 n. 40. This note of Landauer's also confuses Marx's articles in the *NRZ* with Engels' articles in the *NYDT* on "Revolution and Counterrevolution in Germany"; Marx's references to dictatorship were in the former.
24. Miquel's letter is the subject of Chap. 14, Sec. 1.
25. Karl Marx Chronik, 84.
26. E. Bernstein: Die Briefe J. Miquels an K.M., *Neue Zeit*, Apr. 3, 1914.
27. Mommsen:J.M., 1:38-39 fn.
28. New Mega III, 3:1324.
29. Dommanget: Idées Polit. et Soc, 396f.
30. Cf. Chap. 9, Sec. 3.
31. Vaillant, "Propos Blanquistes," in *LeSocialiste* (Paris), Jan. 1-8, 1911, page I.
32. Seilhac: Le Monde Socialistc, 86.
33. Dommanget: Idées Polit. et Soc, 380.
34. Ibid., 115,396.
35. See the footnotes in Chap. 10, pp. 158 and 161.
36. See Chap. 10, p. 158.
37. ME: [Review] "Les Conspirateurs [etc.]," in MEW 7:269 [MECW 10:314].
38. Ibid., MEW 7:271 [MECW 10:316].
39. Ibid., MEW 7:273,274 [MECW 10:318,319].
40. Ibid., MEW 7:273 [MECW 10:318].

BIBLIOGRAPHY
(WORKS CITED)

This list provides bibliographic data for writings referred to in the Reference Notes or in the text.

In the first three sections—writings by Marx & Engels, writings by Marx, writings by Engels—titles are given first in English, followed by the original language (in italics) or by a double degree sign (∞) if the original was in English. Original German titles are usually given as they appear in MEW; the statement "No title" means that the title as given has been conferred by editors, not by M/E. In these three sections, the form of citation is the same for articles, books, or whatever. The following information is provided for individual writings: date of writing (W) or dateline (D); date of first publication by the author (P) or posthumous publication (P/P). The CAPITALIZED titles are for published books, mainly collections of writings, as distinct from individual writings.

In the fourth section of this list (Writings by Others), entries list the edition used in this book. For abbreviations, see the note introducing the Reference Notes; other abbreviations are identified in the Index.

WRITINGS BY MARX & ENGELS

(The symbol M/E = Marx *or* Engels, i.e., authorship not ascribed as between these two.)

Address of the Central Committee to the Communist League, March 1850. *Ansprache der Zentralbehörde an den Bund vom März 1850.* (W) 1850: Mar. (P) Same, as circular to CL members; 1851, in German bourgeois press; 1885, by Engels.

Address of the Central Committee, to the Communist League, June 1850. *Ansprache der Zentralbehörde an den Bund vom Juni 1850.* (W) 1850: ca. beginning of June. (P) Same, as circular CL members; extracts in some German papers; 1885, by Engels.

Address of the German Democratic Communists of Brussels to Mr. Feargus O'Connor.∞ Signed: The Committee, Engels, Ph. Gigot, Marx. (D) 1846: July 17. (P) July 25, in *Northern Star.*

The Alliance of the Socialist Democracy and the International Working Men's Associa-

tion. *L' Alliance de la Dèmocratie Socialist et l'Association Internationale des Travailleurs.* (W) 1873: Apr.-July, mostly by Engels and Lafargue, conclusion by Marx; using material sent in by others. (P) Aug., as a GC pamphlet, no personal signatures.
Arrests. *Verhaftungen.* (D) 1848: July 3; by M/E, authorship not ascribed. (P) July 4, in *NRZ.*
Circular Against Kriege. *Zirkular gegen Kriege.* Signed: by seven names incl. M&E.; no title. (D) 1846: May 11. (P) May, as circular by Communist Correspondence Committee.
Circular Letter to Bebel et al. *Zirkularbriefe an Bebel, Liebknecht, Bracke, u.a.* (W) 1879: Sept. 17-18; n.d. (P/P) 1931.—Drafted by Engels; sent as circular to German party leadership.
COLLECTED WORKS. (Abbrev.: MECW.) Edited by IML (Moscow) in collaboration with Progress Pub. (Moscow), L A W (London), and Intl. Pub. (NY); there are three editorial commissions (Russian, British, American). Volume f was published 1975; 50 volumes are planned, serially numbered but divided into three series: Vols. 1-28 (writings in chronological order); Vols. 29-37 *(Capital* and economica); Vols. 38-50 (correspondence). To date, we have Vols. 1-14, 16-18, 38-39; Volume 15 has so far been skipped, no doubt because of Marx's *Revelations of the Diplomatic History of the 18th Century.*
The Communist Manifesto. *Also & originally* Manifesto of the Communist Party. *Das Kommunistische Manifest.* Or: *Manifest der kommunistischen Partei.*(W) 1847-48: Dec. to last part of Jan.; final form written by M. (P) 1848: Feb. (last half), as pamphlet.
[Communist Manifesto] Draft Plan for Section III. *Planentwurf zum dritten Absehnitt.* (W) 1847: Dec. or next month. (P/P) 1932.
[Communist Manifesto] Preface to the German Edition of 1872. *Vorwort...* (D) 1872: June 24. (P) July, in the edition.
CORRESPONDANCE. Publiee sous la resp. de. G. Badia et J. Mortier. Paris: Editions Sociales, 1971- . Last volume published to date is Tome 10 (1984) covering to June 1870.
LA CORRISPONDENZA DI MARX E ENGELS CON ITALIANI 1848-1895. A cura di G. Del Bo. (Istituto G. Feltrinelli. Testi e Document! di Storia Moderna e Con ternporanea, 11) Milan: Feltrinelli, 1964.
The German Ideology. Critique of the Latest German Philosophy . . . *Die deutsche Ideologie. Kritik der neuesten deutschen Philosophic...* (W) 1845-46: Nov. to Aug.; no title. (P/P) 1932.
GESAMTAUSGABE. For the old *Marx-Engels Gesamtausgabe,* see *MEGA.* For the new edition now being published, see *NEW MEGA.*
The Great Men of the Emigration. *Die grossen Männer des Exits.* (W) 1852: May-June; intended as a brochure. (P/P) 1930 in Russian; 1960 in orig. German.
The Holy Family, or Critique of Critical Critique. Against Bruno Bauer &. Co. *Die heilige Familie, oder Kritik der kritischen Kritik. Gegen Bruno Bauer & Consorten.* (W) 1844: Sept. to Nov.; foreword dated Sept. (P) 1845: Feb. ca. 24, as a book. Signed: by Friedrich Engels & Karl Marx. —Each author wrote separate sections independently, not in collaboration.
Introductory Note [to the leaflet of Blanqui's toast]. *Vorbemerkung [zur deutschen Übersetzung des Toastes von L.-A. Btanqui].* (W) 1851: Mar. 3-6. (P) latter part of Mar., prefacing a flysheet bearing German translation of the "toast" (statement) sent by Blanqui to the so-called Banquet of the Equals.
Letter to Etienne Cabet, and Statement Against the German Democratic Society in Paris. [In French; no.title] (W) 1848: Mar. (P/P) 1940 in Eng.; 1970 in orig. French.
Letter to the Brunswick Committee. *See* next entry.

Letter to the Executive Committee of the Social-Democratic Workers Party. *Brief an den Ausschuss der Sozialdemokratischen Arbeiterpartei.* (W) 1870: Aug. 22-30; n.d. (P) Sept. 5, as a quotation in a leaflet issued by the Executive Committee; Sept. 11, in *Volksstaat.*

Marrast and Thiers. *Marrast und Thiers.* (W) 1848: July 2, by M/E, authorship not ascribed. (P) July 3, in *NRZ*.

MEGA. The title page reads, in full: *Karl Marx / Friedrich Engels / Historisch-kritische Gesamtausgabe/Werke/Schriften/Briefe,* im Auftrage des Marx-Engels-Instituts Moskau [herausgegeben von D. Ryazanov], Marx-Engels-Verlag GMBH, Berlin, 1927-35 (unfinished). Ryazanov's name appeared only on the first volume; Vol. 5 and 7 bore a Moscow-Leningrad imprint. Only seven volumes were published in Series *(Abteilung)* I, offering writings in a chronological order; only four volumes, the letters between M and E themselves, in Series III, the correspondence. Series II was going to be the Economica; Series IV, index volumes. Some volumes consist of two physical volumes *(Halbbände),* for ex., *MEGA* I, 1.1 and 1.2. An unnumbered volume *(Sonderausgabe)* was published in 1935 containing *Anti-Dühring* and *Dialectics of Nature.* Otherwise Series I goes to the end of 1848.

NEW MEGA. (This is our own designation, used to avoid confusion; see also MEGA.) The title page reads: *Karl Marx / Friedrich Engels / Gesamtausgabe / (MEGA),* Hrsg. vom IML beim ZK der KP der Sowjetunion und vom IML beim ZK der SED [Berlin]. Published by: Dietz Verlag Berlin, 1975- (in progress). —There are four series *(Abteilungen)* of volumes: I. Works, articles, drafts; II. *Capital* and preparatory writings; III. Correspondence; IV. Excerpts, notes, marginalia. Every volume consists of two physical volumes, the first containing the text, the second the "Apparat" (editorial apparatus, annotation, etc.). The set will consist of 100 volumes (hence, apparently, 200 physical volumes).

Programs of the Radical-Democratic Party and of the Left at Frankfurt. *Programme der radikal-demokratischen Partei und der Linken zu Frankfurt.* (D) 1848: June 6; by M/E, authorship not ascribed. (P) June 7, in *NRZ.*

Review. May to October [1850]. *Revue. Mai bis Oktober.* (W) 1850: ca. Oct.-Nov. 1; probably mostly by M. (D) Nov. 1. (P) Nov. 29, in *NRZ Revue,* No. 5/6, dated May-Oct. —In 1895 Engels used part of this review to constitute Part IV of M's *Class Struggles in France.*

[Review of] "Le Socialisme et l'Tmpôt," par Emile de Girardin. [In German, with this title] (W) 1850: Mar./Apr. (P) May ca. 20, in *NRZ Revue,* No. 4.

[Review of] "Les Conspirateurs," par A. Chenu... "La Naissance de la République en Février 1848," par Lucien de la Hodde ... [In German, with this title] (W) 1850: Mar.-Apr. (P) May ca. 20, in *NRZ Revue,* No. 4.

SCRITTI ITALIANI. A cura di G. Bosio. (Saggie e Documentazioni, 1) Milan/Rome: Ed. Avanti, 1955.

The Sevastopol Hoax—General News.$^{\infty}$ (W) 1854: Oct. 5-6. (D) Oct. 6. (P) Oct. 21, in *NYDT.*

To the Workers of Cologne. *An die Arbeiter Kölns.* (W) 1849: May 18; by M/E, authorship not ascribed; probably by M. (P) May 19, in *NRZ;* signed by the edit. board.; on front page of last issue.

Valdenaire's Arrest—Sebaldt. *Valdenaires Haft—Sebaldt.* (W) 1848: June 18; by M/E, authorship not ascribed. (P) June 19, in *NRZ.*

WERKE. (Abbrev.: MEW.) Institut für Marxismus-Leninismus beim ZK der SED. Berlin: Dietz Verlag, 1956-68. 39v 4 + suppl. vol. (Ergänzungsband); in actuality, 43 physical volumes, exclusive of the index volumes titled *Marx-Engels Verzeichnis.* Volumes 1-22: chronological series of writings (incl. unpublished notes and miscel-

laneous documents); Volumes 23-25 cover *Capital,* the three-volume Volume 26 covers *Theories of Surplus Value* (called Volumes 26.1, 26.2, 26.3); Volumes 27-39 present the complete correspondence. An unnumbered Supplementary Volume *(Ergänzungsband)* comprises two physical volumes (Eb. I, Eb. 2).
WRITINGS ON THE PARIS COMMUNE. Ed. by Hal Draper. NY: Monthly Review Press, 1971.

WRITINGS BY MARX

[Affairs in Prussia] (D) 1858: Dec. 4. (P) Dec. 27, in *NYDT;* no title.
The Attack on Francis Joseph—The Milan Riot—British Politics—Disraeli's Speech—Napoleon's Will.$^{\infty}$ (D) 1853: Feb. 22. (P) Mar. 7-8, in *NYDT.*
Banquet Speech. *See* Speech at the Seventh Anniversary Celebration ... Bonaparte's Present Position.$^{\infty}$ (D) 1858: Mar. 18. (P) Apr. 1, in *NYDT.*
The Bourgeoisie and the Counterrevolution. *Die Bourgeoisie und die Kontrerevolution.*(D) 1848: Dec. 9-29. (P) Dec. 10-31, in *NRZ,* 4 installs.
Camphausen's Statement at the Session of May 30. *Camphausen's Erklärung in der Sitzung vom 30. Mai.* (D) 1848: June 2. (P) June 3, in *NRZ.*
Capital. Critique of Political Economy. Volume 1 (Book I: The Process of Production of Capital). *Das Kapital. Kritik der politischen Oekonomie. Erster Band (Buck 1: Der Produktionsprocess des Kapitals).* (W) Feb. 1866 to Aug. 1867: for final preparation of this volume for publication. (P) 1867: Sept. 14, by Meissner (Hamburg). 1890: fourth German ed., edited & rev. by Engels. (Tr) 1887: authorized English tr. by Moore & Aveling, ed. by Engels, based on 3d German ed. This tr. revised to accord with 4th ed.: for Kerr ed. by E. Untermann (1906); for FLPH, Moscow, by IML editors (ca. 1954). Best independent tr. is by Ben Fowkes, 1977 (Pelican Marx. Lib. or Vintage Books).
The Civil War in France. Address of the G.C. of the I.W.M.A.$^{\infty}$ (W) 1871: latter half of May; adopted May 30. (P) June ca. 13, as pamphlet; 2d ed., end of June; 3d ed., Aug.
[The Civil War in France) First Draft. (W) 1871: Apr.-May. (P/P) 1934, in *Arkhiv M-E;* reproduced in ME: Writings on the Paris Commune, 103+. (A new IML reading of the original ms has appeared in New Mega 1, 22:15+.)
[The Civil War in France] Second Draft. (W) 1871: May. (P/P) Same as preceding entry.
The Civil War in the United States. *Der Bürgerkrieg in den Vereinigten Staaten.* (W) 1861: June-July, finished Oct. (P) Nov. 7, in *Die Presse.*
The Class Struggles in France 1848 to 1850. *Die Klassenkämpfe in Frankreich 1848 bis 1850.* (W) 1850: Jan. to Nov. 1. (P) Mar. to Nov., in *NRZ Revue.* The first three parts, published in No. 1-3, were titled "1848 to 1849" *(1848 bis 1849)* or simply "1848-1849"; for the fourth part, see above, ME: Review / May to October. 1895: first published in book form under present title, ed. by Engels.
The Coming Election in England.$^{\infty}$(D) 1857: Mar. 13. (P) Mar. 31, in *NYDT.*
Comments on the Latest Prussian Censorship Instruction. *Bemerkungen über die neueste preussische Zensurinstruktion.* (W) 1842: Jan. 15-Feb. 10. (P) 1843:Feb. in *Anekdota zur neuesten deutschen Philosophie und Publicistik* (Switz.), Bd. 1. Signed: Von einem Rheinländer.
Confidential Communication. *Konfidentielle Mitteilung.* (W) 1870: Mar. ca. 28, sent to German party executive with covering letter dated Mar. 28 (P/P) 1902, in *Neue Zeit.*

Conspectus of Bakunin's Book *Statism and Anarchy. Konspekt von Bakunins Buch "Staatlichkeit und Anarchie."* (W) 1874 to early 1875; no title; summaries and excerpts with scattered comments. (P/P) 1962, in *MEW*.
The Constitution of the French Republic Adopted November 4, 1848.$^{\infty}$ (W) 1851: May-June. (P) June 14, in *Notes to the People*, Vol. 1, No. 7. —The ed., Ernest Jones, may have translated M's article into English.
Contribution to the Critique of Political Economy. *Zur Kritik der politischen Ökonomie*. (W) Aug. 1858 to Jan. 1859, from economic mss of 1857-58. (P) 1859: June 11, as book (Berlin: Duncker).
The Crisis and the Counterrevolution. *Die Krisis und die Kontrerevolution*. (D) 1848: Sept. 11-13,15. (P)Sept. 12-14,16, in *NRZ*, in 4 installs.—This title headed only the first article; others titled "The Crisis" *(Die Krisis)*.
Critical Notes on the Article "The King of Prussia and Social Reform. By a Prussian." *Kritische Randglossen zu dem Artikel "Der König von Preussen und die Sozialrefotm. Von einem Preussen"* (D) 1844: July 31. (P) Aug. 7,10, in *Vorwärts* (Paris), in 2 installs.
Critique of Hegel's Philosophy of Right: Introduction. *Zur Kritik der Hegelschen Rechtsphilosophie. Einleitung.* (W) End of 1843 to Jan. 1844. (P) 1844: Feb., in *D.F.J.*
Critique of Hegel's Philosophy of Right (Manuscript). *Kritik des Hegelschen Staatsrechts.* (W) 1843: summer; no title. (P/P) 1927, in *MEGA*. —Various forms of this title are found in both German and English.
Critique of the Gotha Program. Notes on the Program of the German Workers' Party. *Kritik des Gothaer Programms. Randglossen zum programm der deutschen Arbeiterpartei.*(W) 1875: Apr.-May; no title. (P/P) 1891:Jan.,in *Neue Zeit*, Jg.9,Bd. 1,No. 18; edited by Engels. 1932: complete original ms published.—In original publication and many reprints, the title "Critique..." covered a group of documents, with the title "Notes..." heading Marx's critique.
The Czar's Views—Prince Albert.$^{\infty}$ (D) 1854: Jan. 24. (P) Feb. 11, in *NYDT;* no title.
A Decree of Eichmann's. *Ein Erlass Eichmanns.* (D) 1848:Nov. 18. (P)Nov. 19, in *NRZ*.
The Defeat of Cobden, Bright and Gibson.$^{\infty}$ (D) 1857: Mar. 31. (P) Apr. 17, in *NYDT*.
Defeat of the Palmerston Ministry.$^{\infty}$ (D) 1857: Mar. 6. (P) Mar. 25, in *NYDT*.
The Derby Cabinet— Palmerston's Deceptive Resignation.$^{\infty}$ (W) 1858: Feb. 26. (P) Mar. 15, in *NYDT;* no title. —The conferred title above is based on M's workbook title.
Economic and Philosophic Manuscripts of 1844. *Ökonomisch-philosophische Manuskripte aus dem Jahre 1844.* (W) 1844: Apr.-Aug.; no title. (P/P) 1932, in *MEGA*, with conferred title above. —Often called the "Paris manuscripts of 1844."
The Eighteenth Brumaire of Louis Bonaparte. *Der achtzehnte Brumaire des Louis Bonaparte.* (W) Dec. 1851. to Mar. 1852. (P) 1852: May, in *Die Revolution* (NY), No. 1, titled "Der 18te Brumaire des Louis Napoleon." 1869: July, second ed., somewhat revised. 1885: ca. June, third ed.
The English Election.$^{\infty}$ (D) 1857: Mar. 20. (P) Apr. 6, in *NYDT*.
Erfurt Echoes in 1859. *Die Erfurterei im Jahre 1859.* (W) 1859: July. (P) July 9, in *Das Volk.* —The MECW title is "Erfurtery in the Year 1859."
Espartero.$^{\infty}$ (W) 1854: Aug. 4. (P) Aug. 19, in *NYDT* (heavily edited, last sentence added).
Fair Professions.$^{\infty}$ (W) 1859: May. (P) May 18, in *NYDT*.
Fall of the Aberdeen Ministry.$^{\infty}$ (D) 1855: Feb. 2. (P) Feb. 17, in *NYDT*.
Foreword to Engel's *Socialism, Utopian and Scientific*, French Edition of 1880. *Avant-propos à "Socialisme Utopique et Socialisme Scientifique,"1880* (W) 1880: May 4/5, in consultation with Engels, as foreword to a pamphlet ed. planned by Lafargue. (P) late May, in the pamphlet; signed P. L. (for P. Lafargue), with slight editorial changes.
From the "Memoires de R. Levasseur (de la Sarthe) ... " *Kampf der Montagnards und*

426 Bibliography of Works Cited

Girardins (Exzerpte aus R. Levasseurs Memoiren). (W) End of 1843 & early 1844; excerpts and notes; no title. (P/P) in full, 1932: in *MEGA*.

Gatherings from the Press. [In German, despite title] (W) 1859: June-July, in collaboration with E. Biskamp. (P) June 4, 25, July 9, 16, in *Das Volk.* —A series of spoofs against Kinkel's weekly *Hermann.*

Herr Vogt. *Herr Vogt.* (W) 1860: Jan. to Nov. 8; preface dated Nov. 17. (P) Dec. 1, as book (London: A. Petsch & Co.).

The India Bill.∞ (W) 1858: July 9. (P) July 24, in *NYDT;* no title. —Title above is from M's workbook.

Indifference to Political Affairs. *L'Indifferenza in Materia Politica.* (W) Nov./Dec. 1872 to Jan. 1873. (D) 1873: Jan. (P) Dec, in *Almanacco Repubblicano per l'Anno 1874* (Lodi), ed. by E. Bignami.

Interesting from Sicily. / Garibaldi's Quarrel with La Farina. / A Letter from Garibaldi.∞ (D) 1860: July 23. (P) Aug. 8, in *NYDT.*

Intervtew(s) in the Chicago Daily Tribune. *See* under author, H., in section "Writings by Others."

DIE KLASSENKÄMPFE IN FRANKREICH 1848 BIS 1850. Mil Einleitung von F. Engels, und einem Vorwort von August Bebel. Berlin: Buchh. Vorwärts, Paul Singer G.m.b.H., 1911. [This edition defective.]

The Knight of the Noble Consciousness. *Der Ritter von edelmüthigen Bewusstsein.* (W) 1853: Nov. (D) Nov.28(P) 1854: Jan., as pamphlet; published in NY by M's friends Cluss and Weydemeyer, bearing no publisher's name.

Kossuth and Mazzini—Intrigues of the Prussian Government—Austro-Prussian Commercial Treaty—The *Times* and the Refugees.∞ (D) 1853: Mar. 18. (P) Apr. 4, in *NYDT;* no title.

Letters from Napier—Roebuck's Committee. *Briefe von Napier—Roebucks Komitee.* (D) 1855: June 15. (P)June 18, in *NOZ.*

LETTRES ET DOCUMENTS DE KARL MARX 1856-1883. In: Istituto G. Feltrinelli (Milan), *Annali,* Anno I, p. 149+.

Manteuffel's Speech—Religious Movement in Prussia—Mazzini's Address—London Corporation—Russell's Reform—Labor Parliament.∞ (D) 1853: Nov. 29. (P) Dec. 12, in *NYDT;* no title.

MANUSKRIPTE ÜBER DIE POLNISCHE FRAGE (1863-1864). Hrsg. und eingeleitet von Werner Conze und D. Hertz-Eichenrode. (Quellen und Untersuchingen zur Gesch. d. deut. u. öster. Arbeiterbewegung, 4) IRSH, Amsterdam. The Hague: Mouton, 1961.

Moralizing Criticism and Critical Morality. Contribution to German Cultural History versus Karl Heinzen. *Die moralisierende Kritik und die kritisierende Moral. Beitrag zur deutschen Kulturgeschichte gegen Karl Heinzen.* (W) 1847: Oct. (P) Oct. 28 to Nov. 25, in *DBZ,* in 5 installs.

The New English Budget.∞ (D) 1857: Feb. 20. (P) Mar. 9, in *NYDT*

Notebook on the Paris Commune. Press Excerpts and Notes [March-April 1871] . (W) 1871 March-Apr. (P/P) 1934, in *Arkhiv M-E,* Vol. 3(8), p. 92-238. —Excerpts from English and French newspapers from Mar. 18 to Apr. 30. For reprint and tr., see next entry.

NOTEBOOK ON THE PARIS COMMUNE. PRESS EXCERPTS & NOTES. Ed. by Hal Draper. Berkeley: Independent Socialist Press, 1971. —This publication covers the preceding entry, not the following entry.

Notebook on the Paris Commune. Press Excerpts, April-May 1871. (W) 1871: Apr.-May. (P/P) 1963, in *Arkhiv M-E,* Vol. 15, p. 22-302. —Excerpts from French newspapers covering Apr. 1 to May 23, 1871, and also a section covering Aug. 28 and Sept. 16-22,1870.

ON THE FIRST INTERNATIONAL. Ed. by Saul K. Padover. (The KM Library, 3) NY: McGraw-Hill, 1973.
On the Jewish Question. *Zur Judenfrage.* (W) 1843: autumn. (P) 1844: Feb., in *DFJ.*
Outline of a Report on the Irish Question to the German Workers Educational Association in London, Dec. 16, 1867. *Entwurf eines Vortrages zur irisches Frage* ... (W) 1867: Dec., part German & English notes. (P/P) 1962, in *MEW.*
Palmerston. *Palmerston.* (D) 1855: Feb. 27. (P) Mar. 3, in *NOZ.*
Parliamentary Affairs. *Parlamentarisches.* (D) 1855: Jan. 27. (P) Jan. 30, in *NOZ.* —MECW title is "Parliamentary News."
Pélissier's Mission to England.∞ (D) 1858: Mar. 27. (P) Apr. 15, in *NYDT.*
Plan of the "Library of the Best Foreign Socialist Writers." (W) 1845: Mar.; no title in notebook. (P/P) 1932, in *MEGA.* —This is a list of names, plus one German phrase.
Poland, Prussia and Russia. *Polen, Preussen und Russland.*(W) 1863: Feb. -Mar., perhaps, finished May; ms notes. (P/P) 1961, in M: *Manuskripte über die poln. Frage* (which see).
Political Parties in England—The Situation in Europe.∞ (W) 1858: June 11. (P) June 24, in *NYDT*; no title.
The Poverty of Philosophy. Reply to The Philosophy of Poverty by M. Proudhon. *Misère de la Philosophie. Réponse à La Philosophie de la Misère de M. Proudhon.* (W) 1847: first half; foreword dated June 15. (P) July, as book (Paris: A. Frank; Bruxelles: C. G. Vogler).
Revelations Concerning the Communist Trial in Cologne. *Enthüllungen über den Kommunisten-Prozess zu Köln.* (W) 1852: Oct.-Dec. 2. (P) 1853: Jan., unsigned, as pamphlet (Basel: Chr. Krüsi); Apr., in *Neu-England-Zeitung,* in installs., and then as pamphlet. 1875: as brochure (Leipzig: Genossenschaftsbuchdruckerei), with added "Afterword" *(Nachwort),* dated Jan. 8,1875.
The Rhein- und Mosel-Zeitung as Grand Inquisitor. *Die Rhein- und Mosel-Zeitung als Grossinquisitor.* (D) 1843: Mar. 11. (P) 12, in *Rheinische Zeitung.*
The Situation in Prussia.∞ (D) 1858: Dec. 4. (P) Dec. 27, in *NYDT;* no title.
Speech at the Anniversary of the *People's Paper.*∞ (W) 1856: speech delivered Apr. 14, in English. (P) Apr. 19, in *People's Paper.*
Speech at the Seventh Anniversary Celebration of the International in London.∞ (W) 1871: delivered at banquet Sept. 24 or 25 (for dating, see Chap. 20, Sec. 2). (P) Paraphrase of M's speech included in dispatch in *N.Y. World,* Oct. 15,1871, headed "The Reds in Session ...," datelined "London, Sept. 26."—This dispatch reprinted in *New Politics* (NY), summer 1963, p. 130-32.
Speeches at the Meeting of the Central Committee of the Communist League, Sept. 15, 1850. [In German] (W) 1850: Sept. 15; M spoke twice at the meeting, aside from short remarks also noted in the Minutes. (P) The Minutes of this meeting were published 1956 in *IRSH* (Amsterdam); 1960: in *MEW.* Marx's own report of his first speech was given in his pamphlet *Revelations Concerning the Communist Trial in Cologne* (see above).
The Suppression of the Neue Rheinische Zeitung under Martial Law. *Die standrechtliche Beseitigung der "Neuen Rheinischen Zeitung."* (D) 1849: May 18. (P) May 19, in *NRZ;* no title.
Szemere—The Duke of Norfolk—The Western Powers and Turkey.∞ (D) 1854: Jan. 10. (P) Jan. 28, in *NYDT;* no title.
To the Editor of the *People's Paper.*∞ (D) 1853; in Sept. 7. (P) Sept. 10, in *People's Paper.*
To the Editor of the *Times.*∞ (D) 1871: Apr. 3. (P) Apr. 4, in *Times.*
Victory of the Counterrevolution in Vienna. *Sieg der Kontrerevolution zu Wien.* (D) 1848: Nov. 6. (P) Nov. 7, in *NRZ.*
The Western Powers and Turkey—Imminent Economic Crisis—Railway Construction in India.∞ (D) 1853: Sept. 20. (P) Oct. 4 in *NYDT;* no title.

428   Bibliography of Works Cited

WRITINGS OF THE YOUNG MARX ON PHILOSOPHY AND SOCIETY. Tr. & ed. by L. D. Easton & K. H. Guddat. Garden City: Doubleday, 1967.

WRITINGS BY ENGELS

The Antwerp Death Sentences. *Die Antwerper Todesurteile.* (D) 1848: Sept. 2. (P) Sept. 3, in *NRZ.*
The Assembly at Frankfurt. *Die Frankfurter Versammlung.* (D) 1848: May 31. (P) June 1, in *NRZ.*
The Bakninists at Work. Memoir on the Uprising in Spain in the Summer of 1873. *Die Bakunisten an der Arbeit...* (W) 1873: Sept.-Oct. (P) Oct. 31, Nov. 2, 5, in *Volksstaat,* in 3 installs.
The Berlin Debate on Revolution. *Die Berliner Debatte über die Revolution.* (D) 1848: June 13, 14. (P) June 14-17, in *NRZ,* in 4 installs.
British Disaster in the Crimea.$^{\infty}$ (W) 1855: Jan. 4. (P) Jan. 22 in *NYDT.*
The Campaign for the German Imperial Constitution. *See The* German Campaign for a Reich Constitution.
Cologne in Danger. *Köln in Gefahr.* (D) 1848: June 10. (P) June 11, in *NRZ.*
The Communists and Karl Heinzen. *Die Kommunisten und Karl Heinzen* (D) 1847: Sept. 26, Oct. 3. (P) Oct. 3, 7, in *DBZ*, in 2 articles.
The Conciliationist Session of July 4. (Second Article.) *Vereinbarungssitzung vom 4. Juli. (Zweiter Artikel.)* (D) 1848: July 9. (P) July 11, in *NRZ—The* MECW title is "The Agreement Session..."
The Condition of England: 1. The Eighteenth Century. *Die Lage Englands: 1. Das achtzehnte Jahrhundert.* (W) 1844: Feb. (P) Aug. 31 to Sept. 11, in *Vorwärts* (Paris), in 4 installs.
The Condition of England: 2. The English Constitution. *Die Lage Englands: 2. Die englische Konstitution,* (W) 1844: Mar. (P) Sept. 18 to Oct. 19, in *Vorwärts* (Paris), in 7 installs.
The Condition of the Working Class in England. *Die Lage der arbeitenden Klasse in England.* (W) Sept. 1844 to Mar. 1845. (P) 1845: May, as book (Leipzig: Wigand); preface *(Vorwort)* dated Mar. 15.
CORRESPONDENCE / FREDERICK ENGELS / PAUL AND LAURA LAFARGUE. Tr. by Y. Kapp. 3v. Moscow: FLPH, 1959-61?—AH letters in English.
CORRESPONDENCE / FRIEDRICH ENGELS / PAUL ET LAURA LAFARGUE. Ed by E. Bottigelli; tr. by P. Meier, 3v. Paris: Eds. Sociales, 1956-59—All letters in French, but English originals are given too.
The Counterrevolutionary Plans in Berlin. *Die kontrerevolutionären Pläne in Berlin,* (I)) 1849: Apr. 30. (P) May 1, in *NRZ*
Critique of the Erfurt Program. *Zur Kritik des sozialdemokratischen Programmentwurfs 1991.* (W) 1891: June 18–29; no title; sent to the German party Executive. (P/P) 1901: in *Neue Zeit*, Bd. 1, No. 1, omitting the appendix *(Beilagen).*
The Defeat of the Piedmontese. *Die Niederlage der Piemontesen.* (W) 1849: Mar. 30 to Apr. 3. (P) Mar. 31, Apr. 1, 4, in *NRZ*, in 3 installs.
Democratic Pan-Slavism. *Derdemokratische Panslawismus.* (D) 1849: Feb. 14, 15. (P) Feb. 15-16, in *NRZ.*
Dialectics of Nature. *Dialektik der Natur.* (W) May 1873 to Mar. 1876; mid-1878 to Mar.

1883; some additions in 1885-86. Drafts and notes, fragments, & c. (P/P) 1925, in *Arkhiv M-E;* 1935, in *MEGA* (Sonderausgabe).
Engels/Lafargue Correspondence. *See* Correspondence / Fr. Engels / P. & L. Lafargue.
England. *England* [in Ger.] (D) 1852: Jan. 23,30. (P/P) 1960, in *MEW.*
The English Ten Hours Bill. *Die englische Zehnstundenbill.* (W) 1850: Mar. (P) May ca.20, in *NRZ Revue,* No. 4.
The Exploits in the Baltic and Black Seas—Anglo-French System of Operations.[∞] (W) 1854: May 22. (D) May 23. (P) May 27, in *People's Paper,* June 9, in *NYDT.*
The Festival of Nations in London. *Das Fest der Nationen in London.* (W) End of 1845. (P) End of 1846, in *Rheinische Jahrbücher z. gesellsch. Reform,* Vol. 2.
For Poland. *Für Polen.* (W) 1875: ca.Mar. (P) Mar. 24, in *Volksstaat.* —Here E reports speeches made by M and himself at a Jan. 23 meeting.
The Foreign Policy of Russian Czarism. *Die auswärtige Politik des russischen Zarentums.* (W) Dec. 1889 to Feb. 1890. (D) "End of Feb." (P) 1890: Feb., Aug., in the Russian *Sotsial-Demokrat,* No. 1 and 2 (in Russian tr.); Apr., May, in *Neue Zeit,* Jg. 8, No. 4,5; Apr., May, in *Time* (London monthly), in English tr. done with Engels' help (he may have done Chaps. 2-3).
From the Banat. [In German] (W) 1849: Feb. 3. (P) Feb. 4, in *NRZ*— English tr. in *MECW;* not included in *MEW.*
The Future Italian Revolution and the Socialist Party [Letter to Turati, in French]. (W) 1894; Jan. 26, as letter for publication (P) Feb. I, in *Critica Sociale* (Milan), in Turati's tr., dated Jan. 26, titled "La Futura Rivoluzione Italiana e il Partito Socialista." July 12, in *Sozialdemokrat* (Berlin), in Ger.
Garibaldi's Progress.[∞] (W) 1860: Sept. Ca. 1 (P) Sept. 2, in *NRZ.*
The General Council to All the Members of the International Working Men's Association.[∞] (W) 1872: Aug. 4-6; adopted by G.C. Aug. 6; sent out as circular to members. (P/P) 1940, in Russian; ca. 1968, in GCFI, Vol. 5.
The German Campaign for a Reich Constitution. *Die deutsche Reichsverfassungskampagne.* (W) Aug. 1849 to Feb. 1850. (P) 1850: Mar.-Apr., in *NRZ Revue,* No. 1,2, 3, in 3 installs.
German Socialism in Verse and Prose. *Deutscher Sozialismus in Versen und Prosa.* (W) 1846 to Jan. 1847. (P) 1847: Sept. 12 to Dec. 9, in *DBZ,* in 8 installs.
Hankering for a State of Siege. *Belagerungsgelüste.* (D) 1849: May 5. (P) May 6, in *NRZ.*
The Housing-Question. *Zur Wohnungsfrage.* (W) May 1872 to Jan. 1873. (P) June 26, 1872 to Feb. 22, 1873, in *Volksstaat,* in 11 installs. Part III was published Feb. 8-22. First published complete in a pamphlet in 1887 in Zurich (called 2d ed.).
Introduction to Marx's Civil War in France. *Einleitung...* (W) 1891: Mar. (D) Mar. 18. (P) Mar., in *Neue Zeit,* Jg. 9, Bd. 2, No. 28, titled "On the Civil War in France" (*Über den Bürgerkrieg in Frankreich);* then as intro to 3d German ed. of Marx's work.
Introduction to Marx's Class Struggles in France. *Einleitung . . .* (W) 1895: Feb. 14-Mar.6. (D) Mar.6.(P) Apr.,in *Neue Zeit,* Jg. 13, Bd. 2, No. 27,28; then as intro to Marx's work; in both cases in bowdlerized form. Engels' original text was first published in 1930 by the IML.
Karl Marx. *Karl Marx* [in German] (W) 1877: June. (P) 1878: in *Volks-Kalender* (an almanac), Brunswick.
The Kölnische Zeitung on the June Revolution, *Die "Kölnische Zeitung" über die Junirevolution.* (D) 1848: June 30. July I, in *NRZ.*
The Late Trial at Cologne.[∞] (D) 1852: Dec. 1. (P) Dec. 22, in *NYDT.*
[Letter from France, I to VIII] [∞] (P) 1850: Jan. to Aug., in *Democratic Review.*—Now erroneously ascribed to Engels by IML, in *MECW* and *New Mega.* See footnote in Chap. 12.

The Magyar Struggle. *De rmagyarische Kampf.* (W) 1849: Jan. ca. 8. (D) Jan. (P) Jan. 13, in *NRZ.*
Marx and the Neue Rheinische Zeitung. *Marx und die "Neue Rheinische Zeitung."* (W) 1884: Feb. to Mar. (P) Mar. 13, in *Sozialdemokrat.*
On Authority. *Dell'Autorià.* (W) 1873: Mar. (P) *Dec,* in *Almanacco Repubblicano per l'Anno 1874,* Anno Terzo; pubblicazione della *Plebe.* Comp. Enrico Bignami. Lodi, 1873.
On the History of Early Christianity. *Zur Geschichte des Urchristentums.* (W) 1894: June 19 to July 16. (P) Sept.-Oct., in *Neue Zeit,* Jg. 13, Bd. 1, No. 1-2.
On the History of the Communist League. *Zur Geschichte des Bundes der Kommunisten.* (D) 1885: Oct. 8. (P) Oct., as intro to 3d German ed. of Marx's *Revelations Conc. the Com. Trial.*
The Peasant War in Germany. *Der deutsche Bauernkrieg.* (W) 1850: summer, perh. also autumn. (P) Nov. 29, in *NRZ Revue,* No. 5/6. 1870: Oct., as a brochure, called "2d printing."
Preface to Marx's Capital, Volume 1, English Edition.$^{\infty}$ (D) 1886: Nov. 5. (P) 1887: Jan., in the published edition.
Principles of Communism. *Grundsätze des Kommunismus.* (W) 1847: summer or autumn; no title. (P/P) 1914, in brochure, ed. by E. Bernstein. Berlin: Vorwärts-Verlag.
Program of the Blanquist Refugees of the Commune. *Programm der blanquistischen Kommuneflüchtlinge.* (W) 1874: June. (P) June 26, in *Volksstaat,* as No. 2 of the series "Refugee Literature" *(Flüchtlingsliteratur),* without title. 1894: in pamphlet *Internationales aus dem "Volksstaat" (1871-75),* titled as above.
Progress of Social Reform on the Continent.$^{\infty}$ (W) 1843: ca. Oct.-Nov. (D) first part only, Oct. 23. (P) Nov. 4, 18, in *New Moral World;* Nov. 11,25, in *Northern Star.*
The Prosecution of Montalembert.$^{\infty}$ (D) 1858: Nov. 6. (P) Nov. 24, in *NYDT.*
Rapid Progress of Communism in Germany.$^{\infty}$ (W) Nov. 1844 to Apr. 1845. (P) Dec. 13, 1844 and May 8, 10, 1845, in *New Moral World,* as 3 articles.
Real Causes Why the French Proletarians Remained Comparatively Inactive in December Last.$^{\infty}$ (W) 1852: Feb. to Apr. (P) Feb. 21, Mar. 27, Apr. 10, in *Notes to the People,* in 3 installs.—The title was probably conferred by editor Ernest Jones.
The Reform Movement in France.$^{\infty}$ (W) 1847: Nov. (P) Nov. 20, in *Northern Star.*
Refugee Literature, III. *Flüchtlingsliteratur, III.* (W) 1875: ca. Feb. to Mar. (P) Mar. 28, Apr. 2, in *Volksstaat,* in 2 installs, as third in the series, without separate title. See the second in the series, "Program of the Blanquist Refugees ...," for republication.
Reply to the Hon. Giovanni Bovio. [Letter sent to Turati in French.] (D) 1892: Feb. 6. (P) Feb. 16, in *Critica Sociate* (Milan), in Italian tr., titled "Federico Engels a Giovanni Bovio."—Engels' ms apparently had the following heading in mixed French-Italian: "Réponse a Pon(orabile) Giovanni Bovio."
Revolution and Counterrevolution in Germany.$^{\infty}$ (W) Aug. 1851 to Sept. 1852; drafted by E, reviewed by M, who sent it in under his own name. (P) Oct. 25,1851 to Oct. 23, 1852, in *NYDT,* in 19 numbered installs; signed Karl Marx. Under the rubric "Germany" the heading was "Revolution and Counter-Revolution." (P/P) 1896, as a book by Marx, ed. by Eleanor Marx Aveling, titled *Revolution and Counter-Revolution; or, Germany in 1848.* This ed. included "The Late Trial at Cologne" (see above). E's authorship became known in 1913, from the published M-E correspondence.
The Rhenish Congress of Municipalities. *Der rheinische Städtetag.* (D) 1849: May 3. (P) May 4, in *NRZ.*
The Role of Force in History. *Die Rolle der Gewalt in der Geschichte.* (W) Dec. 1887 to Mar.

1888; unfinished ms; no title. (P/P) 1896,in *Neue Zeit,* Jg. 14, Bd. 1, No. 22-26, titled "Force and Economics in the Establishment of the New German Empire" *(Gewalt und Ökonomie bei der Herstellung des neuen Deutschen Reichs),* ed. by E. Bernstein. 1946, as a book, titled "On the Force Theory" *(Ueber die Gewaltstheorie)* plus previous title as subtitle.
Social Questions in Russia. *Soziales aus Russland.* (W) 1875: Mar. or Apr. (P) Apr. 16, 18, 21, in *Volksstaat,* in 3 installs, as 5th article in series "Refugee Literature"; then ca. May, as a separate pamphlet, with title as above.—An "Afterword, 1894" *(Nachwort ...)* was added in the 1894 collection *Internationales aus dem "Volksstaat" (1871-75).*— The MESW title is "On Social Relations in Russia."
Socialism, Utopian and Scientific. *Socialisme Utopique et Socialisme Scientifique.* (W) 1880: Jan. to Mar., as a somewhat revised version of three chapters of *Anti-Dühring.* (P) Mar. 20 to May 5, in *Revue Socialiste,* in 3 installs; tr. by P. Lafargue; in May, as a separate pamphlet. 1883: Mar., pamphlet ed. in German, titled *Die Entwicklung des Sozialismus von der Vtopiezur Wissenschaft.* 1892: Sept., first authorized English ed., tr. by E. Aveling.
The State of Germany. (W) Oct. 1845 to Feb. 1846. (P) Oct. 25, Nov. 8,1845 and Apr. 4,1846, in *Northern Star,* as three articles.
The Ten Hours' Question.$^{\infty}$ (W) 1850: Feb. 8-20. (P) March issue, *Democratic Review,* Vol. 1, p. 371+.
The True Socialists. *Die wahren Sozialisten.* (W) 1847: prob. Jan.-Apr., to continue the subject from *The German Ideology;* unfinished ms; no title. (P/P) 1932, in *MEGA.*
The Turkish Question.$^{\infty}$ (W) 1853: Mar. (P) Apr. 19, in *NYDT.*
The 24th of June. *Der24.Juni.* (W) 1848: June 27. (P) June 28, in *NRZ.*
[Two Years of a Revolution; 1848 and 1849]$^{\infty}$ (P) 1850: Apr., May, June, in *Democratic Review,* in 3 installs.—Now erroneously ascribed to Engels by I ML, in *MECW* and New Mega. See footnote in Chap. 12.

WRITINGS BY OTHERS

A la Classe Ouvrierè. Par le Comité Révolutionnaire du Prolétariat. Londres, Delahaye, n.d. (Contents dated Oct. 1,1874).
Académic Franchise. *Dictionnaire de l'Académie Francaise.* Paris, 1694.
Amann, P. "Karl Marx, 'Quarante-Huitard Français'?" In: I.R.S.H. (Amsterdam), 1961, VI, p. 249+.
Andréas, Bert. *Le Manifeste Communiste de Marx et Engels. Histoire et Bibliographic 1848-1918.* (Institut G. Feltrinelli. Bibliographies) Milan: Feltrinelli, 1963.
An Anthology of Chartist Literature [binding title]. *Antologiya Chartistskoi Literatury* [title-page title]. Sostablenie, predislobie i kommentariy Yu. B. Kobaleba. Moscow, 1956.
Archives Bakounine. *See* under Bakunin, Michael.
Arendt, Hannah. *On Revolution.* NY: Viking Press (Compass Books), c. 1963; 1965 (paperback).
Arkhiv K. Marksa if. Engel'sa. Vols. 1-5. Moscow.
Auclair, Marcelle. *La Vie de Jean Jaurès, ou la France d'avant 1914.* Paris: Eds. du Seuil, c!954.
Avineri, Shlomo. *The Social and Political Thought of Karl Marx.* Cambridge Univ. Press, 1968.

Babeuf, François Noël. *The Defense of Gracchus Babeuf before the High Court of Vendôme.* Ed. & tr. by J. A. Scott. With an essay by Herbert Marcuse. Univ. of Massachusetts Press, 1967.

Bakunin, Michael. *Archives Bakounine/Bakunin-Archiv.* Published for the International Institute for Social History, Amsterdam, by A. Lehning, A.J. C. Rüter, P. Scheibert. Leiden: Brill, 1963- (in progress).—Tome III: *Etatisme et Anarchie/1873.* Ed. A. Lehning, 1967. (Orig. Russian + French tr.).

———. *The "Confession" of Mikhail Bakunin.* With the marginal comments of Tsar Nicholas I. Tr. by R. C. Howes. Intro & notes by L. D. Orton. Cornell Univ. Press, 1977.

———. *Gosudarstvennost i Anarkhiya.* Geneva, 1873.

———. Letter to Albert Richard. See Richard, Albert...

———. "Letter to Nechayev of 2 June 1870." In: *Encounter* (London), July and Aug. 1972. Tr. by L. Bott. *(See also* Confino, M.).

———. *The Political Philosophy of Bakunin: Scientific Anarchism.* Compiled & ed. by G. P. Maximoff. Pref. by B. F. Hoselitz. Intro by R. Rocker. Glencoe, Ill.: Free Press, 1953.

———. *Statism and Anarchy. See* under Bakunin: *Archives Bakounine,* Tome III.

Bax, Ernest Belford. *The Last Episode of the French Revolution. Being a History of Gracchus Babeuf and the Conspiracy of the Equals.* London: Grant Richards, 1911.

Becker, Gerhard. *Karl Marx und Friedrich Engels in Köln 1848-1849. Zur Geschichte des Kölner Arbeitervereins.* Berlin (DDR): Rütten & Loening, 1963.

Beer, Max. *A History of British Socialism.* Intro by R. H. Tawney. London: G. Bell, 1923. (First pub. 1919) 2v.

———. "An Inquiry into Dictatorship." In: *Labour Monthly* (London), June, July and Aug. 1922, in 3 installs.

Berlin, Isaiah. *Karl Marx, His Life and Environment.* 2d ed. (Home University Lib. of Modern Knowledge) London: Oxford Univ. Press, 1948, repr. 1949. |Citations are to this ed. unless otherwise specified.|—4th ed., Oxford Univ. Press, 1978, repr. 1981.

Bernstein, Eduard. "Die Briefe Johannes Miquels an Karl Marx." In: *Neue Zeit,* Jg. 32, Bd. 2, No. 1 (Apr. 3,1914) and No. 2 (Apr. 10,1914).

———. *Evolutionary Socialism: A Criticism and Affirmation.* Tr. by E. C. Harvey. (Socialist Lib., 7) NY: B. W. Huebsch, 1909.—Tr. (lacking two chapters) of his *Die Voraussetzungen* |&c|, q.v. *New edition:* Intro, by Sidney Hook. NY: Schocken, 1961; 7th printing 1975.

———. *Ferdinand Lassalle as a Social Reformer.* Tr. by Eleanor Marx Aveling. London: Swan Sonnenschein, 1893.—Tr. of Bernstein's intro to Lassalle's works in German, published in 1892.

———. *Die Voraussetzungen des Sozialismus und die Aufgaben der Sozialdemokratie.* Stuttgart: Dietz Nachf.,1902.—Orig. pub. 1899. For English tr., see his *Evolutionary Socialism.*

Bernstein, Samuel. *Auguste Blanqui and the Art of Insurrection.* London: L& W, 1971.

———. "Marx in Paris, 1848: A Neglected Chapter." In: *Science & Society,* Summer 1939, Vol. 3, No. 3.—And "Marx and Engels in Paris, 1848: Supplementary Documents." Ibid., Spring 1940, Vol. 4, No. 2.

———. |Review of Jellinek's *Paris Commune of 1871*|. In: *Science & Society,* Summer 1938.

Bertrand, Louis. *Histoire de la Démocratie et du Socialisme en Belgique depuis 1830.* Brussels: Dechenne, 1906. 2v.

Blanc, Louis. *1848. Historical Revelations: Inscribed to Lord Normanby.* London: Chapman & Hall, 1858.—Written in English by Blanc; for his French version, see his *Révélations Historiques.*

———. *Pages d'Histoire de la Révolution de Février 1848.* Paris: Bureau du Nouveau Monde, 1850.

———. *Révélations Historiques / en réponse au livre de Lord Normanby...* Brussels: Meline, Cans et Cie., 1859. 2v.—The subtitle states that this work was "first published in English by the author, and, in the French the translation made by himself, enlarged to nearly double its size."

Blanqui, Louis Auguste. *Critique Sociale.* Paris, 1885. 2v.

Blanqui, Louis Auguste. *Instructions pour une Prise d'Arme; L'Eternite par les Astres...* Ed. by M. Abensour and V. Pelosse. Paris: Société Encyclopédique Franҫhise, c1972.

Bougeart, Alfred. *Marat, l'Ami du Peuple.* Paris: Librairie Internationale, 1865. 2v.

Bourgin, Georges, and Hubert Bourgin. *Le Socialisme François de 1789 à 1848.* Paris: Hachette, 1912.

Bulwer-Lytton, Edward. *Rienzi, the Last of the Tribunes.* London: Dent (Everyman's Lib.), n.d.—First pub. 1835.

Der Bund der Kommunisten. Dokumente und Materialien. Band 1: 1836-1849. (Above title: IML beim ZK der SED / IML beim ZK der KPdSU) Berlin: Dietz Verlag, 1970.

Buonarroti, Philippe. *Conspiration pour l'Egalité dite de Babeuf* Paris: Eds. Sociales, 1957.—First pub. 1828.

———. *Buonarroti's History of Babeuf's Conspiracy for Equality.* Tr. & with notes by Bronterre [O'Brien]. London: Hetherington, 1836.

Butler, E. M. *The Saint-Simonian Religion in Germany.* Cambridge, Eng.: University Press, 1926.

Cabet, Etienne. "France.—What Must Be Done After a New Revolution?" In: *Democratic Review,* Sept. 1850, Vol. 2, p. 136+.

———. "The History of the Colony or Republic of Icaria in the United States of America." In: *Iowa Journal of History and Politics,* Vol. 15, Apr. 1917. Tr. by Thomas Teakle, from the 2d ed. (Paris, 1855); here titled "History and Constitution of the Icarian Community."

———. *Voyage en Icarie.* Paris: Au Bureau du Populaire, 1845.—First pub. 1840.

Cadogan, Peter. "Harney and Engels." In: IRSH (Amsterdam), Vol. 10, 1965, p. 66+.

Calvez, Jean-Yves. *La Pensée de Karl Marx.* Septième éd., revue et corrigée. Paris: Eds. du Seuil, c1956.

Carr, Edward Hallett. *The Bolshevik Revolution 1917-1923.* (A History of Soviet Russia) NY: Macmillan, 1951-53. 3v.

———. *Karl Marx. A Study in Fanaticism.* London: Dent, 1934.

———. *Michael Bakunin.* NY: Vintage Books, 1961, c1937.

Caute, David, ed. *Essential Writings of Karl Marx.* Selected, and with an intro and notes, by David Caute NY: Collier Bks., c1967.

Chang, Sherman H. M. *The Marxian Theory of the State.* With an intro by John R. Commons. Phila.: The author, 1931.

Charléty, Sébastien. *Histoire du Saint-Simonisme (1825-1864).* Paris: Hachette, 1896.

Cluseret, Gustave Paul. "L'International et la Dictature. Réponse à la brochure *Internationale et Révolution:*" In: *L'Egalité* (Geneva), Dec. 18, 1872, Quatrième année, No. 22-23, pp. 7-3.

Cobban, Alfred. *Dictatorship. Its History and Theory.* NY: Scribner's, 1939.

Cole, G. D. H. *History of Socialist Thought.* London: Macmillan; NY: St. Martin's Press, 1955-65. 5v. in 7.—Vol. 1: *Socialist Thought: The Forerunners 1789-1850.* 1955; first ed. 1953. Vol. 2: *Socialist Thought: Marxism and Anarchism 1850-1890.* 1957; first ed. 1954.

Collins, Henry, and C. Abramsky. *Karl Marx and the British Labour Movement. Years of the First International.* London: Macmillan, 1965.

The Columbia Encyclopedia. Third edition. Ed. by Wm. Bridgewater and Seymour Kurtz. NY: Columbia Univ. Press, 1963; 9th printing, 1968.
Communist League. "Rules of the Communist League. (Dec. 1847.)" In: *MECW* 6:633+.
Communist League. Central Committee. "Minutes of the Session of Sept. 15, 1850." In: MEW 8:597+; MECW 10:625+.
Confino, Michael. *Violence dans la Violence. Le Débat Bakounine-Necaev.* (Bibliothequè Socialiste, 24) Paris: Maspero, 1973.
Cornu, Auguste. *Moses Hess et la Gauche Hégélienne.* Paris: Alcan, 1934.
Costa, Charles Da. *See* Da Costa, Charles.
Culver, Kenneth Leon. *The Brissotin-Robespierrist Struggle During the Legislative Assembly with Reference to the Fear of a Dictator.* Unpub. diss., Ph.D., Univ. of Calif, Berkeley, 1935.
Cunow, Heinrich. "Marx und die Diktatur des Proletariats." In: *Neue Zeit,* Jg. 38 (1919/20), Bd. 2, p. 152+.
Czobel, A., and C. Kahn. *Karl Marx as Labor Defender (1848-1871).* NY: Labor Defender, n.d. [ca. 1933].
Da Costa, Charles. *Les Blanquistes.* (Histoire des Partis Socialistes en France, ed. A. Zévaès, 6) Paris: Rivière, 1912.
Da Costa, Gaston. *La Commune Vécue... (18mars-28 mai 1871).* Paris: Ancienne Maison Quantin, 1903-05. 3v.
Dan, Theodore. "Les Socialistes Russes et la Dictature du Prolétariat." In: Dan & Martov, *La Dictature du Proletariat* (see below).—This lecture published orig. as a pamphlet: same title; Bibliothèque de la Bataille Socialiste. Paris, 1934.
Dan, Theodore, and J. Martov. *La Dictature du Prolétariat.* Préface de J. Arrès-Lapoque. (Pages Socialistes, 9) Paris: Eds. de la Liberté, 1947.
De Luna, Frederick A. *The French Republic under Cavaignac, 1848.* Princeton Univ. Press, 1969.
Deville, Gabriel. *Gracchus Babeuf und die Verschwörung der Gleichen.* Tr. by E. Bernstein, with an Afterword *(Nachwort)* by him. Hottingen-Zurich: Sozialdemokratische Bibliothek, 1887.
Dézamy, Théodore. *Le Jésuitisme Vaincu et Anéanti par le Socialisme...* Paris, 1845.
Dictionary of the History of Ideas. Studies of Selected Pivotal Ideas. Ed. by Philip P. Weiner. NY: Scribner's, 1968-74. 5v.
Dictionnaire Biographique du Mouvement Ouvrier François. See Maitron, J.
Dictionnaire Universel François et Latin. [Commonly called *Dictionnaire de Trevoux*.] Nouv. ed., Nancy, 1734.
[Diderot, Denis, ed.] *Encyclopédie, ou Dictionnaire Raisonné des Sciences, des Arts et des Métiers.* Paris, 1751-72; Suppl., 1780.
Diehl, Karl. *Die Diktatur des Proletariats und das Rätesystem.* Zweite Auflage. Mit einem Nachtrage "Die Entwicklung des Bolschevismus von 1920-1924." Jena: G. Fischer, 1924.
Dominick, Raymond H., III. *Wilhelm Liebknecht and the Founding of the German Social Democratic Party.* Univ. of N. Carolina Press, 1982.
Dommanget, Maurice. "Les Blanquistes dans l'Internationale . . ." In: *La Première Internationale...* (q.v.).
———. *Les Idées Politiques et Sociales d'Auguste Blanqui.* Paris: Rivière, 1957.
Donoso Cortés, Juan. *Obras.* Ed. by Gavino Tejado. Madrid: Impr. de Tejado, 1854. 3v.—Vol. 3 contains his "Discurso Pronunciado en el Congreso el 4 de Enero de 1849."

Drahn, Ernst. *Karl Marx und Friedrich Engels ueber die Diktatur des Proletariats.* (Der Rote Hahn. Doppelband 51/52) Berlin-Wilmersdorf: Verlag "Die Aktion," 1920.
Draper, Hal. "The Death of the State in Marx and Engels." In: *Socialist Register 1970,* ed. by R. Miliband & J. Saville; p. 281 +. London: Merlin Press, 1970.
———. "Joseph Weydemeyer's 'Dictatorship of the Proletariat.'" In: *Labor History* (NY), Spring 1962, Vol. 3, No. 2, p. 208+.
———. *Karl Marx's Theory of Revolution.* Vol.1: *State and Bureaucracy,* 1977. Vol. 2: *The Politics of Social Classes,* 1978. NY: Monthly Review Press, 1977-.
———. "Marx and the Dictatorship of the Proletariat." In: *Etudes de Marxologie,* No. 6, Sept. 1962 (Cahiers de l'Institut de Science Economique Appliqué, No. 129; Série S, No. 6) Paris.—Same (condensed version). In: *New Politics,* Summer 1962, Vol. 1, Nov. 4, p. 91+.
———. "A Note on the Father of Anarchism." In: *New Politics* (NY), Winter 1969, Vol. 8, No. 1, p. 79+.
Duntan, Graeme. *Marx and Mill. Two Views of Social Conflict and Social Harmony.* Cambridge Univ. Press, 1977; first pub. 1973.
Duveau, Georges. *1848: The Making of a Revolution.* Intro by G. Rudé. Tr. by A. Carter. NY: Vintage Bks., 1968, c1967.
Easton, Loyd D. "August Willich, Marx, and Left-Hegelian Socialism." In: *Etudes de Marxologie,* No. 9, Aug. 1965 (Cahiers de l'I.S.E.A., No. 164) Paris.
Eccarius, J. G. "Legality and Demagoguism," by J. G. E. In: *Notes to the People* (London), Mar.-Apr. 1852, in 5 installs.
Edwards, Stewart, ed. *The Communards of Paris, 1871.* London: Thames & Hudson, 1973.
Eisenstein, Elizabeth L. *The First Professional Revolutionist: Filippo Michele Buonarroti (1761-1837).* A Biographical Essay. (Harvard Historical Monographs, 38) Harvard Univ. Press, 1959.
Encyclopaedia Britannica. 11th edition. NY, 1910-11. 29v.
Encyclopaedia of the Social Sciences. Ed. by E. R. A. Seligman. NY: Macmillan, 1930-35; reissued 1937.15v.
Evans, Michael. *Karl Marx.* (Political Thinkers, 3) London: Allen & Unwin, 1975.
Ex Libris Karl Marx und Friedrich Engels. Schicksal und Verzeichnis einer Bibliothek. Einleitung und Redaktion: Bruno Kaiser. Berlin: Dietz, 1967.
The Federalist Papers. By Alexander Hamilton, James Madison, John Jay. With an intro [etc]... by Clinton Rossiter. NY, 1961—No. 70 (by Hamilton).
Felix, David. *Marx as Politician.* Southern Ill. Univ. Press, 1983.
Fetscher, Iring, ed. *Grundbegriffe des Marxismus. Eine Lexikalische Einführung.* Hamburg: Hoffmann und Campe, c1976.—Thirteen authors are listed at the end as collaborators.
Feuer, Lewis S. *Marx and the Intellectuals. A Set of Post-Ideological Essays.* Garden City: Anchor Bks. (Doubleday), 1969.
Förder, Herwig. *Marx und Engels am Vorabend der Revolution. Die Ausarbeitung der politischen Richtlinien für die deutschen Kommunisten (1846-1848).* (Deutsche Akademie der Wiss. zu Berlin. Institut für Geschichte. Schriften. Reihe I, Band 7) Berlin: Akademie-Verlag, 1960.
Footman, David. *Ferdinand Lassalle, Romantic Revolutionary.* Yale Univ. Press, 1947.— Pub. in Britain as *The Primrose Path.*
Furetière, Antoine. *Dictionnaire Universel...* Nouv. éd. La Haye &c, 1691.
G.C.F.I. *See* General Council of the First International.
Garnier-Pagès, Louis Antoine. *Histoire de la Révolution de 1848.* Paris: Pagnerre, 1872—

436 Bibliography of Works Cited

v.—Tome 11: Journées de Juin.
Gay, Peter. *The Dilemma of Democratic Socialism. Eduard Bernstein's Challenge to Marx.* Columbia Univ. Press, 1952.
The General Council of the First International...(Series: Documents of the First International) Five unnumbered volumes, each title beginning as above, followed by the years covered. Moscow: FLPH (for first vol.), Progress Pub., n.d. (1963-68?).—Vol. [1] GCF! 1864-1866; The London Conference; Minutes. [2] GCFI 1866-68; Minutes. [3] GCFI 1868-1870; Minutes. [4] GCFI 1870-1871; Minutes. [5] GCFI 1871-1872; Minutes.
Girardin, Emile de. *Questions de Mon Temps, 1836à 1856.* Paris: Serrière, 1858-61.13v.
Gottschalk, Louis R. *Jean Paul Marat. A Study in Radicalism.* NY: Greenberg, 1927.
Graham, John T. *Donoso Cortés, Utopian Romanticist and Political Realist.* Univ. of Missouri Press, 1974.
Grünberg, Carl, ed. *Die Londoner Kommunistische Zeitschrift und Andere Urkunden aus den Jahren 1847/1848.* Mit einer einleitenden Abhandlung . . . und Anmerkungen . . . (Hauptwerke des Sozialismus und der Sozialpolitik. N.F., 5. Heft. Leipzig: C. L. Hirschfeid, 1921.
Guérin, Daniel. *Jeunesse du Socialisme Libertaire; Essais.* Paris: Rivière, 1959.
———. *La Lutte de Classes sous la Première République. Bourgeois et "Bras Nus" (1793-1797).* (Collection La Suite des Temps, 16) 6. éd. Paris: Gallimard, c1946.2v.
Guillaume, James. *L'Internationale. Documents et Souvenirs (1864-1878).* Paris, 1905-10. 4v.
———. *Karl Marx Pangermaniste et l'Association Internationale des Travailleurs de 1864 à 1870.* Paris: A. Colin, 1915.
Guizot, François. *De la Démocratie en France (Janvier 1849).* Paris: V. Masson, 1849.
———. *Democracy in France.* By Monsieur Guizot. NY: Appleton, 1849.
Gurvitch, Georges. *Etudes sur les Classes Sociales.* (Bibliothèque Médiations) Paris: Eds. Gonthier, c1966.—Subtitle on cover: *L'Idle de Classe Sociale de Marx à Nos Jours.*
H. "Karl Marx. Interview with the Corner-Stone of Modern Socialism . . . ." *Chicago Tribune,* Jan. 5, 1879, p. 7. (Datelined London, Dec. 18 [1878], "Special Correspondence of the Tribune.") Cited from pamphlet reprint, *An Interview with Karl Marx in 1879* [sic: read 1878], T. W. Porter, ed. (Amer. Inst, for Marxist Studies, Occas. Papers, 10), NY, 1972. This reprint has some inaccuracies. The identity of H. is unknown.
Halévy, Elie. *The Era of Tyrannies. Essays on Socialism and War.* Tr. by R. K. Webb. With note by Fritz Stern. Garden City: Anchor Bks. (Doubleday), 1965.
Hammen, Oscar J. *The Red '48ers; Karl Marx and Friedrich Engels.* NY: Scribner's, 1969.
Hardy, Deborah. *Petr Tkachev, the Critic as Jacobin.* Univ. of Washington Press, 1977.
Harney, George Julian. *The Harney Papers.* Ed. by F. G. Black & R. M. Black. (Publications on Social History, 5) Assen: Van Gorcum, 1969.
Harrington, Michael. *Socialism.* NY: Bantam Bks., 1973, c1972.
Heinzen, Karl. *Erlebtes.* 2. Theil: *Nach meiner Exilirung.* (Gesammelte Schriften, Bd. 4) Boston, 1874.
Heinzen, Karl. *Die Helden des teutschen Kommunismus.* Bern, 1848.
Hess, Moses. *Rome and Jerusalem. A Study in Jewish Nationalism.* Tr. with intra and notes by M. Waxman. NY: Bloch Pub. Co., 1918.
Hillquit, Morris. *From Marx to Lenin.* NY: Hanford Press, 1921.
Hirsch, Helmut. *Denker und Kämpfer. Gesammelte Beiträge zur Geschichte der Arbeiterbewegung.* Frankfurt: Eur. Verlagsanstalt, 1955.
Hoffenstein, Samuel. *The Complete Poetry* . . . NY: Modern Lib., 1954.—Contains his "Poems in Praise of Practically Nothing."

Holcombe, A. N. *Government in a Planned Democracy.* NY, 1935.
Hook, Sidney. *Marx and the Marxists; the Ambiguous Legacy.* Princeton: Van Nostrand (Anvil Original), 1955.
———. *Towards the Understanding of Karl Marx. A Revolutionary interpretation.* NY: John Day, 1933.
Hostetter, Richard. *The Italian Socialist Movement. I: Origins (1860-1882).* Princeton: Van Nostrand, n.d. (c 1958).
Hubert, Charles-Fr "Note Chronologique sur l'Idee Marxiste de Dictature du Prolétariat." In: *Economic et Humanisme* (Eveux, L'Arbresie), No. 19,1945, p. 327+.
Hunt, R. N. Carew. *A Guide to Communist Jargon.* NY: Macmillan, 1957.
———. *Marxism Past and Present.* NY: Macmillan, 1955.
Hunt, Richard N. *The Political Ideas of Marx and Engels.* Vol.1: *Marxismand Totalitarian Democracy, 1818-1850.* Univ. of Pittsburgh Press, 1974.
Internationale et Révolution,à propos du Congrès de la Haye. Par des réfugiés de la Commune. Londres, 1872.
Jaucourt, Chevalier de. "Dictateur." In: Diderot, *Encyclopédie* (q.v.).
Jaures,Jean. *Etudes Socialistes.* 5. éd. Paris: Sociétéd'Eds. Litt. et Artistiques, 1902.
Jeanneret, G. "La Correspondance du Peintre G. Jeanneret," *Le Movement Social,* No. 51, May-June 1965.
Jellinek, Frank. *The Paris Commune of 1871.* NY: Grosset & Dunlap (Universal Lib.), 1965.—With new intro by author. First pub. 1937.
Johnson, Christopher H. *Utopian Communism in France. Cabet and the Icarians, 1839-1851.* Cornell Univ. Press, 1974.
Johnstone, Monty. "The Paris Commune and Marx's Conception of the Dictatorship of the Proletariat." In: *Massachusetts Review,* Summer 1971, Vol. 12, No. 3, p. 447+.
Kandel, E. P., ed. *Marx und Engels und die ersten proletarischen Revolutionäre.* Tr. from Russian by E. Salewski. Berlin: Dietz, 1965.
Karl Marx; Chronik seines Lebens in Ein&ldaten. Zusammengestellt vom Marx-Engels-Lenin-Institut, Moskau. Moscow: Marx-Engels-Verlag, 1934.
Kautsky, Karl. *Bernstein und das sozialdemokratische Programm. Eine Antikritik.* Stuttgart: Dietz Nachf., 1899.
———. *The Dictatorship of the Proletariat.* Intro by John H. Kautsky. [Tr. by H. J. Stenning.] (Ann Arbor Paperbacks) Univ. of Michigan Press, 1964.—Tr. of *Die Diktatur des Proletariats,* Vienna, 1918. This bad tr. was first pub. by I.L.P.: 2d ed., Manchester, National Labour Press, n.d. (1920).
———. *Social Democracy versus Communism.* Ed. & tr. by David Shub & Jos. Shaplen. With intro by Sidney Hook. NY: Rand School Press, 1946.
Koebner, R. "Despot and Despotism: Vicissitudes of a Political Term." In: *Journal of the Warburg & CourtauldInstitutes,* Vol. 4,1951, p. 275+
Koechlin, Heinrich. *Die Pariser Commune des Jahres 1871 in Bewusstsein ihrer Anhänger.* (Inaugural dissertation, Univ. Basel) Mulhouse, 1950.
Kropotkin, Peter. *The Great French Revolution—1789-1793.* Trans, by N. F. Dryhurst. NY: Schocken Bks., 1971.—First pub. 1909.
Kühn, Walter. *Der junge Hermann Becker.* Dortmund, 1934.
Ladendorff , Otto. *Historisches Schlagwörterbuch. Ein Versuch.* Strassburg/Berlin: Trübner, 1906.
Lafargue, Paul, & Wilhelm Liebknecht. *Karl Marx; His Life and Work. Reminiscences...* NY: Intl. Pub., 1943.
———. "Parliamentarianism and Boulangism." In: *Labour Monthly* (London), Aug. 1958, p. 374+.—Tr. of an article pub. in the Russian *Sotsial-Demokrat,* 1888.
Landauer, Carl. *European Socialism.* Univ. of Calif. Press, 1959.2v.

Langer, William L. *Political and Social Upheaval 1832-1852.* NY: Harper & Row, 1869.
[Larousse du XIXe Siecle]*Grand Dictionnaire Universel Francais, Historique [etc.]*... Par Pierre Larousse. Paris: 1865-90. 17v.
Laski, Harold J. *The Socialist Tradition in the French Revolution.* London: Fabian Society; Allen & Unwin, 1930.
Laurat, Lucien. *Marxism and Democracy.* Tr. by Edw. Fitzgerald. London: V. Gollancz, 1940.
Laveaux, Jean Charles Thibaut de. *Nouveau Dictionnaire de la Langue Francaise.* Paris, 1820.
Lefebvre, Georges. *The French Revolution.* Vol. 1: *From Its Origins to 1793.* Tr. by E. M. Evanson. Vol. 2: *From 1793 to 1799.* Tr. by J. H. Stewart & J. Friguglietti. London: Routledge & K. Paul; NY: Columbia Univ. Press, 1962-64.
Leff, Gordon. *The Tyranny of Concepts: A Critique of Marxism.* London: Merlin Press, c1961.
Lehning, Arthur. "Buonarroti's Ideas on Communism and Dictatorship." In: *IRSH* (Amsterdam), Vol. 2, 1957, Part 2.
———. "The International Association (1855-1859)." In: *IRSH* (Amsterdam), Vol. 3, 1938.
Lenin, V. I. *Collected Works.* Moscow: FLPH (Vol. 1-19), Progress Pub., 1960-70. 45v.—The following writings are cited from this set. The numbers after the title give volume and initial page. How the "Spark" Was Nearly Extinguished. 4:333. (W) 1900: Sept. (P/P) 1924. On the Slogan for a United States of Europe. 21:339. (P) 1915: Aug. 23. The Proletarian Revolution and the Renegade Kautsky. 28:271. (W) 1918: Oct.-Nov. (P) 1918, as pamphlet. The State and Revolution. 25:381. (W) 1917: Aug.-Sept.; 2nd ed. dated Dec. 1918. (P) 1918; 2nd ed., 1919. Two Tactics of Social-Democracy in the Democratic Revolution. 9:15. (W) 1905: June-July. (P) July, as pamphlet. The Victory of the Cadets and the Tasks of the Workers' Party 10:199. (W) 1906: Apr. (P) Same, as pamphlet.
Leroy, Maxime. *Histoire des Idées Sociales en France.* Paris: Gallimard, 1946-62. 3v.
Levy, Leonard W. *Jefferson & Civil Liberties; The Darker Side.* Harvard Univ. Press (Belknap Press), 1963.
Lichtheim, George. *From Marx to Hegel.* NY: Seabury Press (Continuum Book), 1974, c1971.
———. *Marxism. An Historical and Critical Study.* NY: Praeger, 1962, c1961.
———. *The Origins of Socialism.* NY: Praeger, 1969.
———. *A Short History of Socialism.* NY: Praeger, 1970.
Lidtke, Vernon L. *The Outlawed Party; Social Democracy in Germany, 1878-1890.* Princeton Univ. Press, 1966.
Liebknecht, Wilhelm. *Briefwechsel mit Karl Marx und Friedrich Engels.* Hrsg. und bearbeitet von Georg Eckert. (Quellen und Untersuchungen zur Geschichte der deutschen und österreichischen Arbeiterbewegung, V. I.I.S.G., Amsterdam) The Hague: Mouton, 1963.
———. *Karl Marx; Biographical Memoirs.* Tr. by E. Untermann. Chicago: Kerr, c1901.
———. *On the Political Position of Social-Democracy... I No Compromises, No Election Deals. I The Spider and the Fly.* Moscow: FLPH, n.d. [after 1958].
———. "Report on the Working-Class Movement in Germany." In: *GCF1* '64-66 [v.1], p.251+.
———. & Paul Lafargue. *See under* Lafargue, P.
Lissagaray, H. P. O. *History of the Commune of 1871.* Tr. by Eleanor. Marx Aveling. NY: Monthly Review Press, 1967.—Tr. first pub. 1886; original pub. 1876.
Littré, Emile. *Dictionnaire de la Langue Francaise.* Paris. 1863.

Longuet, Charles. "Marx et la Commune." In: *Le Mouvement Socialiste*, Jan. 15, 1901, Vol. 5, No. 50.—This is his preface to the forthcoming French tr. of *Civil War in France*.
Lorwin, Lewis L. "Blanqui." In: *Encyclopaedia of the Social Sciences*, Vol. 2.
Loubère, Leo A. *Louis Blanc. His Life and His Contribution to the Rise of French Jacobin-Socialism.* (Northwestern Univ. Studies in History, 1) Northwestern Univ. Press, 1961.
Lougee, Robert W. *Midcentury Revolution, 1848. Society and Revolution in Frame and Germany.* Lexington, Mass.: Heath, 1972.
Machiavelli, Niccolò. "Discourses on the First Decade of Titus Livius." In: his *Chief Works*, Vol. 1. Tr. by Allan Gilbert. Duke Univ. Press, 1965.
MacIver, R. M. *Leviathan and the People.* Louisiana State Univ. Press, 1939.
McLellan, David. *Karl Marx: His Life and Thought.* London: Macmillan, 1973.
———. The Thought of Karl Marx. An Introduction. NY: Harper & Row, 1971.
Madariaga, Salvador de. *Bolivar.* Mexico City, 1951. 2v.—[English ed., in one vol.] London/NY, 1952.
Maitron, Jean, ed. *Dictionnaire Biographique du Mouvement Ouvrier Français.* Publié sous la direction de Jean Maitron. Paris: Eds. Ouvrières, 1964-77. 15v.—This comprises three series of volumes; a fourth series in prep.
Marcuse, Herbert. "Repressive Tolerance." In: Wolff, Robert P. et al. *A Critique of Pure Tolerance.* Boston: Beacon Press, c1965.
———. "Thoughts on the Defense of Gracchus Babeuf." In: Babeuf, F. N. *The Defense of Gracchus Babeuf...* (q.v.).
Martov, Julius. "Marx and the Dictatorship of the Proletariat." In: his *The State and the Socialist Revolution* (q.v.).—First pub. 1918.
———. *The State and the Socialist Revolution.* Tr. by Integer. NY: International Review, 1938.
——— & T. Dan. *See under* Dan, Theodore.
Mason, Edward S. "Blanqui and Communism." In: *Political Science Quarterly*. Dec. 1929, Vol. 44, No. 4, p. 498+.
Mathiez, Albert. *The French Revolution.* Tr. by C. A. Phillips. NY: Grosset & Dunlap (Universal Lib.), 1964.—Tr. first pub. 1928; orig. first pub. 1922.
Mautner, Wilhelm. "Zur Geschichte des Begriffes 'Diktatur des Proletariats.' " In: *Archiv für die Geschichte des Sozialismus und der Arbeiterbewegung* (ed. C. Grünberg), Jg. 12, 1926, p. 280+.
Mayer, Gustav. *Bismarck und Lassalle. Ihr Briefwechsel und ihre Gespräche.* Berlin: Dietz Nachf., 1928.
———. *Friedrich Engels. A Biography.* Intro by G. D. H. Cole. Tr. by Gilbert & Helen Highet; tr. edited by R. H. S. Crossman. NY: Knopf, 1936.—A rewritten condensation of the original.
———. *Friedrich Engels. Eine Biographie.* 2. verbess. Auflage. The Hague: M. Nijhoff, 1934. 2v.
Mayo, Henry B. *Democracy and Marxism.* Foreword by W. B. Smith. NY: Oxford Univ. Press, 1955.—Revised ed.: *Introduction to Marxist Theory*, 1960.
Mehring, Franz, ed. *Aus dem literarischen Nachlass von Karl Marx, Friedrich Engels und Ferdinand Lassalle.* Stuttgart: Dietz Nachf., 1902. 4v.
———. *Karl Marx: The Story of His Life.* Tr. by E. Fitzgerald. Ed. by R. & H. Norden. NY: Covici Friede, 1935.—Orig. pub. 1918.
Merriam, Charles E. *The New Democracy and the New Despotism.* NY, 1939.
Michel, Louise. *La Commune.* 2. éd. Paris, 1898.
Molnár, Miklós. *Le Declin de la Première Internationale. La Conférence de Londres de 1871.*

(Publications de l'Institut Univ. de Hautes Etudes Intles., 42) Geneva: Lib. Droz, 1963.
Mommsen, Wilhelm. *Johannes Miquel.* Stuttgart: Deutsche Verlags-Anstalt, 1928. 2v.
Moore, Stanley W. *The Critique of Capitalist Democracy. An Introduction to the Theory of the State in Marx, Engels, and Lenin.* NY: Paine-Whitman Pub., 1957.
———. *Three Tactics; The Background in Marx.* NY: Monthly Review Press, 1963.
Morton, A. L. *The Life and Ideas of Robert Owen.* NY: Monthly Review Press, 1963.
Müller-Tellering, Eduard von. *Vorgeschmack in die künftige deutsche Diktatur von Marx und Engels.* Von Tellering. Cöln: Selbstverlag des Verfassers, 1850.
Nicolaievsky, Boris, & Otto Maenchen-Helfen. *Karl Marx, Man and Fighter.* Tr. by G. David & E. Mosbacher. Phila.: Lippincott, 1936.—Orig. pub. in German, 1933.— "Revised and extended edition," Penguin Press, 1973; Pelican Bks., 1976. Notes, &c. edited by L. Evrard from contributions by various hands. [Citations are to 1936 ed. unless otherwise specified.]
Nomad, Max. *Apostles of Revolution.* NY: Collier Bks., 1961.—First pub. 1939.
Obermann, Karl. *Joseph Weydemeyer, Pioneer of American Socialism.* NY: Intl. Pub., 1947.
Philipon de La Madelaine, Louis. *Dictionnaire de la Langue Française, abrégé du Dictionnaire de l'Académie.* 4. éd. Paris, 1823.
Pierre, Victor. *Histoire de la République de 1848. Gouvernement Provisoire. Commission Exécutive. Cavaignac. 24 Février-20 Décembre 1848.* Paris: Plon, 1873.
The Pioneer; or, Grand National Consolidated Trades' Union Magaine. Birmingham, then London: Vol. I, no. 1-44; Sept. 7, 1833 to July 5, 1834. Edited by James Morrison.
Plotkin, Norman. "Les Alliances des Blanquistes dans la Proscrition." In: *1848; Revue des Révolutions Contemporaines.* Dec. 1951, Vol. 189, p. 116+.
Postgate, Raymond W. *Out of the Past. Some Revolutionary Sketches.* Boston: Houghton Mifflin, 1923.
La Première Internationale; l'Institution, l'Implantation, le Rayonnement. [Colloque] Paris, 16-18 Novembre 1964. (Colloques Internationaux du C.N.R.S. Sciences Humaines. Actes du Colloque International sur la Première Intle.) Paris: Eds. du C.N.R.S., 1968.
Proudhon, Pierre Joseph. *Carnets de P.-J. Proudhon.* Ed. by P. Haubtmann. Paris: Rivière, 1960-74. 4v.—Unfinished series; so far covers only 1843-51.
———. *Idée Générale de la Révolution au XIXe Siècle.* 2d ed. Paris: Garnier Frères, 1851.
Puech, Jules L. *Le Proudhonisme dans l'Association Internationale des Travailleurs.* Préface de Charles Andler. Paris: Alcan, 1907.
Pyziur, Eugene. *The Doctrine of Anarchism of Michael A. Bakunin.* (Marquette Slavic Studies, 1) Marquette Univ. Press, 1955.
Reminiscences of Marx and Engels. Moscow: FLPH, n.d.—A collection.
Richard, Albert. "Bakounine et l'Internationale à Lyon—1868-1870." In: *Revue de Paris,* Sept. 1, 1896, 3° année, Tome 5, p. 119+.
Richter, Melvin. "Despotism." In: *Dictionary of the History of Ideas* (q.v.), Vol. 2.
Robertson, Priscilla. *Revolutions of 1848; A Social History.* (Harper Torchbooks) NY: Harper & Bros., c1952.
Robespierre, Maximilien. *Discours et Rapports de Robespierre.* Avec une introduction et des notes par Ch. Vellay. (L'Elite de la Révolution) Paris: Libr. Charpentier & Fasquelle, 1908.
Röser, Peter. "From Peter Röser's Evidence." In: MECW 38:550+.
Rosenberg, Arthur. *Democracy and Socialism. A Contribution to the Political History of the Past 150 Years.* Tr. by Geo. Rosen. London: Bell, 1939.
———. *A History of the German Republic.* Tr. by I. F. D. Morrow & L.M. Sieveking. London: Methuen, 1936; reprinted, NY: Russell & Russell, 1965.

Rossiter, Clinton L. *Constitutional Dictatorship. Crisis Government in the Modern Democracies.* Princeton Univ. Press, 1948.

———. *Marxism: The View from America.* (Harvest Book) NY: Harcourt Brace & World, 1960.

Rousseau, Jean Jacques. *TheSocial Contract* and *Discourses.* (Everyman's Lib., 660A) Tr. with an intro by G. D. H. Cole. NY/London: Dutton; Dent, 1950.

Rubel, Maximilien. "LesCahiers de Lecturede Karl Marx." In: *IRSH* (Amsterdam), Vol.2, 1957, Part 3.

Saint-Simon, Claude Henri de Rouvroy de. *Oeuvres de Saint-Simon et d'Enfantin.* Paris: E. Dentu, 1865-78.47v.

Sanderson, John. *An Interpretation of the Political Ideas of Marx and Engels.* London: Longmans, 1969.

Saville, John, ed. *Ernest Jones: Chartist.* Selections from the Writings and Speeches of Ernest Jones with intro and notes. London: L&W, 1952.—Cited for Saville's intro, p. 13-82.

Schapiro, Leonard. *The Communist Party of the Soviet Union.* NY: Random House, 1959.

Schapper, Karl. " Einleitung." In: *Kommunistische Zeitschrift,* Probeblatt, Nr. 1, Sept. 1847. Reprinted in: *Der Bund der Kommunisten* (q.v.), 1:501+.—Printed without signature; Schapper is the probable author.

Schoyen, A. R. *The Chartist Challenge; A Portrait of George Julian Harney.* NY: Macmillan, 1958.

Schraepler, Ernst. *Handwerkerhünde und Arbeitervereine 1830-1853. Die politische Tätigkeit deutscher Sozialisten von Wilhelm Weitling bis Karl Marx.* (Historische Kommission zu Berlin. Veröffentlichungen. Bd. 34.—Publikationen zur Geschichte der Arbeiterbewegung. Bd. 4.) Berlin/NY: Walter de Gruyter, 1972.

Seilhac, Léon de. *Le Monde Socialiste. Les Partis Socialistes Politiques. Les Congris Socialistes Politiques. Les Diverses Formules du Collectivisme.* Paris: Libr. V. Lecoffre, 1904.

Sidney, Algernon. "Discourses Concerning Government." In: his *Works.* London, 1772.

Silberner, Edmund. *Moses Hess; Geschichte seines Lebens.* Leiden: E.J. Brill, 1966.

Simkhovich, Vladimir G. *Marxism versus Socialism.* London: Williams & Norgate, n.d.—First pub. 1912.

Sombart, Werner. *Socialism and the Social Movement.* Tr. from the 6th German ed. by M. Epstein. London: Dent; NY: Dutton, 1909.—First ed. pub. 1896.

Somerhausen, Luc. *L'Humanisme Agissant de Karl Marx.* Préface de Bracke. Paris: Richard-Masse, 1946.

Spencer, Henry R. "Dictatorship." In: *Encyclopaedia of the Social Sciences* (q.v.), Vol. 5.

Spinoza, Baruch. *Tractatus Politicus.* In: his *Opera Postkuma,* 1677.

Spitzer, Alan B. *The Revolutionary Theories of Louis Auguste Blanqui.* (Columbia Studies in the Social Sciences, 594) Columbia Univ. Press, 1957.

Stein, Lorenz [von]. *Geschichte der sozialen Bewegung in Frankreich von 1789 bis aufmsere Tage.* Munich: Drei Masken Verlag, 1921. 3v.—Orig. pub. 1850. This was an expansion of Stein's *Der Sozialismus und Communismus des heutigen Frankreich. Ein Beitrag zur Zeitgeschichte,* 1842 (2d ed., 1848, off the press in 1847).

———. *The History of the Social Movement in France, 1789-1850.* Introduced, ed. & tr. by Kaethe Mengelberg. Totowa, N. J.: Bedminster Press, 1964.—This is a condensation of the 1850 work.

Stenographische Berichte uber die Verhandlungen des Reichstags. VIII. Legislaturperiode. I. Session 1890/91. Dritter Band. 77. Sitzung. Feb. 28,1891. Berlin, 1891. [Bennigsen, Grillenberger speeches.]

Stenographische Berichte über die Verhandlungen des Reichstags. VIII. Legislaturperiode. I.

442 Bibliography of Works Cited

Session 1890/91. Vierter Band. 105. Sitzung, Apr. 21,1891. Berlin, 1891. [Liebknecht speech.]
Tellering. *See* Müller-Tellering, Eduard von.
Testut, Oscar. *Le Livre Bleu de l'Internationale. Rapports et Documents Officiels...* Paris: Lachaud,1871.
Tocqueville, Alexis de. *The Old Régime and the French Revolution.* Trans, by S. Gilbert. Garden City: Doubleday Anchor Books, 1955.
Tucker, Robert C. *The Marxian Revolutionary Idea.* NY: W. W. Norton, c1969.
Turner, John Kenneth. *Challenge to Karl Marx.* NY: Reynal & Hitchcock, 1941.
Ulam, Adam B. *The Unfinished Revolution. An Essay on the Sources of Influence of Marxism and Communism.* NY: Vintage Bks. (Random House), c1960.
Venturi, Franco. *Roots of Revolution. A History of the Populist and Socialist Movements in Nineteenth Century Russia.* With an intro by Isaiah Berlin. Tr. by Francis Haskell. NY: Grosset & Dunlap, 1966.—English tr. first pub. *1960; tr. of Il Populismo Russo,* 1952.
Vérecque, Charles. *Dictionnaire du Socialisme.* Paris: Giard & Brière, 1911.
Vermersch, Eugène. *Opuscules Révolutionnaires,* 1-6. [Series of small pamphlets] London: The author, n.d. [1873].—No. 2: *LaDictature.* No. 3: *LeDroit au Vol.* No. 6: *La Société Secrète.*
Vidal, Gore. "The Second American Revolution?" [Review of Lundberg, *Cracks in the Constitution).* In: *NY. Review of Books,* Feb. 5,1981.
Voden, Alexei Mikhailovich. "Na zare 'Legalnogo Marksizma.' " [At the Dawn of "Legal Marxism."] In: *Letopisi Marksizma,* No. 4, 1927.
———. "Talks with Engels." In: *Reminiscences of Marx and Engels* (q.v.).—Excerpts from Voden's 1927 article.
Vogt, Carl. *Mein Prozess gegen die Allgemeine Zeitung.* Geneva, 1859.
Vogt, William. *La Vie d'un Homme; Carl Vogt.* Paris/Stuttgart, 1896.
Vuillaume, Maxime. *Mes Cahiers Rouges.* (Collection Cahiers de la Quinzaine) Tome 10: *Proscrits.* Paris, n.d. (1913 or 1914).
W. B. "Eduard von Müller-Tellering. Verfasser des ersten antisemitischen Pamphlets gegen Marx." In: *I.I.S.H. Bulletin.* Vol. 6, 1951, No. 3, p.178+.
Webb, Sidney. *What Happened in 1931: a Record.* (Fabian Tract, No. 237) Fabian Society, 1932.
Wittke, Carl. *The Utopian Communist. A Biography of Wilhelm Weitling, Nineteenth-Century Reformer.* Louisiana State Univ. Press, 1950.
Wolfe, Bertram. *Marx and America.* (John Day Pamphlets, No. 38) NY: John Day, 1934.
———. *Marxism. One Hundred Years in the Life of a Doctrine.* NY: Dial Press, 1965.
———. *Three Who Made a Revolution. A Biographical History.* Boston: Beacon Press, 1955; c1948.
Wollstonecraft, Mary. *An Historical and Moral View of the Origin and Progress of the French Revolution; and the Effect It Has Produced in Europe.* Volume the First. Second Edition. London: J. Johnson, 1795.—This was the only volume she wrote.

INDEX

This Index does not cover the Reference Notes or the Bibliography. There is no heading for *Marx* or *Engels*, nor for a number of geographical terms and subject headings which occur so abundantly that a long list of page numbers would be of little use. Topics under these subjects should be sought under headings of a narrower scope. Titles of writings by Marx or Engels are indexed only for substantive references, not if merely quoted or mentioned as a source. The same applies to names of periodicals.

Reference to a page includes relevant footnotes on that page. Reference to a footnote only is indicated by *n;* thus 129n = footnote on page 129. An *f* means "plus page following"; thus 129f = pages 129-130. "Passim" is shown by three suspension points between page numbers; thus 129 . . . 150 = pages 129-150 passim, that is, the subject is explicit or implicit throughout those pages.

A short list of abbreviations is given on page 387f, but this Index includes a general glossary of abbreviations used in this volume.

Alphabetization follows the rules commonly found in American libraries, that is, the so-called Anglo-American code.

A la Classe Ouvrière (Delahaye), 287
AFL-CIO, 204
Abendpost (Berlin), 222
abolition of classes, 225f, 247, 297
absolutism, figleaf of, 318
Adam (Bibl. figure), 360
Adam, 185-87, 189, 192f, 197-200, 202, 207, 209
Address to the Communist League (ME): of March 1850, 141n, 159f, 198, 214, 235, 238, 271n, 334, 340, 344-46, 348f, 352-54, 358, 371-73; of June 1850: 191f, 199, 203, 205, 354, 358

adventurism, 135, 154, 157, 170f
Albert (pseud. of Alexandre Martin), 47, 161
Algeria, 49, 67
Alliance of the Socialist Democracy, 94-97
The Alliance of the Socialist Democracy and the IWMA (Engels, Lafargue, Marx), 94, 97
alliances, allies (classes), 72, 160. *See also* hegemony of the proletariat
Almanacco Repubblicano per l'Anno 1874 (Lodi), 295
Amann, Peter, 135n

443

444 Index

America. *See* United States
Anabaptists, 55, 103
anarchism, anarchists, 43, 47f, 49n, 55f, 58, 80f, 93-95, 101, 116f, 225, 230, 253, 266, 276, 285, 295, 298-300, 354, 374
anarchy, anarchism (old pejorative sense), 24, 69f, 78, 83, 228; 'party of anarchy,' 371
Anneke, Friedrich, 242
Annenkov, Pavel Vasilyevich, 148
Anti-Dühring (Engels), 123
antipoliticalism. *See* anarchism
antireligious propaganda. *See* atheism
anti-Semitism. *See* Jewish question
Anti-Socialist Law (Ger.), 104, 267, 311, 314
Arendt, Hannah, 271n
Aristotle, 68
armed force. *See* force and violence
Arnaud, Antoine, 281
artisans, 339n
ascendancy ("proletarian ascendancy"), 214f
asceticism, 342, 362
ascription to Engels (of material in *Democratic Review*), 164, 179n
assassination, 267
The Assembly. *See* National Assembly (France)
Assi, Adolphe Alphonse, 131, 138
L'Atelier (Paris), 151f
atheism, antireligious propaganda, 37, 228, 283, 287, 363
Athens (Gr.), 71
Atta Troll (Heine), 220
Augustus, Emperor, 13
Australia, 236
Austria, Austria-Hungary, 169, 258, 267, 370. *See also* Hungary
Austrian Social-Democratic movement, 310
Aveling, Edward (Bibbins), 105
Avineri, Shlomo, 332

Babeuf, François Noël, *called* Gracchus, 19, 27, 29, 32f, 35, 112, 120-24, 341f, 348, 353, 357, 362f, 366

Babouvism, Babouvists, 29-31, 33f, 37-40, 52,112,120-24, 212, 341f
Baden movement and government of 1849, 90, 158
Bailly, Jean Sylvain, 25
Bakunin, Michael *(Russ.* Mikhail Alexandrovich), 55-57, 93-97, 101, 116, 262, 266, 290f, 295, 298-301, 345n, 378; his *Confession,* 56
Bakuninists, Bakuninist movement, 94, 96f, 101, 266, 281f, 284, 290-92, 295. *See also* Alliance of the Socialist Democracy; Guillaume
Bakuninists at Work (Engels), 266
Bangya, János *(Ger.* Johann), 192
Banquet of the Equals, 128
Barbaroux, Charles Jean Marie, 23
Barbès, Armand, 34, 47, 124,130f, 159, 164, 384
Barrot, Camille Hyacinthe Odilon, 159
Barth, Paul, 310
Barthélemy, Emmanuel, 132, 189f, 193,197, 204f, 207, 209
Bastide, Jules, 50, 52
Bastille (Paris), 349
Bauer, Bruno, 368
Bauer, Dr. Ludwig (or Louis), 195, 231
Bax, E. Belfort, 18f
Bayswater Tavern (London), 193
Bazard, Saint-Amand, 40
Bebel, August, 103-05, 261, 303, 310, 381
Becker, Hermann, 54, 231, 235
Becker, Gerhard, 155n
Becker, Bernhard, 257
Becker, Johann Philipp, 257f
Beer, Max, 114, 330f
Beesly, Edward Spencer, 105, 132
Belgium and the Belgians, 96,135, 152,154, 192, 209n, 268, 274, 281, 363, 365. *See also* Brussels
Belle-Île (prison), 128, 132, 136
Belleville (Paris), 274
Bennigsen, Rudolf von, 312f
Bentham, Jeremy, 122n, 356
Berkley, Sir John, 17
Berlin, Isaiah, 35, 143n, 333, 353

Index 445

Berlin University, 123
Bernard, Simon, 132
Bernstein, Eduard, 35, 100, 104, 123, 144, 181, 183, 226, 254, 267, 337 ... 344, 353, 355-57, 361n, 381-83
Bernstein, Samuel, 135n, 139n, 187
Bernstein(ian)ism, 148, 221, 223, 225, 254, 331, 337, 343f, 355, 382
Beust, Friedrich, 242
Bielefeld (Ger.), 217
Bignami, Enrico, 295
Billy the Kid, 347
Biskamp (or Biscamp), Elard, 251
Bismarck, Otto von, 53, 85f, 99, 104, 256f, 267, 311
Bismarck(ian)ism, 86, 102, 227, 253, 257f
Blanc, Louis, 45-48, 52, 55, 59, 74, 88f, 91, 117-19, 125, 127f, 135, 151f, 164n, 168, 177-82, 186, 189, 196, 222, 230, 246, 366n
Blanqui, (Louis) Auguste, 4, 34, 40, 47, 120 ... 144, 159, 164, 180-83, 187-90, 194, 203-06, 208, 228, 230, 265, 274f, 279-82, 293, 302, 333f, 336-39, 343f, 345n, 348-54, 356-58, 379-84; his *Instructions pour une Prise d'Armes*, 35, 125. *See also* next four entries
Blanqui & the 'd. of the p.' myth, 34-39, 120
Blanqui's Toast, affair of, 128f, 132
Blanquism, Marx's relation to, 4, 5, 119, 120 ... 144, 145 ... 171, 180, 181, 184 ... 213, 215f, 226, 228f, 264-69, 279-86, 289, 293, 297f, 302f, 307-09, 315f, 333, 337 ... 359, 366, 379, 383f
Blanquists, Blanquist movement. *See preceding entry; also:* 31, 34, 36f, 40, 43, 74, 187, 233, 246, 248, 274-78; pamphlet *Internationale et Ré-volution* (1872), 37, 280, 282-84, 286, 297; pamphlet *Aux Communeux* (1874), 37, 282, 285, 302; social composition, 126f, 343. *See also* Boulangeo-Blanquists
Blind, Karl, 228

Blum, Robert, 217
Bober, M. M., 336
Bobzin, Friedrich, 195
Bohemia (Austria-Hungary), 57, 158
Bolivar, Simon, 6, 84
Bolshevism, 37, 95, 332, 337
Bonaparte, Louis Napoleon (Napoleon III), 53, 55, 71, 78f, 82f, 87f, 100, 105, 129f, 132f, 142, 168, 176f, 239f, 250, 254 ... 262, 277, 309, 364, 373
Bonaparte, Napoleon. *See* Napoleon I
Bonapartism, Bonapartists: *in Bonaparte's regime:* 80, 132, 249, 274, 373; *elsewhere and gen.:* 6, 83f, 85, 91, 99f, 105, 248-50, 253-55, 257-61
Book review ... *See* Review of ...
Bornstedt, Adalbert von, 135, 154
Bottigelli, Emile, 307, 308n
Boulangeo-Blanquists, 308
Boulanger, Georges (Gen.), and Boulangism, 83, 308f
Boulevard de la Villette (Paris), 274
Boulevard Saint-Michel (Paris), 275
bourgeois democracy, bourgeois-democratic regime, 83, 115, 308, 321f
bowdlerization (of Engels), 317, 336
Bradlaugh, Charles, 132
Bremen (Ger.), 232
Brentano, Lorenz Peter, 90
brigandage, 266, 292
Brissot de Warville, Jacques Pierre, 20f, 22n
Brissotins. *See* Girondins
Brousse, Paul, 101f
Browning, Robert, 294n
Brüning, Chancellor Heinrich, 13
Bruhn, Karl [von], 206f
Brussels (Belg.), 123, 132-34, 140, 143, 148f, 151f, 191f, 230, 242f
Brutus, Marcus Junius, 19
Bucher, Lothar, 65
Buchez, Philippe, 151
Bukharin, Nikolai I., 332n
Bulwer-Lytton, Baron Edward, 29
Buonarroti, Filippo Michele *(in France* Philippe), 29-33, 37f, 42, 120-25, 135, 209n, 348

446 Index

Burr, Aaron, 18
CL. *Abbrev. of* Communist League
Cabet, Etienne, 41f, 117-19, 151f, 181f, 342, 356f; his *Voyage en Icarie,* 41
Cabetist movement, Cabetists, 41f, 45, 118, 151, 153, 161, 342, 356f
Cadogan, Peter, 107
Caesar. Julius, 12. 17, 19, 89
Caesarism, 12f, 18, 22n, 62, 100f, 261
Café de la Renaissance (Paris), 126
Cahiers du Bolchévisme (Paris), 186
Cahors (prison), 281
Calvez, Jean-Yves, 333
Camphausen, Ludolf, 61-67
Capital (Marx), 139, 234n, 310, 373
Carbonari, 171
Carey, Henry Charles, 247
Carnot, Lazare Hyppolyte, 130
Carr, Edward Hallett, 153, 333
cartel (relationship), 142f
caste, 222, 226
Castlereagh, Robert Stewart, Lord, 87
Caussidierè, Marc, 189
Caute, David, 333
Cavaignac, General Louis Eugène, 45, 48-53, 62, 66f, 78, 157, 175f, 237-39, 296, 309
Cayenne (Fr. Guiana), 83, 132
Cazavant [Blanquist], 189
censor (Roman official), 18, 22
Center for Socialist History (Berkeley), 6
Center party (Ger.), 85, 314
Central Committee of the European Democracy, 89f, 167, 196
Central Republican Club (Paris), 135
centralization, 266, 315f
Cercle Social, 121f, 361
Champ-de-Mars (Paris), 25, 182
Chang, Sherman H. M., 331
Chartist movement, Chartists, 106, 114, 122, 142f, 150f, 193, 201, 203f, 215, 297f, 344, 350, 356. *See also* Harney; E. Jones; O'Brien
Chastellux, François de, 356
Château du Taureau (Morlaix, Fr.), 281

Chaumette, Pierre Gaspard ("Anaxagoras"), 19
Chenu, Adolphe, 161f, 384
Chicago (Ill.), 243
China, 260
Christian communism, 236
Christian socialism, 151
Ciceronian praeteritio, 341
Cincinnatus, Lucius Quinctius, 89
Circular Against Kriege (ME), 146, 148, 217
civil liberties, 364. *See also* democratic rights
Civil War (U.S.), 82, 243
The Civil War in France (Marx), 78, 105, 139, 265, 269, 271, 273, 281, 292, 373, 377; its drafts, 78f, 91, 272f, 373; Engels' Introduction, 315-17, 386
Clairvaux (Fr.), 281
class rule, concept of, 115-17. *See also* rule of the proletariat
class struggle, 221f, 226, 247f, 356
The Class Struggles in France (Marx), 159, 175-82, 214, 219f, 224, 227f, 232, 251, 271, 296, 330f, 334-36, 351, 356, 371, 379f, 385; Engels' Introduction, 314, 317
Cloots, Jean Baptiste du Val-de-Grâce, Baron de; *called* Anacharsis Cloots, 19
club movement (1848), 135, 348, 352
Cluseret, Gustave Paul, 286
Cluss, Adolf, 247f
coalitionism, coalition government, 87, 91, 106, 165, 321
Cobden, Richard, 88
Coblenz (Ger.), 230f
Cole, G. D. H., 275, 333, 376
Cologne (Ger), 155-58, 165, 167, 191, 229, 231, 235, 255. *See also* Neue Rheinische Zeitung
Cologne Communist trial (1852), 55, 165n, 233, 346, 372
Cologne Workers Association, 156
colonialism. *See* nationalism
Columbia Encyclopedia, 15
Comité Révolutionnaire du Prolétariat, 287f

Commissaire, Sébastien, 42
Committee of Public Safety (French
  Rev.), 21, 26, 32, 245, 365
Committee of Public Safety (Paris,
  1848), 182
Committee of Public Safety (Cologne,
  1848), 156
Committee of Public Safety (1871),
  276f
Commons, John R., 331
Commune of Paris. *See* Paris Commune (1789+)
Commune Révolutionnaire, 282f
Communia colony (Iowa), 55
communism, communist (term), 41,
  356f
Communist Club of New York, 243
Communist Correspondence Committee (Brussels), 140f, 151, 191,
  243
Communist International, 330
Communist League, 98, 112f, 117,
  123f, 126, 135, 141, 148f, 151, 154,
  165-67, 169f, 186, 191-94, 196-
  204, 206f, 209-12, 216f, 221,
  226-28, 231-36, 243, 264, 268,
  340f, 345f, 352-56; Central
  Comm. split, 1850, 232. *See also*
  Cologne Communist trial
Communist Manifesto (ME), 34, 60, 78,
  112-14, 122, 139-41, 149-51, 180,
  195, 224, 234n, 244-46, 254, 271,
  283, 297, 301, 329, 333, 335, 337,
  341f, 353, 358, 371
Communist Party. *See* French Communist Party; German CP
compensation or confiscation, 298
Comte, Auguste, 104f
Comtists (Positivists), 104f. *See also*
  Beesly, Edward S.
Condition of the Working Class in England (Engels), 234n, 242
Condorcet, Marie Jean Antoine, Marquis de, 20
Conservatives (Ger.), 314
Considlrant, Victor, 125
conspiratorialism, secret societies, 34,
  57, 97, 124, 127, 134, 145, 149,
  151, 161f, 168-71, 187, 189, 199-
  202, 212, 265, 287, 291, 307, 315,
  339, 341, 346, 348, 352f, 357,
  384
Constituent Assembly (Fr.), 45, 159
constitutional dictatorship, 53. *See also*
  martial law
The Convention. *See* National Convention (French Rev.)
cooperatives, cooperativism, 43, 296
Corday, Charlotte, 24
Corn Laws (Brit.), 87
Cornu, Auguste, 254
Cossack(s). *See* Russia
Council of Three Hundred (Fr. Rev.),
  25
coup de main (term), 384
Cournet, Frédéric, 281
Crédit Mobilier, 80
Le Cri du Peuple (Paris), 278n
Crimean War, 16, 86
Critique of the Erfurt Program (Engels),
  317-23, 330, 377, 386
Critique of the Gotha Program (Marx),
  103f, 303-05, 307, 309-15, 320f,
  330, 334f, 386; suppression of,
  310f
Cromwell, Oliver, 20, 43, 62, 73, 107,
  194n, 235, 238, 245, 361
Crossman, R. H. S., 376
Cunow, Heinrich, 330
czar. *See* Nicholas I

DBZ. *See* Deutsche-Brüsseler-Zeitung
Da Costa, Charles, 36f, 126f, 274f,
  279f, 339n
Da Costa, Gaston, 276
Dan, Theodore, 344
Dana, Charles A., 245
Danton, Georges Jacques, 19, 23f, 121,
  365
Darmstadt (Ger.), 216f, 243
Darthé, Augustin Alexandre Joseph,
  31f
Debon [given name unknown], 31f
Deflotte. *See* Flotte, Paul de
Delacroix, Jean François, 21
Delahaye, Pierre Louis, 286n
Delahaye, Victor Alfred, 286-88
Delord, Taxile, 47

448 Index

democracy, democratic state forms, 43, 55, 59, 68f, 273, 292, 299, 316, 362; representative democracy, 116, 299. *See also* bourgeois democracy
The Democracy, 54, 59-61, 72, 113-15, 121, 217
Democratic Association (Brussels), 123, 135
Democratic Association (Cologne), 54, 156
Democratic Association (London), 195, 207, 231
Democratic Association (Paris), 135, 154, 170
Democratic Association (Rhineland), 156
Democratic Communists, 140f
Democratic Congress (Ger., 1848), 243
democratic dictatorship. *See* dictatorship (of democratic bodies), *or* dictatorship (of the democracy)
Democratic Party (U.S.), 204
democratic republic, 230, 305, 316-23
Democratic Review (London), 117f, 163, 179, 214f, 376
democratic rights. *See* civil liberties; freedom of the press; right to organize; recall
Demuth, Helene, 80
Denmark and the Danes, 106n
Denonville (pseud.). *See* Watteau, L.
De Paepe, César, 96
Desmoulins, Camille, 19
despotism, 11, 15, 25. 28, 31, 71, 77-79, 81f, 85, 116, 156, 235, 240, 276, 299, 367; class despotism, 77-79; democratic despotism, 69; military despotism, 114; "despotic encroachments," 114; of democracy, 69; parliamentary despotism, 78, 176; popular despotism, 68f
Deutsch-Französische Jahrbücher (Paris), 254
Deutsche Reichszeitung (Frankfurt), 217
Deville, Gabriel, 139, 341
Dézamy, Théodore, 42, 152, 234n, 357

dialectic, 338, 341, 343
dictatorship (term), 4; early meanings, 16-18; *see also* dictatura as Roman term.—As election postponement, 45f, 177; bourgeois dictatorship, 176, 179, 215, 296; class dictatorship, 175f, 178, 180, 186, 212f, 229, 232, 238, 246, 262, 264, 276, 278, 309; by science or scientists, 99, 300; commissioned dictatorship, 176; constitutional dictatorship, 13f; editor's, 80f; educational dictatorship, 30, 33, 37, 47,125,149; in *Class Struggles in France*, 175-78; inner-party, 101-07; intellectual dictators, 80; majority or minority, 47, 59, 286, 302, and *see also* majority rule; military dictatorship), 66, 69-71, 82-84, 90, 175, 235-37, 239, 308f; of democratic bodies, 20f, 28, 41, 62-64, 66f, 239; of the Democracy, 20, 29, 41, 58 . . . 67; of the Central Committee, 233f, 276; of Paris, 31, 38f, 46, 246, 285, 316, 366; of the party (or band), 38, 222, 228f, 233, 264, 302f, 315, 324; 'official' dictatorship, 94, 96; parliamentary dictatorship, 176; secret dictatorship, 33, 55, 57, 93-97, and *see also* Invisible Brotherhood; semidictatorship, 85; social dictatorship (Stein), 73f, 178
dictatorship of the proletariat (selected references):
counterposition of bourgeois and proletarian dictatorship, 240, 272n, 295f, 314, 370; high visibility, 251; 'impersonal d. of the p.,' 281n; list of loci, 385f; meaning (general thesis), 1, 211-13, 269, 289, 293, 298, 305, 322; periodization, 111; published loci, 332, 334-36; 'specific form for,' 318-20
'dictatura' as Roman term, 11-16, 17 . . . 26, 28f, 32, 52f, 70, 73, 77, 178

La Dictature (Vermersch), 291
dictionaries, 17, 28f, 80, 88
Dictionary of the History of ideas, 15
Dictionnaire de l'Acadimie Française, 17, 28
Dictionnaire de Trevoux, 17
Diderot, Denis, 17
Diehl, Karl, 331
Diggers. *See* True Levelers
Directory (Fr.), 123
'disciple' of Marx, 'Marxist,' 243f
discipline, 237f, 265, 279n, 315
Discontogesellschaft, 227
doctrinaire socialism, doctrinaires, 177, 179f. *See also* sectism
Dombrowski, Jaroslaw, 293
Dominick, R. H., 314n
Dommanget, Maurice, 36, 38, 130n, 134-37,139, 187, 190, 204-06, 209, 275, 281n, 302n, 381-83; his tendency, 382f
Donoso Cortés, Juan, 59, 70f, 86
Doppet, François Amédée, 20
Doullens (prison), 136
Dracula myth, 144
Drahn, Ernst, 233n, 330
Draper, Hal (refuted), 350
Dronke, Ernst, 164, 219f
dual power, 64
Düsseldorf (Ger.), 98
dueling, duels, 209, 257
Duncan, Graeme, 333
Dupont [Blanquist], 189
Dupont, Eugène, 296
Duprat, Pascal, 50

E. *Abbrev. of* Engels
Easton, Loyd D., 378
Eccarius, J. G., 89f, 179n, 238f, 245, 296
Economie et Humanisme (Paris), 331
ed. *Abbrev. of* editor, editorial
Egalité (Geneva), 286
Egalité (Paris), 102
Eifel region (Ger.), 235
The Eighteenth Brumaire of Louis Bonaparte (Marx), 78,175f, 280, 310
Eisenachers, Eisenacher party, i.e., German Social-Democratic Workers Party. *See* German Social-

Democratic movement
Eisenstein, Elizabeth L., 33
elections: democratization, 61; direct/indirect voting, 61. *See also* dictatorship (as election postponement)
émeute (riotous outbreak), the term, 162f, 384
Encyclopaedia of the Social Sciences, 11, 334
ends and means, 229
Enfantin, Barthélemy Prosper, 40
Engels, Col. Friedrich; *in full* Karl Friedrich Gottfried Ludwig, 157n
Engels-vs.-Marx myth, 269, 298
English Revolution (Cromwellian), 62, 194, 340n, 361n
'Enragés,' 22, 121, 361-63, 366
equality, as social goal; equalitarianism, 121, 348
Erfurt congress, Erfurt program. *See* Critique of the Erfurt Program
Espartero, Baldomero; Conde de Luchana [etc.], 90
Etudes de Marxologie (Paris), 4n
Eudes, Emile, 274f, 280f
Eurocommunists, 355
European Central Committee. *See* Central Committee of the European Democracy
European Democracy, Central Committee of. *See* Central Comm. . . .
Evans, Michael, 336
ex-Communists, ex-Marxists, 347f
Executive Commission (Fr., 1848), 48f

FBI, i.e., Federal Bureau of Investigation, 144
FD. *Abbrev. of* Fraternal Democrats
Fabians, Fabianism, 60n, 337
'falsifiction' (term), 3
fascism, 48, 308. *See also* Nazism
Fauchet, Abbé Claude, 121
Fazy, James, 90
February Revolution. *See* Revolution of 1848 (France)
feminism. *See* women's emancipation
Ferdinand Lassalle as a Social Reformer (Bernstein), 100
Ferguson, Adam, 70

450   Index

Fetscher, Iring, 292n, 333, 377
Feuer, Lewis S., 375-77
Field of Mars. *See* Champ-de-Mars (Paris)
Filmer, Sir Robert, 17
Finlen, James, 106
First International. *See* International Working Men's Association
Fischel, Eduard, 142
Fleurus (Belg.), 365
Flocon, Ferdinand, 135, 152
Flotte, Paul de, 129, 189
Flourens, Gustave, 130
force and violence, 4, 25, 42, 66, 72f, 85f, 90, 125, 129, 146, 149, 151, 157, 167, 176, 187, 237, 257, 262, 266, 268, 291, 293, 295, 300, 310, 312f, 317f, 340, 343, 353, 366
Ford, Gerald, 29n
Foreign Affairs Committees. *See* Urquhartites
Fouquier-Tinville, Antoine Quentin, 363
Fourier, Charles, 40, 209n, 234n
Fourierist movement, Fourierists, 40, 125
'fourth estate' (as term), 33, 214, 234
Franco-Prussian War, 154, 274
Frankel, Leo, 277
Frankfurt (Ger.), 216f, 227, 243. *Note:* All references are to Frankfurt am Main
Frankfurt Assembly (1848), 62-67, 217, 248, 251
Frankfurt revolt (1848), 156
Fraternal Democrats, 141, 186, 193f, 201, 203, 208
La Fraternité (Paris), 187
Tree state,' 303
freedom of the press, 32, 51f, 56, 58f, 66, 83, 87, 235, 277, 368
Freiligrath, Ferdinand, 245
French Academy, 17, 28
French Branch (of the IWMA). *See* IWMA
French Communist Party, 186, 361, 382
French Republicans. *See* Republicans (Fr.)

French Revolution (1789+), 18 . . . 26, 28, 29n, 30f, 41, 53, 62, 66, 69, 71, 83, 121f, 142n, 194n, 255, 318f, 341, 349, 360 . . . 367, 370; Reign of Terror, *see* terror(ism). *See also* Jacobins
French social-democrats, 74, 78, 117, 127f, 140, 151-53, 177-79, 187, 190, 205, 371. *See also* Blanc, L.
French socialist movement, 130. *See also* Guesdists, Possibilists
French Workers Party. *See* Guesdists
Friedrich Wilhelm IV (King), 71
Friend of the People (London), 238
Frost, John, 107
Furetière, Antoine, 17

GCFI. *Abbrev. of* The General Council of the First International.
GGWA. *Abbrev. of* General German Workers Association
GWEA. *Abbrev. of* German Workers Educ. Assoc.
Garde Mobile (Fr.). *See* Mobile Guard
Garibaldi, Giuseppe, 89, 95, 98
Garnier-Pagès, Louis Antoine, 49
Garrone, Galante, 123
Gatherings from the Press (Marx), 251
Gay, Jules, 357
Gay, Peter, 333, 338, 340
General Council. *See* International W.M.A.
General German Workers Association (Lassallean), 99, 102f, 255-57, 261
general strike, 266
generalship. *See* restraint in revolution
Geneva (Switz.), 90, 96, 220, 248f
Genghis Khan, 341
German Campaign for a Reich Constitution (Engels), 223
German Communist Party, 233n
German Democratic Association. *See* Democratic Association
The German Ideology (ME), 218, 356
German Legion (1848), 135, 154, 155, 357
German National Assembly. *See*

Index   451

Frankfurt Assembly
German Social-Democratic movement, 13, 53, 100, 103f, 222, 233n, 267, 297, 310 . . . 323, 330, 337; Eisenachers (before 1875), 103, 261, 303. *See also* Anti-Socialist Law; Lassalleans; GGWA; Reichstag Fraction
German Workers Club (Paris), 135
German Workers Educational Association (London) (GWEA), 165, 193, 195f, 231, 251, 343
German-American Revolutionary Loan, 171
Gesellschaftsspiegel (Elberfeld), 254
Giessen (Ger.), 248
Girardin, Emile de, 39, 49, 51
Girey-Dupré, 21
Girondins (in French Rev.), 20-23, 39, 121, 181, 361. *See also* Brissot
Gladstone, William Ewart, 107
God as dictator, 71
Godwin, William, 122n
Goegg, Amand, 90
Goethe, Johann Wolfgang von, 217f, 220
Göttingen (Ger.), 227f, 381
Gois, Emile, 280
Gotha congress, Gotha program. *See* Critique of the Gotha Program
Gottschalk, Andreas, 54
Gottschatk, Louis R., 22n
Goudchaux, Michel, 130
government (vs state), 304
Gracchi (i.e., the brothers Tiberius Sempronius Gracchus and Gaius Sempronius Gracchus), 19
Granger, Ernest Henri, 274, 280, 308
Great Men of the Emigration (ME), 90, 128, 171
Greece (ancient), Greek society, 71
Greek Street (London), 195
Grillenberger, Karl, 312-15
Gronlund, Laurence, 243
Grün, Karl, 217f, 242, 254
Guddat, Kurt H., 378
Günther, J. Georg, 217
Guérin, Daniel, 319
Guesde, Jules, 101, 355

Guesdists (Fr.), 102, 305, 307f, 355
Guillaume, James, 101, 290
Guizot, François, 59, 68-70
Gurvitch, Georges, 300n, 378

Hague Congress. *See* IWMA
Hales, John, 287f
Halévy, Elie, 15, 35
Hamburg (Ger.), 206
Hamilton, Alexander, 18
Hamlet, 131
Hamm (Ger.), 243
Hammen, Oscar, 155n
Hardie, Keir, 105f
Harney, George Julian, 106f, 114, 117f, 121, 141, 163, 179, 185f, 189f, 193f, 198, 200-03, 205, 208, 210, 214, 238
Harring, Harro, 90
Harrington, Michael, 334
harsh tone and polemical intolerance, 218, 221
Hasenclever, Wilhelm, 104
Hatzfeldt, Countess Sophie von, 98, 132f
Haupt, Hermann Wilhelm, 166f
Hearst, William Randolph, 39, 49
Hébert, Jacques René, 121f, 290
Hébertists, 366
Hegel, G. W. F., 69, 237, 338
hegemony of the proletariat, 271f
Heine, Heinrich, 220
Heinzen, Karl, 89-91, 196, 199, 230, 232, 247, 252
Helvétius, Claude Adrien, 122n
Hermann (London), 251
Herr Vogt (Marx), 90, 192, 235, 248-50, 255
Herrick, Robert, 17
Herrschaft (term), 1, 112, 215, 300
Herwegh, Georg, 135, 154
Hess, Moses, 5, 43, 130, 217, 253 . . . 263
Hetherington, Henry, 122
Highet, Gilbert and Helen, 376
Hilf Dir (defence force), 258n
Hillquit, Morris, 330
history. *See* materialist conception of history

452 Index

Hitler, Adolf, 41, 83
Hitlerism. *See* Nazism
Hodde, Lucien de la, 161, 384
Hoffenstein, Samuel, 357
Holbach, Paul Henri Dietrich, Baron d', 122n
Holcombe, A. N., 68n
Holmes, Sherlock, 134
The Holy Family (ME), 121, 242f, 356, 362, 364
L'Homme Libre, (Paris), 37
Hook, Sidney, 334, 337
Hôpital Necker. *See* Necker hospital
House of Commons. *See* Parliament
House of Trades, 43
The Housing Question (Engels), 283, 296f, 386
Howard, Leslie, 360, 362
Hubert, Charles-Fr., 331
Hugo, Victor, 52
Hungary and Hungarians, 192f, 278, 369
Hunt, R. N. Carew, 334
Hunt, Richard N., 202, 208, 331, 360n
Hyndman, Henry Mayers, 105, 324

IISH. *Abbrev. of* International Institute for Social History (Amsterdam)
IML. *Abbrev. of* Institute of Marxism-Leninism (Moscow, Berlin)
IRSH. *Abbrev. of* International Review of Social History (Amsterdam)
IWMA. *Abbrev. of* International Working Men's Association
Icar, 41f, 119
Icaria, 41, 117f
Icarians. *See* Cabetist movement
Idée Générale de la Révolution (Proudhon), 239
Imbert, Jacques, 135
impatience, 267f, 274
importing of revolution, 154f
Independent Labour Party (Brit.), 105, 115n
India, 260
industrial army, 234n
insane asylum analogy, 40, 256

Institute of Marxism-Leninism (Moscow, Berlin), 206, 221n, 384
International Labor Conference (Berlin), 287
International Publishers (N.V.), 384
International Working Men's Association (First International), 55, 94, 96f, 101, 104f, 136,140,188,191, 208, 254, 260-62, 277, 279-86, 292f, 355, 386; anarchist IWMA, 101; "French Branch," 136; General Council, 96f, 262, 265, 277-79, 281f, 294f, 319; German Swiss center, 261; Swiss Federal Council, 96. *Congresses:* Geneva Congress (1866), 261, 279f, 296; Lausanne Congress (1867), 261; Brussels Congress (1868), 261, 280; Basel Congress (1869), 261; London Conference (1871), 292; Hague Congress (1872), 266, 281f, 285, 292.
internationalism, international organization, 141,191,193, 208f, 272, 365
interpenetration of ultraleftism and opportunism, 199
L'Intransigeant (Paris), 308
Invisible Brotherhood, Invisible Directors, etc.: Bakunin's, 94-96; Proudhon's, 59
invisible dictators. *See* dictatorship (secret dictatorship)
Ireland and the Irish, 85,105, 107, 373
Isaacs, Bernard, 384
Iserlohn (Ger.), 264
Islam, 142, 236
Israel, 260
Italian War of 1859, 258
Italy and Italian movements, 191, 237, 295f, 320n, 321, 369f. *See also* Garibaldi, Mazzini, Mazzinists

Jacobin-communism, Jacobin-communists, Jacobin-revolutionary, Jacobin-leftist, 29, 33f, 37f, 43, 47, 57,121f, 134, 145, 161, 166, 212, 216, 228f, 264f, 271, 276f,

286, 289, 291, 344, 348, 366. *See also* Blanquism
Jacobins, Jacobinism (in French Rev.), 20, 22, 41, 46, 121, 154f, 193, 194, 319, 335, 348, 361 . . . 366. *See also* names of leaders, Robespierre, Saint-Just, etc.
Jahn, Friedrich Ludwig, 318n
Jászi, Oscar, 334
Jaurès, Jean, 124, 319, 355
Jefferson, Thomas, 18
Jersey (Channel Is.), 194
Jesuits, 33, 102
Jesus, 341
Jewish question, anti-Semitism, 101, 231f, 253f, 259f. *See also* Zionism
Johannard, Jules, 281
John of Leyden, 55, 103
Johnson, Christopher H., 118n
Johnson, Samuel, 3
Johnstone, Monty, 322n
Jones, Ernest, 89. 106f, 114, 117, 132, 143, 240
Jottrand, Lucien, 123, 135
Jourdan, Count Jean Baptiste, 365
Journal des Actionnaires (Paris), 257 -
July monarchy. *See* Louis Philippe
July Revolution. *See* Revolution of 1830
June days (June uprising, etc.) of 1848, 48, 73, 160, 179f, 187, 190, 193, 369f, 373
June days of 1849, 78, 373
Junkers (Ger.), 86, 222, 314

KGB, 352
KMTR. *Abbrev. of* Karl Marx's Theory of Revolution (see Biblio. under Draper)
Kagan (N. Y.), 332
Kallenberg, 195
Kamenev, Lev Borisovich, 332n
Karl Marx, Chronik seines Lebens, 381. *See also* in Biblio.
Karl Marx, Pangermaniste (Guillaume), 101
Kautsky, Karl, 105, 309-11, 317, 329f, 332n, 335, 364f
Kinkel, Gottfried, 89, 171, 199, 251

knee-jerk denunciations, 229-31
Koch, Eduard Ignaz, 244f
Koechlin, Heinrich, 276
Kommunistische Zeitschrift (London), 117, 149
Korff, Hermann, 242
Kościusko, Tadeusz (or Thaddeus Kosciusko), 26, 91
Kossuth, Lajos (or Louis, Ludwig), 89f, 171, 230, 369f
Kriege, Hermann, 147f, 217f. *See also* Circular Against Kriege
Kropotkin, Prince Peter (or Pyotr Alexeyevich), 94
Kühlwetter, Friedrich Christian Hubert von, 62f
Kugelmann, Dr. Louis (or Ludwig), 136

Labour Monthly (London), 330
Labour party (Brit.), 115
Ladendorf, Otto, 363, 367
Lafargue, François, 137f
Lafargue, Laura. *See* Marx, Laura
Lafargue, Paul, 83, 94, 96f, 132, 137-39, 268, 280f, 291, 307-09, 311, 383
Lafayette, Marie Joseph, Marquis de, 20, 25, 40
Lagrange, Charles, 50
Lahautière, Richard, 42
Lamartine, Alphonse de, 47, 181f
Lamennais, Félicité Robert de, 357
Landauer, Carl, 334, 379f
Larabit, Marc, 50
Larousse du XIXe Siècle; Grand Dictionnaire Universel [etc.], 28
Laski, Harold J., 123
Lassalle, Ferdinand, 93, 98-102, 105, 132f, 142, 164n, 254-58, 261, 299, 304, 310-13; his *Open Letter*, 99
Lassallean party organization. *See* General German Workers Association
Lassalleans, Lassallean movement, 253f, 257f, 260-62, 303f, 310f. *See also* GGWA
Laveaux, Jean Charles Thibaut de, 28

Lavrov, Pyotr Lavrovich, 294
League of the Just, 117, 123,134, 141, 146f, 368
Leclerc, Théophile, 121f, 361
Ledru-Rollin, Alexandre Auguste, 59, 89,91,135, 151, 164n, 167, 177, 182, 185f, 188, 196
Leff, Gordon, 334
Lefrançais, Gustave, 276
legality, revolutionary legality, 62f, 70, 86,91,147,159,262,313,318, 323, 343
Legion of Honor (Fr.), 288
Lehning, Arthur, 202
Lelewel, Joachim, 134f
Lenchen. *See* Demuth, Helene
Lenin, V. I., 6, 11n, 295, 319-22, 324, 329-31, 333, 335, 345n
Leninist theory, 320n
Leroux, Pierre, 42, 151, 357
Letter from France (ascribed to Engels), 164
Levasseur, René 21
Levelers, 194, 361
Levraud, Edmond, 280
Lévy-Bing, L., 260
Lewy, Gustav, 98, 264
liberals, liberalism, 69, 71, 84, 88, 114, 117, 154, 155n, 167, 237; British Liberals, Liberal party, 85, 114; German Liberals, National Liberals, 85, 217, 227, 314
libertarians. *See* anarchism
Library of the Best Foreign Socialist Writers, 122
Lichtheim, George, 272n, 334, 343-47, 353-55, 357
Liebknecht, Wilhelm, 80, 99, 104, 138, 261, 290, 303, 310, 313-15, 318n
Lincoln, Abraham, 15f, 273
Littré, Emile, 28f
Longuet, Charles, 137, 139n, 277f, 281f, 383
Longuet, Jenny (Mrs.). *See* Marx, Jenny (m. Longuet)
Lorwin, Lewis L., 35
Loubère, Leo, 46f
Louis Philippe (King), 40, 69, 187 274n

love (supernal), 148
ltr. *Abbrev. of* letter
Lüning, (Heinrich) Otto, 217-26, 229, 242f,246, 248, 251
Lüning, Louise, 216
Luxembourg (Paris), 182
Lyons (Fr.), 42, 94, 266, 339n

M. *Abbrev. of* Marx
ME. *Abbrev. of* Marx and Engels
M/E. *Abbrev. of* Marx or Engels
MECW. *Abbrev. of* ME: Collected Works (see Biblio.). *See also* ascription to Engels; translation problems
MEGA. *Abbrev. of ME:* Gesamtausgabe (old edition, see Biblio.)
MESW. *Abbrev. of ME:* Selected Works in Three Volumes (see Biblio.)
MEW *Abbrev. of ME:* Werke (see Biblio.)
Macaulay, Thomas Babington, 114f
McCarthy, Senator Joseph, and McCarthyism, 343
Macfarlane, Helen, 244f
Machiavelli, Niccolò, 16f, 291
MacIver, Robert Morrison, 15
McLellan, David, 155n, 208, 335
Maenchen-Helfen, Otto, 354
Märker, Friedrich August, 64
Magyars. *See* Hungary and Hungarians
majority rule or minority rule, 68f, 113-15,145,151,178,180,215, 271, 285-87, 302, 318, 356f, 371. *See also* dictatorship (majority or minority)
Majority-Minority split. *See* Paris Commune
Mammon, 148
Manchester (Eng.), 68, 87
Manchester Commercial Association, 68
manual (Blanquist revolutionary manual), 204f
Marat, Jean Paul, 20, 22-26, 121f, 128, 193, 291
Marcuse, Herbert, 33
Marie, Pierre, 181

Marius, Gaius, 43
Marrast, Armand, 62n, 181
martial law (state of siege), 13, 18, 25, 50, 52f, 58, 84, 156, 158, 175f
Martin, Alexandre. *See* Albert
Martin, Constant, 281
Martov, Julius, 344
Marx, Eleanor, 100
Marx, Jenny (Mrs.), 130, 219, 223
Marx, Jenny (m. Longuet), 137, 293f
Marx, Laura (m. Lafargue), 132,137, 268, 307, 308n
marxologist, marxology (term), 11n
Mason, Edward S., 275
materialism, 121, 166, 248, 283
materialist conception of history, 309f, 375
Mathiez, Albert, 361
May Day, 268
Mayer, Gustav, 185n, 375f
Mayo, Henry B., 336
Mazas prison (Paris), 132
Mazzini, Giuseppe, 89,167,169-71
Mazzinists, Mazzinist movement, 169, 191n
Mehring, Franz, 65, 94, 330
Ménard, Louis, 190
Menshevism, 324, 344
Merriam, Charles E., 15
Merriam-Webster dictionary, 3, 375
messiahs, messianism, 39f, 53, 235, 259f
Michelet, Jules, 22n
Middle Ease, 259
Milan (It.), 169f
militarization of labor, 234
military dictatorship. *See* dictatorship
Millerandism. *See* coalitionism
Millière, Jean Baptiste, 295
Milton, John, 17
Milwaukee (Wisc.), 243
Minden (Ger.), 242
minority rule. *See* dictatorship (majority or minority); majority rule or minority rule
Miot, Jules, 276
Miquel, Johannes, 227-29, 251, 318, 321, 381
Mirabeau, Honoré Gabriel Riqueti, Comte de, 21
Misère de la Philosophie (Marx). *See* Poverty of Philosophy
mistranslation. *See* translation problems
mob rule, &c, 294n, 299, 349, 364
Mobile Guard (Fr.), 51
Moilin, Jules Antoine, *called* Tony, 137
Mommsen, Wilhelm, 229, 381
Mont St-Michel (prison), 134
Montagne, Montagnards. *See* French social-democrats
Montesquieu, Charles de Secondat, Baron de, 77
Moore, Samuel, 113n
Moore, Stanley W., 331, 355-57
Moralizing Criticism and Critical Morality (Marx), 230
Morlaix (Fr.), 281
Morley, John, 107
Morris, William, 105
Morrison, James, 42f, 80n
Moses, 341
The Mountain. *See* French social-democrats
Mühlhausen (Ger.), 164
Mülberger, Arthur, 297
Müller-Tellering, Eduard von, 229-32
Münster (Ger.), 55,103, 242
Münzer, Thomas, 164, 372
Murphy's Law, 13

NDZ. *Abbrev. of* Neue Deutsche Zeitung (Darmstadt, Frankfurt)
NOZ. *Abbrev. of* Neue Oder-Zeitung (Breslau)
NRZ. *Abbrev. of* Neue Rheinische Zeitung (Cologne, 1848-49)
NRZ Revue. *Abbrev. of* Neue Rheinische Zeitung, politisch-okonomische Revue (London)
NYDT. *Abbrev. of* New York Daily Tribune
Nachet [French deputy], 50
Naples (It.), 98
Napoleon I, 19, 62, 73, 83, 237, 255, 260, 362n, 363
Napoleon III. *See* Bonaparte, L. N.

Narodniks. *See* Russian Populists
Narváez, Ramón Maria, Duke of Valencia, 70, 90
Le National (Paris), 50, 152
National Assembly (France), 21, 25, 48, 50-53, 87f, 176, 239f. *See also* Constituent Assembly
National Assembly (Ger., in Frankfurt). *See* Frankfurt Assembly
National Assembly (Prussia, 1848), 61, 64
National Charter Association, 106
National Convention (French Rev.), 21, 23, 28, 31f, 41, 66, 88
National Guard (Paris), 25,118,182, 273, 276. *See also* Mobile Guard
National Liberals (Ger.). *See* liberals (Ger.)
National Workshops (Fr.), 48, 52
National-Zeitung (Berlin), 250
nationalism, national problems and movements, 6, 26, 84, 91, 125, 185, 318n. *See also* racism
Nationalverein (Ger.), 217, 227
Nauvoo (Ill.), 118,153
Nazism (Germany), 14f, 41, 232
Nechayev, Sergei G., 95, 97
Necker hospital, 137, 282
Neue Deutsche Zeitung (NDZ) (Darmstadt, Frankfurt), 216-20, 223, 225f, 228, 243, 246, 248, 251, 385
Neue Rheinische Zeitung (Cologne), 54, 60-66, 81, 155-58, 191, 193, 217, 230, 245, 251, 330, 369f, 383
Neue Rheinische Zeitung, politisch-ökonomische Revue (London), 161, 167, 175,184, 190,194,196,215, 219f, 223f, 244, 251
Neue Zeit (Stuttgart), 103f, 310f, 381
Neufchfttel (Switz.), 101
New Mega. *Short form of ME:* Gesamtausgabe—new edition (see Biblio.)
New York Daily Tribune (N.Y.), 68, 86, 88, 168f, 245, 373
New York World (N.Y.), 292-94
New-Yorker Staatszeitung (N.Y.), 236
Nicholas I (Czar), 56f

Nicolaievsky, Boris, 135, 155, 165n, 199-205, 211n, 354f, 358f
Nihilists, 361
North German Reichstag. *See* Reichstag
Notes to the People (London), 240
Nuremberg (Ger.), 41

O'Brien, James, *called* Bronterre, 30, 122, 193
O'Connor, Feargus, 106n, 203
Old Testament, 19
Olympus, 222
On Authority (Engels), 81, 374
On the History of the Communist League (Engels), 123f
On the Jewish Question (Marx), 211n
opportunism. *See* reformism
'organization of labor,' 45, 48
organizational questions, 248. *See also* sectism; splits
Oriental despotism, 43, 77f
Osnabrück (Ger.), 227
ostracism (Greek institution), 71
Owen, Robert, 40, 43, 356f
Owenite movement, Owenites, 43, 120, 217, 357
Oxford English Dictionary, 80, 363

Paderborn (Ger.), 217
Paepe, César de. *See* De Paepe
Palais Royal (Paris), 261
Palatinate (Ger.), 158, 236
Palestine, 260
Palmerston, Viscount; Henry John Temple, 86-88,142
Pan-Slavism, Pan-Slavists, 55f
paraleipsis, 341
Pardigon, François, 190, 193, 195f, 198
Paris. *See* dictatorship (of Paris)
Paris Commune (1789 +), 20f, 23, 66, 245, 319, 365f
Paris Commune (1871), 5, 37, 39, 111, 130f, 136, 248, 265f, 269-79, 281, 284-86, 292-95, 301, 315-17, 321, 322n, 329, 333, 335, 355, 366, 370, 374, 377, 381f; its *Journal Officiel*, 39, 89,91, 271;

Majority-Minority split, 276-78. *See also* Civil War in France (Marx)
Parliament (Brit.), 43, 71, 86, 215
parliamentarism, parliamentary government, 43, 55f, 62, 79, 83, 86, 88, 90, 115, 125, 273. 308f, 343, 377; 'parliamentary idiotism,' 311; revolutionary parliamentarism, 314
Parnell, Charles Stewart, 85, 105, 107
party democracy. *See* dictatorship (inner-party)
La Patrie en Danger (Paris), 275
Payne, Robert, 204
peaceful methods. *See* force and violence
peasant problems, peasantry, 26, 46, 155f, 177, 235, 271, 339n
Peasant War in Germany (Engels), 164, 244, 372
Pennsylvania, University of, 331
Peoples Paper (London), 130, 143
Le Père Duchêne (Paris), 290
Pereire, Isaac, 80
permanent revolution, 60, 160, 167, 180f, 185f, 224, 340, 351n, 356, 379
Peter-and-Paul Fortress (Russ.), 56
Pfänder, Karl, 147
Philipon de La Madelaine, Louis, 28
Piedmontese, 370
Pieper, Wilhelm, 128, 194, 207, 227f
Pillot, Jean Jacques, 40
The Pioneer (Birmingham, London), 43
plagiarism, 358
Plato, 68
La Plebe (Lodi, Milan), 295
Plekhanov, Georgi Valentinovich, 5f, 323f
Plotkin, Norman, 189, 204f, 208
Poland, Polish movements, 26, 91, 134, 154, 192, 193, 293
political action, independent, 297
Poor Man's Guardian (London), 122
pope, "papism," 29, 40, 42, 80, 101, 105, 290
Le Populaire (Paris), 357

popular sovereignty, 61-63, 69
Positivists. *See* Comtists
possibilism, 64; French Possibilists, 101
Post gate, Raymond W., 36, 283
Potsdam (Ger.), 64
The Poverty of Philosophy (Marx), 137, 224f
Prague (now Czecho.), 57
Prairial [May 20-June 19], 42
premature revolution, 164, 267
Priklmajer-Tomanovic, Zorica, 332
Principles of Communism (Engels), 60, 113, 149
The Program of the Blanquist Refugees (Engels), 139n, 145, 266, 283, 302, 315, 381, 386 101
Progress Publishers (Moscow), 383
Le Prolitaire (Paris), 101f
Proletarian League of New York, 243
proletariat (term), 38, 72f, 126. *See also* dictatorship of the proletariat; hegemony of the p.; rule of the p.
"Promethean Complex," 375
Le Proscrit (London), 185
Protot, Eugene, 279
Proudhon, Pierre Joseph, 47, 58f, 164n, 224, 239f, 295, 357, 364
Proudhonists, Proudhonist movement, 126, 153, 188, 191f, 253, 261, 265, 277-80, 295, 297, 315
Provisional Government (Fr., 1848), 45-47, 54, 73, 135, 153, 164, 181f
Provisional Government (Fr., 1870), 91
Prussian Code, 64
Publicola. *See* Valerius Publicola
putsch (term), 158n, 383f
putschism, putsches, 34, 48, 124f, 134, 144-47, 150f, 153, 158f, 161, 169, 171, 199, 215, 264, 266f, 307, 339, 342, 346. *See also* Blanquism
Pyat, Felix, 136, 265

qu. *Abbrev. of* quoted, quotation
Qui Vive! (London), 290

RZ. *Abbrev. of* Revolutionare Zentralisation

racism, 290f. *See also* Jewish problems; nationalism
Radetzky, Gen. Joseph, 169
Radical party: French, 287; Swiss, 91
Radjavi, Kazem, 332
Ranvier, Gabriel, 280f
Raspail, François, 130, 159, 182
Rathbone Place (London), 195f
recall of officials, right to, 316
Reclus, Elie, 276
red party, reds (the term), 177
Die Reform (N.Y.), 243
La Réforme (Paris), 143, 151f
reformism, 5, 43, 103, 125, 148, 165, 167, 170f, 195, 198f, 216, 221, 226, 229, 238, 254, 256f, 261 f, 288, 295, 297, 307, 311f, 317f, 337, 342f, 361n. *See also* Possibilism; social-democracy
refugees, refugee organization, 186–89, 193, 195, 231, 278f, 281
Regnard, Albert, 280f
Reichstag, 13f, 85f, 227, 381; North Ger. Reichstag, 85
Reichstag Fraction (of German S.-D. party), 104, 311-15, 317f, 322
Reign of Terror. *See* French Revolution; terror(ism)
religion. *See* atheism
La Renaissance (Paris), 137f
republicans, republicanism, 20, 79, 130, 236, 308, 365
Republicans, Republican movement (France), 45, 48f, 71
Republik der Arbeiter (N.Y.), 55
restraint in revolution (generalship), 150, 153-58, 267f
Rev. from. *Abbrev. of* Revised from [an extant translation]
Rev. after. *Abbrev. of* Revised after [original text]
Revelations Concerning the Communist Trial in Cologne (Marx), 167, 170
Review of Chenu-Hodde book (ME), 161f, 196, 212
Revisionism. *See* Bernstein(ian)ism
Die Revolution (N.Y.), 243, 245
Revolution and Counterrevolution in Germany (Engels), 66, 89, 168

Revolution of 1830 (Fr.), 29, 40, 124
Revolution of 1848-1849, 68, 107, 289, 340n, 363; *in Bohemia:* 57; *in France:* 19, 45 . . . 59, 72f, 128, 135, 164, 168, 178-83, 193, 205, 224, 267, 319, 369f, and *see also* club movement, June days; *in Germany:* 53f, 60-67, 90, 154-58, 164, 236, 243, 258n, and *see also* Neue Rheinische Zeitung; *in Austria: see* Austria; Vienna; *in Hungary: see* Kossuth; *in Italy: see* Italy; *in Switzerland:* 90
Revolutionare Zentralisation, 192, 203, 236
revolutionary club movement. *See* club movement
revolutionary cretinism, 55, 83, 292, 343
revolutionary parliamentarism. *See* parliamentarism
Revolutions. *See* French Revolution (for 1789 +), Revolution of 1848, Revolution of 1830, etc.
Reynolds, George William MacArthur, 193
Rheinische Zeitung (Cologne), 242, 254
Rhineland and the Rhinelanders (Rhenish), 98, 235, 254, 264. *See also* names of cities
Ricardo, David, 247
Richard, Albert, 94-96
Rienzi, Cola di, 29
Rigault, Raoul, 276
right to organize, 313f
Robespierre, Maximilien de, 11, 19-21, 23-26, 32, 35, 42f, 121f, 128, 146, 193, 194n, 240, 361, 362-65, 366
Robespierrism. *See* Jacobinism; Robespierre
Rochefort, Henri de, 308
Rodrigues, Olinde, 40
Rdser, Peter, 165-67
The Role of Force in History (Engels), 85
Rome (ancient), Roman society, 19, 43, 50, 362. *See also* dictatura as Roman term
Rome (the city), 29, 78

Roosevelt, Franklin D., 87
Rosenberg, Arthur, 14, 188
Rossiter, Clinton, 13-15, 176
Rousseau, Jean Jacques, 17f, 22n, 364
Roux, Jacques, 25, 121f, 361
"Royal Prussian government socialism," 102, 257, 261
Rubel, Maximilien, 4n
Ruge, Arnold, 154,167, 232, 254
rule of the proletariat, 74, 111-14, 212f, 214f, 222f, 226, 233, 244, 248, 263, 269f, 292, 297f, 300, 367; proletariat organized as the ruling class, 301. *See also* dictatorship of the p.
Ruskin, John, 107
Russia (pre-1917) and Russians, 26, 81, 86, 96f, 236f, 255, 266, 303. *See also* Bolshevism; Menshevism; Urquhart; Urquhartites
Russia (USSR), 3. *See also* Russian Revolution, Stalinism
Russian language, 298
Russian Populists, Narodnik movement, 56, 266, 294, 323, 361, 363n
Russian Revolution, 1917, 2, 3, 6
Russian Social-Democratic movement, 6, 308, 322-25, 344
Ryazanov, David (pseud, of D. B. Goldendach), 136
Ryazanskaya, S., 384

SPDS. *Abbrev. of* Société des Proscrits Démocrates-Socialistes
SUCR. *See* Société Universale des Communistes Révolutionnaire
Saint-Just, Louis Antoine Léon de, 19, 22, 121f, 193
St. Louis (Mo.), 243
St. Martin's Hall (London), 191n
Saint-Ouen (Fr.), 287
Saint-Simon, Claude Henri, 39
Saint-Simonism, Saint-Simonians, 39f, 42, 80, 208n, 260
Sand, George, 357
Sanderson, John B., 335
Sarrut, Germain, 50
Satan, 17

Savonarola, Girolamo, 341
Scandinavian socialists-communists, 141
The Scarlet Pimpernel, 360, 363
Schapiro, Leonard, 335
Schapper, Karl, 117,146-50,156, 165-67, 186, 196, 207, 210, 230, 232f. *See also* Willich-Schapper group
Schily, Viktor, 250, 255, 258
Schlamperei, 330
Schmidt, Conrad, 309f, 386
Schoyen, A. R., 179n
Schraepler, Ernst, 202, 208, 216, 357-59
Schramm, Conrad (or Konrad), 89, 128,193f, 206, 209, 235
Schramm, Rudolph, 231f
Schulze-Delitzsch, Hermann, 257
Schwefelbande, 249f
Schweitzer, Johann Baptist von, 102-05,254,257,261f,311
Schweitzerism, 103
science and scientists, 99, 105, 248f, 254f, 300
Sebaldt, 62n
Second Empire. *See* Bonaparte or Bonapartism (Bonaparte's regime)
Second International, 6, 320f, 324f
Secret Directorate. *See* Babouvists
secret societies. *See* conspiratorialism
sectism, sects, 102f, 140, 145,177, 180, 280, 304, 324. *See also* doctrinaire socialism
Seilhac, Leon de, 382
self-restraint. *See* restraint in revolution
semidictatorship. *See* dictatorship
Semmig, Hermann, 258
separation of powers, 62f
September massacre (1792), 23
Serraillier, Auguste, 277
Serrano y Domínguez, Francisco, 82
Sidmouth, Henry Addington, Viscount, 87
Sidney, Algernon, 17
Silberner, Edmund, 253, 255-58, 261
Silesian weavers, 145
Simkhovitch, Vladimir G., 353, 379

460 Index

Slav Congress (Prague), 57
smashing state machinery. *See* state (recasting . . .)
Soboul, Albert, 36In
Social-Democracy, social-democratic movements, 48, 91, 166, 355; the term, 153. *See also* German (or French, or Russian, etc.) social-democratic movement; reformism; Second International
Social Democratic Federation (Brit.), 105
Social-Demokrat (Berlin), 257, 261
social peace, 314
social-reformism. *See* reformism
'social republic,' 270
Socialism, Utopian and Scientific (Engels), 123
socialist government, distinguished from workers' state, 270f
Socialist Labor Party (U.S.), 335
Socialist League (Brit.), 105
Société Démocratique Française (London), 117, 196
Société des Proscrits Démocrates-Socialistes (London), 186-90, 193, 195f, 200f, 203
Société des Saisons (Fr.). *See* Society of the Seasons
La Société Secrète (Vermersch), 291
Société Universelle des Communistes Révolutionnaires (SUCR), 128, 136, 140, 160f, 164, 184 . . . 214, 336, 344, 346, 350f, 353f, 358, 385
Society of the Rights of Man (Paris), 135
Society of the Seasons (Fr.), 124, 134, 268
Solingen (Ger.), 264
Sombart, Werner, 35
Sorge, Friedrich Adolph, 282, 311
Sotsial-Demokrat (Geneva), 308
South America, 84
Southern States. *See* Civil War (U.S.)
sovereignty of the people. *See* popular sovereignty
Der Sozialdemokrat (Zurich, London), 104

Spain and the Spanish, 70f, 89,193. *See also* Donoso Cortés
Spencer, Henry R., 11, 48
Spinoza, Baruch, 17
Spitzer, Alan, 36, 38, 126, 339n
splits, 324
spontaneity, 291
Stalin, Joseph, 3, 41, 222. *See also* Stalinism.
Stalinism, Stalinists, 3, 6,101, 332, 355, 361n, 384
state: autonomy of, 73; recasting the state, 63, 65; state and government forms, 304; theory of, 331. *See also* free state; workers state
state of siege. *See* martial law
statism, 304
Statism and Anarchy (Bakunin), 298f
Steffen, Wilhelm. 235
Stein, Lorenz [von], 59, 71-74, 178, 367-69
Stieber, Wilhelm, 233n
Stirner, Max, 121
Stirnerian(ism), 222
Struve, Gustav [von], 89, 195f, 231f
Der Stürmer (Berlin), 232
Suez Canal, 260
Sulla, Lucius Cornelius, 12, 43, 89
Sun Yat-sen, 331
Switzerland and the Swiss, 90, 96, 101, 188, 192, 203, 236, 243, 249f, 323. *See also* Geneva; Revolutionise Zentralisation; Zurich
syndicalism, 43, 354
Syria, 260

tacit renunciation, 347
Tagwacht (Zurich), 97
Taschereau letter, 182
Tasin, N., 332
tax refusal campaign, 155, 157
taxation, 304
Techow, Gustav, 192, 236-38
Tellering. *See* Müller-Tellering
ten-hour day, 52, 214
The Ten Hours Question (Engels), 376
terror(ism), 5, 25, 46, 53, 79n, 83, 179,245,317, 343f, 360-74; 'anonymous terrorism,' 79; bour-

Index   461

geois terrorism, 179; class terrorism, 79, 373; in Miquel, 228; in Stein, 72; individual terrorism, 361; *Terrorismus* (Gallicized), 362f; terrorization, 363; white terror, 369f
Thermidor, 26
Thiers, Adolphe, 131, 309
Time magazine (N.Y.), 335
Times (London), 68, 273
Tkachev, Peter (*or* Pyotr Nikitich), 266
toasts (political statements), 193. *See also* Blanqui's toast
Tocqueville, Alexis de, 69, 77; his *Democracy in America*, 69
Tolain, Henri, 261
Tories, Tory party (Brit.), 85, 142
Tory socialism, 105
tr. *Abbrev. of* translation, translated in
trade unions, trade-unionism, 43, 102f, 116, 296, 301
transitional period, program, regime, &c, 30, 40f, 42, 45, 60, 63, 67f, 90, 287, 294, 297f, 304-06, 312f, 342
translation problems, 7, 130n, 158n, 161n, 179,181n, 186, 298n, 305, 346, 376, 378-80, 383f
Trevoux. *See* Dictionnaire de Trevoux
tribune, tribunate (Roman office), 18-20, 23f, 29, 255
Tridon, Gustave, 39, 137, 277, 279, 281
Trier (Ger.), 62n
Trier'sche Zeitung (Trier), 242
Tristan, Flora, 208-09n
True Levelers, 361n
'the true people,' 240
True Socialism,' 217f, 242, 253f
Tucker, Robert C, 380
Türr, Istvan (*Ger.* Stefan), 192
Tuileries (Paris), 47
Turkey, 141, 266
Turn-Zeitung (N.Y.), 244-47
Turner, John Kenneth, 336
Turner bund, 244
Two Years of a Revolution (ascribed to Engels), 179n
tyranny, tyrants, 11, 15, 25, 41, 68f, 85

Tzschirner, Samuel Erdmann, 192

Ulam, Adam, 354
Union Sacrée, 275
united fronts, 140-43, 192, 355
United States, 14,18, 29n, 99,117, 149,171, 188,194, 217, 231f, 235, 243 . . . 248, 255, 316, 318, 353. *See also* Civil War
universal suffrage, 43, 59, 85, 114f, 168, 176, 214f, 255, 262, 273, 285, 299, 316, 367
Urquhart, David, 141-43
Urquhartites, Urquhartite movement, 141-43
Utin, Nikolai Isaakovich, 266
utopians, utopianism, 177f

Vaillant, Edouard, 165, 265, 278, 280-83, 285, 307f, 355, 381f
Valdegamas, Marquis de. *See* Donoso Cortés, Juan
Valerius Publicoia, Publius, 19
Varlin, Eugène, 277f
Les VeilUes du Peuple (Paris), 136
Venturi, Franco, 294
Vermersch, Eugenè, 289-92
Vermorel, Auguste, 277
Versailles government (vs Paris Commune), 131, 273, 277f
Versailles prison, 281
Vidal, François, 187
Vidal, G., 186
Vidal, Gore, 60n
Vidil, Jules, 185-87, 190, 192f, 196-200, 202, 204f, 207, 209
Vienna (Austria), 158, 230f, 310, 369f
La Villette (barracks), 274
Vincennes (Paris fort), 274
violence. *See* force and violence
Voden, Alexei Mikhailovich, 323f
Vogt, Karl (or Carl), 248-52, 255. *See also* Herr Vogt
Vogt, William, 251
Das Volk (London), 251
Volksstaat (Leipzig), 297, 302
voluntarism. *See* will
Vorwärts (Berlin), 104, 310f, 318
Vorwärts! (Paris), 254

'vrai peuple,' 240
Vuillaume, Maxime, 289f

Der Wächter am Rhein (Cologne), 54
Wagner, Richard, 29
Waldeck, Benedikt Franz Leo, 65
Walloons (Belg.), 268
war problems, policy, 142, 165, 236f, 363-65, 370; war danger, 83; war powers, 87
warnings against provocation. *See* restraint in revolution
Washington, George, 41, 89
Watteau, Dr. Louis, 129f, 132f, 139, 280
Webb, Sidney, 60n
Webster's dictionary. *See* Merriam-Webster
Weimar Republic, constitution (Germany), 13f
Weitling, Wilhelm, 35, 39f, 53-55, 147-49, 209, 217, 234n, 236, 244, 342,353,356
Wermuth, Karl Georg Ludwig, 233n
Weserdampfboot (Minden), 217
Westdeutsche Zeitung (Cologne), 231
Westphälische Dampfboot (Bielefeld, Paderborn), 217f, 242
Weydemeyer, Joseph, 6, 179n, 216-20, 223, 225f, 242-48, 251, 329, 331, 334,336,385
Whigs, Whig party (Brit.), 86
Wieland, Christoph Martin, 363n
Wiener, Philip P., 15
Wilhelm I (King), 84
Wilhelm II (Kaiser), 82
Wilhelm, Prince Regent. *See* Wilhelm I
will and voluntarism, 32, 55, 59, 69, 93, 166, 168, 146f, 299, 339-41, 362
Willich, August, 128, 165-67, 170f, 184-86,194,196, 198, 207, 209-12, 216, 229, 231-38, 242, 351. *See also* Willich-Schapper group
Willich-Schapper group, 128, 166f, 169-71, 196-99, 207, 212, 228, 232-34, 236, 254. *See also* Schapper; Willich
Windischgrätz, Prince Alfred zu, 57
Wolfe, Bertram, 115f, 204n, 331, 347-53, 354f, 357, 366n, 372n
Wolff, Ferdinand, 193
Wollstonecraft, Mary, 21
women's emancipation (women's equality, rights), 43, 80n
Workers Association. *See* Cologne Workers Association; German Workers Educational Association (London)
workers' councils, 346
workers' state, 1f, 116, 213, 269f, 273, 292, 294, 298, 306, 320. *See also* socialist government
The World. See New York World
World War I, 11,48
Worringen (Ger.), 156
'worse the better' pattern, 239
Wróblewski, Walery, 293

X [friend of Vermersch], 290

youth; young Marx, 344

Zévaès, Alexandre, 139n
Zionism, 253f, 259f
Zurich (Switz.), 97, 311

www.ingramcontent.com/pod-product-compliance
Ingram Content Group UK Ltd.
Pitfield, Milton Keynes, MK11 3LW, UK
UKHW031412070225
454810UK00006B/163